W9-CMS-029

FOR REFERENCE

Do Not Take From This Room

Denise Lowe, MA

An Encyclopedic Dictionary of Women in Early American Films
1895-1930

"This book is more than an impressive work of research and scholarship. It is clearly a tribute to the women in the early days of the American cinema whose stories so often have been forgotten, half-told, or contorted by publicists and promoters.

Yet this is not simply a comprehensive resource that lists for the first time a vast new tableau of history. This volume is also a real page-turner. Writing in a fluid telegraphic style, Denise Lowe continually endeavors to reach beyond the bare facts, conveying to us in thumbnail sketches the psychological underpinnings of the lives she describes—the strengths and frailties, fears and tragic flaws, dreams and demons, personal quirks, and unique inner qualities that made these women remarkable, resilient, and sometimes tragic figures who contributed so much to the evolution of this crucial and distinctly American cultural industry.

What a treat to browse through these myriad true-life tales of drama, inspiration, adventure, melodrama, courage, and achievement. Here are stories of dreams come true, dreams shattered and, more often than expected, dreams regenerated and realized through notable career changes within the same industry.

Surely this is a rare and special achievement. Lowe has created an essential scholarly resource that can be read by film buffs everywhere just for fun. Bravo!"

Brian Damude, MFA
Chair,
School of Image Arts,
Ryerson University

The Haworth Press®
New York • London • Oxford

An Encyclopedic Dictionary of Women in Early American Films
1895-1930

THE HAWORTH PRESS
Titles of Related Interest

An Encyclopedic Dictionary of Women in Early American Films
1895-1930

Denise Lowe, MA

The Haworth Press®
New York • London • Oxford

The Haworth Press, Inc., 10 Alice Street, Binghamton, NY 13904-1580.

Photographs on cover from top to bottom:
Marie Prevost, courtesy of SilentsAreGolden.com.
Mary Philbin, courtesy of author's collection.
Pauline Stark, courtesy of author's collection.

Cover design by Jennifer M. Gaska.

Library of Congress Cataloging-in-Publication Data

Lowe, Denise.
    An encyclopedic dictionary of women in early American films : 1895-1930 / Denise Lowe.
      p. cm.
    Includes bibliographical references and index.
    ISBN 0-7890-1842-X (hard. : alk. paper) — ISBN 0-7890-1843-8 (pbk. : alk. paper)
    1. Motion picture actors and actresses—United States—Biography—Dictionaries. 2. Actresses—United States—Biography—Dictionaries. 3. Women motion picture producers and directors—United States—Biography—Dictionaries. 4. Women in the motion picture industry—United States. I. Title.

PN1998.2.L686 2004
791.43'092'27309041—dc22

                                                      2003025274

CONTENTS

ABOUT THE AUTHOR

Denise Lowe, MA, is the author of *Women and American Television: An Encyclopedia.* Her work has also appeared in the *St. James Encyclopedia of Popular Culture* and the *Encyclopedia of Murder and Violent Crime.*

Preface

At the turn of the century silent films taught what was expected of a person within American culture. They showcased the expectations of both men and women through the characters presented and the treatment these characters received. Early films often acted as educational tools for new immigrants.

Soon, however, the film industry wanted to reach a "better" class of people. Filmmakers started to target middle-class women and made films that would bring women and, hopefully, their children to the previously almost entirely male and immigrant entertainment. Films increasingly focused on love and family. Evil was punished and virtue was rewarded. By 1908, daily attendance had reached 200,000—with almost 67 percent of those attending being women and children.

The filmmakers continued to entice stage performers to their medium to add to the fledgling industry's respectability and legitimacy. Not secondarily, this also improved their profits. The new industry was still wide open, and creative women were welcomed in all areas of the industry with no restrictions. Women became directors and writers, while many others became important and influential stars—some for years and some for only brief periods.

All these pioneer women were important to the industry. Without them the industry would not have evolved into the megaforce that it is today. Yet so many of these women are almost, if not completely, forgotten today. How many people really remember Clara Bow or Lillian Gish or even Mary Pickford?; and those are perhaps the most famous female actors of the era. If you were to mention Billie Burke, Helen Holmes, Nina Mae McKinney, and Pola Negri, you'd probably get only a blank stare.

As a feminist and a popular culture historian, I felt I had to give these early actors a chance to be remembered. The women I wrote about were all popular during their era—sometimes this popularity was brief, but it always influenced the public and the industry. Sometimes the individual was a segue from one style to another; for instance, the Dolly Sisters were the point at which a celebrity switched from being someone famous for being accomplished (actor, writer, politician) to being famous for being famous. After their rise to fame, a new *cult of celebrity* developed, inhabited by the people who are, to this day, famous for going to parties or being seen at the right places.

Many of these women had tragic lives. Many had very short lives. Many were used up by the industry they helped to create and then discarded to an uncertain future. But, because they were pioneers, I believe they deserve our respect and our remembrance.

Because this tribute is so late in coming, many of these women have been totally lost to time. Their stories are gone. Sometimes small bits are known. Sometimes nothing at all of their childhood or early years is known. Sometimes only the life invented by the studio is known, and that is generally totally erroneous. So many of these women of the silent film era could not be included; it is a wrong done to these women by the people in the intervening years who just didn't care. Those people stand convicted, but it is our loss.

The Dictionary

 A

The Academy of Motion Picture Arts and Sciences (1927)

The Academy of Motion Picture Arts and Sciences is a nonprofit organization established to "improve the artistic quality of the film medium, provide a common forum for the various branches and crafts of the industry, foster cooperation in technical research and cultural progress." Membership is by invitation only, and to qualify for membership the prospective member must demonstrate "distinctive achievement" in one of the branches of the motion picture industry, which originally included producers, actors, directors, writers, and technicians. As the industry grew and diversified, other branches were established to represent this progress.

The idea originated during a discussion between Louis B. Mayer, Conrad Nagel (actor), Fred Niblo (director), and Fred Beetson (producer) early in 1927 as an alternative to outside censorship and artistic control. Of the thirty-six founding members of the Academy only three were women—Mary Pickford, Jeanie Macpherson (screenwriter and early actor), and Bess Meredyth (screenwriter).

Adams, Stella (1883 Sherman, TX-1961 Woodland Hills, CA)

Stella Adams appeared in one film while in her teens but really began her film career in 1912 with Nestor just three years after the studio was founded. Like many early stars for independent studios, Adams relocated to California with her studio when Nestor went West to avoid infringement complaints from the Patent Trust.

Once in California, Adams continued to appear in comedies but also began to appear in westerns, which were becoming popular because they were easy to produce in the open spaces available in Cali-

1

fornia. When director Al Christie left Nestor to form his own company to produce comedies, Adams went with him and appeared in the popular "Christie Comedies" during the latter part of the 1910s. She went on to appear the popular "Keeping up with the Joneses" series at Universal and the Imperial Comedies at Fox.

Film Credits

1907   *The Power of the Sultan*

1912   *The Passing Parade; The Lady Barber of Roaring Gulch; The Lucky Loser*

1913   *Four Queens and a Jack; The Girl Ranchers; The Girls and Dad; The God of Girzah; The Golden Princess Mine; Hawkeye's Great Capture; Her Friend the Butler; His Wife's Burglar; A Man of the People; The Power of Heredity; The Prairie Trail; The Raid of the Human Tigers; The Tale of the Hat; A Tale of the West; Teaching Dad a Lesson; To the Brave Belong the Fair; The Unhappy Pair; The War of the Cattle Range; When Cupid Won; When His Courage Failed; A Woman's Way; Under Western Skies*

1914   *Her Husbands; His Royal Pants; Scooped by a Hencoop; Cupid's Close Shave; The Wrong Miss Wright; She Was Only a Working Girl; Those Persistent Old Maids; Twixt Love and Flour; The Way of Life; What a Baby Did; When Bess Got in Wrong; When Eddie Went to the Front; When the Girls Joined the Force; When Ursus Threw the Bull; Could You Blame Her?*

1915   *All Aboard; All in the Same Boat; Behind the Screen; Father's Lucky Escape; Following Father's Footsteps; For the Good of the Cause; The Heart of Sampson; Her Friend the Milkman; His Wife's Husband; It Happened on Friday; Keeping It Dark; A Looney Love Affair; Love and a Savage; A Maid by Proxy; A One Cylinder Courtship; Taking Her Measure; Those Kids and Cupid; Wanted: A Leading Lady; When He Proposed; Where the Heather Blooms; With Father's Help;, Almost a King; A Coat's a Coat*

1916   *Cupid Trims His Lordship; Double Crossing the Dean; Eddie's Night Out; Good Night Nurse; He Almost Eloped; Her Friend the Doctor; Her Hero Maid; Her Steady Carfare;*

The Janitor's Busy Day; A Leap Year Tangle; Mingling Spirits, Mixed Kids; Never Lie to Your Wife; The Newlyweds' Mix-Up; Twixt Love and the Iceman; When Aunt Matilda Fell; The Wooing of Aunt Jemima; The Browns See the Fair; What Could the Poor Girl Do?

1917   *Five Little Widows; A Bold Bad Knight*

1926   *Under Western Skies*

1927   *Showing Off; Keeping in Trim; Passing the Joneses; Society Breaks*

1928   *Reel Life; Indoor Golf; Horse Play; Her Only Husband; A Full House; A Big Bluff; Start Something; Meet the Count; McGinnis vs. Jones; Me, Gangster*

1932   *Bachelor Mother; Sister to Judas*

1933   *The Vampire Bat; Whirlwind; Sing, Sinner, Sing*

1934   *The Tonto Kid; Whom the Gods Destroy*

1936   *Theodora Goes Wild*

Adoree, Renee (1898 Lille, France-1933 Tujunga, CA)

Courtesy of Silents Are Golden at <SilentsAreGolden.com>

The future "Renee Adoree" was born Jeanne de la Fonte in a tent between performances to parents who worked in the circus. She traveled throughout Europe with her parents; by the age of ten she had performed as a toe dancer, bareback rider, and acrobat. Although she was unable to attend a normal school, the children of the circus performers were tutored; by the time she was an adult she spoke five languages.

During her teens she began appearing in small stage productions in France and escaped to England prior to World War I. She came to the United States to appear on Broadway, and her appearances brought her to the attention of American film producers. Her debut film was *The Strongest* (1920).

She continued to appear in films but did not get a breakthrough role until 1925 when she was cast as Melisande in *The Big Parade*. In that year she also appeared in a provocative film, *Man and Maid,* written by Elinor Glyn—soon to be famous for her explanation and exploitation of "It."

Adoree was well on her way to becoming one of the screen's sexiest stars, as well as a true acting talent. However, after a flurry of film appearances at the end of the 1920s, her career stalled. She continued to appear sporadically in films until she became too ill with tuberculosis and was forced to bed for two years in an effort to regain her strength. Although she hoped to be able to return to films, she died before she was well enough to try a comeback.

Film Credits

1920	*Strongest; Mystic Faces*
1921	*Made in Heaven*
1922	*A Self-Made Man; West of Chicago; Honor First; Monte Cristo; Mixed Faces; Day Dreams; The Law Bringers*
1923	*Six-Fifty; The Eternal Struggle*
1924	*Women Who Give; A Man's Mate; Defying the Law; The Bandolero*
1925	*Excuse Me; Man and Maid; Parisian Nights; The Big Parade; Exchange of Wives*
1926	*The Blackbird; La Boheme; Exquisite Sinner; Blarney; Tin Gods; The Flaming Forest*
1927	*The Show; Heaven on Earth; Mr. Wu; On Ze Boulevard; Back to God's Country*
1928	*A Certain Young Man; Forbidden Hours; The Cossacks; Mating Call; Show People; The Spieler; The Michigan Kid*
1929	*Tide of Empire; His Glorious Night; The Pagan*
1930	*Redemption; Call of the Flesh; The Spoiler; Singer of Seville*

Adventures of Kathlyn *(1913)*

Adventures of Kathlyn was the first serial to be featured both in film and in biweekly installments in a newspaper, *The Chicago Tribune.* The narratives of Kathlyn's adventures appeared in the special features section of the Sunday edition. A tremendously successful venture, soon other papers were printing installments of serials, resulting in increased popularity for these plots that often starred females in adventurous, nontraditional roles.

Each installment was a complete story; the only association between episodes was that the same characters and setting were featured. The main character, Kathlyn, had somehow inherited a throne in India, and the episodes dealt with the problems she encountered trying to fulfill her new role. Although the plot was pathetic, the acting and photography kept the audience coming back each week.

Akins, Zoe (1886 Humanville, MO-1958 Los Angeles, CA)

Zoe Akins began her career writing short stories for magazines. In 1915 she moved to stage plays, achieving such success that she had sixteen plays produced in sixteen years. Her string of hits made her the best-known female playwright of the period.

She adapted her play *The Greeks Had a Word for It* in 1932 after writing several scenarios in the late 1920s. She went on to write other screenplays, many of which were adaptations of her stage plays. During the 1930s she excelled at the light comedies popular during the Depression, although she also wrote dramatic screenplays during that period.

She was best at writing woman-centered scripts that expressed the female view. Her major concern in writing was to make her female characters appealing to the audience without giving up strength and individuality.

She won the Pulitzer Prize for Drama in 1935 for her adaptation of Edith Wharton's book *The Old Maid*, which was then made into a 1939 film.

Writing Credits

1925	*Daddy's Gone A-Hunting; Eve's Secret*
1929	*Her Private Life; Declassee*
1930	*Sarah and Son; The Furies; Ladies Love Brutes; Anybody's Woman; The Right to Love; Toda una vida*
1931	*Girls About Town; Working Girls; Women Love Once; Once a Lady*
1932	*Greeks Had a Word for Them*
1933	*Morning Glory; Christopher Strong; A Whole Life*
1934	*Outcast Lady*

1936   *Accused; Lady of Secrets; Camille*
1938   *The Toy Wife; Three Blind Mice*
1939   *Zaza; The Old Maid*
1947   *Desire Me*
1953   *How to Marry a Millionaire*
1958   *Stage Struck*
1959   *The Sad Horse*

Alden, Mary (1883 New York City-1946 Woodland Hills, CA)

Originally appearing on the stage, Mary Alden moved into movies in 1913 in her late twenties, but her age guaranteed her only supporting roles. However, she assured her place in film history when she appeared as Lydia Brown, the mulatto housekeeper in D. W. Griffith's 1915 controversial masterpiece *The Birth of a Nation*.

Although in her later films her appearances were often uncredited, her career spanned three decades.

Film Credits

1913   *The Better Way*
1914   *The Battle of the Sexes; Home, Sweet Home; A Woman Scorned; The Second Mrs. Roebuck; Lord Chumley; The Little Country Mouse; Another Chance; The Old Maid*
1915   *The Birth of a Nation; The Lucky Transfer; Slave Girl; The Outcast; A Man's Prerogative; Bred in the Bone; The Lily and the Rose; Her Mother's Daughter; Ghosts; Big Jim's Heart; Ghosts*
1916   *Acquitted; The Good Bad Man; Macbeth; An Innocent Magdalene; Hell-to-Pay Austin; Pillars of Society; The Narrow Path; Intolerance; Less Than the Dust; Austin*
1917   *The Argyle Case; Land of Promise*
1918   *The Naulahka; The Narrow Path*
1919   *Common Clay; The Mother and the Law; The Broken Butterfly; Erstwhile Susan; The Unpardonable Sin*
1920   *Parted Curtains; Milestones; Silk Husbands and Calico Wives; Miss Nobody; The Inferior Sex; Honest Hutch; Nobody's Girl*
1921   *The Witching Hour; Snowbird; The Old Nest; Trust Your Wife*

1922   *The Hidden Woman; A Woman's Woman; Notoriety; Man with Two Mothers; The Bond Boy*

1923   *The Tents of Allah; The Empty Cradle; Pleasure Mad; The Steadfast Heart; The Eagle's Feather; Has the World Gone Mad?*

1924   *A Fool's Awakening; When a Girl Loves; Babbitt; Soiled; The Beloved Brute; Painted People*

1925   *The Happy Warrior; The Unwritten Law; Siege; Under the Rouge; The Plastic Age; Faint Perfume*

1926   *The Earth Woman; Brown of Harvard; Lovey Mary; April Fool*

1927   *The Potters; The Joy Girl; Twin Flappers*

1928   *Fools for Luck; The Cossacks; Ladies of the Mob; Sawdust Paradise; Someone to Love*

1929   *Port of Dreams; Girl Overboard*

1931   *Politics*

1932   *Hell's House; Strange Interlude; Rasputin and the Empress*

1935   *One More Spring; The Grand Hotel Murder*

1936   *Legion of Terror; Gentle Julia; Career Woman*

Allen, Phyllis (1861 Staten Island, NY-1938 Los Angeles, CA)

Phyllis Allen began her career in vaudeville before moving into films. Because of her large physical appearance and comic timing, she was excellent in the frantic slapstick comedies of Keystone Studios. She made several films with Charlie Chaplin and often costarred with Mack Swain, another large comedian at Keystone.

Film Credits

1913   *Those Good Old Days; The Riot; Fatty at San Diego; Murphy's I.O.U.; On His Wedding Day*

1914   *The Rounders; Dough and Dynamite; Cursed by His Beauty; Fatty's Jonah Day; Getting Acquainted; Ambrose's First Falsehood; Tillie's Punctured Romance; The Property Man; His Trysting Place; Gentleman of Nerve; A Fatal Sweet Tooth; Caught in a Cabaret; A Busy Day; Shot in the Excitement; Hello Mabel*

1915   *Her Winning Punch; Gussle's Day of Rest; A Submarine Pirate; A Night in the Show; That Little Band of Gold; Hogan's Wild Oats; Gussle's Wayward Path; Gussle Tied to Trouble; Giddy, Gay, and Ticklish; Fickle Fatty's Fall; Gussle Rivals Jonah; Gussle's Backward Way*

1916   *A Movie Star; The Judge; No One to Guide Him*

1917   *The Adventurer*

1919   *Monkey Stuff*

1920   *White Youth; Her First Flame*

1921   *The Kid*

1922   *Pay Day*

1923   *The Pilgrim*

Allison, May (1890 Rising Fawn, GA-1989 Bratenahl, OH)

Courtesy of Silents Are Golden at <SilentsAreGolden.com>

May Allison is remembered as the female lead of one of the first romantic screen couples. During the years of World War I, she and Harold Lockwood appeared in more than twenty romantic films together.

In the 1920s her film output lessened; in 1927 she completely retired to care for her husband, James Quirk, editor of *Photoplay* magazine, which was, perhaps, the most popular fan magazine in history. After his death in 1932, she edited the magazine until a new editor was found.

Film Credits

1915   *David Harum; The Governor's Lady; The Secretary of Frivolous Affairs; The House of a Thousand Scandals; The End of the Road; The Buzzard's Shadow; The Tragic Circles; Pardoned; The Great Question; A Fool There Was*

1916   *The Other Side of the Door; Life's Blind Alley; The Come-Back; The River of Romance; Mister 44; Pidgin Island; The Secret Wire; The Masked Rider; The Man in the Sombrero;*

Lillo of the Sulu Seas; The Gamble; The Broken Cross; Big Tremaine

1917   *The Promise; The Hidden Children*

1918   *Social Hypocrites; The Return of Mary; Her Inspiration; The Winning of Beatrice; The Testing of Mildred Vane; A Successful Adventure*

1919   *In for Thirty Days; Peggy Does Her Darndest; The Island of Intrigue; Castles in the Air; Almost Married; The Uplifters; Fair and Warmer*

1920   *The Cheater; Held in Trust; Are All Men Alike?; The Walk-Offs*

1921   *The Marriage of William Ash; Extravagance; The Last Card; Big Game*

1922   *The Woman Who Fooled Herself*

1923   *The Broad Road*

1924   *Flapper Wives; Youth for Sale*

1925   *I Want My Man; Wreckage*

1926   *The Greater Glory; Men of Steel; Mismates; The City*

1927   *One Increasing Purpose; Her Indiscretion; The Telephone Girl*

Anderson, Mignon (1892 Baltimore, MD-1983 Burbank, CA)

One of the first leading ladies of films when she joined Thanhouser Company in 1910, Mignon Anderson was given the nickname "Filet Mignon," alluding to her attractiveness.

Anderson's parents were actors, and she made her stage debut at six months of age. After finishing high school, she joined the Thanhouser Company at the (then) generous salary of $75 per week. Billed as "the second Mary Pickford," Anderson's only attribute in common with Pickford was her size—she was barely five feet tall and weighed less than 100 pounds.

Her most memorable Thanhouser film was *The Mill on the Floss* (1915) which, like several Thanhouser films, was praised for its handling of a classic story. Anderson left Thanhouser after she married in 1916 and moved West with her husband.

By 1917 she was under contract with Universal where she worked with directors Lois Weber and Ruth Ann Baldwin. She left Universal in 1918 and freelanced until 1922, when she made her final film appearance for Metro.

Film Credits

1911   *The Winter's Tale; The Pied Piper of Hamelin; Silas Marner; David Copperfield*
1912   *Nicholas Nickleby; The Merchant of Venice; Big Sister; As It Was in the Beginning; On the Stroke of Five; At Liberty—Good Press Agent*
1913   *Robin Hood; The Plot Against the Governor*
1914   *Beating Back; A Dog of Flanders; Pamela Congreve; The Harlow Handicap; A Hatful of Trouble; Lucy's Elopement; Naidra, the Dream Woman; The Messenger of Death*
1915   *Milestones of Life; The Price of Her Silence; The Mill on the Floss*
1916   *The Woman in Politics; Her Husband's Wife; Pamela's Past; The City of Illusion; The Knotted Cord*
1917   *A Young Patriot; The Circus of Life; A Wife on Trial; The Phantom's Secret; Even As You and I; Meet My Wife; The Master Spy; The Hunted Man*
1918   *The Claim; The Shooting Party*
1919   *The Midnight Stage; Blind Man's Eyes; The House of Intrigue; The Secret Peril; Marry My Wife*
1920   *Mountain Madness; King Spruce; The Heart of a Woman*
1921   *Cupid's Brand*
1922   *Kisses*

Aoki, Tsuru (1892 Tokyo, Japan-1961 Tokyo, Japan)

The only Japanese female to play leading roles in American films, Tsuru Aoki was the wife of famed Japanese actor Sessue Hayakawa.

She began her acting career on the stage at the age of eight and by the mid-1910s was appearing in American films. An inactive period in the United States spanned thirty-five years, ending with her final film appearance as Mother Une in *Hell to Eternity* (1960).

Film Credits

1913 *The Oath of Tsuru San*
1914 *The Wrath of the Gods; The Typhoon; The Village 'Neath the Sea; The Death Mask*
1915 *The Beckoning Flame; The Chinatown Mystery*
1916 *Alien Souls; The Honorable Friend; The Soul of Tsuru San*
1917 *Each of His Kind; The Call of the East*
1918 *The Curse of Iku; The Bravest Way; His Birthright*
1919 *A Heart in Pawn; The Dragon Painter; Bonds of Honor; The Courageous Coward; Gray Horizon; Ashes of Desire*
1920 *Locked Lips; The Breath of the Gods; A Tokyo Siren*
1921 *Black Roses*
1922 *Five Days to Live; Night Life in Hollywood*
1923 *La Bataille*
1924 *The Danger Line; Sen Yan's Devotion; The Great Prince Shan*
1960 *Hell to Eternity*

Arthur, Jean (1900 Plattsburgh, NY-1991 Carmel, CA)

Born Gladys Georgianna Greene, Jean Arthur began her career as a print advertising model and moved into films with her appearance in *Somebody Lied* (1923). She continued to appear in shorts and B Westerns before appearing in the mystery serial *Masked Menace* (1927), which led to only more less-than-stellar parts.

She made the transition to sound easily, and her first talking part was in *Brotherly Love* (1928); her first completely sound film was *The Canary Murder Case* (1929). After her first sound film, she received heavy promotion from her studio and was selected as a WAMPAS Baby Star in 1929, even though she had been in the industry for six years by that time. She appeared in other films as the ingenue until 1931, when she moved to New York to "learn to act."

She returned to Hollywood in 1933 with new acting confidence, as well as blonde hair, and soon signed a contract with Columbia. With the advent of sound in films, Arthur was able to make use of what some film historians believe was her most memorable feature— a voice that contemporary writers compared to "a thousand tinkling bells."

Her breakthrough film was 1935's *The Whole Town's Talking*, but she became a recognized star in the Frank Capra film *Mr. Deeds Goes to Town* (1936), in which she starred as the hard-boiled, but good-hearted, career woman opposite Gary Cooper's "everyman" character. She appeared in other Capra films and was considered by critics of the period to be the "ideal Capraesque heroine."

She received a Best Actress nomination for her portrayal in *The More the Merrier* (1943), followed by a self-imposed retirement from films soon after. She continued to perform on Broadway but appeared in only two films after 1944—*A Foreign Affair* (1948) and *Shane* (1953).

In 1966 she moved into television with her own series, *The Jean Arthur Show,* in which she played lawyer Patricia Marshall, during a period when the second-wave women's liberation movement was just forming. Unfortunately, the television audience was not ready for a female lawyer and the series lasted only eleven weeks. After the series ended, Arthur taught drama in college.

Film Credits

1923   *Somebody Lied; The Temple of Venus; Cameo Kirby*
1924   *Wine of Youth; Biff Bang Buddy; Fast and Fearless; Bringin'
        Home the Bacon; Thundering Romance; Travelin' Fast; Spring
        Fever; The Powerful Eye; Case Dismissed; Temple of Venus*
1925   *Seven Chances; The Drug Store Cowboy; The Fighting
        Smile; Tearin' Loose; A Man of Nerve; The Hurricane Horse-
        man; Thundering Through; Ridin' Rivals*

1926   *Under Fire; The Roaring Rider; Born to Battle; The Fighting Cheat; Eight Cylinder Bull; Double Daring; Lightning Bill; Twisted Triggers; The Cowboy Cop; The College Boob; The Block Signal; The Mad Racer*

1927   *Hello Lafayette; Winners of the Wilderness; Husband Hunters; The Broken Gate; Horse Shoes; The Poor Nut; Flying Luck; The Masked Menace; Bigger and Better Blondes*

1928   *Wallflowers; Easy Come, Easy Go; Warming Up; Brotherly Love; Sins of the Father*

1929   *The Canary Murder Case; Stairs of Sand; The Mysterious Dr. Fu Manchu; The Greene Murder Case; The Saturday Night Kid; Halfway to Heaven*

1930   *Street of Chance; Young Eagles; Paramount on Parade; The Return of Dr. Fu Manchu; Danger Lights; The Silver Horde*

1931   *The Gang Buster; The Virtuous Husband; The Lawyer's Secret; Ex-Bad Boy*

1933   *The Past of Mary Holmes; Get That Venus*

1934   *Whirlpool; The Most Precious Thing in Life; The Defense Rests*

1935   *The Whole Town's Talking; Party Wire; Public Hero #1; The Public Menace; If You Could Only Cook; Diamond Jim*

1936   *Mr. Deeds Goes to Town; The Ex-Mrs. Bradford; Adventure in Manhattan; More Than a Secretary*

1937   *The Plainsman; History Is Made at Night; Easy Living*

1938   *You Can't Take It with You*

1939   *Only Angels Have Wings; Mr. Smith Goes to Washington*

1940   *Too Many Husbands; Arizona*

1941   *The Devil and Miss Jones*

1942   *The Talk of the Town*

1943   *The More the Merrier; A Lady Takes a Chance*

1944   *The Impatient Years*

1948   *A Foreign Affair*

1953   *Shane*

Arvidson, Linda (1884 San Francisco, CA-1949 New York City)

Although Linda Arvidson appeared in films for only seven years, during that time she made more than 120 films. Best remembered as D. W. Griffith's first wife (1906-1936), she appeared in many of his early films. Griffith attempted to keep their marriage a secret because he felt it reflected badly on him to have a working wife, and once he became more successful he insisted she retire.

After retiring as an actor, she wrote several scenarios between 1911 and 1916. She wrote her memoirs, *When Movies Were Young*, in 1925 (reprinted 1968), which included a wealth of information on Griffith and his early work.

Film Credits

1907   *Mr. Gay and Mrs.*

1908   *Classmates; The Princess in the Vase; King of Cannibal Island; The King's Messenger; When Knights Were Bold; The Stage Rustler; The Adventures of Dolly; The Red Man and the Child; A Calamitous Elopement; The Greaser's Gauntlet; The Man and the Woman; The Fatal Hour; Balked at the Altar; For a Wife's Honor; Betrayed by a Handprint; The Red Girl; Where the Breakers Roar; A Smoked Husband; Father Gets in the Game; Ingomar, the Barbarian; The Vaquero's Way; The Planter's Wife; Concealing a Burglar; After Many Years; The Pirate's Gold; The Taming of the Shrew; The Song of the Shirt; The Clubman and the Tramp; The Feud and the Turkey; The Test of Friendship; An Awful Truth; The Helping Hand; When Knighthood Was in Flower; At the French Ball; At the Crossroads of Life; Bandits Waterloo; Stolen Jewels; A Woman's Way*

1909   *The Sacrifice; A Rural Elopement; Those Boys!; The Fascinating Mrs. Francis; The Welcome Burglar; Those Awful*

Hats; The Cord of Life; Tragic Love; The Curtain Pole; The
Politician's Love Story; At the Altar; A Fool's Revenge; The
Salvation Army Lass; The Voice of the Violin; The Deception;
The Medicine Bottle; A Drunkard's Reformation; Confidence;
The Eavesdropper; The French Duel; A Baby's Shoe; Resur-
rection; Jones and the Lady Book Agent; The Cricket on the
Hearth; Her First Biscuits; The Faded Lilies; The Peachbasket
Hat; The Country Doctor; The Cardinal's Conspiracy; A
Convict's Sacrifice; Pranks; The Mills of the Gods; Leather
Stockings; The Hessian Renegades; Comata, the Sioux; In Old
Kentucky; A Child Wanted; Pippa Passes; Lines of White on a
Sullen Sea; The Restoration; The Death Disc; Through the
Breakers; A Corner in Wheat; In a Hamper Bag; To Save Her
Soul; Edgar Allen Poe; The Day After; One Touch of Nature;
Mrs. Jones Entertains; Love Finds a Way; The Criminal Hyp-
notist; Mr. Jones Has a Card Party; A Wreath in Time; The
Joneses Have Amateur Theatricals; The Golden Louis; His
Wife's Mother; The Roue's Heart; The Lure of the Gown; I Did
It; Jones and His New Neighbors; The Winning Coat; The
Drive For Life; Twin Brothers; Lucky Jim; 'Tis an Ill Wind
That Blows No Good; The Sealed Room

1910   The Rocky Road; The Dancing Girl of Butte; The Last Deal;
The Cloister's Touch; The Duke's Plan; The Converts; Gold
Is Not All; Thou Shalt Not; The Gold Seekers; The Unchang-
ing Sea; The Face at the Window; A Midnight Cupid; The
Call to Arms; A Salutary Lesson; The Usurer; In Life's Cy-
cle; The Broken Doll; A Child's Stratagem; White Roses;
A Lucky Toothache; The Honor of His Family; The Woman
from Mellon's; The Englishman and the Girl; The Thread of
Destiny; Two Brothers; The Way of the World

1911   The Two Paths; His Trust; His Trust Fulfilled; Fate's Turning; Heart Beats of Long Ago; Fisher Folks; His Daughter;
In the Days of '49; Enoch Arden: Part 1 and 2; The Last Drop
of Water; The Miser's Heart

1912   A String of Pearls; A Child's Remorse

1913   The Scarlet Letter

1914   The Wife; A Fair Rebel; Mission Bells; House That Jack Built

1915   The Gambler of the West

1916   Charity

Writing Credits

1911   *How She Triumphed; Enoch Arden: Part 1 and 2*
1912   *A Blot on the 'Scutcheon*
1916   *Charity*

Arzner, Dorothy (1900 San Francisco, CA-1979 La Quinta, CA)

Although not the first female film director, Dorothy Arzner was the most successful during the years prior to World War II, and at one time was the only female director at any of the large Hollywood studios. Besides being the first woman to join the Directors Guild of America, she was also the only female director to make the transition from silent films to sound.

Through her father, who operated the Hoffman Café, one of the favorite eating-places of the Hollywood set, she was exposed to the film industry early in her life. This exposure, however, did not endear the entertainment industry to her, and she attended The University of Southern California for two years as a premed student. Her interest in medicine led her to volunteer as a driver for the Los Angeles Emergency Ambulance Corps during World War I.

While working with that group she met William de Mille who supervised the ambulance drivers. At de Mille's invitation in 1919 she visited a set at Paramount Studios and became interested in film direction. It was this initial introduction that Arzner later credited with beginning her interest in learning all phases of film production.

Arzner began her career in films as a script typist, but she was a horrible typist and moved on after only three months. Soon she was working as a script girl, now known as a continuity director, for an Alla Nazimova production. From there she moved to film editing, where her editing ability was recognized when she was made chief editor. After working on approximately thirty-two pictures in one year at Realart, she moved to Paramount where she edited such films as *Blood and Sand* (1922) and *The Covered Wagon* (1923).

Arzner then tackled adapting scenarios from stories such as Adela Rogers St. Johns's fact-based *Red Kimono* (1925) before getting the opportunity to direct. She purportedly threatened to leave Paramount if she was not allowed to direct a film. Her directorial debut was Esther Ralston's starring vehicle *Fashions for Women* (1927), a comedy in which Ralston played the dual roles of fashion model and cigarette girl.

She worked on several other projects before directing Katherine Hepburn in *Christopher Strong* (1933) and Rosalind Russell in *Craig's Wife* (1936), which many believe to be Arzner's best film. Arzner worked only sporadically in the early 1940s, and her films were neither critical nor popular successes. Her final commercial film was *First Comes Courage* (1943).

During World War II she directed training films for the newly created Women's Army Corps (WACs) and after the war became involved in teaching film production at UCLA, producing stage plays, and producing approximately fifty television commercials for Pepsi-Cola.

Late in her lifetime she received several honors for her groundbreaking career. She was honored at the first International Festival of Women's Films in New York in 1972, as well as being honored by the Directors Guild of America in 1975 for her "unique contributions within Hollywood cinema" as the first female member of the organization. Sadly, she was not awarded a star on the Walk of Fame until 1986, seven years after her death.

Directing Credits

1927	*Fashions for Women; Ten Modern Commandments; Get Your Man*
1928	*Manhattan Cocktail*
1929	*The Wild Party*
1930	*Sarah and Son; Paramount on Parade; Anybody's Woman*
1931	*Working Girls; Honor Among Lovers*
1932	*Merrily We Go to Hell*
1933	*Christopher Strong*
1934	*Nana*
1936	*Craig's Wife*
1937	*The Bride Wore Red*
1940	*Dance, Girl, Dance*
1943	*First Comes Courage*

Editing Credits

1920	*The Six Best Cellars*
1922	*Blood and Sand*

1923   *The Covered Wagon*
1924   *Inez of Hollywood*
1926   *Old Ironsides*

Writing Credits

1924   *The No-Gun Man; The Breed on the Border*
1925   *The Red Kimono; When Husbands Flirt*
1926   *Old Ironsides*

Asian Actors

Very few Asian actors appeared in silent films, due to both the limited number of actors available and the practice of using white actors made up to look Asian. However, Anna Mae Wong was a popular and highly visible actor from that period. Because mainstream studios did not make films focusing on Asian topics, Marion E. Wong created a production company, Mandarin Film Company, that made films for Asian audiences.

Astor, Gertrude (1887 Lakewood, OH-1977 Woodland Hills, CA)

Gertrude Astor began her acting career on the stage at the age of thirteen. A versatile performer, at one point in her career she played trombone on a Mississippi showboat. She moved to films in 1914, appearing in one- and two-reelers before joining the newly formed Universal Studio the following year as one of their first contract players.

Astor was gracefully tall in an era when the most popular actresses were petite (Pickford, Marsh, and Gish), so she easily stood out. Her height and elegant carriage made her a natural to play both "other" women and refined ladies, although she most often appeared as a vamp. Although she never reached the same height of popularity as some of the other actresses of the silent era, she was a respected figure in Hollywood for many years and was regularly named one of the industry's best-dressed women. Most important, her career spanned six decades, although in her later years she appeared as a supporting player rather than as the headliner.

Film Credits

1916   *The Janitor's Vacation; Bombs and Banknotes; The Shadow of Suspicion*

1917   *The Little Orphan; The Devil's Pay Day; The Scarlet Crystal; Polly Redhead; The Gray Ghost; The Rescue; Cheyenne's Pal; The Girl Who Won Out; Bondage; The Price of a Good Time; The Lash of Power; The Startling Climax; Some Specimens; Heart of Gold; The Golden Heart; Follow the Tracks; A Darling Buckskin; By Speshul Delivery*

1918   *The Girl Who Wouldn't Quit; Mum's the Word; The Lion's Claw; The Brazen Beauty; Vamping the Vamp; Shot in the Dumbwaiter; Pink Pajamas; The Guy and the Geyser; Great Sea Scandal; After the War*

1919   *The Wicked Darling; Destiny; Pretty Smooth; Loot; The Lion Man; Tapering Fingers; Lay Off!; Missing Husband; Mixed Tales; The Red Glove; The Wife Breakers; Shut in the Dumb Waiter; The Trembling Hour; What Am I Bid?*

1920   *Occasionally Yours; The Great Lover; Burning Daylight; The Branding Iron*

1921   *The Concert; Through the Back Door; Her Mad Bargain; Lucky Carson; The Spenders; Fascinating Widow; The Great Moment; Who Am I?*

1922   *Seeing's Believing; Beyond the Rocks; Lorna Doone; The Impossible Mrs. Bellew; You Never Know; The Ninety and Nine; The Wall Flower; Skin Deep; The Kentucky Derby; Hurricane's Gal*

1923   *Alice Adams; The Ne'er-Do-Well; Rupert of Hentzau; The Six-Fifty; Flaming Youth; The Wanters; Hollywood*

1924   *Secrets; Broadway or Bust; Daring Love; The Torrent; The Silent Watcher; Ridin' Kid from Powder River; Robes of Sin; All's Swell on the Ocean; Fight and Win* (ten episodes)

1925   *Easy Money; The Reckless Sex; The Verdict; The Charmer; Pursued; Kentucky Pride; The Wife Who Wasn't Wanted; Satan in Sables; Stage Struck; Laughing Ladies; Ship of Souls; Borrowed Finery*

1926   *Kiki; The Boyfriend; Don Juan's Three Nights; Old Soak; Sin Cargo; Tell 'Em Nothing; Too Many Women; Dame Chance; The Strong Man; Behind the Front; Dizzy Daddies*

1927   *The Cheerful Fraud; Taxi Dancer; The Cat and the Canary; Pretty Clothes; Shanghaied; Irresistible Lover; Uncle Tom's Cabin; The Small Bachelor; Oh; What a Man!; Ginsberg the Great*

1928   *Rose-Marie; Five and Ten Cent Annie; Stocks and Blondes; The Butter and Egg Man; The Naughty Duchess; The Cohens and the Kellys in Paris; Cheerful Fraud; Hit of the Show; Pay As You Enter; A Woman of Affairs*

1929   *Synthetic Sin; Two Weeks Off; The Fall of Eve; Twin Beds; Frozen Justice; Untamed; She Goes to War; Chasing Husbands*

1930   *Dames Ahoy; Be Yourself; Over the Radio; The Doctor's Wife; Live and Learn; The Boss's Orders*

1931   *Come Clean; Hell Bound; Finger Prints*

1932   *In Walked Charley; The Western Limited; They Never Came Back; Running Hollywood; While Paris Sleeps; Hesitating Love*

1933   *Frisco Jenny; Wine; Women and Song; Ship of Wanted Men; I Have Lived; Carnival Lady; Crook's Tour*

1934   *I'll Take Vanilla; Now I'll Tell; Washee Ironee; The Chases of Pimple Street; Tailspin Tommy; The Mighty Barnum; Guilty Parents*

1935   *The Northern Frontier; Okay Toots; Four Hours to Kill; Border Brigands; Dante's Inferno; Bad Boy; Manhattan Monkey Business; I Live for Love; I Don't Remember; The Drunkard; No More Ladies; Honeymoon Limited; Here Comes the Band*

1936   *The Milky Way; San Francisco; Magnificent Brute; Postal Inspector; His Brother's Wife; Great Guy; Empty Saddles; Our Relations*

1937   *Rich Relations; The Man Who Cried Wolf; Easy Living; All Over Town; Wells Fargo*

1938   *The Big Broadcast of 1938*

1939   *Dust Be My Destiny; The Women; $1000 a Touchdown*

1940   *Misbehaving Husbands*

1941   *Hold Back the Dawn; Lady for a Night*

1942   *Reap the Wild Wind; Sleepytime Gal; Rough on Rents; Moontide*

1944   *The Scarlet Claw*

1945   *Swinging on a Rainbow; Dick Tracy; Guest Wife; An Angel Comes to Brooklyn*
1946   *Dragonwyck; Sister Kenny*
1948   *Sitting Pretty; Jinx Money; Music Man; Joe Palooka in Winner Take All; My Dear Secretary*
1949   *Jolson Sings Again; The Story of Seabiscuit*
1950   *Father Makes Good; Montana; Sunset Blvd; The File on Thelma Jordan; Again . . . Pioneers*
1951   *A Place in the Sun; Crazy Over Horses; When Worlds Collide*
1952   *Paula; Angel Face*
1953   *Loose in London*
1954   *A Star Is Born*
1955   *Daddy Long Legs; At Gunpoint*
1956   *Around the World in Eighty Days; Everything But the Truth; The Boss*
1957   *The Oklahoman*
1961   *All in a Night's Work*
1962   *The Man Who Shot Liberty Valance; The Devil's Hand*

Astor, Mary (1906 Quincy, IL-1987 Woodland Hills, CA)

Mary Astor was born Lucille Vascincellos (or Vasconcellos) Langhanke to parents who began entering her in beauty contests while she was still a young child. When she was fourteen she placed second in a contest sponsored by the fan magazine *Shadowland,* which brought her a Hollywood contract and an appearance in her first film, *Scarecrow* (1920). After this film she moved to Hollywood under contract to Famous Players-Lasky and began appearing in small roles.

Her first big break came as Lady Margery Alvanley opposite John Barrymore in *Beau Brummel* (1924). In 1926 she was selected as a WAMPAS Baby Star as an actor that held the promise of stardom; in fact, she had little interest in becoming a star but was pushed before the cameras by her starstruck father. In spite of her reluctance, by the end of the decade she was making $3,750 per week.

Her father had always been overbearing, especially after he became her manager, so Astor tried to break ties with her parents in 1928 by marrying director Kenneth Hawks. Unfortunately, her husband died only eighteen months after their marriage. In 1934 her parents, who had become accustomed to living off their daughter's labors, sued her in an attempt to force her to support them—the suit was settled out of court.

When she moved into talkies her popularity with fans grew, as did her, purportedly, active love life. Her tell-all diary was used as evidence in her 1936 divorce from her second husband and the resulting custody battle over their daughter. The gossip fodder did not affect her creative output. She won the Oscar for best supporting actress for her role in *The Great Lie* (1941). That year she also appeared in *The Maltese Falcon* as the lovely but lethal Brigid O'Shaughnessy opposite Humphrey Bogart.

Although she appeared in around 123 films, her recurring problems with alcohol and a suicide attempt resulted in poor health, smaller parts in films, and eventually small roles in the dramatic plays of television's Golden Age. Her last film appearance was in 1964, after which she retired to write moderately successful, but now forgotten, novels.

She wrote two books about her often-tempestuous life—*My Story: An Autobiography* (1959), followed by *A Life on Film* (1971).

Film Credits

1920   *The Scarecrow; Hope*
1921   *Sentimental Tommy; The Beggar Maid; The Lady o' the Pines; Bullets or Ballots; Brother of the Bear; The Bashful Suitor*
1922   *The Man Who Played God; The Young Painter; John Smith; Hope; The Angelus; The Rapids*
1923   *Second Fiddle; Success; The Bright Shawl; Puritan Passions; The Marriage Maker; Woman-Proof; To the Ladies; Hollywood*

1924   *The Fighting Crowd; Beau Brummel; The Fighting American; Unguarded Woman; The Price of a Party; Inez of Hollywood*

1925   *Oh, Doctor!; Playing with Souls; Don Q, Son of Zorro; The Pace That Thrills; Scarlet Saint; Enticement*

1926   *High Steppers; The Wise Guy; Don Juan; Forever After*

1927   *The Sea Tiger; The Sunset Derby; Two Arabian Knights; Rose of the Golden West; The Rough Riders; No Place to Go*

1928   *Sailor's Wives; Dressed to Kill; Three-Ring Marriage; Heart to Heart; Dry Martini; Romance of the Underworld*

1929   *New Year's Eve; The Woman from Hell; The Show of Shows*

1930   *The Runaway Bride; Ladies Love Brutes; Holiday; The Lash*

1931   *The Royal Bed; Other Men's Women; Smart Woman; White Shoulders; Behind Office Doors; The Sin Ship*

1932   *The Lost Squadron; Red Dust; Those We Love; A Successful Calamity; Men of Chance*

1933   *The Little Giant; The World Changes; The Kennel Murder Case; Jennie Gerhardt; Convention City*

1934   *Return of the Terror; The Case of the Howling Dog; Upperworld; The Man with Two Faces; The Hollywood Gad-About; Easy to Love; I Am a Thief*

1935   *Page Miss Glory; Man of Iron; Straight from the Heart; Red Hot Tires; Dinky*

1936   *Trapped by Television; The Murder of Dr. Harrigan; Lady from Nowhere; Dodsworth; And So They Were Married*

1937   *The Hurricane; The Prisoner of Zenda*

1938   *There's Always a Woman; Listen Darling; Woman Against Woman; Paradise for Three; No Time to Marry*

1939   *Midnight*

1940   *Turnabout; Brigham Young, Frontiersman*

1941   *The Great Lie; The Maltese Falcon*

1942   *In This Our Life; Across the Pacific; The Palm Beach Story*

1943   *Thousands Cheer; Young Ideas*

1944   *Meet Me in St. Louis; Blonde Fever*

1945   *Claudia and David*

1946   *Fiesta; Desert Fury; Cynthia; Cass Timberlane*

1948   *Act of Violence*

1949   *Little Women; Any Number Can Play*

1956   *The Power and the Prize; A Kiss Before Dying*

1957   *The Devil's Hairpin*
1958   *This Happy Feeling*
1959   *A Stranger in My Arms*
1961   *Return to Peyton Place*
1964   *Hush . . . Hush, Sweet Charlotte; Youngblood Hawke*

Ayres, Agnes (1898 Carbondale, IL-1940 Los Angeles, CA)

Agnes Ayres made her screen debut in 1915 in *His New Job* for Essanay Studios and achieved moderate popularity with movie audiences. However, her popularity soared when she appeared opposite Rudolph Valentino in *The Sheik* (1921) and, later, *Son of the Sheik* (1926).

She continued to make films into the mid-1930s, although the parts she played became smaller until the proliferation of the sound films brought an end to her career.

Film Credits

1915   *His New Job*
1917   *Motherhood; Mrs. Balfame; The Debt; Hedda Gabler; The Mirror; The Dazzling Miss Davison; Richard the Brazen; The Defeat of the City; The Bottom of the Well; The Renaissance at Charleroi; The Ventures; The Furnished Room; O. Henry* (series); *Enchanted Profile*
1918   *One Thousand Dollars; Mammon the Archer; Springtime a la Carte; Transients in Arcadia; Tobin's Palm; Sisters of the Golden Circle; The Rubaiyat of the Scottish Highball; A Ramble in Aphasia; The Purple Dress; The Girl and the Graft; The Enchanted Profile; A Bird of Baghdad; Bottom of the Well*
1919   *A Girl Problem; A Stitch in Time; In Honor's Web; The Gamblers; Sacred Silence; The Ghost of a Chance; Shocks of Doom; The Guardian of the Accolade; The Buried Treasure*

1920   *Go for It; Held by the Enemy; A Modern Salome; The Inner Voice; The Furnace*

1921   *The Love Special; Too Much Speed; Cappy Ricks; The Affairs of Anatol; The Sheik; Forbidden Fruit*

1922   *The Lane That Had No Turning; Bought and Paid For; The Ordeal; Borderland; Clarence; A Daughter of Luxury*

1923   *The Heart Raider; Racing Hearts; The Marriage Maker; The Ten Commandments; Hollywood*

1924   *Don't Call It Love; When a Girl Loves; Bluff; The Guilty One; The Story Without a Name; Worldly Goods; Go and Get It*

1925   *Tomorrow's Love; Her Market Value; The Awful Truth; Morals of Men; My Favorite Wife*

1926   *Son of the Sheik*

1927   *Eve's Love Letters*

1928   *Into the Night; The Lady of Victory; Napoleon and Josephine*

1929   *Broken Hearted; The Donovan Affair; Eve's Love Letters (II); Bye, Bye, Buddy*

1936   *Small Town Girl*

1937   *Maid of Salem; Souls at Sea; Morning Judge*

Baclanova, Olga (1896 Moscow, Russia-1974 Vesey, Switzerland)

Olga Baclanova was the daughter of a wealthy businessman who lost everything in the Bolshevik Revolution and died soon afterward. She began her career on the stage in Russia with the renowned Moscow Art Theater. She fared better than most Russians after the revolution because as an actor with the state-sponsored theater she was given an apartment paid for by the new government.

Baclanova appeared in some of Russia's early films, including *Symphony of*

Love and Death (1914), *When Strings of the Heart Sound* (1914), and *Belated Flowers* (1917). Some of these films were released in the United States and Europe, because during the silent film era there was really no such thing as a "foreign" film. All films depended on facial expressions and actions and it was a simple matter to change the language of the narrative title cards.

In 1923, Baclanova accompanied the theater's touring company to the United States for a seven-month appearance on Broadway. When the company returned to the Soviet Union, Baclanova stayed in the United States, dividing her attention between the stage and, later, films.

Her first American film appearance was a small role in the Norma Talmadge film *The Dove* (1927). She was soon signed to a Paramount contract, and a publicity blitz was started to inform the public of her glamorous, and often fictionalized, history. Her first Paramount outing was as one of the leads in Josef von Sternberg's film *Street of Sin* (1928), a dark film in which she played a prostitute trying to keep her boyfriend from being reformed by Fay Wray's do-gooder character.

Her next appearance was as a no less depressing character—an immoral wife and neglectful mother in *Forgotten Faces* (1928). Neither film found an audience due to the depressing topics. In their next poor choice, Paramount cast her in *The Docks of New York* (1928), another dismal story of love and death, although her acting was favorably reviewed. Three more badly chosen roles followed with *The Three Sinners; Avalanche!;* and *The Man Who Laughs* (all 1928).

Sometimes billed only as "Baclanova" (à la Garbo), her first sound role was in *The Wolf of Wall Street* (1929), but Paramount seemed doomed to choosing good dramatic roles in really badly handled films. In disgust she moved to Fox, where she appeared in musicals showcasing her theatrical talents, but she soon left there for MGM where she was reduced to supporting roles.

Some of her roles allowed her to display her singing talent, although generally she played an icy blonde villain or a statuesque aristocrat. Sadly, for all her talent, her studios consistently failed to choose a vehicle that would exhibit her talents adequately. American audiences were not attracted to the incredibly dark characters that she was chosen to portray, and as a result she never had an opportunity to achieve the stardom that some believe her talent deserved.

She continued to work on stage and appeared in several dramatizations on radio programs late in the 1930s. In the early 1940s she toured the nightclub circuit before her final film appearance in the film adaptation of the Broadway play *Claudia*, reprising her stage role. In the 1960s she moved to Vesey, Switzerland, after her divorce from her third husband.

Film Credits

1927   *The Dove*
1928   *The Three Sinners; Street of Sin; The Man Who Laughs; Avalanche; Forgotten Faces; The Docks of New York; The Woman Disputed*
1929   *The Wolf of Wall Street; A Dangerous Woman; The Man I Love*
1930   *Cheer Up and Smile; Are You There?*
1931   *The Great Lover*
1932   *Downstairs; Freaks*
1933   *Billion Dollar Scandal*
1935   *Telephone Blues*
1943   *Claudia*

Baird, Leah (1883 Chicago, IL-1971 Hollywood, CA)

Leah Baird was born to German immigrant parents and educated in a Catholic convent. She went to business school and trained for the only business-related job open to women—that of a secretary. While completing secretarial training, she became interested in acting and in a short time had become popular among stock performers in the Buffalo, New York, area.

One of her stage performances opposite Douglas Fairbanks (*The Gentleman from Mississippi*) brought her to the attention of the film producers, and she moved to the emerging film industry. In 1911, she was signed to a contract with the Vitagraph Company; her debut film was opposite Maurice Costello in *The Wooing of Winifred.*

She left Vitagraph after two years and signed with IMP Studios as a leading lady, often appearing in period pieces such as *Ivanhoe* (1913) and *Absinthe* (1914). She returned to Vitagraph in late 1914, where she starred in a series of domestic dramas. Her most productive years were between 1918 and 1920, during which she appeared in the successful serial *Wolves of Kultur* and several social dramas with various studios.

She became involved behind the scenes in filmmaking and briefly had her own studio in New Jersey. By 1925 she was concentrating on script writing and did not return to acting until the 1940s, when she was relegated to bit or uncredited parts.

When Baird died in 1971, she was survived by her husband of more than fifty-five years, Arthur F. Beck.

Film Credits

1911   *The Wooing of Winifred*
1912   *The Old Silver Watch; Counsel for the Defense; The Foster Child; The Black Sheep; The Adventures of the Italian Model; Lord Browning and Cinderella; Stenographers Wanted; The Red Barrier; The Gamblers; The Dawning; Chumps; All for a Girl; Adam and Eve; The Diamond Mystery; The College Life; Two Sets of Furs; Leah the Forsaken; A Cure for Pokeritis; Mrs. Carter's Necklace; Working for Hubby; The Way of a Man and a Maid; The Spider's Web; The Nipper's Lullaby; The Extension Table; The Miracle; The Adamless Eden; The Voice or the Face; A Leap Year Proposal; The Night Before Christmas; Sue Simpkin's Ambition; A Woman*
1913   *The Heart of Mrs. Robins; Ivanhoe; The Kiss of Retribution; A Soul in Bondage; Red and White Roses; My Lady of Idleness; The Locket; Hearts of the First Empire; Bunny and the Bunny Hug; The Anarchist; Days of Terror; Tiger Lily; The Vampire of the Desert; Time Is Money; The Child Stealers of Paris; Love and a Throne; Mr. and Mrs. Innocence Abroad; Mona; The Two Purses; That College Life; A Birthday Gift; The House in Suburbia*

1914   *Absinthe; Neptune's Daughter; On the Chess Board of Fate; The Man That Might Have Been; An Affair for the Police; Out of the Far East; Time Is Money; Love and a Lottery Ticket; The Old Rag Doll; The Watchdog of the Deep; His Last Chance; The Silver Loving Cup; The Price of Sacrilege; Senator Jim Webb; The Great Universal Mystery; The Flaming Diagram; When the World Was Silent; Across the Atlantic; The Upper Hand; His Dominant Passion*

1915   *The Dawn of Understanding; The Romance of a Handkerchief; Dorothy; The Ruling Power; The Gods Redeem; Saints and Sinners; A Question of Right or Wrong; Tried for His Own Murder; His Wedded Wife; Hearts to Let; The Return of Maurice Donnelly; When Lizzie Went to Sea*

1916   *Lights of New York; The Bond of Blood; The People vs. John Doe; Would You Forgive Her?; The Road of Many Turnings; The Return of Maurice Donnelly; The Primal Instinct; The Harbor of Happiness; The Slightly Worn Gown; The Voice Upstairs; Love or an Empire; The Eyes of Love; So This Is Paris?; A Caliph of the New Bagdad; The Price of Sacrilege*

1917   *The Devil's Pay Day; One Law for Both; Sins of Ambition; The Fringe of Society; A Sunset; The Blazing Secret; The Eyes in the Dark; The Doctor's Deception; Lost in the Streets of Paris; Old Faithful; The Old Toy Maker; A Woman of Clay*

1918   *Moral Suicide; Wolves of Kultur; Life or Honor?*

1919   *The Echo of Youth; As a Man Thinks; The Volcano; The Capitol*

1920   *Cynthia of the Minute*

1921   *The Heart Line*

1922   *Don't Doubt Your Wife; When the Devil Drives; When Husbands Deceive; The Bride's Confession*

1923   *Is Divorce a Failure?; Destroying Angel; The Miracle Makers*

1924   *The Law Demands; The Radio Flyer; Fangs of the Wolf*

1925   *The Unnamed Woman*

1941   *One Foot in Heaven; Manpower; Blues in the Night; The Body Disappears; Bullets for O'Hara; Bad Men of Missouri*

1942   *Dangerously They Live; Buses Roar; Secret Enemies; Lady Gangster; Kings Row*

1943   *Air Force; This Is the Army; Watch on the Rhine; Thank Your Lucky Stars; The Desert Song*

1944   *The Last Ride; Make Your Own Bed*
1945   *Mildred Pierce; Pillow to Post*
1946   *My Reputation; Shadow of a Woman*
1956   *Around the World in Eighty Days*

Writing Credits

1912   *The Dawning; A Woman*
1913   *The Kiss of Retribution; A Soul in Bondage; The Moulding*
1916   *The Road of Many Turnings*
1920   *Cynthia of the Minute*
1922   *Don't Doubt Your Wife; When the Devil Drives; When Husbands Deceive*
1923   *Is Divorce a Failure?; Destroying Angel; The Miracle Makers*
1925   *Barriers Burned Away; The Primrose Path; The Unnamed Woman*
1926   *Shadow of the Law; Devil's Island; The False Alarm; Spangles*
1927   *Stolen Pleasures; The Return of Boston Blackie*
1933   *Jungle Bride*

Baker, Josephine (1906 St. Louis, MO-1975 Paris, France)

Remembered for her risqué flamboyance, dancer Josephine Baker epitomized the Jazz Age and its climate of experimentation and freedom.

Born into extreme poverty, she began dancing in the streets of St. Louis for change from pedestrians. She moved from the streets onto the stage and at fifteen married. She left St. Louis and her husband in 1923 and began performing in vaudeville to unenthusiastic reviews.

Her future changed in 1925 when she went to France with *Le Revue Negre*. The French embraced her "dans sauvage" style with its frantic movements and sensual appeal. Soon she moved to the *Folies-Bergere,* becoming the symbol for the idealized beauty of the natural world, and in 1925 for the first time performed her famous "banana dance."

In addition to being a creative force, Baker was a masterful self-promoter. She endorsed Josephine dolls and wrote a revealing autobiography. She held regular open houses to allow reporters to photograph her with her pet tiger. Soon, like many celebrities, her private life merged with her public persona.

Although she had made a short French film during the 1920s, more than ten years later Baker made two more moderately successful films—*ZouZou* (1934) and *Princess TamTam* (1935). As her popularity began to wane in Europe, she returned to the United States to attempt to duplicate her earlier French success. Unfortunately, the American audiences were no more favorable than earlier in her career.

She returned to France and retired, becoming a French citizen in 1937. During World War II she worked with the Resistance and in 1961 was awarded the Legion of Honor, France's most prestigious medal, for her work during World War II.

After the war, she became concerned with the problems of war orphans and ultimately adopted twelve children from different ethnic backgrounds. Her "Rainbow Tribe" brought her some attention, but financial difficulties plagued her and she was forced to return to the stage in 1973.

In 1974 she made a command performance at the summer ball in Monaco at Princess Grace's request and was a tremendous hit. Princess Grace also offered her a home in Monaco to ease her financial problems. Baker was working on a new revue to celebrate her fifty years on the stage when she collapsed and lapsed into a coma from which she never regained consciousness.

In February 2001 the mayor of Paris dedicated a square near the Montparnasse Cemetery to Baker to be called Place Josephine Baker.

Film Credits

1927   *Sirene des tropiques* [Siren of the Tropics]
1934   *ZouZou*
1935   *Princess TamTam*
1940   *Moulin Rouge*
1944   *Moulin Rouge* (II)
1945   *Fausse alerte* [The French Way (U.S. release, 1952)]
1954   *An jedem Finger zehn* [Ten on Every Finger]
1955   *Carosello del varieta*

Baldwin, Ruth Ann (unknown)

Ruth Ann Baldwin, one of the early female screenwriters, was born in Connecticut, but the location or year is unknown, as is any information about her death; she, like so many silent film pioneers, has been lost to history.

She came to screenwriting by way of a career in journalism and public relations. Her first major script credit was for a serial for Universal, *The Black Box* (1915). By 1916 she had her own company of actors, and her first solo film was *The Mother Call* (1916). Her first feature film was *A Wife on Trial* (1917), written by and starring her husband, Leo O. Pierson. However, directing was not to her liking and she returned to writing in 1919. She continued working at Universal as "film critic, editor, and writer" until 1921 when she retired.

Writing Credits

1914   *A Prince of Bavaria; The Vagabond; Traffic in Babies; Damon and Pythias; Big Sister's Christmas*

1915   *The Temptation of Edwin Shayne; Pawns of Fate; A Double Deal in Pork; The Blank Page; An Arrangement with Fate; The Black Box*

1916   *The Mother Call*

1917   *'49-'17; The Rented Man; It Makes A Difference; Twixt Love and Desires; A Soldier of the Legion; The Woman Who Would Not Pay; Is Money All?*

1919   *The Sneak; Cheating Herself; Chasing Rainbows; The Broken Commandments*

1920   *The Devil's Riddle*

1921   *The Marriage of William Ash; Puppets of Fate*

Directing Credits

1916   *The Mother Call; End of the Rainbow*

1917   *A Wife on Trial; '49-'17; The Woman Who Would Not Pay; A Soldier of the Legion; Three Women of France; Twixt Love and Desires; It Makes a Difference; The Rented Man; Is Money All?*

Ballin, Mabel (1885 Philadelphia, PA-1958 Santa Monica, CA)

Courtesy of Silents Are Golden at
<SilentsAreGolden.com>

Her grandparents raised Mabel Ballin after her parents died when she was two years old. Her grandmother was a social worker with the less privileged in Philadelphia's tenements, and Ballin's first stage experience was on stage at a Salvation Army hall pounding a tambourine to bring in donations.

Raised in the poverty of the tenements, Ballin was working as an apprentice dressmaker when a wealthy customer paid for her tuition to an industrial arts school. Before graduating, however, Ballin became enamored with acting and moved to New York City.

She worked in musical comedy prior to World War I and married artist Hugo Ballin. The war brought the art world to a halt, so to survive the couple turned to the film industry. She played various supporting roles until 1919, when she was given the lead in *The Quickening Flame*. She and her husband went on to form the Ballin Independent Company with her as actor and him as art director, producer, and scenarist.

Although their films were occasionally complimented as "artistic," their productions were not successful; so when the company failed, Ballin went back to supporting roles in westerns before retiring from the screen in 1925.

Film Credits

1917   *The Spreading Dawn; For Valour*
1918   *The Danger Game; The Service Star; The Glorious Adventure; The Turn of the Wheel; Laughing Bill Hyde*
1919   *Quickening Flame; The White Feather; Lord and Lady Algy; The Illustrious Prince*
1920   *Under Crimson Skies; Pagan Love*

1921   *The Journey's End; Jane Eyre; East Lynne*
1922   *Other Women's Clothes; Married People*
1923   *Vanity Fair; Souls for Sale*
1925   *Barriers Burned Away; Riders of the Purple Sage; Beauty and the Bad Man; The Shining Adventure; Code of the West*

Bankhead, Tallulah (1902 Huntsville, AL–1968 New York City)

Although Tallulah Bankhead was never a great star, during her own period she was extremely well known—perhaps for her lifestyle more than for her talent. Even after her death she continued as a popular culture icon as comics parodied her deep voice and dramatic mannerisms.

She was born into a powerful political family—her father was a U.S. congressperson and Speaker of the House for four years. A temperamental child, she decided that acting was a logical outlet for her "emotions." She went to New York and had small roles in a few plays before appearing in two less-than-successful films—*When Men Betray* (1918) and *Thirty a Week* (1918). She returned to stage work but still did not garner the acclaim she wanted, so she signed to do a play in London.

In London, she was a huge success in *The Dancer* (1923) and became a popular favorite with audiences. She soon became an international celebrity, with women imitating her hairstyle and her clothing while voraciously reading about her newest escapade.

She returned to Hollywood in triumph and was signed by Paramount, where she was put in sophisticated, world-weary roles that did not add to her reputation. For whatever reasons, her characterizations still didn't take with the filmgoing audience.

Once again she left Hollywood, but this time for the New York stage, intent on repeating her British successes on this side of the Atlantic. Before long she had regained her previous stature as an actor. She was lured back to Hollywood when Alfred Hitchcock asked her to play the journalist in *Lifeboat* (1944). She won the New York Critics Best Actress award for her portrayal, but she realized that film was still not her medium.

She once again returned to the stage and occasionally appeared on the cabaret circuit. In the late 1940s she had an extremely popular radio show, *The Big Show,* which lead to her catchphrase, "Hello Daaawlings," entering the popular culture lexicon.

She wrote her autobiography, *Tallulah,* in 1952. In her final days, she became a regular guest star on a variety of television programs, including the camp favorite *Batman* as the Black Widow (1967).

Film Credits

1918   *Thirty a Week; When Men Betray; Who Loved Him Best?*
1919   *The Trap*
1927   *Woman's Law*
1928   *His House in Order*
1931   *Tarnished Lady; My Sin; The Cheat*
1932   *Make Me a Star; Faithless; Thunder Below; Devil and the Deep*
1943   *Stage Door Canteen*
1944   *Lifeboat*
1945   *A Royal Scandal*
1953   *Main Street to Broadway*
1965   *Fanatic*
1966   *The Daydreamer* (voice only)

Banky, Vilma (1898 Nagyrodog, Hungary-1991 Los Angeles, CA)

Courtesy of Silents Are Golden at <SilentsAreGolden.com>

Born Vilma Lonchit, Vilma Banky starred in twelve Austrian, French, and Hungarian films between 1920 and 1925. In 1925 Samuel Goldwyn signed her to a contract and brought her to the United States.

The exquisite blonde was promoted as "The Hungarian Rhapsody," and her beauty made her one of Goldwyn's biggest stars during the late 1920s. She made two films with Rudolph Valentino and several with Ronald Colman during this period. In the event of the season, she married actor Rod La Rocque in 1927.

Her first talkie was *This Is Heaven* (1929), followed by *A Lady to Love* (1930), but the audience found it difficult to understand her heavy Hungarian accent. She retired from U.S. films after it was suggested in one review that with her accent and mispronunciations of English she could excel in comedies.

She toured with her husband in the play *Cherries Are Ripe* (1930-1931) before going to Germany with him to make her final movies. Wise investments in real estate allowed the couple's retirement to be comfortable and allowed Banky to indulge her enthusiasm for golf—a game she played well into her eighties.

Film Credits (United States)

1925   *The Dark Angel; The Eagle*
1926   *Son of the Sheik; The Winning of Barbara Worth*
1927   *The Night of Love; The Magic Flame*
1928   *Two Lovers; The Awakening*
1929   *This Is Heaven*
1930   *A Lady to Love*

Bara, Theda (1885 Cincinnati, OH-1955 Los Angeles, CA)

Born Theodosia Goodman, the daughter of a tailor, Theda Bara went on to become a "female fiend incarnate" who heartlessly lured men to tragedy. Her interest in dramatics began at an early age, supposedly because she never fit in with her more staid classmates. As a teen she exhibited her flair for the dramatic by dressing all in black, often accessorizing her outfits with swirling capes, and dabbling in the newly popular mysticism.

After two years at the University of Cincinnati, she went to New York to break into show business. In 1908 she appeared on stage in *The Devil,* billed as Theodosia de Coppett, and then joined a touring company in 1911. By 1914 she was ready to try films; she appeared in her first film, *The Stain,* in 1915 as an extra in a crowd scene.

Later that year she appeared in *A Fool There Was* in the role that became her legacy and her curse. She appeared as a vampire. During that era a vampire was a "not quite human" woman who enthusiastically destroyed men for the fun of it by luring respectable men to their doom and, often, to their death. She was irresistible. She was magical—a woman who controlled men by manipulating their baser instincts, the kind of woman the film audience had never seen before.

After appearing in *A Fool There Was;* Bara was voted the "most expressive actress on the screen" by the leading deaf-mute institute in New York. In addition, she was voted number five in overall popularity in a contest held by the fan magazine *Motion Picture.* As a result of her popularity the income from her films virtually built and supported Fox Studios.

Her vamp character was so successful that the persona, as created by her studio, took over her life. The studio sent out press releases claiming that Bara was the daughter of an artist (or desert sheik) and an Egyptian princess (or French actress). Her name was said to be an anagram for "Arab death." Her studio contract forbade her to appear during the day, and she could ride only in white limousines with the drapes drawn and "Nubian" footmen in attendance. She gave interviews in darkened rooms heavy with incense and perfume. Other clauses stated that she could not marry or appear in public with a date.

The public loved the myth. Bara became one of the most popular actors between 1915 and 1919, ranking just behind Mary Pickford and Charlie Chaplin. Her salary reached over $4,000 per week. She appeared in twelve films in 1915, nine in 1916, eight in 1917, seven in 1918, and seven in 1919, but the myth did not have staying power.

After World War I, her persona of sexual exaggeration lost favor with the newly jaded public. Her career was one of the first to be destroyed by overexposure and typecasting. She made only two movies after marrying director Charles Brabin in 1921; the last was a less-than-successful thriller titled *Madame Mystery* (1926), although she was listed as "available" for roles until her death. Although her career was over, her marriage lasted until her husband's death in 1957; Bara became a Hollywood hostess known for her cooking skill.

Film Credits

1915	*The Stain; The Devil's Daughter; The Two Orphans; Sin; Carmen; The Galley Slave; Destruction; Lady Audrey's Secret; The Kreutzer Sonata; A Fool There Was; The Clemenceau Case; Siren of Hell*
1916	*The Serpent; Gold and the Woman; The Eternal Sappho; Under Two Flags; Her Double Life; Romeo and Juliet; The Vixen; East Lynne; The Fire of Hate*
1917	*The Tiger Woman; Her Greatest Love; Heart and Soul; Camille; Cleopatra; Madame Du Barry; The Rose of Blood; The Darling of Paris*
1918	*The Forbidden Path; Salome; When a Woman Sins; Under the Yoke; The Soul of Buddha; The She Devil; The Message of the Lilies*
1919	*The Light; Kathleen Mavourneen; La Belle Russe; A Woman There Was; When Men Desire; The Siren's Song; The Lure of Ambition*
1921	*The Prince of Silence*
1925	*The Unchastened Woman*
1926	*Madame Mystery*

Barriscale, Bessie (1884 Hoboken, NJ-1965 Kentfield, CA)

Bessie Barriscale, born Elizabeth Barry Scale, was one of the most popular actors from 1913 to 1920. Originally a stage actor, Barriscale began appearing in films after her cousins, Mabel and Edith Taliaferro, entered the industry.

A very talented actor, Barriscale worked for several studios and at one point had her own production company. Because of her stage training, she made the transition to talkies easily but retired from films in the early 1930s.

Courtesy of Silents Are Golden at
<SilentsAreGolden.com>

Film Credits

1913　*Eileen of Erin*

1914　*The Making of Bobby Burnit; Ready Money; Rose of the Rancho*

1915　*The Devil; The Cup of Life; The Reward; The Mating; The Golden Claw; The Painted Soul*

1916　*The Green Swamp; Honor's Altar; Bullets and Brown Eyes; The Last Act; Not My Sister; The Sorrows of Love; The Payment; Plain Jane; A Corner in Colleens; Bawbs o' Blue Ridge*

1917　*The Snarl; The Hater of Men; Borrowed Plumage; Wooden Shoes; Those Who Pay*

1918　*Madam Who; Within the Cup; Blindfolded; Rose o' Paradise; Patriotism; Maid o' the Storm; The White Lie; The Heart of Rachael; Two-Gun Betty; The Cast-Off*

1919　*All of a Sudden Norma; A Trick of Fate; Hearts Asleep; Josselyn's Wife; Tangled Threads; The Woman Michael Married; Her Purchase Price; Kitty Kelly, M.D.; Beckoning Roads*

1920　*The Luck of Geraldine Laird; A Woman Who Understood; The Notorious Mrs. Sands; Life's Twist; The Broken Gate*

1921　*The Breaking Point*

1928   *Show Folks*
1933   *Secrets; Above the Clouds*
1934   *Beloved; The Man Who Reclaimed His Head*

Barrymore, Ethel (1879 Philadelphia, PA-1959 Beverly Hills, CA)

Born into the Barrymore-Drew acting dynasty, Ethel Barrymore initially wanted to become a concert pianist but accepted a future in acting. Prior to making her stage debut opposite her uncle John Drew Jr. in a play when she was fifteen years old, Barrymore was educated at a convent.

Her first starring role on stage was in *Captain Jinks of the Horse Marines* (1900-1901), and she became known as "the first lady of the American theater." She made her film debut in *The Nightingale* (1914), but returned to the stage in 1919 because she was not comfortable working in films, where there was no feedback from an audience.

Although she was not exempt from the "Barrymore curse" of over-indulgence in alcohol, she never let it affect her performances. She was very popular with the social leaders of the period and supposedly even turned down a marriage proposal from the then up-and-coming British politician Winston Churchill.

She was brought back to films by the prospect of appearing with her two brothers, John and Lionel. The three co-starred in *Rasputin and the Empress* (1932) in which she played the Czarina Alexandra, with Lionel playing Rasputin and John playing Prince Paul Chegodieff, one of the conspirators in Rasputin's death.

After several unsuccessful plays, she again returned to films, achieving success and comfort playing supporting roles. In 1944 she won the Oscar for Best Supporting Actress for her portrayal of Ma Mott in *None but the Lonely Heart*. She received three other Oscar nominations for *The Spiral Staircase* (1946), *The Paradise Case* (1947), and *Pinky* (1949).

She was the longest-lived of the "Fabulous Barrymores" and lived long enough to break into the newest entertainment medium—television. In addition to appearing on some of the dramatic anthology programs, she had her own series, *The Ethel Barrymore Theater* (1956), which she hosted, as well as occasionally starring in the plays that were presented.

Her autobiography, *Memories,* was published three years before her death.

Film Credits

1914	*The Nightingale*
1915	*The Final Judgment*
1916	*The Kiss of Hate; The Awakening of Helena Ritchie*
1917	*The White Raven; The Call of Her People; The Greatest Power; The Lifted Veil; Life's Whirlpool; The Eternal Mother; An American Widow; National Red Cross Pageant*
1918	*Our Mrs. McChesney*
1919	*The Divorcee*
1932	*Rasputin and the Empress*
1935	*All at Sea*
1943	*Show Business at War*
1944	*None but the Lonely Heart*
1946	*The Spiral Staircase*
1947	*The Farmer's Daughter; The Paradine Case; Moss Rose*
1948	*Night Song; Moonrise; Portrait of Jennie*
1949	*The Great Sinner; Pinky; That Midnight Kiss; The Red Danube*
1951	*It's a Big Country; The Secret of Convict Lake; Kind Lady*
1952	*Deadline—U.S.A.; Just for You*
1953	*The Story of Three Loves; Main Street to Broadway*
1954	*Young at Heart*
1957	*Johnny Trouble*

Basquette, Lina (1907 San Mateo, CA-1994 Wheeling, WV)

Courtesy of Silents Are Golden at
<SilentsAreGolden.com>

Dubbed "The Screen Tragedy Girl" by Adela Rogers St. Johns, Lina Basquette had a father who was a dance instructor and a stepsister who was an actor, so it seemed natural for her to enter show business. She appeared at the 1915 San Francisco World's Fair with a children's ballet troupe, and as a result she signed a contract with Universal to appear in a series of child-centered films.

She tired of films and went to Broadway; she was appearing in a Broadway revue, *The Nifties of 1923,* when she signed with Florenz Ziegfeld. She headlined the 1923 *Ziegfeld Follies* and two years later married studio mogul Sam Warner and moved back to Hollywood.

After her husband's death in 1927, she returned to films but could find work only in westerns or low-budget melodramas, even though she had been selected as a WAMPAS Baby Star in 1928. She blamed her lack of success on her in-laws with whom she was engaged in a bitter battle over her husband's estate and custody of their child. She eventually lost custody of their child and left Hollywood.

She formed an orchestra, The Hollywood Aristocrats, and toured with them for several years. She also claimed to be a spy for the OSS during World War II, alleging that Adolph Hitler had been a big fan. Having suffered during her bitter court battles with the Warner family, Basquette was further traumatized when a serviceman raped her in 1943. After the trial, she retired from the public eye to breed champion Great Danes, becoming one of the foremost dog show judges and writing two dog care books.

In the 1950s she appeared on the popular television game show *The $64,000 Question* as a dog expert and got to $16,000 before missing a question. Her autobiography, published in 1990, was titled *Lina, DeMille's Godless Girl.*

Film Credits

1916   *The Dumb Girl of Portici; Brother Jim; The Grip of Crime; The Human Cactus; The Juvenile Dancer; The Dance of Love; Shoes*

1917   *The Gates of Doom; The Black Mantilla; A Dream of Egypt; A Romanov Rose; Little Marian's Triumph; Amelita's Friend; His Wife's Relations; The Star Witness; A Prince for a Day; Polly Put the Kettle On*

1918   *The Weaker Vessel*

1922   *Penrod*

1927   *Serenade; Ranger of the North*

1928   *The Noose; Wheel of Chance; Celebrity; Show Folks*

1929   *The Younger Generation; The Godless Girl; Come Across*

1930   *The Dude Wrangler*

1931   *Goldie; Trapped; Arizona Terror; Hard Hombre; Morals for Women; Mounted Fury; Pleasure*

1932   *Arm of the Law; Hello Trouble; The Phantom Express; Screen Snapshots; Pleasure; The Midnight Lady; Big City Interlude*

1934   *The Chump*

1935   *Stolen Harmony*

1936   *The Final Hour*

1937   *Souls at Sea; Ebb Tide*

1938   *The Buccaneer; Rose of the Rio Grande; Four Men and a Prayer*

1943   *A Night for Crime*

1991   *Paradise Park*

Bauchens, Anne (1882 St. Louis, MO-1967 Woodland Hills, CA)

Anne Bauchens was one of the most respected film editors during the early years of the film industry. Called "Trojan Annie" by her co-workers at Paramount because of her habitual fourteen-hour days and the workload she regularly carried, Bauchens started as a script editor for William de Mille, who taught her editing techniques.

After Cecil B. DeMille finished *The Squaw Man* (1918), Bauchens edited it; although DeMille had said that he would never allow anyone else to edit one of his films, he liked her job so much that she spent the next forty years working almost exclusively for him. In fact, if a studio wanted DeMille to produce a film, he had it written into his contract that Anne Bauchens would be the film editor. DeMille stated in an interview in 1959 that Bauchens was the best editor he knew.

She was the first recipient of the Life Achievement Award given by the American Cinema Editors.

Editing Credits

1918	*The Squaw Man; We Can't Have Everything; Till I Come Back to You*
1919	*Don't Change Your Husband; For Better, for Worse; Male and Female*
1920	*Why Change Your Wife?; Something to Think About*
1921	*Forbidden Fruit; The Affairs of Anatol; Fool's Paradise*
1922	*Saturday Night; Manslaughter*
1923	*Adam's Rib; The Ten Commandments*
1924	*Triumph; Feet of Clay*
1925	*The Golden Bed; The Road to Yesterday*
1926	*The Volga Boatman*
1927	*The King of Kings; Chicago*
1928	*Craig's Wife; Ned McCobb's Daughter*
1929	*Noisy Neighbors; The Godless Girl; Dynamite*
1930	*Lord Byron of Broadway; This Mad World; Madam Satan*
1931	*Guilty Hands; The Squaw Man*
1932	*The Beast of the City; The Wet Parade; The Sign of the Cross*
1933	*Cradle Song; This Day and Age*
1934	*Four Frightened People; Cleopatra; Menace*
1937	*This Way Please; The Plainsman*
1938	*The Buccaneer; Bulldog Drummond in Africa; Sons of the Legion; Hunted Men*
1939	*Union Pacific; Television Spy*
1940	*North West Mounted Police; Women Without Names*
1942	*Reap the Wild Wind; Mrs. Wiggs of the Cabbage Patch; Commandos Strike at Dawn*
1944	*The Story of Dr. Wassell; Tomorrow the World*
1945	*Love Letters*
1947	*Unconquered*
1949	*Samson and Delilah*

1950   *History Brought to Life*
1952   *The Greatest Show on Earth*
1956   *Ten Commandments*

Bayne, Beverly (1894 Minneapolis, MN-1982 Scottsdale, AZ)

Courtesy of Silents Are Golden at SilentsAreGolden.com

Beverly Bayne was half of one of the most successful romantic couples in early films. She began her film career with Essanay in Chicago, starring with Francis X. Bushman. Their film pairing was so popular that they moved together to Metro; their most popular film period was 1916 to 1918 when they starred in what was called "Ruritanian romances," romantically charged films set in fictional places.

Bayne began her film career in 1912 after being noticed by a casting director, while attending school in Chicago, and offered a contract. She was soon appearing with Bushman, and their films were the financial rock of their studio.

Their film chemistry carried over into real life, and they were secretly married in 1918. Their union ended in a divorce in 1924 which also brought the end to Bayne's leading lady status.

Bayne retired from films in 1925 but continued to do stage work and vaudeville until the late 1940s when she retired completely from the entertainment industry and moved to Arizona.

Film Credits

1912   *A Good Catch; White Roses; The Understudy; The New Church Organ; The Old Wedding Dress; The Magic Wand; House of Pride; The Penitent; The Loan Shark; Billy McGrath's Love Letters; A Soul Reclaimed; The Rivals; A Legacy of Happiness; Billy Changes His Mind; The Mis-Sent Letter; Springing a Surprise; The Butterfly Net; The Adamless Eden; The Re-*

turn of Becky; The Hermit of Lonely Gulch; Back to the Old Farm; Well Matched; The Redemption of Slivers; The Grassville Girls; The Thrifty Parson; Miss Simkim's Summer Boarder; The Iron Heel; The Supreme Test

1913   The Farmer's Daughter; White Rose; A Brother's Loyalty; The Power of Conscience; For Old Times Sake; Dear Old Girl; The Toll of the Marshes; The Stigma; The Snare; Love Lute of Romany; Seeing Is Believing; When Soul Meets Soul; What George Did; Hypnotism in Hicksville; Love and Lavallieres; The Girl in the Case; Teaching Hicksville to Sing; The Gum Man; The Tale of the Clock; The Trail of the Itching Palm; The Will-Be Weds; The Wardrobe Lady; The Rival Salesman; Cousin Jane; Tango Tingle; The Same Old Story; Phillip March's Engagement; Hilda Wakes; The Divided House; Witness 'A-3 Center'; Re-Tagged; The Forbidden Way; Tit for Tat; Good Night, Nurse; The Whip Hand; Sunlight; The Right of Way; Smithy's Grandma Party; The Way Perilous; The Death Weight; The Little Substitute; What's the Matter with Father?

1914   Through the Storm; The Girl at the Curtain; Fable of the Brash Drummer and the Nectarine; The Countess; His Stolen Fortune; One Wonderful Night; The Masked Wrestler; Under Royal Patronage; The Plum Tree; In the Glare of Lights; The Private Officer; The Fable of the Bush League Lover Who Failed to Qualify; Every Inch a King; Any Woman's Choice; Three Little Powders; Oh, Doctor; A Foot of Romance; The Epidemic; Curing A Husband; One-to-Three; The Loose Change of Chance; The Volunteer Burglar; The Prince Party; Bridget Bridges It; Making Him Over—For Minnie; This Is the Life; The Man Who Found Out; The Fable of Napoleon and the Bumps; A Gentleman of Leisure; Two Men Who Waited; The Devil's Signature; Love's Magnet; Scars of Possession; The Verdict; Through Eyes of Love

1915   The Ambition of the Baron; Thirteen Down; The Great Silence; Graustark; Providence and Mrs. Urmy; The Crimson

Wing; Pennington's Choice; The Accounting; An Opal Ring; The Mystery of a Silent Death; The Conspiracy at the Chateau; Thirty; Manners and the Man; The Leather Goods Lady; The Counter Intrigue; A Bag of Gold; Eyes That See Not; Hearts and Roses; A Mansion of Tragedy; On the Dawn Road; Whose Was the Shame?

1916   *Man and His Soul; The Red Mouse; The Wall Between; A Million a Minute; In the Diplomatic Service; Romeo and Juliet; A Virginia Romance*

1917   *The Great Secret; Their Compact; The Adopted Son; Red, White, and Blue Blood; The Voice of Conscience*

1918   *Under Suspicion; The Brass Check; With Neatness and Dispatch; Social Quicksands; A Pair of Cupids; The Poor Rich Man; Cyclone Higgins; D.D.*

1919   *God's Outlaw; Daring Hearts*

1920   *Smiling All the Way*

1923   *Modern Marriage*

1924   *Her Marriage Vow; The Age of Innocence*

1925   *Who Cares; The Tenth Woman; Passionate Youth*

1948   *The Naked City*

Beavers, Louise (1902 Cincinnati, OH-1962 Hollywood, CA)

Louise Beavers started her entertainment career as a minstrel performer before coming to Hollywood to get into films. While occasionally appearing as an extra, she earned her living as a maid for actor Leatrice Joy.

Although the first film in which she appeared in the cast credits was *Uncle Tom's Cabin* (1927), she didn't begin getting regular roles until 1929. Arguably her most memorable role was as Delilah Johnson in *Imitation of Life* (1934), a role many believed might have been recognized with an Oscar if she had not been black. Her performance did win her critical acclaim, but she was still forced to accept the stereotypical black roles that were available during that time to support herself.

She briefly replaced Ethel Waters on the television series *Beulah* (1952-1953), then returned to films until she once again appeared in a television series, *Swamp Fox* (1959). Her final film appearance was in *All the Fine Young Cannibals* (1960).

Film Credits

1923   *The Gold Diggers*
1927   *Uncle Tom's Cabin*
1929   *Election Day; Coquette; Glad Rag Doll; Gold Diggers of Broadway; Barnum Was Right; Wall Street; Nix on Dames*
1930   *Wide Open; She Couldn't Say No; True to the Navy; Safety in Numbers; Our Blushing Brides; Manslaughter; Bright Lights; Paid; Outside the Law; Back Pay; Second Choice; She Can't Say No; Recaptured Love*
1931   *Millie; Don't Bet on a Woman; Six Cylinder Love; Up for Murder; Party Husband; Annabelle's Affairs; Sundown Trail; Girls About Town; Heaven on Earth; Ladies of the Big House; Reckless Living; Good Sport; Scandal Sheet*
1932   *The Greeks Have a Word for Them; The Expert; It's Tough to Be Famous; You're Telling Me; Young America; Night World; Street of Women; The Dark Horse; Unashamed; Wild Girl; Too Busy to Work; Old Man Minick; Freaks; Divorce in the Family; What Price Hollywood?; The Midnight Lady; The Strange Love of Molly Louvain; Hell's Highway; Hesitating Loved; Ladies of the Big House; We Humans; Jubilo*
1933   *She Done Him Wrong; Girl Missing; 42nd Street; The Phantom Broadcast; Central Airport; Hold Your Man; Her Bodyguard; Notorious but Nice; Her Splendid Folly; Bombshell; Only Yesterday; A Shriek in the Night; Pick-Up; In the Money; What Price Innocence?; The Big Cage; The Story of Temple Drake; Midnight Mary; The Midnight Patrol; Jimmy and Sally; Grin and Bear It; I'm No Angel*
1934   *Palooka; Registered Nurse; Glamour; A Modern Hero; Beggar's Holiday; Imitation of Life; Merry Wives of Reno; The Merry Frinks; I've Got Your Number; I Give My Love; I Believed in You; Hat, Coat, and Gloves; Dr. Monica; Cheaters;*

Bedside; Gambling Lady; Woman Condemned; Million Dollar Baby

1935 *West of the Pecos; Annapolis Farewell*

1936 *Bullets or Ballots; The Gorgeous Hussy; General Spanky; Wives Never Know; Rainbow on the River*

1937 *Love in a Bungalow; The Last Gangster; Wings Over Honolulu; Make Way for Tomorrow*

1938 *Life Goes On; Brother Rat; Scandal Street; Peck's Bad Boy with the Circus; The Headleys at Home; Reckless Living*

1939 *Reform School; Made for Each Other; Prison Bait; The Lady's from Kentucky*

1940 *Parole Fixer; No Time for Comedy; Women Without Names; I Want A Divorce*

1941 *Sign of the Wolf; The Vanishing Virginian; Virginia; Shadow of the Thin Man; Kisses for Breakfast; Belle Starr*

1942 *Reap the Wild Wind; Holiday Inn; The Big Street; Young America; Tennessee Johnson; Seven Sweethearts*

1943 *Good Morning Judge; All by Myself; DuBarry Was a Lady; There's Something About a Soldier; Top Man; Jack London*

1944 *Follow the Boys; South of Dixie; Dixie Jamboree; Barbary Coast Gent*

1945 *Delightfully Dangerous*

1946 *Young Widow; Lover Come Back*

1947 *Banjo*

1948 *Mr. Blandings Builds His Dream House; Good Sam; For the Love of Mary; A Southern Yankee*

1949 *Tell It to the Judge*

1950 *My Blue Heaven; The Jackie Robinson Story; Girls' School*

1952 *Never Wave at a WAC; I Dream of Jeannie; Colorado Sundown*

1956 *Good-bye My Lady; You Can't Run Away from It; Teenage Rebel*

1957 *Tammy and the Bachelor*

1958 *The Goddess*

1960 *The Facts of Life; All the Fine Young Cannibals*

Bellamy, Madge (1899 Hillsboro, Texas-1990 Upland, CA)

Born Margaret Philpott, Madge Bellamy went on to be called "Miss Firecracker" by fan magazines because of her habit of plain-speaking no matter who the listener—often to the detriment of her career. Bellamy began dancing as a child to help eliminate a posture problem, and she dreamed of being on the stage. She made her debut in *Aida;* when the nine-year-old was called into court for violating child labor laws, she pointed out that she was breaking no laws because she was not paid.

Before graduating from high school, Bellamy moved to New York to become a dancer. Soon she joined the chorus of *The Love Mill* (1917) on Broadway and then, encouraged to broaden her talent base, began acting. Unfortunately, her impetuous manner led to her being labeled as unreliable and difficult to handle.

Through perseverance she was given her first speaking role with a touring company's version of *Pollyanna* (1918) and garnered favorable reviews that enabled her to replace Helen Hayes in *Dear Brutus* (1920). While appearing in this play she made her film debut in *The Riddle: Woman* (1920).

When the tour ended for *Dear Brutus,* Bellamy joined a stock company based in Washington, DC, where she was required to perform a different play every week. During this period she did a screen test for Thomas Ince that resulted in her being offered a contract.

Her first film in Hollywood was *Passing Through* (1921), and she appeared in several films before appearing in her breakout role in *Lorna Doone* (1922). In her autobiography, *Darling of the Twenties,* Bellamy stated that her favorite acting experience was in *The Iron Horse* (1924), produced by John Ford.

Bellamy turned down the opportunity to appear in *Ben-Hur* and engaged in several "artistic differences" with studio heads and producers. She began to appear in a series of inconsequential flapper roles and then suddenly married a stockbroker—a marriage that lasted six days.

Her career waned due to several very ill-advised decisions that were often made in a fit of temper. After appearing in a number of low-budget films, Bellamy retired from the screen. Her habit of spending left her with little to fall back on after her retirement, so her lifestyle took a definite downward turn.

In 1943 she made headlines for shooting at a former boyfriend. She claimed that they had decided to get married but had never gone through with it. When, after a four year "engagement," the man subsequently married someone else, she claimed he was a bigamist.

Although she claimed in her autobiography to have suffered "abject poverty," she did own property and a retail store in which she worked to support herself while she wrote novels and screenplays that were never sold. Finally, in the early 1980s, someone bought her store for "twice as much" as she ever earned while making films and her final years were spent in comfort if not satisfaction.

Film Credits

1920	*The Riddle: Woman*
1921	*The Cup of Life; Passing Through; Blind Hearts; Love Never Dies; The Call of the North; Hail the Woman*
1922	*Lorna Doone; The Hottentot*
1923	*Garrison's Finish; Soul of the Beast; Are You a Failure?*
1924	*No More Women; Do It Now; The White Sin; Love's Whirlpool; His Forgotten Wife; The Fire Patrol; The Iron Horse; Secrets of the Night; On the Stroke of Three; Love and Glory*
1925	*A Fool and His Money; The Dancers; The Parasite; The Reckless Sex; Wings of Youth; The Man in Blue; Havoc; Thunder Mountain; The Golden Strain; Lazybones; Lightnin'*
1926	*The Dixie Merchant; Sandy; Black Paradise; Summer Bachelors; Bertha, the Sewing Machine Girl*
1927	*Ankles Preferred; The Telephone Girl; Very Confidential; Silk Legs; Colleen*
1928	*Soft Living; The Play Girl; Mother Knows Best*
1929	*Fugitives; Tonight at Twelve*
1932	*White Zombie*
1933	*Gordon of Ghost City; Riot Squad; Gigolettes of Paris*
1934	*Charlie Chan in London*

1935   *The Great Hotel Murder; The Daring Young Man; Metropolitan*

1936   *Crack-Up; Under Your Spell; Champagne Charlie*

1945   *Northwest Trail*

Bennett, Belle (1891 Milcoon Rapids, IA-1932 Los Angeles, CA)

Belle Bennett got her start in show business as a youngster performing vaudevillian skits on her family's showboat. She appeared in bit parts before moving to films full-time in 1914, where she specialized in portraying caring, selfless women.

From 1919 to 1924 she divided her time and talent between stage and film work. In 1925 she portrayed Stella Dallas (in the film by the same name) and was awarded star status for the rest of her career.

Courtesy of Silents Are Golden at <SilentsAreGolden.com>

Film Credits

1913   *An Accidental Clue; The Little Peacemaker; The Death Stone of India; Three Soldiers; A Man's Awakening; The Vortex; Who Is Savage?*

1914   *Mrs. Wiggs of the Cabbage Patch*

1915   *The Reckoning Day; Hearts and Clubs; Mignon*

1916   *Not My Sister; Sweet Kitty Bellairs; Jerry in the Movies; A Capable Lady Cook; Around the World; His Golden Hour; A Lucky Leap; The Fascinating Model; Sweedie, the Janitor; Where Is My Husband?*

1917   *Fires of Rebellion; The Charmer; The Devil Dodger; Bond of Fear; Ashes of Hope; The Fuel of Life; Because of a Woman; The Jewel of Death; Fat and Foolish; The Taming of Lucy*

1918   *The Lonely Woman; The Last Rebel; The Atom; The Reckoning Day* (II); *A Soul in Trust; Bruin Trouble; There and Back*

1919   *The Mayor of Filbert*

1920   *Monkey Shines*

1922   *Your Best Friend; Flesh and Spirit*
1924   *In Hollywood with Potash and Perlmutter; Hello Frisco*
1925   *Playing with Souls; His Supreme Moment; If Marriage Fails; Stella Dallas; East Lynne*
1926   *The Reckless Lady; Fourth Commandment; The Amateur Gentleman; The Lily*
1927   *Mother; The Way of All Flesh; Wild Geese*
1928   *Mother Machree; The Devil's Skipper; The Sporting Age; The Battle of the Sexes; The Power of Silence; The Devil's Trademark*
1929   *The Iron Mask; Molly and Me; My Lady's Past; Their Own Desire*
1930   *The Woman Who Was Forgotten; Courage; Recaptured Love; Big Money*
1931   *The Big Shot*

Bennett, Enid (1893 York, Australia-1969 Malibu, CA)

Courtesy of Silents Are Golden at <SilentsAreGolden.com>

Enid Bennett appeared on the stage in Australia before arriving in the United States with a touring company soon after the end of World War I. She began in films as a protégé of Thomas Ince and was an extremely popular star from 1917 to 1924.

Her diminutive size made her a natural in "young maiden" roles. Two of her most memorable roles were as Maid Marion in *Robin Hood* (1922) and as Lady Rosamund in *The Sea Hawk* (1924). However, after these triumphant portrayals she virtually disappeared from the screen, possibly as a result of her marriage to director Fred Niblo.

She worked as her husband's assistant during filming in Italy on the epic *Ben-Hur* (1925), and after returning to the United States she appeared occasionally on screen through the 1930s.

Film Credits

1916   *The Aryan; Officer 666; Get-Rich-Quick Wallingford*
1917   *Princess of the Dark; The Little Brother; Happiness; The Girl Glory; The Mother Instinct*
1918   *Keys of the Righteous; The Biggest Show on Earth; A Desert Wooing; The Vamp; The Marriage Ring; Coals of Fire; Naughty! Naughty!; Fuss and Feathers; When Do We Eat?; They're Off*
1919   *Happy Though Married; Partners Three; The Law of Men; The Haunted Bedroom; Stepping Out; The Virtuous Thief; What Every Woman Wants*
1920   *The Woman in the Suitcase; The False Road; Hairpins; Her Husband's Friend; Silk Hosiery*
1921   *Keeping Up with Lizzie*
1922   *Bootlegger's Daughter; Robin Hood; Scandalous Tongues*
1923   *Your Friend and Mine; Strangers of the Night; The Bad Man; The Courtship of Miles Standish*
1924   *A Fool's Awakening; The Sea Hawk; The Red Lily*
1926   *A Woman's Heart*
1927   *The Wrong Mr. Wright; The Flag*
1929   *Good Medicine*
1932   *Skippy; Waterloo Bridge; Sooky*
1939   *Intermezzo; Meet Dr. Christian*
1940   *Strike Up the Band*

Beranger, Clara (1886 Baltimore, MD-1956 Hollywood, CA)

Clara Beranger was educated at Goucher College before embarking on a career in journalism, writing for various popular magazines. She entered show business as a scriptwriter on Broadway before turning her sights on Hollywood where she then worked as a screenwriter for more than thirty years.

She freelanced before being hired by Fox as a screenwriter and continuities writer. She wrote several scripts for the popular child star "Baby Marie" Osborne and adapted *A Tale of Two Cities* for the screen. She became the exclusive screenwriter for director William de Mille, her future husband, from 1921 to her retirement in the 1930s. After her retirement, she lectured on screenwriting at the University of Southern California and wrote the classic screenwriting text *Writing for the Screen* (1950).

Writing Credits

1913　*Memories of His Youth*
1914　*The Master Mind; Cameo Kitty*
1915　*Anna Karenina; The Galley Slave; Her Mother's Secret; Princess Romanoff; From the Valley of the Missing*
1917　*The Greater Woman; A Tale of Two Cities; Motherhood; The Debt; The Mirror; Mary Moreland; The Dormant Power; The Slave Market*
1918　*The Way Out; Dolly Does Her Bit; The Interloper; The Golden Wall; The Beloved Blackmailer; By Hook or Crook; Appearance of Evil; The Grouch; The Love Nest; Winning Grandma; Milady o' the Beanstalk; The Voice of Destiny*
1919　*The Bluffer; Heart of Gold; The Hand Invisible; Hit or Miss; The Little Intruder; Come Out of the Kitchen; Phil-for-Short; Girls; The Firing Line; Dust of Desire; Bringing Up Betty; The Praise Agent; Sadie Love; Wanted: A Husband; The Unveiling Hand*
1920　*The Fear Market; Judy of Rogue's Harbor; Dr. Jekyll and Mr. Hyde; The Cost; Civilian Clothes; Half an Hour; Blackbirds; White Youth; Flames of the Flesh*
1921　*The Gilded Lily; Exit the Vamp; The Wonderful Thing; Sheltered Daughters; Miss Lulu Bett; A Heart to Let*
1922　*Bought and Paid For; Clarence; Nice People; Her Husband's Trademark*
1923　*The World's Applause; Grumpy; Only 38; The Marriage Maker*
1924　*Don't Call It Love; Icebound; The Bedroom Window; The Fast Set*
1925　*Locked Doors; Men and Women; Lost: A Wife; New Brooms*
1926　*Don Juan's Three Nights*
1927　*Nobody's Widow; The Little Adventuress; The Forbidden Woman; Almost Human*
1928　*Craig's Wife*

1929   *The Idle Rich*
1930   *This Mad World*
1933   *Buried Alive; His Double Life*
1934   *The Social Register*

Bernhardt, Sarah (1844 Paris, France-1923 Paris, France)

When Sarah Bernhardt, possibly the most famous actor of the nineteenth century, exclaimed, "This is my one chance at immortality" and agreed to appear on film in *Queen Elizabeth* (1912), her acceptance of the medium legitimized it in the eyes of many people. During her lifetime there were, as Mark Twain once observed, five kinds of actresses, "bad, fair, good, great—and then there is Sarah Bernhardt."

Bernhardt was born Henriette-Rosine Bernard to a Dutch-Jewish courtesan and grew up amid the Parisian demimonde, never knowing the identity of her father. After being labeled an enfant terrible, she was sent to a series of boarding schools before being introduced to the theater by one of her mother's protectors, Duc de Morny, Emperor Napoleon III's half brother. She threw herself into her studies at the Conservatoire de Musique et Declamation in 1859, and with the assistance of de Morny she entered the Comédie-Française at the age of seventeen.

Although her stage debut was less than stellar, her persistence and love of the theater were rewarded in 1869 when she played a male troubadour in the play *La Passant* and became a star. Her fame spread throughout the Western world, and she made ten tours of the United States between 1880 and 1918. She was, arguably, the first international megastar.

Bernhardt created a persona that the public loved. She lived larger than life; in addition to being an actor she was also an author, a painter, and a sculptor. She engaged in high-profile love affairs; one with the Belgian Prince de Ligne resulted in her only child, Maurice.

In 1900 Bernhardt became interested in the new technology of film making and filmed the dueling scene from Hamlet. After several less-than-successful attempts, she starred in *Camille* (1911), which was a monetary and artistic success for her. Her biggest success, however, was *Queen Elizabeth* (1912), and she came to the United States for promotional appearances that resulted in mass hysteria among her fans.

Her next major success was *Jeanne Dore* (1915), which was filmed only months after her right leg had to be amputated. Her lack of mobility made her rely on facial expression to communicate with the audience, thus eliminating her tendency toward excessive posturing and gestures learned in her years in the theater.

As she was filming *The Fortune Teller* in her townhouse she collapsed and died in the arms of her son. Thousands of mourners lined the streets to pay their respects as her funeral procession wove through Paris. On her simple granite tomb are the words "The Divine: Sarah Bernhardt."

Film Credits

1900	*Hamlet* (one scene)
1911	*Camille* (one scene)
1912	*Adrienne Lecouvreur, Queen Elizabeth*
1915	*Jeanne Dore*
1919	*It Happened in Paris*

Bertsch, Marguerite (1889 New York City-1967)

Marguerite Bertsch was one of several successful female scenarists that wrote during the silent film era. Before joining Vitagraph's scenario department in 1913 she was a successful playwright. Bertsch became interested in writing while attending Columbia University, and it was there that she began writing plays.

As head of Vitagraph's scenario department she was responsible for every major production done at Vitagraph from 1913 to 1916. After working at Vitagraph for several years, she was given the opportunity to direct with the film *The Law Decides* (1916), which she co-directed with William Earle.

The first film she directed by herself was *The Devil's Prize,* which was released late in 1916. Bertsch was also the scenario writer for this drama about a man who blames everyone else for his misfortunes. In 1917, Bertsch directed two other features, *The Glory of Yolanda* and *The Soul Master,* as well as a short titled *Captain Jinks and Himself.*

When asked by the fan magazine *Moving Picture Stories* the difference between writing a film and directing a film, she stated that for her there was no difference because, "I never wrote a picture that I did not mentally direct."

She was active in mentoring other women interested in the film industry and taught classes in writing. In addition, she authored the contemporary "how-to" bestseller *How to Write for Moving Pictures* (1917).

Writing Credits

1912   *The Troublesome Step-Daughters; The Indian Mutiny; Nothing to Wear; Una of the Sierras*
1913   *The Tiger; The Wreck; The Trap; Getting up a Practice; The Flirt; The Diver; The Carpenter; The Call; Cutey and the Twins*
1914   *The Vavasour Ball; My Official Wife; Wife Wanted; Uncle Bill; Shadows of the Past; The Painted World; He Never Knew; A Florida Enchantment; Captain Alvarez*
1915   *The Silent Plea; Mortmain; The Cave Man; The Man Behind the Door; The Enemies*
1916   *For a Woman's Fair Name; The Vital Question; Salvation Joan; The Law Decides; The Dawn of Freedom; Through the Wall; The Devil's Prize; Writing on the Wall*
1917   *The Soul Master*
1919   *The Painted World*

Directing Credits

1916   *The Law Decides; The Devil's Prize*
1917   *The Glory of Yolanda; The Soul Master; Captain Jinks and Himself*

Besserer, Eugenie (1868 Watertown, NY-1934 Los Angeles, CA)

A Christmas baby, Eugenie Besserer did not begin her film career until she was forty-two years old, appearing in *The Wonderful Wizard of Oz* (1910). She excelled in character roles and, because she would take on almost any type of role, was in demand for many films over the next two decades.

Film Credits

1910   *The Wonderful Wizard of Oz*
1911   *George Washington's Escape; The Profligate; The Mother; The Still Alarm; Stability vs. Nobility; One of Nature's Noblemen; A Sacrifice to Civilization; The Craven Heart; It Happened in the West; Slick's Romance; Their Only Son; The Regeneration of Apache Kid; The Blacksmith's Love; Old Billy; The Bootlegger; An Evil Power*
1912   *The Millionaire Vagabonds; Monte Cristo; The Indelible Stain; The Governor's Daughter; The End of the Romance; Sammy Orpheus; The Last of Her Tribe; The Lake of Dreams*
1913   *The Spanish Parrot-Girl; Love Before Ten; Woman: Past and Present; The Probationer; Phantoms; Lieutenant Jones; The Fighting Lieutenant; Diverging Paths; The Girl and the Judge; In God We Trust; The Acid Test*
1914   *Memories; Elizabeth's Prayer; The Salvation of Nancy O'Shaughnessy; The Story of the Blood Red Rose; The Tragedy That Lived; His Fight*
1915   *The Carpet of Bagdad; The Rosary; The Circular Staircase; I'm Glad My Boy Grew Up to Be a Soldier; The Crisis; Ingratitude of Liz Taylor; Poetic Justice of Omar Khan*
1916   *Thou Shalt Not Covet; The Garden of Allah; Twisted Trails*
1917   *Beware of Strangers; Little Lost Sister; The Curse of Eve; Who Shall Take My Life?*
1918   *The City of Purple Dreams; A Hoosier Romance; The Road Through the Dark; Little Orphant Annie; The Eyes of Julia Deep; The Still Alarm; The Sea Flower*
1919   *Ravished Armenia; Turning the Tables; Scarlet Days; The Greatest Question*
1920   *The Fighting Shepherdess; For the Soul of Rafael; Fickle Women; What Happened to Rosa; The Scoffer; The Gift Supreme; 45 Minutes from Broadway; The Brand of Lopez; Seeds of Vengeance*
1921   *Good Women; The Sin of Martha Queed; The Light in the Clearing; Molly O'; The Breaking Point*

1922   *The Rosary; Penrod; Kindred of the Dust; The Hands of Nara; June Madness; The Strangers' Banquet*
1923   *The Lonely Road; The Rendezvous; Anna Christie; Enemies of Children; Her Reputation*
1924   *Bread; The Price She Paid*
1925   *A Fool and His Money; Confessions of a Queen; Wandering Footsteps; Bright Lights; The Circle; Friendly Enemies; The Coast of Folly*
1926   *The Skyrocket; The Millionaire Policeman; The Fire Brigade; Flesh and the Devil; Winning the Futurity*
1927   *Wandering Girls; When a Man Loves; Captain Salvation; Slightly Used; The Jazz Singer*
1928   *Drums of Love; Two Lovers; Yellow Lily; Lilac Time; A Lady of Chance*
1929   *The Bridge of San Luis Rey; Thunderbolt; Madame X; Speedway; Fast Company; Illusion; Seven Faces; Whispering Winds; Mister Antonio*
1930   *A Royal Romance; In Gay Madrid; DuBarry, Woman of Passion*
1932   *Scarface; Six Hours to Live*
1933   *To the Last Man*

Billington, Francelia (1895 Dallas, TX-1934 Glendale, CA)

Francelia Billington epitomized the "leading lady" of silent films— she was willing to try anything from riding a horse to diving off a cliff if it added to a film's narrative. When she was not working in front of the cameras, she was working behind the scenes as camera person— a job she preferred to acting.

After her family moved to Los Angeles in 1905, Billington continued her education at Sacred Heart Convent. At the convent she began to appear in the plays that the school presented.

Without any formal training, she made her debut in 1912 for Kalem Company. She remained with Kalem for only six months before becoming a member of Thanhouser's West Coast company. After receiving a very favorable review for a bit part in *Carmen,* she was offered a contract with Reliance-Majestic Company in 1913.

While at Reliance she appeared in a series of short dramas and comedies, before getting leading roles in *A Child of God* and *Strathmore* (both 1915). She moved to Universal in 1916, where her success and popularity continued until she parlayed these successes into a contract as William Russell's leading lady in his American Film Company films.

Her most memorable role, according to many film historians, was as Mrs. Armstrong in *Blind Husbands* (1919). However, heavy drama was not to her liking and she returned to westerns for the remainder of her career.

She appeared with Tom Mix in several of his 1920 films. While starring in *The Terror* she met her husband, Lester Cuneo, a perennial western villain. She starred with Cuneo in several films before the marriage ended in divorce; Cuneo killed himself after the decree became final. The tragedy shadowed her career and, since camera operating was now a male-dominated field, she was unable to fall back on the job that she had preferred earlier in her life. As her career faltered, her health was weakened by tuberculosis.

Film Credits

1912   *The Mayor's Crusade; The Two Runaways*
1913   *The Wedding Right Up; Told in the Future; The Pride of Angry Bear; The Message of the Flowers; A Life in the Balance; Legally Right; Hearts and Hoofs; The Fraternity Pin; Dora; The Banker's Sons; The Userer; The Boomerang; Carmen; The Widow's Stratagem; The Mountain Witch; The Missing Bonds*
1914   *The Portrait of Anita; The Reform Candidate; The Peach Brand; Through the Dark; Turned Back; Broken Nose Bailey; Runaway Freight; The Tardy Cannon Ball; The Kaffir's Skull; Who Shot Bud Walton?; The Beat of the Year; The Final Verdict*
1915   *A Child of God; Strathmore*
1916   *Naked Hearts; Bettina Loved a Soldier; The Evil Women Do; The Black Sheep of the Family; The Mainspring; The Right To Be Happy; The Best Man's Bride; The Fur Trimmed Coat; Her Wedding Day; The Price of Victory*
1917   *My Fighting Gentleman; High Play; The Frame-Up; The Shackles of Truth; The Masked Heart; Pride and the Man; New York Luck; The Sea Master; Sands of Sacrifice; Heartstrings; Money's Mockery; The Wrong Man; Snap Judgment*

1918   *In Bad; The Midnight Trail*
1919   *Blind Husbands; The Day She Paid*
1920   *The Great Air Robbery; Hearts Are Trumps; Desert Love;
        The Terror*
1921   *The Ranger and the Law; The Truant Husband; High Gear
        Jeffrey*
1922   *Blue Blazes; Restless Souls; Blazing Arrows; Trapped in the
        Air; Silver Spurs*
1923   *What a Wife Learned; The Vengeance of Pierre; The Zero
        Hour; Fighting Jim Grant*
1924   *The White Sin*
1925   *Hearts of the West; Two Fisted Thompson*
1926   *Tex*
1927   *A Rough Shod Fighter*
1930   *The Mounted Stranger*

Binney, Constance (1896 New York City-1989 Queens, NY)

Because of her bobbed hair and exuberance Constance Binney was considered by many to be the ideal flapper, but her first love was dancing; she began her training when she was only four years old. She attended private schools in Connecticut and France and, as befitted her family's social standing, appeared in charity fundraisers after graduation.

Taking the advice of a theatrical producer, she debuted on the stage in the musical comedy *Oh, Lady! Lady!* (1918). While appearing in this play she was offered the part of Norah Cavanagh in *The Sporting Life* (1918).

She was disappointed by her performance, so she returned to the stage in the play *Saturday to Monday* (1918) which, in Binney's words, "lasted about that long." She appeared in *The Test of Honor* with John Barrymore, but it was her success in *39 East* on Broadway in 1919 that earned her a film contract—first with Realart, then with Paramount.

After appearing in several films in the United States and in the British version of *Bill of Divorcement* (1922), she returned to the stage to appear sporadically until she finally retired in 1947.

Film Credits

1918   *Sporting Life; Tom's Little Sister*
1919   *Test of Honor; Erstwhile Susan*
1920   *The Stolen Kiss; Something Different; 39 East*
1921   *Room and Board; The Case of Becky; Such a Little Queen;*
       The Magic Cup; First Love
1922   *Midnight; Sleepwalker; A Bill of Divorcement*
1923   *Three o'Clock in the Morning*

Binney, Faire (1898 New York City-1957 Hollywood, CA)

Faire Binney and her sister, Constance, symbolized the free-spirited flapper era for many movie fans during the 1920s. Born into an affluent New England family, Faire received her education in private schools before beginning her film career in *The Sporting Life* (1918) with her sister.

She appeared with John Barrymore in *Here Comes the Bride* (1918), which garnered much praise for her talent. She portrayed ingenues and flappers throughout the 1920s and appeared on stage in the lead of two Broadway plays—*He and She* (1920) and *The Teaser* (1921).

She became, with her sister, one of the most popular film flappers. But like today, there are always younger women waiting for their chance to be stars, and Faire retired in the mid-1920s.

Film Credits

1918   *Sporting Life; Woman*
1919   *Here Comes the Bride; Open Your Eyes*
1920   *The Wonder Man; Madonnas and Men; The Blue Pearl*
1921   *Frontier of the Stars; The Girl from Porcupine; A Man's Home*
1922   *What Fools Men Are; A Wide Open Town*
1923   *Loyal Lives*
1924   *Second Youth; The Speed Spook; The Man Without a Heart*
1925   *The Lost Chord*
1926   *False Pride*

1951   *Love Nest*
1952   *Monkey Business*
1953   *Dream Wife*

The Birth of a Nation *(1915)*

For all the controversy that surrounds this film, it is *the* pivotal film in the history of motion pictures. It was the first to emotionally place the audience in the midst of vast battle scenes. With its release it brought the film industry an element of legitimacy and elevated films to the status of art.

At three hours in length, the film was the longest produced to that time. It chronicled the events surrounding the Civil War in spectacular fashion. The first part examined the introduction of slavery into the United States and the rise in the abolitionist movement as well as the events of the Civil War, Lee's surrender, and President Lincoln's assassination.

During the second part of the film, the events and climate after the war in the South are portrayed. The damage done to the South by unscrupulous Northern politicians and carpetbaggers is shown. In addition, the creation of the Ku Klux Klan to save the South from complete destruction is depicted; this part of the film, as well as its stereotypical depiction of freed blacks, has caused the controversy encompassing the film since its first showing.

The film, while basically accurate historically, is biased by modern standards; critics often forget that a Victorian Southern gentleman did, after all, produce it at the turn of the century. Although politically incorrect by late twenty-first-century standards, it does depict the prevailing feelings and views of the period in which it was made. Sadly, stereotypical characterizations are still a problem in films, and the so-called problems of the film should not minimize the accomplishment by Griffith in producing the first film spectacle.

Black Actors

Black actors were a part of motion pictures from the inception of the industry. Edison, especially, featured black people in his "everyday life" kinetoscopes as early as 1895.

There is some argument among historians over which film was the first to feature an all-black cast. Some sources say it was *The Pullman Porter* (1910) or *The Railroad Porter* (1912), while others cite *Darktown Jubilee* (1914). But these early films often made the characters clumsy and people to be laughed at by the, mostly white, audience.

The stated purpose of the Lincoln Motion Picture Company (1916-1921) was to make films to "encourage black pride" while upholding the social order of the period. The goals of many of the early black film companies were to correct the distortions portrayed in white films while accurately depicting black reality and fostering a positive black image.

Although the title of the first film has not been firmly established, several small production companies made films featuring black performers which played in theaters in black communities throughout the country. Some of the longer-lasting companies included Ebony Film Corporation, Foster Photoplay Company, the Lincoln Motion Picture Company, Colored and Indian Film Company, Gate City Film Corporation, and Norman Film Manufacturing Company. Other production enterprises would shoot a few films then go out of business since backing was often difficult to find and profits were low.

One of the most remembered production companies was the Micheaux Corporation headed by producer Oscar Micheaux. Established in 1919, the Micheaux Corporation was one of the most artistically refined and longest lasting of the black independents continuing into the 1940s, although during his career Micheaux made only forty-four films.

Estimates of the number of black theaters in existence in the 1920s range from 461 to 700, and there was definitely a market for films starring black performers. These theaters were found in large urban centers such as New York and Los Angeles as well as smaller rural communities in Texas (with fifty-four) and Florida (with fifty-one).

In spite of the difficulties encountered by these production companies, between 1917 and 1930 approximately fifty films were made with all-black casts. The first sound film is believed to have been *Melancholy Dame* (1929) featuring Roberta Hyson in a comedy about black "high society" in Birmingham, Alabama.

The Scar of Shame (1927), produced by Colored Players Film Corporation of Philadelphia, is often cited by historians as a classic silent film. The film dealt with the social structure existing in black society that was based on both class and skin color. The film chronicled the doomed marriage between a light-skinned concert pianist and the dark-skinned lower-class woman he married. The film condemned the rigid discrimination upon which the story was based, even as it tried to analyze it.

With the exception of Louise Beavers, few black females went on to long-lasting careers or made the transition to sound films. Nellie Conley (1873-1959) adopted the name Madame Sul-Te-Wan and appeared in several films, from her debut in the infamous *The Birth of a Nation* (1915), to her final film, *The Buccaneer* (1958).

Anita Bush (1883-1974), an actor who got her training in black vaudeville and appeared before King Edward VII in London, founded the Anita Bush Stock Company. She produced the first black western in 1921 in the all-black town of Boley, Oklahoma.

Evelyn Preer (1896-1932) toured the vaudeville circuit before debuting in *The Homesteader* (1919) produced by Oscar Micheaux. She continued to appear in many of the films he produced, such as *The Brute* (1920), *Deceit* (1923), and *Birthright* (1924), before her final, uncredited, role in *The Blonde Venus* (1932).

Margaret Quimby (1905-1965) appeared in eighteen films in the silent and early sound eras. Gertrude Howard (1892-1934) debuted in *The Circus Cyclone* in 1925 and continued in films until *Peck's Bad Boy* (1934). Other actors can be found only in cast listings, their life stories lost—actors such as Julia Russell who appeared in several Micheaux productions, Edna Morton and Evelyn Ellis who appeared in films from Reol Productions, and Anita Thompson who appeared in Lincoln Motion Picture Company films. Sadly, many of the performers who appeared in black films were listed only as "players."

"Black Maria"

Built in 1893 to produce Thomas Edison's kinetoscope films, "Black Maria" was the precursor to all the later studios and led the way for the cult of the movie star to follow. Designed by W. K. Laurie Dickson, the building was on a revolving mechanism so that it could be moved to follow the natural lighting of the sun.

Located in the garden of Edison's West Orange, New Jersey, home it was made of blackened tin that was connected in such a way that no light could come through to the interior. It was made up of two "rooms"—one with the stage for the performers and one for the camera and darkroom. There were only two windows in the darkroom section and these could be sealed to completely block out any light. The building was called "Black Maria" supposedly because of its sinister look rather than for its color.

Blane, Sally (1910 Salida, CO-1997 Los Angeles, CA)

Courtesy of Silents Are Golden at <SilentsAreGolden.com>

Sally Blane was one of four sisters who entered the film industry as youngsters. Although generally considered less talented than her younger sister, Loretta Young, her career spanned more than two decades.

She danced professionally and appeared in child roles in films in 1917 and 1921. She returned in 1927 as an ingenue and changed her name from Elizabeth Jane Young to Sally Blane. She starred in the popular "Collegians" series and appeared in several westerns with Tom Mix. She was named as a WAMPAS Baby Star in 1929 along with her sister Loretta.

She appeared with her sister Loretta in a dance number, "Meet My Sister," in the film *The Show of Shows* (1929). In 1939 Polly Ann, Sally, Loretta, and half-sister Georgianna all appeared in *The Story of Alexander Graham Bell* (1939).

Film Credits

1917   *Sirens of the Sea*
1921   *The Sheik*
1927   *Casey at the Bat; Rolled Stockings; Shootin' Irons; Flashing Oars*
1928   *Wife Savers; Dead Man's Curve; Her Summer Hero; A Horseman of the Plains; Fools for Luck; The Vanishing Pioneer; King Cowboy*
1929   *Outlawed; Wolves of the City; Eyes of the Underworld; The Very Idea; Half Marriage; The Vagabond Lover; Tanned Legs; The Show of Shows*
1930   *Little Accident*
1931   *Annabelle's Affairs; The Star Witness; X Marks the Spot; Women Men Marry; Ten Cents a Dance; The Spirit of Notre Dame; Shanghaied Love; Good Sport; Arabian Knights; Once a Sinner; A Dangerous Affair; Law of the Sea*
1932   *The Circus Show-Up; Local Bad Man; Disorderly Conduct; The Phantom Express; Heritage of the Desert; Pride of the Legion; I Am a Fugitive from a Chain Gang; Wild Horse Mesa; The Reckoning; Probation; Forbidden Company; Escapade; Cross Examination; Running Hollywood; Boys Will Be Boys; Who Me?*
1933   *Trick for Trick; Night of Terror; Mayfair Girl; Crime on the Hill; Advice to the Lovelorn; Hello Everybody!*
1934   *City Limits; Half a Sinner; No More Women; She Had to Choose; Stolen Sweets; City Park; Against the Law; The Silver Streak*
1935   *This Is the Life*
1937   *Great Hospital Mystery; One Mile from Heaven; Angel's Holiday*
1938   *Numbered Woman; Sunday Night at the Trocadero; Crashing Through Danger*
1939   *The Story of Alexander Graham Bell; Fighting Mad; Way Down South; Charlie Chan at Treasure Island*
1944   *La Fuga*
1955   *A Bullet for Joey*

Blythe, Betty (1893 Los Angeles, CA-1972 Woodland Hills, CA)

Betty Blythe began her show business career on the stage in both Europe and the United States before making her film debut in 1916. She quickly became one of Vitagraph's most popular stars, appearing in the hugely successful film *The Queen of Sheba* (1921). Of her part in the film Blythe said, "I wear twenty-eight costumes and if I put them on all at once, I couldn't keep warm."

While popular in the United States, Blythe continued to appear in European productions as well, notably *She* (1925). With the advent of talkies, she moved into sound films but was relegated to supporting roles. She was active through the 1940s and made her final cinematic appearance in the ballroom segment in *My Fair Lady* (1964).

Film Credits

1916   *Slander*

1917   *His Own People*

1918   *A Mother's Sin; Over the Top; The Business of Life; The Little Runaway; A Game of Fate; All Man; The Green God; The King of Diamonds; Miss Ambition; Hoarded Assets; Tangled Lives; The Brief Debut of Tildy*

1919   *Silent Strength; Fighting Destiny; Beating the Odds; Beauty-Proof; The Man Who Won; Dust of Desire; The Undercurrent*

1920   *Burnt Wings; The Silver Horde; Occasionally Yours; Nomads of the North; The Third Generation*

1921   *Just Outside the Door; The Queen of Sheba; Mother o'Mine; Charge It; Disraeli; The Truant Husband*

1922   *Fair Lady; His Wife's Husband; How Women Love; The Darling of the Rich*

1923   *The Truth About Wives; Sinner or Saint; Chu Chin Chow*

1924   *The Recoil; The Spitfire; The Breath of Scandal; Southern Love; In Hollywood with Potash and Perlmutter; Folly of Vanity*

1925   *Percy; Speed; She; Le Puits de Jacob*

1927   *Snowbound; A Million Bid; The Girl from Gay Paree; Eager Lips*

1928   *Domestic Troubles; Glorious Betsy; In No Man's Land; Stolen Love; Sisters of Eve; Daughters of Israel*

1931   *Stars of Yesterday*

1932   *Tom Brown of Culver; Back Street; Lena Rivers*

1933   *Pilgrimage; Only Yesterday; The King's Vacation; Before Midnight*

1934   *Money Means Nothing; A Girl of the Limberlost; Two Heads on a Pillow; The Scarlet Letter; Night Alarm; Ever Since Eve; Badge of Honor; I've Been Around*

1935   *Cheers of the Crowd; Western Courage; The Spanish Cape Mystery; The Perfect Clue; Anna Karenina*

1936   *Yours for the Asking; The Gorgeous Hussy; Rainbow on the River; Murder at Glen Athol*

1937   *Conquest; Espionage; Topper; What Do You Think?*

1938   *Hold the Kiss; Man-Proof; Gangster's Boy; Romance of the Limberlost; Delinquent Parents*

1939   *The Women*

1940   *Misbehaving Husbands; Earl Puddlestone*

1941   *Federal Fugitives; Our Wife; Tuxedo Junction; Top Sergeant Mulligan; Sis Hopkins; Honky Tonk; The Miracle Kid*

1942   *Freckles Comes Home; House of Errors; Piano Mooner; Dawn on the Great Divide; Yokel Boy; Inflation; Dawn on the Great Divide*

1943   *Girls in Chains; Spotlight Revue; Farmer for a Day; Mr. Muggs Steps Out; Bar 20; Where Are Your Children?; Presenting Lily Mars; Crime Doctor; Sarong Girl*

1944   *Charlie Chan in The Chinese Cat; A Fig Leaf for Eve*

1945   *Docks of New York; Her Highness and the Bellboy; They Were Expendable; Adventure; Abbott and Costello in Hollywood; Love, Honor and Goodbye*

1946   *Kid from Brooklyn; The Postman Always Rings Twice; Undercurrent; The Undercover Woman; The Hoodlum Saint; Joe Palooka, Champ*

1947   *Something in the Wind; The Secret Life of Walter Mitty; Jiggs and Maggie in Society; Songs of Love; Cass Timberlane*

1948   *Madonna of the Desert; Luxury Liner; Letter from an Unknown Woman*

1949   *The Barkleys of Broadway; Jiggs and Maggie in Jackpot Jitters*

1950   *Jiggs and Maggie Out West*

1951   *Hollywood Story*

1955   *The Lonesome Trail*

1956   *Lust for Life*

1957   *The Helen Morgan Story*

1964   *My Fair Lady*

Boardman, Eleanor (1898 Philadelphia, PA-1991 Santa Barbara, CA)

Known as much for her off-camera behavior as her acting talent, Eleanor Boardman was born into a strict Presbyterian family that viewed films as wicked. Ignoring her family's admonitions, Boardman began modeling while still as teenager, and soon her face became so associated with the Eastman Kodak Company that she became known as the "Kodak Girl."

She entered show business by way of musical comedy and vaudeville. Then, in her early twenties, she moved to New York to pursue a career in the film industry. Tall and blonde, she was soon approached by the Goldwyn Picture Company with a contract; she went to Hollywood, remaining with the studio when it became Metro-Goldwyn-Mayer. She was named as a WAMPAS Baby Star in 1923.

She portrayed characters that were elegant and sophisticated—traits that she had in abundance. King Vidor, whom she married in

1926, directed her most successful films. One of her best performances, however, was not a glamorous role but that of a plain-look-
ing woman in a failing marriage in Vidor's experimental film *The
Crowd* (1928).

She divorced Vidor in 1933 and, after her film contract expired
later that year, moved with her two daughters to Europe. While in
France she met and married director Harry d'Abbadie d'Arrast, returning with her new husband to Hollywood. After d'Arrast was
virtually blackballed because of disagreements with both Samuel
Goldwyn and Joseph Schenck, the couple returned to Europe where
d'Arrast continued to direct films.

Because of her remarriage, a bitter custody battle ensued between
Vidor and Boardman. She enrolled her two daughters in a Swiss
boarding school to keep them away from their father during the legal
proceedings. Finally, with rumors of war throughout Europe, Vidor
took the girls back to the United States in 1940.

Boardman followed her daughters and for some time lived in the
gatehouse on the estate of her friend Marion Davies. When the war
broke out d'Arrast, too, returned to Hollywood but was still unable to
find work with the studios. When the war ended he returned to Europe and divorced Boardman.

Briefly after World War II she worked as a fashion commentator
for the Paris bureau of *Harper's Bazaar*. She continued to divide her
time between the United States and Europe until the late 1960s when
she returned to California and eventually settled in Montecito, a sub-
urb of Santa Barbara in the central coastal region of California.

Film Credits

1922   *The Strangers' Banquet*
1923   *Gimme; Vanity Fair; Souls for Sale; Three Wise Fools; The
        Day of Faith*
1924   *True As Steel; Wine of Youth; Sinners in Silk; The Turmoil;
        The Wife of the Centaur; The Silent Accuser; So This Is Mar-
        riage?*
1925   *The Way of a Girl; Proud Flesh; The Circle; The Only Thing;
        Exchange of Wives*
1926   *Memory Lane; The Auction Block; Bardelys the Magnificent;
        Tell It to the Marines*
1928   *The Crowd; Diamond Handcuffs*

1929   *She Goes To War*
1930   *Mamba; Redemption*
1931   *The Great Meadow; The Flood; The Squaw Man; Women Love Once*
1932   *The Phantom President*
1933   *The Big Chance*
1934   *The Three Cornered Hat*

Boland, Mary (1880 Philadelphia, PA-1965 New York City)

Mary Boland acted in various regional stock companies before beginning to get roles in Broadway plays. She specialized in dramatic roles and once played seven characters in one play.

She was successful enough on the stage that when she entered films in 1915, she was given lead roles in several films before returning to the stage in 1920. When she again began to appear in films in 1931, she concentrated on character roles and even appeared in some comedies, with one of her most memorable roles being that of the befuddled yet determined Mrs. Bennet in *Pride and Prejudice* (1940). After her comeback in films, she continued to alternate between stage work and films until her final film, *Guilty Bystander* (1950).

Film Credits

1914   *The Penitentes; The Edge of the Abyss*
1915   *The Price of Happiness; The Stepping Stone*
1916   *Mountain Dew*
1917   *A Woman's Experience; The Prodigal Wife*
1918   *The Perfect Lover*
1919   *His Temporary Wife*
1931   *Personal Maid; Secrets of a Secretary*
1932   *Trouble in Paradise; Night After Night; If I Had a Million; The Night of June 13th; Evenings for Sale*
1933   *The Solitaire Man; Three-Cornered Moon; Mama Loves Papa*
1934   *Four Frightened People; Stingaree; Here Comes the Groom; The Pursuit of Happiness; Six of a Kind; Melody in Spring; Down to Their Last Yacht*

1935   *Ruggles of Red Gap; People Will Talk; Two for Tonight; The Big Broadcast of 1936*

1936   *College Holiday; Wives Never Know; A Son Comes Home; Early to Bed*

1937   *Marry the Girl; There Goes the Groom; Mama Runs Wild; Danger—Love at Work*

1938   *Little Tough Guys in Society; Artists and Models Abroad*

1939   *The Women; Night Work; The Magnificent Fraud; Boy Trouble*

1940   *New Moon; Hit Parade of 1941; One Night in the Tropics; Pride and Prejudice; He Married His Wife*

1944   *Nothing but Trouble; In Our Time*

1945   *Forever Yours*

1948   *Julia Misbehaves*

1950   *Guilty Bystander*

Booth, Margaret (1898 Los Angeles, CA)

Margaret Booth entered show business as a "patcher," or the person who spliced film together, for D. W. Griffith right after graduating from Los Angeles High School. She soon moved to Paramount where she assembled tinted sections of film prior to their theatrical release.

She was made first assistant to director John Stahl, where she worked with editing and script continuity. She was finally made editor in 1921 and after working with Irving Thalberg was considered one of the best "cutters" at Metro-Goldwyn-Mayer (MGM). She eventually rose to the position of editor in chief at MGM and worked as supervising editor for more than thirty years (1937-1968).

She received an Oscar nomination for her editing of *Mutiny on the Bounty* (1935) and edited the film, *The Boy Ten Feet Tall,* which won at the Cannes Film Festival in 1963. After her retirement from MGM, she continued to edit on a freelance basis.

In 1977 she received a Lifetime Achievement award from the American Cinema Editors (ACE) for her contribution to the field of film editing.

Editing Credits

1923   *The Wanters*

1924   *Why Men Leave Home; Husbands and Lovers*

1925   *Fine Clothes; The Merry Widow*

1926   *Memory Lane; The Gay Deceiver*

1927   *In Old Kentucky; The Enemy; Lovers?*

1928   *Bringing Up Father; Telling the World; The Mysterious Lady; A Lady of Chance; Our Dancing Daughters*

1929   *The Bridge of San Luis Rey; Wise Girls*

1930   *Redemption; Strictly Unconventional; The Rogue Song; The Lady of Scandal; A Lady's Morals; New Moon*

1931   *It's a Wise Child; Five and Ten; Susan Lennox; The Prodigal; The Cuban Love Song*

1932   *Smilin' Through; Strange Interlude; The Son-Daughter; Lovers Courageous*

1933   *Peg o' My Heart; Bombshell; Dancing Lady; The White Sister; Storm at Daybreak*

1934   *The Barretts of Wimpole Street; Riptide*

1935   *Reckless; Mutiny on the Bounty*

1936   *Romeo and Juliet; Camille*

1938   *A Yank at Oxford*

1963   *The Boy Ten Feet Tall*

As Supervising Editor

1938   *A Yank at Oxford*

1939   *The Wizard of Oz*

1951   *The Red Badge of Courage*

1963   *The V.I.P.s*

1970   *The Owl and the Pussycat*

1972   *Fat City*

1973   *The Way We Were*

1976   *Murder by Death*

1977   *The Goodbye Girl*

1978   *California Suite*

1979   *Chapter Two*

1980   *The Hunter*

1982   *Annie*

Producing Credits

1978   *The Cheap Detective*
1979   *Chapter Two*
1982   *The Toy*
1985   *The Slugger's Wife*

Borden, Olive (1907 Richmond, VA-1947 Los Angeles, CA)

Courtesy of Silents Are Golden at <SilentsAreGolden.com>

Olive Borden's legacy, if she has one, has been a cautionary tale of what might happen to an individual when she works in an industry that often can't tell fact from fiction. For years in reference books on the film industry, Olive Borden was noted as the stage name for Sybil Tinkle, but in the 1990s it was revealed that these two individuals had been confused for years.

Olive Borden was raised in Virginia by her widowed mother. She entered the film industry in the early 1920s. At one time she was called the "joy girl of the silent screen," in recognition of a role she played in *The Joy Girl* (1927), one of her most popular movies.

Her first films were made with Mack Sennett and she was, supposedly, one of his "bathing beauties." She also worked with Hal Roach, appearing in his Christie Comedies, before being selected as a WAMPAS Baby Star in 1925. Her breakout role in *Three Bad Men* (1926) is considered by many historians to be her best role.

She was signed with Fox and spent the remainder of the silent era portraying the carefree flapper that was the epitome of the Jazz Age. But with the advent of sound pictures, the flapper character became obsolete, resulting in her being dropped by Fox when she refused a salary cut. At the same time, her long engagement to actor George O'Brien, who had starred with her in *Three Bad Men,* ended.

She continued to appear sporadically in films through the early part of the 1930s but became dependent on alcohol; her personal life eroded, as did her professional life. When war broke out she joined the Women's Army Corps before she dropped from sight.

Having spent her money as fast as she made it, after the war she was nearly destitute. Eventually, she moved into the Sunshine Mission where her mother worked, but the years of alcoholism had done their damage and she died of liver disease before her forty-first birthday.

Film Credits

1924   *Air Pockets*
1925   *The Dressmaker from Paris; The Happy Warrior; The Overland Limited; Should Husbands Be Watched; Bad Boy*
1926   *The Yankee Senor; My Own Pal; Yellow Fingers; 3 Bad Men; Fig Leaves; The Country Beyond*
1927   *The Money Talks; Secret Studio; The Joy Girl; Pajamas; Come to My House*
1928   *The Albany Night Boat; Virgin Lips; Gang War; Stool Pigeon; Sinners in Love*
1929   *Love in the Desert; The Eternal Woman; Half Marriage; Dance Hall; Wedding Rings*
1930   *Hello Sister; The Social Lion*
1932   *The Divorce Racket*
1933   *Hotel Variety; The Mild West; Leave It To Me*
1934   *Chloe, Love Is Calling You; The Inventors*

Bow, Clara (1905 Brooklyn, NY-1965 Los Angeles, CA)

Courtesy of Silents Are Golden at <SilentsAreGolden.com>

Clara Bow, known as the "It" Girl, was *the* sex symbol of the film industry in the 1920s. Although a huge star, she was a consummate actor with no star temperament who willingly helped new actors just starting in films.

The third child born to a mentally ill (probably schizophrenic) mother, Sarah, and a grim abusive father, Robert, Bow was the only one of their children to survive beyond infancy. Her father had dreams but no ambition, and her mother married to get away from an unsavory home life, only to end in a more difficult and depressing situation.

Since Robert refused to support his family, Clara had to drop out of school to go to work before finishing the eighth grade. In 1921 Bow entered the Fame and Fortune Contest sponsored by Brewster Publications, the publisher of *Motion Picture, Motion Picture Classic,* and *Shadowland,* and she won a part in a film. Although her part was edited out before the release of the film; *Beyond the Rainbow,* Bow was determined to continue in films.

She made a few low-budget films on the East Coast before she went to Hollywood to appear in *Maytime* for Preferred Pictures. She made twenty-one films in 1924, and each successive picture added to her reputation as an actor. In 1924 she was also selected as a WAMPAS Baby Star. In 1925 Bow appeared in fourteen films. She portrayed one of the most popular characters of her career the following year when she appeared in *Dancing Mothers* (1926), as the fun loving but irresponsible daughter Kittens.

Her reputation as a femme fatale was solidified after the son of a well-to-do Eastern family tried to commit suicide when Bow refused to marry him after their initial meeting. He milked his fifteen minutes of fame into two weeks of lurid headlines before Bow leveled him at his sanity hearing by saying that if he truly had intended to kill himself he would have "used pistols."

Even as her fame grew, Bow remained as unpretentious as she had ever been. She did not see any reason to buy a huge mansion when a smaller home would be sufficient. She lived her life on her terms, but she knew that underneath her self-confident exterior was the lonely, fearful little girl from the tenements.

Her next major role was in *Wings,* awarded the first Academy Award for Best Picture. Although her part was limited since it was a combat movie, she had the most controversial scene in the film when two men burst into her character's room and her topless torso is briefly revealed before she has time to cover herself.

Then she appeared in *It*—a film that came to define both a generation and Clara Bow herself. "It," in the words of originator Elinor Glyn, was "an inner magic, an animal magnetism, a self confidence" that pulled others to the possessor. In the film she plays shop girl Betty Lou Spence, who sets her sights on the son of her new boss. It was during this period that the director of the film, Clarence Badger, stated that the best way to direct Bow was to explain the concept of the scene to her and "just let her go."

It became the most popular film to that time, breaking records in every city in which it played. *Variety* stated, "This Bow girl . . . just runs away with the film." Bow became the ideal Jazz Baby of the Jazz Age.

F. Scott Fitzgerald defined Bow as "the quintessence of what the term flapper signifies . . . pretty, impudent, superbly assured, as world-wise [and] briefly-clad" as any of her followers. Bow became the premiere sex symbol of the 1920s. She began to believe that she did have "It," which gave her real confidence for the first time.

Her studio came to realize that no matter what the picture was about, the audience wanted to see Bow behave flippantly and outrageously. So they developed a formula for her films. First, the studio did not have to worry about plot—just showcase Bow. Second, the male lead was of no concern to the audience—they would pay attention only to Bow and her antics. Finally, make the screen character as close to Bow's publicized character as possible and tie in her supposed off-screen exploits whenever possible.

But her overwhelming success brought problems, not the least of which was the schedule that the studio set for her—often having her work ninety hours per week. Added to her grueling schedule was the fact that Bow slept very little because of the trauma she had experienced when she awoke years earlier to find her mother standing over her with a knife ready to kill her during one of her mother's "spells." Eventually, Bow collapsed under the extreme pressure and was finally given a chance to rest between pictures.

Two of her most endearing and captivating traits to her fans were her simplicity and genuineness in an industry of fabrication and fantasy. Unfortunately, these traits also caused her problems within the movie community because her behavior reminded everyone of their own less-than-stellar beginnings. Many people in Hollywood distanced themselves from her so that they would not be branded "common" by association. Sadly, Bow was often alone and confused by social rules that made no sense to her.

At the height of her popularity, in 1928, Bow received over 10,000 fan letters each week. In May 1928 the postmaster of Los Angeles announced that in just one month almost 45,000 fan letters came through his office for Bow. However, when she tried to move from comedies to more serious films, the fans rebelled. She was the happy flapper and they wanted her to remain the symbol of happiness and light for them.

While her naïveté and genuineness caused less authentic people to distance themselves from her, talkies dealt the final blow to Bow's career. Afflicted by a stammer since childhood that was accentuated by stress, her voice was viewed by the studio as a whine. However, her fans loved "their star's" first talkie, *The Wild Party,* although only major cities had converted to sound capability.

Eventually her fear and feelings of inferiority made it too difficult for Bow to say her lines. Too many words were beyond her limited education. Films, in her words, were "just no fun anymore." Perhaps the final killing blow to Bow's career came from a friend, who after failing in an attempt to blackmail Bow, held the actor up to ridicule at her trial. Now the spending of its favorite star appalled the country that had loved Bow's frivolousness and extravagance.

Ridiculed and ostracized by the only people who mattered to her, her fans, Bow became prey to "shattered nerves" and went to a sanitarium to rest and regain her strength. In the summer of 1931, Bow removed her belongings from her dressing room—which had since been assigned to someone else—and at twenty-five years old became a has-been.

After a long rest, Bow returned to films and changed studios. Her first film was *Call Her Savage* (1932), a strange film that dealt with just about every forbidden topic known to censorship at that time— including homosexuality, prostitution, and sadism. When her new studio sent her on a publicity tour of Europe, she encountered many of her die-hard fans, including Adolph Hitler. Tired of the same type of roles, Bow retired permanently in 1934.

She centered her retirement on her two sons, but she was never able to achieve the happiness and peace she so craved. After years of instability, she went through a battery of psychological tests and it was determined that the unpredictable behavior that had drawn so many fans to her was a result of schizophrenia. Inherited from her mother, who died in a sanitarium, Bow now had a reason for her dissatisfaction and reaction to stress. Further psychotherapy revealed both the tortured childhood Bow had endured and that her father had raped her at sixteen.

Bow's unstable behavior took its toll on her marriage; since Bell had political aspirations, a mentally ill wife was a liability. The couple separated, with Bell retaining custody of their two sons and Bow retiring to Los Angeles where she lived in seclusion for most of her life. She took up painting and foreign languages, among other hobbies, until her sudden death from a heart attack. Before her death she reflected that silent stars "had individuality. Today they're more sensible . . . but we had more fun."

Film Credits

1922   *Beyond the Rainbow; Down to the Sea in Ships*
1923   *Enemies of Women; The Daring Years; Maytime*
1924   *Grit; Poisoned Paradise; Daughters of Pleasure; Wine; Empty Hearts; Helen's Babies; Black Lightening; Black Oxen; This Woman; Black*
1925   *Capital Punishment; The Adventurous Sex; Eve's Lover; Lawful Cheater; The Scarlet West; Parisian Love; Kiss Me Again; The Keeper of the Bees; The Primrose Path; Free to Love; The Best Bad Man; The Plastic Age; The Ancient Mariner; My Lady's Lips; My Lady of Whims; The Boomerang; The Great Sensation*
1926   *Shadow of the Law; Two Can Play; Dancing Mothers; Fascinating Youth; Mantrap; Kid Boots; The Runaway; Dancing Madness*
1927   *It; Children of Divorce; Rough House Rosie; Wings; Hula; Get Your Man*
1928   *Red Hair; Ladies of the Mob; The Fleet's In; Three Weekends*

1929   *The Wild Party; Dangerous Curves; The Saturday Night Kid; Hollywood Snapshots #11*
1930   *Paramount on Parade; True to the Navy; Her Wedding Night; Love Among the Millionaires*
1931   *No Limit; Kick In*
1932   *Call Her Savage*
1933   *Hoopla*

Brady, Alice (1892 New York City-1939 New York City)

Alice Brady, a future winner of the Best Supporting Actress Oscar, was born into a show business family. Her father was a Broadway producer and her mother was a French dancer. She was educated in convents, where she began training her clear soprano voice.

Although her father did not want her to go into show business, he consented to her attending the Boston Conservatory of Music. While attending the conservatory she was given the opportunity to appear in a stage musical and accepted, using the name Marie Rose. After two years, a reporter discovered her true identity and she finally told her father of her budding stage career. Her father reluctantly accepted her career choice and told her if she was going to be an actor to use her own name.

After creating a name for herself on the stage, she made her film debut in *As Ye Sow* (1914). She worked steadily for the next few years, but personal tragedies brought her to the brink of a nervous breakdown, so she left films in 1923. After an extended rest she returned to the stage.

She returned to films in 1932 and received critical as well as popular recognition in 1936, when she was nominated for the first time in the Best Supporting Actress category for her appearance as the befuddled mother in the screwball classic *My Man Godfrey*. The following year she won the Best Supporting Actress statuette for her portrayal of Mrs. O'Leary in the drama *In Old Chicago* (1937). She continued to work in films until her death.

Film Credits

1914   *As Ye Sow*
1915   *The Boss; The Lure of Woman; The Cup of Chance*
1916   *The Ballet Girl; The Woman in 47; Then I'll Come Back to You; Tangled Fates; La Vie de Boheme; Miss Petticoats; The Gilded Cage; Bought and Paid For; The Rack*
1917   *A Woman Alone; A Hungry Heart; The Dancer's Peril; Darkest Russia; Maternity; The Divorce Game; A Self-Made Widow; Betsy Ross; A Maid of Belgium; Her Silent Sacrifice*
1918   *The Spurs of Sybil; The Trap; At the Mercy of Men; The Whirlpool; Woman and Wife; The Ordeal of Rosetta; The Knife; In the Hollow of Her Hand; Her Great Chance; The Death Dance; The Better Half*
1919   *The Indestructible Wife; The End of the Road; Marie Ltd.; The Redhead; His Bridal Night; The World to Live In*
1920   *The Fear Market; Sinners; A Dark Lantern; The New York Idea*
1921   *Out of the Chorus; Little Italy; The Land of Hope; Hush Money; Dawn of the East*
1922   *Missing Millions; Anna Ascends*
1923   *The Leopardess; The Snow Bride*
1933   *When Ladies Meet; Beauty for Sale; Broadway to Hollywood; Stage Mother; Should Ladies Behave?*
1934   *Gay Divorcee; Miss Fane's Baby Is Stolen*
1935   *Gold Diggers of 1935; Lady Tubbs; Metropolitan; Let 'em Have It*
1936   *My Man Godfrey; Go West Young Man; Three Smart Girls; The Harvester; Mind Your Own Business*
1937   *Mama Steps Out; Call It a Day; Mr. Dodd Takes the Air; Merry Go Round of 1938; One Hundred Men and a Girl; In Old Chicago*
1938   *Joy of Living; Goodbye Broadway*
1939   *Young Mr. Lincoln; Zenobia*

Brent, Evelyn (1899 Tampa, FL-1975 Los Angeles, CA)

Courtesy of Silents Are Golden at <SilentsAreGolden.com>

Known for her "smoldering eyes" and bad-girl roles, Evelyn Brent had an erratic career that never resulted in lasting stardom, but she was popular during the early years of her career. Born to a single mother who was only fourteen, Brent's life was one of hardship and poverty.

While she was still in high school, she began modeling in New York. When her friends started going to Fort Lee, New Jersey, to get work in films, she accompanied them and was soon getting work as an extra. In 1915 she signed a contract with Metro Studios and was publicized as the studio's new ingenue under the name "Betty Riggs."

Her career had become stagnant when she, like much of the entertainment business, fell victim to the influenza pandemic of 1918-1919. After nearly dying, she went to London with a friend to recuperate. While in London she had the opportunity to appear in a play that became one of the hits of the season; she was soon receiving film offers from British producers. She appeared in several British films with moderate success.

However, she once more became ill and soon was nearly destitute. She was able to return to the United States only by appearing in a newsreel advertising the Cunard Steamship Lines. Upon returning to New York, she married a childhood friend, Bernie Fineman, who was also an executive at Paramount Pictures.

Although she had been in films for years, with the help of her husband she was declared a WAMPAS Baby Star in 1923. That year she appeared in *Held to Answer,* in which she played the type of role she was best at—an angry woman with few morals.

She continued to appear in films, but it was not until she was cast in several Josef von Sternberg films that she truly reached her potential as an actor. In the first film, *Underworld* (1927), she portrayed the character that she is most remembered for—Feathers McCoy, a gangster's girlfriend considered by many film historians to be the first modern femme fatale. The following year she appeared in two other von Sternberg films—*The Last Command* and *The Dragnet*. In each her portrayals were critically acclaimed, but she was unable to capitalize on the popularity that the roles brought her.

Although she made the transition to sound easily—her deep, throaty voice seemed matched to the type of characters she most often played—by the 1930s she was freelancing at lesser studios known as Poverty Row. In 1932 she began appearing on the vaudeville circuit. Although she was a popular attraction, she still could not capitalize on her popularity.

With the advent of television, she turned to that medium, her last appearance being in a 1959 episode of *Wagon Train*. In the early 1960s she left the entertainment industry and worked as an artist's representative. She lived out her days in a small apartment in Westwood Village, California.

Film Credits

1913　*The Pit; The Gentleman from Mississippi*
1914　*The Heart of a Painted Lady*
1915　*The Shooting of Dan McGrew; When Love Laughs*
1916　*The Lure of Heart's Desire; The Soul Market; Playing with Fire; The Spell of the Yukon; The Weakness of Strength; The Iron Woman; The Iron Will*
1917　*The Millionaire's Double; To the Death; Raffles, the Amateur Cracksman; Who's Your Neighbor?*
1918　*Daybreak*
1919　*Fool's Gold; The Other Man's Wife; The Glorious Lady; Help! Help! Police!*
1920　*The Shuttle of Life; The Law Devine*
1921　*Laughter and Tears; Sybil; Sonia; The Door That Has No Key; Demos; Circus Bill*
1922　*The Spanish Jade; Trapped by the Mormons; The Experiment; Pages of Life; Married to a Mormon*

1923   *Held to Answer*
1924   *Loving Lies; The Shadow of the East; Arizona Express; The Plunderer; The Lone Chance; The Desert Outlaw; The Cyclone Rider; The Dangerous Flirt; My Husband's Wives; Silk Stocking Sal*
1925   *Midnight Molly; Forbidden Cargo; Alias Mary Flynn; Smooth As Satin; Lady Robinhood; Three Wise Crooks; Broadway Lady*
1926   *Queen o' Diamonds; Secret Orders; The Impostor; The Jade Cup; Flame of the Argentine; Love 'Em and Leave 'Em*
1927   *Blind Alleys; Underworld; Woman's Wares; Love's Greatest Mistake*
1928   *The Showdown; A Night of Mystery; The Mating Call; Interference; The Last Command; His Tiger Wife; The Dragnet; Beau Sabreur*
1929   *Broadway; Fast Company; Darkened Rooms; Dark Skies; Woman Trap; Why Bring That Up?*
1930   *Slightly Scarlet; Framed; Paramount on Parade; The Silver Horde; Madonna of the Streets*
1931   *Pagan Lady; The Mad Parade; Traveling Husbands*
1932   *High Pressure; The Crusader; Attorney for the Defense*
1933   *The World Gone Mad*
1935   *Home on the Range; Symphony of Living; Speed Limited; The Nitwits; Without Children*
1936   *Song of the Trail; Hopalong Cassidy Returns; The President's Mystery; Penthouse Party; Jungle Jim; It Couldn't Have Happened—But It Did*
1937   *The Last Train from Madrid; Night Club Scandal; Sudden Bill Dorn; King of Gamblers; Daughter of Shanghai*
1938   *Tip Off Girls; Mr. Wong; Detective; Law West of Tombstone*
1939   *Panama Lady; Daughter of the Tong; The Mad Empress*
1941   *Emergency Landing; Dangerous Lady; Wide Open Town; Forced Landing; Holt of the Secret Service*
1942   *Wrecking Crew; Westward Ho; The Payoff*
1943   *Spy Train; The Seventh Victim; Silent Witness*
1944   *Bowery Champs; Raiders of the South*
1947   *Robin Hood of Monterey*

1948   *The Golden Eye; Stage Struck*
1950   *Again; Pioneers*

Brian, Mary (1906 Corsicana, TX-2002 Del Mar, CA)

Courtesy of Silents Are Golden at <SilentsAreGolden.com>

Mary Brian, called "The Sweetest Girl in Pictures," entered the film industry by way of winning the Miss Personality award in a beauty contest. Her first film was *Peter Pan* (1924) in which she played Wendy Darling.

The following year she was selected as a WAMPAS Baby Star and worked at Paramount Studios from 1926 to 1931, generally in roles that required little of her but to look virginal. After leaving Paramount she freelanced at various studios but never got beyond leading roles in "B" movies.

Her career waned by the end of the 1930s, and she made films in England as well as danced on the vaudeville circuit and did regional theater. During World War II she entertained troops with the USO.

After the war she disappeared from films only to reappear in the 1950s in the syndicated version of one of the first situation comedies in television, *Meet Corliss Archer* (1954-1955), as the main character's mother, Janet Archer. When this series was cancelled, she retired to paint and, as of 2000, lived quietly in Studio City in the same apartment she had moved into in 1953. In December 2002 she died of natural causes at the age of ninety-six.

Film Credits

1924   *Peter Pan*
1925   *The Air Mail; The Street of Forgotten Men; A Regular Fellow; The Little French Girl*
1926   *The Enchanted Hill; Behind the Front; Paris at Midnight; Brown of Harvard; More Pay—Less Work; Beau Geste; Prince of Tempters; Stepping Along*
1927   *Her Father Said No; High Hat; Knockout Reilly; Running Wild; Man Power; Shanghai Bound; Two Flaming Youths*
1928   *Under the Tonto Rim; Harold Teen; Varsity; Someone to Love; Partners in Crime; Forgotten Faces; The Big Killing*
1929   *Black Waters; The Man I Love; River of Romance; The Virginian; The Marriage Playground; Navy Blues*
1930   *The Kibitzer; Burning Up; Only the Brave; The Light of Western Stars; Paramount on Parade; The Social Lion* (I); *Only Saps Work; The Royal Family of Broadway*
1931   *Captain Applejack; The Front Page; Gun Smoke; Homicide Squad; The Runaround; Hollywood Halfbacks*
1932   *It's Tough to Be Famous; Blessed Event; The Unwritten Law; Screen Snapshots; Manhattan Tower*
1933   *Hard to Handle; Girl Missing; Song of the Eagle; Moonlight and Pretzels; The World Gone Mad; One Year Later; Fog*
1934   *Monte Carlo Nights; College Rhythm; Star Night at the Cocoanut Grove; Shadows of Sing Sing; Private Scandal; Fog; Ever Since Eve*
1935   *Charlie Chan in Paris; Weekend Millionaire; Man on the Flying Trapeze*
1936   *Two's Company; Three Married Men; Spendthrift; Once in a Million; Killer at Large; The Amazing Quest of Ernest Bliss*
1937   *Navy Blues; The Affairs of Cappy Ricks*
1942   *Calaboose*
1943   *I Escaped from the Gestapo; Danger! Women at Work*
1945   *I Was a Criminal*
1946   *Dragnet*

Brockwell, Gladys (1894 Brooklyn, NY-1929 Hollywood, CA)

Courtesy of Silents Are Golden at
<SilentsAreGolden.com>

Considered by contemporaries to be one of the most talented character actors of the silent era, Gladys Brockwell began her career on the stage before appearing in several two-reel films for film pioneer Siegmund Lubin in 1913. She freelanced at East Coast studios before graduating to lead roles, often as vamps, with Fox Studios in 1916.

Throughout the 1920s she appeared as characters much older than her actual years in several films that are considered silent era classics such as *Stella Maris* (1925) and *Seventh Heaven* (1927). She was praised for her work in the first all-dialogue feature, *The Lights of New York* (1928), which was almost unanimously panned except for the favorable review she received.

Because of her stage training, she had no difficulty making the transition to sound films. However, peritonitis contracted after an automobile accident ended her life and a promising career.

Film Credits

1913   *The Harmless One; The Evil Eye; The Evil One; The Rattlesnake; His Blind Power*

1914   *The Wrath of the Gods; The Typhoon; The Worth of a Life; A Relic of Old Japan; A Political Feud; The Play's the Thing; One of the Discard; Narcotic Spectre; The Geisha; Divorce; The Ambassador's Envoy*

1915   *A Man and His Mate; On the Night Stage; Up from the Depths; Double Trouble*

1916   *The Price of Power; The Crippled Hand; The End of the Trail; The Fires of Conscience; Sins of Her Parent; The She-Devil; Flames of the Flesh; The Scarlet Road; The Purple Maze; The Woman Who Followed Me*

1917   *One Touch of Sin; The Honor System; Her Temptation; To Honor and Obey; Conscience; A Branded Soul; For Liberty; The Soul of Satan; The Price of Her Soul*

1918   *The Moral Law; The Devil's Wheel; Her One Mistake; The Scarlet Road; The Bird of Prey; Kultur; The Strange Woman*

1919   *The Call of the Soul; The Forbidden Room; Pitfalls of a Big City; The Divorce Trap; The Sneak; Chasing Rainbows; The Broken Commandments; Thieves*

1920   *White Lies; A Sister to Salome; Rose of Nome; The Mother of His Children; Flames of the Flesh; The Devil's Riddle*

1921   *The Sage Hen*

1922   *Oliver Twist; Double Stakes; Paid Back*

1923   *Penrod and Sam; The Darling of New York; The Hunchback of Notre Dame; His Last Race; The Drug Traffic*

1924   *Unmarried Wives; The Foolish Virgin; So Big*

1925   *The Reckless Sex; Chickie; The Necessary Evil; The Splendid Road; Stella Maris; The Ancient Mariner*

1926   *The Skyrocket; The Carnival Girl; The Last Frontier; Her Sacrifice; Spangles; Twinkletoes*

1927   *Long Pants; Seventh Heaven; The Satin Woman; The Country Doctor; Man, Woman, and Sin*

1928   *A Girl in Every Port; Lights of New York; The Home Towners; The Woman Disputed; My Home Town; The Law and the Man; Hollywood Bound*

1929   *Hardboiled Rose; From Headquarters; The Hottentot; The Argyle Case; The Drake Case*

Broken Blossoms *(1919)*

Broken Blossoms is noteworthy on several points. This film was the first film directed by D. W. Griffith for United Artists, the studio that he, Douglas Fairbanks, Mary Pickford, and Charlie Chaplin formed in 1919. It was also his last major film production.

The film is a poignant masterpiece in which a Chinese immigrant befriends and attempts to protect a young girl from her abusive father. If viewed by today's standards, it is politically incorrect, as are most silent films that deal with racial or social situations. If viewed as a historical document of its time, the story is touching yet deeply sad.

It starred Richard Barthelmess as the immigrant called only "Yellow Man" on the title cards and Lillian Gish as the young girl. After a particularly violent beating by her father, the young girl runs away and is found by the Yellow Man, who has fallen in love with the girl from afar. He takes her to his room and nurses her back to health.

Her father hears that his daughter is living with a Yellow Man and "rescues" her, only to beat her to death in a drunken rage. The Yellow Man arrives too late to save her but kills her father. He then takes the girl's body back to his room where, sitting next to the object of his doomed love, he kills himself.

First called a "masterpiece" in a contemporary review in *The New York Times*, the film was both a commercial and critical success.

Bronson, Betty (1906 Trenton, NJ-1971 Pasadena, CA)

Courtesy of Silents Are Golden at <SilentsAreGolden.com>

Betty Bronson's career lasted only a few years, but while she was popular she was incredibly influential on the film audience. Her film career began when she was still in high school, as she and friends traveled to New Jersey to get jobs as extras on weekends.

While appearing as an extra, Bronson was chosen to star as Peter Pan in the 1924 version of J. M. Barrie's classic story, beating out several Hollywood stars, including Gloria Swanson and Mary Pickford. After the release of the film, the American public was struck with "Bronson-mania" and could not get enough of their new sweetheart.

Her studio attempted to capitalize on her popularity by releasing another fantasy film, *A Kiss for Cinderella* (1925). However, in the time it had taken to get the film ready for release, the tastes of the viewing audience had changed, making sentimental fantasy passé.

The new rage was flappers, and Bronson tried to fit into that mold with moderate success but never attained the degree of success of her first film. Her real talent was as a pantomimist, which, although necessary for silent films, was superfluous when the new medium of sound came to films.

She retired from films when she married in 1932 and later appeared only rarely in supporting roles.

Film Credits

1922   *Anna Ascends*

1923   *Go-Getter; The Eternal City; Java Head; His Children's Children; Twenty-One*

1924   *Peter Pan*

1925   *Not So Long Ago; The Golden Princess; A Kiss for Cinderella; Ben-Hur; Are Parents People?*

1926   *The Cat's Pajamas; Paradise; Everybody's Acting*

1927   *Paradise for Two; Ritzy; Open Range; Brass Knuckles*

1928   *The Singing Fool; Companionate Marriage*

1929   *Bellamy Trial; One Stolen Night; Sonny Boy; The Locked Door; A Modern Sappho*

1930   *The Medicine Man*

1931   *Lover Come Back*

1932   *The Midnight Patrol*

1937   *Yodelin' Kid From Pine Ridge; Jungle Menace*

1961   *Pocketful of Miracles*

1962   *Who's Got the Action*

1964   *The Naked Kiss*

1968   *Blackbeard's Ghost*

1971   *Evel Knievel*

Brooks, Louise (1906 Cherryvale, KS-1985 Rochester, NY)

Courtesy of Silents Are Goldent at
<SilentsAreGolden.com>

Louise Brooks is rarely remembered as the gifted actor she was but merely as *the* flapper of late 1920s films. Her bobbed hair—her "black helmet"—created a new fad in women's hairstyles. Although her film output was not excessive, her effect on popular culture of the period was immense. She is, quite simply, an icon of her time.

Brooks began entertaining people at very early age—she was four when she appeared as Tom Thumb's wife in a church fundraiser. From the age of ten she gave dance recitals throughout Kansas with her mother as chaperone and accompanist.

At fifteen she went to New York to join the avant-garde Denishawn Dance Company, the leading modern dance troupe in the United States at that time. But after a short time she left Denishawn because the director felt she lacked commitment. Soon she was hired to dance in the chorus in the play *Scandals* (1924).

She sailed to Europe and found work at a leading nightclub in London, the Café de Paris. Her act was a hit and she became the first person to dance the Charleston in London. Buoyed by this success, she returned to the United States where she joined the Ziegfeld Follies in 1925 and was christened one of Ziegfeld's "Glorified Girls."

At Ziegfeld's request, Alberto Vargas, a renowned artist of that time, painted her portrait for his office wall. Although known for her beauty, she was also accepted into New York's "smart set" where her friends numbered among the most creative and learned of the city.

Her film debut was in *The Street of Forgotten Men* (1925), and she soon signed a long-term contract with Paramount. She received much critical acclaim for her acting in her next major role in *The American Venus* (1926) then later that year appeared in *A Social Celebrity* in her first flapper role prior to marrying director Eddie Sutherland.

Brooks became so much a symbol of the time that a syndicated comic strip, *Dixie Dugan,* began in 1929 purportedly using events in her life while a chorus girl as the basis of the events in the main character's life. She continued to be popular at the box office and starred in *The Canary Murder Case,* the first film featuring William Powell as Detective Philo Vance.

Two years later she went to Europe to star in director G. W. Pabst's film *Pandora's Box* (1929), after leaving Paramount over a salary issue. In this film, which Brooks thought was her best, she played Lulu, a nymphomaniac who marries an older man only to fall in love with his son and is eventually murdered by Jack the Ripper. It did not fare well with critics or audiences, possibly because of the controversial subject, but she would be forever after compared to the character that she played in this film.

She returned briefly to New York but refused to rejoin Paramount. She once more traveled to Europe where she made two other films—*Diary of a Lost Girl* (1920) and *Beauty Prize* (1930). Upon returning to Hollywood she wasn't offered the types of roles she wanted, so she retired from films.

She married wealthy playboy Deering Doyle in 1933 and formed a dance team with him, but the team and the marriage didn't last. After leaving Doyle, she teamed with Dario Borzani and the team of Dario and Louise toured to excellent reviews for two years.

Brooks returned to Hollywood to open a dance studio, but the enterprise proved to be unsuccessful, so she returned to Kansas and opened another studio in Wichita. She also wrote a booklet, *The Fundamentals of Good Ballroom Dancing.*

She returned to New York in 1943 where she did a variety of jobs—from appearing on radio shows to working at Saks Fifth Avenue as a sales clerk. Five years later she began her autobiography, *Naked on My Goat,* but destroyed it before it was published.

In 1956 she moved to Rochester, New York, where she studied film—seeing her own for the first time—and began a writing career. Her works appeared in many film journals, and a collection of her essays was published in *Lulu in Hollywood* (1983).

Although little remembered in the United States, the films Brooks made in Europe remain popular in revivals. She made several trips to Europe to introduce her works to later generations of viewers, but as her health failed, she became more reclusive.

Film Credits

1925   *The Street of Forgotten Men*
1926   *The American Venus; A Social Celebrity; It's the Old Army Game; The Show Off; Love 'Em and Leave 'Em; Just Another Blonde*
1927   *Ten Years Only; Evening Clothes; Rolled Stockings; Now We're in the Air; The City Gone Wild*
1928   *A Girl in Every Port; Beggars of Life*
1929   *Pandora's Box; The Canary Murder Case; Diary of a Lost Girl*
1930   *Prix de Beaute (The Beauty Prize)*
1931   *It Pays to Advertise; God's Gift to Women; Windy Riley Goes Hollywood*
1936   *Empty Saddles*
1937   *When You're in Love; King of Gamblers*
1938   *Overland Stage Raiders*

Bruce, Kate (1858 undisclosed-1946 New York City)

Kate Bruce began her career as an actor with a traveling troupe of players that performed throughout the eastern United States. She appeared in her first movie, *The Greaser's Gauntlet,* in 1908, at the age of fifty. The following year she appeared in thirty-eight films—an output that was not unusual during the period of simplicity in film production.

She joined D. W. Griffith's stock company at American Biograph and became his preferred maternal character actor. She appeared in almost very Griffith film until 1924. Although she made 158 films, she made only one talkie, *The Struggle* (1931), which was also her last film.

Film Credits

1908   *The Greaser's Gauntlet; Betrayed by a Handprint; Behind the Scenes; An Awful Moment; The Fight for Freedom*
1909   *One Touch of Nature; The Girls and Daddy; The Golden Louis; At the Altar; Trying to Get Arrested; Confidence; A Baby's Shoe; His Duty; The Way of Man; The Country Doctor; The Cardinal's Conspiracy; The Slave; A Strange Meeting;*

They Would Elope; The Better Way; The Hessian Renegades; The Broken Locket; In Old Kentucky; A Fair Exchange; A Child Wanted; The Awakening; The Little Teacher; A Change of Heart; His Love Lost; Lines of White on a Sullen Sea; What's Your Hurry?; The Light That Came; Two Women and a Man; A Midnight Adventure; The Open Gate; The Mountaineer's Honor; In the Watches of the Night; In the Window Recess; Through the Breakers; A Corner in Wheat; In a Hempen Bag; To Save Her Soul; Choosing a Husband; The Gibson Goddess; The Restoration; The Trick That Failed; The Red Man's View; A Trap for Santa Claus; In Little Italy

1910   *The Rocky Road; All on Account of the Milk; The Cloister's Touch; The Woman from Mellon's; One Night and Then; The Englishman and the Girl; His Last Burglary; The Newlyweds; The Converts; The Twisted Trail; Gold Is Not All; As It Is in Life; A Romance of the Western Hills; The Two Brothers; Ramona; A Knot in the Plot; The Impalement; A Child of the Ghetto; May and December; What the Daisy Said; An Arcadian Maid; Her Father's Pride; The Usurer; Willful Peggy; The Modern Prodigal; Muggsy Becomes a Hero; Examination Day at School; The Iconoclast; A Gold Necklace; The Broken Doll; Two Little Waifs; Waiter No. 5; The Fugitive; Simple Charity; A Plain Song; His Sister-in-Law; The Masher; The Call; The Honor of His Family; The Duke's Plan; The Faithful; The Gold Seekers; The Unchanging Sea; Love Among the Roses; The Affair of an Egg; How Hubby Got a Raise; That Chink at Golden Gulch; A Lucky Tooth Ache; The Message of the Violin; The Song of the Wildwood Flute; Effecting a Cure; Happy Jack; a Hero; White Roses; His Wife's Sweethearts*

1911   *His Trust; His Trust Fulfilled; The Poor Sick Men; A Wreath of Orange Blossoms; What Shall We Do with Our Old?; His Mother's Scarf; How She Triumphed; Fighting Blood; The Baron; The Squaw's Love; Her Awakening; The Midnight Marauder; The Italian Barber; Help Wanted; Three Sisters; Heart Beats of Long Ago; Teaching Dad to Like Her; The Spanish Gypsy; Priscilla and the Umbrella; Paradise Lost; A Night of the Road; The Two Sides; In the Days of '49; The New Dress; The Manicure Lady; The Crooked Road;*

A Country Cupid; The Last Drop of Water; The Ruling Passion; The Rose of Kentucky; Swords and Hearts; The Adventures of Billy; The Long Road; The Battle; Through Darkened Vales; A Terrible Discovery; The Voice of the Child

1912 *The Eternal Mother; The Sunbeam; The Engagement Ring; Hot Stuff; The Punishment; Just Like a Woman; The Brave Hunter; One Is Business, the Other Crime; Fickle Spaniard; The Old Actor; The Furs; When Kings Were the Law; Home Folks; Lena and the Geese; The Spirit Awakened; A Dash Through the Clouds; The School Teacher and the Waif; An Indian Summer; Tragedy of the Dress Suit; A Feud in the Kentucky Hills; The One She Loved; The Painted Lady; The Informer; My Hero; Won by a Fish; His Own Fault; The Baby and the Stork; With a Kodak; The Transformation of Mike; A String of Pearls; Iola's Promise; The Leading Man; When the Fire Bells Rang; A Close Call; The Would Be Shriner; A Child's Remorse; Heredity; The New York Hat; A Cry for Help*

1913 *The Telephone Girl and the Lady; The Tender Hearted Boy; Drink's Lure; A Girl's Stratagem; The Sheriff's Baby; The Little Tease; A Misunderstood Boy; The Yaqui Cur; Just Gold; Death's Marathon; The Mothering Heart; For the Son of the House; The Perfidy of Mary; An 'Uncle Tom's Cabin Troupe; A Frightful Blunder; The Wanderer; A Stolen Loaf; The House of Darkness; Olaf, an Atom; The Reformers; The Enemy's Baby; The Work Habit; The Strong Man's Burden; The Stopped Clock*

1914 *Judith of Bethulia; The Battle of Elderbush Gulch; A Nest Unfeathered; A Mother's Way; The Mystery of the Milk*

1915 *After the Storm; A Mystery of the Mountains; East Lynne; When Hearts Are Young*

1916 *Betty of Greystone; Susan Rocks the Boat; Civilization; The Marriage of Molly-O; Gretchen the Greenhorn; Intolerance; The Microscope Mystery; The House Built Upon Sand*

1917 *Betsy's Burglar; A Woman's Awakening; Souls Triumphant; Madame Bo-Peep; Time Locks and Diamonds; The Stainless Barrier*

1918   *Hearts of the World; The Hun Within; The Greatest Thing in Life*

1919   *A Romance of Happy Valley; The Girl Who Stayed at Home; True Heart Susie; The Fall of Babylon; The Mother and the Law; Scarlet Days*

1920   *Mary Ellen Comes to Town; The Idol Dancer; Way Down East; Flying Pat*

1921   *The City of Silent Men; Experience; Orphans of the Storm*

1923   *The White Rose*

1924   *His Darker Self*

1925   *I Want My Man*

1927   *Secret Studio; Ragtime; A Bowery Cinderella*

1929   *The Flying Fool*

1931   *The Struggle*

Buffington, Adele (1900 St. Louis, MO–1973 Woodland Hills, CA)

Adele Buffington spent three years as a cashier at a movie theater studying films and characters before writing her first script, *La Petite* (1919), which she immediately sold to an independent studio. Later in 1919, she went to work for Thomas Ince as an assistant before once more writing on her own.

She wrote many westerns, even though the popular thought of the day held that women could not write westerns. However, she wrote westerns for some of the most popular silent era cowboys, including Tom Mix, Buck Jones, and Tim McCoy.

She continued working in the sound era, sometimes writing under a male pseudonym. In fact, it was as "Jess Bowers" that she wrote the first of the popular "Rough Rider" series, *Arizona Bound* (1941). Sadly, most of her sound work was done under a male name, perhaps as a result of women being pushed out of behind the scenes work, as films became a big business that men wanted to control.

She was a founding member of the Screen Writers Guild. Although by her death in 1973 she was credited with having written more than 150 films, much of the information about her career has been lost.

Writing Credits

1919 *La Petite; Apache*
1924 *Empty Hearts*
1925 *The Bloodhound; The Lawful Cheater; Love on the Rio Grande; The Fighting Cub; That Man Jack!*
1926 *The Cowboy and the Countess; The Test of Donald Norton; The Galloping Cowboy*
1927 *Blood Will Tell; Eager Lips; Broadway After Midnight*
1928 *Coney Island; Bare Knees; Queen of the Chorus; The Chorus Kid; Devil Dogs; Midnight Life; The Avenging Rider; The River Woman; The Phantom City; Man Higher Up; The Broken Mask*
1929 *Times Square*
1930 *The Swellhead; Extravagance; Just Like Heaven*
1931 *Aloha; Freighters of Destiny; Forgotten Women; Arizona Territory;*
1932 *Single-Handed Sanders; High Speed; A Man's Land; Ghost Valley; Haunted Gold*
1933 *West of Singapore; The Iron Master; The Eleventh Commandment*
1934 *Marrying Widows; The Moonstone; When Strangers Meet; The Hell Cat; Cheaters; Picture Brides; Beggar's Holiday*
1935 *Keeper of the Bees; Powdersmoke Range; His Gaucho*
1936 *Any Man's Wife*
1937 *The Sheik Steps Out; Michael O'Halloran; The Duke Comes Back; Circus Girl; Prison Nurse*
1938 *Tenth Avenue Kid*
1941 *Arizona Bound; The Gunman from Bodie; Forbidden Trails*
1942 *Below the Border; Ghost Town Law; Down Texas Way; Riders of the West; West of the Law; Dawn on the Great Divide*
1943 *The Ghost Rider; Outlaws of Stampede Pass; The Texas Kid; The Stranger from Pecos; Six-Gun Gospel*
1944 *Raiders of the Border*
1945 *The Navajo Trail; Flame of the West; The Lost Trail; Frontier Feud; Stranger from Santa Fe*
1946 *Drifting Along; Wild Beauty; Bad Men of the Border; Shadows of the Range*

1948   *Overland Trails; Crossed Trails; The Valiant Hombre*
1949   *Crashing Thru; Haunted Trails; Riders of the Dusk; Western Renegades; West of El Dorado; Streets of San Francisco; Shadows of the West; Range Land*
1950   *West of Wyoming; Gunslingers; Jiggs and Maggie Out West; Arizona Territory; Six Gun Mesa*
1951   *Overland Telegraph*
1953   *Cow Country; Born to the Saddle*
1958   *Bullwhip*

Burke, Billie (1885 Washington, DC-1970 Los Angeles, CA)

Given the birth name Mary William Ethelbert Appleton Burke, it seemed ordained that Billie Burke would not be an ordinary girl. Show business seemed a natural outlet since her father was an internationally known clown with Barnum and Bailey Circus. As a child she traveled with her father throughout the United States and Europe prior to the family settling in London.

She made her stage debut in a British musical in 1903 and became a hit with London audiences. She returned to the United States in 1907 to star opposite John Drew in *My Wife* on Broadway, and the play was a huge success. She continued to appear in hit Broadway plays, many by Charles Frohman, as well as take productions on the road throughout the country.

Her stage successes as well as her marriage to Florenz Ziegfeld in 1914 brought her to the attention of the film community, and she made her lead debut in *Peggy* (1916). A few months later she appeared in *Gloria's Romance* and continued working, appearing in both films and Broadway productions, until 1921 when she retired after starring in the film *The Education of Elizabeth.*

The Depression necessitated her coming out of retirement and re-entering the world of film, which now revolved around talkies. Ziegfeld became ill and was unable to work so, although they were estranged, Burke moved him to Hollywood where she was getting back into films. He died there in 1932.

Her stock character was a ditzy woman who had little common sense or imagination. She appeared in several popular films from the period including *A Bill of Divorcement* (1932) and *Dinner at Eight* (1933). In 1937 she starred in the first of three *Topper* films as the befuddled Mrs. Topper whose husband is haunted by three ghosts—a couple killed in a car accident and their alcoholic St. Bernard. The next year she received an Oscar nomination for her work in *Merrily We Live*.

Her defining role—or at least the one that she would be remembered for by generations of children—was that of Glinda the Good Witch of the North in *The Wizard of Oz* (1939). Although not popular with contemporary audiences, the film became a children's television classic.

She continued to appear in films throughout the 1940s, but as she grew older she found parts more difficult to find. She wrote her autobiography, titled *With a Feather on My Nose* (1949). Her final film appearance was in *Sergeant Rutledge* (1960), after which she permanently retired.

Film Credits

1914   *Our Mutual Girl*
1916   *Peggy; Gloria's Romance*
1917   *Arms and the Girl; The Land of Promise; The Mysterious Miss Terry*
1918   *Eve's Daughter; Let's Get a Divorce; In Pursuit of Polly; The Make-Believe Wife*
1919   *Good Gracious, Annabelle; The Misleading Widow; Sadie Love; Wanted: A Husband*
1920   *The Frisky Mrs. Johnson; Away Goes Prudence*
1921   *The Education of Elizabeth*
1929   *Glorifying the American Girl*
1932   *A Bill of Divorcement*
1933   *Dinner at Eight; Only Yesterday; Christopher Strong*
1934   *Where Sinners Meet; We're Rich Again; Forsaking All Others; Finishing School Society Doctor; After Office Hours; Becky Sharp; Splendor; She Couldn't Take It; A Feather in Her Hat; Doubting Thomas*
1936   *Piccadilly Jim; Craig's Wife; My American Wife*
1937   *Parnell; The Bride Wore Red; Navy Blue and Gold; Topper*
1938   *Merrily We Live; Everybody Sing; The Young At Heart*

1939   *The Wizard of Oz; Topper Takes a Trip; Zenobia; Bridal Suite; Eternally Yours; Remember?*

1940   *And One Was Beautiful; Irene; The Captain Is a Lady; Hullabaloo; The Ghost Comes Home; Dulcy*

1941   *Topper Returns; The Wild Man of Borneo; One Night in Lisbon*

1942   *In This Our Life; They All Kissed the Bride; Girl Trouble; What's Cookin'?; The Man Who Came for Dinner*

1943   *Hi Diddle Diddle; You're a Lucky Fellow, Mr. Smith; So's Your Uncle; Gildersleeve on Broadway*

1944   *The Laramie Trail*

1945   *The Cheaters; Swing Out Sister*

1946   *Breakfast in Hollywood; The Bachelor's Daughters*

1948   *Silly Billy; Billie Gets Her Man*

1949   *The Barkleys of Broadway; And Baby Makes Three*

1950   *Father of the Bride; The Boy from Indiana*

1951   *Father's Little Dividend; Three Husbands*

1953   *Small Town Girl*

1959   *The Young Philadelphians*

1960   *Sergeant Rutledge; Pepe*

C

Caprice, June (1899 Arlington, MA-1936 Los Angeles, CA)

Fox Studios predicted that by the end of 1916 June Caprice "would be the best known woman of the screen." Caprice was the epitome of the World War I heroine—youthful, beautiful and virginal. Unfortunately few ingenues could maintain a career as they aged since they became famous for their look of dewy innocence. Furthermore, after the war the audience was no longer interested in Victorian innocence but turned to the worldliness of the Jazz Age flapper.

Caprice was educated in Boston and entered films when she won a Mary Pickford look-alike contest held at a Boston theater. She soon moved to New York where Fox Studios quickly put her under contract. Her film debut was *Caprice of the Mountains* (1916) and she adopted her character's name as her own last name.

Her popularity skyrocketed, and soon she was a favorite topic in fan magazines. She was one of Fox's most profitable stars during the last years of the 1910s, but as she grew older her popularity waned. By 1921 she had retired from films after having married her director, Harry Millarde. She became a Hollywood hostess and mother until her untimely death after a lengthy illness.

Film Credits

1916	*Caprice of the Mountains; Little Miss Happiness; The Ragged Princess; The Mischief Maker*
1917	*A Modern Cinderella; A Child of the Wild; The Small Town Girl; Patsy; Every Girl's Dream; Unknown 274; The Sunshine Maid; Miss U.S.A.*
1918	*The Heart of Romance; A Camouflage Kiss; Blue-Eyed Mary; Miss Innocence*
1919	*The Love Cheat; A Damsel in Distress; Oh Boy!*
1920	*In Walked Mary; Rogues and Romance*
1921	*The Sky Ranger*

Carmen, Jewell (1897 Danville, KY-1984 San Diego, CA)

Courtesy of Silents Are Golden at <SilentsAreGolden.com>

A popular star from 1916 to 1921, the facts of Jewell Carmen's early life were always unclear. Articles in contemporary fan magazines habitually contained contradictions such as where she was born and where she went to school.

She began her film career as an extra at the Keystone Company in 1913 under the name Evelyn Quick. She soon moved up to being a stock player after successfully appearing in *A Life in Balance* (1913) and then *The Professor's Daughter* (1913). But just as quickly she left Keystone under a cloud of gossip and innuendo and for the next two years appeared as an uncredited extra.

In 1916 she appeared as an extra in Griffith's *Intolerance* and in the Lillian Gish vehicle *Daphne and the Pirate*. About this time she changed her name to Jewell Carmen and moved to the Triangle-Fine Arts Studio where they promoted her as the studio's leading starlet. It was also in 1916 that she starred with Douglas Fairbanks in four of his films—*The Half-Breed, Flirting with Fate, Manhattan Madness*, and *American Aristocracy*.

After appearing in his films, she again changed studios and continued her career as a leading lady. When she married filmmaker Roland West in 1918, she retired from acting except for an occasional part in one of her husband's films.

In 1935 she was once more in the headlines when her husband was implicated in Thelma Todd's death. The tragedy ended her marriage, and after selling her house, she left Hollywood to live quietly in the San Diego area.

Film Credits

1913	*The Professor's Daughter; Professional Jealousy; He and Himself; Four Queens and a Jack; A Life in Balance*
1916	*Daphne and the Pirate; Sunshine Dad; The Children in the House; The Half-Breed; Flirting with Fate; Manhattan Madness; American Aristocracy; Intolerance*
1917	*A Tale of Two Cities; American Methods; The Conqueror; Les Miserables; When a Man Sees Red; To Honor and Obey; The Kingdom of Love*
1918	*The Girl with the Champagne Eyes; The Bride of Fear; Confession; Fallen Angel; Lawless Love*
1921	*The Silver Lining; Nobody*
1926	*The Bat*

Carol, Sue (1906 Chicago, IL-1982 Los Angeles, CA)

Sue Carol entered the film industry in 1927 at 20 years old. Supposedly signed as the "new" Clara Bow to keep Bow "towing the line" at the studio, Carol portrayed the same type of character—flappers who were really old-fashioned girls at heart, or college girls looking for fun as well as an education. She was reportedly the inspiration for the 1920s song "Sweet Sue."

Chosen as a WAMPAS Baby Star in 1928, Carol was a talented actor as well as popular with directors. After her selection as a Baby Star, her roles became more substantial, but she never achieved stardom or appeared in any groundbreaking films. She made the transition to sound films, but by the 1930s the flapper parts she excelled at were no longer popular.

She remained in films until the late 1930s, when she left to become a talent agent. Her most important client was her third husband, Alan Ladd. After Ladd's death she briefly worked as a producer with his old studio, Paramount.

Film Credits

1927   *Slaves of Beauty; Soft Cushions*
1928   *Skyscraper; Walking Back; Beau Broadway; Win That Girl; The Air Circus; Captain Swagger; The Cohens and the Kellys in Paris*
1929   *It Can Be Done; Girls Gone Wild; Fox Movietone Follies of 1929; Chasing Through Europe; The Exalted Flapper; Why Leave Home?*
1930   *The Lone Star Ranger; The Golden Calf; Dancing Sweeties; She's My Weakness; Check and Double Check; The Big Party*
1931   *Graft; In Line of Duty*
1933   *Secret Sinners; Straightaway*
1937   *A Doctor's Diary*

Carr, Mary (1874 Germantown, PA-1973 Woodland Hills, CA)

Born Mary Kennean near Philadelphia, Mary Carr worked as a teacher before joining a touring company. Soon she married William Carr, a fellow actor, and appeared with his troupe while raising six children.

When her husband began directing films, she made her film debut in *The City of Failing Light* (1916). Her portrayal of the mother beaten down by poverty in *Over the Hill to the Poorhouse* (1920) brought her to the viewing audience's enthusiastic attention and typecast her in mother roles.

Although she appeared in many films in the 1920s, the advent of sound virtually ended her career. She appeared sporadically in films, generally in supporting roles in films directed by her son Thomas Carr, until her death.

Film Credits

1916   *The City of Failing Light; Souls in Bondage; Her Bleeding Heart; The Flames of Johannis; Love's Toll; The Light at Dusk*

1917   *The Barrier*

1918   *My Own United States; The Birth of a Race; To the Highest Bidder; The Beloved Rogue; The Sign Invisible*

1919   *Mrs. Wiggs of the Cabbage Patch; The Lion and the Mouse; Calibre 38; The Spark Divine*

1920   *Over the Hill to the Poorhouse*

1921   *Thunderclap*

1922   *Silver Wings*

1923   *Custard Cup; The Daring Years; Broadway Broke; Three O'Clock in the Morning; You Are Guilty; On the Banks of the Wabash; Loyal Lives*

1924   *Roulette; Damaged Hearts; Why Men Leave Home; The Spirit of the USA; For Sale; A Self-Made Failure; The Mine with the Iron Door; Three Women; East of Broadway; On the Stroke of Three; Painted People; The Woman on the Jury*

1925   *Easy Money; Capital Punishment; The Parasite; The Night Ship; The Re-Creation of Brian Kent; Go Straight; Drusilla with a Million; Wizard of Oz; The Fighting Club; A Slave of Fashion; The Red Kimono; Hogan's Alley; Flaming Waters; His Master's Voice; The Gold Hunters; Big Pal; School for Wives*

1926   *Stop; Look and Listen; The King of the Turf; The Night Watch; The Night Patrol; Somebody's Mother; Fourth Commandment; The Wise Guy; Frenzied Flames; The Midnight Message; The False Alarm; Dame Chance; Atta Boy; Whom Shall I Marry; Pleasures of the Rich; The Hidden Way; Her Own Story*

1927   *Blonde or Brunette; God's Great Wilderness; Paying the Price; Special Delivery; The Swell-Head; Better Days; Jesse James; On Your Toes; The Show Girl; False Morals*

1928   *A Million for Love; Lights of New York; Love Over Night; Dame Care*

1929   *Some Mother's Boy; Sailor's Holiday*

1930   *Second Wife; Ladies in Love; Hot Curves; The Utah Kid; Just Imagine; Trailing Trouble; Midnight Special*

1931   *Kept Husbands; One Good Turn; The Fighting Marshal; Law of the Tong; Primrose Path; Honeymoon Lane; Beyond Victory*

1932   *The Fighting Fool; Pack Up Your Troubles; Forbidden Trail; Stout Hearts and Willing Hands; Running Hollywood; Young Blood*

1933   *Gun Law; The Power and the Glory; Police Call; The Moonshiner's Daughter; Bombshell; Flying Devils*

1934   *The Loudspeaker; Whom the Gods 'Destroy; Love Past Thirty; Change of Heart; The World Accuses*

1935   *Silk Hat Kid; I Don't Remember; The Fighting Lady; Go into Your Dance*

1936   *The Country Doctor; Gentle Hulia; The Sea Fiend*

1937   *Rich Relations; Music for Madame*

1938   *West of Rainbow's End*

1939   *East Side of Heaven*

1940   *The Shop Around the Corner; Manhattan Heartbeat*

1941   *Model Wife*

1942   *Eagle Squadron*

1945   *Oregon Trail*

1946   *Devil Monster*

1956   *Friendly Persuasion*

Cassinelli, Delores (1888 Chicago, IL–1984 New Brunswick, NJ)

Like many early film stars, Delores Cassinelli's real life is difficult to ascertain amid the publicity churned out by the studios. Publicized by the studios as having been born in Italy, the "land of sunshine and flowers," her death certificate cited her birthplace as the less-picturesque Chicago.

After becoming interested in drama, she left the convent that she had entered as a novice and embarked on a show business career. Her first documented film connection was when she joined Essanay Studios in 1911 and appeared in the one-reel comedy *Bill Bumper's Bargain* with Francis X. Bushman.

She remained with Essanay for several years before moving to the Emerald Company and becoming known as the "Cameo Girl." Unfortunately, since her best work was with smaller independent production companies, she never attained the stardom that many historians believe that her talent deserved.

In the early 1920s she was being offered only supporting roles and by the mid-1920s she decided to retire. She moved to New York and disappeared into obscurity.

Film Credits

1911   *Bill Bumper's Bargain; Two Men and a Girl*
1912   *Napatia, the Greek Singer; The Laurel Wreath of Fame; Billy and the Butler; The Virtue of Rags; Giuseppe's Good Fortune; From the Submerged; Billy McGrath's Love Letters; The Lemon; Our Neighbor's Wife; Out of the Night; The Old Wedding Dress; The Tale of the Cat; The Adamless Eden; A Corner in Whiskers; Her Adopted Father; Well Matched; The Redemption of Slivers; Miss Simkin's Summer Boarder; The Fisherman's Luck; House of Pride; Mr. Up's Trip Tripped Up; Billy McGrath's Art Career; Mr. Hubby's Wife; A Little Louder Please; Do Dreams Come True?*
1913   *When Soul Meets Soul; The Broken Heart; The Girl at the Brook; Love and Lavallieres; Don't Lie to Your Husband; The Girl in the Case; The Misjudging of Mr. Hubby; The Price of Gold; A Wolf Among Lambs; The Capture; The Unknown; Cinderella Gloves; The Divided House*
1918   *The Million Dollar Dollies; Lafayette, We Come; Zongar; Lest We Forget*
1919   *Unknown Love; The Virtuous Model; The Right to Lie*
1920   *The Web of Deceit; Tarnished Reputations*
1921   *Forever; Anne of Little Smoky; The Hidden Light*
1922   *Secrets of Paris; The Challenge; Do Dreams Come True?*
1923   *Columbus; Jamestown*
1924   *Lend Me Your Husband; Dangerous Money*
1925   *The Midnight Girl; The Unguarded Hour*

Castle, Irene (1893 New Rochelle, NY-1969 Eureka Springs, AR)

Irene Castle and her husband, Vernon, were the most famous exhibition dancers of the early 1900s. Born Irene Foote, she was the daughter of a successful New Rochelle doctor, but the show business bug bit her after she fell in love with vaudeville performer Vernon Castle.

After their marriage they traveled to Paris where they became a popular dancing act. They became worldwide celebrities. Castle's hairstyles were copied into wigs and she had her own signature line of cosmetics. Returning to the United States, they opened their first dancing studio in 1914 and operated several other clubs and studios in the New York area. In addition, they wrote an instructional dance book, *Modern Dancing* (1914).

In the mid-1910s they joined the vaudeville circuit and gave dancing exhibitions throughout the United States and Canada. At one point they were said to have charged $1,000 per hour for dancing lessons. Both she and her husband appeared on Broadway in Irving Berlin's musical *Watch Your Step* and in a film on their lives, *The Whirl of Life* (1915).

During World War I Vernon Castle was a flight instructor, and he died in a crash shortly before the end of the war. Thereafter, Irene Castle continued to appear in both musicals and dramatic films. In 1939 she acted as writer, costume designer, and technical advisor on the film *The Story of Vernon and Irene Castle* which starred Ginger Rogers and Fred Astaire, the last RKO film made by the reigning dance team of films. The film was based on her autobiographical book *My Husband* (1919). Later she wrote *Castles in the Air* (1958) which further documented her life.

Film Credits

1915 *The Whirl of Life*
1917 *Stranded in Arcady; Vengeance Is Mine; Patria; Sylvia of the Secret Service; The Mark of Cain*
1918 *Convict 993; The Hillcrest Mystery; The Mysterious Client; The First Law; The Girl from Bohemia*
1919 *The Firing Line; The Invisible Bond*
1921 *The Broadway Bride*
1922 *French Heels; No Trespassing; Slim Shoulders*
1924 *Broadway After Dark*

Celebrity

The term *celebrity* was first used in reference to a person when Emerson spoke of "celebrities of wealth and fashion" in 1848, but the manifestation of "celebrity" didn't become widespread until the advent of the movie star.

Once their studios publicized individual actors, the age of the celebrity began in earnest. In fact, between 1901 and 1914 articles about people that appeared in *Saturday Evening Post* and *Collier's* were generally about politicians, businesspeople, or other professionals. After 1922, however, more than 50 percent of the articles featuring individuals focused on people from the entertainment industry.

A celebrity is known for his or her image. That image, in turn, is created by publicity departments and nurtured by the media. Once that image is properly "packaged," it is sold to the public.

Clair, Ethlyne (1904 Talladego, AL-1996 Los Angeles, CA)

After winning a beauty contest in Atlanta, Georgia, Ethlyne Clair attended the National Academy of Fine and Applied Arts in Washington, DC. While still a student she went to visit her brother in New York and was introduced to an agent who secured her a contract with Walter Kane Productions.

While attending a social function at the Astor Hotel, Clair met Julius Stern who offered her a contract with his studio to appear in a new comedy series in development. The series would follow the lives and marital tribulations of young newlyweds. During 1927 she appeared in twenty-seven "Newlywed" comedies and nine "Snookums" comedies.

Before her contract ended she appeared in her first serial, *The Vanishing Rider* (1928) which ran for ten episodes. When her contract ended she went to Pathe and appeared in *Queen of the Northwoods*

(1929). Unfortunately, she entered serials after their heyday, when most studios were abandoning that genre.

Although she was named as a WAMPAS Baby Star in 1929, her career did not last beyond 1931. She retired when she married makeup artist Ernie Westmore; they had a daughter before the marriage ended in divorce. Later she enjoyed a lasting second marriage.

Film Credits

1924   *Sandra*
1925   *Chickie*
1926   *Be My Wife; Early to Wed; Dancing Fools; All for Uncle; There's a Will; No Blondes Allowed; What a Party!;* Four *"Snookums"* films
1927   *The Hero on Horseback; Three Miles Up; Painted Ponies; George Runs Wild;* twenty-seven *"Newlywed"* films; nine *"Snookums"* films
1928   *Riding for Fame; Guardians of the Wild; Taking the Count; Vanishing Rider* (ten episodes); *Broke Out; Cash Customers; Hey Rube!*
1929   *Wild Blood; Gun Law; From Headquarters; The Pride of Pawnee; The Show of Shows; Queen of the Northwoods; This Way Please; Just the Type*
1930   *Second Choice*
1931   *God's Gift to Women*

Clark, Marguerite (1883 Avondale, OH-1940 New York City)

Marguerite Clark, who became one of the most popular and highest paid actors of the early 1910s, was born on a farm in rural Ohio and educated in convent schools. Her mother died when she was ten, followed four years later by her father. She left school at sixteen and made her stage debut in Baltimore, Maryland, as a member of the Skra Kosch Opera Company before going to New York.

Her first Broadway job was as an understudy in *The Belle of Bohe-*

mia, but by 1910 she was starring in some of the most popular plays on Broadway. While appearing on Broadway, Sarah Bernhardt attended one of her performances and praised the younger woman for her talent and delivery.

Her success on the stage brought her to the attention of a talent agent from the Famous Players Company; she signed a contract and prepared to move to California. Her film debut was *Wildflowers* (1914) with Jack Pickford, Mary Pickford's younger brother. In fact, although both she and Mary Pickford worked for the same studio at the same time, she was a supposed rival of "America's Sweetheart" for the hearts of audiences. Her popularity was second only to Pickford in much the same type of roles—waifs and child-women characters. She was able to continue these roles until she was in her late thirties because of her diminutive size and doll-like face.

Her most memorable films dealt with fairy or folk tales such as *The Goose Girl* (1915), *Snow White* (1916), and *The Seven Swans* (1917). In a rare show of loyalty in an era when actors jumped from one studio to another, she stayed with Famous Players for her entire acting career.

Her performances always ranked high in polls of viewers by fan magazines, and she was voted the most popular actor of 1920 in a Quigley Publications poll. She created her own production company in 1921 and released her first (and only) film, *Scrambled Wives*.

After this film received tepid reviews and little audience interest, she retired from films and moved to her husband's plantation outside of New Orleans. The governor soon appointed her to Louisiana's Motion Picture Censorship Board. In 1925 she was crowned the Queen of the Mardi Gras in recognition of her tireless charitable work, including sending several students to college from her community each year.

After her husband's death in 1936, she returned to New York to live a secluded life until her death.

Film Credits

1914   *Wildflower; The Crucible*
1915   *The Goose Girl; Gretna Green; The Pretty Sister of Jose; The Seven Sisters; Helene of the North; Still Waters; The Prince and the Pauper*

1916   *Mice and Men; Out of the Drifts; Molly Make-Believe; Silks and Satins; Little Lady Eileen; Miss George Washington; Snow White*
1917   *The Fortunes of Fifi; The Valentine Girl; The Amazons; Bab's Diary; Bab's Burglar; Bab's Matinee Idol; The Seven Swans*
1918   *Rich Man; Poor Man; Prunella; Out of a Clear Sky; Little Miss Hoover; Uncle Tom's Cabin*
1919   *Mrs. Wiggs of the Cabbage Patch; Let's Elope; Come Out of the Kitchen; Girls; Widow by Proxy; Luck in Pawn; A Girl Named Mary; Three Men and a Girl*
1920   *All of a Sudden Peggy; Uncle Tom's Cabin* (II); *Easy to Get*
1921   *Scrambled Wives*

Clayton, Ethel (1882 Champaign, IL-1966 Oxnard, CA)

Like many young women of the period, Ethel Clayton was convent educated before venturing into films. She made her film debut in 1909 in the one-reel comedies for the Essanay studios before going to the Lubin Studios in 1912. Sadly, all documentation for these early films has been lost. While at Lubin she appeared in many films directed by her husband, Joseph Kaufman, before his death in 1919.

She finally signed with Paramount, where her preferred genres were romances and domestic dramas. Her final appearance as the lead character was in *The Call of the Circus* (1930), but she continued to appear in supporting roles into the 1940s.

Film Credits

1909   *Justified; Gratitude; The Brothers; The Twelfth Juror*
1910   *The Tout's Remembrance*
1912   *For the Love of a Girl; A Romance of the Coast; The Doctor's Debt; The Last Rose of Summer; Just Maine Folk; The Wonderful One-Horse Shay; Home Sweet Home*

1913   *Art and Honor; His Children; Friend John; Heroes One and All; The Faith of One Girl; A Hero Among Men; Price Demanded; The New Gown; When Tony Pawned Louisa; Mary's Temptation; The Burning Rivet; A Deal in Oil; The Doctor's Romance; When the Earth Trembled; His Code of Honor*

1914   *The Daughters of Men; The Gamblers; The Wolf; Mazie Puts One Over; The Lion and the Mouse; The House Next Door; The Fortune Hunter*

1915   *The College Widow; The Sporting Duchess; The Great Divide; Darkness Before Dawn*

1916   *Dollars and the Woman; His Brother's Wife; A Woman's Way; Husband and Wife; The Hidden Scar; Beyond the Wall; The New South*

1917   *The Bondage of Fear; The Web of Desire; Man's Woman; The Stolen Paradise; The Dormant Power; Easy Money; The Volunteer; Yankee Pluck; The Woman Beneath; Souls Adrift*

1918   *Journey's End; The Man Hunt; The Girl Who Came Back; The Mystery Girl; Woman's Weapon; The Witch Woman; The Whims of Society; Stolen Hours; A Soul Without Windows*

1919   *Maggie Pepper; Pettigrew's Girl; The Woman Next Door; Men, Women, and Money; A Sporting Chance; More Deadly Than the Male; Vicky Van*

1920   *The Thirteenth Commandment; A Lady in Love; The Ladder of Lies; Crooked Streets; The City Sparrow; Young Mrs. Winthrop; The Sins of Rosanne*

1921   *The Price of Possession; Sham; Wealth; Beyond; Exit the Vamp*

1922   *The Cradle; For the Defense; If I Were Queen; Her Own Money*

1923   *The Remittance Woman; Can a Woman Love Twice?*

1925   *The Mansion of Aching Hearts; Wings of Youth; Lightnin'*

1926   *Bar-C Mystery; Sunny Side Up; Risky Business; His New York Wife*

1927   *The Princess from Hoboken; The Princess of Broadway*

1928   *Mother Machree*

1930   *The Call of the Circus; Hit the Deck*

1932   *The Crooked Circle; The All-American; Thrill of Youth; Hotel Continental*

1933 *The Whispering Shadow; Secrets; Private Jones*
1936 *Hollywood Boulevard; Easy to Take*
1937 *Artists and Models; Souls at Sea; Rich Relations; Make Way for Tomorrow; King of Gamblers; Hold 'Em Navy; Exclusive; Easy Living; Bulldog Drummond's Revenge; Blonde Trouble; Partners in Crime; Wells Fargo*
1938 *The Buccaneer; The Big Broadcast of 1938; If I Were King; Artists and Models Abroad; Men with Wings; Cocoanut Grove; Scandal Street; Bulldog Drummond's Peril; You and Me; Sing You Sinners; Ride a Crooked Mile; Tom Sawyer; Detective*
1939 *The Sap Takes a Wrap; Café Society; Ambush; Paris Honeymoon; Boy Trouble; St. Louis Blues; King of Chinatown; I'm from Missouri; Grand Jury Secrets; Geronimo*
1941 *West Point Widow*
1942 *The Major and the Minor; Lucky Jordan*
1943 *Dixie; Lady Bodyguard; True to Life*
1944 *Henry Aldrich's Little Secret*
1947 *The Perils of Pauline*

Clifford, Ruth (1900 Pawtucket, RI-1998 Woodland Hills, CA)

Ruth Clifford began her career in films in the one- and two-reelers produced at Edison, although these titles do not survive. She eventually moved to Universal in 1917 and became a star after appearing in *A Kentucky Cinderella* (1917).

She remained a popular star throughout the silent era, but the advent of sound found her in supporting roles. She later appeared in small parts in several of John Ford's 1950 films as well as on various early television programs.

Film Credits

1916 *Her Wedding Day; A Hero by Proxy; In the Dead of Night; The Penalty of Treason; Behind the Lines; Polly Put the Kettle On; Ashes; Should She Have Told?*
1917 *The Bubble of Love; The Keeper of the Gate; Mary of America; The Melody of Death; A Kentucky Cinderella; Mother o' Mine; The Mysterious Mr. Tiller; The Desire of the Moth; The*

Door Between; The Savage; Eternal Love; Polly Put the Kettle On

1918   *Hands Down; The Kaiser, the Beast of Berlin; Hungry Eyes; The Red, Red Heart; The Guilt of Silence; Midnight Madness; The Lure of Luxury; The Cabaret Girl; Fires of Youth*

1919   *The Game's Up; The Millionaire Pirate; The Black Gate*

1920   *The Invisible Ray; The Amazing Woman*

1921   *Tropical Love*

1922   *My Dad*

1923   *The Face on the Bar-Room Floor; The Dangerous Age; Truxton King; Daughters of the Rich; Mothers-in-Law; Hell's Hole; April Showers; Ponjola*

1924   *The Whispered Name; The Dramatic Life of Abraham Lincoln; Butterfly; The Tornado*

1925   *As Man Desires; Her Husband's Secret; The Storm Breaker; The Love Hour; The Phantom of the Opera*

1926   *Brooding Eyes; Lew Tyler's Wives; Typhoon Love*

1927   *The Thrill Seekers; Don Mike*

1929   *The Devil's Apple Tree; The Eternal Woman; The Show of Shows*

1932   *The Sign of the Cross*

1933   *The Constant Woman; Only Yesterday; On Ice; The Hitchhiker; Let's Live Tonight; Stolen Harmony*

1934   *Stand Up and Cheer; Whom the Gods Destroy; Elmer and Elsie; Stand Up and Cheer*

1935   *Ginger; Dante's Inferno; She Married Her Boss; Paddy O'Day; Hold 'Em Yale*

1936   *The Return of Jimmy Valentine; To Mary, with Love; Hollywood Boulevard; The Crime of Dr. Forbes*

1938   *Four Men and a Prayer; Keep Smiling*

1939   *Wife, Husband and Friend*

1940   *The Man Who Wouldn't Talk; Sailor's Lady*

1941   *How Green Was My Valley; Along the Rio Grande; We Go Fast; Mr. Celebrity*

1942   *It Happened in Flatbush; The Postman Didn't Ring*

1943   *Coney Island*

1944   *The Lodger; The Keys to the Kingdom; In the Meantime, Darling*

1945   *The Spider; Leave Her to Heaven*

1947   *Mickey's Delayed Date* (voice)
1948   *Mickey Down Under* (voice); *Cry of the City; 3 Godfathers; Unfaithfully Yours; The Luck of the Irish; Walls of Jericho*
1949   *You're My Everything; Not Wanted; Father Was a Fullback; Everybody Does It; Prejudice; Slattery's Hurricane; Free for All*
1950   *Wagonmaster; Sunset Boulevard*
1952   *Pluto's Party* (voice); *Stars and Stripes Forever; Pluto's Christmas Tree* (voice)
1955   *A Man Called Peter; The Cobweb; Prince of Players*
1956   *The Searchers; Man in the Gray Flannel Suit*
1958   *The Last Hurrah*
1961   *Two Rode Together*
1964   *I'd Rather Be Rich*

Coffee, Lenore J. (1896 San Francisco, CA-1984 Woodland Hills, CA)

Granddaughter of General John Coffee who had been Andrew Jackson's chief of staff during the Battle of New Orleans, Lenore J. Coffee entered the film industry by submitting a screenplay to Garson Studios for which she eventually was paid $100 and received a six-month writing contract. She went on to work steadily for the next thirty-five years, specializing in writing romances and melodramas.

Her first successful film was *The Volga Boatman* (1926). In the 1930s she was known for writing mystery-adventures and "women's pictures," otherwise known as romantic dramas, at Universal. She is one of the few writers who was successful in two very different genres—one that is fast paced and plot driven (mystery), while the other is character driven and focused on relationships (romances).

In 1938 she was nominated for an Academy Award for *Four Daughters,* written while at Warner Brothers. After receiving that nomination she was Warner's reigning expert on women's films. Unfortunately, as the viewing audience's tastes changed, Coffee's career waned; her last writing credit was for *Cash McCall* (1959).

Regarding her career during Hollywood's studio system, Coffee said, "They pick your brains, break your heart, ruin your digestion—and what do you get for it? Nothing but a lousy fortune."

Writing Credits

1919   *The Better Wife*
1920   *The Forbidden Woman; The Fighting Shepherdess; For the Soul of Rafael*
1921   *Hush; Alias Ladyfingers*
1922   *The Right That Failed; The Face Between; Sherlock Brown*
1923   *The Dangerous Age; Temptation; Wandering Daughters; Daytime Wives; Strangers of the Night; Thundering Dawn; The Age of Desire; The Six-Fifty*
1924   *Bread; The Rose of Paris; Fools' Highway*
1925   *The Great Divide; The Swan; Graustark; Hell's Highroad; East Lynne*
1926   *The Volga Boatman; For Alimony Only; The Winning of Barbara Worth*
1927   *The Night of Love; The Love of Sunya; Lonesome Ladies; The Angel of Broadway; Chicago*
1928   *Ned McCobb's Daughter*
1929   *Desert Nights*
1930   *The Bishop Murder Case; Street of Chance; Mothers Cry*
1931   *The Squaw Man; Possessed; Honor of the Family*
1932   *Arsene Lupin; Downstairs; Rasputin and the Empress; Night Court*
1933   *Torch Singer*
1934   *Four Frightened People; Evelyn Prentice; Such Women Are Dangerous; All Men Are Enemies*
1935   *David Copperfield; Vanessa: Her Love Story; Age of Indiscretion*
1936   *Suzy*
1937   *Parnell*
1938   *Four Daughters; White Banners*
1939   *Good Girls Go to Paris; Four Wives; Stronger than Desire*
1940   *My Son, My Son; The Way of All Flesh*
1941   *The Great Lie*
1942   *We Were Dancing; The Gay Sisters*
1943   *Old Aquaintance*

1944   *Till We Meet Again; Marriage Is a Private Affair*
1946   *Tomorrow Is Forever*
1947   *The Guilt of Janet Ames; Escape Me Never*
1949   *Beyond the Forest*
1951   *Lightning Strikes Twice*
1952   *Sudden Fear*
1954   *Young at Heart*
1955   *The End of the Affair; Footsteps in the Fog*
1958   *Another Time; Another Place*
1959   *Cash McCall*

Collier, Constance (1878 Windsor Berks, England-1955 New York City)

Courtesy of Silents Are Golden at <SilentsAreGolden.com>

Constance Collier was an accomplished actor on both the British and American stages before appearing in D. W. Griffith's 1916 classic *Intolerance*. After making several films in both England and the United States, she became an acting coach to such stars as John Barrymore and Colleen Moore.

During the 1920s and 1930s she wrote scenarios and adapted several plays for film. In addition, she appeared in several films for MGM after being chosen by the studio in the hopes that she could fill the void left by Marie Dressler's death. This was, of course, impossible, but Collier claimed her own fans and appeared in films into the 1940s.

Film Credits

1916   *The Code of Marcia Gray; MacBeth; Intolerance; The Tongues of Man*
1919   *The Impossible Woman*
1920   *Bleak House*
1922   *The Bohemian Girl*

1935   *Shadow of Doubt; Anna Karenina; Professional Soldier*
1936   *Little Lord Fauntleroy; Girls' Dormitory*
1937   *Thunder in the City; Wee Willie Winkie; Stage Door; A Damsel in Distress; She Got What She Wanted; Clothes and the Woman*
1939   *Zara*
1940   *Susan and God; Half a Sinner*
1945   *Week-end at the Waldorf; Kitty*
1946   *Monsieur Beaucaire; The Dark Corner*
1947   *The Perils of Pauline; An Ideal Husband*
1948   *Rope; The Girl from Manhattan*
1949   *Whirlpool*

Writing Credits

1921   *Forever*
1925   *The Rat*
1927   *Downhill*
1936   *Peter Ibbetson* (adaptation)

Compson, Betty (1897 Beaver City, UT-1974 Glendale, CA)

Courtesy of Silents Are Golden at
<SilentsAreGolden.com>

Betty Compson began her entertainment career in vaudeville, billed as "The Vagabond Violinist" at the age of fifteen after spending several years playing musical accompaniment for films. Three years later, while playing a show in Los Angeles, she took time to make a screen test before completing the tour.

When the tour ended she was offered a job as a comedian at Christie Studios. However, a disagreement over her responsibility to make personal appearances to promote her films resulted in her being fired in 1918.

She was nearing destitution when she was offered a role in the serial *The Terror of the Range* (1919). Her breakout film was *The Miracle Man*, the 1919 film in which she costarred with Lon Chaney.

As the result of this film, she signed a contract with Paramount in 1920, but poor choices of films by the studio resulted in Compson not being offered a contract renewal two years later. Compson moved to England and made several successful films there from 1922 to 1924. Her overseas success motivated Paramount to offer her another contract and she appeared in *The Enemy Sex* (1924). The following year she married director James Cruze.

After her marriage, Compson began freelancing, but most of the larger studios considered her a has-been and she began appearing in the quick, low-budget films of the smaller studios. During this same period, her marriage was undergoing serious problems and the couple decided to divorce. Soon after, Cruze declared bankruptcy and his creditors attached all of Compson's finances, even what she had made before her marriage to Cruze.

Compson appeared with Lon Chaney again in *The Big City* and then in *The Docks of New York* (both 1928). Later that year, she was nominated for an Academy Award for Best Performance by an Actress for her role of Carrie in *The Barker.* She continued to appear sporadically in films throughout the 1930s and 1940s. In addition, she appeared on the stage and even on the vaudeville circuit. She also started a cosmetic line that capitalized on her film career.

By now she was on her third marriage and, with her husband, she started a business that made personalized ashtrays for businesses such as hotels and restaurants. The business was highly successful and, because of her wise investments, she stated in a later interview "there would never be a benefit for Betty Compson." She ran this business alone after her husband's death.

Film Credits

1914   *He Loved the Ladies*
1915   *Where the Heather Blooms; Wanted: A Leading Lady; Those Primitive Days; Love and a Savage; Almost a Widow; Some Chaperone; Their Quiet Honeymoon*
1916   *His at Six O'Clock; All Over a Stocking; The Browns See the Fair; Cupid Trims His Lordship; The Deacon's Waterloo; Eddie's Night Out; He Almost Eloped; His Celluloid Hero; Her Steady Carfare; He's a Devil; A Quiet Supper for Four; The Janitor's Busy Day; Jed's Trip to the Fair; A Leap Year*

Tangle; Lem's College Career; The Wooing of Aunt Jemima; When Lizzie Disappeared; Wanted: A Husband; Love and Vaccination; Mingling Spirits; The Newlyweds Mix-Up; Potts Bungles Again; When the Losers Won; Her Friend, the Doctor

1917 *Five Little Widows; Many a Slip; A Bold, Bad Knight; Those Wedding Bells; Almost a Scandal*

1918 *Out West; Border Raiders; Betty Wakes Up*

1919 *The Prodigal Liar; The Light of Victory; The Little Diplomat; The Devil's Trail; The Miracle Man; Terror of the Range*

1921 *Prisoners of Love; At the End of the World; The Little Minister; A Smoky Love Affair; Ladies Must Live; For Those We Love; Betty's Big Ideas*

1922 *The Green Temptation; Over the Border; The Bonded Woman; To Have and To Hold; The Law and the Woman; Kick In; Always the Woman*

1923 *The White Flower; The Rustle of Silk; The Woman with Four Faces; Woman to Woman; The White Shadow; The Royal Oak; Hollywood*

1924 *Miami; The Enemy Sex; Ramshackle House; The Female; The Fast Set; The Garden of Weeds; The Stranger; The Prude's Fall*

1925 *Locked Doors; New Lives for Old; Eve's Secret; Paths to Paradise; Beggar on Horseback; The Pony Express; Counsel for the Defense*

1926 *The Palace of Pleasure; The Wise Guy; The Belle of Broadway*

1927 *Say It with Diamonds; Temptations of a Shop Girl; Cheating Cheaters; The Ladybird*

1928 *Love Me and the World Is Mine; The Desert Bride; Masked Angel; Life's Mockery; Court Martial; The Docks of New York; The Big City; The Barker; Scarlet Seas*

1929 *Weary River; On with the Show; The Time, the Place and the Girl; Street Girl; Skin Deep; The Great Gabbo; Woman to Woman; Blaze o' Glory; The Shows of Shows*

1930 *Case of Sergeant Grischa; Isle of Escape; Those Who Dance; Czar of Broadway; Midnight Mystery; Inside the Lines; The Spoilers; The Boudoir Diplomat; She Got What She Wanted*

1931 *The Lady Refuses; The Virtuous Husband; Woman Pursued; Three Who Loved; The Gay Diplomat; Hollywood Halfbacks*

1932   *The Silver Lining; Guilty or Not Guilty*
1933   *Destination Unknown; Notorious but Nice; West of Singapore*
1934   *No Sleep on the Deep; Manhattan Butterfly*
1935   *False Pretenses*
1936   *August Weekend; Hollywood Boulevard; Bulldog Edition; The Millionaire Kid; Laughing Irish Eyes; Killer at Large; The Drag-Net*
1937   *Federal Bullets; Two Minutes to Play; God's Country and the Man; Circus Girl*
1938   *Port of Missing Girls; A Slight Case of Murder; Two Gun Justice; Torchy Blane in Panama; Blondes at Work; Under the Big Top; The Beloved Brat*
1939   *Hotel Imperial; News Is Made at Night; Mystic Circle Murder; The Cowboys from Texas; They Asked for It*
1940   *Strange Cargo; Laughing at Danger; Mad Youth*
1941   *The Watchman Takes a Wife; Mr. and Mrs. Smith; College Sweethearts; Roar of the Press; Invisible Ghost; Escort Girl*
1943   *Danger! Women at Work; Confessions of a Vice Baron*
1946   *Claudia and David; Her Adventurous Night*
1947   *Hard Boiled Mahoney; Second Chance*
1948   *Here Comes Trouble*

Compton, Joyce (1907 Lexington, KY-1997 Los Angeles, CA)

Joyce Compton made a career of playing that Hollywood staple the "dumb blonde." In her more than twenty-five years as a film actor she appeared in some true Hollywood classics.

Born Eleanor Hunt, Compton spent her childhood moving among several cities throughout the United States and even living for a brief period in Toronto, Canada. After her graduation from high school, she won a national beauty contest and, like so many other girls, decided her future lay in Hollywood.

She was given a contract with First National Pictures and made her screen debut in *What Fools Men* (1925). She continued to appear in light comedic roles and in 1926 was selected as a WAMPAS Baby Star. The following year she made *A Border Cavalier*, her first western—a genre that she continued to appear in with such heart throbs as Tim McCoy, Johnny Mack Brown, and Roy Rogers.

In 1929 she moved to Fox Studios where she was given better roles. She appeared with Clara Bow in her first sound picture, *Dangerous Curves* (1929). It was during a period when she was freelancing that she portrayed Una Mellon in *The White Parade* (1934), which was one of her favorite characters.

She continued to be a popular supporting actor through the 1950s, although she seemed fated to play characters who all tended to be a variation on the dumb blonde characterization. But she was able to play that character in a variety of genres, excelling in comedies and light musicals.

A multitalented individual, Compton also enjoyed painting and writing as well as playing a number of musical instruments. She even gave clothing design a try. In fact, she designed the home that she lived in with her parents. Her final appearance was in the television series *Pete and Gladys*.

Film Credits

1925   *The Golden Bed; Sally; What Fools Men; Broadway Lady*
1926   *Syncopating Sue*
1927   *Ankles Preferred; The Border Cavalier*
1928   *Soft Living*
1929   *The Wild Party; Dangerous Curves; Salute*
1930   *The Sky Hawk; The Three Sisters; Wild Company; High Society Blues; Lightnin'*
1931   *Three Rogues; Three Girls Lost; Annabelle's Affairs; Woman of All Nations; Up Pops the Devil; Good Sport; Not Exactly Gentlemen*
1932   *Westward Passage; Unholy Love; Beauty Parlor; Lady and Gent; A Parisian Romance; False Faces; Fighting for Justice; Afraid to Talk; If I Had A Million; Lena Rivers; Hat Check Girl; Madison Square Garden; Under Eighteen*
1933   *Only Yesterday; Sing, Sinner, Sing; Dream Stuff; Luxury Liner; Roadhouse Queen; Knockout Kisses; The Big Fibber*
1934   *Affairs of a Gentleman; Million Dollar Ransom; King Kelly of the U.S.A.; Imitation of Life; The White Parade; The Trumpet Blows; Hollywood Hobbies; Caravan; Everything's Ducky*
1935   *Mister Dynamite; Go Into Your Dance; Manhattan Monkey Business; Life Hesitates at 40; Public Ghost No. 1; Magnifi-*

cent Obsession; Suicide Squad; Rustlers of Red Dog; Let 'Em Have It; College Scandal

1936 *Valley of the Lawless; Country Gentleman; Under Your Spell; Trapped by Television; Star for a Night; Sitting on the Moon; Murder with Pictures; Love Before Breakfast; The Harvester; Ellis Island; Three Smart Girls*

1937 *Top of the Town; Pick a Star; Kid Galahad; Born Reckless; The Toast of New York; Small Town Boy; The Awful Truth; Wings over Honolulu; We Have Our Moments; She Asked for It; Sea Racketeers; China Passage; Rhythm in the Clouds; How to Watch Football*

1938 *You and Me; Artists and Models Abroad; Women Are Like That; Trade Winds; Spring Madness; Man-Proof; Love on a Budget; Going Places*

1939 *Rose of Washington Square; Reno; Balalaika; Escape to Paradise; Hotel for Women; The Flying Irishman; The Last Warning*

1940 *I Take This Oath; They Drive by Night; City for Conquest; The Villain Still Pursued Her; Turnabout; Sky Murder; Honeymoon Deferred; I Take This Woman; Who Killed Aunt Maggie?*

1941 *Manpower; Ziegfeld Girl; Moon over Her Shoulder; Blues in the Night; Blonde Menace; Bedtime Story; Let's Make Music; Scattergood Meets Broadway*

1942 *Too Many Women; Thunder Birds*

1943 *Silver Spurs; Silver Skates; Let's Face It; A Gentle Gangster; Swing Out the Blues*

1945 *Christmas in Connecticut; Mildred Pierce; Roughly Speaking; Pillow to Post; Hitchhike to Happiness; Danger Signal*

1946 *Dark Alibi; Behind the Mask; Rendezvous with Annie; Night and Day; The Best Years of Our Lives*

1947 *Scared to Death; Linda Be Good; Exposed*

1948 *A Southern Yankee; Sorry, Wrong Number; Luxury Liner*

1949 *Mighty Joe Young; Grand Canyon; Incident*

1957 *The Persuader; Jet Pilot*

1958 *Girl in the Woods*

Cooper, Miriam (1891 Baltimore, MD-1976 Charlottesville, VA)

Miriam Cooper was educated in convents in Baltimore and New York before becoming a model for painter and photographer Harrison Fisher. Although records indicate that Cooper appeared in *The Duke's Plan* (1910), she didn't consistently appear in films until 1912 when she joined the Kalem Company.

She was brought to the attention of Kalem's producers by former model Alice Joyce who was Kalem's leading lady during the period when Cooper entered films. At first she was relegated to extra or walk-on roles, but soon she was appearing in ingenue roles and dramatic leads. In her first year, she made moe than 100 one- and two-reel films.

In December 1913, D. W. Griffith invited her to join his stock company at Reliance-Majestic Studios. Her first film for him was *Home, Sweet Home* (1914) in which she played the Easterner who leads Mae Marsh's man astray. She continued appear in various productions until 1915 when she appeared as Margaret Cameron in Griffith's *The Birth of a Nation.*

During the filming of *The Birth of a Nation,* Cooper met director Raoul Walsh whom she married after completing another Griffith epic, *Intolerance* (1916), in which she played "the friendless one" in the contemporary story. Cooper had planned to retire after her marriage but instead appeared in several of her husband's films between 1916 and 1921.

In 1924 she divorced Walsh and, according to her memoirs, before retiring to Virginia, appeared in her last film, *Is Money Everything?* However, records indicate that *Is Money Everything?* was released in 1923, so perhaps she appeared in the film at the end of 1923 and then divorced Walsh. At any rate, a film she appeared in prior to her "final" film was released after it was, so she has a film credit after her retirement, further confusing her filmography.

She wrote her autobiography in 1973, *Dark Lady of the Silent: My Life in Early Hollywood.*

Film Credits

1910   *The Duke's Plan*
1912   *A Blot on the 'Scutcheon; The Water Rights War; Victim of Circumstances; Tide of Battle; The Soldier Brothers of*

Susanna; The Siege of Petersburg; Saved from Court Martial; A Railroad Lochinvar; A Race with Time; The Pony Express Girl; His Mother's Picture; The Girl in the Caboose; The Drummer Girl of Vicksburg; The Darling of the CSA; The Confederate Ironclad; The Colonel's Escape; The Bugler of Battery B; The Battle of Wits; Battle of Pottsburg Bridge; Battle in the Virginia Hills; War's Havoc; The Filibusters; The Prison Ship; "Fighting" Dan McCool; The Grit of the Girl Telegrapher; The Rival Engineers; The Peril of the Cliffs; The Farm Bully; The Toll Gate Raiders

1913   *The Turning Point; A Treacherous Shot; A Sawmill Hazard; Prisoners of War; Infamous Don Miguel; The Exposure of the Land Swindlers; A Desperate Chance; Captured by Strategy; The Battle of Bloody Ford; The Woe of Battle; Across the Continent*

1914   *A Diamond in the Rough; The Dishonored Medal; Home, Sweet Home; The Stolen Radium; The Horse Wrangler; The Gunman; When Fate Frowned; Their First Acquaintance; The Odalisque; For His Master; The Double Deception*

1915   *The Birth of a Nation; The Slave Girl; The Story of a Story; The Burned Hand; The Fatal Black Bean; His Return; The Artist's Wife; The Greaser*

1916   *Intolerance*

1917   *Betrayed; The Silent Lie; The Honor System; The Innocent Sinner*

1918   *The Prussian Cur; The Woman and the Law*

1919   *The Mother and the Law; Evangeline; Should a Husband Forgive?*

1920   *The Deep Purple*

1921   *The Oath; Serenade*

1922   *Kindred of the Dust*

1923   *Her Accidental Husband; Daughters of the Rich; The Broken Wing; The Girl Who Came Back; Is Money Everything?*

1924   *After the Ball*

Copyright Laws

In the early years of film, when one film was successful other companies would rush to produce an almost identical story. Or, if a book was successful, the production companies would film the screenplay without the writer's permission. At the time there were no protections for "intellectual" works.

In 1907 writer Gene Gauntier adapted the novel *Ben-Hur* for the screen for Kalem Film Company without notifying the book's author, Lew Wallace. In 1912 Wallace sued for infringement because he had not given permission for the production.

The resulting decision required that all films produced in the United States had to be registered for copyright, thereby requiring film adaptations to have the original author's permission to be filmed and leading the way to the multimillion dollar film deals of today.

Corbin, Virginia Lee (1910 Prescott, AZ-1942 Winfield, IL)

Courtesy of Silents Are Golden at <SilentsAreGolden.com>

Called the "Dresden Doll of the Movies," Virginia Lee Corbin was one the most popular child stars of the silent era. Supposedly talking at the age of eleven months, Corbin entered show business before she was three, appearing with her mother who was a stage actor.

Although her exact means of entering the film industry is not clear, she was appearing in films by 1916 and had a contract with the Fox Film Company. Touted for her ability to exhibit emotions in her roles, she was also called "the youngest emotional star" and promoted extensively by the Fox publicity department.

In addition to the fairy-tale movies she appeared in, Corbin co-starred with Tom Mix in two westerns in 1918 and then seemed to disappear from films for several years. During this absence she continued to appear throughout the vaudeville circuit.

Her next film appearance was in *Enemies of Children* (1923). In 1924 Corbin appeared in her first adult role, as a flapper in the Eleanor Boardman vehicle *Wine of Youth*. She continued to represent the younger generation as a flapper in several, mostly comedy, films throughout the next few years.

Although by 1925 Corbin had been in the industry for nine years, she had just begun to appear in adult roles. As Corbin neared eighteen, her private life started to garner publicity as she began fighting with her mother over the mismanagement of the money Corbin made as a child actor. In fact, in 1929, Corbin married Chicago stockbroker Theodore Krol, several years her senior, in what some believed to be an effort to escape her mother's control.

After spending a year in England with her husband to acquire a more sophisticated accent for sound pictures, Corbin returned to Hollywood to appear in only four films in 1931. She retired from films to start a family and had two sons by 1935. Sadly, by 1936 her marriage was over and she was involved in a custody fight for her children, with her husband charging that she was an "unfit mother" due to her "excessive use of alcohol." After a short reconciliation, the Krols were divorced and her husband was awarded custody of the children—both under five years old. She married another stockbroker only months later.

After an abortive comeback attempt in 1940, Corbin was not heard from again until her death was announced at the age of thirty-one from tuberculosis.

Film Credits

1916   *Behind Life's Stage; By Conscience's Eye; The Castle of Despair; The Chorus Girl and the Kid; Nannette; Intolerance; Pidgin Island*

1917   *The Light of Love; The Old Toy Maker; Somebody Lied; The Terror; Three Women of France; Heart Strings; Jack and the Beanstalk; Aladdin and the Wonderful Lamp; Babes in the Woods; Vengeance of the Dead; A Modern Jack and the Bean Stalk*

1918   *Treasure Island; Six-Shooter Andy; Ace High; Fan Fan*

1919   *The Forbidden Room*

1920   *The White Dove*

1923   *Enemies of Children*

1924   *Wine of Youth; Sinners in Silk; All's Swell On the Ocean; Fight and Win* (ten episodes); *City That Never Sleeps; Broken Laws; The Chorus Lady*

1925   *The Three Keys; The Cloud Rider; Lilies of the Streets; Head-lines; The Handsome Brute; North Star*

1926   *The Whole Town's Talking; The Honeymoon Express; Ladies at Play; Hands Up!*

1927   *The Perfect Sap; Driven from Home; Play Safe; No Place to Go; Chasing Choo Choos*

1928   *Bare Knees; The Little Snob; The Head of the Family; Jazzland*

1929   *Footlights and Fools; Jazz Mamas; Knee High*

1931   *Morals for Women; Shotgun Pass; Forgotten Women; X Marks the Spot*

Costello, Delores (1905 Pittsburgh, PA-1979 Fallbrook, CA)

Delores Costello and her sister, Helene, appeared as children in many films starring their father, Maurice Costello. As she reached her teens, Costello left films to concentrate on a career in the theater and occasionally moonlighted as a model.

In the early 1920s, feeling that she had learned her craft, Costello returned to films and became one of the loveliest leading ladies of the period. Because of her patrician looks she was most often cast as aristocrats or virtuous heroines. She was given a few opportunities to show her acting teeth in such films as *When a Man Loves*.

She was named as a WAMPAS Baby Star in 1926 the same year she made one of her most memorable films, *The Sea Beast* (1926), the first film version of the classic *Moby Dick*. Although the original had no love interest, one was de rigueur in a John Barrymore film and the couple lit up both the screen and their off-screen lives. Costello and Barrymore married in 1928.

She continued to appear in leading roles until the 1930s when she retired to devote herself to her growing family—daughter Delores Ethel Mae (DeDe) and son John Barrymore Jr. After her divorce from Barrymore in 1935, she returned to films and appeared in mature character roles that revealed her true depth of talent. Shortly after appearing in *The Magnificent Ambersons* (1942), she retired from films and moved to her avocado farm, Fall Brook Ranch, in California.

Film Credits

1909 *A Midsummer's Night Dream*
1910 *The Telephone*
1911 *A Geranium; The Child Crusoes; His Sister's Children; A Thief in the Night; Some Good in All; Consuming Love; A Reformed Santa Claus*
1912 *The Meeting of the Ways; Captain Jack's Dilemma; Lulu's Doctor; The Troublesome Step-Daughters; The Money Kings; A Juvenile Love Affair; Wanted: A Grandmother; Vultures and Doves; Captain Barnacle's Legacy; The Toymaker; Ida's Christmas; For the Honor of the Family; She Never Knew; Her Grandchild; Bobby's Father; The Irony of Fate*
1913 *A Birthday Gift; The Hindoo Charm; In the Shadow; Fellow Voyagers*
1914 *Some Steamer Scooping; Etta of the Footlights; Too Much Burglar*
1915 *The Evil Men Do; The Heart of Jim Brice; How Cissy Made Good*
1923 *The Glimpses of the Moon; Lawful Larceny*
1925 *Bobbed Hair; Greater Than a Crown*
1926 *The Sea Beast; Mannequin; Bride of the Storm; The Little Irish Girl; The Third Degree*
1927 *When a Man Loves; A Million Bid; Old San Francisco; The Heart of Maryland; The College Widow*
1928 *Tenderloin; Glorious Betsy*

1929   *The Redeeming Sin; Glad Rag Doll; The Madonna of Avenue A; Hearts in Exile; The Show of Shows; Noah's Ark*

1930   *Second Choice*

1931   *Expensive Women*

1937   *Little Lord Fauntleroy; Yours for the Asking*

1938   *The Beloved Brat; Breaking the Ice*

1939   *King of the Turf; Whispering Enemies; Outside These Walls*

1942   *The Magnificent Ambersons*

1943   *This Is the Army*

Costello, Helene (1903 New York City–1957 Los Angeles, CA)

The elder of the two Costello sisters who worked in the film industry during its early years, Helene Costello got her start by appearing with her father, Maurice Costello, in his films. Although their name sounds Spanish or Italian, the family traced its roots to Ireland.

Costello appeared in films as a child but then left the industry in 1915. She worked in both the theater and on the vaudeville circuit until she was approached to appear on her own in films in the early 1920s. Although only an average actor, her beauty made her a popular costar through the latter part of the 1920s. She was chosen as a WAMPAS Baby Star in 1927.

The year after her selection as a "future star," she was released from her Warner Bros. contract because, she claimed, she did not want to be Rin Tin Tin's leading lady. She continued to work in films for a few years in bit parts and as an extra, but her career as a leading lady was over. However, contemporary writing of the period indicated that her voice was considered inadequate for recording techniques used at that time.

After four failed marriages, an extended child custody battle over the daughter born during her fourth marriage, and years of ill health, Costello died in poverty in a mental hospital where she had been committed for her drug and alcohol addictions. A friend eulogized her by saying that she wanted "love and understanding more than anything else in life—but receiving very little of either. She wanted something better from the world than she ever got."

Film Credits

1909   *The Galley Slave; A Midsummer Night's Dream; Les Miserables*

1911   *Courage of Sorts; A Quaker Mother; A Geranium; Captain Barnacle's Baby; Her Crowning Glory; The Child Crusoes; Her Sister's Children; Regeneration; Auld Lang Syne; The Old Doll; Consuming Love*

1912   *Captain Jack's Dilemma; Tom Tilling's Baby; Captain Barnacle's Messmates; The First Violin; She Never Knew; At Scrogginses' Corner; The Greatest Thing in the World; Lulu's Doctor; The Troublesome Step-Daughters; The Church Across the Way; The Black Sheep; Wanted: A Grandmother; Rip Van Winkle; In the Garden Fair; The Night Before Christmas; Two Women and Two Men; Meeting of the Ways; Cleopatra; The Toy Maker; Five Senses; Days of Terror; The Money Kings; Captain Barnacle's Legacy; The Irony of Fate; The Servant Problem*

1913   *Mr. Bolter's Niece; Buttercups; Tim Grogan's Founding; One Good Turn; Mystery of the Stolen Child; Fortune's Turn; The Hindoo Charm; The Other Woman; Heartbroken Shep; Matrimonial Manoeuvres; The Doctor's Secret; Fellow Voyagers; A Christmas Story; Beau Brummell; Just Show People*

1914   *Some Steamer Scooping; The Memories That Haunt; Etta of the Footlights; The Mysterious Lodger; How Cissy Made Good; The Barrel Organ; The Blood Ruby; Too Much Burglar; By the Governor's Order*

1915   *Lifting the Ban of Coventry; The Evil Men Do*

1925   *Ranger of the Big Pines; The Man in the Box; Bobbed Hair*

1926   *The Love Toy; Wet Paint; Don Juan; The Honeymoon Express; Millionaires; While London Sleeps*
1927   *Finger Prints; The Broncho Twister; The Heart of Maryland; In Old Kentucky; Good Time Charley; The Fortune Hunter; Husbands for Rent*
1928   *Comrades; Burning Up Broadway; Phantom of the Turf; Lights of New York; The Midnight Taxi; The Circus Kid; Broken Barriers*
1929   *The Fatal Warning; When Dreams Come True; The Show of Shows; Innocents of Paris*
1935   *Public Hero No. 1*
1936   *Riffraff*
1942   *The Black Swan*

Courtot, Marguerite (1897 Summit, NJ-1986 Long Beach, CA)

Marguerite Courtot won a beauty contest at the age of four and her future in show business was established. Her mother used the prize money to pay for dancing lessons, and Courtot danced and modeled locally until she was sent to Switzerland to finish her education.

Once she returned to the United States, Courtot returned to modeling and a friend suggested that she audition for the Kalem Company. She impressed the studio, but her mother would not allow her to travel to Florida with the company, preferring that she stay at home and continue her education. During the summers, however, she was allowed to work at the New Jersey studio and by the age of sixteen was one of Kalem's most popular players.

She enjoyed making costume dramas but also had a talent for non-slapstick comedies. When she was only fifteen she played the lead in *The Octoroon* (1913), a part that was considered extremely demanding. In 1915 she appeared in sixteen one-reel episodes of an ongoing series, *The Ventures of Marguerite.*

Although she considered Kalem her "family," Courtot moved to Famous Players-Lasky and made *Rolling Stones* (1916), in which she portrayed the good girl who turns a young man from the wrong path in life. She costarred with Owen Moore; their pairing was so successful that they immediately made another film, *The Kiss* (1916).

Once World War I was declared, Courtot shelved her film work to work in a marine recruiting office, then to tour selling war stamps. When the war ended she returned to films and soon starred in the serial that made her famous, *Bound and Gagged* (1919). Over the next two years three other serials followed this successful series.

While filming *Down to the Sea in Ships* (1922), Courtot met Raymond McKee; soon after the completion of the film, they were married. Courtot made a few films after her marriage but soon retired to devote herself to her family. The McKees were married more than sixty years before Raymond McKee died in 1984—just two years before his wife.

Film Credits

1912   *The Swamp Fox*
1913   *The War Correspondent; The American Princess; The Grim Toll of War; The Wartime Siren; The Fire-Fighting Zouaves; The Fighting Chaplin; Shenandoah; Breaking Into the Big League; The Fatal Legacy; The Riddle of the Tin Soldier; The Vampire; The Octoroon; Man's Greed for Gold*
1914   *A Celebrated Case; Francis Marion, the Swamp Fox; Through the Flames; The Show Girl's Glove; Kit, the Arkansas Traveler; Barefoot Boy; The Green Rose; Fate's Midnight Hour; The Girl and the Stowaway; The Riddle of the Green Umbrella; The Girl and the Explorer; The Prodigal; The Black Sheep; Home Run Baker's Double; The Hand Print Mystery*
1915   *The Adventures of Briarcliff; The Cabaret Singer; The Secret Room; The First Commandment; Poison; The Girl and the Bachelor; The Third Commandment; The Black Ring; Prejudice; The Seventh Commandment; In Double Harness; Playing for High Stakes; The Vanderhoff Affair; The Ventures of Marguerite; By Whose Hand?; The Pretenders*
1916   *The Fate of America; The Sealskin Coat; The Tricksters; The Lurking Peril; The Trail's End; The Dead Alive; Feathertop; Rolling Stones; The Kiss*
1917   *Crime and Punishment; The Natural Law*

1918   *The Unbeliever*
1919   *The Perfect Lover; Bound and Gagged; Teeth of the Tiger; The Undercurrent*
1920   *Pirate Gold; Rogues and Romance; Velvet Fingers*
1921   *The Yellow Arm; The Sky Ranger*
1922   *Beyond the Rainbow; The Cradle Buster; Down to the Sea in Ships; Silar Marner*
1923   *Jacqueline, or Blazing Barriers; Outlaws of the Sea; The Steadfast Heart*
1924   *Men, Women, and Money*

Crawford, Joan (1908 San Antonio, TX-1977 New York City)

Born into severe poverty to a divorced mother, Joan Crawford was originally named Lucille Le Sueur. After tiring of the menial jobs she was forced to take because of her lack of education, Crawford entered dancing contests in an attempt to enter show business.

After winning a Charleston contest, she began appearing in nightclubs as well as the chorus of first regional, then Broadway shows. She was discovered while appearing in the chorus on Broadway and signed to a short-term contract with MGM.

In her first film, she was a stand-in double for Norma Shearer in *Lady for a Night* (1925), but she was soon appearing in both supporting and minor lead roles. During her first year with MGM the studio sponsored a contest in the fan magazine *Movie Weekly* to find a screen name for Le Sueur. After being christened "Joan Crawford," she appeared in a succession of predictable, but often popular, films and was selected as a WAMPAS Baby Star in 1926.

Her breakthrough film was *Our Dancing Daughters* (1928). in which she played the virtuous flapper Diana Medford. Her first sound film was *Untamed* (1929). after which she began to appear in a several "working-girl-makes-good-but-doesn't-necessarily-achieve-happiness" roles which were extremely popular with audiences and earned Crawford a place among the most popular actors of the 1930s.

By the mid-1930s she was known as much for her clothing style as for her film appearances. Some critics complained that her roles were just excuses for her to parade in front of the camera in gorgeous Adrian-designed clothes. Although she epitomized the idealized movie star in her off-screen life, by the end of the decade her popularity had waned to the point that MGM let her go after eighteen years.

After two years in which she made only two pictures and played housewife to her third husband, she signed with Warner Bros. and soon appeared in her seminal role, *Mildred Pierce* (1945), which brought her the Best Actress Oscar. She continued to appear in films, although her popularity was never what it had been in the 1930s.

With the advent of television she made some appearances on the small screen. In 1962 she appeared with Bette Davis in *Whatever Happened to Baby Jane?* which began a series of appearances in horror/science fiction films. After she retired from the screen she remained before the public as the spokesperson for Pepsi-Cola, the company for which her fourth husband, Alfred Steele, served as chairman of the board.

Sadly, after her death, her long-running film career, including three Oscar nominations, and her loyalty to friends and support of charities were overshadowed by the malicious tell-all book *Mommie Dearest,* written by her adopted daughter, Christina. The book is nothing less than a character assassination and was written *after* Christina found out that she was not an heir to Crawford's estate.

Film Credits

1925	*Lady for a Night; Proud Flesh; A Slave of Fashion; Pretty Ladies; Old Clothes; The Circle; Sally; Irene and Mary; The Merry Widow; The Midshipman; The Only Thing*
1926	*Tramp, Tramp, Tramp, The Boob; Paris*
1927	*Winners of the Wilderness; The Taxi Dancer; The Understanding Heart; The Unknown; Twelve Miles Out; Spring Fever*
1928	*The Law of the Range; Rose-Marie; Across to Singapore; Four Walls; Our Dancing Daughters; Dream of Love; West Point; Tide of Empire*

1929   *The Duke Steps Out; Our Modern Maidens; Untamed; The Hollywood Revue of 1929*
1930   *Montana Moon; Our Blushing Brides; Paid; Great Day*
1931   *Dance, Fools, Dance; Laughing Sinners; This Modern Age; Possessed (I); The Slippery Pearls*
1932   *Letty Lynton; Grand Hotel; Rain; Screen Snapshots*
1933   *Today We Live; Dancing Lady*
1934   *Sadie McKee; Chained; Forsaking All Others*
1935   *I Live My Life; No More Ladies*
1936   *The Gorgeous Hussy; Love on the Run*
1937   *The Last of Mrs. Cheyney; The Bride Wore Red; Mannequin*
1938   *The Shining Hour*
1939   *Women; Ice Follies of 1939*
1940   *Strange Cargo; Susan and God*
1941   *A Woman's Face; When Ladies Meet*
1942   *They All Kissed the Bride; Reunion in France*
1943   *Above Suspicion*
1944   *Hollywood Canteen*
1945   *Mildred Pierce*
1946   *Humoresque*
1947   *Possessed; Daisy Kenyon*
1949   *Flamingo Road; It's a Great Feeling*
1950   *The Damned Don't Cry; Harriet Craig*
1951   *Goodbye My Fancy*
1952   *This Woman Is Dangerous; Sudden Fear*
1953   *Torch Song*
1954   *Johnny Guitar*
1955   *Queen Bee; Female on the Beach*
1956   *Autumn Leaves*
1957   *The Story of Esther Costello*
1959   *The Best of Everything*
1962   *Whatever Happened to Baby Jane?*
1963   *The Caretakers*
1964   *Four Days in November; Strait-Jacket; Della*
1965   *I Saw What You Did*
1968   *The Karate Killers; Berserk*
1970   *Trog*

Cripple Creek Bar Room *(1898)*

This short was probably directed by W. K. Laurie Dickson for showing on Edison's Kinetoscope machines and has been called the first movie western. The small saloon is called Miner's Arms and has only one table, a wood stove, and a short bar. Three miners are playing cards at the table, and an old man is sleeping near the stove when an uncouth miner comes in and tries to clear the bar. The robust bar maid finally has enough and throws the bully out of the bar. Then the original patrons gather at the bar for a drink on the house.

Crowell, Josephine (1849 Halifax, Canada-1932 Amityville, NY)

Called "the wickedest woman in pictures" after appearing as Catherine de Medici in *Intolerance* (1916), Josephine Crowell had a career in stage comedies before starting her film career.

Her first film is believed to be *The School Teacher and the Waif* (1912) at the Biograph studios. She worked several years for Biograph and other studios before being cast as de Medici in the D. W. Griffith classic. Her segment of the film depicted de Medici's efforts to plot the massacre of the Huguenots.

Although she portrayed other less diabolical characters such as caring mothers and supportive elder relatives, she was more often called upon to, in her own words, "poison a little child." In another of her more memorable parts, she exceeded her de Medici evil by whipping Lillian Gish and threatening her with a gun as she chased her throughout a house in *The Greatest Question* (1919). She retired from films in the early 1930s, just a few years before her death.

Film Credits

1912   *The School Teacher and the Waif; The Painted Lady*
1913   *His Mother's Son; The Mothering Heart*
1914   *Home, Sweet Home; The Avenging Conscience; The Tear That Burned; The Mountain Rat*
1915   *The Birth of a Nation; A Man and His Mate; The Penitentes; A Yankee from the West; The Three Brothers*
1916   *Martha's Vindication; A Child of the Streets; The Little School Ma'am; Pillars of Society; Intolerance; The Old Folks at Home; The Wharf Rat; The House Built Upon Sand; The She-Devil*

1917   *The Bad Boy; Betsy's Burglar; Cheerful Givers; Rebecca of Sunnybrook Farm; The Fair Barbarian*

1918   *Stella Maris; Heart of the World; The Bravest Way; Women's Weapons; Me und Gott (When America Awoke)*

1919   *Puppy Love; Diane of the Green Van; Josselyn's Wife; The Woman Next Door; Rose o' the River; The House of Intrigue; The Greatest Question; Peppy Polly*

1920   *The Six Best Cellars; White Lies; Crooked Streets; Held by the Enemy; Half a Chance; Flames of the Flesh; Dangerous to Men*

1921   *Home Stuff; Live and Let Live; Don't Neglect Your Wife; The Snob; Bunty Pulls the Strings*

1922   *Shattered Idols; A Homespun Vamp; Seeing's Believing; Lights of the Desert; Minnie*

1923   *Nobody's Money; Main Street; Rupert of Hentzau; Yesterday's Wife; Ashes of Vengeance*

1924   *Flowing Gold; Hot Water*

1925   *The Sporting Venus; Welcome Home; The Merry Widow; New Brooms; No Father to Guide Him*

1926   *The Splendid Crime; Yellow Fingers; Mantrap; For Wives Only; Padlocked; Bred in Old Kentucky; Dog Shy*

1927   *Fighting Love; The King of Kings; Dad's Choice*

1928   *Speedy; The Man Who Laughs*

1929   *Wrong Again*

Cunard, Grace (1893 Columbus, OH–1967 Woodland Hills, CA)

Called "the Serial Queen," Grace Cunard was one of the most popular serial stars of the silent era. Cunard was born Harriet Mildred Jeffries and became interested in acting at an early age. At thirteen she joined a touring stock company with her mother as chaperone and made her debut in *Dora Thorne* (1906).

Her debut film is believed to be *The Duke's Plan* (1910), directed by D. W. Griffith at Biograph Studios. However, she didn't get along with Griffith, so she moved to Lubin

Studios. During this time she met Francis Ford, older brother of director John Ford, who became her creative partner.

When she was asked to work at Universal, she brought Ford with her and they began their creative partnership—he as director/actor and she as writer/actor. They produced a series of historical dramas, westerns, and melodramas from 1912 to 1913 that were extremely popular with film audiences.

In 1914, the team produced a two-reel film on spies in the Philippines, which became the basis of *Lucille Love, Girl of Mystery* and was expanded to a fifteen chapter serial. Cunard played the heroine chased around the world by the villain (Ford) who was trying to steal a map from her. This serial's success led to Universal's participation in serial production for the next thirty-two years.

The success of *Girl of Mystery* was followed by *Broken Coin* (1915, twenty-three episodes), *The Adventures of Peg o' the Ring* (1916, fifteen episodes), and *The Purple Mask* (1916, sixteen episodes). At the height of her popularity, Cunard made $450 per week plus 25 cents per foot of film and 10 percent of the net profits of each film she wrote.

Unfortunately, *The Purple Mask* was not as successful as Universal had hoped; because it did not recoup its high production costs, the Cunard-Ford team was broken up. The films Cunard appeared in afterward were less than stellar. After writing and acting in *Elmo; the Mighty* (1919, eighteen episodes), she had a physical and emotional breakdown. Universal took this opportunity to not renew her contract.

After her recovery, she did some freelancing, but she was often relegated to supporting roles. Her last major role was in *Last Man on Earth* (1924), a science fiction comedy that featured Cunard's character trying to ransom the last man on Earth.

She appeared in *Blake of Scotland Yard* (1927) before being relegated to mostly character roles in the 1930s and 1940s. Realizing that roles were becoming harder to find, Cunard retired from films in 1945. Her second marriage in 1925 to stuntman Jack Shannon lasted until her death in 1967.

Film Credits

1911   *Before Yorktown*
1912   *The Indian Massacre; Custer's Last Raid; Sundered Ties; An Indian Legend; Custer's Last Fight; His Squaw*

1913   *The Battle of Bull Run; The She Wolf; The Madonna of the Slums; Wynona's Vengeance; The Light in the Window; The Stars and Stripes Forever; Taps; War; The Battle of San Juan Hill; The Black Masks; Captain Billie's Mate; The Coward's Atonement; The Darling of the Regiment; From Dawn to Dusk; From Rail Splitter to President; The Half Breed Parson; His Brother; The Favorite Son; The Telltale Husband; The Sharpshooter; Texas Kelly at Bay; An Orphan at War; The Belle of Yorktown; The White Vaquero*

1914   *Washington at Valley Forge; The Great Universal Mystery; The Mysterious Rose; The Phantom Violin; Lucille Love, Girl of Mystery; Won in the First; A War Time Reformation; The Mystery of the White Car; How Green Saved His Mother-in-Law; How Green Saved His Wife; In the Fall of '64; The Man of Her Choice; The Mysterious Leopard Lady; The Mad Hermit; The Unsigned Agreement; Their Vacation; The Tangle; A Study in Scarlet; Roll Your Peanut; The Return of the Twins' Double; Be Neutral; The Bride of Mystery; The Ghost of Smiling Jim; Sheridan's Pride; The Twins' Double; The Mysterious Hand; The District Attorney's Brother; The Call of the Waves; A Study in Scarlet*

1915   *Smuggler's Island; Three Bad Men and a Girl; The Hidden City; The Broken Coin; The Campbells Are Coming; And They Called Him Hero; The Call of the Waves; The Curse of the Desert; The Girl of the Night; The Girl of the Secret Service; The Heart of Lincoln; The Madcap Queen of Gredshoffen; The Mystery of the Throne Room; Nabbed; Old Peg Leg's Will; The Reward; One Kind of a Friend*

1916   *The Adventures of Peg o' the Ring; The Purple Mask; The Bandit's Wager; Brennon o' the Moor; Behind the Mask; Born of the People; The Elusive Enemy; Her Better Self; Her Sister's Sin; The Heroine of San Juan; Lady Raffles Returns; The Madcap Queen of Crona; The Phantom Island; The Powder Trail; The Princely Bandit; The Sham Reality; The Strong Arm Squad; The Unexpected; His Majesty Dick Turpin; Peg o' the Ring; The Mad Hermit*

1917   *Society's Driftwood; Unmasked; The Little Rebel's Sacrifice; The Puzzle Woman; The Rebel's Nest; The Terrors of War; True to Their Colors; In Treason's Grasp; The Mad Hatter* (I)

1918   *Hell's Crater; After the War; The Silent Mystery*
1919   *Elmo, the Mighty*
1920   *The Woman of Mystery; The Mad Hatter* (II)
1921   *The Girl in the Taxi; A Daughter of the Law; Her Western Adventure; A Daughter of the Law* (II)
1922   *The Heart of Lincoln*
1924   *Emblems of Love; The Last Man on Earth; The Elk's Tooth*
1925   *The Kiss Barrier; Outwitted*
1926   *Exclusive Rights; The Winking Idol; Strings of Steel; Fighting with Buffalo Bill*
1927   *The Denver Dude; The Return of the Riddle Rider; Blake of Scotland Yard*
1928   *A Trick of Hearts; Masked Angel; The Price of Fear; Haunted Island; The Chinatown Mystery*
1929   *The Ace of Scotland Yard; Untamed*
1930   *A Lady Surrenders; Little Accident*
1931   *Heroes of the Flames; Ex-Bad Boy; Resurrection*
1932   *Heroes of the West; The Fourth Horseman*
1933   *Ladies They Talk About*
1934   *Man Who Reclaimed His Head; Ladies They Talk About*
1935   *Rustlers of Red Dog; Call of the Savage; Bridge of Frankenstein; Alias Mary Dow*
1936   *Dangerous Waters; Show Boat; Magnificent Brute; The Rest Cure; Night Waitress*
1937   *Wings Over Honolulu*
1938   *Crashing Hollywood*
1940   *Winners of the West; A Little Bit of Heaven*
1942   *Gang Busters; The Mummy's Tomb; Pittsburgh*
1943   *The North Star; Adventures of Smilin' Jack*
1944   *Casanova Brown; Firebrands of Arizona; The Climax*
1945   *Easy to Look At; Great Stagecoach Robbery; Behind City Lights; Girls of the Big House*
1946   *Magnificent Doll*

Writing Credits

1912   *A Soldier's Honor*
1913   *The Madonna of the Slums; The Battle of Manila; The Black Masks; Captain Billie's Mate; The Capture of Aguinaldo; The Coward's Atonement; The Darling of the Regiment; The Half*

Breed Parson; His Brother; From Dawn Till Dusk; From Rail Splitter to President; The Light in the Window; The She Wolf; The Stars and Stripes Forever; Taps; The White Vaquero; The Toll of War; War; Texas Kelly at Bay; The Battle of San Juan Hill

1914   *The Twin's Double; Washington at Valley Forge; The Mysterious Rose; The Phantom Violin; Lucille Love, Girl of Mystery; The Bride of Mystery; The District Attorney's Brother; The Ghost of Smiling Jim; How Green Saved His Wife; How Green Saved His Mother-in-Law; In the Fall of '64; The Mad Hermit; The Man of Her Choice; The Mysterious Hand; The Mysterious Leopard Lady; The Mystery of the White Car; Pay the Rent; The Return of the Twins' Double; Roll Your Peanut; Sheridan's Pride; A Study in Scarlet; The Tangle; Their Vacation; The Unsigned Agreement; Won in the First; Universal Ike in Mary Green's Husband; The Call of the Waves*

1915   *Smuggler's Island; Three Bad Men and a Girl; The Hidden City; The Doorway of Destruction; The Broken Coin; The Call of the Waves; The Curse of the Desert; The Girl of the Secret Service; The Heart of Lincoln; The Madcap Queen of Gredshoffen; The Mystery of the Throne Room; Nabbed; Old Peg Leg's Will; One Kind of Friend; And They Called Him Hero; The Campbells Are Coming*

1916   *The Adventures of Peg o' the Ring; Born of the People; Brennon o' the Moor; The Dumb Bandit; The Elusive Enemy; Her Better Self; Her Sister's Sin; The Heroine of San Juan; Behind the Mask; The Unexpected; Peg o' the Ring; The Mad Hermit; The Bandit's Wager; Lady Raffles Returns; The Madcap Queen of Crona; Good Morning Judge; Mr. Vampire; The Phantom Island; Poisoned Lips; The Powder Trail; The Princely Bandit; The Purple Mask; The Sham Reality; The Strong Arm Squad; The Unexpected*

1917   *The Puzzle Woman; The Rebel's Nest; The Little Rebel's Sacrifice; The Terrors of War; True to Their Colors; Unmasked*

1928   *The Scrappin' Ranger*

Curley, Pauline (1895 Holyoke, MA-2000 Santa Monica, CA)

Pauline Curley, whose mother was a stage actress, entered show business at a very young age. Curley worked on the stage as a child and by five years of age had appeared in both stock productions and vaudeville. As she got older, and when she was not touring, she was educated at the Professional Children's School in New York City.

She moved to films in 1912 and became popular with the movie audience after appearing opposite Douglas Fairbanks Sr. in *Bound in Morrocco* in 1918. She then appeared in several popular serials, most notably *The Invisible Hand* and *The Veiled Mystery* (both in 1920). She also appeared regularly in westerns, becoming the heroine in the Range Rider western series.

Although she made the transition from silents to sound, after 1928 she had only one uncredited appearance in a film. As parts became more scarce, she retired to her other life of being a wife to cinematographer Kenneth Peach and concentrated on raising her sons.

Note: Depending on the source, her year of birth has been reported as 1895, 1903, and 1905.

Film Credits

1912   *Tangled Relations*

1913   *The Better Way; The Call of the Road*

1915   *The Unbroken Road; Life Without Soul*

1917   *Intrigue; The Fall of the Romanoffs; Cassidy; A Case of Law; The Square Deceiver; The Girl Philippa*

1918   *Her Boy; His Daughter Pays; The Landloper; Mr. Fix-It; Lend Me Your Name; Bound in Morocco*

1919   *The Man Beneath; The Solitary Sin; The Turn in the Road*

1920   *The Veiled Mystery; The Valley of Tomorrow; The Invisible Hand; Love Apple*

1921   *Hands Off; Judge Her Not; The Vengeance Trail*

1922   *The Prairie Mystery; Border Law*

1923   *Smoked Out; Double Cinched; Lost; Strayed or Stolen*

1924   *Midnight Secrets; Shackles of Fear; The Trial of Vengeance; The Desert Secret*

1925   *His Greatest Battle; Ridin' Wild; Cowboy Courage; Smoked Out; Double Cinched*

1926   *Walloping Kid; Twin Six O'Brien; The Millionaire Orphan; Prince of the Saddle; Two-Fisted Buckaroo; West of the Rainbow's End; Pony Express Rider; Lost, Strayed or Stolen*

1927   *Where the North Holds Sway; The Laffin' Fool; Code of the Range; Thunderbolt's Tracks*
1928   *Devil Dogs; Power*
1929   *Locked Door*

Dalton, Dorothy (1893 Chicago, IL-1972 Scarsdale, NY)

Dorothy Dalton was the type of actor directors dream of working with on a picture. She could play any woman—naive or naughty, generous or self-centered—and make the audience believe in her character. Her characters were always independent and strong—much like Dalton herself.

Her father was a successful businessman and Dalton adored him. From an early age she confided to her parents that she wanted to be an actor. Her father required that she get an education before she tried acting, but when she graduated she still wanted to be an actor. Her father wanted her to study law, so they struck a bargain: he would send her to school to study acting, but if she could not get an acting job, she would go to law school.

Since her father was an honorable man, he made sure that she got the best acting education possible at the American Conservatory of Chicago. She made her theatrical debut in Holyoke, Massachusetts, in 1910 with the Empire Stock Company. Later, her father saw her in a play in Denver and conceded the wager.

After achieving success in the theater, Dalton joined the vaudeville circuit, writing, directing, and starring in *The Smuggler*, which was a huge success. She alternated between the stage and vaudeville until 1914 when she saw her first film and decided that she wanted to try acting before the cameras.

Her screen debut was as Jen in Edgar Selwyn's production of *Pierre of the Plains* (1914), and Dalton set her sights on continuing in films. She decided that she wanted to work with Thomas Ince and traveled to Hollywood to meet with him. Surprisingly, he agreed to see her. Although he thought her "mad as a hatter," he did hire her to appear opposite William S. Hart in *The Disciple* (1915).

Her portrayal of the errant wife was so sympathetically believable that Ince undertook fostering her career. She became known as "Ince's Girl" but maintained that their relationship was strictly professional. In 1917 the release of *Flame of the Yukon,* in which Dalton played a dancehall girl known to all as "The Flame," made her a top star. It was a success that she was never able to match.

She was her best in dramatic roles and at the end of World War I even made two popular spy melodramas, *The Kaiser's Shadow* and *Vive la France.* She continued to appear in roles as diverse as the sympathetic wife and the tough owner of a gambling den.

In 1919 Dalton had her Broadway debut in Morris Gest's production of *Aphrodite,* as the wanton Chrysis who dies after taunting the goddess with her own beauty. The play was a hit and Dalton won critical and popular acclaim. The play ran for more than a year, and during that time Dalton appeared in several films produced at Paramount's East Coast studios.

When she returned to Hollywood she continued to be a top star on the Paramount lot and was still a sought-after actor in 1924 when a vacation to Florida changed her life and career. While in Palm Beach she met Arthur Hammerstein, famed theatrical producer and father of actor Elaine Hammerstein. Although Hammerstein was seventeen years older than Dalton, the couple married and Dalton retired from films and the theater.

Although the marriage was often stormy, it lasted until Hammerstein's death in 1955. The remainder of Dalton's life was spent traveling and visiting her daughter, Carol, and her granddaughter, as well as her far-flung family of friends.

Film Credits

1914   *Pierre of the Plains; Across the Pacific*
1915   *The Disciple*

1916   *The Three Musketeers; The Raiders; Civilization's Child; The Captive God; The Jungle Child; The Vagabond Prince; A Gamble in Souls; The Female of the Species*

1917   *The Weaker Sex; Chicken Casey; Back of the Man; The Dark Road; Wild Winship's Widow; The Flame of the Yukon; Ten Diamonds; The Price Mark; Love Letters*

1918   *Flare-Up Sal; Love Me; Tyrant Fear; The Mating of Marcella; The Kaiser's Shadow; Green Eyes; Vive la France; Quicksand; Unfaithful*

1919   *Hard Boiled; Extravagance; The Homebreaker; The Lady of Red Butte; Other Men's Wives; L'Apache; His Wife's Friend; The Market of Souls*

1920   *Black Is White; The Dark Mirror; Half an Hour; A Romantic Adventuress; Guilty of Love*

1921   *The Idol of the North; Behind Masks; Fool's Paradise*

1922   *Moran of the Lady Letty; The Crimson Challenge; The Woman Who Walks Alone; The Siren Call; On the High Seas*

1923   *Dark Secrets; Fog Bound; Law of the Lawless*

1924   *The Lone Wolf; The Moral Sinner*

Dana, Viola (1897 Brooklyn, NY-1987 Woodland Hills, CA)

Courtesy of Silents Are Golden at <SilentsAreGolden.com>

Born Virginia Flugrath, Viola Dana was one of three sisters in her family who entered show business during the early years of films. Her mother was determined that her daughters would become actors, so she started them taking dancing lessons while very young. The sisters began appearing in touring companies and local entertainment venues before they reached adolescence.

Dana was the first to find work in films when she appeared in Edison's version of *A Christmas Carol* (1910) under her birth name, which she continued to use until she changed her name to Viola Dana for the film *Molly the Drummer Boy* (1914).

While at Edison she met future director John H. Collins, and they were married when she was only sixteen years old. Afterward, Collins became the director as well as the writer for many of her films and she became one of Edison's most popular performers.

The couple moved to Metro in 1916, and her success continued under her husband's guidance. In the midst of this success, sadly, Collins became a victim of the 1918 flu pandemic and Dana was a widow at twenty-one.

Dana later starred in numerous productions, most notably *Bred in Old Kentucky* (1926) as Katie O'Doone. She retired in 1929 after appearing in *One Splendid Hour,* one of the many silent stars who did not make the transition to sound films. Her final public appearance was in 1987 for a television documentary about Buster Keaton titled *A Hard Act to Follow.* She died just months later.

Film Credits

1910	*A Christmas Carol*
1912	*The Lord and the Peasant; Children Who Labor; The Butler and the Maid; How Father Accomplished His Work*
1914	*Molly the Drummer Boy; The Blind Fiddler; Who Goes There?; The Adventure of the Hasty Elopement*
1915	*House of the Lost Court; Cohen's Luck; On Dangerous Paths; Gladiola; Children of Eve; Lena; The Slavey Student; The Portrait in the Attic*
1916	*The Innocence of Ruth; The Flower of No Man's Land; The Light of Happiness; The Gates of Eden; The Cossack Whip*
1917	*Lady Barnacle; Threads of Fate; Rosie O'Grady; The Mortal Sin; God's Law and Man's; Aladdin's Other Lamp; The Girl Without a Soul; Blue Jeans*
1918	*The Winding Trails; A Weaver of Dreams; Breakers Ahead; Riders of the Night; The Only Road; Opportunity; Flowers of the Dusk*
1919	*The Gold Cure; Satan Junior; The Parisian Tigress; False Evidence; Some Bride; The Microbe; Please Get Married*
1920	*The Willow Tree; The Chorus Girl's Romance; Blackmail; Cinderella's Twin; Dangerous to Men*
1921	*The Off-Shore Pirate; Puppets of Fate; Home Stuff; Life's Darn Funny; There Are No Villains; The Match-Breaker*

1922   *Fourteenth Lover; Glass Houses; Seeing's Believing; They Like 'Em Rough; The Five Dollar Baby; June Madness; Love in the Dark*

1923   *Crinoline and Romance; Her Fatal Millions; Rouged Lips; In Search of a Thrill; A Noise in Newsboro; The Social Code; Hollywood*

1924   *Heart of a Bandit; Don't Doubt Your Husband; The Beauty Prize; Revelation; Open All Night; Merton of the Movies; Along Came Ruth*

1925   *As Man Desires; Forty Winks; The Necessary Evil; The Great Love; Winds of Change*

1926   *Wild Oats Lane; Bigger Than Barnum's; Kosher Kitty Kelly; The Ice Flood; The Silent Lover; Bred in Old Kentucky*

1927   *Home Struck; Salvation Jane; Naughty Nanette; Lure of the Night Club*

1928   *That Certain Thing*

1929   *Two Sisters; The Show of Shows; One Splendid Hour*

Daniels, BeBe (1901 Dallas, TX-1971 London, England)

Courtesy of Silents Are Golden at <SilentsAreGolden.com>

BeBe Daniels was born into a theatrical family—her father managed a touring company and her mother was an actress. Her first theatrical appearance was supposedly at ten weeks of age in her mother's play *Jane*. By the age of three she appeared as one of the ill-fated princes in *King Richard III* and was a show business veteran before she reached the age of four. She was billed as "the world's youngest Shakespearean actress."

She made her screen debut in *The Common Enemy* in 1910. She later played comedic leads in roles featuring warm, sincere young women. At thirteen she became comedian Harold Lloyd's costar in his *Lonesome Luke* series and went on to be his costar as he developed his "glasses" character. For years she and Lloyd were a couple both on and off screen, but when their romance stalled, Daniels went on to another studio to pursue a dramatic career.

Her first feature film was in Cecil B. DeMille's *Male and Female* (1919). In 1920 she finished sixth in a competition for "favorite actress" sponsored by the fan magazines *Motion Picture Magazine* and *Motion Picture Classic.*

She had a beautiful singing voice and had no difficulty making the transition to sound films. In fact, the advent of sound films led to her appearing in several successful musicals including *Rio Rita* (1929) and *Love Comes Along* (1930).

In 1930 she moved to England with her husband, actor Ben Lyon, and they became successful musical-comedy stars appearing on stage and touring music halls throughout the country. In the early 1940s, they starred together in a successful radio show, *Hi Gang,* which ran for twelve years before moving to television for another four years and spawning two films.

During World War II Daniels entertained both British and U.S. troops and was instrumental in organizing shows to tour in England and throughout the rest of Europe. In addition, she wrote dispatches about the American war effort and landed on Omaha Beach when the Allies were still securing their beachhead. In 1946 Daniels was awarded the U.S. Medal of Freedom for her work in battle zones during the war.

After the war she and Lyon returned to Hollywood but found that after living in London for so many years they did not feel "at home" in America. So they returned to England where they created a new radio show, *Life with the Lyons.* This show also moved to television and spawned two feature films.

Film Credits

1910   *The Wonderful Wizard of Oz; The Common Enemy; The Courtship of Miles Standish; Justinian and Theodora*
1914   *Anne of the Golden Heart*
1915   *Giving Them Fits; Bughouse Bellhops; Great While It Lasted; Ragtime Snap Shots; A Foozle at the Tee Party; Peculiar Patients' Pranks; Lonesome Luke; Social Gangster*
1916   *An Awful Romance; Luke's Society Mix-up; Luke's Movie Muddle; Luke's Washful Waiting; Luke and the Mermaids;*

Luke's Speedy Club Life; Lonesome Luke Leans to the Literary; Luke Lugs Luggage; Lonesome Luke Lolls in Luxury; Luke, the Candy Cut-Up; Luke Foils the Villain; Luke and the Rural Roughnecks; Luke Pipes the Pippins; Lonesome Luke; Circus King; Luke's Double; Luke and the Bomb Throwers; Luke's Late Lunchers; Luke Laughs Last; Luke's Fatal Flivver; Luke Rides Roughshod; Luke, Crystal Gazer; Luke's Lost Lamb; Luke Does Midway; Luke Joins the Navy; Luke and the Bang-Tails; Luke, the Chauffeur; Luke's Preparedness Preparations; Luke, the Gladiator; Luke, Patient Provider; Luke's Newsie Knockout; Luke, Rank Impersonator; Luke's Fireworks Fizzle; Luke Locates the Loot; Luke's Shattered Sleep; The Flirt (I); Them Was the Happy Days!

1917 *Lonesome Luke's Lively Life; Over the Fence; Lonesome Luke on Tin Can Alley; Lonesome Luke's Honeymoon; Lonesome Luke's Wild Women; Birds of a Feather; Stop! Luke! Listen!; Pinched; Bliss; Rainbow Island; The Flirt (II); Fireman Save My Child; All Aboard; We Never Sleep; Luke's Lost Liberty; Luke's Busy Day; Drama's Dreadful Deal; Luke's Trolley Troubles; Lonesome Luke, Lawyer; Luke Wins Ye Ladye Faire; Lonesome Luke, Plumber; Lonesome Luke, Messenger; Lonesome Luke, Mechanic; Lonesome Luke Loses Patients; By the Sad Sea Waves; Lonesome Luke from London to Laramie; Love, Laughs and Lather; Clubs Are Trump; Move On; Bashful; Step Lively; Lonesome Luke's Lovely Rifle*

1918 *The Lamb; Here Come the Girls; Somewhere in Turkey; An Ozark Romance; Bride and Gloom; Nothing but Trouble; Hello Teacher; Back to the Woods; Hear 'Em Rave; Take a Chance; She Loves Me Not; The Non-Stop Kid; The City Slicker; Hey There; Why Pick On Me?; The Tip; Two-Gun Gussie; Fireman, Save My Child; Swing Your Partners; Are Crooks Dishonest?*

1919 *Ask Father; Young Mr. Jazz; Ring Up the Curtain; The Marathon; Off the Trolley; Spring Fever; Just Neighbors; Be My Wife; Heap Big Chief; The Rajah; Soft Money; Bumping Into Broadway; Male and Female; Captain Kidd's Kids; Everywoman; Count Your Change; On Fire; Look Out Below; Billy Blazes, Esq.; At The Stage Door; A Jazzes Honeymoon; Chop Suey & Co.; Pay Your Dues*

1920   *The Dancin' Fool; Sick Abed; You Can Never Tell; She Couldn't Help It; Oh, Lady, Lady!; The Fourteenth Man; Why Change Your Wife?*

1921   *The Affairs of Anatol; Two Weeks with Pay; The Speed Girl; One Wild Week; The March Hare; Ducks and Drakes*

1922   *Nancy from Nowhere; A Game Chicken; North to the Rio Grande; Singed Wings; Pink Gods; Nice People*

1923   *The World's Applause; The Glimpses of the Moon; The Exciters; His Children's Children; Hollywood*

1924   *Daring Youth; Unguarded Women; Monsieur Beaucaire; Sinners in Heaven; Argentine Love; The Heritage of the Desert; Dangerous Money; Hello Frisco*

1925   *Miss Bluebeard; The Crowded Hour; The Manicure Girl; Wild, Wild Susan; Lovers in Quarantine*

1926   *The Splendid Crime; Miss Brewster's Millions; The Palm Beach Girl; The Campus Flirt; Stranded in Paris; Volcano*

1927   *A Kiss in a Taxi; Swim, Girl, Swim; She's a Sheik; Senorita*

1928   *The Fifty-Fifty Girl; Hot News; Take Me Home; Feel My Pulse; What a Night!*

1929   *Rio Rita*

1930   *Love Comes Along; Alias French Gertie; Dixiana; Lawful Larceny; Reaching for the Moon*

1931   *My Past; The Maltese Falcon; The Slipper Pearls; Honor of the Family*

1932   *Radio Girl; Silver Dollar*

1933   *42nd Street; A Southern Maid; The Song You Gave Me; Hollywood on Parade No. 9; Cocktail Hour; Counselor at Law*

1934   *Registered Nurse*

1935   *Music Is Magic*

1936   *Treachery on the High Seas*

1938   *The Return of Carol Deane*

1939   *Not Wanted on Voyage*

1941   *Hi Gang!*

1948   *The Fabulous Joe*

1955   *The Lyons in Paris*

1956   *Life with the Lyons*

Darmond, Grace (1898 Toronto, Canada-1963 Los Angeles, CA)

Grace Darmond has the distinction of having starred in the first film using the Technicolor process, *The Gulf Between* (1918). Her father was a violinist and she received a traditional education but privately dreamed of being an actress. After her father's death, she and her mother moved to Chicago and it was here that she overcame her naturally shy personality to begin appearing in front of an audience.

The possessor of all the traits admired in young women at the turn of the century, she represented the societal female norms of compassion, shyness, and diffidence. She was given a contract by Selig Company and was naturally cast in ingenue roles, with her first film being a comedy titled *When the Clock Went Wrong* (1914).

Since she personified these traits that were typically seen as dependent, it is interesting that she found a career in the fast-paced world of movie serials. In 1916 she left Selig to appear in her first serial at Pathe, *The Shielding Shadow,* about the fight to possess a cloak of invisibility. Two years later she had moved again, this time to Vitagraph; by 1919 she was freelancing.

Although she did appear in some features, most of her work was done in the serial genre until the mid-1920s when she began to be cast in flapper roles. With the advent of sound she retired to lead a reclusive life.

Film Credits

1914   *When the Clock Went Wrong; Your Girl and Mine*
1915   *The Millionaire Baby; A Texas Steer; The House of a Thousand Candles; A Black Sheep*
1916   *Temperance Town; The Shielding Shadow; The Black Orchid; Badgered*
1917   *In the Balance*
1918   *The Other Man; The Gulf Between; An American Live Wire; The Girl in His House; A Diplomatic Mission; The Man Who Wouldn't Tell; The Seal of Silence; The Crucible of Life*
1919   *The Highest Trump; The Valley of Giants; The Hawk's Trail; What Every Woman Wants*
1920   *So Long Letty; The Invisible Divorce; Below the Surface*

1921   *See My Lawyer; White and Unmarried; The Hope Diamond Mystery; The Beautiful Gambler*

1922   *Song of Life; Handle with Care; I Can Explain; A Dangerous Adventure*

1923   *The Midnight Guest; Daytime Wives; Gold Madness; The Hero; The Wheel of Fortune*

1924   *Discontented Husbands; Alimony; The Gaiety Girl; The Painted Flapper*

1925   *Flattery; The Great Jewel Robbery; Where the Worst Begins*

1926   *Her Big Adventure; Midnight Thieves; The Night Patrol; Honesty—the Best Policy; Her Man o' War; The Marriage Clause*

1927   *Wide Open; Wages of Conscience; Hour of Reckoning; Life in Hollywood*

1941   *Our Wife*

Darwell, Jane (1879 Palmyra, MO-1967 Woodland Hills, CA)

Jane Darwell, who won an Oscar as Best Supporting Actress in 1940, came from a wealthy family that claimed to be descended from President Andrew Jackson. Prior to entering show business; she received her education from the best schools in the United States.

She began her entertainment career in the renowned Henry Duffy stock company and after touring for several years made her Broadway debut. She generally was cast in character roles as mothers, midwives, or other matronly characters.

She appeared in several films between 1913 and 1915, often directed by Cecil B. DeMille, but returned to the stage for many years. When she once more returned to films she was cast in supporting character roles in the 1930s, again as motherly types, and appeared in several Shirley Temple movies. It was as Ma Joad in *Grapes of Wrath* (1940) that she won the Oscar as Best Supporting Actress. Upon receiving the award she deadpanned, "Needless to say this is my favorite role."

Although ill and living at the Motion Picture Country Home, she was coaxed out of retirement by Walt Disney to play the part of The Bird Woman in *Mary Poppins* (1964).

Film Credits

1913   *At Shiloh; The Cowboy Magnet; The War of the Cattle Range; The White Squaw; The Head Hunters; The Capture of Aguinaldo*

1914   *The Master Mind; The Only Son; The Man on the Box; Ready Money; Rose of the Rancho*

1915   *Hypocrites; The Goose Girl; After Five; The Rug Maker's Daughter; The Reform Candidate*

1930   *Tom Sawyer*

1931   *Fighting Caravans; Huckleberry Finn; Ladies of the Big House*

1932   *No One Man; Washington Merry-Go-Round; Hot Saturday; Back Street; Women Won't Tell*

1933   *The Past of Mary Holmes; Murders in the Zoo; The Girl in 419; Emergency Call; Bed of Roses; Before Dawn; One Sunday Afternoon; Aggie Appleby, Maker of Men; Only Yesterday; Design for Living; He Couldn't Take It; Roman Scandals; King for a Night; Jennie Gerhardt; Good Housewrecking; Child of Manhattan; Bondage; Ann Vickers; Air Hostess; Roman Scandals*

1934   *Cross Country Cruise; Fashions of 1934; David Harum; Finishing School; Let's Talk It Over; The Most Precious Thing in Life; Million Dollar Ransom; Embarrassing Moments; Blind Date; One Night of Love; The Scarlet Empress; Desirable; Wake Up and Dream; Happiness Ahead; The White Parade; Bright Eyes; Wonder Bar; Once to Every Woman; Journal of a Crime; Heat Lightning; Gentlemen Are Born; The Firebird; Change of Heart; Jimmy the Gent*

1935   *Tomorrow's Youth; One More Spring; Paddy O'Day; Wig-Wag; We're Only Human; Navy Wife; Metropolitan; McFadden's Flats; Life Begins at Forty; Curly Top*

1936   *The Country Doctor; Poor Little Rich Girl; Ramona; Craig's Wife; White Fang; Star for a Night; Private Number; Little Miss Nobody; The First Baby; Captain January; Laughing at Trouble*

1937   *The Great Hospital Mystery; Fifty Races to Town; The Singing Marine; Love Is News; Dangerously Yours; Slave Ship; Nancy Steele Is Missing; Wife, Doctor, and Nurse*

1938   *Change of Heart; The Jury's Secret; Battle of Broadway; Time Out for Murder; Three Blind Mice; Little Miss Broadway; Up the River; Five of a Kind*

1939   *Jesse James; Unexpected Father; 20,000 Men a Year; Gone with the Wind; The Rains Came; The Zero Hour; Miracle on Main Street; Inside Story; Grand Jury Secrets*

1940   *The Grapes of Wrath; Untamed; Chad Hanna; Youth Will Be Served; Brigham Young, Frontiersman*

1941   *Thieves Fall Out; Small Town Deb; Private Nurse; The Devil and Daniel Webster*

1942   *All Through the Night; It Happened in Flatbush; Men of Texas; The Battle of Midway; Highways by Night; Young America; On the Sunny Side; The Loves of Edgar Allan Poe*

1943   *The Ox-Bow Incident; Stage Door Canteen; Family Feud; Tender Comrade; Government Girl; Gildersleeve's Bad Day; The Great Gildersleeve*

1944   *The Impatient Years; Sunny Dinner for a Soldier; She's a Sweetheart; Reckless Age; Music in Manhattan*

1945   *I Live in Grosvenor Square; Captain Tugboat Annie*

1946   *The Dark Horse; My Darling Clementine; Three Wise Fools*

1947   *Keeper of the Bees; The Red Stallion*

1948   *Train to Alcatraz; 3 Godfathers*

1949   *Red Canyon*

1950   *Wagonmaster; The Daughter of Rosie O'Grady; Father's Wild Game; Surrender; The Second Face; Redwood Forest Trail; Caged*

1951   *The Lemon Drop Kid; Journey Into Light; Fourteen Hours; Excuse My Dust; Three Husbands*

1952   *We're Not Married!*

1953   *The Sun Shines Bright; It Happened Every Thursday; The Bigamist; Affair with a Stranger*

1954   *A Life at Stake*

1955   *Hit the Deck*

1956   *There's Always Tomorrow; Girls in Prison*
1958   *The Last Hurrah*
1959   *Hound-Dog Man*
1964   *Mary Poppins*

Davenport, Dorothy (1895 Boston, MA-1977 Woodland Hills, CA)

Dorothy Davenport, who preferred to go by her married name—Mrs. Wallace Reid—throughout her life, was a multitalented individual who was successful at writing, acting, directing, and producing. She came from a theatrical family and made her stage debut at sixteen.

She began appearing in films around 1910 and worked for Biograph, Nestor, and Centaur Studios before moving to Los Angeles. She was publicized as "the classiest and most bewitching" actress of the period. In 1913 she married Wallace Reid, who became one of the first screen idols. She continued work, often starring with her husband, until 1917 when she retired after the birth of their son. In 1923 Reid died while trying to overcome the morphine addiction he had acquired after an accident on a movie set when doctors kept giving him shots so that shooting would not be delayed.

After her husband's death, Davenport became a crusader against drug addiction and a proponent of social reform. She founded the Wallace Reid Foundation Sanitarium in Santa Monica for the treatment of addicts. A month after he died she began work on a film about the horrors of narcotics and addiction, *Human Wreckage* (1923). The film was a success and acclaimed for "forcibly delivering its message."

One of her next productions cost Davenport almost everything she owned. *The Red Kimono* (1925) was based on a true story about a young girl lured into prostitution. When it was filmed the names were not changed, which resulted in a lawsuit by the "young girl" who was now married. The judgment cost Davenport everything she owned including her house.

After her third production, *The Earth Woman* (1926), Davenport returned to appearing before the camera for several years. But in 1929 she once more served as director; the project was *Linda,* a film about a girl forced to marry.

In 1930 she announced her retirement but within three years was back making films—this time as a writer/director/producer for various independent studios. In 1935 she produced and cowrote *Honeymoon Limited* and began a long-standing professional association with director Arthur Lubin. From 1950 to 1956 she and Lubin worked on films about Francis the talking mule, a comedy series for Universal.

Davenport never remarried, and when she retired, she devoted herself to her family until her death.

Film Credits

1910   *A Mohawk's Way; The Fugitive; The Oath and the Man; Examination Day at School; The Iconoclast; A Gold Necklace; The Broken Doll; Two Little Waifs; Waiter No. 5; The Fugitive; The Troublesome Baby; The Golden Supper*

1911   *The Best Man Wins; His Dream*

1912   *Her Indian Hero; The Lost Address; His Only Son; A Matinee Mix-Up; Inbad, the Count; Uncle Bill; The Torn Letter; A Pair of Baby Shoes; The Feudal Debt; A Brave Little Woman; The Bachelor and the Baby; The Boomerang; The Border Parson; Fatty's Big Mix-Up; In the Long Run; Almost a Suicide; Home and Mother*

1913   *The Spark of Manhood; The Cracksman's Reformation; The Fires of Fate; Retribution; A Cracksman Santa Claus; The Lightning Bolt; A Hopi Legend; All Rivers Meet the Sea; A False Friend; Toplitsky and Company; The Failure of Success*

1914   *The Intruder; The Countess Betty's Mine; The Wheel of Life; Fires of Conscious; The Greater Devotion; The Voice of Viola; Heart of the Hills; The Way of a Woman; The Mountaineer; The Spider and Her Web; Women and Roses; Cupid Incognito; A Gypsy Romance; The Test; The Skeleton; The*

Fruit of Evil; The Quack; The Siren; The Man Within; Passing of the Beast; Love's Western Flight; A Wife on a Wager; 'Cross the Mexican Line; The Den of Thieves; A Flash in the Dark; Breed o' the Mountains

1915 *The Explorer; Mr. Grex of Monte Carlo; The Unknown; The Adventurer; One Hundred Years Ago*

1916 *Doctor Neighbor; Black Friday; Barriers of Society; The Devil's Bondwoman; A Yoke of Gold; The Way of the World; The Unattainable; A Miracle of Love; Phantom Island; Her Husband's Faith; Headaches; Two Mothers; Her Soul's Song; Romance at Random; Number 16 Martin Street; The Human Gamble; The Mother Call; The Wrong Heart*

1917 *The Scarlet Crystal; The Girl and the Crisis; The Squaw Man's Son; Treason; Mothers of Men; Buried Alive; It Makes a Difference; Penalty of Silence; Brand of Death*

1920 *The Fighting Chance; Arms and the Gringo*

1921 *Every Woman's Problem*

1922 *The Masked Avenger; The Test*

1923 *Human Wreckage; Adam's Rib*

1924 *Broken Laws*

1925 *The Red Kimono*

1927 *The Satin Woman*

1928 *Hellship Bronson*

1929 *Linda*

1933 *Man Hunt*

1934 *Road to Ruin; Woman Condemned*

Writing Credits

1932 *Racing Strain*

1934 *The Road to Ruin*

1935 *Honeymoon Limited; Women Must Dress*

1938 *Rose of the Rio Grande; Prison Break*

1940 *On the Spot; Haunted House; Drums of the Desert; The Old Swimming Hole; Tomboy*

1941 *Red Head*

1947 *Curley*

1948 *Who Killed Doc Robbin?*

1949 *Impact*

1950 *Rhubarb*

1954   *Francis Joins the WACS*
1955   *Footsteps in the Fog*

Producing Credits

1923   *Human Wreckage*
1924   *Broken Laws*
1925   *The Red Kimono*
1926   *The Earth Woman*
1929   *Linda*
1934   *The Road to Ruin; Red Head*
1935   *Honeymoon Limited; Women Must Dress*
1936   *The House of a Thousand Candles*
1937   *Paradise Isle; A Bride for Henry*
1938   *Rose of the Rio Grande*

Directing Credits

1925   *The Red Kimono*
1929   *Linda*
1933   *Sucker Money*
1934   *The Road to Ruin; Woman Condemned*

Davies, Marion (1897 Brooklyn, NY-1961 Los Angeles, CA)

Marion Davies was born to an upper-class family whose father was a lawyer. While in school she captained the basketball team and displayed an athleticism that would be an asset later as a dancer. She briefly attended a convent high school while modeling for advertising illustrations.

Soon she followed her three older sisters into show business and began her career on Broadway as a chorus girl at the age of sixteen. Not long after her debut she caught the eye of Florenz Ziegfeld and went on to appear as a dancer in the *Ziegfeld Follies* in 1916. The following year she appeared in her first film, *The Runaway Romany,* for which she wrote both the script and the titles.

While generally considered a talented comedienne, after becoming involved with William Randolph Hearst in a long-running relationship, he was determined to see her star in costume pieces and overblown melodramas. Although his vast publishing holdings kept Davies's name before the public, his vision did much to destroy her credibility and undermined her real comedic talent.

While many malign her talent, few argue that she lived a luxurious life that few could aspire to live. She had a fourteen-room bungalow on the MGM lot and alternated between living in a Beverly Hills mansion or a beach house in Santa Monica with 110 rooms and fifty-five baths. Her invitations were the hottest ticket of the period; she threw lavish parties either at one of her homes or at Hearst's retreat up the coast, now called Hearst Castle.

Kind and generous to everyone she knew, at one point she loaned Hearst $1 million to keep his publishing empire going during a financially difficult period during the mid-1930s. She invested in real estate from a young age and acquired considerable holdings in Manhattan and California.

She supported many charities and served as president of the Motion Picture Relief Fund. The Hollywood Chamber of Commerce named her "Woman of the Year" in 1958 in recognition of her charitable works. Always concerned about children, she founded the Marion Davies Children's Clinic at UCLA Medical Center in Los Angeles.

She retired from films in 1940 to care for the ailing Hearst, who was thirty-four years her senior. After his death, Davies learned that she had inherited the majority of his vast empire, but she passed control to his family for the sum of $1.00 per year. Davies married for the first time at the age of fifty-four, but the marriage didn't last.

When the film *Citizen Kane* debuted, it was generally believed that the film was based on Hearst and Davies. Many believed that Davies was as without talent and brains as her supposed film alter ego, Susan Kane. Before his death Orson Welles admitted that he had done Marion Davies "an enormous disservice" by his creation of Susan Kane to achieve his "cinematic goal."

A biography, written from tapes made by Davies before her death, titled *The Times We Had: Life with William Randolph Hearst* was published in 1975.

Film Credits

1917   *The Runaway Romany*
1918   *Cecelia of the Pink Roses; The Burden of Proof; Beatrice Fairfax*
1919   *Getting Mary Married; The Cinema Murder; The Dark Star; The Belle of New York*
1920   *April Folly; The Restless Sex*
1921   *Buried Treasure; Enchantment*
1922   *Bride's Play; Beauty's Worth; The Young Diana; When Knighthood Was in Flower*
1923   *Adam and Eva; Little Old New York; The Pilgrim*
1924   *Yolanda; Janice Meredith*
1925   *Zander the Great; Lights of Old Broadway; Ben-Hur*
1926   *Beverly of Graustark*
1927   *The Red Mill; Tillie the Toiler; Fair Co-Ed; Quality Street*
1928   *The Patsy; The Cardboard Lover; Show People; The Five o'Clock Girl*
1929   *Marianne; The Hollywood Revue of 1929*
1930   *Not So Dumb; The Floradora Girl*
1931   *The Bachelor Father; It's a Wise Child; Five and Ten; The Christmas Party*
1932   *Polly of the Circus; Blondie of the Follies; Jack Cooper's Christmas Party*
1933   *Peg o' My Heart; Going Hollywood*
1934   *Operator 13*
1935   *Page Miss Glory; Pirate Party on Catalina Isle; A Dream Comes True*
1936   *Hearts Divided; Cain and Mabel*
1937   *Ever Since Eve*

Producing Credits

1919   *Getting Mary Married*
1927   *Quality Street*

1928   *Show People*
1929   *Marianne*
1930   *Not So Dumb; The Floradora Girl*
1931   *The Bachelor Father; It's a Wise Child; Five and Ten*
1932   *Blondie of the Follies; Polly of the Circus*
1935   *Page Miss Glory*
1936   *Hearts Divided*

Daw, Marjorie (1902 Colorado Springs, CO-1979 Huntington Beach, CA)

Marjorie Daw was one of Hollywood's golden people for several years then, like many silent film actors, faded completely away. But while she was at the top she was on the film capital's A-list, even serving as Mary Pickford's maid of honor at the Pickford-Douglas wedding.

Daw was orphaned as a teenager and was forced to work to support her younger brother. Eventually moving to Los Angeles, the siblings began appearing in films as bit players at the Universal Company. Originally she used her birth name, Margaret House, while appearing with the Lasky Company in 1915, but she changed her name to Marjorie Daw around 1916.

Her first big part was as the younger sister in *The Warrens of Virginia* (1915), followed the next year by a role in *Joan the Woman*. Soon after these films she became acquainted with Mary Pickford and began appearing as Douglas Fairbanks's leading lady.

The 1920s were especially busy, with Daw being loaned to or freelancing with every major studio in Hollywood. Although popular with her peers and the viewing audiences, she never quite made it beyond leading lady to the pinnacle of stardom. With the advent of sound Daw retired.

After her first marriage ended in divorce, Daw married Myron Selznick, brother of David O. Selznick, in 1925. The far-from-idyllic marriage ended in 1942 and Daw disappeared from Hollywood. When she died in 1979 she had not seen her daughter for more than twenty years.

Film Credits

1915   *The Unafraid; The Captive; The Puppet Crown; The Secret Orchard; Out of the Darkness; The Chorus Lady; The Human Menace*

1916   *The House with the Golden Windows*

1917   *The Jaguar's Claws; Rebecca of Sunnybrook Farm; Conscience; A Modern Musketeer; Joan the Woman*

1918   *Headin' South; Mr. Fix-It; Bound for Morocco; He Comes Up Smiling; Arizona; The Sunset Princess; Say! Young Fellow!*

1919   *The Knickerbocker Buckaroo; His Majesty, the American*

1920   *The River's End; Don't Ever Marry; The Great Redeemer; Dinty*

19213   *Patsy; Bob Hampton of Placer; The Butterfly Girl; Experience; A Motion to Adjourn; Fifty Candles; Cheated Hearts*

1922   *Penrod; The Lying Truth; A Fool There Was; The Long Chance; The Lone Hand; The Pride of Palomar; The Sagebrush Trial; Love Is an Awful Thing*

1923   *Mary of the Movies; Wandering Daughters; Rupert of Hentzau; Barefoot Boy; Going Up; The Dangerous Maid; The Call of the Canyon*

1924   *Gambling Wives; Revelation; Greater Than Marriage; Virginian Outcast; The Passionate Adventure; Notch Number One; Human Desires*

1925   *Fear-Bound; One Way Street; East Lynne; His Master's Voice*

1926   *In Borrowed Plumes; The Highbinders; Redheads Preferred*

1927   *Outlaws of Red River; Topsy and Eva; Home Made; Spoilers of the West; Why Girls Say No*

Day, Alice (1905 Colorado Springs, CO-1995 Orange, CA)

Although Alice Day was chosen as a scantily clad Sennett Bathing Beauty, her expressive eyes made her perfect for old-fashioned girl roles. Her roles were generally the virginal counterpoint to freethinking flappers. The publicity of the day stressed that these roles came naturally to her since she neither smoked nor drank nor associated loosely with men.

Her family moved to Los Angeles from Colorado, and both Day and her younger sister Marceline worked as extras while still in school. After graduating from high school she received her first substantial role as Norma Talmadge's daughter in *Secrets* (1924). During this period she also had her own comedy film series.

In 1928 she was selected as a WAMPAS Baby Star, which proves that the "newcomers" selected were often merely the ingenues that the studios were promoting at the time. Although she was groomed as Sennett's new star, she supposedly left his studio when asked to wear a costume she considered too revealing. By the 1930s she was no longer working with the large studios, and after 1932 she faded from film screens entirely.

Film Credits

1923   *The Temple of Venus; My Pal*
1924   *Picking Peaches; Shanghaied Lovers; Secrets; Flickering Youth; The Cat's Meow; His New Mamma; The First 100 Years; Little Robinson Corkscrew; Riders of the Purple Cows; Should Husbands Marry?; Romeo and Juliet*
1925   *Cold Turkey; Love and Kisses; The Plumber's Daughter; Bashful Jim; The Beloved Bozo; Honeymoon Hardships*
1926   *Gooseland; His New York Wife; Spanking Breezes; The Perils of Petersboro; Pass the Dumplings; Kitty from Killarney; Hesitating Horses; Alice Be Good; The Waiter from the Ritz*
1927   *See You in Jail; Night Life; The Gorilla*
1928   *The Way of the Strong; The Smart Set; Phyllis of the Follies*
1929   *Red Hot Speed; Drag; Skin Deep; Little Johnny Jones; The Show of Shows; The Love Racket; Times Square; Is Everybody Happy?*
1930   *Melody Man; In the Next Room; Ladies in Love; Hot Curves; Viennese Nights*
1931   *The Lady from Nowhere*
1932   *Love Bound; Two-Fisted Law; Gold*

Day, Marceline (1908 Colorado Springs, CO-2000 Cathedral City, CA)

Courtesy of Silents Are Golden at <SilentsAreGolden.com>

Marceline Day was the younger sister of Alice Day and began her career as a department store and illustrator's model. She first appeared on screen as an extra but was soon chosen, like her sister before her, as one of Mack Sennett's Bathing Beauties, which meant her picture was featured prominently in Keystone advertising.

She replaced her sister as Harry Langdon's leading lady and by 1926 was receiving top billing in her films. Briefly, Sennett publicized that she and her sister were twins. She stayed active through the 1920s, appearing in at least six films per year.

She appeared in several of the most-publicized productions of the silent era including *The Beloved Rogue* and *London After Midnight* (both 1927). She made the transition to sound in the 1929 version of *The Jazz Age*. Two years later, she appeared in *The Mad Parade* (1931), supposedly the first movie featuring an all-female cast.

Able to appear in both dramas and comedies, she appeared opposite such stars as John Barrymore, Buster Keaton, Harry Langdon, and Stan Laurel. But the roles became smaller and smaller, and by the mid-1930s she retired, returning briefly to appear in *Damaged Lives* (1937).

Film Credits

1924   *The Luck of the Foolish; The Hansom Cabman; Picking Peaches; Black Oxfords*
1925   *The Taming of the West; The White Outlaw; Discord in A Flat; Heart Trouble; His New Suit; The Party; Short Pants; The Wall Street Whiz; The Splendid Road; Renegade Holmes, M.D.*

1926   *Western Pluck; Hell's 400; The Barrier; Looking for Trouble; The Boy Friend; The Gay Deceiver; Fools of Fashion; That Model from Paris; College Days*

1927   *The Beloved Rogue; Red Clay; Rookies; Captain Salvation; The Road to Romance; London After Midnight*

1928   *Under the Black Eagle; A Certain Young Man; Detectives; The Cameraman; Driftwood; Restless Youth; Stolen Love; Freedom of the Press; The Big City*

1929   *A Single Man; The Jazz Age; Trent's Last Case; The Wild Party; The One Woman Idea; The Show of Shows*

1930   *Temple Tower; Sunny Skies; Paradise Island*

1931   *Mystery Train; The Mad Parade; The Pocatello Kid; The Sky Raiders*

1932   *The Fighting Fool; Arm of the Law; From Broadway to Cheyenne; The King Murder; The Crusader*

1933   *Via Pony Express; The Telegraph Trail; By Appointment Only; The Flaming Signal; The Fighting Parson; Damaged Lives*

Dean, Priscilla (1896 New York City-1987 Las Vegas, NV)

Courtesy of Silents Are Golden at
<SilentsAreGolden.com>

Born into an acting family, Priscilla Dean made her first stage appearance while still an infant. As a seasoned veteran of ten, she was cast in *The Children of Kings* (1906) and began touring on her own. Her first love was always the theater, but in 1910 she appeared in three one-reel films by Phillips Smalley.

Since she did not enjoy the feeling of isolation that was inherent in working in front of cameras, she returned to the theater. While dancing in *The Folies Bergere* (1911), she was approached by D. W. Griffith to join the Biograph Stock Company and was soon convinced to give films another chance.

However, Griffith soon became too busy to work with his protégé, and Dean went to Universal where she appeared in several comedies.

Her performance in the serial *The Gray Ghost* (1917) resulted in her being offered a role in Lois Weber's film *Even As You and I* (1917).

Her excellent performance caused Universal to realize that they had overlooked a gifted actor whose, now obvious, talent had been wasted. For the next two years (1918-1920) Dean was promoted as the next Universal star, with one of her best performances being *The Wildcat of Paris* (1918)—a role many felt was tailor-made for her histrionic personality.

Luckily for Dean she was assigned to director Tod Browning who was able to bring out her best performances. During the years that Dean and Browning worked together, Dean appeared in her best work, including *The Virgin of Stamboul* (1920), *Flame of Life,* and *White Tiger* (both 1923).

However, once Dean no longer worked under Browning's direction, her performances became mundane and her career waned. After several years of supporting roles, she retired from films in the early 1930s.

Film Credits

1912   *He Had but Fifty Cents; A Blot on the 'Scutcheon*
1914   *Mother; The Heiress and the Crook*
1916   *Knocking Out Knock Out Kelly; The Lion Hearted Chief; Bungling Bill's Peeping Ways; Love, Dynamite and Baseballs; More Truth Than Poetry; Heaven Will Protect a Woiking Goil; Igorrotes, Crocodiles and a Hat Box; Bungling Bill, Burglar; The White Turkey; Pass the Prunes; A Political Tramp; A Silly Sultan; Two Small-Town Romeos; Nobody Guilty; Knights of a Bathtub; Love and a Liar; Model 46; All Bets Off; Almost Guilty; The Barfly; The Battle of Chili-con-Carne; Beer Must Go Down; The Boy from the Gilded East; Broke but Ambitious; Caught with the Goods; He Maid Me; It Sounded Like a Kiss; When Spirits Fell; Search Me!; How Do You Feel?; His Own Nemesis; With the Spirit's Help*
1917   *Hand That Rocks the Cradle; The Gray Ghost* (sixteen episodes); *Beloved Jim; Even As You and I; Goin' Straight; Somebody Lied; Treat 'Em Rough; Why, Uncle!*

1918   *The Two-Souled Woman; Kiss or Kill; The Wildcat of Paris; She Hired a Husband; The Brazen Beauty; Which Woman?*

1919   *The Wicked Darling; The Silk-Lined Burglar; The Exquisite Thief; Pretty Smooth; The Forbidden; Klever Kiddies; Paid in Advance*

1920   *The Virgin of Stamboul; Outside the Law*

1921   *The Conflict; Reputation*

1922   *Wild Honey; Under Two Flags*

1923   *The Flame of Life; Drifting; The White Tiger*

1924   *The Storm Daughter; The Siren of Seville; A Café in Cairo; Love and Glory*

1925   *The Crimson Runner*

1926   *The Danger Girl; Forbidden Waters; The Speeding Venus; West of Broadway*

1927   *Jewels of Desire; Birds of Prey; Slipping Wives; The Dice Woman*

1931   *Trapped; Hollywood Halfbacks; The Honorable Mr. Buggs*

1932   *Klondike; Behind Stone Walls*

Del Rio, Dolores (1905 Durango, Mexico-1983 Newport Beach, CA)

Courtesy of Silents Are Golden at
<SilentsAreGolden.com>

Dolores Del Rio, the first female Latin film star, was born into a wealthy banking family in Mexico and educated in convents before her marriage at sixteen. While living in Mexico City, she and her husband hosted director Edwin Carewe who offered her a film contract.

The cousin of Latin heart throb Ramon Novarro, Del Rio was not initially interested in Carewe's offer, but eventually she traveled to Hollywood to launch her film career while her husband attempted to establish himself as a screenwriter. Her first film was *Joanna* (1925) and she appeared in a succession of successful films including *What Price Glory* (1926), the second highest-grossing film of that year, earning over $2 million domestically. She was also honored in 1926 to be selected as a WAMPAS Baby Star.

Unfortunately, with the advent of sound, studios seemed content to relegate her to films that used her as "eye candy" and did not give her an opportunity to act. Disgusted with the films being offered to her, Del Rio returned to Mexico where she was given not only decent dramatic roles but also a percentage of the films' profits.

She became an international star, and while she continued to make films in the United States, the majority of her fame came from her theater and film work in Mexico and in Spain. She won an Ariel, the Mexican equivalent to an Oscar, three times—in 1946 for *Las Abandonadas,* in 1952 for *Dona Perfecta,* and in 1954 *El Nino y la Niebla.*

Her influence and impact on the film industry are remembered by a mural painted in 1990 by Alfredo de Batuc located on Hudson Avenue north of Hollywood Boulevard. In addition, she is one of the life-sized screen goddesses that grace the silver gazebo at the west end of the Hollywood Walk of Fame.

Film Credits

1925   *Joanna*
1926   *High Steppers; Pals First; What Price Glory; The Whole Town's Talking*
1927   *The Loves of Carmen; Resurrection*
1928   *The Gateway of the Moon; Ramona; No Other Woman; The Red Dance; Revenge; The Trial of '98*
1929   *Evangeline*
1930   *The Bad One*
1932   *Bird of Paradise; Girl of the Rio*
1933   *Flying Down to Rio*
1934   *Wonder Bar; Madame duBarry*
1935   *The Widow from Monte Carlo; In Caliente; I Live for Love; A Dream Comes True*
1936   *Accused*
1937   *The Devil's Playground; Lancer Spy; Ali Baba Goes to Town*
1938   *International Settlement*
1939   *The Man from Dakota*
1942   *Journey Into Fear*

1943   *Flor silvestre* [Wild flower]
1944   *Maria Candelaria*
1945   *Las Abandonadas; Bugambilia; La Selva de Fuego* [Jungle fire]
1946   *La Otra* [The other]
1947   *The Fugitive*
1948   *Historia de una mala mujer* [The story of a bad woman]
1949   *La Malquerida; La Casa chica* [The love nest]
1950   *Dona Perfecta*
1951   *Deseada*
1953   *Reportaje; El Nino y la Niebla*
1955   *Senora Ama*
1956   *Torero*
1958   *A donde van nuestros hijos?*
1959   *La Cucaracha*
1960   *El Pecado de una madre*
1962   *Flaming Star*
1964   *Cheyenne Autumn*
1961   *La Dama del Alba* [The lady of dawn]
1966   *Casa de Mujeres* [House of women]
1967   *El Hijo de Todas* [The son of all]; *C'era una Volta*
1978   *The Children of Sanchez*

Dempster, Carol (1901 Duluth, MN-1991 La Jolla, CA)

Courtesy of Silents Are Golden at <SilentsAreGolden.com>

Carol Dempster has not been remembered kindly by the film industry. Whether reviled as being haughty and unfriendly or being accused of bringing about the creative downfall of D. W. Griffith, she was not popular with her contemporaries but had many devoted fans.

Although she appeared as a dancer in the Babylonian segment of *Intolerance* (1916), Dempster started her public career in earnest as a dancer with the Ruth St. Denis troupe but had to withdraw from the tour because of her mother's ill health. Later, Griffith asked her to join his troupe of players.

She was a supporting player in several films before she got her first lead role in a feature film. In *The Girl Who Stayed at Home* (1919) critics commented that she seemed to have trouble finding "her voice" and unsuccessfully imitated other Griffith actors. In fact, the main complaint about her acting was that she was always a distilled version of someone else, be it Lillian Gish, Mae Marsh, or another Griffith actor.

Several Griffith films followed with varying degrees of financial and critical success. It was not until one of her final films, *Isn't Life Wonderful?* (1924), that she finally gave a star performance. Unfortunately, while critics praised the film, the viewing audience found the subject of the realities of postwar Europe out of touch with the fun-seeking twenties.

Ironically, with her final film, *The Sorrows of Satan* (1926), Dempster seemed to come into her own as an actor. The public found the love story appealing while the critics gave mixed reviews. But as Griffith fell further out of favor with audiences and studios, Dempster's career waned.

In 1929 Dempster married a New York banker and officially retired from films. In a rare interview a few years before her death, Dempster wanted to assure her fans that her life "had a happy ending."

Film Credits

1916   *Intolerance*
1918   *The Greatest Thing in Life*
1919   *The Hope Chest; A Romance of Happy Valley; The Girl Who Stayed at Home; True Heart Susie; Scarlet Days*
1920   *The Love Flower; Way Down East*
1921   *Dream Street*
1922   *One Exciting Night; Sherlock Holmes*
1923   *The White Rose*
1924   *America; Isn't Life Wonderful*
1925   *Sally of the Sawdust; That Royle Girl*
1926   *The Sorrows of Satan*

Devore, Dorothy (1899 Fort Worth, TX-1976 Woodland Hills, CA)

Courtesy of Silents Are Golden at
<SilentsAreGolden.com>

Dorothy Devore entered show business at fifteen by staging her own theatricals called "The Dorothy Devore Revue." A multitalented young girl, she wrote both the script and the music for these shows. She appeared on the vaudeville circuit and in nightclubs throughout the Los Angeles area for three years.

Devore entered films with the advent of a new genre—the romantic comedy. In direct contrast to the popular slapstick style of comedy, this new style derived laughs from the realistic situations and story rather than from outlandish behavior. She signed with Al Christie in 1918 and began appearing in his two-reel films as an ingenue lead.

She was chosen as a WAMPAS Baby Star in 1923 and her popularity increased with the viewing audience. As she became more popular Devore asked for a raise, and when Christie could not match Warner Bros.' offer, she signed a seven-year contract with the other studio. With her new studio she began to appear in feature-length comedies, but conflict arose between Devore and Jack L. Warner.

After several disagreements, a final conflict over Devore supporting one of the most popular stars of the time, Rin Tin Tin, led to the end of her association with the studio. Refusing to be second lead to an animal because she believed it would demean her as an actor and stigmatize her career, Devore soon decided to buy out her contract.

After leaving Warner Bros., Devore signed with Educational Comedy Studios and appeared in a series of "Dorothy Devore Comedies" during the last years of her career. For these films Devore was given complete creative control, but only eight were made before she retired with the advent of sound.

During her retirement she traveled extensively and lived for several years in Shanghai with her third husband. Her final years were spent at the Motion Picture Country Home.

Film Credits

1918	*Know Thy Wife; Hazel from Hollywood; Camping Out; The Extra Bridegroom; Frenzied Film; The House Cleaning Horrors; Maid Wanted; Please Hit Me; The Price of a Rotten Time; Swat the Flirt; The Law of the North*
1919	*The Girl Dodger; Love in a Hurry; Lost: A Bridegroom; Kiss the Bride; Anybody's Widow; All in the Swim; Marry My Wife; Sing, Rosa, Sing; How's Your Husband?*
1920	*Man vs. Woman; Should Husbands Dance; The Reckless Sex; Nearly Newlyweds; All Jazzed Up; 45 Minutes from Broadway*
1921	*Magnificent Brute*
1922	*Fair Enough; Oh Promise Me*
1923	*When Odds Are Even; Kidding Katie*
1924	*Hold Your Breath; The Tomboy*
1925	*The Narrow Street; Who Cares; The Prairie Wife; A Broadway Butterfly; How Baxter Butted In; His Majesty, Bunker Bean; Three Weeks in Paris; The Midnight Flyer; Fighting the Flames*
1926	*The Man Upstairs; The Gilded Highway; The Social Highwayman; Senor Daredevil; Money to Burn*
1927	*The Wrong Mr. Wright; Mountains of Manhattan; Better Days; The First Night*
1928	*No Babies Wanted*
1930	*Take the Heir*
1939	*Miracle on Main Street*

Dix, Beulah Marie (1876 Kingston, MA-1970 Woodland Hills, CA)

An unrepentant "blue stocking," Beulah Marie Dix began writing as a child when she created a boy hero and wrote about the exciting life that she wished she could have lived. Luckily her father recognized and encouraged his daughter's intelligence, and at sixteen she was enrolled at Radcliffe. Four years later she graduated summa cum laude, Phi Beta Kappa, and was the first woman to win Harvard's George B. Sohier literary prize.

After graduation Dix became known as a dramatist, and one of her first plays, *Across the Border*, was produced in Boston in 1914. She was a devout pacifist and wrote many plays about war, trying to get her audience to see the futileness of it.

When her ideals did not set well with the playgoing public, she moved west as a writer for Famous Players-Lasky in 1916. At the time there were several women writers at the studio; Dix did not want to fade into the crowd, so she went out of her way to be "one of the boys." She preferred to write for men and was known for her "gift for violence."

She began her film career as a continuity writer—the one who wrote the words on the narrative cards that helped that audience follow the film. In the early years of films everyone did everything, and Dix was also an extra, a lighting technician, a film editor, and a director's assistant.

She wrote only sporadically after the advent of sound, and one of her final films was the adaptation of earlier play *The Life of Jimmy Dolan* (1933). Dix rebelled against the censorship of the day and relished finding ways to swear without the censor's realizing it by using arcane words. Her last film credit was in 1942.

Writing Credits

1917   *The Prison Without Walls; The Cost of Hatred; The Girl at Home; What Money Can't Buy; The Hostage; Ghost House; The Sunset Trail; The Call of the East; Nan of Music Mountain; On Record*

1918   *The Hidden Pearls; Wild Youth; The Girl Who Came Back; Women's Weapons; The Squaw Man*

1919   *Fires of Faith; The Woman Thou Gavest Me; Secret Service; The Heart of Youth; In Mizzoura; Men, Women and Money*

1920   *Held by the Enemy; Sweet Lavender; The Breed of the Treshams*

1921   *The Easy Road; The Affairs of Anatol; Fool's Paradise*

1922   *Crimson Challenge; The Ordeal; For the Defense; Borderland; A Daughter's Luxury*

1923   *Nobody's Money; Children of Jazz; The Fighting Blade; The Spanish Dancer*

1924   *Feet of Clay*

1925   *The Road to Yesterday*

1926   *Silence; Sunny Side Up; Risky Business*

1927   *Fighting Love; The Country Doctor*

1928 *The Leopard Lady; Ned McCobb's Daughter*
1929 *Girls Gone Wild; Trent's Last Case; The Godless Girl; Black Magic*
1930 *Girl of the Port; Midnight Mystery; Conspiracy*
1931 *Three Who Loved*
1933 *The Life of Jimmy Dolan; Even in My Heart*
1935 *College Scandal*
1939 *They Made Me a Criminal*
1942 *Sweater Girl*

The Dolly Sisters
Rosie (1892 Budapest, Hungary-1970 New York City)
Jenny (1892 Budapest, Hungary-1941 Hollywood, CA)

The Dolly Sisters were one of the first celebrities of the early 1900s. They were not great entertainers, but they attracted publicity and became legends for simply existing.

Identical twins Roszika (Rosie) and Janszieka (Jenny) Deutsch came to the United States when they were about five years old. After settling in Brooklyn, their mother sent them to ballet lessons that were the start of their entertainment career.

They made their theatrical debut in 1909, but it was their appearance in the *Ziegfeld Follies of 1911* that really started their careers. They appeared in Asian-inspired headdresses and shared a skirt—the "Siamese Twins" number was a hit. While the epitome of beauty at that time was innocent blondes, the sisters played up their dark exotic features and dressed in flashy outfits.

They moved to the theater and appeared in a succession of "confused identity" plays. They began to appear on the arms of important, or at least famous, men of the day—Diamond Jim Brady was especially fond of them and supposedly took a paternal interest in their lives.

Even after the twins married (Rosie in 1913 and Jenny in 1914), they continued to appear together and, occasionally, separately. Their first film was *The Call of the Dance* (1915). The film was a murder mystery exotically spiced by white slavery. Later Rosie appeared with Lillian Gish in *The Lily and the Rose* (1915) as the other woman that steals Gish's faithless husband.

Several years later the sisters appeared as themselves in *The Million Dollar Dollies* (1918), a bizarre film that had them pretending to be detectives amid a cast of mystics and royalty, all of whom wanted a mysterious "magical" ring. By the early 1920s, the sisters were ready to return to Europe since both had recently gotten divorced from their American husbands.

They appeared in London but found their biggest success in Paris where they were considered chicly exotic. They became the "toasts of two continents" and alternated between appearing in Europe and America. Their renown enabled them to enter society and they soon retired from show business to become society leaders. Actually, they began collecting rich lovers and a large collection of jewelry—a showcase in one of their entry halls displayed a fifty-one-carat square-cut diamond from an appreciative "friend."

In 1927 Rosie married a tobacco heir from Canada and the sisters soon became fixtures in the casinos of the Riviera. Legend has it that Jenny broke the bank in Monte Carlo four times and that Rosie parlayed a $4 loan into $400,000. While living in Europe, Jenny adopted two Hungarian orphans.

By 1931 Rosie was divorced again, but the following year she married a Chicago department store heir and moved with him to Illinois. Sadly, soon after she left Jenny was badly injured in an automobile accident in France that resulted in extensive scars to her face that even plastic surgery could not completely repair.

Jenny moved to Chicago to be near Rosie and married a friend of her brother-in-law, but the marriage did not last. Hoping to get her adopted daughters into films, Jenny moved to Hollywood in 1940. But she had never really recovered from her accident and described herself as "a broken shell."

After calling her aunt to say she didn't feel well, Jenny fashioned a noose from her dressing gown belt and hung herself from an iron curtain rod in her living room. Her aunt arrived too late to help her—Jenny was dead at age forty-eight. It is unclear what happened to her daughters after her death.

Rosie sold the rights to the sisters' life stories to Twentieth Century Fox with the stipulation that Jenny's suicide would not be mentioned nor would her adopted daughters. The film that was produced was a complete fabrication which had nothing to do with the actual individuals—except the name, *The Dolly Sisters* (1945).

Rosie's husband died in the early 1950s and she was in the news in 1962 after a suicide attempt. She lived out her life in Manhattan.

Film Credits

Rosie
1915 *The Call of the Dance; The Lily and the Rose*
1918 *The Million Dollar Dollies*
Jenny
1915 *The Call of the Dance*
1918 *The Million Dollar Dollies*

Dove, Billie (1900 New York City-1997 Woodland Hills, CA)

Courtesy of Silents Are Golden at
<SilentsAreGolden.com>

Billie Dove, at the height of her fame, surpassed all other actors as a box-office draw including Mary Pickford, Greta Garbo, and Clara Bow. Called "the American Beauty," she was known for her patrician features and perfect complexion.

Billie Dove was the daughter of Swiss immigrants and decided on a film career while still in school. Once her decision was made she regularly made the trip to Fort Lee, New Jersey, in search of work as an extra or bit player. While waiting for her film break, she appeared in Ziegfeld's *Follies* and was the girl used to introduce the Irving Berlin standard "A Pretty Girl Is Like a Melody."

As she became more popular in the *Follies* her stage fame grew and she was given lead roles in films shot in the New York area. In 1922 she traveled to Hollywood after signing a one-year contract with Metro. Two of her films were shot in experimental two-color Technicolor—*Wanderer of the Wasteland* (1924) and *The Black Pirate* (1926).

In 1926 Dove also started working with director Lois Weber who was able to coax the best performance of Dove's career from her in *The Marriage Clause*. The film was so popular that they immediately filmed *Sensation Seekers* that had Dove in a flapper role.

These two successes lead to Dove being considered a true leading lady and bankable at the box office. During this period Dove began a romance with the scion of a wealthy family who enjoyed dabbling in films, Howard Hughes. Although the couple was reportedly on the verge of marriage many times, the relationship came to an end after three and a half years.

She made the transition to sound and appeared in a variety of roles that emphasized her versatility as an actor. In *Cock of the Air* (1932), whose final version was decimated by the Hays Office, Dove got her first real chance to shine in a comedy.

In 1933 she retired from films, at the height of her popularity, to have a family. Her second marriage ended after thirty-seven years, but during that time she had two children. Never jaded by her success, Dove remained accessible and unaffected until her death.

Film Credits

1921	*Get-Rich-Quick Wallingford; At the Stage Door*
1922	*Polly of the Follies; Beyond the Rainbow; Youth to Youth; One Week of Love*
1923	*All the Brothers Were Valiant; Madness of Youth; Soft Boiled; The Lone Star Ranger; The Thrill Chaser*
1924	*On Time; Try and Get It; Yankee Madness; Wanderer of the Wasteland; The Roughneck; Folly of Vanity*
1925	*The Air Mail; The Light of Western Stars; The Lucky Horseshoe; Wild Horse Mesa; The Fighting Heart; The Ancient Highway*
1926	*The Black Pirate; The Marriage Clause; Kid Boots; The Lone Wolf Returns*
1927	*An Affair of the Follies; Sensation Seekers; The Tender Hour; The Stolen Bride; American Beauty; The Love Mart*
1928	*The Heart of a Follies Girl; Yellow Lily; Night Watch; Adoration*
1929	*Careers; The Man and the Moment; The Painted Angel; Her Private Life*
1930	*A Notorious Affair; Sweethearts and Wives; One Night at Susie's; The Other Tomorrow*
1931	*The Lady Who Dared; The Age for Love*
1932	*Cock of the Air; Screen Snapshots; Blondie of the Follies*
1964	*Diamond Head* (walk-on)

Dresser, Louise (1878 Evansville, IN-1965 Woodland Hills, CA)

Louise Dresser made her theatrical debut in Columbus, Ohio, in 1895. Although her real name was "Kerlin," she took the name "Dresser" after songwriter Paul Dresser, who was trying to get her a job, introduced her as his younger sister.

She became a popular star of both stage and vaudeville, touring throughout the United States in sold-out venues. She introduced the popular standard of the period "My Gal Sal" while on tour and starred in the Broadway hit *Matinee Idol* during the 1910-1912 seasons.

She entered films in 1922 and achieved a success in *The Goose Woman* (1925). While she was top billed in some films or generally well up in the cast listings, she was mainly known for her portrayal of matronly characters. She is perhaps best know for the films she made with Will Rogers throughout the 1930s in which she played his nagging wife and, once, his sister.

She retired from films at the end of 1937 because, although she came from the theater, her voice did not record well and her age had begun to catch up with her. Later in her life she moved to the Motion Picture Country Home where she died after surgery for an intestinal illness.

Film Credits

1922	*The Glory of Clementina; Enter Madame; Burning Sands*
1923	*Prodigal Daughters; Salomy Jane; The Fog; Ruggles of Red Gap; Woman-Proof; To the Ladies*
1924	*The Next Corner; The City That Never Sleeps; Cheap Kisses; What Shall I Do?*
1925	*Percy; The Eagle; The Goose Woman; Enticement*
1926	*Fifth Avenue; The Blind Goddess; Broken Hearts of Hollywood; Everybody's Acting; The Third Degree; Padlocked; Gigolo*
1927	*White Flannels; Mr. Wu*
1928	*A Ship Comes In; The Garden of Eden; The Air Circus; Mother Knows Best*
1929	*Not Quite Decent; Madonna of Avenue A*
1930	*Mammy; This Mad World; The Three Sisters; Lightnin'*

1931   *Caught*
1932   *Stepping Sisters*
1933   *State Fair; Song of the Eagle; Doctor Bull; Cradle Song*
1934   *David Harum; The World Moves On; The Scarlet Empress; A Girl of the Limberlost; Servants' Entrance; Hollywood on Parade*
1935   *The County Chairman*
1937   *Maid of Salem*

Dressler, Marie (1868 Cobourg, Ontario-1934 Santa Barbara, CA)

Marie Dressler, one of the most popular comics of the late 1920s and early 1930s, entered show business while a teenager because her father could barely support his family as a n'er-do-well musician. She got her first taste of audience laughter when she fell from her pedestal while portraying Cupid in a church play.

She claimed to have realized early in life that what she lacked in the looks department she could make up for with humor: she would never be called pretty, but she was often praised for being funny. She entered show business at fourteen by joining a barnstorming stock company and then moved to other more successful and professional companies. By the time she was twenty-four years old she was supporting her entire family—including a brother-in-law.

Her first major stage part was in *Under Two Flags* (1886), and she made her New York debut in *The Robber of the Rhine* (1892) with Maurice Barrymore. While starring with Barrymore he suggested that she try comedy. She subsequently began appearing in vaudeville where her size and mannerisms played well with the physicality of slapstick comedy. After her initial success, Dressler claimed she continued to "bump into scenery to amuse the customers."

As a comic vaudevillian, Dressler became one of the country's biggest stars as well as appearing in several successful Broadway musicals. She traveled to London in 1907 where she made several successful appearances before returning to New York. Arguably her most popular characterization during the early 1910s was that of Tillie in *Tillie's Nightmare* (1910) in which she popularized the song, "Heaven Will Protect the Working Girl."

Mack Sennett, having seen the play, convinced Dressler to reprise her role in the first full-length comedy film *Tillie's Punctured Romance* (1914) with supporting actors Charlie Chaplin and Mabel Normand. The film was a hit, and in 1917 she formed her own production company to produce more "Tillie" films. Although she did produce a few more "Tillie" films, none were accepted as well as the first film.

When Dressler could not find a good film in which to appear, she returned to vaudeville and the musical comedy that was her forte. But after having supported a chorus-girl strike, Dressler was blackballed by stage management and by 1926 was destitute.

As Dressler was working as a hostess in a dinner club in New York and considering life as a domestic servant, her old friend Frances Marion wrote a script for her and secured funding for the film from Irving Thalberg. *The Callahans and the Murphys* (1927) was the first pairing of Dressler with Polly Moran, and they created a successful comedy team. Although praised by critics, the film supposedly insulted Irish-Americans with its stereotypical depiction of the Irish as feuding drunks, so the film was pulled from theaters.

She joined a theatrical stock company in Los Angeles but soon returned to film because by now "talkies" had taken over. She established herself as a comedic supporting actor by combining tragedy with her comedic mannerisms. One of her greatest roles was as the downtrodden Marthy in Garbo's *Anna Christie* (1930).

It was in *Min and Bill,* a film in which she costarred with gruff Wallace Beery, that Dressler hit gold—both financially and by winning the 1930 Best Actress Oscar. She followed this with an equally impressive portrayal of the housekeeper who marries her boss in *Emma* (1932) and as Carlotta Vance in *Dinner at Eight* (1933). Another pairing with Beery in 1933, *Tugboat Annie,* was also a box-office smash.

The 1930s were successful years for Dressler. For three years in a row Dressler was voted the most popular box office attraction in polls conducted by the *Motion Picture Herald.* She also was named "most popular star" in a survey conducted by the *Hollywood Reporter*. Of her Oscar win she said it was "a crown for all the years of suffering and hardship."

Always considering herself homely, she titled her autobiography *The Life Story of an Ugly Duckling* (1924) and a second volume, simply, *My Own Story* (1934). In summing up her career she said, "I was born homely (but) I have earned my bread by making other people laugh. . . . When everything else fails I . . . make a face."

Film Credits

1910   *Actors' Fund Field Day*
1914   *Tillie's Punctured Romance*
1915   *Tillie's Tomato Surprise*
1917   *Tillie Wakes Up; The Scrub Lady*
1918   *The Agonies of Anges; The Cross Red Nurse; Fired*
1927   *The Callahans and the Murphys; The Joy Girl; Breakfast at Sunrise*
1928   *Bringing Up Father; The Patsy*
1929   *The Hollywood Revue of 1929; The Vagabond Lover; Dangerous Females; The Divine Lady; Voice of Hollywood* (I and II)
1930   *Anna Christie; Chasing Rainbows; One Romantic Night; Caught Short; Let Us Be Gay; Min and Bill; Derelict; The March of Time; The Girl Said No*
1931   *Reducing; Politics; The Christmas Party*
1932   *Emma; Prosperity*
1933   *Dinner at Eight; Broadway to Hollywood; Going Hollywood; Tugboat Annie; Christopher Bean*

DuBrey, Claire (1892 Bonner's Ferry, ID-1993 Los Angeles, CA)

Claire DuBrey began her career in films as an extra after answering an ad for "society women types to work in motion pictures." She made her screen debut in *Peggy* (1916). Her films for 1917 show a combination of westerns and society melodramas in which she was cast as a vamp, a sexually predatory female character that flourished for a short time in the 1910s. In fact, one critic wrote that the characters she played were not happy unless they wrecked "at least one home per picture."

By 1918 she was a frequent leading lady opposite western star Harry Carey, and when the film called for it, she did her own stunts. She once noted that luckily she had never been hampered in her acting by being typecast. At various times she had been called the perfect "princess type," "Mexican spitfire type," and "western heroine type"—leaving her a large range of characters to portray.

As roles began to become more scarce she turned to the Los Angeles stage for employment. She alternated between the stage and films for the remainder of the 1920s. In 1928 she met Marie Dressler, and when Dressler's popularity rose, DuBrey was hired by her friend to handle her fan mail and personal correspondence.

While she worked for Dressler she wrote a memoir of the star, but the book was never published. As Dressler became ill DuBrey, who had nursing training, took care of her until vicious rumors about the two being lovers caused DuBrey to leave her old friend. After Dressler's death, DuBrey returned to films and was in demand for supporting roles through the 1950s. She even voiced a character in Walt Disney's *Cinderella* (1950).

Ill health and deafness caused her to retire in 1959. She lived simply for the remainder of her life and died a month before her 101st birthday.

Film Credits

1916   *Peggy; Civilization*
1917   *The Piper's Price; The Reward of the Faithless; The Fighting Gringo; The Rescue; Follow the Girl; Pay Me; Triumph; Anything Once; The Winged Mystery; Red Saunders Plays Cupid; The Almost Good Man; The Drifter; A 44 Caliber Mystery; Hair Trigger Burke; The Surprise Honeymoon; The Honor of an Outlaw; Six-Shooter Justice*
1918   *The Human Target; Madame Spy; The Magic Eye; Midnight Madness; Modern Love; Prisoner of the Pines; The Risky Road; Social Briars; Up Romance Road; Border Raiders; Brace Up*
1919   *The Wishing Ring Man; A Man and His Money; The Sawdust Doll; When Fate Decides; The Devil's Trail; The World*

Aflame; The Spite Bride; What Every Woman Wants; The Old Maid's Baby; A Man in the Open; The Ghost Girl; Modern Husbands

1920   *Dangerous Hours; The Heart of a Child; The Green Flame; Life's Twist; The Walk-Offs; A Light Woman; The House of Whispers; Perilous Valley*

1921   *The Bronze Bell; That Girl from Montana; My Lady's Latch-key; I Am Guilty; The Hole in the Wall*

1922   *Glass Houses; Only a Shop Girl; The Ordeal; To Have and To Hold; When Love Comes; You Never Know; Sure Shot Morgan*

1923   *Ponjola; The Voice from the Minaret*

1924   *Borrowed Husbands; The Sea Hawk*

1925   *Drusilla with a Million; The Girl of Gold; Infatuation*

1926   *Exquisite Sinner; Miss Nobody*

1927   *The Devil Dancer*

1929   *Two Sisters*

1930   *For the Love o' Lil*

1931   *Politics*

1932   *Prosperity; Divorce in the Family*

1933   *Gabriel Over the White House; Broadway to Hollywood; Night Flight; The Sin of Nora Moran; Made on Broadway; Ever in My Heart; Shadows of Sing-Sing; Beauty for Sale; Women in His Life*

1934   *Among the Missing; Bachelor of Arts; Blind Date; Coming Out Party; Glamour; Jane Eyre; Now I'll Tell; This Side of Heaven; Viva Villa!*

1935   *Life Begins at 40; Vagabond Lover*

1936   *The Devil-Doll; Ramona*

1937   *Dangerously Yours; Nothing Sacred; Wife, Doctor, and Nurse; Outcast; Mountain Justice; Blossoms On Broadway; Man of the People*

1938   *The Baroness and the Butler; Miracle Money; Marie Antoinette; Little Miss Broadway; The Strange Case of Dr. Meade;*

That Certain Age; Men with Wings; One Wild Night; Walking
Down Broadway

1939   Sergeant Madden; Everybody's Baby; Within the Law; Tell
No Tales; When Tomorrow Comes; The Story of Alexander
Graham Bell; See Your Doctor; South of the Border; Hotel
for Women; The Forgotten Woman; Chicken Wagon Family;
Coast Guard; Four Wives; Jesse James; Three Smart Girls;
Grow Up; Juarez

1940   The Shop Around the Corner; The Blue Bird; Virginia City;
Andy Hardy Meets a Debutante; All This and Heaven Too;
Black Diamonds; Youth Will Be Served; High School; Charlie Chan's Murder Case; Brigham Young, Frontiersman; The
Girl from Avenue A

1941   Blondie in Society; Blossoms in the Dust; Private Nurse; Rise
and Shine; Ellery Queen and the Murder Ring

1942   A Close Call for Ellery Queen; Bells of Capistrano; Now,
Voyager; The Magnificent Dope; Juke Box Jenny; The Gay
Sisters

1943   Heaven Can Wait

1944   Oh, What a Night; Lights of Old Santa Fe; Dragon Seed; Casanova Brown

1945   Dakota; A Song to Remember; Star in the Night

1946   The Invisible Informer; Cloak and Dagger; Don Ricardo Returns; The Best Years of Our Lives; Secret of the Whistler;
The Catman of Paris

1947   The Bells of San Fernando; The Homestretch; Ivy; Unconquered; The Bishop's Wife

1948   Lightnin' in the Forest; French Leave; Out of the Storm; The
Loves of Carmen; Every Girl Should Be Married; Killed Doc
Robbin?

1949   Abbott and Costello Meet the Murderer; Boris Karloff;
Streets of San Francisco; Samson and Delilah; Dear Wife

1950   Mr. Music; Destination Big House; Cinderella

1951   The Big Carnival; Double Dynamite; Ace in the Hole

1952   Jack and the Beanstalk

1953   Raiders of the Seven Seas

1954   *Phantom of the Rue Morgue*
1958   *Escort West; Frontier Gun; Hot Rod Gang*
1959   *Girls Town*

Durfee, Minta (1891 Los Angeles, CA-1975 Woodland Hills, CA)

Minta Durfee began her career as a chorus girl and appeared in musical comedy revues in vaudeville and on the stage before moving into motion pictures. In 1908 she married comedian Roscoe "Fatty" Arbuckle and together they joined Mack Sennett's Keystone Company. She appeared opposite her husband in many of his early movies as well as appearing with Charlie Chaplin in his early Keystone films. Her films were mostly one- or two-reelers, and although most of them are from this period, she was one of the most popular of the early comedians.

She left Arbuckle in 1918 but did not become legally separated until 1921 and was not divorced until 1925. When she left Arbuckle she also left the film industry. However, she did begin appearing in an occasional film after 1935 and did some television guest appearances.

Although she was no longer living with Arbuckle when he became involved in the Virginia Rappe murder trial, she was unwavering in her support of him. In fact, much of her later life was dedicated to clearing his name and promoting his work.

Film Credits

1913   *A Quiet Little Wedding; Fatty at San Diego; Wine; Fatty Joins the Force; Fatty's Flirtation; Fatty's Day Off*
1914   *A Misplaced Foot; A Flirt's Mistake; Making a Living; A Film Johnnie; Tango Tangles; A Suspended Ordeal; The Alarm; The Knockout; Fatty and the Heiress; Fatty's Finish; The Rounders; The New Janitor; Fatty's Debut; Fatty Again;*

Fatty's Wine Party; Leading Lizzie Astray; Fatty's Magic Pants; Ambrose's First Falsehood; Tillie's Punctured Romance; Fatty and Minnie He-Haw; Twenty Minutes of Love; The Star Boarder; The Masquerader; His New Profession; Cruel, Cruel Love; Caught in a Cabaret

1915 *When Love Took Wing; A Village Scandal; Our Dare Devil Chief; Mabel; Fatty and the Law; Love; Speed and Thrills; The Home Breakers; Hearts and Planets; Fickle Fatty's Fall; Fatty's Tintype Tangle; Fatty's Reckless Fling; Fatty's Faithful Fido; Fatty's Chance Acquaintance; Fatty and Mabel at the San Diego Exposition; Dirty Work in a Laundry; Court House Crooks; A Bird's a Bird; Ambrose's Little Hatchet; Fatty and the Broadway Stars; He Wouldn't Stay Down; Ambrose's Fury*

1916 *The Other Man; His Wife's Mistakes; The Great Pearl Tangle; Bright Lights*

1918 *Mickey*

1926 *Skinner's Dress Suit*

1935 *Naughty Marietta*

1940 *The Man with Nine Lives; Glamour for Sale*

1941 *How Green Was My Valley; The Devil and Miss Jones; The Miracle Kid*

1942 *Blondie for Victory*

1943 *The Chance of a Lifetime*

1945 *Eve Knew Her Apples*

1947 *Son of Rusty*

1948 *My Dog Rusty*

1956 *Around the World in Eighty Days*

1957 *An Affair to Remember; Will Success Spoil Rock Hunter?*

1963 *It's a Mad, Mad, Mad, Mad World*

1964 *The Unsinkable Molly Brown*

1968 *Savage Intruder*

1971 *Willard; The Steagle; What's the Matter with Helen?*

Dwan, Dorothy (1906 Sedalia, MO-1981 Ventura, CA)

Dorothy Dwan, who claimed Scottish patriot Sir William Wallace (who has been immortalized many times on film—most recently in 1995 by Mel Gibson in *Braveheart*) as an ancestor, was educated in

Philadelphia before beginning her show business career. As was common during the silent era, she was still a teenager when she entered films. This was the practice for women because the lighting used was harsh and added years to the actors' faces so the younger the women, the better they photographed.

Her film debut was in *The Silent Vow* (1922), but she did not appear again in a film until two years later. In 1925 Dwan was selected to be comedian and director Larry Semon's leading lady in *The Perfect Clown,* and she became a rising young star. The following year she also became Semon's wife.

Unfortunately, she too often took her husband's advice and appeared in mundane roles or films. When Semon's business difficulties necessitated a large amount of money, Dwan was forced to accept any role and appeared in a succession of "programmer" (formula) melodramas. Semon never recovered his fortune and the difficulties resulted in his complete breakdown.

Her husband's health continued to decline until he died in 1928. Dwan continued to appear in westerns in support of such stars as Ken Maynard and Tom Mix until the advent of the sound era. In 1930 she married an oil executive and permanently retired from films.

The marriage ended in divorce in 1935 and Dwan moved back to her home state to study nursing. After another marriage ended in divorce, Dwan returned to California and sold real estate.

Film Credits

1922   *The Silent Vow; The Sawmill*
1924   *Sinners in Silk; Her Boy Friend; Kid Speed; The Breed of the Border; Those Who Dance; The Enemy Sex*
1925   *The Wizard of Oz; Bashful Buccaneer; The Perfect Clown; My Best Girl; The Cloudhopper*
1926   *Stop, Look and Listen; The Dangerous Dude; The Call of the Klondike; The Great K & A Train Robbery; A Captain's Courage; The Canyon of Light; Perils of the Coast Guard*
1927   *McFadden's Flats; Hills of Kentucky; The Princess of Broadway; Spuds; The Land Beyond the Law; Tumbling River; Silver Valley*
1928   *Square Crooks; Riders of the Dark; Obey Your Husband; Out with the Tide*

1929 *The Drifter; The California Mail; The Peacock Fan; The Devil Bear*

1930 *The Fighting Legion; Hide-Out*

Eddy, Helen Jerome (1897 New York City-1990 Alhambra, CA)

Helen Jerome Eddy moved to Los Angeles while still a toddler and entered films after graduating from high school. There is disagreement as to whether she began working at Lubin or Vitagraph but during her career she worked for virtually every studio at one time or another. Before she retired from films she had made more than 100 films, although many titles have been lost.

With her aristocratic demeanor and large expressive eyes, Eddy specialized in portraying upper-class characters during the silent era. Although she rarely played lead roles, her performances as supporting characters always garnered her featured billing. She made the transition to sound and continued in supporting roles until 1940, when she retired and began a successful real-estate career.

Film Credits

1915 *As the Twig Is Bent; The Gentleman from Indiana; The Red Virgin*

1916 *Madame la President; The Code of Marcia Gray; Pasquale; Her Father's Son; Redeeming Love; The Tongues of Men*

1917 *His Sweetheart; The Wax Model; As Men Love; The Marcellini Millions; The Cook of Canyon Camp; Lost in Transit; Rebecca of Sunnybrook Farm; The Fair Barbarian*

1918 *Jules of the Strong Heart; The Spirit of '17; One More American; Breakers Ahead; Old Wives for New; Winner Takes All*

1919 *The Turn in the Road; The Boomerang; The Blinding Trail; The Man Beneath; A Very Good Young Man; The Trembling Hour; The Tong Man*

1920 *Pollyanna; The House of Toys; Miss Hobbs; The County Fair; A City Sparrow; The Forbidden Thing; A Light Woman*

1921   *The First Born; One Man in a Million; The Other Woman; The March Hare; The Ten Dollar Raise*

1922   *When Love Comes; The Flirt*

1923   *An Old Sweetheart of Mine; The Country Kid; To the Ladies; An Old-Fashioned Sweetheart of Mine*

1924   *The Fire Patrol*

1925   *Marry Me; The Dark Angel*

1926   *Padlocked; Camille*

1927   *Quality Street*

1928   *13 Washington Square; Chicago After Midnight; Two Lovers; The Speed Classic*

1929   *Blue Skies; The Divine Lady; Small Talk; Midstream; Railroadin'*

1930   *War Nurse; Reaching for the Moon; So Big*

1931   *The Great Meadow; Girls Demand Excitement; Skippy; Sooky; Mata Hari*

1932   *Impatient Maiden; No Greater Love; Make Me a Star; The Night of June 13th; A Parisian Romance; Madame Butterfly; Frisco Jenny*

1933   *The Bitter Tea of General Yen; Strictly Personal; The Masquerader; Torch Singer; Night Flight; Man's Castle; Broadway Through a Keyhole*

1934   *Riptide; Unknown Blonde; Dr. Monica; A Girl of the Limberlost*

1935   *Helldorado; A Shot in the Dark; Rendezvous at Midnight; Carnival; Bride of Frankenstein; The Girl from 10th Avenue; Keeper of the Bees*

1936   *Klondike Annie; The Country Doctor; Show Boat; The Garden of Allah; Winterset; Stowaway; The Crime of Dr. Forbes*

1937   *Jim Hanvey, Detective; The Soldier and the Lady; Women Men Marry; Nancy Steele Is Missing!*

1938   *The Strange Case of Dr. Meade; City Streets; Crime Ring; Tarnished Angel*

1939   *Burn 'Em Up O'Connor; Mr. Smith Goes to Washington; Good Girls Go to Paris; Blondie Brings Up Baby*

1940   *Strike Up the Band*

1947   *The Secret Life of Walter Mitty*

Electric Theater (1902)

The Electric Theater in Los Angeles was one of the first structures established specifically to exhibit films. Prior to the Electric Theater, films were shown in vaudeville houses between live performances and in storefronts that were temporarily converted to show films.

Using the term *theater* was reaching a bit, since the establishment was more tent than building in its early years. Under large lettering proclaiming "Electric Theater" were the words, "Where you see all the latest life size moving pictures." Near the entrance the management assured its clientele that the establishment was "moral and refined" as well as "pleasing to the ladies . . ."

During the early years of the film industry, exhibition sites regularly projected admonitions such as "Gentlemen, please refrain from Smoking, Spitting or Using Profane Language During the Performance" and "Don't Spit on the floor. . . . Remember the Johnstown Flood." In addition, the squeamish were reassured that the premises were "Ventilated and Disinfected Every Day." When studios and exhibitors sought to attract female viewers, women were assured that even "Women Without Escorts Cordially Invited."

Eyton, Bessie (1890 Santa Barbara, CA-1965 Thousand Oaks, CA)

Bessie Eyton got into show business by way of her father, who was a musician. As was common during that period, she married quite young and used her married name throughout her career, even after her divorce.

She signed with the Selig company's Los Angeles branch in 1910 and remained with them through 1918. Although she had no formal training on the stage, as did many early film actors, she was talented and soon rose to be one of Selig's most popular performers. Most of the films she appeared in were melodramas, but she made sure that each film had enough action and stunts to keep the viewers' interest.

Although she had always been popular with the audience, it was her portrayal of Virginia Carvel in *The Crisis* (1916) that won her critical acclaim. However, once Selig went out of business in 1918, Eyton never regained her former popularity. She appeared in bit parts and as a supporting actor through the 1930s.

Later, a tremendous argument with her mother motivated Eyton to disappear. For years her family heard nothing from her until they were notified of her death.

Film Credits

1911   *The Totem Mark; George Washington's Escape; The Sheriff of Tuolomne; Saved from the Snow; In the Shadow of the Pines; Kit Carson's Wooing; McKee Rankin's '49'; An Indian Vestal; Coals of Fire; A Painter's Idyl; Captain Brand's Wife; Lieutenant Grey of the Confederacy; Blackbeard; The Right Name, but the Wrong Man; An Evil Power; A Diamond in the Rough; The Chief's Daughter; For His Pal's Sake*

1912   *A Waif of the Sea; The Hobo; The End of the Romance; The Price of Art; Sammy Orpheus; The Lake of Dreams; The Indelible Stain; Monte Cristo; An Old Actor; The Last of Her Tribe*

1913   *When the Circus Came to Town; Until the Sea; The Three Wise Men; The Hopeless Dawn; A Wild Ride; The Wordless Message; Alone in the Jungle; Hope*

1914   *The Uphill Climb; Smuggler's Sister; The Salvation of Nancy O'Shaughnessy; The Spoilers; In the Days of the Thundering Herd; The Abyss; Playing with Fire; Shotgun Jones; In Defiance of the Law; The Wilderness Mail; Etienne of the Glad Heart; The White Mouse; When the West Was Young; The Gang of the White Swan; The Dream Girl; The Test; The Fifth Man*

1915   *The Adventure Hunter; The Man from Texas; The Jungle Lovers; His Fighting Blood; Red Blood of Courage; The Great Experiment; The Flashlight*

1916   *The Cycle of Fate; The Prince Chap; Twisted Trails; The Crisis; The Cycle of Fate; Angel of Poverty Row; The Sole Survivor*

1917   *Beware of Strangers; The Heart of Texas Ryan; Little Lost Sister; Who Shall Take My Life?*

1918   *The City of Purple Dreams; Lend Me Your Name; The Way of a Man with a Maid; The Still Alarm*

1919   *The Usurper; A Man of Honor; Children of Banishment*
1924   *Cheap Kisses*
1925   *The Girl of Gold*

Fairfax, Marion (1875 Richmond, VA-1970 Los Angeles, CA)

Marion Fairfax was raised in Chicago and attended Emerson College in Boston before briefly attempting a stage career. She turned to writing instead and became a successful Broadway playwright with her first play, *The Triumph of Love,* debuting in February 1904. During the early part of her writing career she also appeared in her plays, but by 1908 she was devoting herself full time to writing. She worked closely with director Marshall Neilan during this period.

In 1915, after several years of New York success, she moved to Hollywood and began writing scenarios for the Lasky Feature Play Company. The first film that she wrote to be produced was *The Chorus Lady* (1915). While at Lasky she not only wrote but also supervised the editing and production of many of her films as well as other productions.

In 1922 Fairfax formed her own production company to produce, write, and direct *The Lying Truth,* a film dealing with the horrors of drug addiction. Interestingly, this film was written after Fairfax had worked with Wallace Reid on one of her earlier films and predates the film made by Dorothy Davenport Reid in response to her husband's death by at least a year. In an interview for *Moving Picture World* in 1921 Fairfax said that she wanted her films to be "human and clean, my characters natural . . . [people] that really exist in our own lives."

Fairfax continued writing through the 1920s, working with several well-known directors including James Cruze and William de Mille. Perhaps her most famous film was the early science fiction thriller *The Lost World* (1925). Her final film credits were during 1926.

Writing Credits

1915	*The Chorus Lady; Mr. Grex of Monte Carlo; The Immigrant*
1916	*Tennessee's Partner; The Blacklist; The Sowers; The Clown; Common Ground; Anton the Terrible; The Chaperon*
1917	*The Primrose Ring; Freckles; The Crystal Gazer; Hashimura Togo; On the Level; The Secret Game*
1918	*The Widow's Might; The Honor of His House; The White Man's Law; Less Than Kin; The Mystery Girl*
1919	*The Secret Garden; You Never Saw Such a Girl; The Roaring Road; Putting It Over; A Daughter of the Wolf; Love Insurance; The Valley of the Giants*
1920	*The River's End; Don't Ever Marry; Go and Get It; Dinty*
1921	*The Mad Marriage; Bob Hampton of Placer; Through the Back Door; The Lotus Eater*
1922	*The Lying Truth; Sherlock Holmes; Fools First; The Snowshoe Trail*
1924	*A Lady of Quality; Torment; Lilies of the Field*
1925	*As Man Desires; The Lost World; The Talker; Clothes Make the Pirate*
1926	*Old Loves and New; The Blonde Saint*

Supervisory Credits

1924	*Painted People; The Perfect Flapper; For Sale; Single Wives; Flirting with Love; Sundown; So Big; The Woman on the Jury*
1925	*The Lost World; If I Marry Again; The Making of O'Malley; The Knockout; Clothes Make the Pirate*

Fan Magazines

Once actors started being known by their own names, the desire to know more about them individually exploded. The fan magazine was developed to answer this demand. The first two magazines, *Motion Picture Story* and *Photoplay,* were founded in 1911. When these two publications proved popular and profitable, *Motion Picture Classic*

(1915), *Picture-Play* (1915), *Shadowland* (1919), and many others followed them.

The most successful of the fan magazines, and the longest lasting, was *Photoplay*. Its original format consisted of plot synopses of newly released films and star portraits, along with popularity contests, real (and fabricated) letters to the editor, and editorial columns that were thinly disguised star promotions.

In 1915 James R. Quirk became vice president of the magazine and revised its format, taking over full editorial control in 1920. He eliminated the synopses and made the magazine a critical and informational volume. He hired Adela Rogers St. John to provide the star profiles and interviews that the readers wanted, while he continued the film criticism that he felt was necessary to improve the medium. It was within the pages of *Photoplay* that Terry Ramsaye wrote the first film industry history, *A Million and One Nights* (1926).

Although fan magazines were very popular with their readers, the articles were often not very well written and the writers and other individuals employed by the periodicals were often looked down upon by employees of "legitimate" magazines. Many of the fan magazines' writers even agreed with other writers' assessment of the "uncultured" nature of their work. One anonymous fan magazine writer said in a 1943 issue of *American Mercury,* "We dish out gossip just short of slander . . .we attribute lowbrow profundities to actors who have never been within hailing distance of an idea . . .we glorify clothes-horses . . ."

The publications created an illusion of constant availability of the stars to their fans—a communication of sorts. One popular gambit was the article written by a popular star. These articles were meant to keep the actors' names before their fans and encourage interest in their latest work. The articles were seldom illuminating but always self-promoting in one way or another. In 1919 Theda Bara wrote "How I Became a Vampire," while Bebe Daniels wrote "One Lesson the War Has Taught." Pauline Frederick wrote "The Story of My Life" for *Motion Picture Magazine* (1919). In 1922 Marion Davies regaled *Photoplay* readers with "How I Keep in Condition" a year after Corinne Griffith wrote the same type of article.

While fan magazines were popular with the film going audience, another favorite source of "information" were gossip columns found in magazines and newspapers. Although many such columns were in publication during the silent era, there were two first-tier gossip columnists—Louella Parsons and former actress Hedda Hopper. In keeping with the time and nature of their work, they never said anything outright but hinted at the truth by innuendo and suggestion.

Parsons got her start in 1914 with *Chicago Record-Herald*. In the 1920s she had a popular New York radio show called *The Hollywood Hotel* where her fawning coverage of Marion Davies brought her to the attention of William Randolph Hearst. She was subsequently offered a job with the *San Francisco Examiner* and was syndicated throughout the Hearst publishing empire.

Parsons reveled in the power her position gave her and made no attempt at journalistic integrity. She was completely biased: if she liked someone she praised them, but if she didn't she could (and did) damage careers out of spite. She attributed almost national significance to every "scoop" she wrote about and regaled her readers with the cloak-and-dagger lengths she went to in bringing her readers the top information.

Hopper was Parsons's favorite foil, target, and chief competitor. Although she never had the power that Parsons wielded because of Hearst's backing, she was a force to be reckoned with for many years. Hopper worked for the *Los Angeles Times,* and together with Parsons, they were *the* sources of information on Hollywood for more than thirty years. The two columnists tried to out-scoop each other and contradict whatever the other wrote. And, although Hopper was less obvious about it, she too was biased and given to holding grudges.

The age of the fan magazine ended in the 1960s, although other types of magazines quickly tried to fill the gap. Teen magazines and women's magazines started to include more coverage of entertainment stars—articles on their lives and outlooks on life, as well as their careers. But then a different type of magazine—one with some news but mostly driven by personalities—appeared. Such magazines as *People, Entertainment Weekly,* and *Us Weekly* filled the void left by the end of the older style of fan magazine.

Farrar, Geraldine (1882 Melrose, MA-1967 Springfield, CT)

Geraldine Farrar was one of the most famous women of her time and arguably the finest operatic talent of the early 1900s. She was amazingly popular with the public, even non-opera buffs, and had a legion of fans known as "Gerry-flappers."

Her talent was recognized while she was still quite young, and she studied in Boston and New York as well as Paris and Berlin. She made her debut in 1901 in Berlin as Marguerite in *Faust*. After several years of success in Europe, she made her U.S. debut at The Metropolitan Opera House in New York in 1906 as Juliet in *Romeo and Juliet*.

When World War I made it impossible for her to tour Europe, Farrar accepted an offer to appear in a series of films for Jesse Lasky and directed by Cecile B. DeMille. Her collaborations with DeMille were successful and resulted in several well-done films, most memorably *Carmen* (1915) and *Joan the Woman* (1916).

Unfortunately, about this time Farrar married an egotistical, no-talent actor who eventually ruined her film career, from either incredibly poor judgment or outright jealousy, and then divorced her when her money ran out. She retired from films in 1920 and wrote her autobiography, *Such Sweet Compulsion*, in 1938.

Film Credits

1915 *Carmen; Temptation*
1916 *Maria Rosa*
1917 *The Woman God Forgot; The Devil-Stone; Joan the Woman*
1918 *The Turn of the Wheel; The Hell Cat*
1919 *Shadows; The Stronger Vow; The World and Its Woman; Flame of the Desert*
1920 *The Woman and the Puppet; Riddle: A Woman*
1931 *The Movie Album*

Faye, Julia (1893 Richmond, VA-1966 Hollywood, CA)

Julia Faye began her entertainment career in touring companies before making her film debut in 1915. She briefly worked with D. W. Griffith in 1916 before moving to Famous Players-Lasky. While with Famous Players she met the man who would determine her career—Cecil B. DeMille. She was his mistress for many years, and DeMille supposedly remained devoted to her even after their romantic relationship ended. He featured her in all of his films from 1918 to 1956.

Courtesy of Silents Are Golden at
<SilentsAreGolden.com>

Film Credits

1915   *The Lamb; Don Quixote*

1916   *The Surf Girl; His Auto Ruination*

1917   *A Roadside Impresario; The Woman God Forgot*

1918   *The Whispering Chorus; Old Wives for New; Sandy; Till I Come Back to You; Mrs. Leffingwell's Boots; The Squaw Man*

1919   *Venus in the East; Don't Change Your Husband; A Very Good Young Man; Stepping Out; Male and Female; It Pays to Advertise*

1920   *The Six Best Cellars; Something to Think About; Life of the Party*

1921   *Forbidden Fruit; The Great Moment; The Affairs of Anatol; Fool's Paradise; The Snob*

1922   *Saturday Night; Manslaughter; Nice People*

1923   *Nobody's Money; Hollywood; Adam's Rib; The Ten Commandments* (I)

1924   *Don't Call It Love; Triumph; Changing Husbands; Feet of Clay*

1925   *The Golden Bed; Hell's Highroad; The Road to Yesterday*

1926   *The Volga Boatman; Bachelor Brides; Meet the Prince; Corporal Kate*

1927   *The Yankee Clipper; The King of Kings; His Dog; The Fighting Eagle; Turkish Delight; The Main Event; Chicago*

1929   *The Godless Girl; Dynamite; The Voice of Hollywood No.3*

1930   *Not So Dumb*

1931   *The Squaw Man*

1933   *Only Yesterday*

1936   *Till We Meet Again*

1938   *You and Me*

1939   *The Spellbinder; Union Pacific*

1940   *Remember the Night; North West Mounted Police*

1941   *Pacific Blackout*

1942   *Reap the Wild Wind*

1943   *So Proudly We Hail*

1944   *The Story of Dr. Wassell; Casanova Brown*

1945   *Masquerade in Mexico*

1947   *Fear in the Night; Blaze of Noon; Welcome Stranger; The Perils of Pauline; Unconquered; California; Easy Come, Easy Go*

1948   *Joan of Arc; Night Has a Thousand Eyes; The Big Clock*

1949   *A Connecticut Yankee in King Arthur's Court; Chicago Deadline; Song of Surrender; Samson and Delilah; Red Hot and Blue; Alias Nick Beal*

1950   *Where Danger Lives; Sunset Blvd.; The Lawless; Copper Canyon*

1951   *Here Comes the Groom*

1952   *The Greatest Show on Earth*

1956   *The Ten Commandments* (II)

1958   *The Buccaneer*

Fazenda, Louise (1895 Lafayette, IN-Beverly Hills, CA)

Courtesy of Silents Are Golden at
<SilentsAreGolden.com>.

Louise Fazenda, a talented early comedian, had the distinction of being one of the only actors in Hollywood to be well thought of by the entire film community both during her career and after her retirement. Considering the competition and jealousy of Hollywood, this was not an inconsequential achievement.

Fazenda moved to Los Angeles with her family when she was about two years old and originally planned to be either a teacher or a writer. But when her father's business failed, she did odd jobs until she found work as a film extra. Since she was helping to support her family, when she could not find an acting job she did stunt work.

She began to appear as a stock player for Universal's Joker Comedy unit in 1913 then moved to Mack Sennett's Keystone Company in 1915, where she became one of his most popular stars. Although attractive enough to be chosen one of Sennett's first "Bathing Beauties," she was one of the few actors of the period who would deliberately downplay her looks in order to portray gawky "bumpkin" characters, a characterization that she perfected while attending Sennett's comedy training known as the "Komedy Kollege." In fact, her bumpkin characters were so popular that Sennett once insured her pigtails for $10,000 as a publicity stunt.

She became known for her willingness to do anything if it caused the audience to laugh and to try any stunt regardless of the risk. By the mid-1920s, when she moved into feature films, she was a sought-after character actor who could coax a laugh from the audience with any character she portrayed. Although still playing the country girl, she also became known for her society dowager characterization in several social comedies of the period.

In 1927 she married famed producer Hal B. Wallis—a marriage that lasted until her death. Both she and Wallis worked for Warner Bros. studios, and it was often quipped around the lot that Wallis was "the prisoner of Fazenda." She made the transition to sound and continued to appear in films throughout the 1930s.

Fazenda retired from films after 1939 and became a social leader of Hollywood as well as a tireless worker for and contributor to numerous charities. In addition, she became known as an art collector, amassing many museum-quality paintings and sculpture over the years.

Film Credits

1913   *The Cheese Special; Poor Jake's Demise; Almost An Actress; Mike and Jake at the Beach; Mike and Jake at the Oil Fields; Mike and Jake in the Wild Wild West; Thou Shalt Not Rubber; Mike and Jake at College; Mike and Jake Go Fishing; Mike and Jake in Mexico; Mike and Jake in Society; For Art and Love; Hilda of the Mountains; The Joy Riders; Mike and Jake Among the Cannibals; Mike and Jake As Heroes; Mike and Jake As Pugilists; She Should Worry*

1914   *The Sharps Want a Flat; Some Nightmare; The Tender Hearted Sheriff; That's Fair Enough; Their First Anniversary; What Happened to Schultz?; When Their Wives Join the Regiment; Wifie's Busy Day; Jam and Jealousy; Love and Electricity; Love and Graft; Love and Politics; Love Disguised; A Mexico Mix; Love, Roses and Trousers; The Midnight Alarm; Mike and Jake Join the Army; The New Butler; Mike Searches for His Long Lost Brother; The Mystery of the Taxi Cab; The Polo Champions; Schultz the Barber; Schultz the Paper Hanger; Across the Court; The Baseball Fans of Fanville; The Battle of the Nations; The Bucket Sharpers; Saving the Child; Captain's Kid's Priceless Treasure; The Chicken Chasers; The Head Waiter; Cruel, Cruel World; The De-Feet of Father; The Diamond Nippers; A Dream of a Painting; The Fatal Letter; He Married Her Anyhow; Heaven Will Protect the Working Girl; His Doctor's Orders; His Wife's Family; In the Clutches of the Villain; Oh, What's the Use!; Mike and Jake in the Clutch of Circumstances; Well! Well!*

1915   *Hubby's Cure; A Hash House Fraud; The Water Cure; Won with Dynamite; A Game Old Knight; The Blank Note; Ambrose's Fury; Ambrose's Lofty Perch; Ambrose's Nasty Temper; The Great Vacuum Robbery; Willful Ambrose; A Versatile Villain; A Rascal's Foolish Way; Fatty's Tintype Tangle; Crossed Love and Swords; A Bird's a Bird; A Bear Affair; Ambrose's New Hatchet; When Ambrose Dared Walrus; Stark Mad*

1916   *His Hereafter; The Marble Heart; The Judge; A Bath House Blunder; Maid Mad; A Love Riot; Her Marble Heart; The Feathered Nest; Bombs!*

1917   *Her Torpedoed Love; Maggie's First False Step; His Precious Life; Her Fame and Shame; The Betrayal of Maggie; Are Waitresses Safe?*

1918   *The Village Chestnut; The Summer Girls; The Kitchen Lady; Her First Mistake*

1919   *Hearts and Flowers; Back to the Kitchen*

1920   *Married Life; Down on the Farm; The Quack Doctor; The Star Boarder; It's a Boy; You Wouldn't Believe It; Let 'er Go*

1921   *A Small Town Idol; Astray from Steerage; Bungalow Troubles; Dizzy Daisy*

1922   *The Beauty Shop; Quincy Adams Sawyer; Bow Wow; The Beautiful and the Damned*

1923   *The Spoilers; The Spider and the Rose; Tea with a Kick; The Fog; The Gold Diggers; The Wanters; Main Street; Mary of the Movies; The Old Fool*

1924   *The Dramatic Life of Abraham Lincoln; The Galloping Fish; True As Steel; Listen Lester; Being Respectable; The Lighthouse by the Sea; This Woman*

1925   *The Price of Pleasure; Bobbed Hair; Broadway Butterfly; Compromise; Hogan's Alley; Cheaper to Marry; The Love Hour; The Night Club; Déclassé; Grounds for Divorce*

1926   *The Bat; Footloose Widows; Miss Nobody; The Passionate Quest; Millionaires; The Old Soak; The Lady of the Harem; Ladies at Play; Tin Gods*

1927   *The Red Mill; The Gay Old Bird; A Texas Steer; A Sailor's Sweetheart; The Cradle Snatchers; Finger Prints; Babe Comes Home; Simple Sis; Ham and Eggs at the Front*

1928   *Heart to Heart; The Terror; Pay As You Enter; Tillie's Punctured Romance; Outcast; Riley the Cop; Vamping Venus; Domestic Troubles; Noah's Ark; Five and Ten Cent Annie*

1929   *Show of Shows; Hot Stuff; The Desert Song; Stark Mad; Hard to Get; The Broadway Hoofer; On with the Show; Faro Nell; House of Horror; Hot Lemonade; Noah's Ark; Night Club*

1930   *No, No, Nanette; Wide Open; Loose Ankles; Spring Is Here; Bride of the Regiment; Rain or Shine; Leathernecking; Viennese Nights; High Society Blues; So This Is Paris Green; Bearded Lady*

1931   *Misbehaving Ladies; The Mad Parade; Newly Rich; The Cuban Love Song; Gun Smoke; The Itching Hour*

1932   *Racing Youth; Once in a Lifetime; The Unwritten Law; Running Hollywood; Union Wages; Hesitating Loves*

1933   *Alice in Wonderland; Out of Gas; Stung Again*

1934   *Wonder Bar; Caravan; Mountain Music* (I)

1935   *Bad Boy; The Casino Murder Case; Broadway Gondolier; The Winning Ticket; A Dream Comes True; The Widow from Monte Carlo*

1936   *Colleen; I Married a Doctor; Doughnuts and Society*

1937   *Ever Since Eve; Merry-Go-Round of 1938; Ready, Willing and Able; First Lady; The Road Back; Mountain Music* (II)

1938   *Down on the Farm; Swing Your Lady*

1939   *The Old Maid*

1943   *Happy Times and Jolly Moments*

Female Impersonation

Males impersonating females is a standard comedy gambit. The practice can trace its history from the ancient Greeks to modern films and television. In fact, the fame of some actors of the late twentieth century hinged on their female personas, such as RuPaul and Dame Edna Everage.

Silent film comedians made use of this stock-in-trade in several movies. Often the impersonation was a warning to women under the guise of comedy and often showed the "woman" flaunting the status quo. Occasionally the actor would undertake the impersonation as a convenient means of deception to allow the male access to places that would normally be closed to him, such as a harem or a girls school. Other times the impersonator used "her" feminine wiles to make a fool of the unsuspecting male characters in the films.

Charlie Chaplin appeared as a woman in *The Masquerader* (1914), *A Busy Day* (1914), and *A Woman* (1915). In *A Busy Day,* Chaplin played a militant suffragette who is pushed in the ocean by her disgusted male companion and is allowed to drown.

A partial list of female impersonators during the silent era includes Stan Laurel, Oliver Hardy, Syd Chaplin, John Bunny, Lupino Lane, and Wallace Beery. Fatty Arbuckle appeared as a female in two of his popular films—*Miss Fatty's Seaside Lovers* (1915) and *The Butcher Boy* (1917).

Ferguson, Helen (1900 Decatur, IL-1977 Clearwater, FL)

Helen Ferguson, one of the earliest and most successful publicists in the film industry, starred in three popular serials of the 1920s and was one of the first "promising" starlets chosen as a WAMPAS Baby Star in 1922. Although a complete filmography is not available, it is believed that she began her film career with Essanay Studios in Chicago around 1914, where she made more than 100 one- and two-reel films.

Her first recorded film credit is from mid-1917, and she appeared in many action films and westerns before moving to Fox Studios and starring with Buck Jones in several popular films. She then moved to Pathe and appeared in the serials for which she is best remembered. Her first serial, *Wild West* (1925), brought the elements of circus life to the old west and was relatively successful. Her next serial, *Casey of the Coast Guard* (1926), revolved around the authority's efforts to catch a band of smugglers. Her final Pathe serial was *The Fire Fighters* (1927).

She retired from films in 1930, after marrying a wealthy banker, and decided to concentrate on stage work. She was moderately successful on the stage, but she retired completely in 1933 to become a publicist for the film industry. Among her clients were Henry Fonda, Loretta Young, and Barbara Stanwyck. She was extraordinarily successful as a publicist and was termed "a powerhouse" in the film industry. In 1961 she co-wrote the book titled, *The Things I Had to Learn* with Loretta Young. She retired from publicity work in 1967 and settled briefly in Palm Desert, California.

In 1976 she moved to Clearwater, Florida, where she died a year later. She was buried at Forest Lawn Cemetery in Glendale, California—the final resting place for many famous celebrities.

Film Credits

1917   *Sundaying in Fairview; Filling His Own Shoes; The Golden Idiot; The Gift o' Gab; The Small Town Guy; Fools for Luck*
1918   *Life's Greatest Problem*
1919   *The Gamblers; The Lost Battalion; The Great Victory*
1920   *Shod with Fire; Burning Daylight; Going Some; The Romance Promoters; The Challenge of the Law; Just Pals; The Mutiny of the Elsinore*
1921   *The Right Way; The Freeze-Out; Straight from the Shoulder; To a Finish; Making the Grade; Desert Blossoms; Miss Lulu Bett; The Call of the North*
1922   *According to Hoyle; Roughshod; The Crusader; Hungry Hearts; The Flaming Hour*
1923   *The Famous Mrs. Fair; Brass; Within the Law; Double Dealing; The Unknown Purple*
1924   *The Right of the Strongest; Racing Luck; The Valley of Hate; Never Say Die; Chalk Marks; Why Get Married?*
1925   *The Cloud Rider; My Neighbor's Wife; The Scarlet West; Nine and Three-Fifths Seconds; The Isle of Hope; Wild West; Spook Ranch*
1926   *Casey of the Coast Guard*
1927   *The Fire Fighters; Cheaters; Jaws of Steel; Taxi! Taxi!*
1929   *In Old California; Finders Keepers; Trusting Wives*
1930   *Scarlet Pages*
1934   *Kid Millions*

Finch, Flora (1868 Surrey, England-1940 Los Angeles, CA)

Flora Finch spent several successful years in the theater on both sides of the Atlantic before entering the infant film industry during a lull in theater work. Her first film was *Mrs. Jones Entertains* (1908), which costarred John Compson and was directed by D. W. Griffith. This film was the first in a series of collaborations among the three that lasted for several films and featured some of the few comedies directed by Griffith.

In 1910 she began appearing as Mrs. Bunny in a long-running Vitagraph series with popular comic John Bunny. The appreciative audience called these short subjects, numbering more than 260, "Bunnyfinches." Sadly, the series ended with Bunny's sudden death in 1915.

In 1917 Finch created her own production company, Flora Finch Film Company. It is unclear how long her company survived, but by the early 1920s she was once more working for various studios. Finch was a popular character actor throughout the 1920s and easily made the transition to sound at the end of the decade. She continued to appear in supporting and bit roles until 1939.

Film Credits

1908   *The Helping Hand*
1909   *Mr. Jones Has a Card Party; Those Awful Hats; His Wife's Mother; Jones and His New Neighbors; Schneider's Anti-Noise Crusade; A Sound Sleeper; Jones and the Lady Book Agent; What Drink Did; Her First Biscuits; The Way of Man; Mrs. Jones Entertains; A Wreath in Time*
1910   *All on Account of the Milk; Muggsy's First Sweetheart; Uncle Tom's Cabin* (I); *The Troublesome Baby; Davy Jones and Captain Bragg*
1911   *The Misses Finch and Their Nephew Billy; The New Stenographer; Captain Barnacle's Courtship; The Wooing of Winnifred; The Derelict Reporter; Two Overcoats; The Woes of a Wealthy Widow; The Subduing of Mrs. Nag; Intrepid Davy; Her Crowning Glory; Her Hero; Selecting His Heiress; The Politician's Dream; The Ventriloquist's Trunk; The Midnight Marauder; The Gossip; Tim Mahoney, the Scab; The Sleep Walker; In Northern Forests; Treasure Trove; In the Clutches of a Vapor Bath*

1912 *The First Violin; The Old Silver Watch; The Troublesome Step-Daughters; The Foster Child; The Awakening of Jones; Bachelor Buttons; Lord Browning and Cinderella; A Vitagraph Romance; Umbrellas to Mend; The Suit of Armor; Suing Susan; Red Ink Tragedy; Pseudo Sultan; A Persistent Lover; Pandora's Box; Martha's Rebellion; Leap Year Proposals; The Jocular Winds of Fate; Irene's Infatuation; In the Flat Above; How He Papered the Room; Her Old Sweetheart; Freckles; The First Woman Jury in America; Diamond Cut Diamond; A Cure for Pokeritis; The Church Across the Way; Bunny's Suicide; Bunny and the Twins; The Browns Have Visitors; Stenographer Wanted; Her Forgotten Dancing Shoes; The Governor Who Had a Heart; Thou Shalt Not Covet; Professor Optimo; Saving an Audience; Captain Barnacle's Legacy; An Elephant on Their Hands; Bunny All at Sea; An Expensive Shine; The Hand Bag; The Professor and the Lady; The Unusual Honeymoon; The Servant Problem; Doctor Bridget; Planting the Spring Garden*

1913 *Mr. Bolter's Niece; Horatio Sparkins; No Sweets; When the Press Speaks; Father's Hatband; The Wonderful Statue; When Mary Grew Up; Three Black Bags; Those Troublesome Tresses; There's Music in the Hair; Stenographer Troubles; The Schemers; The Pickpocket; One Good Joke Deserves Another; A Millinery Bomb; Love's Quarantine; Love Laughs at Blacksmiths or Love Finds a Way; The Locket; John Tobin's Sweetheart; Hubby's Toothache; Hubby Buys a Baby; His Honor the Mayor; He Answered an Ad; The Golf Game and the Bonnet; The Girl at the Lunch Counter; A Gentleman of Fashion; The Fortune; The Feudists; Fatty's Affair of Honor; Cupid's Hired Man; The Classmates Frolic; Bunny's Dilemma; Bunny's Birthday Surprise; The Brown's Study Astrology; The Autocrat of Flapjack Junction; And His Wife Came Back; Which Way Did He Go?; The Little Minister; A Trap to Catch a Burglar; Suspicious Henry; The Way Out; The Dog House Builders; The Wonderful Statue; When Women Go on the Warpath; The Lady and Her Maid; Cutey and the Chorus Girls; Bunny As a Reporter; Bingles' Nightmare; Bingles Mends the Clock*

1914 *Bunny's Birthday; A Train of Incidents; Bunny's Little Brother; How Cissy Made Good; The Vases of Hymen; Tangled Tangoists; Sweeney's Christmas Bird; Such a Hunter; The Rocky Road to Love; Private Bunny; Polishing Up; The Old Maid's Baby; The Old Firehouse and the New Fire Chief; The New Secretary; Mr. Bunny in Disguise; Love's Old Dream; The Locked House; Hearts and Diamonds; Fixing Their Dads; Father's Flirtation; A Change in Baggage Checks; Bunny's Swell Affair; Bunny's Scheme; Bunny's Mistake; Bunny Buys a Hat for His Bride; Bunny Buys a Harem; Bunny Backslides; Cutey's Wife; Cutey's Vacation; Bunco Bill's Visit*

1915 *A Night Out; Two and Two; The Starring of Flora Finchurch; A Mistake in Typesetting; The Lady of Shalott; Conquest of Constantia; Between Two Fires*

1916 *Prudence and the Pirate; The Brown Derby*

1917 *War Prides; Flora the School Teacher; Flora the Manicure Girl; Flora the Life-Saver; Flora the International Spy; Flora the Dressmaker; Flora Joins the Chorus; Flora in the Movies*

1918 *The Great Adventure; Boodle and Bandits*

1919 *Dawn; Oh Boy!*

1920 *The She-Male Sleuth; Birthright*

1921 *Orphans of the Storm; Lessons in Love*

1922 *Man Wanted; When Knighthood Was in Flower; Orphan Sally*

1923 *Luck*

1924 *Roulette; Monsieur Beaucaire*

1925 *The Early Bird; The Midnight Girl; Men and Women; The Adventurous Sex; The Wrongdoers; The Live Wire; His Buddy's Wife; A Kiss for Cinderella; Lover's Island*

1926 *Fifth Avenue; The Brown Derby; Morning Judge; Oh, Baby!*

1927 *Captain Salvation; The Cat and the Canary; Rose of the Golden West; Quality Street*

1928 *The Wife's Relations; Five and Ten Cent Annie; The Haunted House*

1929 *The Faker; Come Across*

1930 *Sweet Kitty Bellairs; The Matrimonial Bed*

1931   *I Take This Woman*
1934   *The Scarlet Letter; The Painted Veil*
1936   *Show Boat; San Francisco; Postal Inspector*
1937   *Way Out West; Mama Steps Out; When Love Is Young; Bad Guy; A Night at the Movies*
1939   *The Women*

Fischer, Margarita (1886 Missoury Valley, OH-1975 Encinitas, CA)

Margarita Fischer, one of the many popular stars of the pre-World War I era, was born to a show business family and toured with her parents in the company managed by her father. She made her stage debut at age eight; known as "Babe Fischer," she appeared in repertoire, stock, and vaudeville throughout her youth.

She entered films after becoming tired of the rigors of constant touring. She appeared briefly with the Selig Polyscope Company before moving to IMP in 1911 and then the Bison Company in 1912. After she married fellow actor Harry Pollard, he became her manager-director and she soon became a popular leading lady.

After freelancing for a few years, she joined the American Film Company where her husband wrote and directed several of her short films before moving to the longer feature format. Her career stalled by the early 1920s and she retired completely from films after a disastrous remake of *Uncle Tom's Cabin* in 1927.

Film Credits

1911   *Over the Hills; A Lesson to Husbands; The Girl and the Half-Back*
1912   *The Tribal Law; The Worth of a Man; Romance and Reality; The Rights of a Savage; The Parson and the Medicine Man; On the Shore; The Old Folks' Christmas; A Melodrama of Yesterday; Love War and a Bonnet; Jim's Atonement; The Exchange of Labels; The Dove and the Serpent; The Call of the Drum; Big-Hearted Jim; Better Than Gold; Betty's Bandit; Employer's Liability; A Fight for Friendship; The Hand of Mystery; Hearts in Conflict; An Indian Outcast; Nothing*

Shall Be Hidden; On the Border Line; Trapped by Fire; Rose of California; Squnk City Fire Company; The Baby; Where Paths Meet

1913   *In Slavery Days; How Men Propose; Shon the Piper; The Thumb Print; Uncle Tom's Cabin; A Wrong Road; A Woman's Folly; When the Prince Arrived; The Wayward Sister; The Turn of the Tide; The Stolen Idol; The Shadow; Robinson Crusoe* (I); *Sally Scraggs, Housemaid; The Tale of a Lonely Coast; The Boob's Dream Girl; The Diamond Makers; The Fight Against Evil; The Great Ganton Mystery; His Old-Fashioned Dad; Like Darby and Joan; The Missionary Box; Paying the Price; The Power of Heredity; The Primeval Test*

1915   *The Quest; The Lonesome Heart; The Girl from His Town; Infatuation; The Miracle of Life*

1916   *The Dragon; The Pearl of Paradise; Miss Jackie of the Navy*

1917   *The Butterfly Girl; The Devil's Bait; The Girl Who Couldn't Grow Up; Miss Jackie of the Army; The Devil's Assistant; The Brand of Death; Defiance; The Diamond Thieves; The Human Flames; A Sin Unatoned; Robinson Crusoe* (II)

1918   *Molly Go Get 'Em; Jilted Janet; Ann's Finish; The Primitive Woman; The Square Deal; Impossible Susan; Money Isn't Everything; Fair Enough; The Mantle of Charity*

1919   *Molly of the Follies; Charge It to Me; Trixie from Broadway; The Tiger Lily; The Hellion; Put Up Your Hands!*

1920   *The Dangerous Talent; The Week-End; The Thirtieth Piece of Silver; Their Mutual Child; The Gamesters*

1921   *Beach of Dreams; Payment Guaranteed*

1924   *K: The Unknown*

1925   *Any Woman*

1927   *Uncle Tom's Cabin*

Flappers

The flapper was the rebellious young woman of the Jazz Age. The term supposedly came from the sound of the unbuckled galoshes that the fashionable girl of the period wore. Immortalized in popular culture from the cartoons of illustrator John Held Jr. to the movies of the

1920s to the novels of F. Scott Fitzgerald, flappers became the symbol of the modern New Woman of the post–World War I era.

With bobbed hair and short skirts, the younger generation was no longer relegated to the home or shackled by family obligations. The flapper wore dresses that exposed more of her body than any "good" girl had ever exposed—bare arms and legs with nothing from the knee down!

Youth and the young were all the rage after the end of the "war to end all wars." Flappers socialized with both men and women and seemed to have only one simple goal—to live life to the fullest while having fun. Social sophistication was the style of the day, yet there was an underlying pessimism beneath the gaiety. The world had lost its innocence in the years of the war and people no longer believed that the future would necessarily be better.

The flapper first appeared in film reviews in 1921, and in 1923 Colleen Moore was called "The Perfect Flapper," after her role in *Flaming Youth*. The flapper became a staple character in 1920s films—a girl who could do anything during the course of the scenario as long as she returned to her "place" in society by the end of the film.

Long forgotten by film audiences, the flapper filled the void during the confusing transition from Edwardian old-fashioned girls to the modern woman of postwar America.

Flugrath, Edna (1893 Brooklyn, NY-1966 San Diego, CA)

The eldest of the Flugrath sisters, Edna Flugrath began her entertainment career in vaudeville, stage performances, and even ballet. A life on the road grew tiresome, so after several years of touring, Flugrath returned to New York to seek employment in films.

She was signed as a stock player with the Edison Film Company and by 1912 was one of the company's leading ladies, appearing in a variety of one- and two-reel films. While at Edison she met her future husband, director Harold Shaw, and when he moved to England to direct, she finished her contract and followed him. She appeared in several of his films before they were married in 1917, after which Flugrath briefly retired from films. She returned in 1920 to appear in several of her husband's films, with both the London Film Company and the Stoll Film Company.

Upon returning to the United States, Flugrath was unable to engineer a film comeback, so she opened a beauty salon in Hollywood. Not long after their return to Hollywood Shaw was killed in an automobile accident and Flugrath further disappeared from public attention. She also became estranged from her sisters, Viola Dana and Shirley Mason, to the point that they learned of her death from a stranger.

Film Credits

1912   *Annie Crawls Upstairs; A Proposal Under Difficulties; The Dam Builder; Hearts and Diamonds; Like Knights of Old; The New Member of the Life Saving Crew; On Donovan's Division; Outwitting the Professor; The Third Thanksgiving*

1913   *Uncle Mun and the Minister; Between Orton Junction and Fallonville; The Undesirable Relatives; Mother's Lazy Boy; The Photographer and the Blotter; A Race to New York; A Tardy Recognition; The Widow's Suitors; A Perilous Cargo; At Bear Track Gulch; Nursery Favorites*

1914   *The King's Minister; A Christmas Carol; Child o' My Heart; England's Menace; The Two Columbines; The King and the Rajah; Turtle Dove* (all in the United Kingdom); *Trilby; Liberty Hall; Duty; Bootle's Baby*

1915   *The Incomparable Bellairs; Lil o' London* (both in the United Kingdom); *Mr. Lyndon at Liberty; The Third Generation; The Heart of Sister Ann; The Firm of Girdlestone; The Derby Winner; Ashes of Revenge*

1916   *You; The Two Roads*

1917   *Me and m' Pal; The Man Without a Soul*

1920   *London Pride; True Tilda; The Land of Mystery; The Pursuit of Pamela*

1921   *Kipps; A Dear Fool; A Case of Identity*

1922   *False Evidence*

1923   *The Social Code*

1924   *Winning a Continent* (originally filmed in 1916)

Frederick, Pauline (1883 Boston, MA-1938 Beverly Hills, CA)

Courtesy of Silents Are Golden at
<SilentsAreGolden.com>

Pauline Frederick was a successful stage actor and singer before being lured to the film industry. Her New York stage debut was in 1902 in *The Rogers Brothers in Harvard,* and her Broadway debut was a few years later in *It Happened in Nordland.*

Her film debut was in 1915 in the Famous Players production *The Eternal City,* shot on location in Rome and finished just days before war broke out in Europe. Because of her fame from the stage, she was an immediate success; between 1915 and 1917 she appeared in almost twenty features for Famous Players.

She moved briefly to the Samuel Goldwyn production company, but after an unrivaled performance in *Madame X,* Frederick spent several years appearing in mundane productions. After completing her final film contract, she returned to the stage.

She continued to appear in occasional films while maintaining her stage career and made the transition to sound films with ease. In 1926 she revived her most memorable role in a stage production of *Madame X* that toured both the United States and Europe. Her final screen appearance was in 1937, less than one year before she died of asthmatic complications.

Film Credits

1915 *The Eternal City; Sold; Zaza; Bella Donna; Lydia Gilmore*
1916 *The Spider; Audrey; The Moment Before; The World's Great Snare; The Woman in the Case; Ashes of Embers; Nanette of the Wilds; The Slave Island*
1917 *The Slave Market; Sapho; Sleeping Fires; Her Better Self; The Love That Lives; Double Crossed; The Hungry Heart*

1918   *Mrs. Dane's Defense; Madame Jealousy; La Tosca; Resur-rection; Her Final Reckoning; Fedora; A Daughter of the Old South*

1919   *Out of the Shadow; The Woman on the Index; Paid in Full; One Week of Life; The Fear Woman; The Peace of Roaring River; Bonds of Love; The Love of Letty*

1920   *The Paliser Case; Madame X; A Slave of Vanity; The Woman in Room 13*

1921   *The Mistress of Shenstone; Salvage; The Sting of the Lash; The Lure of Jade; Roads of Destiny*

1922   *Two Kinds of Women; The Glory of Clementina; The Woman Breed*

1924   *Three Women; Married Flirts; Let Not Man Put Asunder*

1925   *Smouldering Fires*

1926   *Devil's Island; Josselyn's Wife; Her Honor, the Governor*

1927   *The Nest; Mumsie*

1928   *On Trial*

1929   *The Sacred Flame; Evidence*

1931   *This Modern Age*

1932   *Wayward; The Phantom of Crestwood; Self Defense*

1934   *The Social Register*

1935   *My Marriage*

1936   *Ramona*

1937   *Thank You Mr. Moto*

1938   *The Buccaneer*

Friganza, Trixie (1870 Grenola, KS-1955 Flintridge, CA)

When Trixie Friganza decided to join a musical touring company in 1889 because it paid five times what she made as a salesgirl, her appalled family sent the sheriff after her. But after deciding that Friganza was not at risk, the sheriff convinced her mother to let her remain with the company. By the 1890s she was established as a star of musical comedy in the United States and traveled to London to make her European debut. Although she had started her career as a chorus girl, she soon gained weight to the point that when she made her vaudeville debut in 1906 she did a Marie Dressler impersonation.

By 1912 she was a vaudeville headliner and often appeared at the Palace Theater in New York in an act she billed as "My Little Bag o'

Trix" and was always, as noted in *Variety,* a "riotous hit." One of her most popular characterizations was that of the man chaser who bemoaned, "Won't someone kindly stake me to a man."

She made fun of her size and her supposed social ineptness with songs such as "No Wedding Bells for Me" (which she refused to sing once she got married) and "I'm Not Having Birthdays Any More." She increased her apparent size by wearing several costumes at the same time and removing them during the course of her act. When questioned about her size, she replied that when she started her career "you could blow me through a keyhole. Now you have to take down the whole door to get me through."

She moved to films in the 1920s, appearing in character roles and making the transition to sound. However, her roles were becoming smaller so she retired in 1939. After her retirement she sold all her possessions and donated the money to the Sacred Heart Academy near Pasadena, California. After some discussion with convent officials, she moved into the convent, where she taught drama classes until she became bedridden due to severe arthritis.

Film Credits

1923   *Mind Over Motor*
1925   *The Charmer; Proud Flesh; The Coming of Amos; The Road to Yesterday; Borrowed Finery*
1926   *Monte Carlo; Almost a Lady; The Whole Town's Talking; The Waiter from the Ritz*
1927   *A Racing Romeo*
1928   *Gentlemen Prefer Blondes; Thanks for the Buggy Ride*
1930   *Free and Easy; The Unholy Three; Strong and Willing; My Bag o'Trix*
1933   *Myrt and Marge*
1935   *Wanderer of the Wasteland*
1936   *Silks and Saddles*
1937   *A Star Is Born; How to Undress in Front of Your Husband*
1940   *If I Had My Way*

Fuller, Dale (1885 Santa Ana, CA-1948 Pomona, CA)

Dale Fuller grew up in an agricultural area of Southern California before attending Mills College for Women in Oakland, California. In the early 1900s it was unusual for any girl to attend college, and it is unclear whether she graduated before starting her show business career.

She joined a stock company and traveled throughout the western states. She also played the vaudeville circuit in addition to performing in musical comedy revues. After tiring of touring in 1916, she decided to turn her sights to a film career.

She joined Mack Sennett's Triangle-Keystone Company, where she served her apprentice years in the studio's frantic comedies. She interspersed theater work with her film appearances and never settled at one studio for long. She still managed to appear in some of the silent era's classic films by Erich von Stroheim and the briefly popular exaggerated romances of Elinor Glyn.

Her final film appearance was in 1935. She retired to a rural area of Southern California, not far from where she was born, and lived in anonymity until her death thirteen years later.

Film Credits

1915   *Crooked to the End*
1916   *The Surf Girl; A Scoundrel's Tale; Bath Tub Perils*
1917   *Dodging His Dream; Dodging His Doom; His Bitter Fate; An Innocent Villain; Their Domestic Deception; His Baby Doll; A Noble Fraud; A Dog's Own Tale*
1922   *Foolish Wives; Borderland; Manslaughter; One Wonderful Night*
1923   *Souls for Sale; Tea: What a Kick; Reno; Merry-Go-Round*
1924   *Three Weeks; The Marriage Circle; Babbitt; His Hour; Husbands and Lovers; House of Horrors; Greed*
1925   *Tomorrow's Love; The Devil's Cargo; Lady of the Night; The Woman Hater; The Merry Widow; The Unchastened Woman; The Only Thing; Ben-Hur; The Shadow on the Wall*
1926   *Memory Lane; Her Second Chance; The Speeding Venus; Midnight Lovers; The Canadian; Volcano*
1927   *The Beauty Shoppers; The King of Kings*
1928   *Fazil; The Cossacks* (I); *The Wedding March*
1929   *Glad Rag Doll; The Sacred Flame*
1930   *The Man from Blankley's; The Office Wife*
1931   *The Great Meadow*

1932   *Emma; Rasputin and the Empress*
1934   *House of Mystery; Twentieth Century; We Live Again*
1935   *A Tale of Two Cities*

Fuller, Mary (1888 Washington, DC-1973 Washington, DC)

Courtesy of Silents Are Golden at
<SilentsAreGolden.com>

Mary Fuller, who starred in the first serial in film history, was supposedly a descendent of a family who had come to America on the Mayflower. Born into a wealthy Washington, DC, family, she quit high school after her first year to embark on an acting career with a touring company.

She moved into films early and worked as a stock player for Vitagraph from 1906 to 1909 before moving to Edison Films for two years. It was while working at Edison that she appeared in *What Happened to Mary?* (1912). What Happened to Mary? was a joint project between Edison Films and *McClure's Ladies World* magazine. The one-reel films were released simultaneously with the publication of the associated stories in the magazine. The series catapulted Fuller to stardom and resulted in her being named one of the top five film stars of 1914 by *Motion Picture Magazine.*

She moved to Universal in 1914 and made her feature film debut with *Under Southern Skies* (1915). But at the height of her fame, Fuller retired from films and virtually disappeared.

After Fuller retired there was uncertainty as to what had happened to her, and over the years several stories were put forth. One had her retiring after a failed romance and a resulting nervous breakdown only to fail in an attempt at a film comeback years later. Another had her forced to live with her mother as her mental condition deteriorated. Regardless of which scenario is correct, if either is, Fuller did die in a mental hospital and was buried in an unmarked grave.

Film Credits

1907 *The Ugly Duckling*
1908 *Leah the Forsaken; The Stage-Struck Daughter; The Flower Girl of Paris*
1909 *A Sister's Love; Jessie, the Stolen Child; King Lear; The Foundling; Betty's Choice; A Rose of the Tenderloin; Lochinvar; The House of Cards; Hansel and Gretel; Fuss and Feathers; A Child of the Forest; Bluebeard*
1910 *Frankenstein; Michael Strogoff; Sisters; The Princess and the Peasant; Ononko's Vow; The Luck of Roaring Camp; The Lady and the Burglar; The House of Seven Gables; From Tyranny to Liberty; For Her Sister's Sake; An Engineer's Romance; Elektra; Carminella; Arms and the Woman; The Peacemaker; Uncle Tom's Cabin; The Farmer's Daughter; A Modern Cinderella* (I)
1911 *A Stage Romance; Aida; In the Days of Chivalry; The Star Spangled Banner; Trading His Mother; The Switchman's Tower; Two Officers; The Modern Dianas; The Professor and the New Hat; The Surgeon's Temptation; The Silent Tongue; Three Musketeers (Part 1 and 2); Foul Play; At the Threshold of Life; A Conspiracy Against the King; The Reform Candidate; A Modern Cinderella* (II); *The Daisy Cowboy; An International Heart Breaker; The Stuff That Dreams Are Made Of; The Story of the Indian Ledge; The Awakening of John Bond; The Lure of the City; The Girl and the Motor Boat; The Ghost's Warning; Three Men and A Maid; The Resurrection of John; Nell's Last Deal; A Card of Introduction; Turned to the Wall; Madeline's Rebellion; A Sane Fourth of July; The Cardinal's Edict; The Wager and the Wage Earners; Her Brother's Photograph; A Thoroughbred; Sir George and the Heiress*
1912 *Thirty Days at Hard Labor; A Question of Seconds; The Bachelor's Waterloo; The Stolen Nickel; The Jewels; The Dumb Wooing; The Little Woolen Shoe; An Unusual Sacrifice; The Convict's Parole; The Little Bride of Heaven; Master and Pupil; Partners for Life; The Harbinger of Peace; Mr. Pickwick's Predicament; Martin Chuzzlewit; The Governor; Sally Ann's Strategy; His Mother's Hope; Fog; For Her;*

Treasure Island; The Insurgent Senator; For the Common-wealth; A Cowboy's Stratagem; Children Who Labor; What Happened to Mary?; More Precious Than Gold; The Cub Reporter

1913 *The Ambassador's Daughter; A Woodland Paradise; With the Eyes of the Blind; When the Right Man Comes Along; When Greek Meets Greek; A Tudor Princess; The Translation of a Savage; The Romance of Rowena; The Robbers; The Prophecy; The Princess and the Man; The Pied Piper of Hamelin; The Minister's Temptation; Mercy Merrick; Mary Stuart; A Light on Troubled Waters; Leonie; Kathleen Mavoureen; Joyce of the North Woods; It Is Never Too Late to Mend; The Girl and the Outlaw; A Face from the Past; Elsie the Forester's Daughter; The Dean's Daughters; A Daughter of the Wilderness; An Almond-Eyed Maid; All on Account of a Portrait; The Elder Brother; A Lonely Road; Who Will Marry Mary?; Alexia's Strategy; Fortune Smiles*

1914 *The Active Life of Dolly of the Dailies; The Necklace of Rameses; The Perfect Truth; The Ghost of Mother Eve; Comedy and Tragedy; An Affair of Dress; Putting One Over; A Princess of the Desert; On the Heights; When East Met West in Boston; Frederick the Great; The End of the Umbrella; A Tight Squeeze; Lost: A Pair of Shoes; A Terror of the Night; Dolly Plays Detective; Dolly at the Helm; The Last Assignment; The Viking Queen; His Big Chance; A Girl of the People; The Heart of the Night Wind; A Lonely Salvation; Heart of the Hills; The Virtuoso; The Witch Girl; The Phantom Cracksman; The Man of Destiny; The Chinese Fan; A Lonely Road*

1915 *Under Southern Skies; The Woman Who Lied; A Witch of Salem Town; The Unhidden Treasure; The Taming of Mary; The Tale of the "C"; The Rustle of a Skirt; The Bribe; The Counterfeit; My Lady High and Mighty; The Master Mummer; Mary's Duke; The Little White Violet; Li'l Nor'wester; The Laugh That Died; The Judgment of Men; Jeanne of the Woods; The Honor of the Ormsbys; His Guardian Angel; The Golden Spider; The Girl Who Had a Soul; Everygirl; A Daughter of the Nile; Circus Mary; The Woman Who Lied*

1916　*A Sea Mystery; The Heart of a Mermaid; Madame Cubist; Thrown to the Lions; The Little Fraud; The Girl Who Feared Daylight; The Huntress of Men; The Three Wishes; The Limousine Mystery; The Scarlet Mark; Behind the Veil; The Garden of Shadows; A Splash of Local Color; The Trail of Chance; Stolen Honors; The Strength of the Weak; Mother's Guiding Hand; Love's Masquerade; Cheaters*

1917　*The Long Trail; The Untamed; Public Be Damned; The Beautiful Imposter; To the Highest Bidder*

Garbo, Greta (1905 Stockholm, Sweden-1990 New York City)

Courtesy of Silents Are Golden at
<SilentsAreGolden.com>

The actor later idolized by Hitler and called simply "The Face" was born Greta Lovisa Gustafson into an extremely poor family whose father, a laborer, died when she was only fourteen. She left school to help support her family and held several menial jobs, including soap latherer at a barbershop, before she began working in a department store. Her employers at the department store capitalized on her beauty by having her appear in short advertising promotions, which eventually led to her appearance in a comedy short, *Luffarpetter* [Peter the Tramp] (1922).

She applied for a scholarship to the Royal Stockholm Theatre School, and while studying there she appeared as an ingenue in Mauritz Stiller's film *Gosta Berlings Saga* [The Atonement of Gosta Berling] (1924). The film impressed Louis B. Mayer, who offered Stiller a contract, but Stiller would not accept unless Garbo was also put under contract. Although Mayer thought Garbo "too fat," he acquiesced and Garbo traveled to America with Stiller.

The woman who arrived in America was not the sophisticated en-chantress that would become a film legend. She was given a studio makeover and given a part that no one else wanted—that of a peasant girl who becomes a vamp and avenges herself on the man who rav-ished her as a child. Although Garbo thought that the part was rather silly, the resulting film, *The Torrent* (1926), brought her rave reviews.

Variety exclaimed that she had "looks, acting ability and personal-ity." Her next two films were equally successful, and audiences were mesmerized by her passionate portrayals. After these three film suc-cesses, she demanded a raise to $5,000 per week. MGM held out against her demands for seven months but eventually capitulated. The studio promoted her first talking role with the banner headline "Garbo Speaks!" and the film was a hit. Her accent, which the studio originally feared would end her career, only added to her enigmatic personality and the audience loved her.

At the height of her popularity, she received more than 20,000 fan letters per month. Rumor had it that an Arab sheik offered her $50 million just to attend his dinner party—which she turned down. Her temperament and whims became as famous as the star herself. She shunned publicity, and her remark "I want to be left alone," became the famous, if misquoted, line "I want to be alone."

She grew tired of playing vampish parts, so when her contract ex-pired in the early 1930s, in addition to demanding more money, she held out for the power to choose one of her films. Her choice was *Queen Christina* (1933), for which she received her highest praise; her portrayal was voted the year's best female performance in Britain.

Although her appeal in America was lessening, she was still a ma-jor draw in Europe, so MGM renewed her contract in 1935 at a salary of $250,000 per picture. The first picture under the new contract was *Anna Karenina* (1935), for which Garbo won the New York Critics Award for Best Actress. Her next film, *Camille* (1936), is often cited as her best performance—she again won the New York Critics' Award but lost her bid for an Oscar.

In 1939 Garbo was awarded the Litteris and Artibus medal, Swe-den's highest honor, but in America her career was again in flux. For her next film the studio proclaimed, "Garbo Laughs!" and Garbo was a hit in *Ninotchka* (1939), for which she was again nominated for an Academy Award. But mishandling by MGM and the outbreak of World War II brought an end to her career.

In her sixteen-year career she made only twenty-seven films. Still, the mystique that surrounded her has never truly faded and some believe that her image is still the standard by which all female actors are compared. Her fame grew even as she granted no interviews, signed no autographs, and attended none of her own premieres.

Upon retiring, Garbo moved to New York and traveled for a time before going into complete seclusion in her seven-room apartment in New York's Upper East Side. Although during World War II she was accused of being pro-German, she became a U.S. citizen in 1951 and it was later revealed that she had helped the British by providing intelligence and acting as a courier during the war.

In 1954 she received a special Oscar for her "unforgettable screen performances," but even this honor did not bring her out of her self-imposed seclusion. Years later *The Guiness Book of World Records* voted her "the most beautiful woman who ever lived." A few years before her death, when asked by a fan "Are you Garbo," she replied enigmatically, "I was Greta Garbo."

Film Credits

1922	*Luffarpetter [Peter the Tramp]*
1924	*Gosta Berlings Saga [The Atonement of Gosta Berling]*
1925	*Die Freudlosegasse [Viennese love]*
1926	*The Torrent; The Temptress; Flesh and the Devil*
1927	*Love*
1928	*The Divine Woman; The Mysterious Lady; A Woman of Affairs*
1929	*Wild Orchids; A Man's Man; The Single Standard; The Kiss*
1930	*Anna Christie; Romance*
1931	*Love Business; Susan Lenox (Her Rise and Fall); Mata Hari; Inspiration; Anna Christie*
1932	*Grand Hotel; As You Desire Me*
1933	*Queen Christina*
1934	*The Painted Veil*
1935	*Anna Karenina*
1936	*Camille*
1937	*Conquest*
1939	*Ninotchka*
1941	*Two-Faced Woman*

Garon, Pauline (1901 Montreal, Quebec-1965 San Bernardino, CA)

The eleventh child of a French-Canadian family, Pauline Garon moved to New York to find fame in the film industry before she was twenty years old. Her debut film was *A Manhattan Knight* (1920), and she had appeared in only a few films before being chosen as a WAMPAS Baby Star in 1923.

She turned down a contract offer from Paramount Studios, saying that she wished the freedom to work with any studio. Luckily for her career she became a favorite with Cecil B. DeMille and appeared in many of his silent films, including *Adam's Rib* (1923) and *Passionate Youth* (1925).

Garon became identified with the short-lived sensation of the 1920s—the flapper. Flappers were the icons of the era for the younger generation, and Garon was very popular with them. She achieved a measure of fame for her portrayals, but her dependence on one character type boded ill for her career future.

While appearing in American films Garon also starred in French language remakes of popular English films often shot in the Paris MGM studios. However, with the advent of sound and the fall from grace of the flapper character, Garon's career waned. As the sound era progressed Garon moved from supporting roles to bit parts. For the remainder of her career she was relegated to small parts such as maids or a speaking member of a crowd.

Film Credits

1920 *A Manhattan Knight*
1921 *Doubling for Romeo; The Power Within*
1922 *Polly of the Follies; Reported Missing; Sonny*
1923 *The Man from Glengarry; You Can't Fool Your Wife; Children of the Dust; Forgive and Forget; Adam's Rib; The Marriage Market; The Critical Age*
1924 *Pal o' Mine; The Average Woman; The Spitfire; Wine of Youth; The Turmoil; The Painted Flapper; What the Butler Saw*
1925 *Speed; Fighting Youth; The Love Gamble; The Great Sensation; Compromise; Satan in Sables; Rose of the World; The*

Splendid Road; Flaming Waters; Passionate Youth; Where Was I?; Der Farmer aus Texas (German)

1926   *Christine of the Big Tops*

1927   *Driven from Home; The Love of Sunya; The Princess of Broadway; Naughty; Ladies at Ease; Temptations of a Shop Girl; Eager Lips; The College Hero*

1928   *The Girl He Didn't Buy; Dugan of the Dugouts; The Devil's Cage; Riley of the Rainbow Division; The Heart of Broadway; The Candy Kid; Must We Marry?*

1929   *Redskin; The Gamblers; In the Headlines; The Show of Shows; Lover's Delight*

1930   *The Thoroughbred; Letters; Jack White Talking Pictures; Garde la bombe; We! We! Marie!; Oh La-La; Spectre vert; Parlez Vous*

1931   *Echec au roi*

1933   *The Phantom Broadcast; Easy Millions; One Last Year; By Appointment Only*

1934   *Lost in the Stratosphere; Wonder Bar; La Veuve Joyeuse*

1935   *Becky Sharp; Dangerous; The White Cockatoo; Going Highbrow; Folies-Bergère de Paris*

1936   *Colleen; King of Hockey; It Had to Happen; Colleen; Folies-Bergère*

1937   *Her Husband's Secretary; Shall We Dance?*

1938   *Bluebeard's Eighth Wife*

1941   *How Green Was My Valley*

Gauntier, Gene (1885 Kansas City, MO-1966 Cuernavaca, Mexico)

Gene Gauntier was set on a show business career early in life. She attended the Kansas City School of Oratory and, unlike many young people interested in acting, was encouraged by her parents to enter show business. One of her first acting jobs was with Lois Weber's repertory touring company, and she was not yet twenty when she joined the Kalem Film Company in New York.

She found it easy to transition to films and was popular with the viewing audience. However, although she liked the action in some of the films in which she appeared, she found that she preferred to write. Kalem was having trouble keeping up with the demand for new movies, so Gauntier was asked to write a scenario. Although her first attempt was not accepted, she persevered and soon was writing as many as three one-reel films in a day.

By 1906 she was an established scenario writer. In 1907 she was given two days to write an adaptation of *Ben-Hur* for production. This scenario made her a part of cinema history because the publisher of the book sued Kalem for copyright infringement and won. This case established copyright law as it pertained to the film industry.

She was lured away from Kalem by Biograph and became their scenario editor and studio manager. While there she supposedly was the person who recommended that newcomer D. W. Griffith be given the opportunity to direct. But overall she found the work at Biograph unfulfilling, so she returned to Kalem in 1908 as both an actor and scenarist.

One of her first scenarios after her return was a film in which she starred, titled *The Adventures of a Girl Spy* (1908). It was the first of many films featuring the intrepid Nan who for several years was involved in every kind of adventure that Gauntier could conceive. The series was popular with audiences and established Gauntier as a scenarist.

By now one of the most sought after writers in films, Gauntier was given the opportunity to direct. In 1909, Gauntier went to Europe to make films on location and the production group remained overseas for several years. In 1911, while touring through Egypt, Gauntier wrote the first major film version of Christ's life, *From the Manger to the Cross* (1912). Gauntier portrayed the Virgin Mary in the film and edited the finished product.

Although she had turned down the opportunity to have her own company several years earlier, when Kalem did not give Gauntier and director Sidney Olcott the proper credit for *From the Manger to the Cross,* they left Kalem and created their own company, Gene Gauntier Feature Players. Sadly, the larger studios were edging out independent film studios, and the company lasted only three years. However, the Gauntier/Olcott team soon signed with Universal.

By 1918, Gauntier had had enough of the film industry and retired to become a war correspondent. After World War I, Gauntier was employed as a drama and acting critic for a Kansas City newspaper. Later she added the title "novelist" to her resume when she published the novel *Sporting Lady* in 1933.

The last years of her life were spent traveling, and she was visiting her sister in Mexico when she died.

Writing Credits (Unfortunately since so many of her scenarios were written for one- and two-reel movies many of the titles have been lost.)

1907   *Tom Sawyer; Ben-Hur; The Days of '61; Why Girls Leave Home*

1908   *The Adventures of a Girl Spy; Evangeline; The Scarlet Letter; Hulda's Lovers; Washington at Valley Forge; The Japanese Invasion; Hiawatha; As You Like It; Dolly; The Circus Queen; Way Down East*

1909   *The Grandmother; The Wayward Daughter; The Slave to Drink; The Man Who Lost; The Girl Spy: An Incident of the Civil War*

1910   *The Castaways; The Girl Spy Before Vicksburg; The Little Spreewald Maiden; A Lad from Old Ireland; The Stepmother; The Romance of a Trained Nurse; The Forager; Confederate Spy*

1911   *A Hitherto Unrelated Incident of the Girl Spy; Colleen Bawn; Captured by the Bedouins; Down Through the Ages; Fighting Dervishes of the Desert; An Irish Honeymoon; Rory O'More; Arrah-Na-Pogue*

1912   *From the Manger to the Cross; The Shaughraun; The O'Neill; You Remember Ellen; Winning a Widow; The Kerry Gow; Ireland, the Oppressed*

1913   *A Daughter of the Confederacy; The Octoroon; Lady Peggy Escapes*

1914   *The Fight for a Birthright; A Celebrated Case*

1915   *Gene of the Northland*

Film Credits

1906   *The Paymaster*

1907   *Way Down East; Dolly the Circus Queen*

1908   *Evangeline; The Scarlet Letter; Thompson's Night Out; The Romance of an Egg; The Man in the Box; As You Like It; The Adventures of a Girl Spy; Thompson's Night Out; The Stage Rustler; Betrayed by a Handprint; The Girl and the Outlaw; The Taming of the Shrew*

1909   *The Wayward Daughter; The Slave to Drink; The Man Who Lost; The Cracker's Bride; The Girl Spy: An Incident of the Civil War*

1910   *The Castaways; A Child's Faith; The Girl Spy Before Vicksburg; The Little Spreewald Maiden; A Lad from Old Ireland; Confederate Spy; The Further Adventures of the Girl Spy; The Bravest Girl in the South; The Egret Hunter; A Colonial Belle; The Perversity of Fate; The Cow Puncher's Sweetheart; The Heart of Edna Leslie; The Stranger; The Stepmother; The Romance of a Trained Nurse; The Forager*

1911   *A Hitherto Unrelated Incident of the Girl Spy; Colleen Bawn; An Irish Honeymoon; A War Time Escape; The Lass Who Couldn't Forget; In Old Florida; The Fiddle's Requiem; To the Aid of Stonewall Jackson; The Romance of a Dixie Belle; Special Messenger; Rory O'More; The Fishermaid of Ballydavid; Arrah-Na-Pogue*

1912   *From the Manger to the Cross; The Shaughraun; O'Neill; His Mother; The Vagabonds; Far from Erin's Isle; You Remember Ellen; Captain Rivera's Reward; Victim of Circumstance; The Belle of New Orleans; Fighting Dervishes of the Desert; Missionaries in Darkest Africa; An Arab Tragedy; Winning a Widow; A Prisoner of the Harem; Down Through the Ages; The Kerry Gow; The Mayor of Ireland; Ireland, the Oppressed*

1913   *Lady Peggy Escapes; The Wives of Jamestown*

1915   *The Mad Maid of the Forest; Gene of the Northland*

1920   *Witch's Lure*

Gaynor, Janet (1906 Philadelphia, PA-1984 Palm Springs, CA)

Courtesy of Silents Are Golden at
<SilentsAreGolden.com>

Janet Gaynor had an engagingly youthful demeanor that was a hit with audiences for many years. She won the first Best Actress Award given by the Academy of Motion Picture Arts and Sciences in 1928 for her accumulated work in *Seventh Heaven* (1927), *Sunrise* (1927), and *Street Angel* (1928). She was the first and only actor to receive the award for more than one performance.

Although she originally moved to Los Angeles to attend secretarial school, she was soon making the rounds of the studios in search of movie work. She got her first acting experience in Hal Roach's comedy shorts and bit parts in formula westerns. In 1926 she was cast as Anna Burger in her first feature-length film, *The Johnstown Flood,* which resulted in an offer of a five-year contract with Fox Studios. That year she was also chosen as a WAMPAS Baby Star.

After winning the Academy Award, she was paired with Charles Farrell as "America's favorite love-birds" in a series of ten films. She and Farrell starred in *Sunny Side Up* (1929), supposedly the first musical written for film. She made the transition to sound as one of the biggest stars at Fox Studios. She was one of the most popular actors in the 1930s tying Marie Dressler in 1931-1932 as the top box office star; in 1934, after Dressler's death, Gaynor held that title alone.

After several years of mediocre films, she had a huge hit with *A Star Is Born* (1937). She was nominated for another Academy Award for her portrayal of Vicki Lester/Esther Blodgett but was edged out by Luise Rainer. She next starred in *The Young in Heart* (1938) but retired in 1939 after marrying costume designer (Gilbert) Adrian. She made occasional appearances during the early years of television and appeared as Pat Boone's mother in the 1957 film *Bernardine.*

During her retirement she indulged her interest in painting until she was injured in an automobile accident along with Mary Martin in 1982. She never fully recovered from her injuries, and she died from complications of those injuries in 1984. Prior to her death she told a reporter, "I think I had a wonderful career. . . . I enjoyed it all."

Film Credits

1924   *Cupid's Rustler; Young Ideas; All Wet*
1925   *The Haunted Honeymoon; Dangerous Innocence; The Burning Trail; The Teaser; The Plastic Age; Crook Buster*
1926   *The Beautiful Cheat; The Johnstown Flood; Ridin' for Love; Skinner's Dress Suit; The Shamrock Handicap; The Galloping Cowboy; The Fire Barrier; The Man in the Saddle; Don't Shoot; The Blue Eagle; The Midnight Kiss; The Return of Peter Grimm; Martin of the Mounted; Lazy Lightning; The Stolen Ranch; Pep of the Lady J; Forty-Five Minutes from Hollywood; Fade Away Foster; Oh, What A Nurse!*
1927   *Seventh Heaven; The Horse Trader; Two Girls Wanted; Sunrise*
1928   *Street Angel; 4 Devils*
1929   *Lucky Star; Christina; Sunny Side Up*
1930   *High Society Blues; Happy Days*
1931   *The Man Who Came Back; Daddy Long Legs; Merely Mary Ann; Delicious*
1932   *Tess of the Storm Country; The First Year*
1933   *Adorable; Paddy the Next Best Thing; State Fair*
1934   *Servants' Entrance; Change of Heart; Carolina*
1935   *One More Spring; The Farmer Takes a Wife*
1936   *Small Town Girl; Ladies in Love*
1937   *A Star Is Born*
1938   *Three Loves Has Nancy; The Young in Heart*
1957   *Bernardine*

George, Maude (1888 Riverside, CA-1963 Sepulveda, CA)

Although she never achieved stardom, Maude George, the niece of stage actor Grace George, was one of the silent era's best character actors, excelling at world-weary sophisticates. After completing school, she worked in stock and touring companies before embarking on a film career.

George signed with the Universal Company in 1915 and became popular for her dramatic performances. After appearing in Lois Weber's production of *Idle Wives* (1916), she achieved lead status and began writing scenarios—her first was *The Eagle's Wings* (1916).

George joined Erich von Stroheim's company of players in 1920 and appeared in some of her best work over the next eight years. She retired from films as the sound era was beginning in 1929. After her retirement she lived quietly with her second husband until her death.

Film Credits

1915	*A Little Brother of the Rich; Business Is Business; The Frame-Up; Both Sides of Life; A Cigarette—That's All; When a Queen Loved O'Rourke; The Palace of Dust; The Road to Paradise*
1916	*The Target; The Gay Lord Waring; A Youth of Fortune; Hulda the Silent; A Son of the Immortals; The Iron Hand; The Silent Battle; The Pool of Flame; The Beckoning Trail; The Social Buccaneer; Beyond the Wall; The People vs. John Doe; Idle Wives; The Moving Finger; The Shadows of Suspicion; Langdon's Legacy*
1917	*The Piper's Price; Barbary Sheep; Magda; Heart Strings; Even As You and I; The Melody of Death*
1918	*Blue Blazes Rawden; The Marriage Ring*
1919	*The Midnight Stage; The Lamb and the Lion; A Rogue's Romancy*
1920	*Devil's Passkey; Madame X*
1921	*Roads of Destiny*
1922	*Foolish Wives; Monte Cristo; The Power of a Lie*
1923	*Merry-Go-Round; Temporary Marriage; Six Days; The Drums of Jeopardy*
1924	*Torment; Soiled; Worldly Goods*
1925	*Confessions of a Queen*

1926   *The Love Toy*
1927   *Altars of Desire*
1928   *The Garden of Eden; After the Storm; Isle of Lost Men; The Wedding March; The Woman from Moscow*
1929   *The Veiled Woman*

Writing Credits

1916   *The Eagle's Wings*
1917   *The Fighting Gringo; Mary from America*

Geraghty, Carmelita (1901 Rushville, IN-1966 New York City)

Carmelita Geraghty came from a true show business family—her father, Thomas, was an early scenario writer and her two brothers, Maurice and Gerald, both followed their father and became screenwriters. Geraghty honed her acting talents with a Los Angeles stock company before working as a script girl for Mack Sennett and other directors.

Because of her dark coloring and exotic features, when she was finally offered an acting role in a film directed by George Fitzmaurice her character was a "foreigner." She continued to play "exotic" roles in several Sennett comedies over the next two years. In 1924 she was selected as a WAMPAS Baby Star.

Geraghty left Sennett to begin a feature career in westerns and melodramas. Her roles were small in the beginning, but she was soon playing second leads and, occasionally, lead roles. One of her best roles was as Mary Pickford's irresponsible sister in *My Best Girl* (1927). She made the transition to sound easily and continued to appear in supporting roles. She also appeared in the serial *The Jungle Mystery* (1932).

She married writer-producer Carey Wilson in 1934, and the marriage lasted until his death. After her marriage she made only one film before going into permanent retirement. While retired she devoted herself to painting and was talented enough to have several of her canvases exhibited in galleries.

Film Credits

1923   *Jealous Husbands; Bag and Baggage*
1924   *Through the Dark; Discontented Husbands; Trouble Brewing; High Speed; Geared to Go; Black Oxen; All's Swell on the Ocean; Fight and Win*
1925   *Brand of Cowardice; The Mysterious Stranger; Under the Rouge; The Pleasure Garden; Passionate Youth; My Lady of Whims; Cyclone Cavalier*
1926   *The Flying Mail; The Lily; Josselyn's Wife; The Canyon of Light; The Great Gatsby*
1927   *What Every Girl Should Know; Venus of Venice; My Best Girl; The Small Bachelor; The Slaver; The Last Trial*
1928   *The Good-Bye Kiss; South of Panama; The Campus Carmen; Object: Alimony; His Unlucky Night; Motorboat Mamas; The Bargain Hunt; Hubby's Weekend Trip*
1929   *Paris Bound; Mississippi Gambler; This Thing Called Love; After the Fog; Clunked on the Corner; Don't Get Jealous; A Close Shave*
1930   *Men Without Law; Rogue of the Rio Grande; Fightin' Thru; What Men Want; Pick 'Em Young*
1931   *Millie; The Texas Ranger; Graft; Forgotten Women; The Devil Plays; Night Life in Reno; Fifty Million Frenchmen*
1932   *Prestige; Jungle Mystery; Malay Nights; Escapade*
1933   *The Flaming Signal; Broadway Bad*
1935   *Manhattan Butterfly*
1936   *Phantom of Santa Fe*

Gerber, Neva (1894 Argenta, IL-1974 Palm Springs, CA)

Neva Gerber was one of the top ten serial queens of the silent era and appeared in the first all-sound serial, *The Voice from the Sky* (1930). Although her father's family was well-to-do, her parents separated while Gerber was quite young. She was raised by nuns at the College of the Immaculate Heart in Los Angeles after her mother moved with her daughter to California. When her father died suddenly, his family made sure that his estranged widow and child received no money.

With no means to support her child adequately, Gerber's mother gave guardianship of her only child to an attorney who tried to force the Midwestern Gerber clan to settle the estate. Although she never received a "fair" inheritance, when she turned eighteen Gerber did receive $15,000; when her grandfather died, in a belated attack of conscience, he left her a farm in Illinois.

Upon graduating from high school, Gerber got started in films and by 1915 was the star of several one-reelers. Around this time, Gerber became engaged to ill-fated director William Desmond Taylor, although a marriage never took place because she was still married to her first husband. By 1917 she became a serial star, appearing in such popular serials as *The Mystery Ship* and *The Voice on the Wire*. In 1918 she appeared opposite western star Harry Carey in several of his films.

When Taylor was killed she was one of the few actors involved in his murder investigation to withstand the scandal with her career intact. She continued in films after the scandal, making some of the most successful serials of the period under the direction of Ben Wilson. When Wilson died in 1930, Gerber's career stalled and she did not make the transition to sound. She married three more times, but when she died she had to be buried by the state in a pauper's grave.

Film Credits

1912 *The Flower Girl's Romance; The Water Right War; The Detective's Sister*
1913 *Redemption*
1914 *The Judge's Wife; The Criminal Code; Bill's Wife; The Detective's Bureau; The Fringe of the Glove*
1915 *Alias James, Chauffeur; The High Hand; An Eye for an Eye; Naughty Henrietta; The Redemption of the Jasons; The Stay-at-Homes; The Mollycoddle; A Deal in Diamonds; The Madonna; Applied Romance; Cupid Takes a Taxi; His College Wife; Betty's First Sponge Cake; Jimmy on the Job; Plot and Counterplot; Green Apples; The Honeymooners; The Mysterious Passion; Incognito; Love, Mumps and Bumps; Mother's Busy Week; Billie, the Hillbilly; Touring with Tillie; One to the Minute; Almost a Widow; Anita's Butterfly; Cupid Beats Father; Nobody's Home; Making Over Father; Two Hearts and a Thief; Getting It Wrong; Mischief and a Mirror; That Country Gal; Life's Staircase; When War Threatened; His*

Mysterious Profession; Everyheart; Tricks of Fate; The Country Girl

1916	*The Impersonation; Idle Wives; The Castle of Despair; Honor Thy Country; The Mansard Mystery; Raccoons; The Shadow; Society Hypocrites; Ella Wanted to Elope; Mammy's Rose; Won by One; Getting It Wrong; Walk This Way*

1917	*Caught in the Act; Even As You and I; The Prodigal Widow; The Voice on the Wire; Like Wildfire; Mr. Opp; The Spindle of Life; The Mystery Ship; The Great Secret*

1918	*The Beautiful Liar; Let's Fight; Hell Bent; Three Mounted Men; The Great Torpedo Secret*

1919	*Roped; A Fight for Love; Pitfalls in a Big City; The Trail of the Octopus; Bill's Anniversary; Bill's Finish; Bill's Hat; Them Eyes; When a Woman Strikes; Tailor Made*

1920	*Bill's Wife; The Screaming Shadow; The Branded Four*

1921	*A Yankee Go-Getter; The Mysterious Pearl; Dangerous Paths*

1922	*The Price of Youth; Impulse*

1923	*In the West; The Santa Fe Trail; The Seventh Sheriff*

1924	*Trouble Trail; Sagebrush Gospel; Western Fate; The Whirlwind Ranger; Days of '49; California in '49*

1925	*Vic Dyson Pays; Warrior Gap; Tonio, Son of the Sierras; The Mystery Box; A Daughter of the Sioux; The Power God*

1926	*The Power God; The Sheriff's Girl; Wolves of the Desert; Officer 444; West of the Law; Fort Frayne; The Fighting Stallion; Baited Trap; Hell Hounds of the Plains*

1927	*A Yellow Streak; Riders of the West; The Range Riders; The Mystery Brand*

1928	*The Odd Code; The Lone Patrol; The Phantom Pinto*

1929	*The Saddle King; Thundering Thompson*

1930	*The Voice from the Sky*

Gertie, the Dinosaur (1909/1904)

As with so much of the silent era, the debut year of *Gertie, the Dinosaur* is not completely agreed upon. Early printed reference sources state 1909, while more recent sources indicate 1914. The consensus of most current historians is that the debut was 1914, but the fact the more contemporary historians put the date at 1909 causes some disagreement.

Billed as "the greatest animal act in the world," Gertie was the first animated cartoon animal and predated Disney's *Steamboat Willie* by at least fourteen years. Created by comic strip artist Winsor Z. McCay, Gertie interacted with her creator on the screen and "responded" to his commands. Gertie was a friendly herbivore that walked through the picture eating a tree, tried to eat a train, and took the man who had created her for a ride on her back. The film lasted twelve minutes and included 10,000 drawings of Gertie.

Gibson, Helen (1892 Cleveland, OH-1977 Roseburg, OR)

Helen Gibson joined the ranks of serial stars when she took over the starring role in *The Hazards of Helen* in 1914 when Helen Holmes changed studios. Although her natural athleticism and fearlessness when doing stunts made her a natural for the rough-and-tumble serials, it was her close resemblance to Holmes that assured her the role. In fact, at the time many fans were not aware that there had been a change in actors.

Gibson was born Rose August Wenger to Swiss-German parents. Her love of horses and riding led to appearances with Miller Brothers' Wild West Show as a rodeo rider. When the show closed in Los Angeles in 1911, the troupe signed to appear in films.

In 1913 she married Hoot Gibson who was years away from his success in western films, and her own success caused friction within the marriage. Before taking over *The Hazards of Helen,* she had a successful career in westerns; this success continued when the serial ended in 1916 after 199 episodes. In 1920, the year she divorced Gibson, she created Helen Gibson Productions, but the venture failed and she was left virtually penniless.

In 1921, while appearing in a film for Spencer Productions, her appendix ruptured and the resulting surgery forced the company to replace her. She continued to appear in films after her recovery, but by the mid-1920s her popularity with fans had waned. She appeared in vaudeville between 1926 and 1927 before returning to films, where she became known as one of the best stuntwomen in the business. She remained in films, appearing in supporting and bit parts, until the 1950s. Her final appearance was a small, uncredited role in *The Man Who Shot Liberty Valance* (1962).

Film Credits

1914	*The Hazards of Helen* (through 1916)
1917	*Fighting Mad; The Dynamite Special; The End of the Run; The Perilous Leap; Saving the Fast Mail; The Wrong Man*
1918	*Bawled Out; The Branded Man; Captured Alive; Danger Ahead; The Dead Shot; The Fast Mail; The Midnight Flyer; Play Straight or Fight; The Robber; The Silent Sentinel; Under False Pretenses; Wolves of the Range*
1919	*Loot; The Black Horse Bandit; The Canyon Mystery; Down but Not Out; Gun Law; The Rustlers; Riding Wild; The Secret Peril*
1921	*No Man's Woman; The Wolverine*
1922	*Nine Points of the Law; Thorobred*
1928	*The Vanishing West; The Chinatown Mystery*
1931	*The Lightning Warrior; The Cheyanne Cyclone*
1932	*Human Targets; The Silver Lining; Law and Lawless*
1933	*King of the Arena*
1934	*Wheels of Destiny; 365 Nights in Hollywood; The Way of the West; Rocky Rhodes*
1935	*Cyclone of the Saddle; Bride of Frankenstein; The Drunkard; Fighting Caballero*
1936	*Custer's Last Stand; Lady of Secrets; Last of the Warrens*
1937	*Danger Valley*
1938	*Flaming Frontiers*
1939	*Stagecoach; The Oregon Trial*
1940	*The Covered Wagon*
1941	*The Sheriff of Tombstone*
1942	*The Valley of Vanishing Men*
1949	*Cheyenne Cowboy*
1950	*Fast on the Draw; Crooked River*
1951	*Hollywood Story*
1953	*City That Never Sleeps*
1954	*Ma and Pa Kettle at Home*
1962	*The Man Who Shot Liberty Valance*

Gish, Dorothy (1898 Massillon, OH-1968 Rapallo, Italy)

Courtesy of Silents Are Golden at <SilentsAreGolden.com>

Called by her sister "the most talented of the Gishes," when Dorothy Gish's father deserted his family, her mother turned to acting to support her children. As soon as Dorothy and her sister were old enough, they joined their mother on the stage. By 1902 Dorothy was a seasoned performer.

In 1912, their friend Mary Pickford took the Gish sisters to Biograph Studios and the girls were given jobs as extras. Not long after their arrival, D. W. Griffith cast Dorothy and Lillian as the stars of *An Unseen Enemy* (1912), the first of over 100 films in which Dorothy Gish would appear. At first Griffith found the sisters so close in appearance to each other he had Dorothy wear a red ribbon and Lillian wear a blue ribbon to tell them apart. She occasionally starred with Lillian, and although Dorothy was a talented dramatic actor, her forte was light comedy.

By 1914 she was a popular Biograph star and regularly appeared in the fan magazines of the time. In fact, Laura Lee Hope wrote a series of juvenile books—*The Moving Picture Girls*—based on the Gish sisters. Dorothy was known around the Biograph lot as a prankster and was one of the few people able to make even the austere Griffith smile.

In 1918 she appeared in *Hearts of the World* as a madcap French peasant—one of her best performances. Later that year she signed a contract with Paramount Studios, where she made fourteen films over the next four years. During her years at Paramount she married fellow actor James Rennie, but the couple separated in 1930 and eventually divorced in 1935.

In 1921 she starred with her sister in *Orphans of the Storm*, directed by Griffith. Although she enjoyed comedies, she was careful not to be typed as a "comedian," because the audiences sometimes felt that female comics were "unfeminine." She worked steadily throughout the 1920s and starred in her sister's only directing attempt, *Remodeling Her Husband* (1920), as well as the first internationally successful British film, *Nell Gwyn* (1926).

With the advent of sound, Gish returned to the stage and appeared in the successful play *Young Love,* in both New York and London. Her first sound film was not successful and she decided to concentrate on her stage career. In addition to her stage work she made several guest appearances on the radio in broadcasts of popular plays of the day.

She returned to films for the comedy *Our Hearts Were Young and Gay* (1944) and appeared in three more films over the next twenty years. But in 1964 she again retired from films, stating that "making movies used to be fun." She made appearances on a few of the dramatic anthology series on television in the early 1950s, such as *The Ford Theatre Hour* and *The Philco Television Playhouse,* and appeared for several more years on the stage before her final appearance, with her sister, in *Chalk Garden* (1956).

After her retirement, she traveled extensively, but when her health began to fail she settled on the Italian Riviera until her death in 1968. Earlier her sister had written of her, "she is laughter . . .nothing saddens her or concerns her lastingly . . . trouble . . . is banished with a shrug of a shoulder."

Film Credits

1912   *An Unseen Enemy; The Painted Lady; The Musketeers of Pig Alley; Gold and Glitter; My Baby; The Informer; Brutality; The New York Hat; My Hero; A Cry for Help; The Burglar's Dilemma; So Near, Yet So Far*

1913   *Oil and Water; The Perfidy of Mary; The Lady and the Mouse; Just Gold; Her Mother's Oath; The Widow's Kid; The Vengeance of Galora; Those Little Flowers; Pa Says; The Lady in Black; The House of Discord; Almost a Wild Man; The Adopted Brother; Broken Ways; His Mother's Son; Red Hicks Defies the World; Almost a Wild Man; The Reformers; Papa's Baby; The Suffragette Minstrels; A Cure for Suffragettes; By Man's Law*

1914   *Judith of Bethulia; Home, Sweet Home; The Wife; Their First Acquaintance; The Tavern of Tragedy; The Suffragette's Bat-*

tle in Nuttyville; The Sisters; Silent Sandy; The Saving Grace; Sands of Fate; The Rebellion of Kitty Belle; The Old Man; The Newer Woman; The Mysterious Shot; The Mountain Rat; Liberty Belles; A Lesson in Mechanics, Her Old Teacher, Her Mother's Necklace, Her Father's Silent Partner, Granny, The Floor Above, A Fair Rebel, A Duel for Love, Down the Road to Creditville, The City Beautiful, The Better Way; Back to the Kitchen; The Availing Prayer, Arms and the Gringo; The Warning (I)

1915   *How Hazel Got Even; Bred in the Bone; Old Heidelberg; The Warning* (II); *Jordan Is a Hard Road; Victorine; Out of Bondage; An Old-Fashioned Girl; The Mountain Girl; Minerva's Mission; The Lost Lord Lowell; The Little Catamount; Her Mother's Daughter; Her Grandparents*

1916   *Betty of Greystone; Little Meena's Romance; Susan Rocks the Boat; The Little School Ma'am; Gretchen the Greenhorn; Atta Boy's Last Race; Children of the Feud*

1917   *The Little Yank; Stage Struck; Her Official Fathers*

1918   *Hearts of the World; The Hun Within; Battling Jane*

1919   *The Hope Chest; Boots; Peppy Polly; I'll Get Him Yet; Nugget Nell; Nobody Home; Turning the Tables*

1920   *Mary Ellen Comes to Town; Remodeling Her Husband; Little Miss Rebellion; Flying Pat*

1921   *Orphans of the Storm; The Ghost in the Garret*

1922   *The Country Flapper*

1923   *Fury; The Bright Shawl*

1924   *Romola*

1925   *Night Life of New York; Clothes Make the Pirate; The Beautiful City*

1926   *Nell Gwyn; London*

1927   *Tiptoes; Madame Pompadour*

1930   *Wolves*

1944   *Our Hearts Were Young and Gay*

1946   *Centennial Summer*

1951   *The Whistle at Eaton Falls*

1963   *The Cardinal*

Gish, Lillian (1893 Springfield, OH-1993 New York City)

Lillian Gish, called the "First Lady of the Silent Screen," was perhaps the finest female actor of the silent era. Her career spanned seventy-five years and over 100 productions. She received numerous awards during her stage and film career; during her lifetime she was one of the most respected actors in the industry.

Both she and her sister, Dorothy, got their start in show business when very young. By the age of seven, Gish was a seasoned performer and appeared successfully on stage for more than ten years. She was well on her way to becoming one of the best stage actors of the era when she turned her sights on the film industry. D. W. Griffith directed her first film, *An Unseen Enemy* (1912), in which she starred with her sister as two youngsters who are locked in a room and threatened by a gun-wielding housekeeper. She appeared in eleven other films for him in that first year and continued to work with him for ten years. She was his ideal ethereal Victorian beauty, "the quintessential Griffith heroine."

She was regularly featured in Biograph films over the next few years. In 1915 she starred in Griffith's infamous *The Birth of a Nation,* as Elsie Stoneman. The following year she appeared in another Griffith epic, *Intolerance* (1916), as the "eternal mother." The list of her films with Griffith over the years they worked together is a listing of silent era classics, including *Broken Blossoms* (1919) and *Orphans of the Storm* (1921).

Although she looked fragile, she was a hard bargainer when it came to her contracts. In 1923 she received an unheard-of 15 percent of the profits of her film *The White Sister* (1923). But for all her power and popularity during the first part of the decade, by the mid-1920s newer faces were getting all the attention from film audiences.

She directed only once, *Remodeling Her Husband* (1920), a film that starred her sister, Dorothy. Gish finished the film under budget and it made more than $460,000, but she found that she did not enjoy working behind the scenes. Several years passed without her appearing in any film, but when she wasn't working in Hollywood she returned to the stage. She continued her earlier stage success and received both popular and critical acclaim. In 1920 John Barrymore claimed that she was an artist "worthy to rank with Bernhardt."

Gish did not welcome the advent of sound. She felt that silent films could have a greater impact on audiences and were "wonderfully expressive." Eventually she was forced by her contract to make the transition, although films had lost their appeal for her. After a role in *His Double Life* (1933), Gish did not appear on screen again until 1943.

But no matter how long she had been away from the screen, Gish was always able to command the audience's attention. No longer the fresh ingenue, Gish had matured in her craft. In 1946 she received an Academy Award nomination for Best Supporting Actress for her role as the mother (Laura Belle McCanles) in *Duel in the Sun*.

One of her best performances was as the spinster Rachel Cooper with whom two children find refuge in *The Night of the Hunter* (1955), a story of greed set in the South during the Depression. The film was not received well by critics or audiences at the time, but it has become a cult classic. She continued to divide her time between the stage and films, and when television evolved she appeared on several of the dramatic anthologies of the 1950s, as well as in several made-for-television movies. She appeared with Helen Hayes in the 1969 version of *Arsenic and Old Lace,* and her last appearance on television was the PBS series *The Adventures of Huckleberry Finn* (1986).

She wrote three books about her life and career, starting with *Life and Lillian Gish* (1932). In *The Movies, Mr. Griffith, and Me* (1969) she made sure to credit Griffith, whom she always called "Mr. Griffith," for his pioneering work. She never turned her back on Griffith, even when the industry that he helped to create did; she helped to care for him until his death in 1948. Theirs was a relationship of mutual respect and admiration. Griffith once said that she had "the best mind of any woman I have ever met." Her final book of memoirs was titled, *Dorothy and Lillian Gish* (1973).

In 1970 she received a special Academy Award for "superlative artistry and for distinguished contribution to the progress of motion pictures." Bowling Green State University dedicated and named a theater on campus the Dorothy and Lillian Gish Film Theater in 1976. In 1982 she was one of the artists honored by The Kennedy Center, and two years later she received the twelfth Lifetime Achievement Award from the American Film Institute (1984). In addition, each year at the Museum of Modern Art in New York City an exhibition of one of her films is held on the anniversary of her birthday, October 14.

Three years after she was honored by the AFI she made her last motion picture, *The Whales of August* (1987). The film was delayed because her costar, Bette Davis, demanded top billing that should, by rights, have gone to Gish. Finally, Gish gave in to the demand, (supposedly) commenting, "Let her have it if it means that much to her."

Film Credits

1912   *An Unseen Enemy; Two Daughters of Eve; In the Aisles of the Wild; The One She Loved; The Painted Lady; Musketeers of Pig Alley; Gold and Glitter; My Baby; The Informer; The New York Hat; A Cry for Help; The Burglar's Dilemma; So Near, Yet So Far; Brutality*

1913   *Oil and Water; The Unwelcome Guest; A Misunderstood Boy; The Left Handed Man; The Lady and the Mouse; The House of Darkness; Just Gold; A Timely Interception; The Mothering Heart; During the Round-Up; An Indian's Loyalty; A Woman in the Ultimate; A Modest Hero; So Runs the Way; Madonna of the Storm*

1914   *Judith of Bethulia; The Battle of Elderbush Gulch; The Battle of the Sexes; The Quicksands; Home, Sweet Home; The Tear That Burned; The Sisters; The Rebellion of Kitty Belle; Lord*

Chumley; The Hunchback; A Duel for Love; The Angel of Contention
1915 *The Birth of a Nation; The Lost House; Enoch Arden; Captain Macklin; The Lily and the Rose*
1916 *Daphne and the Pirate; Sold for Marriage; An Innocent Magdalene; Intolerance; Diane of the Follies; The Children Pay; The House Built Upon Sand*
1917 *Souls Triumphant*
1918 *Hearts of the World; The Great Love; The Greatest Thing in Life*
1919 *A Romance of Happy Valley; Broken Blossoms; True Heart Susie; The Greatest Question*
1920 *Way Down East*
1921 *Orphans of the Storm*
1923 *The White Sister*
1924 *Romola*
1925 *Ben-Hur*
1926 *The Scarlet Letter; La Boheme*
1927 *Annie Laurie; The Enemy*
1928 *The Wind*
1930 *One Romantic Night*
1933 *His Double Life*
1942 *Commandos Strike at Dawn*
1943 *Top Man*
1946 *Miss Susie Slagle; Duel in the Sun*
1948 *Portrait of Jennie*
1955 *The Night of the Hunter; The Cobweb; Film Fun*
1958 *Orders to Kill*
1960 *The Unforgiven*
1962 *The Great Chase*
1966 *Follow Me, Boys!*
1967 *Warning Shot; The Comedians*
1978 *A Wedding*
1984 *Hambone and Hillie*
1986 *Sweet Liberty*
1987 *The Whales of August*

Glaum, Louise (1900 Baltimore, MD-1970 Los Angeles, CA)

Louise Glaum belongs on the list of women who capitalized on the brief popularity of Theda Bara's vamp characterization. Nicknamed by publicists during her vamp period either "The Spider Woman" or "The Tiger Woman," she began appearing in films as early as 1912 at the Nestor Studio, which three years later became Universal Studios.

By 1915 she was appearing opposite William S. Hart in a succession of western films directed by Thomas Ince. She moved into feature films in 1917 and left her western period behind. The following year she began appearing in vamp roles and was credited by one contemporary critic as "the best actress of all screen vamps." However, by the end of World War I the vamp persona was no longer popular with the film audience and Glaum, too strongly associated with the role, faded from the screen.

Film Credits

1912   *When the Heart Calls; The Girls and the Chaperone; Hearts and Skirts; Her Friend the Doctor; The Lady Barber of Roaring Gulch; Making a Man of Her; Sharps and Chaps; A Stubborn Cupid; The $2500 Bride; Those Lovesick Cowboys; Love and a Lemon*

1913   *The Quakeress; The Girls and Dad; The Seal of Silence*

1914   *The Great Universal Mystery;* Fifteen *Universal Ike* shorts; Eighteen *Universal Ike Junior* shorts

1915   *The Cup of Life; The Renegade; The Darkening Trail; The Reward; The Toast of Death; Keno Bates, Liar; The Iron Strain; Matrimony; The Forbidden Adventure*

1916   *Hell's Hinges; The Three Musketeers; The Aryan; Honor Thy Name; Home; The Wolf Woman; The Return of Draw Egan; Somewhere in France*

1917 *The Weaker Sex; Love or Justice; Golden Rule Kate; Idolators; A Strange Transgressor*

1918 *An Alien Enemy; Shackled; Wedlock; A Law Unto Herself; The Goddess of Lost Lake; Staking His Life*

1919 *The Lone Wolf's Daughter; Sahara*

1920 *Love Madness; Sex; The Leopard Woman; Sweetheart of the Doomed; Love*

1921 *Greater Than Love; I Am Guilty*

1925 *Fifty-Fifty*

Glyn, Elinor (1864 Jersey, England-1943 London, England)

Raised in frugality by her widowed mother the Glyn family's poverty was relieved only by infrequent gifts from wealthy relatives. As a result of her upbringing, Elinor Glyn vowed to join the world represented by her rich relatives. Her mother's remarriage to a well-to-do Scotsman was to have been the family's salvation from poverty, but her stepfather was miserly. The stepfather's health made it necessary for the family to move to Jersey, where Glyn joined in the social life of the island. But life on the island was not exciting enough, and Glyn convinced a vacationing Frenchwoman to take her back with her to Paris in 1880. When her sister, Lucy, went to live on an English estate, Glyn went to visit and ingratiate herself with the lesser aristocracy.

Years of planning were rewarded in 1892 when Glyn married into the life she craved—that of comfort and ease. But her husband was a disappointment, so Glyn continued to collect clothes, many designed by her sister, and acquire an elegant polish.

In 1898 she began writing a fashion column in the magazine *Scottish Life.* The magazine was short-lived, but Glyn continued to write. While recovering from rheumatic fever Glyn wrote the manuscript that became the serialized *Letters of Elizabeth,* concerning a married woman's illicit affair. The next year, the "letters" were published into a book that became a moderate success, probably because many late-Victorian critics labeled it as "shocking." *Three Weeks* (1907) brought her fame, and the book's "unbridled lust" continued to make it a hit twenty-five years after it was first published.

During World War I, she worked as a war correspondent, first for the newspaper *News of the World,* then for the Hearst newspapers.

After the war she wrote *The Philosophy of Love* (1920), one of the first books to outline a campaign to get and keep a man.

In the fall of 1920 studio head Jesse Lasky offered her $10,000 per picture, so she traveled to the United States to begin a career in screenwriting. Her first production was *The Great Moment* (1920) starring Gloria Swanson. A self-styled authority on romance, she adapted her novels to the screen. The resulting films were extremely successful, but soon her career hit a slump.

However, her career and reputation were revived with the publication of her novel *It*. She adapted the novel for the screen and the film, starring Clara Bow, became the sensation of 1926. She began writing articles for magazines advising readers on "all things amorous," but especially on how to use "It"—her euphemism for sex appeal.

Unquestioningly a part of the 1920s wild-spirited jazz age, Madame Glyn (as she styled herself) became obsolete as the decade drew to a close. She returned to England in 1929, leaving behind a large unpaid tax bill in the United States. After a short-lived and unsuccessful attempt at film production, Glyn returned to novel writing with the publication of *Love's Hour* (1932). She wrote her autobiography, *Romantic Adventure,* in 1936.

Writing Credits

1921   *The Great Moment*
1922   *Beyond the Rocks; The World's a Stage*
1924   *Three Weeks; How to Educate a Wife; His Hour*
1925   *Man and Maid; The Only Thing; Soul Mates*
1926   *Love's Blindness*
1927   *Ritzy; It*
1928   *Mad Hour; Red Hair; Three Weekends*
1929   *The Man and the Moment*
1930   *Such Men Are Dangerous; Knowing Men*

Producing/Directing Credits

1927   *It*
1930   *Knowing Men; The Price of Things*

Gonzalez, Myrtle (1891 Los Angeles, CA-1918 Los Angeles, CA)

Born into one of the founding families of Spanish California, Myrtle Gonzalez was educated in Los Angeles and, from a young age, showed singing talent. She appeared in many local revues before going on the stage in juvenile roles.

When the film studios began moving to California, Gonzalez readily applied for work to avoid the rigours of touring. She joined the Vitagraph troupe of players in 1912 and began appearing in western films. She became very popular with the audience and, when her contract with Vitagraph expired, she moved to Universal. While at Universal she was promoted as "the virgin lily of the screen" and was poised in 1918 to become one of the studio's premiere performers.

Sadly, she was one of the first victims of the Spanish influenza pandemic of 1918. Although known for her energetic and active roles, she had suffered from a heart ailment since childhood and was unable to fight off the disease.

Film Credits

1913	*Any Port in a Storm*
1914	*His Wife and His Work; Captain Alvarez; The Yaqui's Revenge; Anne of the Mines*
1915	*The Chalice of Courage; The Bride of the Nancy Lee; The Terrible Truth; Through Troubled Waters*
1916	*It Happened In Honolulu; The Secret of the Swamp; The Girl of Lost Lake; A Romance of Billy Goat Hill; The End of the Rainbow; Missy; Her Dream Man; The Wise Man and the Fool; Her Greatest Story; The Heart of Bonita; The Windward Anchor; Lonesomeness; The Secret Foe; Bill's Wife; The Brink; The Gambler; Miss Blossom; The Thief of the Desert; Her Great Part; Grouches and Smiles; Fool's Gold; The Unexpected Scoop*
1917	*Mutiny; Southern Justice; The Greater Law; The Show Down; God's Crucible*

Goudal, Jetta (1891 Amsterdam, the Netherlands-1985 Los Angeles, CA)

Jetta Goudal, who remained a "European" although she lived for years in the United States, was a talented actor who protected her privacy with as much enthusiasm as she put into her screen roles. Nothing is known about her early life prior to her arriving in the United States.

She appeared on the New York stage after leaving Europe in 1918, and one of her most memorable parts was as Marthe Roche in *The Hero;* during the 1921 season. Her first screen appearance was a bit part in *Timothy's Quest* (1922) as the hopelessly ill mother whose drunken husband had no interest in caring for their children. She entered films in earnest with her next roles in *The Bright Shawl* (1923) as a Spanish spy and in *The Green Goddess* (1923) as a Hindu servant. Both roles, although very small, won her much attention from the film community and critics.

Her first lead role was in *Open All Night* (1924), directed by Paul Bern. The following year she appeared in her first financially and critically successful film, *Salome of the Tenements,* based on an Anzia Yezierska novel. When her contract with Paramount was cancelled before its expiration, Goudal signed with Cecil B. DeMille and appeared in *The Coming of Amos* (1925) as a tragic Russian princess. Although she had signed a lucrative contract with DeMille, Goudal sued Paramount for terminating her contract eighteen months before it was due to expire.

Two of her most successful films were made while she was under contract with DeMille. Both *White Gold* and *The Forbidden Woman* were selected by the National Board of Review as two of the best films of 1927. However, her insistence on portraying her characters as she felt best resulted in another lawsuit—this time against DeMille. Citing her "temperamental" outbursts that had cost the studio "thousands," DeMille terminated her contract three years early. Although Goudal won the case and was given a monetary settlement, she remained on good terms with DeMille.

After the court battle, Goudal did not appear in another film until 1930, when she starred in the American-made film for European distribution *Le Spectre Vert* [The Green Specter]. This was the first film made in the United States expressly for a European audience.

The advent of sound brought new difficulties to Goudal's career because of her pronounced accent. Relegated to auditioning for supporting roles of "foreigners," Goudal developed her flair for interior decoration. As a result she met and married her husband, Harold Grieve, a former art director and set designer turned decorator.

She retired from films and went into business with her husband, working in the Los Angeles area until ill health forced her to retire. Goudal is credited today with establishing a star's rights within the film industry and as a founding member of Actors' Equity.

Film Credits

1923   *The Bright Shawl; The Green Goddess*
1924   *Open All Night*
1925   *Salome of the Tenements; The Spaniard; The Coming of Amos; The Road to Yesterday*
1926   *Three Faces East; Paris at Midnight; Her Man o' War*
1927   *Fighting Love; White Gold; The Forbidden Woman*
1928   *The Cardboard Lover*
1929   *Lady of the Pavements*
1930   *Le Spectre Vert*
1932   *Business and Pleasure*

Grandin, Ethel (1894 New York City-1988 Woodland Hills, CA)

Ethel Grandin's parents were involved in show business, as were several members of her father's family. With these family connections she made her stage debut at age seven in *Rip Van Winkle* (1901) and later that year appeared as "Eros" in the stage production of *Ben-Hur.*

She toured for three years with Chauncey Olcott's company along with Lottie Pickford, Mary Pickford's younger sister. But she did not enjoy the traveling necessary for touring, so Grandin decided to look for work in films. Her first choice of studio was Biograph, but after an unpleasant encounter with D. W. Griffith, Grandin signed with Carl Laemmle's Independent Motion Picture Company (IMP) and worked under the direction of Thomas Ince and Herbert Brenon.

When Ince moved west in 1911, Grandin came with him as leading lady and appeared in many of his western productions. In 1912 Grandin married cameraman-director Ray Smallwood and returned with him to New York the next year to rejoin Laemmle's studio. In 1914 she and her husband formed the Smallwood Film Corporation, with herself as the leading lady. Although the company did not last long, Grandin later cited the films they made with pride.

After the demise of her company, Grandin retired to care for her growing family. She did return briefly to the screen to appear in a popular sixteen-chapter serial, *The Crimson Stain Mystery,* and then appeared in a few films in the early 1920s before retiring completely.

Film Credits

1911   *The Toss of a Coin; Uncle's Visit; Bar Z's New Cook; The Colonel's Ward; Cowgirl's Pranks; Dorothy's Family; Behind the Times; By the House That Jack Built; A Biting Business*

1912   *The Crisis; The Law of the West; The War on the Plains; Blazing the Trail; The Deserter; The Sergeant's Boy; The Invaders; The Reckoning; The Colonel's Peril; The Desert; The*

Doctor's Double; His Message; The Lieutenant's Last Fight; A Soldier's Honor; The Vengeance of Fate; The Ranch Girl's Love; The Kid and the Sleuth; Love and Jealousy; A Tenderfoot's Revenge; Broncho Bill's Love Affair; The Deputy's Sweetheart; His Double Life; The Gambler and the Girl; The Garrison Triangle

1913   *Traffic in Souls; A Black Conspiracy* (II); *Love vs. Love; The Gold Mesh Bag; The Bachelor Girl's Club; The Coward's Atonement; The Fatal Verdict; King, the Detective in the Jarvis Case; The Manicure; The Miser's Son; None but the Brave; The Toll of War; Wynona's Vengeance; Texas Kelly at Bay*

1914   *Jane Eyre; The Adopted Daughter; Adventures of a Girl Reporter; Papa's Darling; Where There's a Will There's a Way; Forgetting; The Opal Ring; Love's Victory; Beneath the Mask; The Box Couch; The Dawn of Romance; The Dawn of a New Day; The Great Universal Mystery; Temper vs. Temper*

1915   *Affinities*

1916   *The Crimson Stain Mystery*

1917   *The Little Rebel's Sacrifice; The Silent Prisoner; Tit for Tat*

1921   *Garments of Truth; The Hunch*

1922   *A Tailor-Made Man*

Gray, Gilda (1898 Krakow, Poland-1959 Hollywood, CA)

Courtesy of Silents Are Golden at <SilentsAreGolden.com>

Gilda Gray was eight when her family fled Poland to escape the advancing Russian Army. The family lived briefly in New Jersey before settling in Wisconsin. To further his dreamed-of political career, her father arranged her marriage to his political backer's son when she was only fourteen years old. The following year she had a son and began singing in saloons to help support her family.

It was during this time that she supposedly created "the shimmy," a dance in which she moved her upper body and hips, actually a reaction to her nervousness while trying to sing. It was an instant local sensation (the dance was revived in the 1960s). The story is that the name came from her mispronunciation of "chemise."

With her newfound success, Gray left her family and moved to Chicago where she appeared in a vaudeville act with her "sister." Soon she moved to New York where she appeared in USO shows for the soldiers while she tried to find stage work. Through these USO appearances she met Sophie Tucker who took Gray under her wing and helped her to find a job in the theater.

When Gray was appearing in *The Gaieties of 1919,* she was offered a job as the headliner at a popular New York nightclub. While appearing at the nightclub she also began appearing in *The Ziegfeld Follies.* Because of her popularity and her ability to bring in crowds, Ziegfeld called her "his golden girl."

Gray became the symbol of the age—the Roaring Twenties. With her growing renown the origins of the shimmy became more exotic. It was now a South Seas dance to honor the god of love. She embarked on a vaudeville tour, rumored to be making $47,000 per week, and divorced her husband. When the tour reached Hollywood, she was offered a contract with Famous Players. Her first film for them, *Aloma of the South Seas* (1926), supposedly made $3 million in its first three months.

After a messy divorce from her second husband and manager, Gray left the film industry about the time the stock market crashed in 1929. Gray returned to vaudeville and weathered the economic storm.

While on a visit to Poland in 1939, Gray was put in the situation of needing to once more escape her homeland. She supposedly caught the last flight out of Warsaw before the Nazis invaded. She unwaveringly supported Polish causes during the war, for which she was later awarded the Polish Legion of Honor Cross.

In 1946 she sued Columbia, claiming that their film *Gilda* was based on her life. Even though the film wasn't based on her life, she received an out-of-court settlement that allowed her to purchase a ranch in Colorado.

A few years prior to her death she was featured on the television program *This Is Your Life.* Apparently she lost the ranch at some point, because when she died there was no money for her burial until the Motion Picture Relief Fund stepped in to pay for the service.

Film Credits

1919	*A Virtuous Vamp*
1921	*The Girl with the Jazz Heart*
1923	*Lawful Larceny*
1926	*Aloma of the South Seas*
1927	*Cabaret; The Devil Dancer*
1929	*Piccadilly*
1936	*Rose-Marie; The Great Ziegfeld*

Greeley, Evelyn (1888 Austria-1975 West Palm Beach, FL)

Evelyn Greeley was one the beauties of the silent era and, possibly (as reported in publicity of the period), the granddaughter of famed journalist Horace Greeley. Like many silent actors, the truth about her life is in doubt.

She began her career in stock and toured with the Poli Players Stock Company before leaving the stage for films. She first worked for the Essanay Company in Chicago, eventually signing with World Film Corporation, where she achieved her greatest success between 1917 and 1919. She lost her contract with World Film in 1920 and freelanced for a few years before retiring in 1923 to become a housewife. When she died in 1975, her third husband survived her.

Film Credits

1915	*The Second in Command*
1916	*Tempest and Sunshine; Just a Song at Twilight*
1917	*The Social Leper; The Price of Pride; The Brand of Satan; The Burglar; The Good for Nothing; The Volunteer*
1918	*The Beautiful Mrs. Reynolds; His Royal Highness; Leap to Fame; The Golden Wall; The Beloved Blackmailer; By Hook or Crook; The Road to France; Hitting the Trail*
1919	*Love in a Hurry; Courage for Two; Hit or Miss; Three Green Eyes; Phil-for-Short; Bringing Up Betty; The Oakdale Affair; Me and Captain Kidd*
1921	*His Greatest Sacrifice; Diane of Star Hollow*
1922	*The Pasteboard Crown; Just a Song at Twilight; Bulldog Drummond*

Greenwood, Winifred (1885 Geneseo, NY-1961 Woodland Hills, CA)

Winifred Greenwood was a popular featured player for two early silent film companies—Selig in Chicago and the American Flying-A Company in Santa Barbara, California. As film shorts moved into feature-length films, Greenwood moved into character roles.

Her mother raised Greenwood alone after her father died when she was eight years old. Educated to become a teacher, she left New York Normal School to tour the vaudeville circuit throughout the United States and Canada. After a few years in vaudeville, she moved to the stage, appearing in both musical comedies and melodramas. She toured with various well-known stock companies and for a brief period had her own touring company.

Although she never completely abandoned the stage, she began appearing in one- and two-reel films in 1910, with her debut being Selig's version of *The Wizard of Oz*. Between 1910 and 1913 she was one of Selig's leading stars and her popularity helped to build the studio's million-dollar production complex.

After three years with Selig, Greenwood moved to California and joined the American Flying-A Company, where she met her future husband, actor George Field. Still working in the short-film arena, many of her film titles have been lost, but she averaged three films per week for two years.

Greenwood appeared in her first feature-length films in 1916 and left Flying-A to freelance with various small studios throughout California. When she was unable to find work in films, Greenwood returned to the stage. After her divorce in the early 1920s she regularly alternated between the two venues.

It is unclear whether she continued in films after 1927, since bit players and extras were almost never credited. Eventually failing health forced her to move to the Motion Picture Country Home where she died in 1961.

Film Credits

1910   *The Wizard of Oz*
1911   *Maud Miller; Brown of Harvard; The Two Orphans; Tempted by Necessity; Under Suspicion; His Chance to Make Good;*

A Novel Experiment; The Visiting Nurse; The Mission Worker; The Tale of a Soldier's Ring; A Fair Exchange; A Tennessee Love Story; How They Stopped the Run on the Bank; His Better Self; His First Long Trousers; Getting Married; The Plumber

1912 *The Last Dance; A Detective's Strategy; The Prosecuting Attorney; Belle Boyd, Confederate Spy; The Adopted Son*

1913 *Pauline Cushman, the Federal Spy; The Understudy; The Millionaire Cowboy; The Drummer's Honeymoon; The Shriner's Daughter; What Her Diary Told; The Broken Barrier; The Derelict; Down by the Sea; Dixieland; The Man Who Might Have Been*

1914 *The Little House in the Valley; The Lure of the Sawdust; The Silent Way; A Slice of Life; The Guiding Light; High Cost of Flirting; Key to the Past; The Wishing Stone; The Archeologist*

1915 *Saints and Sinners; Alice of Hudson Bay; The Truth of Fiction; Out of the Ashes; The Water Carrier of San Juan; The Zaca Lake Mystery; The Clear Up; When a Woman Waits; The Alarm of Angelon; Ancestry*

1916 *Lying Lips; Reclamation; The Inner Struggle; Dust; A Woman's Daring; The Voice of Love*

1917 *The Crystal Gazer; Lorelei of the Sea; The Inspiration of Harry Larrabee; The Alien Blood*

1918 *M'Liss; Danger Within; The Deciding Kiss; Believe Me, Xantippe; The Goat; Too Many Millions*

1919 *Come Again Smith; Maggie Pepper; Putting It Over; Men, Women, and Money; The Lottery Man; An Adventure in Hearts*

1920 *Young Mrs. Winthrop; Sick Abed; The Life of the Party; Are All Men Alike?*

1921 *The Faith Healer; Dollar a Year Man; Sacred and Profane Love; Love Never Dies; Leap Year; Don't Call Me Little Girl*

1923 *To The Last Man*

1926 *The Flame of the Yukon*

1927 *The King of Kings*

1936 *The Music Goes 'Round*

Griffith, Corinne (1894 Texarkana, TX-1979 Santa Monica, CA)

Courtesy of Silents Are Golden at <SilentsAreGolden.com>.

Corinne Griffith, known at the height of her popularity as "The Orchid Lady" of the silent screen, began her career as a dancer on stage and the vaudeville circuit. She made her first film in 1916 for Vitagraph when she replaced Anita Stewart as their female lead and proved to be popular with the early viewing audiences.

She moved to First National in the mid-1920s and became one of their most popular actors, known for her elegance and beauty. Her popularity allowed her to produce some of her own films, and she reigned as a top star in both comedies and melodramas. For one of her final silent films, *The Divine Lady,* she received an Oscar nomination in 1929. She made a few sound films, but her voice did not record well and she retired in 1932.

After her retirement she invested in real estate and became quite wealthy from these investments. She was an outspoken opponent to income tax when it was first proposed and was politically active on many other issues. In addition, she wrote several books including, *Papa's Delicate Condition* (1952) and her 1972 autobiography, *This You Won't Believe.*

Film Credits

1916   *Through the Wall; The Last Man; The Yellow Girl*
1917   *The Stolen Treaty; Transgression; The Love Doctor; I Will Repay; Who Goes There?*
1918   *The Menace; Love Watches; The Clutch of Circumstance; The Girl of Today; Miss Ambition*
1919   *The Adventure Shop; The Girl Problem; The Unknown Quantity; Thin Ice; A Girl at Bay; The Climbers; The Bramble Bush*

1920	*Deadline at Eleven; Babs; The Whisper Market; The Tower of Jewels; Human Collateral; The Garter Girl; The Broadway Bubble*
1921	*Moral Fibre; The Single Track; It Isn't Being Done This Season; What's Your Reputation Worth?*
1922	*Received Payment; A Virgin's Sacrifice; Divorce Coupons; Island Wives*
1923	*Six Days; The Common Law*
1924	*Lilies of the Field* (I); *Single Wives; Love's Wilderness; Black Oxen*
1925	*Déclassée; The Marriage Whirl; Classified; Infatuation*
1926	*Mademoiselle Modiste; Into Her Kingdom; Syncopating Sue*
1927	*The Lady in Ermine; Three Hours*
1928	*The Garden of Eden; Outcast*
1929	*Saturday's Children; Prisoners; The Divine Lady*
1930	*Lilies of the Field* (II); *Back Pay*
1931	*Lily Christine*
1961	*Paradise Alley*

Producing Credits

1924	*Single Wives; Love's Wilderness*
1925	*Déclassée; The Marriage Whirl; Infatuation*
1926	*Mademoiselle Modiste; Into Her Kingdom; Syncopating Sue*
1927	*The Lady in Ermine; Three Hours*

Gulliver, Dorothy (1908 Salt Lake City, UT-2001 Valley Centre, CA)

Courtesy of Silents Are Golden at <SilentsAreGolden.com>.

Dorothy Gulliver got her start in films after being crowned "Miss Salt Lake City" and winning a talent contest sponsored by Universal Pictures in 1926. After a successful screen test, she was given a contract and began to regularly appear in Universal's films.

One of her first successes was the series *The Collegians* (1926-1930), which featured three friends who were attending the fictional Calford

College together. The films were released over a four-year period, duplicating the time it would take to actually graduate from college. She also had supporting roles in two 1926 Eileen Sedgwick serials, *The Winking Idol* and *Strings of Steel*.

In 1928, after two years in the film industry, Gulliver was selected as a WAMPAS Baby Star. Although she never reached the pinnacle of stardom, Gulliver made the transition to sound easily and continued to appear in westerns and serials through the early 1930s—in one, *Shadow of the Eagle* (1932), she costarred with newcomer John Wayne.

Her career was cut short by a serious accident that made it impossible for her to work for a year. Once she recovered, roles were harder to find and she decided to retire from films in the early 1940s. Upon her retirement she occasionally appeared in local stage plays and then moved into television when it was created. In 1968, after more than twenty-five years of retirement, she appeared in *Faces;* her performance was so good that many felt she should have received an Academy Award nomination for Best Supporting Actress.

Film Credits

1926   *The Winking Idol; Strings of Steel; The Collegians; Benson at Calford; Backyard George; Fighting to Win; Hook or Crook; The Last Lap; Making Good; One Wild Time; The Shoot 'Em Up Kid; And George Did It!*

1927   *The Shield of Honor; One Glorious Scrap; A Dog of the Regiment; The Rambling Ranger; Breaking Records; The Cinder Path; Crimson Colors; The Dazzling Co-Ed; The Dude Desperado; A Fighting Finish; Flashing Oars; Samson at Calford; Splashing Through; Winning Five; The Winning Punch; Running Wild; Around the Bases; The Fighting Spirit; The Relay; Shield of Honor*

1928   *Good Morning, Judge; The Wild West Show; Paddling Co-Eds; Honeymoon Flats; The Bookworm Hero; Calford in the Movies; Calford on Horseback; Calford vs. Redskins; Dear Old Calford; The Junior Year; Kicking Through; Clearing the Trail; Fighting for Victory; Sliding Home; The Winning Goal*

1929   *Night Parade; Painted Faces; College Love; Cross Country Run; Farewell; The Winning Point; King of the Campus; The*

Rivals; On Guard; Junior Luck; Sporting Courage; The Varsity Drag; Flying High; On the Sidelines; Use Your Feet; Splash Mates; Graduation Daze; Speeding Youth

1930   *Troopers Three; Under Montana Skies; Voice of Hollywood #7; Big Hearted; Mind Your Own Business*

1931   *The Phantom of the West; In Old Cheyenne; The Galloping Ghost; The Fighting Marshal*

1932   *Shadow of the Eagle; The Honor of the Press; The Last Frontier; Outlaw Justice; The Black Ghost; The Phantom Express*

1933   *King Kong; Revenge at Monte Carlo; Cheating Blondes*

1934   *Stand Up and Cheer; The Pecos Dandy*

1935   *The Fighting Caballero*

1936   *Custer's Last Stand*

1938   *In Early Arizona*

1939   *Lone Star Pioneers; North of Shanghai*

1941   *Borrowed Hero; Appointment for Love*

1942   *A Tragedy at Midnight*

1944   *Sweethearts of the U.S.A.*

1968   *Faces*

1976   *Won Ton Ton, the Dog Who Saved Hollywood*

Guy, Alice (1875 Saint-Mande, France-1968 Mahwah, NJ)

Alice Guy is generally acknowledged as the first female director and was, in fact, one of the first directors to work with "talking" films. Noted in *Photoplay* in 1912 as a "striking example of the modern woman in business who is doing a man's job," Guy was the best known behind-the-scenes woman in silent films.

Born into a middle-class family outside of Paris, her father moved his family and business to Chile when Guy was still very young. When she was older, she attended convent schools in France; after graduation she was hired as secretary to photographer and groundbreaking filmmaker Leon Gaumont around 1895.

Gaumont was working to develop the cameras and projectors for use with motion pictures, and since filmmaking was not yet considered a "business," he allowed Guy to write, direct, and produce her first film, *La Fee aux Choux* [The Cabbage Fairy] in 1896. The short was shown at the International Exhibition in Paris and was, arguably, the first fictional film ever made.

The film was successfully received and she continued to work for Gaumont as a director through 1905, during which time she made more than 400 short subjects. In 1905 Guy was made production director for Gaumont and began directing films using Gaumont's "chronophone," which synchronized pictures with a sound recording, thereby becoming the first person to direct a "talking" picture. In fact, between 1905 and 1906 she made over one hundred "talkies."

In 1906 she met her future husband, Englishman Herbert Blaché-Bolton, who was also working for Gaumont. They married in 1907 just prior to sailing to America so that her husband could head Gaumont's distribution operations in the United States. Upon arriving, Guy settled into being a housewife and gave birth to her daughter, Simone.

After several years Guy formed a production company, Solax, in 1910 with herself as president and director-in-chief. Over the four years of Solax's existence, Guy oversaw more than 330 one-reel films. In 1912, after the birth of her second child, Reginald, Guy designed and had built a new studio to house her company—the first woman to do so. The glass-roofed studio was dominated by her acting mandate, "Be Natural." Sadly, the studio was destroyed by fire in 1923.

She also directed a science fiction film in 1912, titled *The Year 2000,* in which women ruled the world. Her talent and success brought her respect but also resentment from less-talented males within the industry. Her standing in the industry was made evident when she appeared in an article on "Prominent Independent Film Manufacturers" in the February 1912 issue of the *Clipper,* an early trade publication. In it Guy stated that she believed that films should educate as well as entertain.

In 1914 Solax was dissolved and Guy's professionally jealous husband forced her into the position of assistant director to him at the newly formed Blaché Features. But his work was clearly inferior, and both the viewing public and critics made this fact known. In the summer of 1917, Guy gave a series of lectures at Columbia University on filmmaking and, in spite of her husband's attempt to sabotage her career, Guy was still an acknowledged talent; the films that she produced were both critical and popular successes.

However, as the film industry became more "sophisticated" (i.e., more morally relaxed) Guy's Victorian attitudes made her style outdated. She returned to France in 1922, after divorcing her husband, to try to reenter the industry she had virtually created, but work was difficult to find. She was forced into retirement and, thereafter, divided her time between France and the United States, where her daughter worked for the U.S. Foreign Service.

In 1953 Guy was honored at the Cinematheque Francais in Paris as the first woman filmmaker in the world and made a Knight of the Foreign Legion of Honor. Yet when she died in 1968, for all her successes and innovations, few papers carried her obituary.

Directing Credits (for the United States)

1910   *A Child's Sacrifice*

1911   *The Violin Maker of Nuremberg; Rose of the Circus; The Doll; Road Leads Home; The Little Rangers; His Mother's Hymn; Five O'Clock; The Cure*

1912   *Playing Trumps; Phantom Paradise; Mignon; In the Year 2000; Fra Diavolo; The Face at the Window; The Blood Stain; Canned Harmony; Falling Leaves; A Fool and His Money; Making an American Citizen; Mickey's Pal; Blighted Lives; Algie, the Miner; God Disposes; A Terrible Lesson; Mrs. Cranston's Jewels; Child of the Tenements*

1913   *The Roques of Paris; Shadows of the Moulin Rouge; A Terrible Night; The Pit and the Penduylum; The Little Hunchback; A House Divided; Matrimony Speed Limit; Dick Whittington and His Cat*

1914   *The Monster and the Girl; The Woman of Mystery; The Lure; The Tigress; The Dream Woman; Beneath the Czar*

1915   *The Vampire; The Song of the Wage Slave; My Madonna; The Heart of a Painted Woman*

1916   *The Ocean Waif; What Will People Say?*

1917   *The Adventurer; The Empress; A Man and the Woman; House of Cards; Behind the Mask; When You and I Were Young*

1918   *The Great Adventure*

1920   *Vampire; Tarnished Reputations*

1938   *Charlie Chaplin Festival*

H

Hall, Ella (1896 New York City-1982 Los Angeles, CA)

Ella Hall appeared on the stage as a youngster and, at one point, understudied Mary Pickford in *The Warrens of Virginia*. When she entered the film industry, she first worked with Biograph and D. W. Griffith before moving to Reliance Studios.

While at Reliance Studios she was one of the first actors to work in Kinemacolor, one of the first attempts to film in color. During her tenure at Reliance, Hall met Lois Weber and became one of her protégés. When Weber moved to Universal, she arranged for Hall to follow as one of her featured players.

At Universal, Hall appeared in several serials, including *The Master Key* (1914) and *The Great Universal Mystery* (1914). She continued in films until the early 1930s.

Film Credits

1912   *Hot Stuff; The School Teacher and the Waif*

1913   *Memories; The Haunted Bride; The Blood Brotherhood; James Lee's Wife; The Mask; The Jew's Christmas*

1914   *The Female of the Species; A Fool and His Money; The Coward Hater; Woman's Burden; The Weaker Sister; A Modern Fairy Tale; The Man Who Slept; An Episode; The Career of Waterloo Peterson; The Triumph of the Mind; The Stone in the Road; The Pursuit of Hate; Lost by a Hair; The Master Key; The Spy; An Awkward Cinderella; The Boob's Legacy; The Boob's Nemesis; The Bowl of Roses; The Decision; For the Secret Service; The Great Universal Mystery; The Hedge Between; His Uncle's Will; The Little Sister; The Mistress of Deadwood Basin; Olaf Erickson, Boss; Out of the Darkness; The Sherlock Boob; The Symphony of Souls; When Fate Disposes; White Roses*

1915   *The Silent Command; At the Foot of the Stairs; Heritage; Jewel; Betty's Dream Hero; The Boob's Romance; Both Sides of Life; Christmas Memories; The Heart of Lincoln* (I);

Idols of Clay; The Little Blonde in Black; Mavis of the Glen; Shattered Memories

1916   *The Crippled Hand; The Love Girl; Little Eve Edgarton; The Burglar of Algiers; A Boob's Victory; The Heart of a Show Girl; In the Heart of New York; Secret Love; The Silent Man of Timber Gulch; The Silent Member; The Unfinished Case; The Winning of Miss Construe; Child of Circumstances; Just from Sweden*

1917   *Her Soul's Inspiration; The Little Orphan; Polly Redhead; A Jewel in Pawn; The Charmer; The Spotted Lily; My Little Boy*

1918   *New Love for Old; Beauty in Chains; A Mother's Secret; The Heart of Rachael; Which Woman?; Three Mounted Men*

1919   *Under the Top*

1921   *The Great Reward*

1922   *In the Name of the Law; The Heart of Lincoln* (II); *The Third Alarm*

1923   *The Flying Dutchman; Westbound Limited*

1930   *Madam Satan*

1933   *The Bitter Tea of General Yen*

Hall, Lillian (1896 Brooklyn, NY-1959 Los Angeles, CA)

After initially planning a career in business, Lillian Hall left her conventional career for acting—first on the stage and then in films. Although her career spanned only a few years, during that period she appeared in several film classics.

She began her career with the Norma Talmadge Company but apparently freelanced among several studios. She appeared as Beth Marsh in William Brady's production of *Little Women* (1918) and as Alice Munro in Maurice Tourneur's seminal production of *The Last of the Mohicans* (1920).

She retired from the screen when she married in 1924. Little is known of her life after she retired, except that she committed suicide in 1959.

Film Credits

1918   *The Safety Curtain; Little Women; Wanted for Murder*

1919   *Taxi; My Little Sister; Coax Me*

1920   *Sherry; Fickle Women; An Arabian Knight; The Last of the Mohicans; Going Some*
1921   *Oliver Twist; The Secret of the Hills; A Shocking Night; Hearts of Youth*
1922   *The Forest King*
1924   *The Elk's Tooth; Leatherstocking*

Hammerstein, Elaine (1897 Philadelphia, PA-1948 Mexico)

The granddaughter of composer Oscar and the daughter of theatrical producer Arthur, Elaine Hammerstein seemed fated to a career in entertainment. She started her show business career on the stage in *High Jinks,* a musical comedy, but decided that she did not enjoy appearing on the stage and eventually gravitated to films.

Because of her parentage and theatrical connections, she was welcomed into an industry that was still seeking legitimacy. She was a true professional but at the same time did not lose sight of the fact that acting was a job of make-believe, thereby keeping her fame in a perspective lost on many stars—both from the early days and from future generations.

She preferred to appear in melodramas in which she could wear extravagant costumes and became known off screen as a clotheshorse and style leader. One of her favorite film appearances was the Ruritanian romance and elaborate costume piece *Rupert of Hentzau* (1923).

She retired from films to travel the world after she married insurance executive James Kays. While touring Mexico in 1948, she was killed in an automobile accident.

Film Credits

1915   *Moonstone; The Face in the Moonlight*
1916   *Beatrice Fairfax*

1917 *Mad Lover; The Co-Respondent; The Argyle Case; The Silent Master*
1918 *Wanted for Murder; Accidental Honeymoon; Her Man*
1919 *The Country Cousin; Love or Fame*
1920 *Shadow of Rosalie Byrnes; Whispers; Greater Than Fame; The Woman Game; Point of View; Pleasure Seekers; The Daughter Pays*
1921 *The Miracle of Manhattan; The Girl from Nowhere; Handcuffs and Kisses; The Way of a Maid; Poor Dear Margaret Kirby; Remorseless Love*
1922 *Reckless Youth; Evidence; Under Oath; One Week of Love; Why Announce Your Marriage?*
1923 *Rupert of Hentzau; Broadway Gold; Souls for Sale; Drums of Jeopardy*
1924 *The Foolish Virgin; Daring Love; The Midnight Express; One Glorious Night*
1925 *The Unwritten Law; Every Man's Wife; Parisian Nights; After Business Hours; Paint and Powder; S.O.S.; Perils of the Sea*
1926 *Ladies of Leisure; The Checkered Flag*

Hansen, Juanita (1895 Des Moines, IA-1961 West Hollywood, CA)

Juanita Hansen started appearing in small roles in films as soon as she graduated high school in Los Angeles. The first film for which she received billing credit was *The Love Route* (1915), produced by Famous Players-Lasky.

She appeared in D. W. Griffith's *The Martyrs of the Alamo* (1915) before being chosen as a Mack Sennett "Bathing Beauty." Although she wanted to become a dramatic actor, she appeared mostly in Keystone comedies between 1915 and 1917.

She was finally offered an opportunity to appear in dramatic films and signed with Universal in 1918.

That year she appeared in her first serial, *The Brass Bullet,* made up of eighteen two-reel episodes. She continued to appear with some of the leading actors of the era, including William S. Hart and Tom Mix, before winning her campaign to be chosen to take Pearl White's place at Pathe in 1920.

One of the first items she acquired as a star was a Chalmers speedster that she raced throughout the Los Angeles area, much to the consternation of the local police. In fact, she was arrested for speeding so often that it became a normal occurrence for the studio to have to bail her out of jail.

However, before long she was feeling the results of her demanding filming schedule and her love of Hollywood's nightlife. To help her keep up with the demands on her time, she turned to drugs; by the end of 1921 she was a cocaine addict and her health deteriorated quickly. When she became unreliable on the set, Pathe dropped her contract to avoid any unwanted publicity concerning her addiction, which was becoming more and more evident to those around her.

She went through several attempts at rehabilitation without success. One time after kicking her habit, an accident on the set necessitated her taking painkillers and she was re-addicted before the completion of the film project. Finally, in 1928, after years of failed attempts, she was completely drug free, but by then she could get few film jobs. After a final film in 1934 she was lowered to appearing on the carnival circuit until she finally got a clerical job with Southern Pacific Railroad.

Film Credits

1914   *The Patchwork Girl of Oz; The Magic Cloak of Oz*
1915   *The Love Route; The Failure; Betty in Search of a Thrill; The Martyrs of the Alamo; The Absentee; The Failure; The Secret of the Submarine*
1916   *His Pride and Shame; The Finishing Touch; Black Eyes and Blue; The Mediator*
1917   *Glory; A Royal Rogue; Dangers of a Bride; Cactus Nell; A Clever Dummy; A Noble Fraud; When Hearts Collide; His Busy Day; Whose Baby?*
1918   *The Rough Lover; Fast Company; The Risky Road; The Mating of Marcella; The Brass Bullet; The Sea Flower; Broadway Love*

1919 *Breezy Jim; The Poppy Girl's Husband; A Midnight Ro-mance; Rough-Riding Romance; Lombardi Limited; Taking Things Easy; Devil McCare*
1920 *The Lost City; The Phantom Foe*
1921 *The Yellow Arm; The Red Snow*
1922 *The Eternal Flame; The Broadway Madonna*
1923 *The Jungle Princess; Girl from the West*
1934 *Sensation Hunters*

Harlow, Jean (1911 Kansas City, MO-1937 Los Angeles, CA)

Jean Harlow, who went on to become *the* platinum blonde bomb-shell of the 1930s, got her start in silent films. She was born into a well-to-do family headed by a successful dentist and therefore received a privileged upbringing. At the age of sixteen she eloped with the heir of a wealthy Chicago family, but the marriage did not last. It did, however, get Harlow to Hollywood. Within a year she was working as an extra in films starring Laurel and Hardy and Clara Bow.

After appearing in two successful Laurel and Hardy shorts—*Double Whoopee* and *The Saturday Night Kid* (both 1929), Harlow was cast in the talking version of Howard Hughes's World War I film *Hell's Angels* (1930). Although the film had been in production for two years, when the decision was made to continue in sound several roles had to be recast, including the female lead. When the film was finally released it was one of the top ten grossing films of the year.

The film made Harlow famous and the hottest new property in Hollywood. She was a talented comedian and is part of one of the most famous dialogues in early film. In *Dinner at Eight* (1933), Harlow portrays a gold-digging trophy wife whose appearance and behavior hint at an amoral background. As Harlow's character complains that one of the men had expressed the belief that machinery would one day replace humans in every profession, Marie Dressler's character replies, "Oh, my dear, that's something *you* need never worry about."

Her less-than-intelligent vampish persona was established, and Harlow made the most of it. She moved to MGM where she signed a contract at $1,250 weekly for all fifty-two weeks of the year, rather than the standard thirty-nine weeks. Her third film at her new studio was gold—*Red Dust* (1932) opposite Clark Gable firmly established her star status.

After *Red Dust* she returned to comedies again and scored another hit with the satirical *Bombshell* (1933). After this hit, it was not until she, Gable, and Wallace Beery were paired again that she hit box-office gold with *China Seas* (1935). Although the studio tried to transition her to dramas, her best performances were in comedies.

While making *Saratoga,* Harlow became extremely ill. Within days she died of acute nephritis. When the film was released after her death, it made in excess of $2 million. The year of her death, Harlow became the first female film actor to appear on the cover of *Life* magazine (May 1937).

Like Marilyn Monroe after her, Harlow has never been allowed to rest in peace. At regular intervals her life is examined for possible flaws and her name maligned to various degrees. She was subject of two mediocre films in 1965 purporting to tell the story of her life. But through it all, she remains a fine, if underrated, actor and comedian.

Film Credits

1928   *Moran of the Marines; Chasing Husbands*
1929   *Liberty; Fugitives; Close Harmony; Double Whoopee; The Unkissed Man; Thundering Toupees; Bacon Grabbers; The Saturday Night Kid; The Love Parade; This Thing Called Love; Weak but Willing; New York Nights; Why Be Good?; Why Is a Plumber?*
1930   *Hell's Angels*
1931   *City Lights; The Public Enemy; The Secret Six; Iron Man; Goldie; Platinum Blonde; Beau Hunks*
1932   *Three Wise Girls; The Beast of the City; Red-Headed Woman; Red Dust; Talking Screen Snapshots*
1933   *Hold Your Man; Dinner at Eight; Bombshell*
1934   *The Girl from Missouri*
1935   *Reckless; China Seas*
1936   *Riffraff; Wife vs. Secretary; Suzy; Libeled Lady*
1937   *Personal Property; Saratoga*

Henry, Gale (1893 Bear Valley, CA-1972 Palmdale, CA)

Gale Henry began her entertainment career as an opera singer with the Temple Opera Company in Los Angeles where she sang for three years prior to her switch to films. In 1914 she joined the Joker Comedy Company at Universal and was featured in at least one film per week. She perfected the character of the overbearing wife ever ready to chastise her errant husband.

Soon she was the lead female comic. After 1915 she divided her time between Joker and Powers Comedies, both of which released films through Universal. Notable during this period was the two-reel comedy series featuring Lady Baffles and Detective Duck in which Henry costarred with Max Asher.

In 1918 she organized her own production company, Gale's Model Comedies, where she made two-reel comedies. Her first film, *A Wild Woman* (1919), was a hit and was the first of a series of comedies that her company released. Although the troupe had scripts, they were not above improvising if a good gag came to them while filming, so the films were often more spontaneous than scripted. The company produced films for three years before its distributor went bankrupt; rather than restructuring, Henry began working for other studios.

Although she began appearing in features, she continued to occasionally appear in short comedies. She gravitated to supporting roles until she retired shortly after the advent of sound. Sadly, most of the titles to her early film shorts have been lost.

Film Credits

1914 *Across the Court; The Midnight Alarm; The Tender Hearted Sheriff; Universal Ike Has His Ups and Downs; Schultz the Barber; Love and Electricity; Universal Ike Junior Is Kept from Being an Actor; The Fatal Letter; Captain Kid's Priceless Treasures; Love, Roses and Trousers; His Wife's Family; The Polo Champions; Wifies' Busy Day; That's Fair Enough; The Diamond Nippers; Well! Well!; Oh, What's the Use?; What's Happened to Schultz? Jam and Jealousy; In the Clutches of the Villain; The Baseball Fans of Fanville; Cruel, Cruel World!; When Their Wives Joined the Regiment; The De-Feet of Father; Battle of Nations; A Dream of a Painting; Love Disguised*

1915   *No Babies Allowed; Lady Baffles and Detective Duck* (thirteen films); *Hubby's Cure; Fools and Pajamas; He Fell in Love with His Mother-in-Law; The Blank Note; Wanted—A Piano Tuner; The Plumber Wins the Girl; Won with Dynamite; Fooling Father; Love and Law; Saved by a Shower; The Water Cure; School Days; Back to School Days; Schultz's Lady Friend; The Rejuvenation of Liza Jane; Wedding Bells Shall Ring; The Way He Won the Widow; The Fatal Kiss; Over the Bounding Waves; Cy Perkins in the City of Delusions; A Day at the San Diego Zoo; The Lady Doctor of Grizzly Gulch; Hiram's Inheritance; How Billy Got His Raise; The Lover's Lucky Predicament; A Duke for a Day; At the Bingville Booster's Barbeque; The Wrong Label; Right Off the Reel; When Schultz Led the Orchestra; Freaks; A Duel at Dawn; Their Bewitched Elopement; A Dip in the Water; The Bravest of the Brave; When Hiram Went to the City; At the Beach Incognito; He Couldn't Fool His Mother-in-Law; He Couldn't Support His Wife; A Millionaire for a Minute; Pete's Awful Crime; Twentieth Century Susie; Chills and Chickens; Mrs. Prune's Boarding House; Slightly Mistaken; Stage Struck; The Village Smithy*

1916   *You Want Something; Lemonade Aids Cupid; Those Female Haters; Leap and Look Thereafter; Mrs. Green's Mistake; Love Laughs at the Law; Muchly Married; It Nearly Happened; His Highness; The Janitor; Hubby Puts One Over; The Jitney Driver's Romance; Perfect Match; A Wife for a Ransom; A Raffle for a Husband; A Stage Villain; A Dark Suspicion; Love Quarantined; The Fall of Deacon Stillwater; Bashful Charley's Proposal; The Harem Scarem Deacon; She Was Some Vampire; An All Around Cure; I've Got Your Number; Kate's Lover's Knots; She Wrote a Play and Played It; Soup and Nuts; A Marriage for Revenge; The Deacon Stops the Show; In Onion There Is Strength; Musical Madness; The Inspector's Double; Father Gets It Wrong; A Crooked Mix-Up; A Shadowed Shadow; In Love with a Fireman; Their First Arrest; Jags and Jealousy; A Janitor's Vendetta; Scrappily Married; The Tramp Chef; Their Dark Secret*

1917   *Some Nurse; One Damp Day; Mines and Matrimony; Love in Suspense; Cross-Eyed Submarine: Or, 20,000 Peeks Under the Sea; Who Done It?; Love in Suspense; Barred from the Bar; Love me, Love my Biscuits; His Coming Out Party; Out for the Dough; Mule Mates; Rosie's Rancho; Passing the Grip; Wanta Make a Dollar?; Art Aches; Whose Baby?; A Boob for Luck; The Careless Cop; Take Back Your Wife; Left in the Soup; The Last Scent; Simple Sapho; A Burglar's Wife; The Twitching Hour; Kitchenella; The Soubrette; The Stinger Stung; The Vamp of the Camp; Mrs. Madam, Manager; Busting Into Society; A Gale of Verse; Back to the Kitchen; Short Skirts and Deep Water; Nearly a Queen; Hawaiian Nuts; Circus Sarah; Marble Heads; The Fountain of Trouble; The Masked Marvels; Her Naughty Choice; The Wart on the Wire; Tightwad, I Quit!; The Shame of the Bullcon; Water on the Brain; What the—?; Secret Servants; The Cross Eyed Submarine; The Man with a Package; The Boss of the Family; When Damon Fell for Pythias*

1918   *Cave Man Stuff; A Flyer in Folly; Cooks and Crooks; Nothing But Nerve; Gowns and Girls; Saved from a Vamp; A Rural Riot; It's a Cruel World; Her Movie Madness; Butter Again; The Borrowed Baby; Who's Your Wife?*

1919   *The Detectress; Wild Woman; A Model Husband; How's Your Husband?*

1920   *Her First Flame; What! No Spinach?*

1921   *The Hunch*

1922   *Night Life in Hollywood; Quincy Adams Sawyer*

1923   *Held to Answer; Hollywood; Tea: What a Kick!*

1924   *The Fire Patrol; Open All Night; Merton of the Movies; Along Came Ruth*

1925   *New Lives for Old; Déclassée; Youth's Gamble; Soup to Nuts; His Wooden Wedding; All Tied Up*

1926   *Mighty Like a Moose*

1927   *Two-Time Mama; Love 'Em and Weep; Stranded; What Women Did to Me; A One Mama Man; Bigger and Better Blondes*

1928   *The Wild West Show; All Parts*

1929   *The Love Doctor; The Big Squawk; Darkened Rooms*

1931   *Skip the Maloo!*

1932   *Now We'll Tell One; Mr. Bride*

1933   *Luncheon at Twelve*

Holloway, Carol (1892 Williamstown, MA-1979 Los Angeles, CA)

Carol Holloway's father was a college professor, and she enjoyed a middle-class upbringing. She began her career on the stage in the Carleton Stock Company and appeared on Broadway in the production *Everywoman*.

When she entered films she first worked at Lubin, but she moved among several studios working on a number of serials before signing a contract with Vitagraph in 1917. The remainder of her career was spent appearing in action-adventure films and westerns. In 1926 she wrote the scenario for a western titled *The Shoot 'Em Up Kid*.

She made the transition to sound films, but her career was on the downslide. By the late 1930s she had retired from the screen and disappeared from the public eye.

Film Credits

1914	*A Strange Melody; A Game of Wits; The Violinist; Till the Sands of the Desert Grow Cold*
1915	*A Gentleman of Leisure; Her Mother's Secret; The Secretary of Frivolous Affairs; Aided by the Movies; Kiddees, Kids, and Kiddo; The Drummer's Trunk; Making a Man of Johnny; An Auto-Bungalow Fracas; A Gentleman of Leisure*
1916	*The Waifs; Billy Van Deusen's Egg-Spensive Adventure; Dare-Devils and Danger; The First Quarrel; Billy Van Deusen's Operation; Adjusting His Claim; Johnnie's Birthday*
1917	*Dead Shot Baker; The Tenderfoot; Vengeance and the Woman; The Fighting Trail; The Prodigal*
1918	*The Iron Test*
1919	*Perils of Thunder Mountain*
1920	*The Saphead; Two Moons; The Deceiver; Dangerous Love; "If Only" Jim; A Good Bad Man*
1921	*The Sea Lion; Trailin'*
1922	*Up and Going; Rich Men's Wives*
1923	*Gossip; Cordelia the Magnificent; The Ramblin' Kid; Why Women Remarry; The Love Pirate; One of Three*
1924	*Beau Brummel*
1925	*The Rainbow Trail*
1927	*Jake the Plumber; The Cherokee Kid*
1928	*Chicken a la King*
1932	*The Sign of the Cross*
1935	*The Whole Town's Talking; Stolen Harmony; One Hour Late*

1937   *Maid of Salem; Thunder Trail; Oh; Doctor!; Way Out West*
1938   *The Big Broadcast of 1938; Scandal Street*
1939   *The Lady's from Kentucky; St. Louis Blues*
1940   *The Emergency Squad*
1941   *There's Magic in Music*
1946   *The Crime of Dr. Forbes; F-Man*

Holmes, Helen (1893 Chicago, IL-1950 Burbank, CA)

Courtesy of Silents Are Golden at <SilentsAre Golden.com>.

Helen Holmes, called "queen of the iron horse dramas," worked as a photographer's model while still in high school to help support her family.* When her family moved to Death Valley in the hopes of improving her brother's health, Holmes moved with them. There she lived an "old west" lifestyle and even briefly prospected for gold.

After her brother's death, Holmes moved to New York and found work on the stage. In 1911, her friend Mabel Normand advised her to come west to appear in films. While waiting for her break, Holmes continued to work as a model and was featured as "The Santa Fe Girl" on a railroad poster.

She worked at Keystone for about a year then moved to Kalem where she was cast in lead roles. While at Kalem, Holmes met her future husband, director J. P. McGowan, whom she married in 1914. Together they worked on her most popular serial, *The Hazards of Helen* (1914).

After completing *Hazards,* the couple moved to Universal where they continued to work together on serials and western dramas. During this time she also worked with some of the independent studios in both serials and westerns. However, working with independents often meant fewer theaters showed the films, regardless of their quality.

In 1920 Holmes created the Holmes Producing Corporation with release rights through Warner Bros. However, she never regained her previous hold on the filmgoing audience. In 1925 Holmes and

---

*Various sources list her place of birth as Chicago, Louisville, Kentucky, or South Bend, Indiana. Chicago is cited here because it is the city most often listed in references.

McGowan divorced and the following year Holmes retired from films except for an occasional appearance.

After her retirement she bought a ranch with her second husband but had to sell it after several financially draining years. In the mid-1940s Holmes returned to the film industry with a menagerie of trained dogs and cats that appeared in various films. When her husband died, she opened an antique business that she operated until her death.

Film Credits

1912   *Kings Court*
1913   *Brought to Bay; Barney Oldfield's Race for Life; The Smuggler; The Flying Switch; A Demand for Justice; The Battle at Fort Laramie; The Hermit's Ruse; The Runaway Freight; The Alibi; Hide and Seek; A Fight to a Finish; Birds of Prey*
1914   *The Stolen Rembrandt; A Man's Soul; The Conductor's Courtship; A String of Pearls; The Identification; The Operator at Black Rock; The Car of Death; Near Death's Door; Grouch, the Engineer; The Demon of the Rails; The Hazards of Helen; His Nemesis; The Rajah's Jewels; The Refrigerator Car's Captive; The Pay Train; Under Desperation's Spur; Fast Freight 3205; A Flaw in the Alibi*
1915   *The Mettle of Jerry McGuire; A Desperate Leap; When Rogues Fall Out; The Girl and the Game; A Fight to the Finish*
1916   *Whispering Smith; Medicine Bend; Judith of the Cumberlands; The Manager of the B&A; The Lass of the Lumberlands; The Diamond Runners*
1917   *The Railroad Raiders; The Lost Express* (I)
1919   *The Fatal Fortune*
1920   *The Tiger Band*
1921   *Ghost City; A Crook's Romance*
1922   *Hills of Missing Men; The Lone Hand*
1923   *One Million in Jewels; Stormy Seas*
1924   *40-Horse Hawkins; Fighting Fury; The Riddle Rider; Battling Brewster*
1925   *Outwitted; Barriers of the Law; Duped; Blood and Steel; Webs of Steel; The Train Wreckers; Sign of the Cactus*

1926   *Whispering Smith; Mistaken Orders; The Open Switch; The Lost Express* (II); *Crossed Signals; Perils of the Rail; The Fast Freight*
1936   *Poppy*
1937   *Way Out West; The Californian*
1941   *Dude Cowboy*
1943   *The More the Merrier*

Hope, Gloria (1899 Pittsburgh, PA-1976 Pasadena, CA)

Just like one of the characters she portrayed on film, Gloria Hope met a dashing hero, married him, and lived happily ever after as one of Hollywood's golden couples of the silent era.

Prior to entering college to become a teacher, Hope visited an aunt in Hollywood and toured Ince Studios. At the time, the studio needed a young woman to fill a role in a film they were shooting, so they hired her on the spot. Her debut film was *Free and Equal* in 1917, but the film was not released until 1925. Her first film released to theaters was the drama *Time Locks and Diamonds* (1917), and her favorable reception by audiences led to additional roles.

Hope continued to be one of the busiest young actors of the period, appearing in films with most of the studios in Hollywood, but it was her marriage to fellow actor Lloyd Hughes in 1921 that made her the darling of the fan magazines. Amazingly, for all the attention and scrutiny the couple received, the marriage was successful. Hope curtailed her film appearances until, in 1926, she retired to raise her family. The marriage lasted until Hughes's death in 1958.

Film Credits

1917   *Time Locks and Diamonds*
1918   *$5000 Reward; The Great Love; The Law of the North; The Heart of Rachael; The Guilty Man; Naughty, Naughty!*
1919   *The Hushed Hour; Bill Apperson's Boy; The Outcasts of Poker Flat; Burglar by Proxy; Rider of the Law; The Gay Lord Quex*
1920   *The Desperate Hero; Seeds of Vengeance; Prairie Trails; Too Much Johnson; The Third Woman; The Texan*
1921   *Colorado; The Grim Comedian; Courage*
1922   *Tess of the Storm Country; Trouble*
1924   *The Devil Quemado; Free and Equal*
1925   *Sandy*

Hopper, Hedda (1885 Hollidaysburg, PA-1966 Hollywood, CA)

Although mostly remembered as a Hollywood gossip columnist, Hedda Hopper began her career in show business as an actor. Raised in a strict Quaker household, she left her family quite early to pursue a career on Broadway. She is never praised for her acting ability, but she did get a part on Broadway, where she met and married a popular actor of the period, DeWolf Hopper, who was thirty-two years her senior. The marriage did not last, but through it she was brought to Hollywood and began appearing in films in 1916.

Films did not remain her focus for long. By 1936 her nose for gossip and scandal earned her a stint on the radio reporting the goings-on of the Hollywood set. By 1938 she had her own syndicated column and she was challenging Louella Parsons for the title of Queen of the Gossipmongers.

She created her own larger-than-life persona and established her trademark—outlandish hats. Her favorite thing in the world was a real—or fabricated—feud. She had a long-running one with Parsons and Ed Sullivan, as well as other personalities that she delighted in putting in a bad light.

As her fame and reputation grew, she appeared in films as herself—a representative of Hollywood glamour. She wrote an autobiography titled, *The Whole Truth and Nothing But* (1963) and followed that up with *From Under My Hat* (1964). She retired in 1965, and even her enemies admitted that there would never be another to match her. She had been, as one article put it, "alone on the throne."

Film Credits

1916   *The Battle of Hearts*
1917   *Her Excellency the Governor; Nearly Married; Seven Keys to Baldpate*
1918   *The Beloved Traitor; Virtuous Wives; By Right of Purchase*

1919   *The Third Degree; Sadie Love; The Isle of Conquest*

1920   *The Man Who Lost Himself; The New York Idea*

1921   *Heedless Moths; The Inner Chamber; Conceit*

1922   *Women Men Marry; Sherlock Holmes; What's Wrong with the Women?*

1923   *Reno; Has the World Gone Mad!*

1924   *Gambling Wives; Why Men Leave Home; Happiness; Miami; Sinners in Silk; The Snob; Another Scandal*

1925   *Her Market Value; Declassee; Dangerous Innocence; Zander the Great; Raffles; The Teaser; Borrowed Finery*

1926   *The Caveman; Skinner's Dress Suit; Lew Tyler's Wives; Don Juan; Fools of Fashion; Obey the Law; The Silver Treasure; Pleasures of the Rich; Dance Madness*

1927   *Orchids and Ermine; Venus of Venice; Matinee Ladies; Children of Divorce; Black Tears; The Cruel Truth; Wings; Adam and Evil; One Woman to Another; The Drop Kick; A Reno Divorce; French Dressing*

1928   *Love and Learn; The Whip Woman; The Chorus Kid; Harold Teen; Green Grass Widows; Runaway Girls; Undressed; The Port of Missing Girls; Companionate Marriage*

1929   *Girls Gone Wild; The Last Mrs. Cheyney; Cat, Dog and Company; His Glorious Night; Half Marriage; A Song of Kentucky; The Racketeer*

1930   *Such Men Are Dangerous; Murder Will Out; Our Blushing Brides; Holiday; Let Us Be Gay; War Nurse; High Society Blues*

1931   *The Easiest Way; Men Call It Love; The Slippery Pearls; The Common Law; Mystery Train; West of Broadway; A Tailor Made Man; Shipmates; Rebound; The Prodigal; Good Sport; Flying High*

1932   *The Man Who Played God; Night World; As You Desire Me; Skyscraper Souls; Downstairs; Speak Easily; The Unwritten Law*

1933   *Men Must Fight; The Barbarian; Pilgrimage; Beauty for Sale*

1934   *Bombay Mail; Let's Be Ritzy; No Ransom; Little Man, What Now?*

1935   *One Frightened Night; Alice Adams; Three Kids and a Queen; I Live My Life; Ship Café; Lady Tubbs; Society Fever*

1936   *The Dark Hour; Dracula's Daughter; Bunker Bean; Dough-nuts and Society*
1937   *Vogues of 1938; Artists and Models; Nothing Sacred; You Can't Buy Luck; Topper; Dangerous Holiday*
1938   *Tarzan's Revenge; Maid's Night Out; Thanks for the Memory; Dangerous to Know*
1939   *Midnight; Laugh It Off; The Women; What a Life; That's Right—You're Wrong*
1940   *Cross Country Romance; Queen of the Mob*
1941   *I Wanted Wings; Life With Henry; Hedda Hopper's Hollywood (No. 1 and 2)*
1942   *Hedda Hopper's Hollywood (No. 3-6); Reap the Wild Wind*
1946   *Unusual Occupations* (as herself); *Breakfast in Hollywood* (as herself)
1950   *Sunset Boulevard* (as herself)
1960   *Pepe*
1964   *The Patsy* (as herself)
1966   *The Oscar* (as herself)

Horton, Clara (1904 Brooklyn, NY-1976 Encino, CA)

Clara Horton was *the* youthful leading lady of her time. She began posing for artists and illustrators when she was still a toddler and was appearing in films by the time she was eight years old. After signing with the Éclair Company, she was known as "the Éclair Kid" and was one of the most popular child stars to appear in films.

As she grew older, she moved into youthful lead roles for a variety of studios in her early teens. She appeared opposite Jack Pickford in several films before being teamed with Cullen Landis in a series of films. She limited her film appearances between 1922 and 1924 but returned to films in an adult flapper role in 1925. However, flapper roles had a limited life and she appeared in films sporadically after 1927.

Her second marriage was lasting and she retired to the "ordinary" life that she had said she craved in interviews in the early 1920s.

Film Credits

1912	*Because of Bobbie; Dolls; The Passing Parade; Making Uncle Jealous; The Darling of the Mounted; Filial Love; The Homecoming*
1913	*The Return of Lady Linda; The Spectre Bridegroom; The Little Mother of Black Pine Trail; The Crimson Cross; For Better or Worse; The Sons of a Soldier; The Faith Healer; The Trail of the Hanging Rock; Why Aunt Jane Never Married; The Banker's Daughter; Big Hearted Jim; Clara and Her Mysterious Toys; The Detective Santa Claus; For His Child's Sake; The Key; A Puritan Episode; A Son's Devotion; A Wise Judge*
1914	*At the Court of Prince Make Believe; Auntie's Money Bag; Coming Home; The Dupe; Grandfather's Romance; The Greatest of These; In an Old Trunk; In the Days of Old; Just Kids; The Violinist; Willie and the Muse; A Friend in Need*
1915	*The Vengeance of Guido; The Long Shift; Shadows of the Harbor; A Soul's Tragedy; The Answer; The Little Band of Gold*
1916	*Under the Lion's Paw; Us Kids; A Jungle Hero*
1917	*Tom Sawyer; The Plow Woman*
1918	*Huck and Tom; The Whirlwind Finish; The Yellow Dog*
1919	*The Winning Girl; In Wrong; Almost a Husband; The Girl from Outside; Everywoman*
1920	*The Little Shepherd of Kingdom Come; Blind Youth; It's a Great Life; The Heart of a Woman; Nineteen and Phyllis*
1921	*Prisoners of Love; The Servant in the House; Action; The Light in the Clearing*
1922	*Penrod*
1923	*Mind Over Motor*
1924	*Wrongs Righted*
1925	*Makers of Men; The Wheel; Speed Madness; All Around the Frying Pan*
1926	*Winning the Futurity; The Broadway Gallent; Beyond the Trail*
1927	*The Fortune Hunter; The Fightin' Come Back, Sailor Izzy Murphy*

1936   *Bengal Tiger*
1938   *Girls on Probation*
1942   *Just Off Broadway; Who Is Hope Schyler?*
1943   *Time to Kill*

Hotely, Mae (1872 Maryland-1954 Coronado, CA)

Mae Hotely derived her stage name from her married name, Hotaling. Like many of the early female comedians, she has been overlooked by historians in favor of her male counterparts. However, when she was appearing in comedies during the silent era, her antics caused as much laughter as any of the male comedians.

The facts of her early life are not known, but it is believed that she started her show business career in vaudeville before the advent of motion pictures. She got her start in films when her husband was hired as cinematographer for the Lubin Company's Jacksonville, Florida, site.

Hotely appeared in roles ranging from blushing ingenue to crotchety old lady, but she was at her best in comedies where her talent for the ridiculous was allowed to blossom. Her portrayals were so popular with audiences that she was voted one of the most popular actors of 1915, but between 1917 and 1928 there is no record of her appearing in a film.

Finally, after appearing in a film in 1929, her brand of physical comedy had lost favor with audiences and Hotely retired. After her divorce from writer/cinematographer Arthur Hotaling, she virtually disappeared.

Film Credits

1911   *A Wise Detective; A Stage Door Flirtation; Some Mother-in-Law; A Question of Modesty; A Gay Time in Washington; A Gay Time in New York City; A Gay Time in Atlantic City; The Human Torpedo; A Nearsighted Chaperone; A Hot Time in Atlantic City*

1912　*Nora the Cook; The New Constable; His Father's Choice; A Gay Time in Quebec; A Gay Time in Jacksonville, Florida; All in the Wash; His Vacation; Man Wanted; Meeting Mamie's Mother; Down with the Men*

1913　*The Actress and Her Jewels; The Widow's Wiles; Training a Tightwad; Stage-Struck Sally; She Must Elope; She Must Be Ugly; The Missing Jewels; Minnie the Widow; A Master Mix-Up; Lucky Cohen; Kate the Cop; An Interrupted Courtship; Her Wooden Leg; His Widow; His First Experience; Giving Bill a Rest; Fixing Auntie Up; The Female Detective; The Fake Soldiers; The Engaging Kid; Building a Trust; Fooling Their Wives; A Ten Acre Gold Brick*

1914　*Casey's Birthday; The Substitute; Building a Fire; The Female Cop; Long May It Wave; What He Forgot; Who's Boss?*

1915　*The Twin Sister; A Lucky Strike; Matilda's Legacy; Her Choice; A Ready-Made Maid; Out for a Stroll; His Wife's New Lid; A Day on the Force; The Clubman; Baby; An Awful Artist; What He Forgot*

1916　*Nora the Cook*

1929　*Girls Who Dare*

Howell, Alice (1888 New York City-1961 Los Angeles, CA)

Alice Howell started her career in vaudeville and touring companies traveling throughout the East before moving to Los Angeles to work with her vaudeville buddy Mack Sennett. In her many films she portrayed the "ugly funny woman"—one with outlandish makeup, fuzzy hair, and no feminine attributes.

Her first major film was the classic *Tillie's Punctured Romance* (1914), and she worked with such talents as Mabel Normand, Charlie Chaplin, and Fatty Arbuckle while at Keystone. Tiring of the same types of roles, Howell moved to Lehrman Knock-Out (L-KO) in 1915, where she played leading roles in Keystone-type comedies.

Howell remained with L-KO until 1917 when she moved to Century Comedies. Although she received star billing, she left two years later when the studio's focus turned to animal acts rather than human comics. Her move took her to a little-known production company in Chicago called Emerald Motion Picture Company.

Soon after she signed with Emerald in 1919 it merged with Bulls Eye to form Reelcraft, a merger that was hoped would improve both studios' profitability. In 1920, however, Howell moved back to Hollywood with her own production company, which targeted the neighborhood theaters where her brand of comedy burlesque was still popular.

Luckily, Howell left Reelcraft for Universal before it went bankrupt. At Universal Howell joined Neely Edwards and Bert Roach to form a successful comedy trio. Their films were among the most successful for Universal during the early 1920s.

Although a talented comedian, she continued to work in film only through the mid-1920s. During her career Howell had invested her money in real estate and she retired from films to manage her property. Her talent was verified by no less than Stan Laurel years after her retirement when he ranked her as one of the top ten female comedians of all time.

Film Credits

1914   *Knockout; Mabel's Married Life; Laughing Gas; Cursed by His Beauty; Tillie's Punctured Romance; His Musical Career; Caught in the Rain; Caught in the Cabaret*
1915   *Under New Management; Tears and Sunshine; Cupid and the Scrub Lady; From Beanery to Billions; Her Ups and Downs; In the Claw of the Law; Life and Moving Pictures; Lizzie's Shattered Dreams; Room and Board: A Dollar and a Half; Rough but Romantic; Their Last Haul; Silk Hose and High Pressure; Sin on the Sabbath*
1916   *A Busted Honeymoon; Alice In Society; Dad's Dollars and Dirty Doings; The Doubles Troubles; The Great Smash; Her Naughty Eyes; How Stars Are Made; Lizzie's Lingering Love; Pirates of the Air; Tattle-Tale Alice; Unhand Me, Villain!*
1917   *Balloonatics; Hey; Doctor!; Automaniacs*
1918   *Bawled Out; The Cabbage Queen; Her Unmarried Life; Hoot Toot; In Dutch; Untamed Ladies*
1919   *The Beauty and the Boob; Society Stuff*
1920   *Distilled Love; Cinderella Cinders*
1922   *Love Is an Awful Thing*
1923   *Wandering Daughters*

1924   *One Wet Night; Fair and Windy; The Game Hunter; Green Tees; Marry When Young; Patching Things Up; Spring of 1964; That's the Spirit; Way Up North; Why Be Jealous?; Why Pay Your Rent?; Women's Rights*

1925   *Under a Spell; Papa's Pet; Sleeping Sickness; Tenting Out*

I

Intolerance *(1916)*

One of D. W. Griffith's classic productions, *Intolerance* examined the effects of prejudice and intolerance during four periods of history. The Babylon sequence centered on a mountain girl caught in the religious events that destroyed the city. In Judea, the sequence followed the Pharisees that condemned Christ. The Paris sequence concerned two Huguenots preparing for their marriage prior to the Saint Bartholomew's Day massacre of 1572. The final sequence was set in modern America where zealot reformers ruin the lives of a young couple in a retelling of a prominent legal case.

The film was lavish and the structure was innovative. Each segment was independent but linked together by editing and the general theme. At a cost of $2 million, it was one of the most expensive films of the silent era—and one of the longest at thirteen reels. Generally cited as being uneven because not all segments were developed equally, the film did advance the use of film techniques such as tracking and close-ups.

Sadly, for all the film's technical innovation it did not do well commercially. For years Griffith worked to repay the money lost by this film and as a result lost his creative freedom, as he was forced to work on any film to make money.

Ivers, Julia Crawford *(1867 Los Angeles, CA-1930 Los Angeles, CA)*

Unfortunately, like so many of the women from the silent era, nothing is known about Julia Crawford Ivers's early life other than she was born in Los Angeles in 1867. In a contemporary magazine interview, of which there are few, Ivers stated that she had been working in films for nine years as of the publication date in 1922. That would mean that she entered the film industry around 1913, and that, in turn, would mean she had been working in the industry for approximately two years before she was named general manager of Bosworth Studios in 1915.

While at Bosworth she was in complete charge of all aspects of the studio—from running the business and managing finances to writing and directing films. Although Bosworth was originally created to produce film versions of successful Broadway plays, it was soon producing everything from westerns to costume melodramas. All productions were copyrighted as "produced under the direction of Julia Crawford Ivers."

Ivers worked for several years (1916-1922) in collaboration with William Desmond Taylor, making approximately twenty films together before his murder. After his death she wrote an article in which she criticized those who repeated gossip or otherwise blackened his name. Although Ivers had been a prolific writer for many years, after Taylor's death she was credited with working on only three more films.

Reportedly a woman who did not like publicity for herself, in an interview she downplayed her job as a writer as "only a helper" and cautioned other writers to not try to control a production. This subservient attitude is interesting considering that she had been in control of a studio as well having been both a producer and a director. In addition to her film work, Ivers was a regular contributor to various popular magazines of the period.

Writing Credits

1915	*The Rug Maker's Daughter; The Majesty of the Law; Fatherhood; The Gentleman from Indiana; The Reform Candidate; Nearly a Lady*
1916	*The Call of the Cumberlands; He Fell in Love with His Wife; Ben Blair; The Heart of Paula; David Garrick; The American Beauty; The Stronger Love; The Parson of Panamint; The Intrigue; A Son of Erin; The Right Direction*
1917	*Her Own People; The World Apart; The Cook of Canyon Camp; Tom Sawyer*
1918	*The Spirit of '17; Huck and Tom; His Majesty Bunker Bean; Viviette; Good Night, Paul; The Gypsy Trail; Up the Road with Sallie; A Lady's Name; Sauce for the Goose*

1919   *The Final Close-Up; The Veiled Adventure; Widow by Proxy; More Deadly Than the Male; Who Cares?*
1920   *Huckleberry Finn; Easy to Get; Nurse Marjorie; Jenny Be Good; The Soul of Youth; The Furnace*
1921   *The Witching Hour; Sacred and Profane Love; Wealth; Beyond; Morals*
1922   *The Green Temptation*
1923   *The White Flower*
1924   *Married Flirts*
1927   *In a Moment of Temptation*

Directing Credits

1915   *The Majesty of the Law*
1916   *The Heart of Paula; A Son of Erin*
1923   *The White Flower*

Producing Credits

1917   *Lost in Transit; A Kiss for Susie; The Trouble Buster; The Bond Between; The Wax Model*

J

Jean (approximately 1907-1916)

Jean, arguably the first animal star in films, began her career in 1909 and became known as the "Vitagraph dog." A collie, she was very intelligent and could even untie knots, thereby saving her hapless human co-stars. Her owner-trainer, Laurence Trimble, later handled another silent-film dog star, Strongheart.

Film Credits

1910   *Jean and the Calico Doll; Jean Goes Fishing; Where the Wind Blows; A Tin-Type Romance; Jean the Matchmaker; Jean Goes Foraging; Jean and the Waif*
1911   *Jean Rescues*
1912   *Jean Intervenes; The Stumbling Block*

Johnson, Edith (1894 Rochester, NY-1969 Los Angeles, CA)

Edith Johnson, called "the most photographed girl in the world," began her career as a model; while in college she was appointed the "Kodak Girl," resulting in her picture appearing in all of Kodak's print advertisements. Upon graduating from Vassar she accepted a film contract with Selig, where she worked until 1916 when she moved to Universal.

She began making serials, and for the next few years she alternated her films between Universal and Vitagraph with her husband, William Duncan, directing and costarring. Having invested her money wisely, she retired from films in 1924 and embarked on a vaudeville tour with her husband before settling down to raise their three children.

Film Credits

1913   *Dixieland*
1914   *Nan's Victory; Out of Petticoat Lane; The Lure of the Windigo; The Dream Girl; The Flower of Faith*
1915   *Heart's Desire; The Van Thornton Diamonds; The Mystery of Dead Man's Isle; At the Flood Tide; The Circular Staircase; Sweet Alyssum*
1916   *The Cycle of Fate; The Valiants of Virginia; Behind the Lines; For Love and Gold; Guilty; The Five Franc Piece; The Gold Ship; The Black Orchid; Badgered; Giant Powder; The Lost Lode*
1917   *The Scarlet Crystal; A Brother's Sacrifice; The Scarlet Car; Steel Hearts; Hands in the Dark; The Right Man*
1918   *The Fighting Grin; The Shuttle; A Fight for Millions*
1919   *Man of Might; Smashing Barriers* (I); *A Fight for Love*
1920   *The Silent Avenger*
1921   *Fighting Fate; No Defense; Steelheart; Where Men Are Men*

1922   *The Silent Vow; When Danger Smiles; The Fighting Guide*
1923   *Playing It Wild; The Steel Trial; Smashing Barriers* (II)
1924   *The Fast Express; Wolves of the North*

Johnston, Julanne (1900 Indianapolis, IN-1988 Grosse Pointe, MI)

Julanne Johnston began her career as a dancer on the vaudeville circuit as well as with the famous Ruth St. Denis dance troupe. She entered films as a dancer, debuting in *Joan the Woman* (1916) directed by Cecil B. DeMille.

She moved to Fox to appear in short comedies, but most of those film titles have been lost. Her breakthrough role was as the princess in *The Thief of Bagdad* (1924) opposite Douglas Fairbanks. That year she was also selected as a WAMPAS Baby Star.

As was often the case, she did not live up to her hype as a Baby Star and never achieved true stardom. She traveled to Europe to make several films, but by the end of the 1920s her career had waned. Her good friend Colleen Moore featured Johnston in some of her films, and she appeared in some sound films but in very small roles.

Johnston married a wealthy automobile executive and retired from films in 1934. She became a socialite wife and mother of three.

Film Credits

1916   *Joan the Woman*
1919   *Better Times*
1920   *Miss Hobbs; Fickle Women; Seeing It Through*
1923   *The Brass Bottle; Madness of Youth; Tea: What A Kick!*
1924   *The Thief of Bagdad; The Prude's Fall*
1925   *Big Pal; The City of Temptation; The Big Parade*
1926   *Dame Chance; Twinkletoes; Pleasures of the Rich; Aloma of the South Seas*
1927   *Venus of Venice; Good Time Charley; Her Wild Oat*
1928   *The Whip Woman; Name the Woman; The Olympic Hero; Oh Kay!*
1929   *Synthetic Sin; The Younger Generation; Prisoners; Smiling Irish Eyes; The Show of Shows*
1930   *General Crack; Strictly Modern; Golden Dawn; Madame Satan*

1932   *Stepping Sisters*
1933   *Midnight Club; Morning Glory*
1934   *Bolero; The Scarlet Empress; Cleopatra*

Johnstone, Justine (1895 Englewood, NJ-1982 Santa Monica, CA)

Justine Johnstone, once known as "the most beautiful blonde on Broadway," was also a highly intelligent woman. She began her career as a model after winning a beauty contest sponsored by the First International Exposition of Photographic Arts.

Her frequent appearances in print material brought her to the attention of film producers and she was offered a contract with Famous Players. Her film debut was as the self-centered Amelia in *The Crucible* (1914). Soon after that film was released she had her stage debut and appeared in Ziegfeld's *Follies* of 1915. By the end of 1917, she was considered one of Broadway's brightest musical-comedy stars.

However, she realized that she would never be taken seriously as an actor if she continued to appear in musical comedies, so she joined a stock company to gain dramatic acting experience. After her marriage in 1919 to stage producer Walter Wanger, Johnstone signed a film contract with the Realart company.

She soon tired of the roles she was offered—that of wide-eyed ingenues and helpless maidens—and left the film industry. She went to London with her husband and appeared in the long-running play *Polly Preferred*. She appeared in only one more film before retiring from show business completely.

When she became restless as a mother and social leader, Johnstone entered medical school and went into pathological research of sexually transmitted diseases. After her divorce she dedicated herself to medical research, developing the modern intravenous drip device used by the medical profession, as well as developing resuscitation techniques for electric shock victims and the use of cryogenic therapy to combat cancer cells.

Film Credits

1914   *The Crucible*
1920   *Blackbirds; Nothing but Lies*
1921   *Sheltered Daughters; The Plaything of Broadway; Moonlight and Honeysuckle; A Heart to Let*
1925   *Never the Twain Shall Meet*

Joy, Leatrice (1893 New Orleans, LA-Riverdale, NY)

Courtesy of Silents Are Golden at
<SilentsAreGolden.com>

Leatrice Joy, often cited as the innovator of the bobbed-hair craze of the 1920s, started her show business career by touring with the Virginia Brissac Stock Company, appearing in the obligatory ingenue roles, after graduating from Sacred Heart Academy. She moved to films and worked with several small, short-lived studios and in local stock companies before moving to Hollywood in 1917.

By 1921 she had a contract with Goldwyn Studios and was chosen as a protégé of Cecil B. DeMille. She appeared in several of his lavishly produced films, including *Manslaughter* (1922) and *The Ten Commandments* (1923). Under his tutelage she went from comedian to sophisticated leading lady. In fact, she was before her time with her portrayals of independent women who held their own in business and in love.

Once she left DeMille in 1928 her career lost much of its luster, but she continued to appear sporadically in films and on the stage into the 1950s. When she retired from show business, she became active in community affairs and charity work.

Although she was married three times, she maintained that the love of her life was the ill-fated John Gilbert with whom she had her only child, a daughter. As late as 1983 a large portrait of Gilbert dominated her living room.

Film Credits

1915   *His Turning Point*
1916   *The Folly of Revenge; The Other Man*

1917   *The Pride of the Clan; A Girl's Folly; Wits and Fits; The Wishbone; The Window Dresser's Room; Susie's Scheme; Susie the Sleepwalker; Susie of the Follies; Speed; The Slave; The Rejuvenator; The Magic Vest; Her Iron Will; Her Fractured Voice; Getting the Evidence; Auto Intoxication; The Candy Kid*

1918   *One Dollar Bid; Wedlock; Her Man; Three X Gordon; His Day Out; The City of Tears; The Stranger; The Orderly; The Scholar; The Messenger; The Handy Man*

1919   *The Man Hunter; The Water Lily; Shackled*

1920   *The Right of Way; Smiling All the Way; Just a Wife; The Invisible Divorce; Down Home; Blind Youth*

1921   *A Tale of Two Worlds; The Ace of Hearts; Voices of the City; The Poverty of Riches; Ladies Must Live; Bunty Pulls the Strings*

1922   *Saturday Night; The Bachelor Daddy; Manslaughter; Minnie; The Man Who Saw Tomorrow*

1923   *You Can't Fool Your Wife; The Silent Partner; The Ten Commandments; Java Head; Hollywood*

1924   *The Marriage Cheat; Triumph; Changing Husbands*

1925   *The Dressmaker from Paris; Hell's Highroad; The Wedding Song*

1926   *Eve's Leaves; For Alimony Only; Made for Love; The Clinging Vine*

1927   *Nobody's Widow; Vanity; The Angel of Broadway*

1928   *The Blue Danube; Man-Made Woman; Tropic Madness; Show People*

1929   *Bellamy Trial; Strong Boy; A Most Immoral Lady*

1930   *The Love Trader*

1939   *First Love*

1940   *The Old Swimmin' Hole*

1949   *Red Stallion in the Rockies; Air Hostess*

1951   *Love Nest*

Joyce, Alice (1890 Kansas City, MO-1955 Hollywood, CA)

Nicknamed "the Madonna of the Screen," Alice Joyce first entered the working world at thirteen when she got a job as a telephone operator to help support her mother after her parents' divorce. She also worked as a model for artists and photographers and, as one of the top models in New York, she soon applied for work in the movies.

She signed with Kalem Film Company in 1910 and became one of their most popular and prolific young actors, known for her aristocratic grace and refinement. She was soon known as "The Kalem Girl" during the period when studios would not release their actors' names.

She placed among the top five most popular stars in a poll conducted by *Motion Picture Story Magazine* in 1913 and was earning $3,000 per week after Vitagraph bought Kalem Studios. Her classic features were not suitable for comic or western roles, so she played ingenue parts in social dramas well into her twenties. She turned to more mature roles in the mid-1920s, including the role of Clara Bow's mother in *Dancing Mothers* (1926).

With each of her three marriages, she briefly retired from the screen only to return a few years later. Her final retirement came in the 1930s, after which she concentrated on working with women's charitable groups.

Film Credits

1910   *The Deacon's Daughter; The Heart of Edna Leslie; The Engineer's Sweetheart; The Education of Elizabeth; The Roses of the Virgin; The Rescue of Molly Finney; The Engineer's Sweetheart*

1911   *The Trail of the Pomos Charm; The Engineer's Daughter; The Wasp; The Temptation of Rodney Vane; Slim Jim's Last*

Chance; Slabsides; The Peril of the Plains; Peggy the Moonshiner's Daughter; Over the Garden Wall; The Loyalty of Don Luis Verdugo; The Love of Summer Morn; The Lost Ribbon; The Carrier Pigeon; The Branded Shoulder; The Alpine Lease; The Mission Carrier; Tangled Lives; A Cattle Herder's Romance; Reckless Reddy Reforms; The Badge of Courage; The Indian Maid's Sacrifice; Don Ramon's Daughter; When Two Hearts Are Won; The Blackfoot Halfbreed; The Mistress of Hacienda del Cerro; A Prisoner of Mexico; For Her Brother's Sake; When California Was Won; How Betty Captured the Outlaw; The Long Arm of the Law; Too Much; Realism; The Higher; Between Father and Son; The Badge of Courage

1912   *The Alcalde's Conspiracy; The Young Millionaire; The Suffragette Sheriff; The Street Singer; The Strange Story of Elsie Mason; The Stolen Invention; The Spanish Revolt of 1836; Saved from Court Martial; Saved by Telephone; The Russian Peasant; Rube Marquard Marries; A Race with Time; A Princess of the Hills; The Outlaw; The Organ Grinder; The Mystery of Grandfather's Clock; The Mexican Revolutionist; Freed from Suspicion; Fantasca the Gypsy; A Daughter's Sacrifice; The County Fair; A Business Buccaneer; The Bell of Penance; The Battle of Wits; An American Invasion; The Adventures of American Joe; Mrs. Simms Serves on the Jury; An Interrupted Wedding; The Defeat of the Brewery Gang; Jean of the Jail; The Secret of the Miser's Cave; The Gun Smuggler; The Bag of Gold; The Colonel's Escape; The Family Tyrant; The Soldier Brothers of Susanne; The Wondering Musician; The Finger of Suspicion*

1913   *When Fate Decrees; A Victim of Deceit; An Unseen Terror; A Thief in the Night; The Streak of Yellow; The Sneak; The Senator's Dishonor; The Riddle of the Tin Soldier; The Power of Blacklegs; The Pawnbroker's Daughter; Our New Minister; The Octoroon; The Nurse at Mulberry Bend; A Midnight Message; In the Grip of a Charlatan; The Hunchback; The Heart of an Actress; For Her Sister's Sake; The Flag of Freedom; The Exposure of the Land Swindlers; The Cub Reporter's Temptation; The Cloak of Guilt; The Christian; A Bolt from the Sky; The Attorney for the Defense; The*

Artist's Sacrifice; The American Princess; The Adventure of an Heiress; The $20,000 Carat; Perils of the Sea

1914   *Nina of the Theatre; The School for Scandal; The Weakling; The Viper; The Vampire's Trail; The Theft of the Crown Jewels; The Show Girl's Glove; The Shadow; The Riddle of the Green Umbrella; The Price of Silence; The Old Army Coat; Mystery of the Sleeping Death; The Mayor's Secretary; The Lynbrook Tragedy; In Wolf's Clothing; The Hand Print Mystery; The Green Rose; The Girl and the Stowaway; Fate's Midnight Hour; The Dance of Death; A Celebrated Case; The Cabaret Dancer; The Brand; The Beast*

1915   *The White Goddess; Unfaithful to His Trust; The Swindler; The Leech; Her Supreme Sacrifice; The Girl of the Music Hall; The Face of the Madonna; Cast Up by the Sea*

1916   *Whom the Gods Destroy*

1917   *The Courage of Silence; Womanhood, the Glory of the Nation; Within the Law; Her Secret; The Question; Richard the Brazen; An Alabaster Box; The Fettered Woman*

1918   *The Song of the Soul; The Business of Life; The Triumph of the Weak; Find the Woman; To the Highest Bidder; Everybody's Girl; The Woman Between Friends*

1919   *The Captain's Captain; The Lion and the Mouse; The Cambric Mask; The Third Degree; The Spark Divine; The Vengeance of Durand; The Winchester Woman*

1920   *Slaves of Pride; The Sporting Duchess; Dollars and the Woman; The Vice of Fools; The Prey*

1921   *The Inner Chamber; The Scarab Ring; Her Lord and Master; Cousin Kate*

1923   *The Green Goddess* (I)

1924   *White Man; The Passionate Adventure*

1925   *Daddy's Gone A-Hunting; Headlines; Stella Dallas; The Home Maker; The Little French Girl*

1926   *Mannequin; Dancing Mothers; Beau Geste; The Ace of Cads; So's Your Old Man*

1927   *Sorrell and Son*

1928   *The Noose; The Rising Generation; 13 Washington Square*

1929   *The Squall*

1930   *The Green Goddess* (II); *He Knew Women; Song o' My Heart*

K

Keener, Hazel (1904 Fairbury, IL-1979 Pacific Grove, CA)

Hazel Keener, who was crowned "Iowa's Most Beautiful Girl" in 1921, started her career in traveling stock companies that toured throughout the Midwest. After winning her title, she began a modeling career posing for magazine illustrators. Two years later she won the title "Miss Hollywood" in Atlantic City, New Jersey, and was dubbed "The Most Photographed Girl in the World." She soon moved to Hollywood and began appearing in local theater productions.

She made the rounds of the film studios and began appearing in comedies and westerns, often opposite Fred Thomson. During the early years of her film career she often appeared under the name "Barbara Worth," but by the mid-1930s she received billing only under her real name.

She was named a WAMPAS Baby Star in 1924. Her most popular silent film was *The Freshman* (1925) opposite Harold Lloyd. Although she never attained the stardom predicted for her, she did remain in films through the early 1950s, but often in uncredited or walk-on parts.

After her retirement from films she reportedly became a minister in the Church of Religious Science.

Film Credits

1922   *The Married Flapper*
1923   *The Brass Bottle; Tea: What a Kick!*
1924   *The Mask of Lopez; North of Nevada; Galloping Gallagher; His Forgotten Wife; The Silent Stranger; The Dangerous Coward; The Fighting Sap; Empty Hands; Hard Hittin' Hamilton*
1925   *Ports of Call; Ten Days; Parisian Love; The Freshman*
1926   *Vanishing Hoofs*
1927   *The First Night; One Hour of Love; Whispering Sage; The Gingham Girl*
1937   *Wells Fargo*
1938   *Gateway*
1940   *I Love You Again; That Gang of Mine; Untamed*

1941   *Murder by Invitation*
1943   *So Proudly We Hail!*
1944   *The Story of Dr. Wassell; And Now Tomorrow*
1946   *Undercurrent*
1947   *A Double Life*
1948   *Joan of Arc*
1950   *The Great Jewel Robber; The Milkman; Caged*
1951   *The Racket; The Blue Veil*

Keller, Helen (1880 Tuscumbia, AL-1968 Westport, CT)

Most people are aware of the story of Helen Keller's triumph over blindness and deafness to lead a full and vibrant life, but few realize that she was also briefly involved in the film industry. In 1918 she came to Hollywood to make a silent film, *Deliverance,* based on her life and success over her seemingly insurmountable disabilities. Although the critics praised the film, it was not financially successful so Keller left Hollywood.

Keller then joined the vaudeville circuit and for two years was one of the most successful acts to tour. Annie Sullivan, her teacher and companion, would give an introductory speech, then Keller would give a short talk (translated by Sullivan) and answer questions from the audience.

In 1952 Keller helped to adapt her previously published work *The Story of My Life* (1904) as a Broadway play. Later it became a successful film and, still later, a television movie. In 1955 she accepted the Academy Award for Best Feature-Length Documentary for *Helen Keller in Her Story.* Keller maintained a busy schedule of personal appearances and continued to represent the American Foundation for the Blind until she suffered her first stroke in 1961. In 1964 she was honored with the Presidential Medal of Freedom.

Film Credits

1919   *Deliverance*
1954   *Helen Keller in Her Story*

Writing Credits

1952   *The Miracle Worker*

Kellerman, Annette (1887 Sydney, Australia-1975 Southport, Australia)

Annette Kellerman, called "the most beautifully formed woman in modern times," was the first swimmer to turn movie star, and she remained a controversial free spirit in the process.

Kellerman was born in Australia and began swimming to help regain her strength after a childhood illness. Soon she was winning swimming competitions and, when the family moved to England, her father began promoting her in swimming exhibitions and long-distance trials.

After becoming a swimming star in England, Kellerman traveled to the United States for a vaudeville tour in 1907. That summer she was arrested at Revere Beach in Boston for "indecent exposure" for wearing a one-piece bathing suit that left her arms, legs, and neck exposed. Upon learning that the tightness of the suit was not what deemed the costume as "indecent" but the exposure of her arms and legs, Kellerman sewed sleeves and legs onto the suit and was able to return to the beach—in the form-fitting knit suit.

She completed her vaudeville tour and became a regular attraction at the Hippodrome Theatre in New York as "The Diving Venus" for the enormous salary of $5,000 per week. It was while appearing at the Hippodrome that Kellerman supposedly developed synchronized swimming.

Kellerman entered films in 1909 and is one of the two women in contention for the title "first woman to appear in film in the nude." Going strictly by release date, Kellerman's *Neptune's Daughter* (1914) edged out Audrey Munson's *Inspiration* (1915) by a year. However, there is no clear consensus among film historians as to which actor was the first nude actor. In fact, a French short titled *After the Ball, the Bath* (1897) showed the back view of a woman taking a bath, so the recipient of the title depends on the definition of "film."

Over fifteen years Kellerman made eight films, and in 1918 she wrote a book titled *Physical Beauty: How to Keep It*. In 1952 Kellerman's life story was made into a film, *The Million Dollar Mermaid*, which starred another swimming champion, Esther Williams.

Film Credits

1909   *The Bride of Lammermoor; The Gift of Youth; Jepthah's Daughter: A Biblical Tragedy; Entombed Alive*
1911   *Sirens of the Sea; The Mermaids*
1914   *Neptune's Daughter*
1916   *A Daughter of the Gods*
1917   *Coney Island*
1918   *Queen of the Sea*
1920   *The Art of Diving; What Women Love*
1924   *Venus of the South Seas*

Kennedy, Madge (1891 Chicago, IL-1987 Woodland Hills, CA)

Madge Kennedy, a popular star of the 1920s, originally set her sights on an art career. She moved to New York in 1906 to attend the Art Students League with the hopes of becoming an illustrator. However, soon after her arrival she appeared in a student musical that changed her career dream and resulted in her signing a contract with a traveling stock company. Within five years she was back in New York appearing on Broadway in the comedy *Little Miss Brown* (1912) and being touted as the next great Broadway ingenue.

Kennedy was one of the first actors that Samuel Goldwyn signed after the formation of Goldwyn Studios. He publicized Kennedy as "winsome and sweet" and starred her in light romantic comedies. Kennedy made more than twenty-one films for Goldwyn Studios.

After her marriage to producer Harold Bolster, Kennedy left Goldwyn to appear in several films produced by her husband. After her divorce and for the next few decades, Kennedy worked on Broadway but did not appear on the screen. In the 1950s she began a new career as a character actor which lasted into the 1970s. Also during this period, Kennedy appeared on television in the recurring role of "Aunt Martha" on *Leave It to Beaver* (1957-1963) and on several episodes of *Alfred Hitchcock Presents* (1955-1965).

Film Credits

1917   *Baby Mine; Nearly Married*
1918   *Our Little Wife; The Danger Game; The Fair Pretender; The Service Star; Friend Husband; The Kingdom of Youth; A Perfect Lady*
1919   *Day Dreams; Daughter of Mine; Leave It to Susan; Through the Wrong Door; Strictly Confidential*
1920   *The Blooming Angel; Dollars and Sense; The Truth; Help Yourself*
1921   *The Girl with the Jazz Heart; Oh! Mary Be Careful; The Highest Bidder*
1923   *The Purple Highway*
1924   *Three Miles Out*
1925   *Scandal Street; Bad Company; Lying Wives*
1926   *Oh Baby!*
1928   *Walls Tell Tales*
1952   *The Marrying Kind*
1953   *Main Street to Broadway*
1955   *The Rains of Ranchipur*
1956   *The Catered Affair; Three Bad Sisters; Lust for Life*
1958   *A Nice Little Bank That Should Be Robbed; Houseboat*
1959   *Plunderers of Painted Flats; North by Northwest*
1960   *Let's Make Love*
1969   *They Shoot Horses Don't They?*
1970   *The Baby Maker*
1975   *The Day of the Locust*
1976   *Marathon Man*

Kenyon, Doris (1897 Syracuse, NY-1979 Beverly Hills, CA)

Courtesy of Silents Are Golden at <SilentsAreGolden.com>

Doris Kenyon was a true Renaissance woman. She was not only an actor (on stage, in films, on radio, and on television) and vaudeville performer, but also a poet, writer, and singer. She was born into a talented family. Her father was a minister and writer/poet protégé of Longfellow, in addition to serving on the editorial staff of *The National Encyclopedia of American Biography.* Her brother became a New York legislator.

She attended both Packer College Institute and Barnard College and published several books of poetry—one with her father *(Spring Flowers and Rowan)* and several of her own. After singing at an author's luncheon, she was signed to appear in a musical comedy, *The Princess Pat,* which ran for 158 performances on Broadway.

The play led to an offer of a film contract with World Films in 1915. Her debut film was the short *The Pawn of Fate,* while her feature debut was *The Rack* (1916) in which she played a desperate wife who takes her own life. She continued to appear in World releases but also worked for Paramount and starred in a fifteen-episode serial for Pathe titled *The Hidden Hand* (1917). In 1918 she created her own studio, Deluxe Pictures, and made at least three features.

As her father's health declined, she continued to live on the East Coast, enabling her to continue her stage career as well as appear in films. She alternated between stage and films until after her father's death in 1924, when she began to concentrate on films. Her first film after her father's death was the Valentino comeback effort *Monsieur Beaucaire.* Her performance brought a contract offer from First National and a move to Hollywood. She was paired with actor Milton Sills, upon whom she had a crush when she was younger, and their films were highly successful.

Kenyon and Sills were married in 1926 and had a son soon after their marriage. They personally designed their Bel Air home, built while the couple divided their time between the East and West Coasts production centers. However, the pace took its toll on Sills and he retired to a New York sanitarium to recover from a breakdown.

While staying near her husband, Kenyon began a career as a singer on the nightclub circuit. Her act included "talks" that she wrote and published under the title *Doris Kenyon's Monologues—Humorous and Dramatic*. When her husband was well enough to leave the hospital in 1930, the family returned to their Bel Air home. The couple prepared to return to their careers, only to have Sills suddenly die while playing tennis a few months after coming home.

Kenyon was inconsolable but now had sole responsibility for her son. In 1931 she appeared in four successful films for First National but decided that she wanted to pursue her singing rather than continue in films. She studied and toured in Europe before returning to the United States for her vaudeville debut.

She toured briefly and then returned to film work so that she would not have to leave her son in the care of other people. However, when her film work would allow she occasionally embarked on limited tours to sold-out houses throughout the United States.

She married twice after Sills's death, but both unions lasted less than five months combined. Her next venture was into the world of radio—first as a singer then as an actor on two early soap operas—*Crossroads* and *Saturday's Child*.

In 1947 her fourth marriage, to musicologist Bronislaw Mylnarski, proved lasting and continued until his death in 1971. Sadly, her only son also died in 1971.

Film Credits

1916	*The Pawn of Fate; The Feast of Life; The Man Who Stood Still; The Ocean Waif; The Traveling Salesman; The Rack*
1917	*The Man Who Forgot; A Girl's Folly; The Empress; Jimmy Dale Alias the Great Seal; Great White Trail; On Trial*
1918	*The Street of Seven Stars; The Inn of the Blue Moon; Wild Honey*
1919	*Twilight; The Bandbox*
1920	*The Harvest Moon*

1921   *The Conquest of Canaan; Get-Rich-Quick Wallingford*

1922   *Shadows of the Sea; The Ruling Passion; Sure-Fire Flint*

1923   *Bright Lights of Broadway; The Last Moment; Are You Guilty?*

1924   *Restless Wives; The Love Bandit; The New School Teacher; Lend Me Your Husband; Monsieur Beaucaire; Born Rich; Idle Tongues*

1925   *A Thief in Paradise; If I Marry Again; I Want My Man; The Half-Way Girl; The Unguarded Hour*

1926   *Men of Steel; Mismates; Ladies at Play; The Blonde Saint*

1927   *The Valley of Giants*

1928   *Burning Daylight; The Hawk's Nest; The Home Towners; Interference*

1930   *Beau Bandit*

1931   *The Bargain; Alexander Hamilton; The Road to Singapore; The Ruling Voice*

1932   *Young America; The Man Called Back*

1933   *No Marriage Ties; Counselor at Law; Voltaire*

1934   *Whom the Gods Destroy; The Human Side*

1936   *Along Came Love*

1938   *Girls' School*

1939   *The Man in the Iron Mask*

King, Mollie (1895 New York City-1981 Fort Lauderdale, FL)

Courtesy of Silents Are Golden at <SilentsAreGolden.com>

Mollie King, called "Mollie of Manhattan" after achieving success on the musical comedy stage, was a star of two popular serials until flappers became the feminine rage on film and her movie career began to fade.

Born into a theatrical family, her parents and both older siblings were all on the stage. Her show business debut was in vaudeville before she was one year old, and her first "important" stage role was in *Her Own Way* when she was seven years old. When not appearing on the stage, she and her sister and brother toured the vaudeville circuit as "The Three Kings."

She appeared at the Winter Garden and in Ziegfeld's *Follies* before she had graduated high school. After appearing in several successful plays, she was offered a film contract by the World company. Her film debut was in *A Woman's Power* (1916).

She appeared in several dramatic films before being cast in two popular serials in 1917—*The Mystery of the Double Cross* and *The Seven Pearls*. After a final appearance in *Human Clay,* King returned to the stage, appearing only sporadically in films after 1918.

In 1919 her marriage to socially prominent Kenneth Alexander was one of the "must attend" events of the New York season. She curtailed her appearances after her marriage, until finally retiring completely in 1922. Unfortunately, the stock market crash severely lessened the Alexanders' wealth. Little is known about her life after she faded from the social register except that after her marriage to Alexander ended, her second marriage lasted until her death.

Film Credits

1916   *A Woman's Power; A Circus Romance; Fate's Boomerang; The Summer Girl; All Man*
1917   *Kick In; Blind Man's Luck; The On-the-Square Girl; The Seven Pearls; The Mystery of the Double Cross*
1918   *Human Clay*
1919   *Suspense; Greater Than Love*
1920   *Women Men Forget*
1921   *Suspicious Wives*
1922   *Her Majesty*
1924   *Pied Piper Malone*

Kingston, Natalie (1905 Vallejo, CA-1991 West Hills, CA)

Natalie Kingston is best remembered as Tarzan's love interest, Mary Trevor, in the fifteen-chapter Universal serial *Tarzan, the Mighty* (1928). With the popularity of the first serial, she next appeared as the more familiar character Jane Parker in the subsequent fifteen-chapter serial *Tarzan, the Tiger* (1929).

She received her early acting training on the stage after having been a dancer with the Fanchon and Marco troupe. She entered films in the early 1920s when she appeared in several Mack Sennett comedies. In 1927 she was chosen as a WAMPAS Baby Star but was never able to capitalize on the publicity her selection created for her. She faded from the screen soon after the film industry's transition to sound.

Film Credits

1923	*The Daredevil*
1924	*Yukon Jake; All Night Long; The Reel Virginian; Feet of Mud; Romeo and Juliet*
1925	*His Marriage Wow; Plain Clothes; Framed* (I); *Lucky Stars; Don't Tell Dad; Remember When?*
1926	*Wet Paint; Lost at Sea; Don Juan's Three Nights; Kid Boots; The Silent Lover; Gooseland; Soldier Man*
1927	*The Night of Love; Love Makes 'Em Wild; Long Pants; His First Flame; Lost at the Front; Framed* (II); *Figures Don't Lie; The Harvester*
1928	*A Girl in Every Port; The Port of Missing Girls; Street Angel; Painted Post; Tarzan, the Mighty*
1929	*River of Romance; Pirates of Panama; Hold Your Man; Tarzan, the Tiger*
1930	*The Swellhead; Her Wedding Night; Under Texas Skies; The Chumps*
1932	*Doctor's Orders*
1933	*Forgotten; His Private Secretary; Only Yesterday*

Kirkham, Kathleen (1895 Menominee, MI-Santa Barbara, CA)

Kathleen Kirkham was one of the many actors who carried the vamp torch in the film industry after Theda Bara lost favor with film audiences. Like so many actors who owed their fame to vamp roles, her career was not long.

After completing her education, Kirkham joined a stock company and traveled the stock circuits of the western United States. Ending up in Los Angeles, Kirkham attended drama school before making her film debut in *Strathmore* (1915). But it was her role in *The Eyes of the World* (1917) that forever typed her as an "evil" woman.

Kirkham freelanced among the Hollywood studios, appearing with such stars as Douglas Fairbanks, Elmo Lincoln, and Colleen

Moore. During the early 1920s Kirkham was in demand to play the heavy in various films. However, after her marriage, Kirkham became tired of playing essentially the same role in all her films and retired from films. At the time of her death her occupation was listed as cook.

Film Credits

1915   *Strathmore*
1916   *The House of Lies*
1917   *The Eyes of the World; His Sweetheart; The Devil's Bait; The Masked Heart; The Calendar Girl; A Modern Musketeer; The Phantom Shotgun; The Devil's Assistant; The Clean Gun; Brand's Daughter*
1918   *Tarzan of the Apes; The Seal of Silence; For Husbands Only; He Comes Up Smiling; A Diplomatic Mission; The Romance of Tarzan; Arizona; Social Ambition; The Married Virgin*
1919   *Josselyn's Wife; The Master Man; Upstairs and Down; The Third Kiss; The Beauty Market; The Gay Lord Quex; The Pleasant Devil; In Search of Arcady; Hornet's Nest*
1920   *The Triflers; Dollar for Dollar; Number 99; Parlor, Bedroom and Bath; The Little 'Fraid Lady; When Dawn Came; Her Five-Foot Highness*
1921   *Beau Revel; The Sky Pilot; Nobody's Kid; The Foolish Matron; Pilgrims of the Night; The Innocent Cheat; The Adventures of Tarzan*
1922   *A Homespun Vamp; One Eighth Apache; Back to Yellow Jacket*
1923   *The Bolted Door; The Lonely Road; Other Men's Daughters*
1924   *The White Moth; Leave It to Gerry*
1925   *Sackcloth and Scarlet; A Regular Fellow*
1926   *King of the Turf; The Isle of Retribution; Her Honor the Governor*

Kirtley, Virginia (1888 Bowling Green, MO–1956 Sherman Oaks, CA)

Charlie Chaplin's first leading lady, Virginia Kirtley was touted as the next big comedy star by fan magazines, but this prediction never materialized. Her first experience in show business was on the stage and with touring companies in the Los Angeles area.

Originally signing with IMP Studios, Kirtley left to work with Mack Sennett at his Keystone Company. While there she appeared in Chaplin's film debut, *Making a Living* (1914). Like many stars during the silent era, Kirtley changed studios often; in 1915 she joined the American Company, appearing with Irving Cummings, Joseph Harris, and Webster Campbell, before moving to the Selig company before the end of the year.

She appeared with various studios until she retired from acting in 1918 to concentrate on her family. When her husband died suddenly in 1926, Kirtley attempted to return to films but was unable to adapt to the new film environment. Little is known about her life after her failed comeback attempt other than that she continued to live in Sherman Oaks until her death.

Film Credits

1913   *Mabel's Dramatic Career; The Girls and Dad*
1914   *A Flirt's Mistake; Making A Living; A Film Johnnie; Tango Tangles; The Woman Haters; Chicken Chasers; Too Many Brides; A Bathing Beauty*
1915   *The Once Over; The Doctor's Strategy; The First Stone; The Haunting Memory; In the Mansion of Loneliness; When the Fire Bell Rang; The Constable's Daughter; Mrs. Cook's Cooking; Dreams Realized; Oh Daddy; Persistence Wins*
1916   *A Law Unto Himself; Evan's Lucky Day; The Comet's Come-Back; Her Careers; Mother's Birthday; Polishing Up Polly; With the Spirit's Help*
1917   *The Voice of Eva; The Framed Miniature; The Girl Detective; The Grinning Skull; Only a Rose; The Nightcap; To Be or Not to Be Married; A Million in Sight; Who Shall Take My Life?*
1918   *The Last of the Clan; The Purchase Price; The Road to Fame*

Writing Credits

1916   *Two Small Town Romeos; The Barfly; With the Spirit's Help*
1917   *A Million in Sight; The Nightcap; To Be or Not to Be Married*

The Kiss *(1896)*

This one-minute "film" originally had a name that almost took longer to say than the film lasted. Originally called *The Kiss Between May Irwin and John Rice,* it featured the stars in a scene from their, then current, Broadway play, *The Widow Jones,* in which the actors kissed. Filmed in close-up, it was decried as "provocative and salacious" and resulted in censorship boards being set up in several states.

Reviewed in the June 15, 1896, issue of a contemporary publication, *The Chap-Book,* the film was condemned, stating that the loose behavior of the stars on stage was bad enough but that "the unbridled kissing, magnified to gargantuan proportions and repeated thrice, is absolutely loathsome." The film's production company, Edison Manufacturing Company, was also condemned as having "displayed very little delicacy" in the subjects it filmed.

La Plante, Laura *(1904 St. Louis, MO-1996 Woodland Hills, CA)*

Courtesy of Silents Are Golden at
<SilentsAreGolden.com>

Born in St. Louis, Laura La Plante moved to San Diego while a child and entered show business at age fifteen as a Christie Comedy Bathing Beauty, a group in competition with the more famous Sennett Bathing Beauties. Extremely attractive, La Plante was also a talented actor with a wide range in the characters that she could portray.

She moved to Universal in 1922, where she appeared in all genres from comedies to period dramas.

She appeared in several Hoot Gibson westerns before she became popular as the love interest in Reginald Denny's comedy features. After appearing in *Sporting Youth* (1924) she received a five-year contract. Two of the more memorable films from her Universal days were the drama *Smouldering Fires* (1925) and the comedy *Skinner's Dress Suit* (1926), which was directed by her then-husband, William A. Seiter.

She was one of the silent stars who made the transition to sound films when she starred as Magnolia in *Show Boat* (1929). She retired from films in 1935, although she did briefly return to appear in two films after that time. Her second marriage to producer Irving Asher was a lasting one, and she lived in Rancho Mirage in California's high desert, occasionally appearing on television and in local plays.

Film Credits

1919	*The Great Gamble*
1920	*813*
1921	*The Old Swimmin' Hole; Big Town Round-up; Play Square; Old Dynamite; Jiggs in Society; Jiggs and the Social Lion; His Four Feathers; Father's Close Shave; Brand of Courage; Back from the Front; The Alarm; The Call of the Blood; Big Town Ideas; Should Husbands Do Housework?; The Deputy's Double Cross*
1922	*The Wallflower; A Treacherous Rival; The Trail of the Wolf; Taking Things Easy; Society Sailors; Perils of the Yukon; Matching Wits; Fighting Back; Easy to Cop; Desperation; The Call of Courage; A Bottle Baby; The Big Ranger; Ranger's Reward*
1923	*Dead Game; Burning Words; Shootin' for Love; Out of Luck; The Ramblin' Kid; Crooked Alley; The Thrill Chaser; Around the World in Eighteen Days*
1924	*Sporting Youth; Ride for Your Life; Excitement; The Dangerous Blonde; Young Ideas; Butterfly; The Fast Worker; The Fatal Plunge*
1925	*Smouldering Fires; Dangerous Innocence; The Teaser*
1926	*The Beautiful Cheat; Skinner's Dress Suit; The Midnight Sun; Poker Faces; Her Big Night; Butterflies in the Rain*
1927	*The Love Thrill; Beware of Widows; The Cat and the Canary; Silk Stockings*

1928 *Finders Keepers; Thanks for the Buggy Ride; Home, James*
1929 *The Last Warning; Show Boat; Scandal; The Love Trap;*
      Hold Your Man
1930 *The King of Jazz; Captain of the Guard*
1931 *Lonely Wives; God's Gift to Women; Men Are Like That; The*
      Sea Ghost; Meet the Wife
1932 *Stout Hearts and Willing Hands*
1933 *Lost in Limehouse; Her Imaginary Lover*
1934 *Widow's Might; The Girl in Possession; Church Mouse*
1935 *Man of the Moment*
1946 *Little Mister Jim*
1957 *Spring Reunion*

LaBadie, Florence (1888 New York City-1917 Ossining, NY)

Courtesy of Silents Are Golden at
<SilentsAreGolden.com>

Florence LaBadie was adopted after her mother was committed to a mental hospital; her wealthy adoptive parents raised her in Canada. She received her education in both New York City and the Convent of Notre Dame in Montreal. Upon graduation, LaBadie became the model for Penrhyn Stanlaws, one of the best-known illustrators of the turn of the century.

She began appearing on stage in 1908 and signed with Olcott theatrical company. For the next year she toured in various plays appearing along the Eastern seaboard and in the southern United States. In 1909 she accompanied her friend Mary Pickford to Biograph Studios and was given a bit part in the film in production that day.

Although she appeared in bit parts over the next few months, she did not sign with Biograph until 1910. However, she was not happy there, so in 1911 she moved to Thanhouser and became one of their most popular stars. She starred in one of the most successful serials of the time, *The Million Dollar Mystery* (1914).

During her tenure at Thanhouser she was not only their most popular star but also their most publicized, appearing regularly in fan magazines of the period. The magazines raved about her many accomplishments, including writing poetry, playing piano, artistic endeavors such as painting, sculpting, and dancing as well as athletics. While hyperbole was normal in these magazines, LaBadie was accomplished in several of these areas.

During World War I she used her celebrity to raise funds for a variety of worthwhile programs and even lectured on the horrors of war to interested organizations such as the Peace Society. She was very active in the Statue of Liberty Illumination Fund and received an automobile for her efforts on behalf of the project.

Sadly, it was her love of cars and speed that brought about her early death. As she was driving in upstate New York her brakes gave out and she was thrown from the car during the crash. One month later she died from an infection resulting from her injuries.

Film Credits

1909   *The Politician's Love Story; The Salvation Army Lass; A Strange Meeting; The Seventh Day; Comata, the Sioux; Getting Even; In the Window Recess; Through the Breakers*

1910   *Taming a Husband; Serious Sixteen; A Gold Necklace; The Troublesome Baby; After the Ball*

1911   *The Two Paths; The Diamond Star; The Spanish Gypsy; The Broken Cross; Paradise Lost; A Knight of the Road; Madame Rex; His Mother's Scarf; How She Triumphed; Enoch Arden (Part I and II); The Primal Call; Her Sacrifice; Fighting Blood; The Thief and the Girl; The Indian Brothers; The Sorrowful Example; The Blind Princess and the Poet; The Rose of Kentucky; Swords and Hearts; The Trail of Books; Dave's Love Affair; Cinderella; The New Dress; Manicure Lady; Bobby; The Coward; The Smuggler; The Buddhist Priestess; In the Chorus; David Copperfield; The Satyr and the Lady; The Trail of Books; The Last of the Mohicans; A Mother's Faith; A Master of Millions; The Baseball Bug; The Tempest; Beneath the Veil*

1912   *Dr. Jekyll and Mr. Hyde; Petticoat Camp; The Star of Bethlehem; Undine; The Merchant of Venice; Lucile; As It Was in the Beginning; The Arab's Bride; Aurora Floyd; East Lynne; Trouble Maker; Extravagance; The Saleslady; Jilted; Jess; The Ring of a Spanish Grandee; Whom God Hath Joined;*

Called Back; Her Ladyship's Page; The Trouble Maker; The Silent Witness; The Guilty Baby; Flying to Fortune; My Baby's Voice; The Girl of the Grove; A Love of Long Ago; Under Two Flags; Big Sister

1913   *Evidence of the Film; Cymbeline; Life's Pathway; The Share of Fate*

1914   *Cardinal Richelieu's Ward; Crossed Wires; Zudora; The Million Dollar Mystery* (I); *Adrift in the City*

1915   *God's Witness; The Country Girl; Monsieur Lecoq; The Price of Her Silence; The Adventures of Florence; Bianca Forgets; All Aboard*

1916   *What Doris Did; The Five Faults of Flo; Master Shakespeare, Strolling Player; The Fugitive; The Fear of Poverty; Saint, Devil, and Woman; The Return of Draw Egan; The Pillory; Divorce and the Daughter*

1917   *The Woman in White; Her Life and His; The Man Without a Country; When Love Was Blind; War and the Woman; The Million Dollar Mystery* (II)

LaMarr, Barbara *(1896 Yakima, WA-1926 Altadena, CA)*

Courtesy of Silents Are Golden at <SilentsAreGolden.com>

Born Reatha Watson, Barbara LaMarr was nicknamed "the girl who was too beautiful." She made her theatrical debut at four years old when she appeared as Little Eva in a stock production of *Uncle Tom's Cabin.*

Although her family moved to California when she was young, LaMarr didn't become involved in films until after a successful vaudeville and dancing career which included dancing at the 1915 San Francisco World's Fair. While her professional life was successful, her personal life was anything but. She went through three failed marriages by the time she was twenty-one, and each one could have been the basis of a soap opera plot.

Her first husband supposedly died of pneumonia contracted while riding around in a rainstorm after an argument with his young, and restless, wife. Her second husband turned out to be a bigamist who died in surgery for a blood clot on his brain. Her third husband was sent to San Quentin for check forgery.

Saddened by her bad luck with men, LaMarr buried herself in her work, appearing on stage in musical revues as a dancer. In addition she wrote stories and entertainment critiques that were often published in newspapers before she segued into scenario writing. After Mary Pickford advised her to move in front of the cameras, she appeared in Louis B. Mayer's production of *Harriet and the Piper* (1920).

Her next film was with Douglas Fairbanks in *The Nut* (1921), and she was an instant success. She also appeared with Fairbanks as Milady de Winter in *The Three Musketeers* (1921). Her first starring role was in *Cinderella of the Hills* (1921).

LaMarr was incredibly popular with audiences and critics. After an accident on the set of *Souls for Sale* (1923), the studio doctors gave her painkillers to ensure that filming remained on schedule; because of their willingness to ignore the possible consequences of heavy use, by the time the film was complete, LaMarr was addicted. Always ready for a good time, she now began living life in the fast lane and burning her candle at both ends.

Finally her lifestyle caught up with her and she passed out on the set of *The Girl from Montmartre*. In her weakened condition she contracted tuberculosis. LaMarr retired to a small house in Altadena, California, to try to regain her failing health, but she died before she could return to the set. More than 40,000 people filed past her open casket, and the mourning fans nearly caused a riot. Her tomb was inscribed, "With God in the Joy and Beauty of Youth." Writer Adela Rogers St. Johns said of her death, "She died because the tale was told."

Years later another film lovely, Hedy LaMarr, was given her last name in honor of "the girl who was too beautiful."

Film Credits

1920   *Harriet and the Piper; Flame of Youth*
1921   *The Nut; The Three Musketeers; Cinderella of the Hills; Desperate Trails*

1922   *Arabian Love; Domestic Relations; Quincy Adams Sawyer; Trifling Women; The Prisoner of Zenda*

1923   *The Hero; The Brass Bottle; Souls for Sale; Mary of the Movies; St. Elmo; The Eternal Struggle; The Eternal City; Poor Men's Wives; Strangers of the Night*

1924   *Thy Name Is Woman; The Shooting of Dan McGrew; The White Moth; Sandra; Hello Frisco*

1925   *The Heart of a Siren; The White Monkey*

1926   *The Girl from Montmartre*

Writing Credits

1920   *The Little Grey Mouse; Flame of Youth; Rose of Nome; The Mother of His Children; The Land Jazz*

1924   *My Husband's Wives*

LaVerne, Lucille (1869 Memphis, TN-1945 Culver City, CA)

Lucille LaVerne began her career on the New York stage where she made her debut when she was sixteen. She was tremendously popular with audiences and by 1895 had established her own touring company that traveled throughout the United States. When she booked her company in Europe, they were called to do several command performances for European royalty.

She made her first film in 1915, and although she never achieved fame, she was a dependable actor specializing in scolding or nagging old women. Her final film was the Disney cartoon *Snow White and the Seven Dwarfs,* in which she voiced the queen/wicked hag character. After her retirement from films she owned a popular Hollywood nightclub.

Film Credits

1915   *Over Night*

1916   *Sweet Kitty Bellairs; The Thousand-Dollar Husband*

1917   *Polly of the Circus*

1918   *The Life Mask; Tempered Steel*

1919   *The Praise Agent*

1921   *Orphans of the Storm*

1923   *The White Rose; Zara*

1924   *America; His Darker Self*
1925   *Sun-Up*
1928   *The Last Moment*
1930   *Abraham Lincoln; Sinner's Holiday*
1931   *The Great Meadow; An American Tragedy; 24 Hours; The Unholy Garden; Little Caesar*
1932   *Union Depot; She Wanted a Millionaire; Alias the Doctor; While Paris Sleeps; Hearts of Humanity; Breach of Promise; Wild Horse Mesa; A Strange Adventure*
1933   *Pilgrimage; The Last Trail*
1934   *Beloved; School for Girls; Kentucky Kernels; The Mighty Barnum*
1935   *A Tale of Two Cities*
1936   *The Blow Out*
1937   *Snow White and the Seven Dwarfs*

Lawrence, Florence (1886 Hamilton, Canada-1938 Hollywood, CA)

Florence Lawrence is often credited as the actor who began the cult of the film star. After Lawrence signed with Carl Laemmle, he devised what might have been the first publicity stunt. He (anonymously) planted the information that Lawrence had been killed in a streetcar accident and then took out full-page advertisements berating those who would say such a terrible thing about his newly signed star, the new IMP girl. The resulting personal appearance frenzy was, according to most historians, very profitable for the studio but an ordeal for Lawrence.

Lawrence was born in Canada into a family in which her father was many years older than her mother; Florence was the youngest of his second group of children. Her mother was an actor, and Lawrence made her debut with her mother in a song and dance routine when she was only three years old. As she got older and could memorize lines she received billing and enjoyed regular employment.

As a traveling actor, Lawrence received little formal schooling, although she did attend school whenever possible. When her mother settled in Buffalo, New York, it was the first time she had stayed in one place long enough to pass from one grade to the next. But soon she was restless and wanted to get on with her career.

Lawrence got into films sometime at the end of 1906, and her first film, *Daniel Boone, or Pioneer Days in America,* was released early in 1907. She was not pleased with her performance but continued to appear in films with the Vitagraph Company. After briefly leaving films to appear in one final play, Lawrence settled into a film career.

She moved to Biograph and began working with D. W. Griffith in 1908. Lawrence was one of many young ingenues who took turns starring in the films produced by the studio. Although she remembered this time fondly, other actors from the same period found the atmosphere "bedlam."

Although individual actors were still not named, fans began calling their favorites by special titles—Lawrence became the "Biograph Girl." When films began to be reviewed, journalists used such titles as ways to differentiate actors. Lawrence was the unrivaled leading lady of Biograph until the appearance of another Canadian, Mary Pickford, in 1909.

Lawrence left Biograph and, when she was unable to secure employment with another studio, returned to the stage. Eventually she signed with IMP and the previously mentioned publicity stunt began. Following its success, Laemmle continued for some time to refute various "rumors" that no one had yet heard. Once the hoopla was over, Lawrence settled into making one or two films per week; these, of course, were only one or two reels lasting between ten to twenty minutes in length.

Lawrence soon tired of IMP; when she tried to move to Lubin in 1910, she was sued for breach of contract by IMP. The lawsuit was never decided in court—it was either dropped or settled out of court—because no record of it exists. Her first film for her new studio, *His Bogus Uncle,* was released at the end of January 1911.

Sadly, as new ingenues entered films many of the previous stars were pushed into the background. This is what happened to Lawrence. She was never able to keep up with Mary Pickford or Lillian Gish who she worked with at Biograph, and she was overlooked for roles in favor of the newer talent.

By 1914 her career was all but over. She continued to appear sporadically in films until 1936, but years often separated the roles. In 1938, she committed suicide by swallowing a mixture of cough syrup and ant paste.

Film Credits

1906   *Daniel Boone, or Pioneer Days in America; The Automobile Thieves*

1907   *Athletic American Girls; The Mill Girl; The Shaughraun; The Dispatch Bearer; The Boy, the Bust and the Bath; Bargain Fiend*

1908   *Macbeth; Romeo and Juliet; Lady Jane's Flight; The Viking's Daughter; The Bandit's Waterloo; A Calamitous Elopement; Salome; Betrayed by a Handprint; The Girl and the Outlaw; Behind the Scenes; The Heart of O'Yama; Where the Breakers Roar; A Smoked Husband; Richard III; The Stolen Jewels; The Devil; The Zulu's Heart; Father Gets in the Game; Ingomar the Barbarian; The Vaquero's Vow; The Planter's Wife; Romance of a Jewess; The Call of the Wild; Concealing a Burglar; Antony and Cleopatra; After Many Years; The Pirate's Gold; The Taming of the Shrew; The Song of the Shirt; The Ingrate; A Woman's Way; The Clubman and the Tramp; Julius Caesar; Money Mad; The Valet's Wife; The Feud and the Turkey; The Reckoning; The Test of Friendship; An Awful Moment; The Dancer and the King; The Christmas Burglars; Mr. Jones at the Ball; The Helping Hand; The Reg Girl; Dispatch Bearer; Cupid's Realm; Love Laughs at Locksmiths; The Red Girl*

1909   *Mrs. Jones Entertains; One Touch of Nature; The Honor of Thieves; The Sacrifice; The Criminal Hypnotist; Mr. Jones Has a Card Party; The Fascinating Mrs. Francis; Those Awful Hats; The Girls and Daddy; The Brahma Diamond; A Wreath in Time; His Ward's Love; The Curtain Pole; The Joneses Have Amateur Theatricals; The Politician's Love Story; The Golden Louis; At the Altar; The Prussian Spy; His Wife's Mother; A Fool's Revenge; The Wooden Leg; The Roue's Heart; The Salvation Army Lass; The Lure of the Gown; I Did It; The Deception; And a Little Child Shall Lead*

Them; The Medicine Bottle; Jones and His New Neighbors; A Drunkard's Reformation; Trying to Get Arrested; The Road to the Heart; Schneider's Anti-Noise Crusade; The Winning Coat; Confidence; A Trouble-Some Satchel; Lady Helen's Escapade; The Drive For Life; Tis an Ill Wind That Blows No Good; The Eavesdropper; The Note in the Shoe; A Baby's Shoe; The Jilt; Resurrection; Jones and the Lady Book Agent; The Judgment of Solomon; Two Memories; Eloping with Auntie; What Drink Did; Her First Biscuits; The Peachbasket Hat; The Way of Man; The Necklace; The Country Doctor; The Cardinals' Conspiracy; Sweet and Twenty; Jealousy and the Man; The Slave; The Mended Lute; Mr. Jones' Burglar; Mrs. Jones' Lover; The Hessian Renegades; The Awakening; Lines of White on a Sullen Sea; Nursing a Viper; Saul and David; Love's Stratagem; Lest We Forget; Her Generous Way; The Forest Ranger's Daughter; The Awakening of Bess; Those Boys!; A Sound Sleeper; Lucky Jim; One Busy Hour; The French Duel; Eradicating Aunty; The Lonely Villa; Tender Hearts

1910   The Call; Mother Love; The Winning Punch (I); The Widow; Two Men; Transfusion; The Taming of Jane; The Stage Note; The Senator's Double; A Self-Made Hero; The Right of Love; The Right Girl; A Reno Romance; Pressed Roses; Once Upon a Time; Old Heads and Young Hearts; The Nichols on Vacation; The New Shawl; The Mistake; The Miser's Daughter; The Maelstrom; Justice in the Far North; Jane and the Stranger; The Irony of Fate; His Sick Friend; His Second Wife; The Governor's Pardon; A Game for Two; The Eternal Triangle; The Doctor's Perfidy; Debt; The Count of Montebello; The Call of the Circus; The Broken Oath; The Blind Man's Tact; Bear Ye One Another's Burden; Among the Roses; All the World's a Stage; The Tides of Fortune; Never Again; The Coquette's Suitors; The Time-Lock Safe; The Rosary; A Discontented Woman

1911   Age versus Youth; The Rosary; Always a Way; The Wife's Awakening; Vanity and Its Cure; The Two Fathers; Through Jealous Eyes; That Awful Brother; The Test; The Story of Rosie's Rose; The State Line; The Snare of Society; The Slave's Affinity; A Show Girl's Stratagem; The Sheriff and the

Man; A Rural Conqueror; Romance on Pond Cove; A Rebellious Blossom; The Professor's Ward; Opportunity and the Man; One on Reno; Nan's Diplomacy; The Matchmaker; The Maniac; The Little Rebel; The Life Saver; The Hoyden; His Friend, the Burglar; His Chorus Girl Wife; His Bogus Uncle; Higgenses versus Judsons; Her Two Sons; Her Humble Ministry; Her Child's Honor; Her Artistic Temperament; A Head for Business; The Gypsy; A Good Turn; A Girlish Impulse; A Game of Deception; A Fascinating Bachelor; During Cherry Time; Duke de Ribbon Counter; A Blind Deception; Aunt Jane's Legacy; Art versus Music; The Actress and the Singer; The Snare of Society; Through Jealous Eyes; The Secret

1912 *Flo's Discipline; After All; The Winning Punch* (II); *A Village Romance; Tangled Relations; Taking a Chance; The Cross-Roads; A Surgeon's Heroism; Sisters; The Redemption of Riverton; The Players; Not Like Other Girls; The Mill Buyers; The Lady Leone; In Swift Waters; Her Cousin Fred; The Chance Shot; Betty's Nightmare; All for Love; The Advent of Jane; Angel of the Studio*

1913 *Unto the Third Generation; Suffragette's Parade in Washington; The Spender; Influence of Sympathy; His Wife's Child; The Girl o' the Woods; The Counterfeiter; The Closed Door; A Girl and Her Money*

1914 *The False Bride; Diplomatic Flo; The Law's Decree; The Little Mail Carrier; A Disenchantment; The Doctor's Testimony; The Great Universal Mystery; Her Ragged Knight; The Honor of the Humble; The Woman Who Won; The Stepmother; A Singular Cynic; The Romance of a Photograph; Pawns of Destiny; A Mysterious Mystery; The Mad Man's Ward; The Honeymooners; The Coryphee; The Bribe; The Man Who Was Never Kissed; Counterfeiters; A Singular Sinner*

1916 *Elusive Isabel*

1917 *Face on the Screen*

1918 *The Love Craze*

1922 *The Unfoldment*

1923 *The Satin Girl*

1924 *Gambling Wives*

1926   *The Johnstown Flood; The Greater Glory*
1930   *Sweeping Against the Winds*
1931   *Homicide Squad; Hard Hombre*
1932   *Sinners in the Sun*
1933   *Secrets*
1934   *The Old-Fashioned Way*
1935   *The Man on the Flying Trapeze*
1936   *One Rainy Afternoon*

Learn, Bessie (1888 San Diego, CA-1987 Burbank, CA)

Although Bessie Learn had a relatively short film career (1911-1915), she was extremely popular with the filmgoing audience. In fact, in 1913 she was voted one of the top favorites of readers of *Motion Picture Story Magazine.*

Learn was born in San Diego but was raised in Chicago. There she began her entertainment career on the stage before she was eight years old. She signed with Edison Studios in 1911 as a member of their company of players and remained at that studio for her short career in films. In 1914 Learn wrote and directed *Her Grandmother's Wedding Dress,* but she did not pursue either writing or directing careers, possibly because of her husband's disapproval.

Learn had married in 1913, and her husband was adamant about wanting a nonprofessional wife. By 1915 he apparently prevailed and Learn retired from films. Film historians disagree about whether she appeared in two final movies—*The Mysterious Miss Terry* (1917) and *The Lost Battalion* (1919)—but there has been no definitive proof to establish her participation.

After her retirement Learn started a successful business that made lampshades. She also was an avid golfer and a staunch Dodger (baseball) fan who attended games well into her eighties.

Film Credits

1911   *Santa Claus and the Clubman*
1912   *Every Rose Has Its Stem; The Winking Parson; When She Was About 16; Von Weber's Last Waltz; The Totville Eye; Romance of the Rails; A Queen for a Day; The Little Organist; Lead Kindly Light; Kitty's Holdup; His Mother's Hope; For the Cause of the South; The Father; Curing the Office Boy; If*

*All Those Endearing Young Charms; Believe Me; Very Much
Engaged; Martin Chuzzlewit; Apple Pies; The Little Organ
Player of San Juan*

1913   *An Accidental Alibi; John Manley's Awakening; The Island
of Perversity; How They Got the Vote; A Cause for Thankful-
ness; An Unsullied Shield; The Actress; The Maid of Honor;
The Dancer; Over the Back Fence; Barry's Break In; Confidence; Superstitous Joe; Bread on the Waters*

1914   *The Unopened Letter; The Temple of Moloch; Story of the
Willow Pattern; Shorty; The Resurrection of Caleb Worth;
A Question of Identity; The Pines of Lory; His Grandchild;
Her Grandmother's Wedding Dress*

1915   *Through Turbulent Waters; The Ploughshare; The Girl of the
Gypsy Camp; According to Their Lights; Across the Great
Divide*

1919   *The Lost Battalion*

Lee, Lila (1901/1902 Union Hill, NJ-1973 Saranac, NY)

Courtesy of Silents Are Golden at
<SilentsAreGolden.com>

Born Augusta Lee, Lila Lee was a vaudeville veteran as Cuddles Lee before entering films at the age of seventeen. Her debut film was *The Cruise of the Make-Believes* (1918).

She was most often cast as a demure young woman—a characterization that capitalized on her gently refined appearance. She signed a five-year contract with Paramount, but her husband's illness necessitated a light film schedule. However, when he recovered she returned to films in the early 1920s.

Her big break, and the role that elevated her to star status, was as the romantic lead opposite Valentino in *Blood and Sand* (1922). That year she was also selected as a WAMPAS Baby Star.

She continued to appear in films throughout the 1930s, but in 1936 she was involved in a scandal that may have brought a quick end to a faltering career. She was a guest in a house where a man was murdered; although she was not involved, the publicity was unfavorable.

Soon after that episode she had a relapse of the tuberculosis that had plagued her all her life. When she had somewhat recovered her health, she went to New York, where she appeared on the stage. One of her final public appearances was as a surprise guest on television's *This Is Your Life* in 1957.

Film Credits

1918   *Such a Little Pirate; The Cruise of the Make-Believes*
1919   *The Lottery Man; Male and Female; A Daughter of the Wolf; The Secret Garden; Puppy Love; Jane Goes A' Wooing; Rose o' the River; The Heart of Youth; Rustling a Bride; Hawthorne of the U.S.A.*
1920   *The Soul of Youth; Terror Island; The Prince Chap; Midsummer Madness*
1921   *The Easy Road; Dollar a Year Man; Gasoline Gus; Crazy to Marry; After the Show; The Charm School; The Fast Freight*
1922   *One Glorious Day; The Dictator; Blood and Sand; Back Home and Broke; Rent Free; The Ghost Breaker; Ebb Tide; Is Matrimony a Failure?*
1923   *The Ne'er-Do-Well; Homeward Bound; Woman-Proof; Hollywood*
1924   *Love's Whirlpool; Wandering Husbands; Another's Man's Wife*
1925   *The Midnight Girl; Old Home Week; Coming Through*
1926   *Broken Hearts; The New Klondike; Fascinating Youth*
1927   *One Increasing Purpose; Million Dollar Mystery*
1928   *Top Secret Mulligan; A Bit of Heaven; United States Smith; Thundergod; The Adorable Cheat; Just Married; Black Butterflies; The Black Pearl; You Can't Beat the Law; The Man in Hobbles; The Little Wild Girl*
1929   *Drag; Dark Streets; The Argyle Case; Flight; Love, Live and Laugh; The Sacred Flame; The Show of Shows; Queen of the Night Clubs; Honky Tonk*

1930	*Second Wife; Murder Will Out; Those Who Dance; Double Cross Roads; The Unholy Three; The Gorilla*
1931	*Woman Hungry; Misbehaving Ladies*
1932	*Unholy Love; False Faces; War Correspondent; Radio Patrol; The Night of June 13th; Exposure; Officer Thirteen*
1933	*The Face in the Sky; The Iron Master; The Intruder; The Lone Cowboy*
1934	*Whirlpool; Stand Up and Cheer; In Love with Life; I Can't Escape*
1935	*The People's Enemy; Marriage Bargain; Champagne for Breakfast*
1936	*Country Gentleman; The Ex-Mrs. Bradford*
1937	*Two Wise Maids; Nation Aflame*
1952	*Scotland Yard Inspector*
1966	*The Emperor's New Clothes*
1967	*The Cottonpickin' Chickenpickers*

Levien, Sonya (1889 Moscow, Russia-1960 Hollywood, CA)

Sonya Levien immigrated to the United States as a child and briefly practiced law after earning a legal degree from New York University. However, she decided that she preferred a writing career and became a staff writer for both the *Metropolitan* and *The Woman's Journal,* the official publication of the women's suffrage movement.

She soon turned to scenario writing and received her first screen credit for *Who Will Marry Me?* (1919). She did not have another credited work until 1921, when she adapted her own short story, *Cheated Love,* for film. After 1921 she wrote in collaboration with various other writers and had regular screen credits until her retirement.

She was especially noted for her female characters that were known for their integrity, intelligence, and independence. She and her collaborator William Ludwig won an Academy Award for Best Writing in 1955 for *Interrupted Melody* which starred Eleanor Parker. She wrote steadily over her career, completing as many as seven scripts a year, for a total of approximately seventy by the end of her career, most of which were produced.

Writing Credits

1919	*Who Will Marry Me?*
1921	*Cheated Love; First Love*
1922	*The Top of New York; Pink Gods*
1923	*The Snow Bride; The Exciters*
1925	*Salome of the Tenements*
1926	*Why Girls Go Back Home; Christine of the Big Tops*
1927	*The Princess of Hoboken; The Heart Thief; A Harp in Hock*
1928	*A Ship Comes In; The Power of the Press*
1929	*The Younger Generation; Trial Marriage; Behind That Curtain; Lucky Star; They Had to See Paris; Frozen Justice; South Sea Rose*
1930	*So This Is London; Song o' My Heart; Liliom; Lightnin'*
1931	*Daddy Long Legs; Surrender; Delicious; The Brat*
1932	*She Wanted a Millionaire; Rebecca of Sunnybrook Farm; Tess of the Storm Country; After Tomorrow*
1933	*The Warrior's Husband; Cavalcade; State Fair* (I); *Mr. Skitch; Berkeley Square*
1934	*The White Parade; Change of Heart; As Husbands Go*
1935	*Here's to Romance; Paddy O'Day; Navy Wife*
1936	*Ramona; Reunion; The Country Doctor*
1937	*In Old Chicago*
1938	*Kidnapped; The Cowboy and the Lady; Four Men and a Prayer*
1939	*The Hunchback of Notre Dame; Drums Along the Mohawk*
1941	*Ziegfeld Girl*
1943	*The Amazing Mrs. Holliday*
1945	*State Fair* (II); *Rhapsody in Blue; The Valley of Decision*
1946	*The Green Years*
1947	*Cass Timberlane*
1948	*Three Daring Daughters*
1951	*The Great Caruso; Quo Vadis*
1952	*The Merry Widow*
1954	*The Student Prince*
1955	*Hit the Deck; Interrupted Melody; Oklahoma!*
1956	*Bhowani Junction*
1957	*Jeanne Eagels*
1960	*Pepe*
1962	*State Fair* (III)

Little, Anna (1891 Mount Shasta, CA-1984 Los Angeles, CA)

Anna Little was raised on a ranch in Northern California, which was perfect training for the future serial and western star. Soon after graduating from high school, Little joined a stock company and made her stage debut in San Francisco. She was a versatile actor, able to appear in dramatic roles as well as sing when required for lighter roles.

The first film credit that survives is from 1911, although it is believed she worked with Broncho Billy Anderson prior to this date. She became known for her accurate and sympathetic characterizations of Native American characters during a period when they were still being portrayed negatively. Her athleticism and strength made her a natural for the sometimes grueling roles in both westerns and serials.

Although she easily adapted to appearing in the westerns and serials that were popular during the period, her first love was dramatic films. Interestingly, although she could cry on cue, she found it difficult to appear happy on cue.

By 1914 Little was under contract to Universal, appearing in a wide variety of roles, but the audience liked her best in westerns, where her knowledge of ranch life brought realism to her parts; she was soon known as "the darling of the plains." She appeared in one serial, *The Black Box* (1915), but went on to other films and did not become typecast as a serial star. In 1917 she went to New York to appear in some films there, acknowledging that Eastern credits "just about doubled" your salary once an actor returned to Hollywood.

After returning to Hollywood Little was signed by Famous Players-Lasky and began appearing opposite Wallace Reid. In 1918 she appeared in, perhaps, her best-remembered role, as Naturich in *The Squaw Man,* Cecile B. DeMille's remake of his earlier hit. She continued to appear in westerns for the remainder of the decade.

She returned to the serial format late in 1919 with the film *Lightning Bryce,* in which Little portrayed one of two offspring who inherit their father's gold mine. The serial was so popular that she immediately made a second titled *The Blue Fox* (1921). For the next few years she made a multichapter serial each year.

She retired from films in 1925 without explanation and drifted into obscurity. When she died in 1984 her obituary observed that she had been involved in Christian Science programs for many years.

Film Credits

1911   A Young Squaw's Bravery; Cowgirls' Pranks; The Indian
        Maiden's Lesson; The Puncher's New Love; The Lucky Card;
        The Broken Trap
1912   Blazing the Trail; The Crisis; The Doctor's Double; Custer's
        Last Raid; His Punishment; The Lieutenant's Last Fight; On
        the Warpath; The Outcast; The Post Telegrapher; The Indian
        Massacre; The Invaders; The Reckoning; For the Honor of
        the Seventh; Custer's Last Fight; The Altar of Death; On Se-
        cret Service; The Civilian; Mary of the Mines; The Prospec-
        tor's Daughter; The Indian Maid's Elopement; The Empty
        Water Keg; The Battle of the Red Men; His Nemesis; The Bu-
        gle Call; For the Honor of the Tribe
1913   The Battle of Gettysburg; The Little Turncoat; The Mosaic
        Law; Smiling Dan; The Sergeant's Secret; With Lee in Vir-
        ginia; Past Redemption; The Greenhorn; The Waif; The Sign
        of the Snake; The Filly; Her Legacy; The Heart of an Indian;
        A Shadow of the Past; Will o' the Wisp
1914   The Voice at the Telephone; Prowlers of the Wild; The Sob
        Sister; The Big Sister's Christmas; The Great Universal Mys-
        tery; Through the Flames; The Prince of Bavaria; As the
        Wind Blows; The Chorus Girl's Thanksgiving; The Opened
        Shutters; Damon and Pythias; Called Back; A Page from
        Life; On the Verge of War; On the Rio Grande; Kid Regan's
        Hands; Circle 17; True Irish Hearts; For the Wearing of the
        Green; The Squire's Son; The Paths of Genius; The House of
        Bondage; The Queen of Hearts
1915   Changed Lives; The Gopher; The Grail; The Great Ruby
        Mystery; Homage; Misjudged; The Social Lion; Man-Afraid-
        of-His-Wardrobe; Broadcloth and Buckskin; The Black Box;
        The Colonel's Adopted Daughter; Two Spot Joe; Playing
        with High Stakes; The Sheriff of Willow Creek; Man to Man;
        The Valley Feud; There's Good in the Worst of Us; The Cac-
        tus Blossom
1916   Land o' Lizards; Immediate Lee; The Awakening; When the
        Light Came; Double Crossed; The Quagmire; The Ranger of
        Lonesome Gulch; Two Bits; Silent Selby; A Flickering Light;
        The Pilgrim; Nugget Jim's Partner; That Gal of Burke's; Nell

Dale's Men Folks; The Forgotten Prayer; Matchin' Jim; According to St. John
1917 *Under Handicap; Nan of Music Mountain; The Silent Master*
1918 *The World for Sale; Rimrock Jones; The House of Silence; Believe Me Xantippe; The Firefly of France; Less Than Kin; The Source; The Man from Funeral Range; The Squaw Man*
1919 *Alias Mike Moran; Something to Do; The Roaring Road; Square Deal Sanderson; Told in the Hills; Lightning Bryce*
1920 *Excuse My Dust; The Cradle of Courage*
1921 *The Blue Fox*
1922 *Chain Lightning; Nan of the North; Hair Trigger Casey*
1923 *The Greatest Menace; The Eagle's Talons*
1925 *Secret Service Saunders*

Lombard, Carole (1908 Fort Wayne, IN-1942 Table Rock Mountain, NV)

Carole Lombard was one of the best comedic talents of the 1930s and held the unofficial title of "screwball comedy queen." She was also known for always being one of the boys in spite of her beauty and was almost universally loved by her co-workers. Her talent was most apparent when she was deftly handling the satirical comedy popular during the late 1930s, but her career was cut short by a plane crash during World War II.

Lombard's parents were divorced when she was young, and her mother moved the family to Los Angeles. She was discovered while playing baseball with the boys in her neighborhood and appeared in *A Perfect Crime* (1921) when she was only twelve. She returned to school and "normal" life until she was fifteen, when she joined a traveling theater group. After touring with the theater group, she appeared in *Gold Heels* in 1924 but did not again appear in a film until the following year in *Marriage in Transit.*

She signed a five-year contract with Fox that same year, but in 1926 she was involved in car accident that left her face scarred. Fox dropped her contract and, after plastic surgery, Lombard moved to Mack Sennett's studio. She worked for various studios for the next few years before getting a seven-year contract with Paramount in 1930.

She appeared in a succession of films in the early 1930s until she was cast opposite John Barrymore in *Twentieth Century* (1934), a role that made her a star. But disputes with Paramount over roles resulted in her being cast in mediocre, if not truly bad, films. Finally, in 1936, she was cast in one of the best comedies of the 1930s—*My Man Godfrey,* opposite her former husband William Powell, as the charmingly air-headed Irene Bullock. The following year she was cast in another great comedy, *Nothing Sacred,* which took a satirical look at the ethics of the press.

With the outbreak of World War II, Lombard accepted the position as honorary national chairman of the war bond drive and became one of many film stars who traveled the country selling bonds. Early in 1942, after selling over $2 million worth of bonds in Indianapolis, the plane carrying Lombard and her entourage crashed outside of Las Vegas. Her death not only devastated her husband, Clark Gable, but also the filmgoing public. President Roosevelt praised her in a cable to Gable: "She brought great joy to all who knew her . . . she is and always will be a star. We shall never . . . cease to be grateful to her."

Film Credits

1921	*A Perfect Crime*
1924	*Gold Heels*
1925	*Dick Turpin; Marriage in Transit; Gold and the Girl; Hearts and Spurs; Durand of the Badlands*
1926	*The Road to Glory*
1927	*Smith's Pony; Gold Digger of Weepah; My Best Girl; The Girl from Everywhere; The Fighting Eagle*
1928	*The Beach Club; Run, Girl, Run; Smith's Army Life; The Best Man; The Swim Princess; The Bicycle Flirt; Smith's Restaurant; The Divine Sinner; The Girl from Nowhere; His Unlucky Night; Power; The Campus Vamp; Motorboat Mamas; Me, Gangster; Show Folks; Hubby' Weekend Trip; The Campus Cavemen; Ned McCobb's Daughter*
1929	*Matchmaking Mamas; Don't Get Jealous; High Voltage; Big News; The Racketeer; Dynamite*
1930	*The Arizona Kid; Safety in Numbers; Fast and Loose*
1931	*It Pays to Advertise; Man of the World; Ladies' Man; Up Pops the Devil; I Take This Woman*
1932	*No One Man; Sinners in the Sun; Virtue; No More Orchids; No Man of Her Own*

1933   *From Hell to Heaven; The Eagle and the Hawk; Supernatural; Brief Moment; White Woman*

1934   *Bolero; We're Not Dressing; Twentieth Century; Now and Forever; Lady by Choice; The Gay Bride*

1935   *Rumba; Hands Across the Table; The Fashion Side of Hollywood*

1936   *Love Before Breakfast; The Princess Comes Across; My Man Godfrey*

1937   *Swing High, Swing Low; Nothing Sacred; True Confessions*

1938   *Fools for Scandal*

1939   *Made for Each Other; In Name Only*

1940   *Vigil in the Night; They Knew What They Wanted*

1941   *Mr. and Mrs. Smith*

1942   *To Be or Not to Be*

Loos, Anita (1888 Mount Shasta, CA-1981 New York City)

Anita Loos, considered by some to be a writing prodigy as a child, was one of the most prolific writers in Hollywood during the early years of the film industry. She wrote over 100 scripts in four years (1912-1915), and only four were not made into movies.

Loos was a teenage actor when she saw a film and decided she could write a better one. She spent a morning writing a scenario then sent it off to the American Biograph Company—an address she found on a film canister. Two weeks later she received an acceptance letter and her writing career began.

D. W. Griffith directed the resulting film, *The New York Hat* (1912), and she worked regularly for Biograph until 1916, during which time she wrote over 100 scenarios and the accompanying title cards. Known for her wit, in 1916 when she wrote the film adaptation of *MacBeth*, the credits read "by William Shakespeare and Anita Loos." She is credited with being the first person to use verbal humor on title cards.

Loos is perhaps best remembered as the author of *Gentlemen Prefer Blondes* (1928), which was made into two films and spawned a sequel-of-sorts in *Gentlemen Marry Brunettes* (1955). In 1926 she also wrote the play *The Whole Town's Talking,* which she later adapted as a film for the screen, titled *The Ex-Bad Boy* (1931).

In addition to her work writing plays and scripts, Loos wrote several books on her life and career, including *A Girl Like I* (1966), *Kiss*

Hollywood Good-Bye (1974), and *Cast of Thousands* (1977). She also wrote two books about working in Hollywood, titled *How to Write Photoplays* (1920) and *Breaking Into the Movies* (1921). Although she supposedly wrote the books in collaboration with her (then) husband John Emerson, later it was discovered that he often made her put his name to works that he did no actual work on.

Although she was an independent woman earning her own way in a "man's world," Loos never aligned with the feminist movement. Her writing, while amusing and satirical, never placed women in roles that were not socially acceptable. Whether she actually believed that women should be subservient to men is not clear, but controlling men populated her personal life.

Less remembered is the fact that Loos produced several films in the last years of the 1910s. Her first production effort was *Come On In* (1918), a film that she also wrote. In the next two years she produced five other films and then, inexplicably, returned to screenwriting.

Writing Credits

1912   *The Earl and the Tomboy; He Was a College Boy; The New York Hat; The Power of the Camera; The Road to Plaindale; My Baby; The Musketeers of Pig Alley*

1913   *The Telephone Girl and the Lady; The Mistake; All for Mabel; All on Account of a Cold; A Bunch of Flowers; A Cure for Suffragettes; Fall of Hicksville's Finest; A Fallen Hero; The Fatal Deception; A Fireman's Love; For Her Father's Sins; Gentlemen and Thieves; The Great Motor Race; A Girl Like Mother; A Hicksville Epicure; His Awful Vengeance; His Hoodoo; A Horse on a Bill; How the Day Was Saved; The Lady in Black; The Making of a Masher; The Mayor Elect; The Mother; A Narrow Escape; Pa Says; The Path of True Love; Queen of the Carnival; The Saving Grace; The Suicide Pact; Two Women; Unlucky Fim; The Wall Flower; The Wedding Gown; When a Woman Guides; The Widow's Kid; Yiddish Love; The Power of the Camera; Highbrow Love; Bink's Vacation*

1914   *At the Tunnel's End; A Balked Heredity; A Blasted Romance; The Chieftain's Daughter; A Comer in Hats; The Deceiver; The Deadly Glass of Beer; A Hicksville Reformer; The Fatal*

Curve; The Fatal Dress Suit; A Flurry in Art; The Girl in the Shack; His Hated Rival; His Rival; How They Met; The Last Drink of Whiskey; A Life and Death Affairs; The Meal Ticket; The Million-Dollar Bride; Mortimer's Millions; Nearly a Burglar's Bride; Nell's Eugenic Wedding; Nellie, the Female Villain; A No Bull Spy; The Saving Presence; The School of Acting; The Sensible Girl; The Stolen Masterpiece; The Style Accustomed; The Suffering of Susan; Where the Roads Part; The White Slave Catchers; The Gangster of New York; For Her Father's Sins; The Hunchback

1915 The Deacon's Whiskers; The Burlesquers; The Cost of a Bargain; The Fatal Fingerprints; The Fatal Fourth; Heart That Truly Loved; How to Keep a Husband; Mixed Values; Mountain Bred; Nellie, the Female Victim; Pennington's Choice; Sympathy Sal; The Tears on the Page; Wards of Fate

1916 American Aristocracy; A Calico Vampire; A Comer in Cotton; French Milliner; The Half-Breed; His Picture in the Papers; Intolerance; Laundry Liz; Manhattan Madness; MacBeth; The Matrimaniac; The Social Secretary; Stranded; The Wharf Rat; Wild Girl of the Sierras; The Mystery of the Leaping Fish; The Children Pay; The Little Liar; The Americano

1917 Down to Earth; In Again, Out Again; Reaching for the Moon; Wild and Wooly; A Daughter of the Poor

1918 Come On In; Goodbye Bill; Hit the Trail Holiday; Let's Get a Divorce

1919 Getting Mary Married; The Isle of Conquest; A Temperamental Wife; A Virtuous Vamp; Under the Top; Oh, You Women!

1920 The Branded Women; In Search of a Sinner; The Love Expert; The Perfect Woman; Two Weeks; Dangerous Business

1921 Mama's Affair; A Woman's Place

1922 Polly of the Follies; Red Hot Romance

1923 Dulcy

1924 Three Miles Out

1925 Learning to Love

1927 Publicity Madness; Stranded

1928 Gentlemen Prefer Blondes (I)

1929 The Fall of Eve

1931 The Struggle; The Ex-Bad Boy

1932 Blondie of the Follies; Red-Headed Woman

1933   *The Barbarian; Hold Your Man; Midnight Mary*
1934   *The Cat and the Fiddle*
1935   *Biography of a Bachelor Girl; The Girl from Missouri; The Social Register*
1936   *San Francisco; Riffraff*
1937   *Mama Steps Out; Saratoga*
1938   *Alaska; The Great Canadian; The Cowboy and the Lady*
1939   *The Women; Babes in Arms; Another Thin Man*
1940   *Susan and God; Strange Cargo*
1941   *Blossoms in the Dust; They Met in Bombay; When Ladies Meet*
1942   *I Married an Angel*
1945   *A Tree Grows in Brooklyn*
1953   *Gentlemen Prefer Blondes*
1955   *Gentlemen Marry Brunettes*
1958   *Gigi*

Producing Credits

1918   *Come On In; Goodbye Bill*
1919   *A Temperamental Wife*
1920   *In Search of A Sinner; The Love Expert; Dangerous Business*

Lorraine, Louise (1901 San Francisco, CA-1981 Sacramento, CA)

Louise Lorraine was one of the most prolific silent era serial actors, appearing in over 150 chapters in which she defied the odds and evil men to persevere. Born to a Spanish father and a French mother, Lorraine was still a teenager when she entered films, after spending years getting her mother to consent to her career choice. She began as a comedian with Century Studios where she costarred with Chinese comic Chai Hong.

After a few years she went to Universal to appear in action films and westerns. She was chosen as a WAMPAS Baby Star in 1922 after appearing in several serials, most notably the eighteen-chapter Universal hit *Elmo the Fearless* (1920) and Jane to Elmo Lincoln's Tarzan in *The Adventures of Tarzan* (1921).

Early in her career she did her own stunts, but as she became more popular studios were less willing to have her take chances and insisted on a stunt double. Lorraine objected to this, but during an argument with a director about using a double in the scene being filmed, the car that was supposed to skid to a stop overturned, killing everyone onboard. After witnessing the accident, Lorraine never balked at using a double again.

She continued to appear in films in which she battled evildoers ranging from gangsters to mad scientists, until she retired from films to devote herself to her second husband and her two children.

Film Credits

1915 *Neal of the Navy*

1920 *Elmo the Fearless; Flaming Disc; Movie Hero*

1921 *The Trigger Trail; The Midnight Raiders; The Knockout Man; The Outlaw; Double Crossed; Valley of the Rogues; The Adventures of Tarzan; The Fire Eater; A Bunch of Kisses; The Guilty Trail; Fighting Blood; Stand Up and Fight; The Danger Man; Sea Shore Shapes; Get-Rich-Quick Peggy*

1922 *With Stanley in Africa; Up in the Air About Mary; The Radio King; True Blue; The Altar Stairs; The White and Yellow; The Channel Riders; The Cabby; Pirates of the Deep; The Law of the Sea*

1923 *The Gentleman from America; The Oregon Trail; McGuire of the Mounted; The Yellow Handkerchief; Sweetie; The Wolves of the Waterfront*

1925 *The Great Circus Mystery; The Verdict; The Wild Girl; Three in Exile; Borrowed Finery; Pals; Little Red Riding Hood; The Silent Guardian*

1926 *The Blue Streak; Exit Smiling; The Silent Flyer; The Stolen Ranch*

1927 *Winners of the Wilderness; Hard Fists; Rookies; The Frontiersman; Legionnaires in Paris*

1928 *Baby Mine; Circus Rookies; Chinatown Charlie; The Wright Idea; Shadows of the Night*

1929 *The Diamond Master; A Final Reckoning*

1930 *The Mounted Stranger; The Jade Box; The Lightening Express; Near the Rainbow's End; Beyond the Law; Moonlight and Cactus*

Love, Bessie (1898 Midland, TX-1986 London, England)

Courtesy of Silents Are Golden at
<SilentsAreGolden.com>

Bessie Love moved with her family from Texas to Hollywood, where her father set up a chiropractic practice. While waiting for the practice to become established, Love applied for film roles to augment the family income. She was nicknamed the "little brown wren" because of her small stature and coloring.

She caught the eye of D. W. Griffith, who cast her in a small role in *The Birth of a Nation* (1915), followed by the role as the Bride of Cana in *Intolerance* (1916). She was soon a popular and sought-after actor able to appear in all genres from comedy to drama. She was chosen as a WAMPAS Baby Star in 1922 and earned an Academy Award nomination in 1929 for her role in *Broadway Melody.*

However, by 1931 she could not get any roles in Hollywood so she moved with her family to England and, after World War II broke out, entertained the troops there. She returned to the United States after the war and found work as a supporting player. She divided her time between work in the United States and England, appearing on stage, on radio, and on television.

In her later years she wrote about the silent era and critiqued later film works for both British and American publications. She wrote her autobiography, *From Hollywood with Love,* in 1977.

Film Credits

1915 *The Birth of a Nation; Georgia Pearce*
1916 *Acquitted; The Flying Torpedo; The Aryan; The Good Bad Man; Reggie Mixes In; Stranded; Hell-to-Pay Austin; Intolerance, A Sister of Six, Heiress at Coffee Dan's, The Mystery of the Leaping Fish*

1917   *Nina the Flower Girl; A Daughter of the Poor; Cheerful Givers; Sawdust Ring; Wee Lady Betty; Polly Ann*

1918   *Little Sister of Everybody; The Dawn of Understanding; The Great Adventure; How Could You, Caroline?*

1919   *The Enchanted Barn; Carolyn of the Corners; The Wishing Ring Man; A Yankee Princess; The Little Boss; Cupid Forecloses; Over the Garden Wall; A Fighting Colleen*

1920   *Bonnie May; Pegeen; The Midlanders*

1921   *Penny of the Top Hill Trail; The Swamp; The Sea Lion*

1922   *The Vermilion Pencil; Forget Mr. Not; The Village Blacksmith; Nightlife in Hollywood; Deserted at the Altar*

1923   *Three Who Paid; The Ghost Patrol; Souls for Sale; Mary of the Movies; Human Wreckage; The Eternal Three; St. Elmo; Slave of Desire; Gentle Julia; Purple Dawn*

1924   *Torment; Those Who Dance; The Silent Watcher; Dynamite Smith; Sundown; Tongues of Flame; The Woman of the Jury*

1925   *Soul-Fire; A Son of His Father; New Brooms; Marqueray's Duel; The Lost World; The King on Main Street; Bulldog Courage*

1926   *The Song and Dance Man; Lovey Mary; Meet the Prince; Young April; Going Crooked*

1927   *Rubber Tires; A Harp in Hock; Dress Parade; The American; Amateur Night*

1928   *The Matinee Idol; Sally of the Scandals; Anybody Here Seen Kelly?*

1929   *The Broadway Melody; Idle Rich; The Girl in the Show; The Hollywood Revue of 1929*

1930   *They Learned About Women; Chasing Rainbows; Conspiracy; Good News; See America Thirst*

1931   *Morals for Women*

1932   *Big City Interlude*

1936   *I Live Again*

1941   *Atlantic Ferry*

1942   *London Scrapbook*

1946   *Journey Together*

1951   *No Highway; The Magic Box*

1953   *The Weak and the Wicked*

1954   *The Barefoot Contessa; Beau Brummell*

1955   *Touch and Go*

1957   *The Story of Esther Costello*
1958   *Nowhere to Go; Next to No Time*
1960   *Too Young to Love*
1961   *The Greengage Summer; The Roman Spring of Mrs. Stone*
1963   *The Wild Affair; Children of the Damned*
1964   *I Think They Call Him John* (voice only)
1965   *Promise Her Anything*
1966   *Poppies Are Also Flowers*
1967   *I'll Never Forget What's 'is Name; Battle Beneath the Earth*
1968   *Isadora*
1969   *On Her Majesty's Secret Service*
1971   *Catlow; Sunday Bloody Sunday*
1973   *Vampyres*
1974   *The Ritz*
1977   *Gulliver's Travels* (voice only)
1981   *Lady Chatterley's Lover; Ragtime; Reds*
1983   *The Hunger*

Loy, Myrna (1905 Helena, MT-1993 New York City)

Myrna Loy, who starred as Nora Charles in the successful *Thin Man* series, began her career in silent films in 1925. After her father's death during the influenza epidemic of 1918, her mother moved the family to Los Angeles. There she attended school and graduated from Venice High School. While attending the high school in 1921 she modeled for the "Spiritual" statue that still stands with two others at the entry of the main building.

After appearing in local productions and dancing in the chorus at Grauman's Chinese Theatre while still in high school, Loy entered films soon after she graduated. She appeared as an extra in several films before she was cast as a chorus girl in the landmark film *The*

Jazz Singer (1927). She continued honing her craft in every role from ingenue to exotic vamp.

By the mid-1930s she was one of MGM's biggest stars and a popular female box office attraction. Her first breakout hit was *Manhattan Melodrama* (1934), the film that John Dillinger was watching before he was gunned down outside a theater. That same year, after a long apprenticeship in silent films, she starred in the first of six Thin Man films, *The Thin Man,* opposite William Powell as the affluent and urbane couple Nick and Nora Charles, who solved murders amid witty repartee. They became the prototype for many later detective couples, including the Harts in the hit television series, *Hart to Hart* (1979-1984).

In 1937 the readers of Ed Sullivan's entertainment column voted Loy the "Queen of Hollywood." During the war, however, Loy turned her back on Hollywood and served as a full-time Red Cross worker. When the war ended she returned to films, and in addition to such classics as *The Best Years of Our Lives* (1946), she appeared as Lillian Gilbreth in another popular series of films based on the book *Cheaper by the Dozen.*

She was never awarded an Oscar for her acting, but in 1991 she received an honorary Oscar "in recognition of her extraordinary qualities both on screen and off, and with appreciation for a lifetime's worth of indelible performances." Unable to attend the ceremony because of failing health, via satellite from New York the actor simply said, "You've made me very happy. Thank you very much."

After her retirement from films, Loy became involved in politics and served as an advisor to the National Committee Against Discrimination in Housing as well as film advisor to UNESCO. She made her Broadway debut in the 1973 revival of *The Women* and appeared in several television productions. Her autobiography, *Myrna Loy: Being and Becoming,* was published in 1987.

Film Credits

1925   *Pretty Ladies; Sporting Life; Ben-Hur; What Price Beauty?*
1926   *The Caveman; The Love Toy; Why Girls Go Back Home; The Gilded Highway; Exquisite Sinner; So This Is Paris; Don Juan; Across the Pacific; The Third Degree*
1927   *Finger Prints; When a Man Loves; Bitter Apples; The Climbers; Simple Sis; The Heart of Maryland; A Sailor's Sweet-*

heart; The Jazz Singer; The Girl from Chicago; If I Were Single; Ham and Eggs at the Front

1928   *Beware of Married Men; A Girl in Every Port; Turn Back the Hours; The Crimson City; Pay As You Enter; State Street Sadie; The Midnight Taxi*

1929   *Fancy Baggage; Hardboiled Rose; The Desert Song; The Squall; The Black Watch; Noah's Ark; The Great Divide; Evidence; The Show of Shows*

1930   *Cameo Kirby; Isle of Escape; Under a Texas Moon; Cock o' the Walk; Bride of the Regiment; The Last of the Duanes; The Jazz Cinderella; The Bad Man; Renegades; Rogue of the Rio Grande; The Truth About Youth; The Devil to Pay!*

1931   *The Naughty Flirt; Consolation Marriage; Arrowsmith; Transatlantic; Skyline; Rebound; Hush Money; A Connecticut Yankee; Body and Soul*

1932   *Emma; The Wet Parade; New Morals for Old; Love Me Tonight; Thirteen Women; The Mask of Fu Manchu; The Animal Kingdom; The Woman in Room 13; Vanity Fair*

1933   *Topaze; Scarlet River; The Barbarian; When Ladies Meet; Penthouse; Night Flight; The Prizefighter and the Lady*

1934   *Men in White; Manhattan Melodrama; Stamboul Quest; Evelyn Prentice; Broadway Bill; The Thin Man*

1935   *Wings in the Dark; Whipsaw*

1936   *Wife vs. Secretary; The Great Ziegfeld; To Mary, with Love; Libeled Lady; After the Thin Man; Petticoat Fever*

1937   *Parnell; Double Wedding*

1938   *Test Pilot; Man-Proof; Too Hot to Handle*

1939   *Lucky Night; Another Thin Man; The Rains Came*

1940   *I Love You Again; Third Finger, Left Hand; Northward Ho!*

1941   *Shadow of the Thin Man; Love Crazy*

1943   *Show Business at War*

1945   *The Thin Man Goes Home*

1946   *The Best Years of Our Lives; So Goes My Love*

1947   *The Bachelor and the Bobby-Soxer; Song of the Thin Man; The Senator Was Indiscreet*

1948   *Mr. Blandings Builds His Dream House*

1949   *The Red Pony; That Dangerous Age*

1950   *Cheaper by the Dozen*

1952   *Belles on Their Toes*

1956   *The Ambassador's Daughter*

1958   *Lonelyhearts*
1960   *From the Terrace; Midnight Lace*
1969   *April Fools*
1974   *Airport 1975*
1978   *The End*
1980   *Just Tell Me What You Want*

Mackaill, Dorothy (1903 Hull, Yorkshire, England-1990 Honolulu, HI)

Courtesy of Silents Are Golden at <SilentsAreGolden.com>

As a teenager, Dorothy Mackaill ran away to London to take acting lessons. She convinced her father to help support her as she broke into show business and soon got a job as a dancer in a chorus. While appearing in Paris, Mackaill met a friend who got her a job with the *Ziegfeld Follies* in New York.

One of the first friends she made in New York was Marion Davies who got her interested in appearing in films. Her first films were in the early 1920s, and it was not until three years later that she received star billing. Her breakthrough film was *The Man Who Came Back* (1924). That year she was also chosen as a WAMPAS Baby Star.

She continued to star in features until the advent of sound, when the studios wanted new faces for the new medium. Accordingly, her contract with First National was not renewed when it expired in 1931. However, Mackaill continued to ppear in independent productions through the mid-1930s.

She retired from films and took care of her ailing mother for many years. In 1955 she moved to Hawaii where she took up permanent residence in the Royal Hawaiian Hotel. She made some appearances in the locally produced television series *Hawaii Five-O* (1968-1980), including a made-for-TV movie in 1968.

Film Credits

1920   *Torchy's Millions; The Face at the Window; Torchy Mixes In; Torchy's Promotion; Torchy*
1921   *Bits of Life; The Lotus Eater*
1922   *Isle of Doubt; A Woman's Woman; The Streets of New York; The Inner Man*
1923   *Mighty Lak' a Rose; The Broken Violin; The Fighting Blade; The Fair Cheat; His Children's Children; Twenty-One*
1924   *The Next Corner; The Man Who Came Back; The Painted Lady; The Mine with the Iron Door; What Shall I Do?*
1925   *The Bridge of Sighs; Chickie; The Making of O'Malley; Shore Leave; One Year to Live; Joanna*
1926   *The Dancer of Paris; Ranson's Folly; Subway Sadie; Just Another Blonde*
1927   *The Lunatic at Large; Convoy; Smile, Brother, Smile; The Crystal Cup; Man Crazy*
1928   *Ladies Night in a Turkish Bath; Lady Be Good; The Whip; Waterfront; The Barker*
1929   *His Captive Woman; Children; Children of the Ritz; Two Weeks Off; Hard to Get; The Great Divide; The Love Racket*
1930   *Strictly Modern; The Flirting Widow; The Office Wife; Man Trouble; Bright Lights*
1931   *Once a Sinner; Kept Husbands; Party Husband; Their Mad Moment; The Reckless Hour; Safe in Hell*
1932   *Love Affair; No Man of Her Own*
1933   *Neighbors' Wives; The Chief*
1934   *Curtain at Eight; Picture Brides; Cheaters*
1937   *Bulldog Drummond at Bay*

Macpherson, Jeanie (1887 Boston, MA-1946 Hollywood, CA)

Although best known as Cecil B. DeMille's chief scriptwriter from 1915 to 1945, Jeanie Macpherson started out in the entertainment industry as an actor. She was raised in upper-class society in Boston. However, before she could leave for Paris to be educated abroad her family went bankrupt and she had to find work to help support the family.

Not finding office work interesting or challenging, Macpherson decided to try her luck in show business. She spent a few years in the chorus line at the Chicago Opera House before moving to New York to tackle Broadway. She appeared in some musical revues but decided that the new film industry had more potential.

She signed with the American Biograph Company in 1908. D. W. Griffith directed her first film, *Mr. Jones at the Ball* (1908), and she became an early Griffith protégé. She stayed with Biograph for two years, playing what she called "emotional roles," before working briefly with the Edison Company, prior to her move west to work at the newly created Universal Studios.

When she arrived at Universal she worked as leading lady, writer, and director. She preferred to appear in adventure films, so these were the type that she wrote most often. In fact, before suffering a nervous breakdown, Macpherson had her own production company for which she wrote, starred in, and directed two-reel films. When she recovered, she left Universal and went to work for DeMille as his assistant in a relationship that was rumored to be both personal and professional.

Soon she was his main scriptwriter in a collaboration that lasted thirty years and produced some of DeMille's best films. Whether there was a romantic aspect to their relationship, Macpherson spent the remaining years of her life dedicated to furthering DeMille's standing within the industry. In fact, she became so important to DeMille that she was always "on call" to help him when he reached an impasse with a film.

As a writer she was known for her piercing wit and clever phrasing, excelling at the genre that would originally be called "sex comedies" but would later be renamed "social comedies" by film censors. In 1945 when he was having difficulty with the script for *The Unconquered* (1947), DeMille called Macpherson to help with the rewrite; however by that time she was in the final stages of terminal cancer and was unable to help her longtime friend and collaborator. Interestingly, DeMille made only four films after her death.

Writing Credits

1913 *The Sea Urchin; Red Margaret: Moonshiner*
1914 *The Lie*

1915 *The Captive; Evidence; Chimmie Fadden Out West; The Cheat; The Golden Chance; The Unafraid; Temptation*

1916 *The Love Mask; The Heart of Nora Flynn; The Dream Girl; Joan the Woman; The Trail of the Lonesome Pine; Maria Rosa*

1917 *A Romance of the Redwoods; The Little American; The Woman God Forgot; The Devil-Stone*

1918 *The Whispering Chorus; Old Wives for New; Till I Come Back to You*

1919 *Don't Change Your Husband; For Better, for Worse; Male and Female*

1920 *Something to Think About*

1921 *Forbidden Fruit; The Affairs of Anatol*

1922 *Saturday Night; Manslaughter*

1923 *Adam's Rib; The Ten Commandments*

1924 *Triumph*

1925 *The Golden Bed; The Road to Yesterday*

1926 *Red Dice; Her Man o' War; Young April*

1927 *The King of Kings*

1929 *The Godless Girl; Evidence; Dynamite*

1930 *Madame Satan*

1933 *The Devil's Brother*

1935 *The Crusaders*

1936 *The Plainsman* (research only)

1938 *The Buccaneer*

1939 *Land of Liberty; Union Pacific*

1940 *North West Mounted Police*

1941 *Washington Melodrama*

1942 *Reap the Wild Wind*

Film Credits

1908 *The Fatal Hour; The Devil; Father Gets in the Game; The Vaquero's Vow; Concealing a Burglar; The Clubman and the Tramp; The Test of Friendship; Mr. Jones at the Ball; The Taming of the Shrew; Money Mad; The Christmas Burglar*

1909 *Mr. Jones Has a Card Party; A Wreath in Time; Tragic Love; The Curtain Pole; The Medicine Bottle; Trying to Get Arrested; A Rude Hostess; Confidence; Lady Helen's Esca-*

pade; *The Faded Lilies; The Peach Basket Hat; The Message; With Her Card; The Seventh Day; Lines of White on a Sullen Sea; A Midnight Adventure; The Death Disc; A Corner in Wheat; In a Hempen Bag; One Touch of Nature; The Criminal Hypnotist; Her First Biscuits; A Sweet Revenge; The Open Gate; The Trick That Failed; In the Window Recess; Through The Breakers; In Little Italy; To Save Her Soul; The Day After; Mrs. Jones Entertains*

1910   *The Call; The Newlyweds; The Way of the World; An Affair of Hearts; The Impalement; A Victim of Jealousy; A Flash of Light; In Life's Cycle; The Iconoclast; A Gold Necklace; Two Little Waifs; Winning Back His Love; The Troublesome Baby; A Child's Faith; A Salutary Lesson; The Usurer; An Old Story with a New Ending; A Summer Idyll; Little Angels of Luck; A Mohawk's Way; In Life's Cycle; The Oath and the Man; The Message of the Violin; Waiter No. 5; The Fugitive; Sunshine Sue; Love in Quarantine; A Plain Song; A Child's Stratagem; The Golden Supper; His Sister-in-Law; The Lesson*

1911   *A Wreath of Orange Blossoms; Heart Beats of Long Ago; Fisher Folks; Enoch Arden (Part I and II); The Last Drop of Water; Out from the Shadow; The Blind Princess and the Poet; The Midnight Marauder; Spanish Gypsy; The Two Paths; The Italian Barber; Help Wanted; His Trust; His Trust Fulfilled; Conscience; Comrades; The Londale Operator; The Broken Cross; The Chief's Daughter; Madame Rex; A Knight of the Road; The New Dress; Bobby; The Coward; The Ruling Passion; The Village Hero; A Man for All That*

1912   *A Man; The Rugged Coast; The Eternal Mother; The Wrecker's Daughter; Mother and Daughters; The Butler and the Maid; Mary Had a Little Lamb; The Wreckers*

1913   *The Sea Urchin; The Awakening; In a Roman Garden; The Proof; The Violet Bride; On Burning Sand; The Rugged Coast*

1914   *The Leper's Coat; Rose of the Rancho; The Ghost Breaker; The Outlaw Reforms; The Merchant of Venice*

1915   *The Girl of the Golden West; The Captive; Carmen; Kindling*

1917   *The Missing Wallet*

Madison, Cleo (1883 Bloomington, IL-1964 Burbank, CA)

Although Cleo Madison is remembered as one of early women directors that flourished during the silent film era, she had a successful career before entering the film industry. She got her start in show business around 1910 when she joined a touring company in Santa Barbara, much to the horror of her strict family. She advanced from lead actor to manager and continued on the stage for several years.

On a break from touring she decided to try the new medium of film and signed a contract with Universal in 1913. Her first film was a short titled *His Pal's Request,* but the most popular type of film was the adventure serial; Madison was cast in *The Trey o' Hearts* (1914), a film in which she played dual roles—that of the good woman (Rose) and her evil twin sister (Judith).

The film made her a star, and in the years that followed she starred in several films with Lon Chaney as well as in another dual-role drama, *A Mother's Atonement* (1915), in which she played both mother and daughter. By 1915, Madison was directing her own films, and although she never achieved the heights that some of the other female directors did, she was moderately successful.

Known as a stern taskmaster, she was both respected and slightly feared by those who worked on her projects. However, her talent— she also wrote scenarios—and audience appeal negated any interpersonal shortcoming.

In 1916 she directed and starred in one of the first five-reel features, *A Soul Enslaved,* which dealt with the problems faced by the working classes. Another film from 1916, *Her Bitter Cup,* often cited as the earliest feminist production as well as being a suffrage classic, also dealt with the working class and the decisions that women are forced to make to survive.

Between 1915 and 1916 Madison worked on more than twenty films as both star and director. *Motion Picture News* (April 1916) noted that Madison's "acting is emotional and strong . . . her work as a director good."

However, the characters that Madison portrayed, often ingenues in need of a man, were the direct opposite of her personality. When asked by *Motion Picture Weekly* if she was scared the first day she directed, Madison replied, "Why should I be? I had seen men with less brains than I have getting away with it . . . so I knew that I could direct."

By 1921 the pace and stress of Madison's schedule brought on a nervous breakdown and she had to remain secluded for a year. However, she returned to the screen in 1922 and made several films before her final retirement in 1929.

Film Credits

1912   *A Business Buccaneer*

1913   *His Pal's Request; The Trap; The Heart of a Cracksman; Captain Kidd; The Buccaneers; Under a Black Flag; Shadows of Life; Cross Purposes*

1914   *The Man Between; Hearts and Flowers; Sealed Orders; Dolores D'Arada, Lady of Sorrow; The Hills of Silence; The Strenuous Life; The Feud; The Last of Their Race; The Love Victorious; The Mystery of Wickham Hall; The Great Universal Mystery; The Severed Hand; The Trey O'Hearts; The Master Key; The Sin of Olga Brandt; Damon and Pythias; The Mexican's Last Raid; Unjustly Accused; The Law of His Kind; The Deadline; Samson; The Gambler's Oath; The Dead End; The Acid Test; Scooped by Cupid*

1915   *A Woman's Debt; The Mystery Woman; The Crystal; Haunted Hearts; Their Hour; The Mother Instinct; Diana of Eagle Mountain; The Duchess; Human Menace; Wild Irish Rose; The Whirling Disk; The Faith of Her Fathers; The Dancer; The Ways of a Man; The People of the Pit; The Flight of the Night Bird; A Fiery Introduction; Extravagance;*

The Pine's Revenge; Agnes Kempler's Sacrifice; The Fascination of the Fleur de Lis; Alas and Alack; A Mother's Atonement; Liquid Dynamite; The Ring of Destiny; The Power Of Fascination; The Sin of Olga Brandt; Alias Holland Jimmy; Jane's Declaration of Independence

1916   *A Soul Enslaved; His Return; Her Defiance; Her Bitter Cup; Eleanor's Catch; Virginia; When the Wolf Howls; Alias Jane Jones; The Crimson Yoke; A Dead Yesterday; Cross Purposes; Priscilla's Prisoner; The Girl in Lower 9; The Guilty One; Tillie the Little Swede; Along the Malibu; Triumph of Truth; To Another Woman; The Chalice of Sorrow; The Mother Instinct*

1917   *The Daring Change; The Girl Who Lost; The Sorceress; The Web; The Woman Who Would Not Pay; Black Orchids; The Severed Hand*

1918   *Flame of the West; The Romance of Tarzan*

1919   *The Great Radium Mystery; The Girl from Nowhere*

1920   *The Price of Redemption*

1921   *The Lure of Youth; Ladies Must Live*

1922   *A Woman's Woman; The Dangerous Age*

1923   *Souls in Bondage; Gold Madness; The Dangerous Age*

1924   *Discontented Husbands; The Lullaby; True As Steel; Unseen Hands; The Roughneck*

Mandarin Film Company

While several film companies produced films for black audiences, there is a record of only one company producing films for Chinese audiences. The Mandarin Film Company was based in Oakland, California, and began production in approximately 1917.

Apparently all employees were Chinese. The company's president was Marion E. Wong, who was also an actress. She and her sister appeared as the female leads in the company's first, and possibly only, production, *The Curse of Quon Qwon* (1917). Unfortunately, little is known about the company and it is unclear how long it operated.

Mansfield, Martha (1899 Mansfield, OH-1923 San Antonio, TX)

Courtesy of Silents Are Golden at <SilentsAreGolden.com>

Called one of "the most beautiful girls in New York City" at the end of World War I, Martha Mansfield had a tragically brief film career. After graduating from high school, Mansfield began her career in the entertainment industry by joining a stock company.

She moved to New York to launch a stage career and, while not working in the theater, augmented her income by posing for artists and photographers. After dancing in the chorus of the 1913 musical *Hop o' My Thumb* and appearing in a Winter Garden revue, Mansfield was discovered by Florenz Ziegfeld and given a part in his production of *The Century Girl* (1916).

Mansfield worked for several of the smaller film companies before signing a contract with Metro Film Corporation in 1918. Mansfield made her final appearance on the stage in Ziegfeld's 1919 production of *Midnight Frolic* before concentrating on her film career.

Her most famous role was as Millicent Carew in the Famous Players-Lasky production of *Dr. Jekyll and Mr. Hyde* (1920) opposite John Barrymore. This role catapulted her to other lead roles. She freelanced for several years before signing a long-running contract with Fox in 1923.

Her second film for Fox was the film version of the Broadway play *The Warrens of Virginia*. She was cast as the Confederate fiancée of a Union soldier—a role that was expected to make her a star. Unfortunately, while walking to her car after completing a scene on location in San Antonio, Mansfield's costume caught on fire, burning her severely; she died the next day.

Film Credits

1917   *Max Comes Across; Max in a Taxi; Max Wants a Divorce*
1918   *Broadway Bill; The Spoiled Girl*

1919   *The Hand Invisible; The Perfect Lover; Should a Husband Forgive?*

1920   *Dr. Jekyll and Mr. Hyde; Civilian Clothes; The Wonderful Chance; Women Men Love; Mothers of Men*

1921   *A Man of Stone; The Last Door; His Brother's Keeper; Gilded Lies*

1922   *Queen of the Moulin Rouge; Till We Meet Again*

1923   *The Woman in Chains; Youthful Cheaters; Fog Bound; The Silent Command; Potash and Perlmutter; Little Red School House; The Leavenworth Case; Is Money Everything?*

1924   *The Warrens of Virginia*

Marion, Frances (1888 San Francisco, CA-1973 Los Angeles, CA)

Frances Marion was perhaps the most successful scenario writer of the silent era and continued her career into the 1950s. At one point during the silent era she was highest-paid scenario writer in films. Throughout her career she wrote more than 130 films and received numerous awards for her writing, including the Academy Award for Writing for *The Big House* (1930), and *The Champ* (1931). She was the first female to win the writing award for best original screenplay.

Marion began her career as an artist and reporter in San Francisco after having been a telephone operator and a store clerk. In 1912 she moved to Los Angeles to work as a poster painter for films. As she was exposed to the film industry, she decided that she wanted to become more of a part of it. She was hired as an assistant to Lois Weber, one of the most success female directors of the era.

In the beginning she wrote press copy, designed sets, and worked in the costume department. She decided that she wanted to write scenarios, but at that time there were no full-time scenario writers. Her friend Mary Pickford hired her as an actor-writer but it was specified that writing would be her chief job.

However, Marion soon signed with World Studio and began churning out five-reel films—as many as six a month. In 1916 Marion was made head of the scenario department at World. She could write in all genres from gangster to action to comedy. Even though they were no longer at the same studio, she maintained her close contact with Pickford by ghostwriting the column *Mary Pickford's Daily Talks*.

One of the more successful films that Marion had written for Pickford was *The Foundling* (1916), and when a similar theme was chosen for a new film, Pickford demanded that Marion write it. After an extended battle with Adolph Zukor and Cecile B. DeMille, Marion was hired and work began on *The Poor Little Rich Girl* (1917). However, when it was completed Zukor declared it "putrid" and Marion went back to World to continue as production supervisor and scenario writer.

Because they had no other film to take its place, the studio released *The Poor Little Rich Girl,* expecting it to be a dismal failure and possibly threaten Pickford's career. To the studio's amazement the audiences loved it and both Pickford and Marion were renewed in their belief in themselves. The film met with unrivaled financial success and critical approval. Shortly after the film's release Famous Players-Lasky hired Marion at $50,000 per year to develop films for Pickford. Marion was the highest-paid scenario writer in Hollywood and she was only twenty-eight years old. Her salary reached $3,500 per week while working at MGM in the early 1930s.

She wrote many of Pickford's most popular films, but she also wrote for other popular actors including Constance Talmadge, Lillian Gish, Marion Davies, and Marie Dressler. She was under contract with MGM for many years and was allowed an unusual amount of creative freedom. In 1946, Marion left Hollywood to concentrate on writing plays and novels; a story she wrote, *The Clown,* was adapted for film in 1952. In 1972 she wrote her autobiography, *Off with Their Heads.*

Writing Credits

1915 *Fanchon, the Cricket; A Daughter of the Sea; Camille* (I); *A Sister's Burden; Esmeralda; Mistress Nell; The Dawn of Tomorrow; Little Pal; Rags*

1916 *The Foundling; A Circus Romance; Then I'll Come Back to You; The Social Highwayman; The Feast of Life; The Battle of Hearts; Tangled Fates; La Boheme; The Crucial Test; A Woman's Way; The Summer Girl; Friday the 13th; The Revolt; The Gilded Cage; The Hidden Scar; The Heart of a Hero; Bought and Paid For; All Man; The Rise of Susan; The Yellow Passport*

1917 *A Woman Alone; On Dangerous Ground; Tillie Wakes Up; A Hungry Heart; A Square Deal; A Girl's Folly; The Web of*

Desire; The Social Leper; As Man Made Her; Forget-Me-Not; Darkest Russia; The Crimson Dove; The Stolen Paradise; The Divorce Game; Beloved Adventuress; The Amazons; Rebecca of Sunnybrook Farm; The Little Princess; The Poor Little Rich Girl (I)

1918   *Stella Maris; Amarilly of Clothesline Alley; M'Liss; The City of Dim Faces; He Comes Up Smiling; Johanna Enlists; The Goat; The Temple of Dusk; How Could You Jean?*

1919   *Captain Kidd Junior; The Dark Star; The Misleading Widow; A Regular Girl; Anne of Green Gables; The Cinema Murder*

1920   *Pollyanna; The Flapper; Humoresque; The World and His Wife; The Restless Sex*

1921   *The Love Light; Straight Is the Way; Just Around the Corner*

1922   *Back Pay; East Is West; The Toll of the Sea; Minnie; Sonny; The Primitive Lover; The Eternal Flame*

1923   *The Voice of the Minaret; The Famous Mrs. Fair; The Nth Commandment; Within the Law; The Love Piker; Potash and Perlmutter; The Song of Love; The French Doll*

1924   *Through the Dark; The Dramatic Life of Abraham Lincoln; The Mask of Lopez; Galloping Gallagher; Secrets* (I); *Cytherea; Thundering Hoofs; Sundown; Tarnish; In Hollywood with Potash and Perlmutter*

1925   *The Lady; Zander the Great; His Supreme Moment; A Thief in Paradise; Ridin' the Wind; Lightnin'; Graustark; The Dark Angel; Thank You; Simon the Jester; Stella Dallas; Lazybones*

1926   *The First Year; The Tough Guy; Partners Again; Paris at Midnight; Hands Across the Border; The Son of the Sheik; The Winning of Barbara Worth; The Scarlet Letter; Lone Hand Saunders*

1927   *The Red Mill; Silver Comes Through; The Callahans and the Murphys; Jesse James; Love; Madame Pompadour; Don Mike*

1928   *Pioneer Scout; Bringing Up Father; The Sunset Legion; Kit Carson; The Cossacks; Excess Baggage; The Masks of the Devil; The Awakening; The Wind*

1929   *Their Own Desire*

1930   *Anna Christie; The Rogue Song; Let Us Be Gay; Good News; El Presidio; Min and Bill; Wu Li Chang; The Big House*
1931   *The Champ; The Secret Six*
1932   *Emma; Blondie of the Follies; Cynara*
1933   *Dinner at Eight; Peg o' My Heart; The Prizefighter and the Lady; Going Hollywood; Secrets*
1936   *Riffraff; Poor Little Rich Girl* (II); *Camille* (II)
1937   *Knight Without Armour; Love from a Stranger*
1940   *Green Hell*
1945   *Molly and Me*
1952   *The Clown*

Producing Credits

1923   *The Nth Commandment*
1925   *Simon the Jester*

Directing Credits

1921   *The Love Light; Just Around the Corner*
1923   *The Song of Love*

Marsh, Mae (1895 Madrid, NM-1968 Hermosa Beach, CA)

Called "the most exquisitely sensitive face" of the silent screen, Mae Marsh was D. W. Griffith's feminine ideal: pure, delicate, and waiflike. For several years she was one of his favorite actors with her natural acting style and gentle beauty.

Marsh entered show business almost by accident. Although she had appeared in a few small productions prior to her move west, in 1912 she accompanied her older sister to Hollywood when her sister, who worked on the stage, decided to try films. The story goes that she was discovered by Griffith while she watched her sister work in a scene during one of the director's winter stays in California before his permanent move to Hollywood.

The first film in which she was more than an extra was *A Siren of Impulse* (1912) and she had her first starring role a few months later in *Man's Genesis* (1912) after both Mary Pickford and Blanche Sweet turned down the part because of the skimpy costume. When Biograph returned to New York, Marsh stayed in California, appearing for various studios before being called to New York to replace Mary Pickford when she left Biograph.

She was generally cast as an adolescent heroine who was forced to grow up after experiencing a dramatically life-changing event. When Griffith left Biograph, Marsh went with him and appeared in several of his later classic films. She appeared in *The Birth of a Nation* (1915) as Flora, the "Little Sister," and in *Intolerance* (1916) as the grief-stricken "Dear One" whose courtroom scenes are considered by many to be among the greatest acting of the silent era.

She continued to work with Griffith when he formed Triangle Studios with Mack Sennett and Thomas Ince. In 1917 she was offered a contract with Goldwyn Studios and left Triangle when Griffith could not match the salary offered. However, the quality of her work at Goldwyn never matched the work she had done with Griffith.

After her marriage in 1918, she announced her retirement, but she was lured back to appear in two films in the early 1920s. During her "retirement," she wrote a highly autobiographical book titled *Screen Acting*. She went to England to appear in two British films as a representative "Griffith actress" before returning to the United States to work with Griffith again in *The White Rose* (1923).

Marsh was completely devoted to Griffith throughout her life and she was, perhaps, his favorite discovery. In 1923 Griffith said in an interview for *Photoplay* magazine, "Every motion picture star I have known was 'made' by long training and much hard work, but Mae Marsh was born a film star."

Although she concentrated on raising her three children after her final appearance for Griffith, she did occasionally appear in films. After the stock market crash, she was forced to return to films full-time but then appeared less frequently when her financial situation improved.

In 1955 the George Eastman House's Festival of Fine Arts named her one of five outstanding female actors of the silent era. In her final years Marsh devoted much of her time to painting and sculpting.

Film Credits

1910   *Serious Sixteen; Ramona*
1911   *Fighting Blood*
1912   *Just Like a Woman; One Is Business, the Other Crime; The Lesser Evil; The Old Actor; A Beast at Bay; When Kings Were the Law; Home Folks; A Temporary Truce; Lena and the Geese; The Spirit Awakened; The School Teacher and the Waif; An Indian Summer; Man's Genesis; The Sands of Dee; The Inner Circle; Two Daughters of Eve; Brutality; The New York Hat; The Kentucky Girl; A Siren of Impulse; A Voice from the Deep; Those Hickville Boys; A Lodging for the Night; His Lesson; A Beast at Bay; The Parasite; For the Honor of the Seventh; The Indian Uprising at Santa Fe*
1913   *Three Friends; The Telephone Girl and the Lady; An Adventure in the Autumn Woods; The Tender Hearted Boy; Love in an Apartment Hotel; Broken Ways; A Girl's Stratagem; Near to Earth; Fate; The Perfidy of Mary; The Little Tease; If We Only Knew; The Wanderer; His Mother's Oath; The Reformers; Two Men of the Desert; Primitive Man; Influence of the Unknown; For the Son of the House; The Lady and the Mouse; His Mother's Son; A Timely Interception; The Mothering Heart; The Sorrowful Shore; By Man's Law; The Girl Across the Way*
1914   *Judith of Bethulia; Battle of Elderbush Gulch; Brute Force; Home, Sweet Home; The Escape; The Avenging Conscience; Moonshine Molly; Great Leap: Until Death Do Us Part; Apple Pie Mary*
1915   *The Birth of a Nation; The Outcast; The Outlaw's Revenge; The Victim; Her Shattered Idol; Big Jim's Heart*
1916   *Hoodoo Ann; A Child of the Paris Streets; A Child of the Streets; A Wild Girl of the Sierras; The Marriage of Molly-O; Intolerance; The Little Liar; The Wharf Rat*
1917   *Polly of the Circus; The Cinderella Man; Sunshine Alley*

1918   *Fields of Honor; The Beloved Traitor; The Face in the Dark; All Woman; The Glorious Adventure; Money Mad; Hidden Fires; The Racing Strain*

1919   *The Bondage of Barbara; Spotlight Sadie; The Mother and the Law*

1920   *The Little 'Fraid Lady*

1921   *Nobody's Kid*

1922   *Till We Meet Again; Flames of Passion*

1923   *The White Rose; Paddy the Next Best Thing*

1924   *Daddies; Arabella*

1925   *Tides of Passion; The Rat*

1928   *Racing Through*

1931   *Over the Hill*

1932   *That's My Boy; Rebecca of Sunnybrook Farm*

1933   *Alice in Wonderland*

1934   *Bachelor of Arts; Little Man, What Now?*

1935   *Black Fury*

1936   *Three Godfathers; Hollywood Boulevard*

1939   *Drums Along the Mohawk*

1940   *The Grapes of Wrath; Young People; The Man Who Wouldn't Talk*

1941   *Tobacco Road; Great Guns; Remember the Day; How Green Was My Valley; Swamp Water; Blue, White and Perfect; Belle Starr*

1942   *Son of Fury; Tales of Manhattan; Quiet Please: Murder; The Loves of Edgar Allan Poe; It Happened in Flatbush; Just Off Broadway*

1943   *The Moon Is Down; The Song of Bernadette; Dixie Dugan*

1944   *Jane Eyre; In the Meantime Darling; The Sullivans*

1945   *Leave Her to Heaven; A Tree Grows in Brooklyn; The Dolly Sisters*

1946   *My Darling Clementine*

1947   *The Late George Appley; Daisy Kenyon*

1948   *Fort Apache; The Snake Pit; 3 Godfathers; Deep Waters*

1949   *The Fighting Kentuckian; Impact; It Happens Every Spring; A Letter to Three Wives*

1950   *When Willie Comes Marching Home; My Blue Heaven; The Gunfighter*

1951   *The Model and the Marriage Broker*
1952   *The Quiet Man; Night Without Sleep*
1953   *Titanic; The Sun Shines Bright; The Robe; A Blueprint for
        Murder*
1954   *A Star Is Born*
1955   *The Tall Men; Prince of Players; Hell on Frisco Bay; Good
        Morning Miss Dove*
1956   *The Searchers; While the City Sleeps; Julie; Girls in Prison*
1957   *The Wings of Eagles*
1958   *Cry Terror!*
1960   *Sergeant Rutledge; From the Terrace*
1961   *Two Rode Together*
1963   *Donovan's Reef*
1964   *Cheyenne Autumn*

Martin, Vivian (1893 Sparta, MI-1987 New York City)

Dubbed the "Dresden china figurine," Vivian Martin was born into a show business family, as her father was an actor in stock companies. She made her stage debut when another child actor became ill and she was on hand watching her father. She quickly became known for her children's roles in stock companies and made her Broadway debut in 1911.

Martin signed a film contract in 1914 and made her debut in the World Picture production of *The Wishing Ring: An Idyll in Old England*. The characters she played were generally the cheerful young waifs who withstood hardship and overcame obstacles to live happily ever after, a popular character type with audiences during the early years of film.

Although she was given little room for growth as an actor in her roles, she was very popular with audiences and briefly headed her own production company. Sadly, the film audience was not receptive to her appearing in any noningenue role, so Martin returned to the stage in the early 1920s.

After a two-year run on Broadway and a successful London tour, Martin toured the vaudeville circuit in her London play, *Just Married*. Later she returned to Broadway where she appeared successfully for many years before retiring after her second marriage to become a benefactor of the New York Professional Children's School.

Film Credits

1914   *The Wishing Ring: An Idyll in Old England*
1915   *Old Dutch; Arrival of Perpetua; The Little Miss Brown; The Little Dutch Girl; The Little Mademoiselle; A Butterfly on the Wheel; Over Night*
1916   *Merely Mary Ann; A Modern Thelma; The Stronger Love; Her Father's Son; The Right Direction*
1917   *The Wax Model; The Spirit of Romance; The Girl at Home; Giving Becky a Chance; Forbidden Paths; A Kiss for Susie; Little Miss Optimist; The Trouble Buster; Molly Entangled; The Fair Barbarian; The Sunset Trail*
1918   *A Petticoat Pilot; Unclaimed Goods; Viviette; Her Country First; Mirandy Smiles*
1919   *Jane Goes a' Wooing; You Never Saw Such a Girl; Little Comrade; The Home Town Girl; An Innocent Adventuress; Louisiana; The Third Kiss; His Official Fiancée*
1920   *The Song of the Soul; Husbands and Wives*
1921   *Mother Eternal; Pardon My French*
1924   *Soiled*

Mason, Shirley (1900 Brooklyn, NY-1979 Los Angeles, CA)

Along with her two sisters, Edna Flugrath and Viola Dana, Shirley Mason went into films. All three of them endured tragic loss in their personal lives. Led by a mother who was obsessed with her daughters becoming actors, Mason was only eleven years old when she appeared in her first film, *At the Threshold of Life* (1911).

She did not appear in another film until she was fifteen; since she was able to play more adult roles, she was signed by Edison Studios. In 1916 she married actor-turned-director Bernard Durning. By 1917 she was an established actor who appeared in thirteen films that year and was finally given lead credit.

In 1922 Mason was widowed when Durning died suddenly of typhoid fever. Recovering sufficiently from her loss, Mason returned to work. She now appeared in fewer films but made up for her lack of exposure by appearing in better films and in more important roles. Still, Mason did not make the transition to sound and appeared in her final film in 1929.

Film Credits

1910   *A Christmas Carol*

1911   *At the Threshold of Life; April Fool; Uncle Hiram's List*

1912   *Children Who Labor; Mary Had a Little Lamb*

1913   *The Risen Soul of Jim Grant; Her Royal Highness; The Dream Fairy; A Youthful Knight*

1915   *Shadows from the Past; Vanity Fair; The Portrait in the Attic; Blade o' Grass*

1916   *Celeste of the Ambulance Corps*

1917   *Envy; Where Love Is; Pride; Greed; Passion; The Law of the North; The Light in the Darkness; The Little Chevalier; The Lady of the Photograph; The Awakening of Ruth; The Apple Tree Girl; Cy Whittaker's Ward; Wrath; The Tell-Tale Step; The Seventh Sin; Sloth*

1918   *Come On In; Goodbye Bill; The Embarrassment of Riches*

1919   *The Final Close-Up; Putting It Over; The Unwritten Code; The Rescuing Angel; The Winning Girl; Secret Service*

1920   *Treasure Island; Love's Harvest; Merely Mary Ann; Flame of Youth; Molly and I; The Little Wanderer; Her Elephant Man; The Girl of My Heart; Dark Skies*

1921   *Wing Toy; The Lamplighter; The Mother Heart; Lovetime; Ever Since Eve; Queenie; Jackie*

1922   *Little Miss Smiles; The Ragged Heiress; Very Truly Yours; Lights of the Desert; The New Teacher; Youth Must Have Love; Shirley of the Circus; Pawn Ticket 210*

1923   *Lovebound; The Eleventh Hour; South Sea Love*

1924   *Love Letters; That French Lady; Great Diamond Mystery; My Husband's Wives; Star Dust Trail; Curlytop*

1925   *The Scarlet Honeymoon; The Talker; Scandal Proof; What Fools Men; Lord Jim*

1926   *Don Juan's Three Nights; Sweet Rosie O'Grady; Sin Cargo;
        Rose of the Tenements; Desert Gold*
1927   *The Wreck; Let It Rain; Rich Men's Sons; Stranded; Sally in
        Our Alley*
1928   *The Wife's Relations; Runaway Girls; Vultures of the Sea; So
        This Is Love?*
1929   *Anne Against the World; The Show of Shows; The Flying
        Marine; Dark Skies*

Mathis, June (1892 Leadville, CO-1927 New York City)

June Mathis, who was both a writer and an editorial director, was the first female head of a scenario department when she accepted that position at Metro in 1918. As logical as it sounds today, she developed the innovation of planning action prior to the beginning of filming. Mathis was instrumental in getting Metro to film *The Four Horseman of the Apocalypse* (1921) and having an unknown extra named Rudolph Valentino to star in the epic. The film earned Metro $4.5 million and was the top-grossing film of the 1920s.

After her success with *The Four Horsemen of the Apocalypse*, Mathis left Metro to work with Famous Players for a few months. Finally she settled into the position of story division director at Goldwyn. During her time at Goldwyn she worked on several of Alla Nazimova's films and wrote *Blood and Sand* (1922) to capitalize on Valentino's popularity. This film was also instrumental in getting its editor, Dorothy Arzner, the opportunity to direct.

Mathis's subtle handling of sex within the films that she wrote was ahead of her time, and she showed all aspects of a relationship—not just the facets approved by a society still recovering from the Victorian age. She was considered to be such a valuable asset to her employer that Samuel Goldwyn insured her life for $1 million at the height of her success. She is also known to have been instrumental in the negotiations for the formation of Metro-Goldwyn-Mayer.

Her next "insurmountable" assignment was to rewrite and reedit the von Stroheim's classic *Greed* (1923). Known for his excess in filming, von Stroheim had shot twenty-four reels, while the studio wanted the film to run only ten reels. To a great degree, Mathis is responsible for the film that many consider to be von Stroheim's crowning achievement.

One of Mathis's final projects was the adaptation of *Ben-Hur* (1926). She also acted as the on-location studio representative. The film is one of the classics of the silent era.

Writing Credits

1916   *The Upstart; Her Great Price; The Purple Lady; God's Half Acre; The Dawn of Love; The Sunbeam*

1917   *Lady Barnacle; Threads of Fate; The Barricade; His Father's Son; The Power of Decision; A Magdalene of the Hills; The Millionaire's Double; The Beautiful Lie; The Call of Her People; Aladdin's Other Lamp; Miss Robinson Crusoe; The Jury of Fate; Draft 258; Red, White and Blue Blood; Blue Jeans; The Trail of the Shadow; Somewhere in America; The Voice of Conscience*

1918   *Daybreak; The Winding Trail; The Eyes of Mystery; The Brass Check; The Claim; Social Hypocrites; With Neatness and Dispatch; Social Quicksands; The House of Gold; A Man's World; The House of Mirth; The Silent Woman; Kildare of Storm; His Bonded Wife; Five Thousand an Hour; Sylvia on a Spree; Eye for Eye; The Winning of Beatrice; A Successful Adventure; The Legion of Death; To Hell with the Kaiser!; The Trial of Yesterday; Toys of Fate; Secret Strings*

1919   *The Divorcee; Out of the Fog; Johnny-on-the-Spot; Satan Junior; Blind Man's Eyes; The Parisian Tigress; The Island of Intrigue; The Red Lantern; The Amateur Adventuress; Almost Married; Some Bride; The Man Who Stayed at Home; The Microbe; The Brat; Fair and Warmer; The Fall of the Hollenzolleerns; Lombardi Ltd.; Way of the Strong*

1920   *The Willow Tree; The Right Way; Old Lady 31; Parlor, Bedroom and Bath; The Price of Redemption; The Saphead; Polly with a Past; Hearts Are Trumps; The Walk-Offs; The Right of Way*

1921   *The Four Horsemen of the Apocalypse; The Man Who; The Conquering Power; A Trip to Paradise; The Idle Rich; Camille*

1922   *The Golden Gift; Turn to the Right; Kisses; Hate; Blood and Sand; The Young Rajah*

1923   *Three Wise Fools; The Spanish Dancer; The Day of Faith; In the Palace of the King*
1924   *Greed*
1925   *Sally; The Desert Flower; Classified; We Moderns; Ben-Hur*
1926   *Irene; The Greater Glory*
1927   *The Masked Woman; An Affair of the Follies; The Magic Flame*
1930   *Reno*

McAvoy, May (1899 New York City–1984 location unknown)

Courtesy of Silents Are Golden at <SilentsAreGolden.com>

Called a "star-eyed goddess" by Carl Sandburg, May McAvoy and her mother had planned for her to become a teacher. Although she originally had no interest in an entertainment career, after being offered a film role, McAvoy began to explore the possibility of a career in films.

As was the case with many silent film stars, McAvoy began her career as a model. After she turned her sights on a film career, she freelanced in New York, appearing with Lionel Barrymore in *The Devil's Garden* in 1920. But it was her performance as Grizel in the box office disaster *Sentimental Tommy* (1921) that brought her star status and a contract with Paramount.

She moved to Hollywood in 1922 and was so popular with film viewers that in 1923 she became the only film star to be crowned queen of the Tournament of Roses Parade, the New Year's Day spectacle in Pasadena, California. Even after being blackballed by her studio for refusing a role that required partial nudity, McAvoy had a successful freelance career and by 1925 was making $3,000 per week.

In 1926 she starred in an early special-effects film involving a prehistoric Nessie look-alike titled *The Savage,* and she appeared with Ramon Navarro in one of the most popular films of the decade, *Ben-Hur* (1925). She made film history when she appeared with Al Jolson in *The Jazz Singer* (1927), and the following year she appeared in her only all-talkie film, *The Terror* (1928).

She was one of the founding members of the Academy of Motion Picture Arts and Sciences in 1927. After appearing in *Caught in the Fog* (1928), McAvoy retired from films to marry United Artists executive Maurice Cleary. After her son was in school, McAvoy returned to play supporting roles into the 1950s.

Film Credits

1917 *Hate*
1918 *To Hell with the Kaiser; A Perfect Lady; I'll Say So*
1919 *Mrs. Wiggs of the Cabbage Patch; The Way of a Woman; The Woman Under Oath*
1920 *My Husband's Other Wife; The Sporting Duchess; Man and His Woman; House of the Tolling Bell; The Forbidden Valley; The Devil's Garden; The Truth About Husbands; Love Wins*
1921 *Sentimental Tommy; A Private Scandal; Everything for Sale; A Virginia Courtship; Morals*
1922 *A Homespun Vamp; Through a Glass Window; The Top of New York; Clarence; Kick In*
1923 *Grumpy; Only 38; Hollywood; Her Reputation*
1924 *West of the Water Tower; The Enchanted Cottage; The Bedroom Window; Three Women; Married Flirts; Tarnish*
1925 *The Mad Whirl; Tessie; Lady Windermere's Fan; Ben-Hur*
1926 *The Road to Glory; My Old Dutch; The Passionate Quest; The Savage; The Fire Brigade; Calf-Love*
1927 *Matinee Ladies; Irish Hearts; Slightly Used; The Jazz Singer; A Reno Divorce; If I Were Single*
1928 *The Little Snob; The Lion and the Mouse; Caught in the Fog; The Terror; May McAvoy in Sunny California* (Vitaphone Short)
1929 *Stolen Kisses; No Defense*
1940 *The New Pupil; Hollywood: Style Center of the World; Two Girls on Broadway; Phantom Raiders; Dulcy; Third Finger, Left Hand*
1941 *Whispers; Ringside Maisie; The Get-Away; 1-2-3 Go!*
1942 *Mr. Blabbermouth; Kid Glove Killer; Born to Sing*
1943 *Assignment in Brittany*

1944   *Movie Pests*
1948   *Luxury Liner*
1950   *Mystery Street*
1954   *Executive Suite*
1957   *The Wings of Eagles; Gun Glory*

McGuire, Kathryn (1903 Peoria, IL-1978 Los Angeles, CA)

Courtesy of Silents Are Golden at
<SilentsAreGolden.com>

Kathryn McGuire did not have a fabulous film career, but her career had several distinguishing facets to it. She was one of the first actors to be an animal's leading lady when she appeared with Strongheart in *The Silent Call* (1921). She also appeared in two of Buster Keaton's most popular films—*The Navigator* and *Sherlock, Jr.* (both 1924).

She began her career as a dancer while still in high school. In fact, the story goes that Thomas Ince discovered her performing in a high school variety program. She first appeared in comedy shorts with Mack Sennett and Lupino Lane in 1920 and by 1921 had graduated to comedy features and westerns. In 1922 she was chosen as one of the first WAMPAS Baby Stars.

In 1923 she appeared in *The Woman of Bronze* as a woman who models for a sculpture titled "Victory." This role led to the rumor that she was the woman depicted in the Columbia Pictures' logo holding the torch aloft, but the company never verified this. Although she continued to appear in supporting roles in films throughout the 1920s, she made only one talkie before retiring from the screen.

Film Credits

1919   *A Lady's Tailor*
1920   *Down on the Farm; Married Life*
1921   *Dabbling in Art; Home Talent; Bucking the Line; The Silent Call; Molly O'; Playing with Fire*
1922   *The Crossroads of New York*

1923   *The Flame of Life; The Shriek of Araby; The Printer's Devil; The Woman of Bronze; The Love Pirate*
1924   *Pioneer's Gold; Sherlock, Jr.; The Navigator; Phantom Justice*
1925   *Tearing Through; Easy Going Gordon; Two-Fisted Jones; The Gold Hunters*
1926   *The Thrill Hunter; Buffalo Bill on the U.P. Trail; Somebody's Mother; Midnight Faces; Stacked Cards; Dashing Thru; Davy Crockett at the Fall of the Alamo; Mystery Pilot; Howdy Duke*
1927   *Naughty but Nice; The Girl in the Pullman; Drama Deluxe*
1928   *Lilac Time*
1929   *Synthetic Sin; Children of the Ritz; The Border Wildcat; The Big Diamond Robbery; The Long Trail; The Lost Zeppelin; He Did His Best*
1930   *Love a la Mode*

McKinney, Nina Mae (1913 Lancaster, SC-1967 New York City)

Called "one of the most beautiful women of our time" by contemporary columnists, Nina Mae McKinney was the first black film star to cross over to white audiences. After appearing as the ill-fated Chick in *Hallelujah* (1929), she was given the title "the screen's first black love goddess."

Little is known of her early life until she made her professional debut in New York in 1928 in *Blackbirds*. The following year she was cast as the "good time girl" in King Vidor's attempt to realistically depict life among the blacks in the South. Although cited as one of the finest films of the early sound era, the film did not open doors for other black performers or, in any real sense, for McKinney herself.

Although McKinney was touted by Irving Thalberg as "one of the greatest discoveries of the age," she found it difficult to find roles after her success in *Hallelljah*. Even with a five-year contract with MGM, McKinney found it impossible to find any role other than stereotypical parts as comic sidekick or domestic worker. After MGM let her contract lapse, McKinney began touring the nightclub circuit.

She was well received in Europe when she took her act there and was dubbed the "Black Garbo." While in England she appeared with Paul Robeson in *Sanders of the River* (1935). She returned to the

United States to appear in *The Duke Is Tops* (1938), but had to be replaced due to an illness.

Once she recovered she appeared as a nurse-turned-singer in *Gang Smashers* (1938), but after that she appeared only in productions made for black theaters for several years. She returned to mainstream films in *Dark Waters* (1944), a successful thriller set in the Louisiana bayou. Later that year she appeared as a maid in *Together Again.*

She again returned to the nightclub circuit and was appearing in New York when she was called to appear in her final film. Finally, after years of supporting roles she was given a prominent role in *Pinky* (1949), although the film itself was almost anti-black with its "passing for white" premise. During the filming of *Pinky,* McKinney divorced her husband and, with her remarriage shortly afterward, retired from films.

Film Credits

1929	*Hallelujah*
1930	*They Learned About Women*
1931	*Safe in Hell*
1932	*Pie-Pie Blackbird*
1934	*Kentucky Minstrels; The Devil's Daughter*
1935	*Reckless; Sanders of the River*
1936	*The Lonely Trail; The Black Network*
1938	*On Velvet; Gang Smashers*
1939	*Straight to Heaven*
1940	*Swanee Showboat*
1944	*Together Again; Dark Waters*
1945	*The Power of the Whistler*
1946	*Night Train to Memphis; Mantan Messes Up*
1947	*Danger Street*
1949	*Pinky*
1950	*Copper Canyon*

McVey, Lucille (1890 Sedalia, MO-1925 Los Angeles, CA)

Little is known about Lucille McVey's early life in Missouri, but she was a stage actor before getting into films and joining the Vitagraph Company in 1913. There she met her future husband, actor

Sidney Drew. After their marriage in 1914 they appeared together in a series of domestic comedies that were very popular with audiences for their subtlety and good taste.

Much of the credit for the films was given to McVey for conceiving of the plots, and *Photoplay Magazine* noted in an article that "she is the team member who selects the idea and builds on it." The couple moved to Metro Studios in 1916 where she not only appeared with her husband but also wrote scenarios and directed films.

Soon after her husband, who was more than twice her age, died in 1919, she retired from acting but continued to write and direct until an illness made her curtail her activities. She died after an unspecified "long illness" in 1925.

Film Credits

1914   *Too Many Husbands; A Florida Enchantment; Auntie's Portrait*

1915   *Playing Dead; A Safe Investment; Fox Trot Finesse; Is Christmas a Bore?; Between the Two of Them; The Story of the Glove; Miss Sticky-Moufie-Kiss; His Wife Knew About It; By the Might of His Right*

1916   *Duplicity*

1917   *One of the Finest; Twelve Good Hens and True; Too Much Henry; Shadowing Henry; Safety First; Rubbing It In; The Pest; The Patriot; Lest We Forget; Hypochondriacs; His Double Life; His Deadly Calm; His Curiosity; Her Lesson; Her First Love; Her Economic Independence; Her Anniversaries; Henry's Ancestors; The Dentist; A Close Resemblance; As Others See Us; Her Obsession; Caveman's Buff*

1918   *A Youthful Affair; Pay Day; Special Today; His First Love; Gas Logic; Before and After Taking; After Henry; Why Henry Left Home; Why They Left Home*

1919   *Romance and Rings; Once a Mason; The Amateur Liar; Harold, the Last of the Saxons; Bunkered; A Sisterly Scheme; Squared; A Gay Old Dog*

1920   *The Charming Mrs. Chase; The Emotional Miss Vaughn*

Writing Credits

1915 *Playing Dead*
1917 *Why They Left Home; Too Much Henry; Shadowing Henry; Safety First; Rubbing It In; The Pest; The Patriot; Lest We Forget; His Curiosity; Her Lesson; Her Anniversaries; A Close Resemblance*
1918 *A Youthful Affair; Pay Day; Special Today; His First Love; Gas Logic; Before and After Taking; After Henry; Why Henry Left Home*
1919 *Romance and Rings; Once a Mason; The Amateur Liar; Harold, the Last of the Saxons; Bunkered; A Sisterly Scheme; A Gay Old Dog; Squared*
1920 *The Charming Mrs. Chase; The Emotional Miss Vaughn*
1921 *Cousin Kate*

Directing Credits

1917 *Why They Left Home; Too Much Henry; Shadowing Henry; Safety First; Rubbing It In; The Pest; The Patriot; Lest We Forget; His Curiosity; Her Lesson; Her Anniversaries; A Close Resemblance*
1918 *Pay Day; Special Today; His First Love; Gas Logic; Before and After Taking; After Henry; Why Henry Left Home*
1919 *Once a Mason; Harold, the Last of the Saxons; Bunkered; A Sisterly Scheme; Squared; Amateur Liar*
1920 *The Charming Mrs. Chase*
1921 *Cousin Kate*

Mercer, Beryl (1862 Seville, Spain-1939 Santa Monica, CA)

Beryl Mercer was born into an entertainment family; her father was a Spanish diplomat, and her mother was the famed actor Beryl Montague. Because she often toured with her mother, Mercer's first stage appearance was made when she was four years old. By the age of ten she had decided that acting was to be her career, and she excelled at "boy" stage roles in London. As she became older she transferred to ingenue roles. Her American stage debut was in 1906 at the Lyric Theatre.

Her American screen debut was in *The Final Curtain* in 1916, but she returned to the stage. Her next screen appearance was in *Broken Chains* (1922), after which she went on to play character roles as charming, if sometimes bewildered, old ladies. She was appearing in films up to her unexpected death in 1939 following a major operation.

Film Credits

1916   *The Final Curtain*
1922   *Broken Chains*
1923   *The Christian*
1928   *We Americans*
1929   *Three Live Ghosts; Mother's Boy*
1930   *Seven Days' Leave; All Quiet on the Western Front; Dumb-bells in Ermine; In Gay Madrid; Common Clay; The Matrimonial Bed; Outward Bound*
1931   *Inspiration; The Public Enemy; Always Goodbye; The Miracle Woman; Sky Spider; Forgotten Woman; Merely Mary Ann; The Man in Possession; East Lynne; Inspiration; Are These Our Children?*
1932   *Lovers Courageous; Devil's Lottery; Young America; Unholy Love; Midnight Morals; Smilin' Through; Six Hours to Live; No Greater Love; Lena Rivers*
1933   *Supernatural; Blind Adventure; Cavalcade; Her Splendid Folly; Broken Dreams; Berkeley Square*
1934   *Change of Heart; Jane Eyre; The Richest Girl in the World; The Little Minister*
1935   *Age of Indiscretion; Magnificent Obsession; Hitch Hike Lady; My Marriage*
1936   *Three Live Ghosts; Forbidden Heaven*
1937   *Call It a Day; Night Must Fall*
1939   *The Little Princess; The Hound of Baskervilles; The Story of Alexander Graham Bell; A Woman Is the Judge*

Meredyth, Bess (1890 Buffalo, NY-1969 Woodland Hills, CA)

Bess Meredyth began her show business career as a singer in vaudeville before she gravitated to the film industry. While visiting the Los Angeles area in the mid-1910s, she decided to try acting. She began working as an extra for D. W. Griffith and appeared in a series of "Bess" comedy films.

She soon realized, however, that her true talents lay in writing, so she left acting to concentrate on scenario writing. Although she had written one film earlier, she didn't start getting regular writing credit until 1914. Between 1917 and 1919 she wrote over ninety features. In addition, during the 1910s she directed some of the films she wrote, such as *The Romance of Tarzan* (1918), but she always returned to writing.

She was one of the thirty-six founding members of the Academy of Motion Picture Arts and Sciences. Although she made the transition to sound, she received her only nomination for the Oscar for Best Writing on the basis of two silent films, *A Woman of Affairs* (1928) and *Wonder of Women* (1929).

Writing Credits

1910   *The Modern Prodigal*
1913   *Cross Purposes; The Gratitude of Wanda; The Mystery of Yellow Aster Mine*
1914   *The Forbidden Room; Cupid Incognito; The Way of a Woman; Woman and Roses; The Countess Betty's Mine; The Love Victorious; The Mystery of Wickham Hall; Passing the Love of Woman; The Trey of Hearts; The Voice of the Viola; The Severed Hand; When Bess Got It Wrong*
1915   *The Blood of the Children; The Fear Within; The Ghost Wagon; The Human Menace; In His Mind's Eye; The Mystery Woman; Putting One Over; Their Hour; The Fascination of the Fleur de Lis; Stronger Than Death; A Woman's Debt; Wheels Within Wheels*
1916   *Spellbound; The Mother Instinct; The Twin Triangle; Pretty Baby; Bringing Home Father; The White Turkey; The Wedding Guest; A Thousand Dollars a Week; The Soda Clerk; The Small Magnetic Hand; A Price on His Head; Pass the Prunes; Number 16 Martin Street; Borrowed Plumes; Breaking Into Society; Cross Purposes; The Decoy; Fame at Last; From the Rogues; He Almost Lands an Angel; He Becomes a Cop; The Heart of a Show Girl; A Hero by Proxy; Hired and Fired; It Sounded Like a Kiss*

1917 *The Little Orphan; The Midnight Man; Pay Me; Scandal; The Girl Who Lost; His Wife's Relatives; The Light of Love; A Million in Sight; One Thousand Miles an Hour; Practice What You Preach; Three Women of France; The Townsend Divorce Case; Treat 'Em Rough; A Five Foot Ruler; Why, Uncle!; A Wife's Suspicion*

1918 *Morgan's Raiders; The Red, Red Heart; The Devil Bateese; The Romance of Tarzan; The Man Who Wouldn't Tell; The Grain of Dust; Pretty Babies*

1919 *Girl from Nowhere; Big Little Person*

1920 *The Man From Kangaroo; The Jackeroo of Coolabong*

1921 *The Fighting Breed; The Shadow on Lightning Ridge; The Grim Comedian*

1922 *The Song of Life; The Woman He Married; Rose o' the Sea; One Clear Call; Grand Larceny; A Macaroni Sleuth*

1923 *The Dangerous Age; Strangers of the Night*

1924 *Thy Name Is Woman; The Red Lily*

1925 *A Slave of Fashion; The Wife Who Wasn't Wanted; Ben-Hur; The Love Hour*

1926 *The Sea Beast; Don Juan*

1927 *When a Man Loves; Irish Hearts; Rose of the Golden West; The Magic Flame*

1928 *Sailor's Wives; The Little Shepherd of Kingdom Come; Yellow Lily; The Scarlet Lady; The Mysterious Lady; A Woman of Affairs*

1929 *Wonder of Women*

1930 *Chasing Rainbows; In Gay Madrid; Our Blushing Brides; Romance; The Sea Bat*

1931 *Laughing Sinners; West of Broadway; The Prodigal; The Phantom of Paris; The Cuban Love Song*

1932 *Strange Interlude*

1933 *Looking Forward*

1934 *The Affairs of Cellini; The Mighty Barnum; The Iron Duke*

1935 *Metropolitan; Folies-Bergère; de Paris*

1936 *Half Angel; Under Two Flags; Charlie Chan at the Opera; The Great Hospital Mystery*

1940 *The Mark of Zorro*

1941 *That Night in Rio*

1947 *The Unsuspected*

Directing Credits

1914   *Cupid Incognito*
1918   *Morgan's Raiders; The Romance of Tarzan*
1919   *Girl from Nowhere*

Film Credits

1912   *A Sailor's Heart*
1913   *Bred in the Bone; Gold Is Not All*
1914   *Stolen Glory; Dangers of the Veldt; Bessie the Detectress in the Dog Watch; The Call Back; The Fascinating Eye; Father's Bride; Her Twin Brother; The Little Autogomobile; When Bess Got in Wrong; When Lizzie Got Her Polish; Willy Walrus and the Awful Confession; Willy Walrus and the Baby; Willy Walrus and the Parisians; Willy Walrus, Detective; The Wooing of Bessie Bumpkin; Bessie the Detectress in the Old Mill at Midnight; Bessie the Detectress in Tick! Tick! Tick!; The Spanish Jade; The Mother Instinct*

Mersereau, Violet (1892 New York City- 1975 Plymouth, MA)

After her father's death, Violet Mersereau's mother, who had been an actor in France, returned to the stage. By the time she was ten, both Violet and her sister had joined their mother as actors. Mersereau was a successful child actor and toured with various companies until she made her film debut in 1908. Since she was a very private person who avoided granting interviews, many of the details of her early life have been lost.

She first worked with D. W. Griffith at Biograph from 1908 to 1911, then signed with the Nestor Company to appear in ingenue roles. With her blond hair and large expressive eyes she made the perfect "helpless" ingenue so popular during the silent era. She continued in this type of role, at one point being IMP's leading ingenue star.

Her career peaked while she was under contract with Universal, and after she left that studio in 1919 her career stalled. Audience tastes had changed and viewers no longer embraced the Victorian girl-women characters that were Mersereau's specialty. Both she and her sister retired from show business in the early 1920s and in the 1940s were reported to be living in New York.

Film Credits

1908   *The Feud and the Turkey; The Test of Friendship*
1909   *The Suicide Club; The Cricket on the Hearth; The Violin Maker of Cremona; The Friend of the Family; One Busy Hour; The Jilt; Eloping with Auntie; Her Duty; The Lonely Villa; Her First Biscuits; Peachbasket Hat; The Way of Men; His First Love; What's Your Hurry?*
1910   *Her Terrible Ordeal; One Night and Then; A Gold Necklace; Sunshine Sue; Not So Bad As It Seemed; The Passing Grouch*
1911   *His Trust; His Trust Fulfilled; Alias Yellowstone Joe; Help Wanted; The Cowpuncher; The Sheriff's Mistake; At Sunset Ranch; Over the Hills*
1912   *An Even Break; Her First Choice; The Shot That Failed; A Western Girl's Dream; The New Clerk*
1913   *Big Sister; Binks, the Hawkshaw; Stranger*
1914   *In Self Defense; Peg o' the Wilds; Redemption; The Tenth Commandment; When the Heart Calls; The Spitfire*
1915   *The Avalanche; The Alibi; The Wolf of Debt; Uncle John; The Treason of Anatole; The Blank Page; The Adventure of the Yellow Curl Papers; The Awaited Hour; Billy's Love Making; Destiny's Trump Card; Copper; The Destroyer; Driven by Fate; Getting His Goat; On Dangerous Ground; She Was His Mother; The Stake; The Supreme Impulse; Uncle's New Blazer; The Unnecessary Sex; Wild Blood; You Can't Always Tell; The Broken Toy; Larry O'Neill, Gentleman; Thou Shalt Not Lie*
1916   *The Path of Happiness; The Great Problem; Autumn; Broken Fetters; The Narrow Path; The Honor of Mary Blake; The Angel in the Attic; The Doll Doctor; The Gentle Art of Burglary; The Girl Who Didn't Tell; The Go-Between; His Picture*

1917   *The Boy Girl; Little Miss Nobody; The Little Terror; The Raggedy Queen; The Girl by the Roadside; Susan's Gentleman; Soul's United*

1918   *The Midnight Flyer; The Mystery of My Lady's Boudoir; Morgan's Raiders; Together*

1919   *The Nature Girl; Klever Kiddies; Proxy Husband*

1920   *Love Wins*

1921   *Out of the Depths; Thunderclap; Finders Keepers*

1922   *Nero*

1923   *Luck*

1924   *Lend Me Your Husband; Her Own Free Will*

1925   *The Shepherd King*

1926   *The Wives of the Prophet*

Miller, Patsy Ruth (1904 St. Louis, MO-1995 Palm Desert, CA)

Patsy Ruth Miller, dubbed "The Most Engaged Girl in Hollywood" by columnists in recognition of her romantic exploits, was multitalented and began her film career as a protégé of famed Russian émigré Alla Nazimova. She appeared in several of the classics of silent films, including Nazimova's *Camille* and *The Sheik* (both 1921). Her first major success was as romantic lead opposite Charles Ray in *The Girl I Loved* (1923).

Prior to her success in this film, Miller was named a WAMPAS Baby Star in 1922. The following year she appeared in the classic *The Hunchback of Notre Dame,* opposite Lon Chaney, as the alluring Esmerelda.

Miller could play both dramatic and comedic roles, and she achieved a moderate success in silent films in their final years. After signing a contract with Warner Bros. in 1925, she was always billed as the female lead. One of her most popular films was the Lubitsch comedy *So This Is Paris* (1926), followed two years later by another hit, *Marriage by Contract* (1928).

She made the transition to sound films, appearing in several comedies during the early years of the new medium. However, by 1931 her film output had dwindled to almost nil and she retired from films. She appeared in regional theater throughout the 1930s, but her major endeavor was as a writer.

Although she published some short stories as early as the 1930s, she began writing in earnest after her retirement in 1932 while she lived abroad prior to World War II. One of her plays, *The Windy Hill*, was produced and she wrote several books on a variety of topics. Her autobiography, *My Hollywood*, was published in 1988, as a combination autobiography and chronicle of the making of *The Hunchback of Notre Dame*.

Miller was a groundbreaker in a completely unrelated field. She received her pilot's license in the days when flying was considered too technical for women.

Film Credits

1921   *One a Minute; The Sheik; Camille*
1922   *Handle with Care; The Fighting Streak; For Big Stakes; Trimmed; Remembrance; Watch Your Step; Omar the Tentmaker; Fortune's Mask; Where's My Wandering Boy Tonight?*
1923   *The Girl I Loved; Souls for Sale; The Drivin' Fool; The Hunchback of Notre Dame*
1924   *Name the Man; Daughters of Today; The Yankee Consul; Singer Jim McKee; The Breaking Point; A Self-Made Failure; Girls Men Forgot; Fools in the Dark; The Wise Virgin; The Breath of Scandal; Those Who Judge; My Man; A Hero for the Night*
1925   *Her Husband's Secret; Back to Life; Head Winds; Lorraine of the Lions; Red Hot Tires; Rose of the World; Hogan's Alley; The Girl on the Stairs*
1926   *The Fighting Edge; The King of the Turf; Why Girls Go Home; Hell-Bent for Heaven; So This Is Paris; Broken Hearts of Hollywood; Private Izzy Murphy; The White Black Sheep; Oh, What a Nurse!*

1927   *Wolf's Clothing; What Every Girl Should Know; The First Auto; Painting the Town; Once and Forever; Shanghaied; South Sea Love; A Hero for a Night*

1928   *The Tragedy of Youth; Red Riders of Canada; We Americans; Hot Heels; Beautiful But Dumb; Marriage by Contract; The Gate Crasher; Tropical Nights*

1929   *The Fall of Eve; Twin Beds; The Hottentot; The Aviator; The Show of Shows; Whispering Winds; So Long Letty; The Sap*

1930   *Wide Open; The Last of the Lone Wolf*

1931   *Lonely Wives; Night Beat; The Great Junction Hotel*

1932   *The Talians*

1951   *Quebec*

Minter, Mary Miles (1902 Shreveport, LA-Santa Monica, CA)

Courtesy of Silents Are Golden at <SilentsAreGolden.com>

Born into a wealthy Southern family, Mary Miles Minter's real name was Juliet, perhaps preordaining her to a show business career. After her parents divorced, she went to New York with her mother where her mother pursued an acting career. Since a stigma was still connected to acting, her mother changed the family name to "Shelby."

Minter was a beautiful child, and soon "Little Juliet Shelby" was one of Broadway's most popular child actors. Because Minter achieved success that her mother could not match, her mother became her daughter's manager and gave up her acting aspirations.

While appearing on Broadway in *The Littlest Rebel,* Minter made her screen debut in *The Nurse* (1912). Because of her youth, Minter came under the scrutiny of the Gerry Society which monitored child actors. To alleviate any interference in her daughter's career, her mother "borrowed" the birth certificate of a dead cousin and Minter was suddenly a seventeen-year-old "midget" instead of a ten-year-old child.

Minter began concentrating on film roles by 1914 and received enthusiastic reviews of her performance as the fairy in *The Fairy and the Waif* (1915). In 1916 Minter signed with the American Film Company and was promoted as "the Crown Princess of the Motion Picture."

In 1918 Minter signed a contract with Paramount to make twenty films over a five-year period with a guaranteed salary of $1.3 million over the period of the contract. The first film made under this contract, *Anne of Green Gables* (1919), directed by William Desmond Taylor, is considered by many historians to be Minter's finest film.

Supposedly because of her estrangement from her father, Minter gravitated to older men as substitute father figures. She was drawn to Taylor as she continued to work with him and eventually declared herself in love. At the prospect of losing control of her daughter, Minter's mother refused to allow her daughter to continue to work with Taylor.

However, Minter continued to see Taylor socially in, perhaps, her first rebellion against her mother's control over her life. But her rebellion became a moot point when Taylor was found shot to death in February 1922. Minter never completely recovered from the tragedy, both personally and professionally.

Once Minter was associated with the murder investigation Paramount did not believe that she would be believable in her normal demurely innocent ingenue roles. Paramount suggested a role in an upcoming western but Minter's mother refused to allow her daughter to appear in an "inferior" film. Her mother demanded that Paramount buy out her daughter's contract and, surprisingly, they did for $350,000. Minter walked out of Paramount Studios and never made another film.

Soon after her retirement she sued her mother over mismanagement of the money she made while in films, resulting in a trust fund being established for her. She later entered into several successful business enterprises including an antique business and a real estate partnership.

After her mother died in 1957, Minter married her real-estate partner and their business allowed for them to live comfortably. After her husband's death, Minter continued to live in the Los Angeles area, but in 1981 tragedy once more struck her. She was left for dead in her home after being severely beaten; a former servant was implicated. She recovered from her injuries but a few years later suffered a fatal heart attack.

After her death, a woman came forward claiming to be Minter's illegitimate daughter and produced a will stating the she was the only beneficiary of the Minter estate. The legal battle lasted almost twenty years before the woman's claims were proved invalid.

Film Credits

1912	*The Nurse*
1915	*The Fairy and the Waif; Always in the Way; Emmy of Stork's Nest; Barbara Frietchie*
1916	*Rose of the Alley; Dimples; Lovely Mary; Sally in Our Alley; Dulcie's Adventure; Faith; A Dream or Two Ago; Innocence of Lizette; Youth's Enduring Charm*
1917	*The Gentle Intruder; Environment; Annie-for-Spite; Her Country's Call; Periwinkle; Melissa of the Hills; Charity Castle; Peggy Leads the Way; The Mate of Sally Ann; Somewhere in America*
1918	*Beauty and the Rogue; Powers That Prey; A Bit of Jade; Social Briars; The Ghost of Rosy Taylor; Wives and Other Wives; Rosemary Climbs the Heights; The Eyes of Julia Deep*
1919	*The Amazing Imposter; The Intrusion of Isabel; A Bachelor's Wife; Yvonne from Paris; Anne of Green Gables; Onze filmsterren* (France)
1920	*Judy of Rogue's Harbor; Nurse Marjorie; Jenny Be Good; A Cumberland Romance; Eyes of the Heart; Sweet Lavender*
1921	*Moonlight and Honeysuckle; The Little Clown; Her Winning Ways; Don't Call Me Little Girl; All Souls' Eve*
1922	*Tillie; The Heart Specialist; South of Suva; The Cowboy and the Lady*
1923	*Drums of Fate; The Trail of Lonesome Pine*
1924	*A Sainted Devil*

Montgomery, "Baby" Peggy (1918 Merced, CA-)

"Baby" Peggy Montgomery, who some historians call the "Shirley Temple of her era," was discovered when she was only nineteen months old. Her father worked with Tom Mix and while visiting a nearby studio with her mother and a neighbor, Montgomery was cast opposite one of the silent era's dog-stars, Brownie.

When the film was a success, Montgomery was put under contract to Century Studios and in the next three years made nearly 150 two-reel films. Sadly, most of these films have been lost. Her first feature-length film was *The Darling of New York* (1923) for her new studio Universal. Her first feature outing was a success and was closely followed by an even bigger film, *Captain January* (1924).

Although only five years old, in 1923 Montgomery was getting as many as 1.7 million fan letters a year and five women worked full time to keep up with the mail volume. But by the end of 1924, Montgomery had lost her star status. During the 1930s she attempted a comeback but was considered a has-been at sixteen.

After many years of "being lost," Montgomery found a new career as a freelance magazine writer in the 1950s, writing under the name Diana Serra Cary. Her new identity gave her the confidence that she had lost with the end of her acting career. In 1975 she published her first book, *Hollywood Posse: The Story of a Gallant Band of Horsemen Who Made Movie History*, about the real cowboys who worked in early film westerns.

Hollywood's Children: An Inside Account of the Child Star Era (1978), a book about the many children who had worked in films, followed her first success and was eventually made into a documentary for PBS. In 1996 Montgomery published her autobiography, *Whatever Happened to Baby Peggy?* She also published a book on a longtime friend, *Jackie Coogan: The World's Boy King—A Biography of Hollywood's Legendary Child Star*, in 2003.

Film Credits

1921   *Her Circus Man; On with the Show; The Kid's Pal; Playmates; On Account; Pals; Third Class Male; The Clean Up; Golfing; Brownie's Little Venus; Sea Shoe Shapes; A Week Off; A Muddy Bride; Brownie's Baby Doll; Get-Rich-Quick Peggy; Teddy's Goat; Chums*

1922   *The Straphanger; Circus Clowns; Little Miss Mischief; Peggy Behave!; The Little Rascal; Tips*

1923   *Peg o' the Movies; Sweetie; The Kid Reporter; Taking Orders; Carmen, Jr.; Nobody's Darling; Hollywood; Miles of Smiles; The Darling of New York; Hansel and Gretel*

1924   *Such Is Life; Peg o' the Mounted; The Law Forbids; Our Pet; The Flower Girl; Stepping Some; Poor Kid; Captain January; Jack and the Beanstalk; The Family Secret; Helen's Babies*

1925   *Little Red Riding Hood; There He Goes*

1926   *April Fool*

1932   *Hollywood on Parade; Off His Base*

1934   *Eight Girls in a Boat*

1935   *Ah, Wilderness!*

1936   *Girls' Dormitory*

1937   *True Confession*

1938   *Having Wonderful Time*

Moore, Colleen (1900 Port Huron, MI-1988 Paso Robles, CA)

Courtesy of Silents Are Golden at <SilentsAreGolden.com>

Called "the Torch of the Flaming Youth" of the 1920s by F. Scott Fitzgerald, Colleen Moore was born into a middle-class family. Moore went to private schools, studying music at the prestigious Detroit Conservatory. The family moved several times, but Moore later stated that she could not remember her parents ever arguing and, unlike many silent film stars, raved about her happy childhood. Enamored with acting as a youth, Moore kept scrapbooks on her favorite stars and dreamed of joining the ranks of the great film actors of the day.

She performed plays on her homemade stage for other neighborhood children, and while still a teenager she entered the film industry with the help of her uncle who was editor of a Chicago newspaper. She began appearing as an extra in 1916, after it was determined that her distinctive eyes—one brown and one blue—would not appear different on film. After starring as Annie in *Little Orphant Annie* (1918), she was on her way to joining her idols.

After appearing in several films opposite cowboy star Tom Mix, Moore appeared in the film that would associate her forever with the disenfranchised youth of the era, *Flaming Youth* (1923). Her character's pageboy-styled hair and long bangs became her trademark and created a hairstyling fad.

By 1927 she was earning $12,500 per week and was the top box-office draw in the United States. She was a gifted comedian as well as a talented dramatic actor, but her success in *Flaming Youth* caused her to be typecast in flapper roles. The films in which she tried to break from that character were not as successful. One of her dramatic roles was as Jeannine in *Lilac Time* (1928). In this film she portrayed a French peasant who fell in love with one of the pilots (Gary Cooper) whose landing field was near her family's home.

Her first talking film was *Smiling Irish Eyes* (1929), and Moore thought that the film was dull and uninteresting—mostly because the technique she used was the same one used in silent films. With the advent of sound, acting methods had to change and this, as much as inappropriate voices, doomed many silent actors. Moore worked on the stage for a few years then tried a comeback in films in the early 1930s.

Unfortunately, the public didn't want their favorite flapper to grow up, so Moore left films. After her retirement in 1934, she traveled widely, often exhibiting her custom-made dollhouses to benefit children's charities. She finally settled on a large ranch outside of Templeton, California. Unlike other stars of the period, Moore handled her money wisely and even wrote two books on investing after she retired. She wrote her autobiography, *Silent Star,* in 1968.

Film Credits

1916   *The Prince of Graustark*
1917   *The Bad Boy; An Old Fashioned Young Man; The Little American; The Savage; Hands Up!*
1918   *A Hoosier Romance; Little Orphant Annie*
1919   *The Busher; The Man in the Moonlight; The Egg Crate Wallop; Common Property; The Wilderness Trail; A Roman Scandal*

1920   *The Devil's Claim; Dinty; When Dawn Came; So Long Letty;
Her Bridal Night Mare; The Cyclone*

1921   *The Sky Pilot; His Nibs; The Lotus Eater*

1922   *Come On Over; Affinities; Broken Chains; The Ninety and
Nine; The Wall Flower; Forsaking All Others*

1923   *Look Your Best; The Nth Commandment; Slippy McGee; The
Huntress; April Showers; Broken Hearts of Broadway;
Flaming Youth*

1924   *Through the Dark; The Perfect Flapper; Flirting with Love;
So Big; Painted People*

1925   *Sally; The Desert Flower; We Moderns; Ben-Hur*

1926   *Irene; Ella Cinders; It Must Be Love; Twinkletoes*

1927   *Orchids and Ermine; Naughty but Nice; Her Wild Oat*

1928   *Happiness Ahead; Lilac Time; Oh Kay!*

1929   *Synthetic Sin; Smiling Irish Eyes; Footlights and Fools; Why
Be Good?*

1933   *The Power and the Glory; Turn Back the Clock*

1934   *The Social Register; Success at Any Price; The Scarlet Letter*

Moran, Polly (1883 Chicago, IL-1952 Los Angeles, CA)

Once called "the most traveled vaudeville performer in the world," Polly Moran quit school and joined a touring company when she was fifteen years old. As she honed her singing and acting skills, she moved to stage musicals and vaudeville, where she continued to appear for twenty years. In her twenties she toured the United States, England, Europe, and South Africa with an act known for its ribald burlesque humor.

Because she was so popular with vaudeville audiences, she made a film, *The Janitor* (1914), to see if she could transfer her popularity to the new medium. She attracted the attention of Mack Sennett and signed a contract with Keystone, becoming one of the studio's most popular comics as, among other characters, "Sheriff Nell."

Her style, like most comics of the period, was physical slapstick, and she was always ready to take a fall for a laugh. She returned briefly to the stage in 1918 but was again making films—this time features—in 1921. She now specialized in comic relief character roles.

In 1927 she was paired with Marie Dressler and together they made several popular films that were the perfect mixture of comedy laced with tragedy. Moran called their collaboration a blending of "two heavyweight hags" but deeply respected the more experienced Dressler whom she called "Queen Marie."

After Dressler's death Moran never achieved the popularity that she had enjoyed while they were teamed, but she continued to appear in films sporadically for several years. She made headlines again in 1936 when her husband tried to shoot her after he was called "Mr. Moran."

Film Credits

1914 *The Janitor*
1915 *Hogan Out West; Ambrose's Little Hatchet; Caught in the Act; The Beauty Bunglers; Their Social Splash; Hash House Fraud; Those College Girls; A Rascal's Foolish Ways; Her Painted Hero; A Favorite Fool; Fatty and the Broadway Stars; The Hunt; Because He Loved Her*
1916 *Love Will Conquer; A Movie Star; The Village Blacksmith; An Oily Scoundrel; By Stork Delivery; A Bathhouse Blunder; Safety First Ambrose; His Wild Oats; Madcap Ambrose; Vampire Ambrose; Pills of Peril*
1917 *Her Fame and Shame; Cactus Nell; She Needed a Doctor; His Uncle Dudley; Roping Her Romeo; The Pullman Bride; Taming Target Center; His Naughty Thought*
1918 *Grauman Special; Sheriff Nell's Tussle; Saucy Madeline; Two Tough Tenderfeet; The Battle Royal; She Loved Him Plenty*
1920 *Sheriff Nell's Comeback*
1921 *Skirts; Two Weeks with Pay; The Affairs of Anatol; High & Dry*
1923 *Luck*

1926   *The Scarlet Letter; The Blackbird; Stranded in Paris*
1927   *Flesh and the Devil; The Callahans and the Murphys; The Thirteenth Hour; Smith's Cook; London After Midnight; Buttons; The Unknown; Are Brunettes Safe?; The Enemy*
1928   *Rose-Marie; The Enemy; Bringing Up Father; The Divine Woman; Telling the World; While the City Sleeps; Beyond the Sierras; Show People; Shadows of the Night; Detective; A Lady of Chance; Honeymoon*
1929   *China Bound; Honeymoon; Speedway; Dangerous Females; Hollywood Revue of 1929; Unholy Night; Hot for Paris; So This Is College?*
1930   *Chasing Rainbows; The Girl Said No; Caught Short; Way Out West; Way for a Sailor; Those Three French Girls; Remote Control; The Rounder; Crazy Horse; Paid*
1931   *Reducing; It's a Wise Child; Politics; Guilty Hands; The Slippery Pearls*
1932   *Jackie Cooper's Christmas; The Passionate Plumber; Prosperity*
1933   *Alice in Wonderland*
1934   *Hollywood Party; Down to Their Last Yacht*
1936   *Oh Duchess!*
1937   *Sailor Maid; Two Wise Maids*
1938   *Ladies in Distress; Red River Range*
1939   *Ambush*
1940   *Tom Brown's School Days; Meet the Missus*
1941   *Petticoat Politics*
1949   *Adam's Rib; Red Light; Prize Maid*
1950   *The Yellow Cab Man*

Motion Picture Patents Company (1908)

By 1908 it was obvious that films were not just a passing fad and could, in fact, become very profitable. To cash in on this trend, many studios were established and put out great quantities of films that were not very well done. To stem the incursion of these studios, or "factories" as they were called, ten established film producers and equipment manufacturers banded together to create the Motion Picture Patents Company (MPPC) in 1908.

These companies—Edison, Vitagraph, Biograph, Lubin, Selig, Kalem, Essanay, Pathe Exchange, Méliès, and Gaumont—assigned all their patents to Edison and proclaimed that no one else could produce, distribute, or exhibit films without being licensed to do so by them. The Trust, as it was called, proclaimed that by their actions they were bringing organization and standardization to a chaotic industry.

They established fees and a royalty schedule that many other companies ignored. This meant that MPPC was often involved in a constant stream of lawsuits trying to enforce their patents. When legal means failed, the Trust was not averse to using muscle to get their point across. In fact, Hollywood supposedly became a popular film production site because Trust violators could easily make it across the border to Mexico if things got rough.

To distribute MPPC members' films, they created the General Film Company in 1910. This new company put many small distributors out of business. William Fox brought suits against General in a legal battle that lasted four years (1913-1917). In 1917 the court ruled that MPPC had to "discontinue (their) unlawful acts" as being a restraint to business, a decision that led to the company's dissolution. However, by the time the ruling went into force only one of the original companies, Biograph, was still in business.

Munson, Audrey (1891 New York City-1996 Ogdensburg, NY)

Audrey Munson was considered to be "the girl with the ideal figure" and was the world's first model-celebrity or "super model." She posed for almost every important Beaux-Arts sculpture in the United States. She can be seen as "Peace" on the New York Appellate Court House and as "Angels" in the stained glass window at the Church of Ascension in New York; she was the model for all the female figures on the monument to the Battleship Maine in Columbus Circle, and she watches over New York City as "Civic Fame" on the top of the Municipal Building in Manhattan.

She was raised in Providence, Rhode Island, where she studied music and dance as a child. When her parents divorced, she moved with her mother to New York City. Soon she was one of the most sought-after models in the city.

Munson hadn't reached the age of sixteen when she posed nude for the first time; the resulting "Three Graces" was the center of the lobby of the lavish Astor Hotel for many years. As the work got under way to create the art for San Francisco's Panama Pacific International Exposition of 1915, Munson posed for 75 percent of the sculpture and 24,000 feet of murals used to adorn the exhibits, as well as the memorial coin to commemorate the exposition. As a result of this exposure she was christened "the Exposition Girl."

She segued this notoriety into a film career and was one of the first women to appear nude on film. Of course, the nudity was justified as "art" and the film, *Inspiration* (1915), premiered before the end of the Exposition. She appeared in three other mundane films made interesting only by her nude scenes.

In 1919 Munson was the focal point of a murder trial when her landlord killed his wife in order to be free to marry the unsuspecting Munson. Although neither she nor her mother were aware of the man's obsession, the lurid details of the crime eventually ruined Munson's career. With the adverse publicity connected to her name, no photographer or artist was willing to have his work damaged by an association with her. In addition, the type of representational sculpture for which she was know was going out of style. Munson found herself living in poverty.

She had her life story as an artist's model ghostwritten, and the installments appeared in many Sunday newspaper supplements throughout the United States. She also received publicity with the announcement that she was looking for the "perfect male" to marry—and she received more than 200 applications. She supposedly wrote her final film, *Heedless Moths* (1921), said to be largely autobiographical.

Munson's behavior became increasingly bizarre, and her neighbors in the small town in which she and her mother lived began calling her "Crazy Audrey." By 1931 she was ordered into a treatment facility and her mother committed her to a state-run institution. Munson spent the remaining sixty-five years of her life institutionalized, although she needed no medication and was no danger to herself or others.

Film Credits

1915   *Inspiration*
1916   *Purity*
1918   *The Girl o' Dreams*
1921   *Heedless Moths*

Murfin, Jane (1892 Quincy, MI-1955 Brentwood, CA)

Jane Murfin was a successful Broadway playwright before moving to Hollywood to work in films. Her forceful style of writing was easily adapted to films. Her first stage play, *The Right to Lie* (1908), was one of her first films when she adapted it for the screen in 1919.

She wrote more than sixty scripts during her career and was known for her strong female characters. During her career she also directed some of the scripts she wrote, although no documentation is available to support this claim except in the case of *Flapper Wives* (1924).

While she is known for her strong female characterizations, she was also the chief writer for a popular male actor of the early 1920s. Over the course of his career, she wrote five films for Strongheart, a German shepherd who was a Red Cross veteran from World War I. Strongheart, Jean, and Rin Tin Tin were the era's big canine stars.

In 1934 she was made supervisor of motion pictures at RKO Studios—the first woman to hold the position at that studio. The following year she signed a long-running contract with Samuel Goldwyn, continuing to write stories with a focus on human interaction and human nature.

During her career she wrote five films for Katherine Hepburn. Their first collaboration was *Little Women* (1934), and their final work was *Dragon Seed* (1944). She wrote the original version of *What Price Hollywood?*—which was the basis of several subsequent adaptation based on the concept, including *A Star Is Born* (1937/1954/1976).

Another contested Murfin claim to fame is that she "discovered" Rudolph Valentino and gave him his start in films. However, several people in Hollywood claimed to have done this after Valentino became a megastar.

Writing Credits

1918	*Daybreak*
1919	*The Right to Lie; A Temperamental Wife; Marie Ltd.*
1920	*The Amateur Wife*
1921	*The Silent Call; Playthings of Destiny*
1922	*Smilin' Through* (I); *Brawn of the North*
1924	*Flapper Wives; The Love Master*
1925	*White Fang; A Slave to Fashion*
1926	*The Savage; Meet the Prince*

1927   *Notorious Lady; The Prince of Headwaiters*
1928   *Lilac Time*
1929   *Street Girl; Half Marriage; Dance Hall; Seven Keys to Baldpate*
1930   *The Runaway Bride; Lawful Larceny; Leathernecking; The Pay-Off*
1931   *White Shoulders; Caught Plastered; Friends and Lovers; Too Many Cooks*
1932   *Young Bride; Smilin' Through* (II); *Rockabye; What Price Hollywood? Way Back Home*
1933   *Our Betters; The Silver Cord; Double Harness; Ann Vickers; After Tonight*
1934   *Spitfire; This Man Is Mine; The Crime Doctor; The Life of Vergie Winters; The Fountain; The Little Minister*
1935   *Romance in Manhattan; Roberta; Alice Adams*
1936   *Come and Get It; That Girl from Paris*
1937   *I'll Take Romance*
1938   *The Shining Hour*
1939   *Stand Up and Fight; The Women*
1940   *Pride and Prejudice*
1941   *Andy Hardy's Private Secretary; Smilin' Through*
1943   *Flight for Freedom; Cry Havoc*
1944   *Dragon Seed*

Murphy, Edna (1899 New York City-1974 Santa Monica, CA)

Courtesy of Silents Are Golden at <SilentsAreGolden.com>

Edna Murphy worked as a photographer's model while still attending high school, and her modeling led to a screen contract. Her first major role was in the twenty-chapter serial *Fantomas* (1920). For a brief time she was the leading serial star.

By 1922 she was starring at Universal in westerns and in an avant-garde, if difficult to follow at times, serial titled *Her Dangerous Path* (1923). Unlike most serials, Murphy played a different character in each episode, in which Fate dictated the path that her type of character would undertake after making a life-altering decision. When

Murphy moved to Pathe she again returned to the serial format in 1924 in two films, *Leatherstocking* and *Into the Net*.

Her final serial appearance was Universal's *Fingerprints* (1931). Murphy married director Mervyn LeRoy in 1930 and retired from the screen in 1933.

Film Credits

1918	*To the Highest Bidder*
1919	*Puppy Love; Easy Money*
1920	*A Philistine in Bohemia; The North Wind's Malice; Over the Hill to the Poorhouse; The Branded Woman; Fantomas*
1921	*Dynamite Allen; Live Wires; Play Square; What Love Will Do; The Jolt*
1922	*Extra! Extra!; The Ordeal; Don't Shoot; Paid Back; The Galloping Kid; Caught Bluffing; Ridin' Wind*
1923	*Nobody's Bride; The Man Between; Her Dangerous Path; Going Up*
1924	*After the Ball; Daughters of Today; Leatherstocking; The King of the Wild Horses; The White Moth; Into the Net*
1925	*A Man Must Live; Lena Rivers; Wildfire; Lying Wives; The Police Patrol; Ermine and Rhinestones; His Buddy's Wife; Clothes Make the Pirate*
1926	*The Little Giant; Wives at Auction; College Days; Obey the Law; Oh! What a Night!; Forty-Five Minutes to Broadway*
1927	*Tarzan and the Golden Lion; McFadden's Flats; The Valley of Hell; Burnt Fingers; All Aboard; Rose of the Bowery; Silver Comes Through; Modern Daughters; The Black Diamond Express; Dearie; The Silent Hero; The Cruise of the Hellion; His Foreign Wife; Willful Youth*
1928	*Across the Atlantic; The Sunset Legion; A Midnight Adventure; My Man*
1929	*The Bachelor's Club; The Greyhound Limited; Stolen Kisses; Kid Gloves; The Sap; Little Johnny Jones; The Show of Shows; The Unkissed Man*
1930	*Second Choice; Lummox; Wide Open; Dancing Sweeties*
1931	*Behind Office Doors; Fingerprints; Anybody's Blonde; Forgotten Women*
1932	*Girl of the Rio*
1933	*Cheating Blondes*

Murray, Mae (1889 Portsmouth, VA-1965 Woodland Hills, CA)

Courtesy of Silents Are Golden at
<SilentsAreGolden.com>

Known as "the girl with the bee-stung lips," Mae Murray had been a dancer in the *Follies* and on Broadway for several years before she replaced Irene Castle in *Watch Your Step* (1908). Soon Murray was the darling of Broadway. A few years later she literally stopped the show as the Persian princess in her harem-inspired dance in the *Follies* of 1915. After another successful year with the *Follies* and appearances at the popular Sans Souci cabaret in New York, Murray signed a film contract with Paramount in 1916.

Her film debut was in *To Have and to Hold,* but Murray did not initially like the film industry which was so different from the dancing life that she knew. Slowly she adapted to the new medium and became more proficient at the mannerisms needed to project her feelings on the screen.

Her sixth film, *The Plow Girl* (1916), began a partnership with director Robert Leonard that resulted in several of her most successful films. With the success of these films and Murray's increased popularity, she and Leonard were given their own production unit. Eventually the couple was married and their professional collaboration continued to be successful until 1925 when they were amicably divorced.

Murray's first major film after her divorce was *The Merry Widow,* directed by Erich von Stroheim. The film was one of the hits of 1925, but the atmosphere on the set with the headstrong Murray battling the perfectionist von Stroheim nearly closed production many times. While Murray wanted romance, von Stroheim wanted realism. By the time the film was completed, everyone involved was near an emotional collapse.

Unfortunately, after this professional success Murray went on to make the biggest personal mistake of her life; in "the" event of 1926 in Hollywood, she married Prince David Mdivani, a slyly charming but penniless Russian aristocrat. He and his two brothers had determined the way to recoup the family fortune was to marry well, which they did so often that they were called "the marrying Mdivanis."

Her personal mistake became a professional blunder as she allowed her new husband to take over the management of her career. Whether out of spite and jealousy or because of poor judgment, Mdivani advised Murray to walk out on her contract with MGM. This action began a chain of events that resulted in Murray virtually being blackballed from films.

In the meantime, Mdivani had transferred all her money from her name to his accounts so that when Murray asked for a divorce she was informed that she was penniless. She proceeded with the divorce, but by 1934 Murray, who had once been one of the wealthiest actors in Hollywood, could not find work in films and was reduced to sleeping in Central Park.

Her film career over, Murray suffered further personal defeats. In 1964 she was found in St. Louis in a confused state saying that she had gotten off her bus thinking she had reached New York. After a stroke that left her mind even more clouded, she was admitted to the Motion Picture Country Home. She continued to sink further into her own private fantasy world. Although she said she had no regrets about how her life had turned out, neither did she ever accept that she was no longer a star.

In an interview many years after she had slipped from the heights of stardom she stated, "You don't have to keep making movies to remain a star. Once you become a star, you are always a star." Her biography was aptly titled, *The Self-Enchanted* (1959).

Film Credits

1916   *To Have and to Hold; Sweet Kitty Bellairs; The Dream Girl; The Big Sister; The Plow Girl*

1917   *On Record; A Mormon Maid; The Primrose Ring; At First Sight; Princess Virtue*

1918   *The Bride's Awakening; Her Body in Bond; Face Value; Modern Love; Danger, Go Slow*

1919   *The Twin Pawns; The ABC of Love; The Scarlet Shadow; Delicious Little Devil; Big Little Person; What Am I Bid?*

1920   *On with the Dance; The Right of Love; Idols of Clay*

1921   *The Gilded Lily*

1922   *Peacock Alley; Fascination; Broadway Rose*
1923   *Jazzmania; Fashion Row; The French Doll*
1924   *Mademoiselle Midnight; Circe the Enchantress; Married Flirts*
1925   *The Merry Widow; The Masked Bride*
1926   *Valencia*
1927   *Altars of Desire*
1928   *Show People*
1930   *Peacock Alley* (II)
1931   *Bachelor Apartment; High Stakes*

Writing Credits

1918   *Modern Love; Danger; Go Slow; Face Value*

Myers, Carmel (1899 San Francisco, CA-1980 Los Angeles, CA)

Courtesy of Silents Are Golden at
<SilentsAreGolden.com>

Her father, a rabbi, helped Carmel Myers into show business. While acting as the biblical researcher on D. W. Griffith's film *Intolerance,* her father suggested that she was attractive enough to appear in the film. As a gesture of thanks for all the rabbi's assistance, Griffith put Myers in a small role. She had, in fact, appeared in a crowd scene in the film *Georgia Pearce* a year earlier.

When Myers decided she wanted to remain in films, she moved to Universal with the exaggerated entrée of "a former Griffith actress." After a year of appearing in films, she landed the role that made her a star in *Sirens of the Sea* (1917).

While at the height of her popularity she met an unknown dancer who she believed had great potential; she began to request that he appear in her films. The dancer, Rudolph Valentino, soon outshined his supposed benefactor. Of course, once Valentino became famous so many people in Hollywood claimed to have given him help that they must have been lined up for miles.

She appeared in a few films in the early 1930s but appeared only intermittently after 1933. When she died, her ashes were scattered in the Rose Garden of Pickfair.

Film Credits

1915 *Georgia Pearce*
1916 *Tough Luck on a Rough Sea; The Jailbird's Last Flight; Ignatz's Icy Injury; The Matrimaniac; Intolerance*
1917 *A Love Sublime; A Daughter of the Poor; Might and the Man; The Haunted Pajamas; Sirens of the Sea; The Lash of Power*
1918 *My Unmarried Wife; The Girl in the Dark; The Marriage Lie; A Broadway Scandal; The Dream Lady; All Night; The Wine Girl; The Wife He Bought; A Society Sensation; The City of Tears*
1919 *The Little White Savage; Who Will Marry Me?*
1920 *In Folly's Trail; The Gilded Dream; Beautifully Trimmed*
1921 *The Mad Marriage; Cheated Love; The Kiss; A Daughter of the Law; The Dangerous Moment; Breaking Through*
1922 *The Love Gambler; The Danger Point*
1923 *The Last Hour; The Famous Mrs. Fair; Goodbye Girls; Mary of the Movies; Slave of Desire; The Dancer of the Nile; Reno; The Love Pirate; The Little Girl Next Door*
1924 *Poisoned Paradise; Beau Brummel; Broadway After Dark; Babbitt*
1925 *Ben-Hur*
1926 *The Devil's Circus; The Gay Deceiver*
1927 *Tell It to the Marines; The Understanding Heart; Sumuru; Sorrell and Son; The Demi-Bride*
1928 *A Certain Young Man; Prowlers of the Sea; Four Walls; Dream of Love*
1929 *The Red Sword; The Ghost Talks; Careers; The Careless Age; Broadway Scandals; The Show of Shows; He Did His Best*
1930 *The Ship from Shanghai; A Lady Surrenders; The Stronger Sex*
1931 *Svengali; Chinatown After Dark; The Mad Genius; The Lion and the Lamb; Pleasure*

1932   *Nice Woman; No Living Witness*
1934   *Countess of Monte Cristo*
1942   *Lady for a Night; Pretty Dolly*
1944   *The Conspirators*
1945   *George White's Scandals*
1946   *Whistle Stop*
1976   *Won Ton Ton, the Dog Who Saved Hollywood*

Naldi, Nita (1897 New York City–1961 New York City)

Courtesy of Silents Are Golden at <SilentsAreGolden.com>

Although of Irish descent, Nita Naldi played women of exotic ancestry throughout her film career. Her dark beauty lent itself to portrayals of European vamps out to steal the men from virtuous American girls. Because vamps were all the rage when she entered films, she was in demand from the beginning of her career.

Naldi got her start in show business as a dancer in New York's Winter Garden after working as an artist's model for several years. She appeared in Ziegfeld's *Follies* before moving to Hollywood to try a film career.

Her film debut was opposite John Barrymore in *Dr. Jekyll and Mr. Hyde* (1920), and she was immediately elevated to lead roles. Her next films solidified her standing as film's newest sexy star, but it was *Blood and Sand* (1922) opposite Rudolph Valentino that elevated her to "sex goddess."

However, once on the top it is too often impossible to stay there. Most of her later films lacked the impact of *Blood and Sand,* with the possible exception of De Mille's first version of *The Ten Commandments* (1923). Unfortunately, the advent of sound doomed her already-faltering film career because she had a heavy New York accent that did not record well and definitely didn't match her sex goddess image. She did continue to appear on stage and even appeared in a few dramatic anthologies during the early years of television.

Film Credits

1920   *Dr. Jekyll and Mr. Hyde; Life; The Common Sin*
1921   *Experience; The Last Door; A Divorce of Convenience*
1922   *The Man from Beyond; Reported Missing; Channing of the Northwest; Blood and Sand; The Snitching Hour; Anna Ascends*
1923   *The Glimpses of the Moon; You Can't Fool Your Wife; Lawful Larceny; The Ten Commandments; Hollywood*
1924   *Don't Call It Love; The Breaking Point; A Sainted Devil; The Hooded Falcon*
1925   *The Lady Who Lied; The Marriage Whirl; The Pleasure Garden; Cobra; Clothes Make the Pirate; What Price Beauty?*
1926   *The Miracle of Life; The Unfair Sex*
1917   *Pratermizzi; The Mountain Eagle; The Model from Montmartre*

Native American Actors

Native Americans were represented in film from its very beginning when Edison recorded various rituals and dances for exhibition on his kinetoscope system in 1894. From the early years of film westerns were a staple in filmmaking. In fact, Thomas Ince moved members of the Oglala Sioux from South Dakota to his production facility known as "Inceville" where they lived and appeared as needed in his films.

Information on individual Native American actors from the silent era is almost nonexistent. Although many Native Americans were used as extras, very few were given billing. However, they numbered enough to have had their own actors' organization in Los Angeles during the 1920s called the War Paint Club.

One female actor whose name was recorded was Beulah Dark Cloud (born Beulah T. Filson); her birth date is unknown, but her death was recorded in 1946. She was a member of the Algonquin tribe and was the daughter of Chief William Dark Cloud. She appeared with her father in some of D. W. Griffith's films. When she retired from films she became active in American Indian political and social issues.

Minnie Ha-Ha (1891-1984), another actor, was born Minnie Provost in Canada and was a recognized comedian who appeared with some of the best comics of the silent era. She shared billing, of sorts, with Fatty Arbuckle in *Fatty and Minnie He-Haw* (1914) and had a prominent role in Buster Keaton's *The Paleface* (1922).

Princess Red Wing (1884-1974), born Lillian St. Cyr, was a member of the Winnebago Nation of Nebraska. She entered films in 1908 and was the first well-known Native American star. She was featured by D. W. Griffith in a series of "Princess Red Wing" films during the 1910s and had a major role in Cecil B. DeMille's *The Squaw Man* (1914). In addition, she was married to actor-director James Young Deer, who directed his wife in several movies that realistically depicted Native American life, including *Red Wing's Gratitude* (1909), *The Red Girl and the Child* (1910), and *The Squaw Man's Sweetheart* (1912). When she retired with the advent of sound, she became an advocate for Native American rights in Washington, DC.

Nazimova, Alla (1879 Yalta, Russia-1945 Los Angeles, CA)

Courtesy of Silents Are Golden at <SilentsAreGolden.com>

Called simply "Madame," Alla Nazimova was a success on stage before she entered films. While on stage, she was instrumental in introducing New York audiences to the works of Ibsen and Chekhov.

Born Mariam Edez Adelaida Leventon in rural Russia to a brutal father and a lovely but indiscreet mother who was eventually divorced by her husband, she led a lonely life. She showed musical talent early and was taking violin lessons by the age of seven. Her father remarried and opened a pharmacy in her hometown of Yalta, where her stepmother considered her a burden.

She got her early theatrical training by impersonating her father's customers to entertain his employees. She continued to study violin, but when she was chosen to appear in a Christmas pageant her father refused to let her use her own name for fear that his neighbors would know that his child was performing on "the stage." She chose the last name of one of her favorite characters from the novel *Children of the Street* and became Adelaida (later changed to her family nickname "Alla") Nazimova.

She was the hit of the pageant, but because she was pleased with her performance, her father beat her—a beating that Nazimova claimed was the basis of her stage fright throughout her career. Luckily for her, when she was fifteen she was sent to boarding school in Odessa, away from her brutish father.

While there she became friends with young girls who performed in the local theater and soon she decided that she wanted to become an actor. However, it was not until she was seventeen that she began to study acting at the Philharmonic School in Moscow, the most prestigious acting school in Russia.

To support herself as she studied she became a part-time prostitute, eventually becoming the kept woman of a local millionaire. She briefly appeared in regional repertory then returned to the city to appear at the Moscow Art Theater, a joint venture of Konstantin Stanislavsky and Vladimir Nemirovich, but soon she left again to join a stock company in Kislovodsk.

In 1904 she went to Berlin to appear with her company in the play *The Chosen People*. Her performances catapulted her to the heights of Berlin theater. She was soon appearing in London and, eventually, New York. The company toured the United States appearing in various Russian plays until 1906 when the company returned to Russia, but Nazimova decided to remain.

She signed with Broadway producer Lee Schubert and began learning English. Nazimova became the toast of New York theater. In 1915, while appearing in *War Brides,* Nazimova was approached by Lewis Selznick to appear in the film version of the play. The success of the film and Nazimova's performance earned her a five-year contract with Metro at $13,000 per week—more than Mary Pickford was earning at that time. Her films for Metro were all successful and she was soon a force to be reckoned with in Hollywood.

She bought a Spanish-style home on Sunset Boulevard and had a pool designed in the shape of the Baltic Sea amid three and a half acres. She named her home the "Garden of Allah," and it was the site of many extravagant parties during the heyday of early Hollywood. When she mortgaged the house to finance a later film that failed, the house became a hotel and she was allowed to retain a room in which to live.

In the early 1920s, after a string of barely-break-even films, Nazimova dropped from #4 in *Photoplay's* annual popularity poll to #20. Nazimova began producing her own films; although while she regained her reputation as a great actor, the films were only moderately successful, resulting in the financial loses that cost her the "Garden of Allah."

Nazimova returned to the theater and appeared in films only sporadically in later years. Interestingly, she was godmother to future First Lady Nancy Reagan.

Film Credits

1916   *War Brides*
1918   *Revelation; Toys of Fate; Eye for Eye*
1919   *Out of the Fog; The Red Lantern; The Brat*
1920   *Stronger Than Death; The Heart of a Child; Madame Peacock; Billions*
1921   *Camille*
1922   *A Doll's House*
1923   *Salome*
1924   *Madonna of the Streets*
1925   *The Redeeming Sin; My Son*
1940   *Escape*
1941   *Blood and Sand*
1943   *Song of Bernadette*
1944   *Since You Went Away; In Our Time; The Bridge of San Luis Rey*

Producing Credits

1918   *Eye for Eye*
1919   *The Brat*

1920　*Stronger Than Death; The Heart of a Child; Madame Peacock*
1922　*A Doll's House*
1923　*Salome*

Writing Credits

1919　*The Brat*
1920　*Madame Peacock; Billions*
1922　*A Doll's House*

Negri, Pola (1894 Janowa, Poland-1987 San Antonio, TX)

Courtesy of Silents Are Golden at
<SilentsAreGolden.com>

Pola Negri, one of the first European stars to be brought to America, was born into poverty in Poland after her father was sent to a Siberian prison camp. In her early teens she auditioned for acceptance into the training program at the Imperial Ballet. A bout with tuberculosis necessitated that she stop dancing, so she transferred her energies to the theater.

She became one of the most popular actors on the European stage, renown for her talent and fiery temperament. When the first of her German films opened in New York in 1920, an estimated 40,000 people vied to attend the initial showing in a theater that seated only 5,500 people. A riot ensued and the police were called to restore order. For the remainder of its run, the film broke all attendance records to that time.

After the successful reception of her films *Passion* and *Gypsy Blood,* Adolph Zukor decided to bring the star to the United States in an effort to funnel some of the huge profits from her films into his studio. Upon her arrival in the United States, Negri, complete with a ninety-eight carat emerald bracelet from "an admirer," was promoted wildly and her wildest promoter was herself.

She refused to ride in a regular car and instead had a stretch Rolls Royce designed for her in white and ivory with solid gold handles and trims. Her car was driven by a chauffeur dressed in white when it was sunny and in black on rainy days. Her traveling companions were a white lap dog and two white Russian wolfhounds. She also made sure everyone knew that in Europe she was *Countess* Domski though her early marriage had not been a happy one, she retained her title.

When her extravagant lifestyle couldn't keep her in the fan magazines, the "magnificent wildcat" could always fall back on her supposed feud with Paramount's other top female star, Gloria Swanson. Both stars were known for their flamboyance and excess in all areas—be it multiple mansions, cars, or men. Although there was no "feud" as such, both women were dedicated to their careers and to maintaining their position before the public.

Negri's most tempestuous and well-publicized affair was with Rudolph Valentino, the silent film's greatest screen lover. Their relationship was tempestuous enough to be the basis of a soap opera— there were fights, reconciliations, fiery recriminations, and abject apologies. The public loved the drama and seemed not to notice that they were engaged before he had divorced his second wife. Rumors abounded of a secret wedding followed closely by rumors of a permanent breakup. Sadly, before any wedding could take place, Valentino died in 1926. Negri suffered a complete breakdown; while some cynics thought her affliction was convenient, others noted that Valentino had never said they would marry—only Negri. At any rate, her hysterics turned many fans from her.

Although supposedly devastated, Negri returned to work and within a year married another European aristocrat, Russian Prince Serge Mdivani, who like his brothers, was known for marrying well. The prince was penniless and had no standing in Communist Russia but did supposedly come from one of the oldest royal lines in Europe. After completing her contractual obligations, Negri and her prince moved to Europe where they lived grandly. The stock market crash of 1929 decimated what was left of her original $5 million estate.

Negri made some films in England before divorcing the possessive prince in 1931 and announcing her return to Hollywood. When film offers did not materialize, Negri returned to Europe with a film contract and became a European film sensation.

Negri burst forth in American papers in the mid-1930s when it was rumored that she was Adolph Hitler's mistress. When the rumors became less beneficial to her career and it was later rumored that Hitler had put her in a concentration camp after an argument, Negri sued saying that she had never met Hitler. Although they had indeed never met, Hitler was a fan of her movies—after it was "proved" that Negri was of Aryan stock.

With the advent of World War II, Negri lost her newly acquired fortune; when she fled to the United States in 1941, she was virtually penniless. Her thick European accent did not play well in the United States about to go to war, so she made only one film in 1943. She became an American citizen in 1951.

During the 1950s Negri began a career in real estate in San Antonio, Texas, which allowed her to live comfortably until she inherited a friend's large estate. However, she always wanted to return to films; she was given her chance when she appeared in the 1964 Disney production of *The Moon-Spinners* as the ruthless Egyptian millionaire Madame Habib. She wrote her autobiography, *Memoirs of a Star,* in 1970.

Film Credits (United States)

1914   *Love and Passion*
1918   *The Eyes of the Mummy; The Devil's Pawn; Love's Surrogates*
1919   *Intoxication*
1920   *One Arabian Night; Camille*
1921   *Wildcat; Sappho; Vendetta*
1922   *The Last Payment*
1923   *Bella Donna; The Cheat; The Spanish Dancer; Mad Love; Hollywood; Montmartre; Passion*
1924   *Men; Lily of the Dust; Forbidden Paradise; Shadows of Paris*
1925   *East of Suez; Flower of Night; A Woman of the World; The Charmer*
1926   *The Crown of Lies; Good and Naughty*
1927   *Hotel Imperial; Barbed Wire; The Woman on Trial*
1928   *The Secret Hour; Three Sinners; Loves of an Actress; The Woman from Moscow*
1929   *The Way of Lost Souls; The Woman He Scorned*
1932   *A Woman Commands*
1934   *Fanatisme*
1935   *Mazurka*
1937   *Madame Bovary*
1943   *Hi Diddle Diddle*
1964   *The Moon-Spinners*

Nilsson, Anna Q. (1888 Ystad, Sweden-1974 Hemet, CA)

Anna Q. Nilsson, one of the first Swedish imports to Hollywood, was one of the era's biggest stars until a riding accident in 1928 caused her to limit her screen appearances, effectively ending her star years. She was twelve and working in a bakery when she was struck with "America fever" after a visit from her employer's sister who had moved to the United States. After five years of pleading, her parents allowed her to travel to America with some friends of the family for a "short" visit.

Upon her arrival she got a job as a maid but was fired when the wife became concerned with her husband's attention to Nilsson. While looking for another job, Nilsson was asked to pose for a portrait and her modeling career began. Like several of her fellow models, including Mabel Normand and Alice Joyce, Nilsson began looking to the film industry as a career alternative. Although she was perhaps the highest-paid model in New York at the time, she gave in to her friends' urgings and appeared as an extra in one of Alice Joyce's films.

The director of the film remembered her, and when he needed a leading lady for another film, *Molly Pitcher* (1911), he called Nilsson. In the film she had the first of many riding accidents to follow—she never learned to ride a horse, although many of her films called for her to ride. She continued to work for Kalem Studios, one of the first studios to give name billing to their company of players. Originally known only as Anna Nilsson, she filled in as the lead in a few *Hazards of Helen* episodes as well as appearing in one of the first horror films, *The Haunted House of Wild Isle* (1915).

At the end of 1915 Nilsson left Kalem to freelance. Well known as a dramatic actor, she began to appear in comedies to enhance her versatility. She became known for her willingness to take any "good" role—no matter how small. Although she did not always choose her films well, she always received good reviews on her performance no matter how poorly the films themselves were reviewed.

Although she enjoyed her career in films, at one point Nilsson and some of her friends, including Bebe Daniels, compared careers and found that Nilsson and Daniels had suffered the most accidents while filming. This was in part because neither Nilsson nor Daniels ever used doubles for the more dangerous scenes. In fact, during the filming of *Hearts Aflame* (1923), Nilsson was caught in the midst of a "forest fire" with three other actors and thought to be lost, but she emerged from the flames to chase the director around the set—threatening to kill him if she caught him. Filming was halted for five hours while the producer and director hid to allow Nilsson to calm down.

Among her more memorable films was the 1923 Samuel Goldwyn production of *The Spoilers* in which Nilsson appeared as saloon keeper Cherry Malotte (the role played by Kathlyn Williams in 1914). In 1924 Nilsson portrayed Inez Laranatta, who was called "the worst woman in Hollywood," in the film *Inez from Hollywood.* In 1927, Nilsson appeared with baseball great Babe Ruth in *Babe Comes Home,* an otherwise unremarkable film in which Nilsson sustained a serious vertebrae injury.

After working almost nonstop for several years Nilsson decided to take a break and bought a house in Malibu in which she lazed for seven months. She returned to films late in 1928, but the comeback did not last. While camping with friends she was thrown from her horse and broke her hip. Incompetent local medical care resulted in later surgeries to repair the damage, effectively ending her star career because of the lengthy convalescence.

Although she occasionally appeared in films after the accident, by 1950 she was completely retired and living in the California desert. Throughout her career she had been well liked by her fellow actors and always willing to help someone in need. *Photoplay* once wrote that she was "hard-headed and soft-hearted," which in a town known for its self-centeredness makes her worth remembering even without her successful career.

The "Q" in her name stood for "Quirentia" which was based on the day she was born, St. Quirinus Day (March 30). Of course, her studios tried to capitalize on it by claiming it stood for the "quality" of her performances.

Film Credits

1911   *Molly Pitcher; The Flash in the Night*

1912   *The Water Rights War; War's Havoc; Victims of Circumstance; Under a Flag of Truce; Tide of Battle; The Soldier Brothers of Susanna; The Siege of Petersburg; Saved from Court Martial; A Railroad Lochinvar; A Race with Time; The Prison Ship; The Pony Express Girl; His Mother's Picture; The Grit of the Girl Telegrapher; The Girl in the Caboose; The Fraud at the Hope Mine; The Drummer Girl of Vicksburg; The Darling of the CSA; The Confederate Ironclad; The Colonel's Escape; The Bugler of Battery B; The Battle of Wits; Battle of Pottsburg Bridge; Battle in the Virginia Hills; Fightin' Dan McCool; The Farm Bully; The Toll Gate Raiders; Two Spies; The Filibusters*

1913   *Retribution; Uncle Tom's Cabin; The Turning Point; A Treacherous Shot; Shipwrecked; Shenandoah; A Sawmill Hazard; Prisoners of War; A Mississippi Tragedy; John Burns of Gettysburg; Infamous Don Miguel; The Grim Toll of War; The Fatal Legacy; A Desperate Chance; The Counterfeiter's Confederate; Captured by Strategy; The Breath of Scandal; The Battle of Bloody Ford; The Gypsy's Brand; A Man in a Man's World*

1914   *The Conquest of Quebec; Tell-Tale Stains; A Shot in the Dark; The Secret of the Will; Perils of the White Lights; The Man with the Glove; The Man in the Vault; The Ex-Convict*

1915   *Regeneration; Barbara Frietchie; Voices in the Dark; A Sister's Burden; The Siren's Reign; The Second Commandment; Rivals; The Night of the Embassy Ball; In the Hands of the Jury; Hiding from the Law; The Haunting Fear; The Haunted House of Wild Isle; The Destroyer; Barriers Swept Aside*

1916   *The Scarlet Road; Her Surrender; Puppets of Fate; The Tight Rein; The Tangled Web; The Silent Shame; Sold Out; Sowing the Wind; Truth Crashed to Earth; Beyond Recall; Weaker Strain; A Trail of Souls; The Lost Paradise; Weighed in the Balance; The Goad of Jealousy; The Irony of Justice; The Supreme Sacrifice*

1917   *Infidelity; The Moral Code; The Inevitable; Over There; The Silent Master; Seven Keys to Baldpate*

1918   *No Man's Land; The Vanity Pool; The Trail to Yesterday; Heart of the Sunset; In Judgment Of*

1919   *Ravished Armenia; Venus in the East; Cheating Cheaters; A Sporting Chance; The Love Burglar; Her Kingdom of Dreams; Soldiers of Fortune; Way of the Strong; A Very Good Young Man*

1920   *The Thirteenth Commandment; The Toll Gate; The Figurehead; One Hour Before Dawn; The Fighting Chance; The Brute Master; The Luck of the Irish; In the Heart of a Fool*

1921   *Without Limit; The Oath; Why Girls Leave Home; Ten Nights in a Bar Room; What Women Will Do; Varmlanningarna; The Lotus Eater*

1922   *Three Live Ghosts; A Trip to Paramountown; Pink Gods; The Man from Home*

1923   *Hearts Aflame; The Isle of Lost Ships; Souls for Sale; The Rustle of Silk; The Spoilers; Adam's Rib; Ponjola; Thundering Dawn; Innocence; Enemies of Children; Hollywood*

1924   *The Judgment of the Storm; Half-a-Dollar Bill; Flowing Gold; Between Friends; Broadway After Dark; The Fire Patrol; The Breath of Scandal; Vanity's Price; Inez from Hollywood; Painted People; The Side Show of Life*

1925   *The Top of the World; If I Marry Again; One Way Street; The Talker; The Splendid Road; Winds of Chance*

1926   *Too Much Money; Her Second Chance; The Greater Glory; Miss Nobody; Midnight Lovers*

1927   *The Masked Woman; Easy Pickings; Babe Comes Home; Lonesome Ladies; The Thirteenth Juror; Sorrell and Son*

1928   *The Whip; Blockade*

1933   *The World Changes*

1934   *School for Girls; The Little Minister*

1935   *Wanderer of the Wasteland*

1937   *Behind the Criminal*

1938   *Prison Farm; Paradise for Three*

1941   *Raiders of the Timberline; They Died with Their Boots On; The Trial of Mary Dugan; The People vs. Dr. Kildare*

1942   *Girl's Town; The Great Man's Lady; I Live on Danger; Crossroads*

1943   *Headin' for God's Country; Cry Havoc*

1945   *The Valley of Decision; The Sailor Takes a Wife*

1946   *The Secret Heart*

1947   *The Farmer's Daughter; It Had to Be You; Cynthia*

1948   *Fighting Father Dunne; The Boy with Green Hair; Every Girl Should Be Married*

1949   *Malaya; In the Good Old Summertime; Adam's Rib*

1950   *The Big Hangover; Sunset Boulevard*

1951   *Show Boat; An American in Paris; The Unknown Man; The Law and the Lady; Grounds for Marriage*

1952   *Fearless Fagan*

1953   *The Great Diamond Robbery*

1954   *Seven Brides For Seven Brothers*

Nixon, Marion (1904 Superior, WI-1983 Los Angeles, CA)

Courtesy of Silents Are Golden at <SilentsAreGolden.com>

Marion Nixon got her start in entertainment as a dancer who toured the vaudeville circuit. In 1922 she entered films, first as an extra and then as a supporting actor in comedies and westerns. Her first big role was as Agnes Evans in *Cupid's Fireman* (1923).

In 1924 she was chosen as a WAMPAS Baby Star and went on to lead billing in standard dramas of the period. Although she never attained the stardom that her WAMPAS selection predicted, she was a competent actor throughout her career. She was never associated with any particular studio but worked for Universal, Warner Bros., and Fox at various times.

She made the transition to sound in the part-talkie *Geraldine* (1929) and continued to appear in films until 1936. While working at Fox she was used as a "threat" to keep the tempestuous Janet Gaynor in line, since Nixon strongly resembled her—a fact that may have limited Nixon's options.

She was married four times—twice ending in divorce and twice ending with the death of her husband. Prior to her retirement from films she was briefly featured on the front pages of newspapers and fan magazines when she was robbed at gunpoint on a Santa Fe train in 1932.

Film Credits

1923   *Rosita; Big Dan; Cupid's Fireman*

1924   *Just Off Broadway; The City of Stars; The Vagabond Trail; The Circus Cowboy; The Last of the Duanes*

1925   *The Hurricane Kid; Riders of the Purple Sage; The Saddle Hawk; Let 'er Buck; I'll Show You the Town; Durand of the Badlands; The Sporting Life; Where Was I?*

1926   *What Happened to Jones; Rolling Home; Devil's Island; Spangles; Hands Up!*

1927   *Heroes of the Night; The Auctioneer; Down the Stretch; Out All Night; The Chinese Parrot; Taxi! Taxi!*

1928   *The Fourflusher; Out of the Ruins; How to Handle Women; Jazz Mad; Red Lips*

1929   *Man, Woman, and Wife; Silks and Saddles; Geraldine; The Red Sword; Rainbow Man; Say It with Songs; In the Headlines; Young Nowheres; The Show of Shows*

1930   *General Crack; Courage; Scarlet Pages; College Lovers; The Pay-Off; The Lash; Ex-Flame*

1931   *Sweepstakes; Women Go on Forever*

1932   *A Private Scandal; After Tomorrow; Winner Take All; Madison Square Garden; Amateur Daddy; Too Busy to Work; Rebecca of Sunnybrook Farm; Charlie Chan's Chance*

1933   *The Face in the Sky; Best of Enemies; Pilgrimage; Doctor Bull; Chance at Heaven*

1934   *We're Rich Again; Embarrassing Moments; By Your Leave; Strictly Dynamite; Once to Every Bachelor; The Lineup*

1935   *Sweepstakes Annie*

1936   *Captain Calamity; Tango; The Drag-Net; The Reckless Way*

Normand, Mabel (1894 Boston, MA-1930 Woodland Hills, CA)

Courtesy of Silents Are Golden at
<SilentsAreGolden.com>

A talented comedian in her own right whose work is often underrated by film historians, Mabel Normand was to many in the silent era the Queen of Comedy. Perhaps best remembered as the damsel that the Keystone Kops ineffectively tried to "save," Normand's characters are often cited as some of the first liberated females in film. Her characters could take care of themselves—nothing could stop them for long. Normand could be whatever the part required—tomboy or glamour queen or slapstick action star.

Born into a family of vaudevillians, Mabel Ethelreid Normand received her education in a convent in southern New York before moving to New York City with her family. Her first job, at thirteen, was as an advertising model and then an illustrator's model for such artists as Charles Dana Gibson and James Montgomery Flagg, appearing on such magazine covers as *The Saturday Evening Post*. This association with artists led her to enroll in an art school in New York after high school.

She began working in movies for Biograph as an extra around 1908 but was not included in the company move to the West Coast in 1909. She moved to Vitagraph, where her first feature role was either *The Indiscretions of Betty* or *Over the Garden Wall* (both 1910). Many of her early films listed her as "Mabel Fortesque," the marquee name used by studios before they realized the money to be made by allowing the public to identify with their favorite actor.

However, when Biograph returned to New York, Normand went back to her original company and made her first film with Mack Sennett, *The Diving Girl* (1911). Her athleticism made her a perfect comedian, while her attractiveness offset the absurdity of early comedy. Sennett once called her "the most gifted player who ever stepped before a camera."

Her comedy technique made use of physical, often slapstick, gestures as well as facial expressions and her very expressive eyes. She always conveyed high energy and a charming innocence. The first Keystone Kop short was made in 1912, and in the first year of production fifty-three one- and two-reelers were made. Throughout her Kop years (roughly 1912-1916), Normand made other films as well, most notably *A Noise From the Deep* (1913), in which Normand flung the first movie "pie-in-the-face" at Fatty Arbuckle, and *Mabel's Blunder* (1914).

Called by many a "female Chaplin," Sam Peeples noted in *Classic Film Collector* that "a study of her films made before Chaplin came to this country show entire routines, gestures, reactions (and) expressions that were later part of Chaplin's characterizations." It is known that she directed at least five of the films that Chaplin made, and they appeared together in the first American feature-length comedy, *Tillie's Punctured Romance* (1914).

In December 1914 it was announced that Normand would direct all her future films, making her one of the first female directors and the first one to direct comedy. This development is often cited as an attempt by Sennett to placate her after finding him in bed with one of her friends just before their wedding was to take place. It was after this crushing event that Normand became the "I-Don't-Care" girl who said in an interview, "I just live (for) today. I never make plans . . . no thought for the morrow."

In 1915 *Motion Picture World* listed her as female comedian in an article on the idealized "Great Cast." In 1916 she moved into feature-length films with the creation of the Mabel Normand Feature Film Company. Her first feature film was *Mickey* (1918), a huge hit for her both commercially and critically. It traced her evolution from tomboy to romantic young woman—a scenario that proved popular with her fans and which she continued to use for many years.

However, her behavior became increasingly erratic and her health increasingly poor. By 1922, when she became embroiled in the William Desmond Taylor murder, the public was becoming less tolerant of her purportedly wild lifestyle. Still, when *The Extra Girl* was released in 1923 it became a moderate hit for her.

Early the next year she was involved in another scandal when her chauffeur shot playboy Courtland Dines. Her films were banned in Ohio and her career began a downward spiral. Her reckless lifestyle and her ill health began to show on her face, and the once vibrant star aged with each film she made. Her final film was *One Hour Married* (1927).

Always troubled by respiratory ailments, she was diagnosed with tuberculosis and died only months after checking into a sanitorium. Her funeral was a who's who of Hollywood, where both her friends and her colleagues grieved for the "I don't care" comedian.

Film Credits

1910   *The Indiscretions of Betty; Over the Garden Wall; Willful Peggy*

1911   *The Diamond Star; Betty Becomes a Maid; The Troublesome Secretaries; Picciola; When a Man's Married His Troubles Begin; His Mother; A Dead Man's Honor; The Changing of Silas Warner; The Subduing of Mrs. Nag; The Diving Girl; How Betty Won the School; The Baron; The Squaw's Love; Her Awakening; The Making of a Man; The Unveiling; Through His Wife's Picture; A Victim of Circumstances; Why He Gave Up; Saved from Himself; A Tale of Two Cities; Two Overcoats; The Strategy of Ann; The Revenue Man and the Girl; Italian Blood; The Investor's Secret; Their First Divorce Case; Saved From Herself*

1912   *The Eternal Mother; The Mender of Nets; The Fatal Chocolate; The Engagement Ring; A Spanish Dilemma; Hot Stuff; Oh, Those Eyes; Help! Help!; The Brave Hunter; The Fickle Spaniard; The Furs; When Kings Were the Law; Helen's Marriage; Tomboy Bessie; Neighbors; Katchem Kate; A Dash Through the Clouds; The Tourists; What the Doctor Ordered; The Tragedy of the Dress Suit; An Interrupted Elopement; Mr. Grouch at the Seashore; He Must Have a Wife; Cohen Collects a Debt; The Water Nymph; The New Neighbor; Pedro's Dilemma; Stolen Glory; The Ambitious Butler; The Flirting Husband; At Coney Island; The Grocery Clerk's Romance; Mabel's Lovers; At It Again; The Deacon's Troubles; A Temperamental Husband; The Rivals; Mr. Fixit; A Desperate Lover; Brown's Séance; Pat's Day Off; A Family Mix-Up; A Midnight Elopement; Mabel's Adventures; The Drummer's Vacation; The Duel; Mabel's Strata-*

gem; Riley and Schultz; The Beating He Needed; A Voice from the Deep; The New Baby; Race for Life; King's Court

1913　The Cure That Failed; The Mistaken Masher; The Deacon Outwitted; Just Brown's Luck; The Battle of Who Run; Mabel's Heroes; Heinze's Resurrection; The Professor's Daughter; A Tangled Affair; A Red Hot Romance; A Doctored Affair; A Rural Third Degree; The Sleuths at the Floral Parade; A Strong Revenge; Foiling Fickle Father; The Rube and the Baron; At Twelve O'Clock; Her New Beau; Hide and Seek; Those Good Old Days; Father's Choice; The Bangville Police; The Ragtime Band; A Little Hero; Mabel's Awful Mistake; Hubby's Job; The Foreman of the Jury; Barney Oldfield's Race for a Life; Passions He Had Three; The Hansom Driver; The Speed Queen; The Waiter's Picnic; For the Love of Mabel; The Telltale Light; A Noise from the Deep; Love and Courage; Professor Bean's Removal; The Riot; Baby Day; Mabel's Dramatic Career; The Gypsy Queen; The Faithful Taxicab; When Dreams Come True; The Bowling Match; The Speed Kings; Love Sickness at Sea; A Muddy Romance; Cohen Saves the Flag; The Gusher; Fatty's Flirtation; Mabel's New Hero; The Champion; Zuzu; The Bank Leader ; For Lizzie's Sake; Brothers; Near to Earth; On His Wedding Day; Fatty at San Diego; Teddy Tetzlaff and Earl Cooper; Love and Pain; Saving Mabel's Dad; Mabel's Stormy Love Affair

1914　Mabel's Blunder; Hello Mabel; Gentleman of Nerve; Lover's Post Office; His Trysting Place; Tillie's Punctured Romance; Fatty's Wine Party; The Sea Nymphs; Getting Acquainted; How Heroes Are Made; A Misplaced Foot; A Glimpse of Los Angeles; Won in a Closet; Mabel's Bare Escape; Mabel's Strange Predicament; Love, Luck and Gasoline; Mack at It Again; Mabel at the Wheel; Where Hazel Met the Villain; Caught in a Cabaret; Mabel's Nerve; The Alarm; The Fatal Mallet; Her Friend the Bandit; Mabel's Busy Day; Mabel's Married Life; Mabel's New Job; Those Country Kids; Mabel's Latest Prank; Fatty's Jonah Day; In the Clutches of the Gang; A Film Johnnie; An Incompetent Hero; A Missing Bride; A Gambling Rube; Between Showers

1915   *Mabel and Fatty's Wash Day; Fatty and Mabel's Simple Life; Fatty and Mabel at the San Diego Exposition; Mabel; Fatty and the Law; Mabel and Fatty's Married Life; That Little Band of Gold; Wished on Mabel; Mabel and Fatty Viewing the World's Fair at San Francisco; Mabel's Willful Ways; Mabel Lost and Won; Small Town Bully; My Valet; Stolen Magic; Their Social Splash; The Little Teacher; Rum and Wall Paper; Fatty's New Role*

1916   *Fatty and Mabel Adrift; He Did and He Didn't; Bright Lights; Gaumont Graphic Newsreel #39*

1918   *Dodging a Million; The Floor Below; Joan of Plattsburg; The Venus Model; Back to the Woods; Mickey; Peck's Bad Girl; A Perfect 36*

1919   *Sis Hopkins; The Pest; When Doctors Disagree; Upstairs; Jinx*

1920   *Pinto; The Slim Princess; What Happened to Rosa*

1921   *Molly O'*

1922   *Oh Mabel Behave; Head Over Heels*

1923   *Suzanna; The Extra Girl*

1926   *Raggedy Rose; The Nickel Hopper*

1927   *Anything Once!; One Hour Married; Should Men Walk Home?*

Novak, Jane (1896 St. Louis, MO-1990 Woodland Hills, CA)

One of the most popular female actors during the post-World War I era, Jane Novak was educated at the Notre Dame Convent in St. Louis before she and her friend Frieda Spitz toured as the "Randolph Sisters" when they were fourteen. Unfortunately, they had begun their show business careers without their parents' permission; their parents brought them home when they caught up with them, but Novak was allowed to study acting.

While visiting a relative in California in 1913 she began appearing in films for Kalem, where she met her future husband, Frank Newburg. After six months she moved to Vitagraph where she remained until 1915 when she was offered lead status with Hal Roach at his Rolin Film Company. The uncertainty of the new company was not lost on Novak, and she soon signed with Universal where she played a variety of roles in an effort not to be typecast. She was one of the few actors who did not care if the role was a lead or supporting part as long as the role was good.

In 1916 she briefly left films after the birth of her daughter. When she was able to return to films later in the year, she decided to freelance. Her first film on her return was *The Spirit of '76,* a controversial film that made headlines when its producer was jailed under sedition laws. When the film was finally released in 1919 it was a box-office failure.

She next appeared in five westerns with William S. Hart as the perfect feminine counterpart to Hart's larger-than-life hero. In 1922 she appeared in her most successful film to date—a love story titled *Thelma.* Two years later she appeared in what some critics believe to be the best film of her career, *The Lullaby,* in which she played three roles.

She opted for semi-retirement in 1928 to spend more time with her daughter but did appear in an occasional film until her final role in *About Mrs. Leslie* (1954). She spent her retirement working for various charities.

Film Credits

1913 *At the Sign of the Lost Angel*
1914 *Ann, the Blacksmith*
1915 *Her Mysterious Escort; Just Nuts; From Italy's Shore; The Scarlet Sin; A Little Brother of the Rich; The Greater Courage; The White Star; Graft; Tainted Money; The Kiss of Dishonor; The Hungry Actor; All on Account of Towser*
1916 *The Iron Hand; The Target*
1917 *Eyes of the World; The Innocent Sinner; The Spirit of '76*
1918 *The Tiger Man; Selfish Yates; The Claws of the Hun; A Nine O'Clock Town; The Temple of Dusk; String Beans*
1919 *The Money Corral; The Fire Flingers; His Debt; Man's Desire; Wagon Tracks; Behind the Door; The Wolf; Treat 'Em Rough*
1920 *The River's End; The Trail's End; The Great Accident; The Golden Trail*

1921   *The Barbarian; Three Word Brand; Kazan; Roads of Destiny; The Other Woman*
1922   *The Rosary; Belle of Alaska; Colleen of the Pines; The Snowshoe Trail; Thelma; The Soul of a Woman*
1923   *Divorce; Jealous Husbands; The Man Life Passed By*
1924   *The Lullaby; Two Shall Be Born; The Prude's Fall; The Man Without a Heart*
1925   *The Danger Signal; The Substitute Wife; The Lure of the Wild; Share and Share Alike; The Blackguard; Lazybones*
1926   *Whispering Canyon; Lost at Sea*
1927   *One Increasing Purpose; Closed Gates; What Price Love?*
1928   *Free Lips*
1929   *Redskin*
1936   *Ghost Town; Hollywood Boulevard*
1940   *Foreign Correspondent*
1942   *Gallant Lady; The Yanks Are Coming*
1943   *Man of Courage*
1947   *Desert Fury*
1950   *Paid in Full; The Furies; The File on Thelma Jordan*
1954   *About Mrs. Leslie*

O'Day, Molly (1911 Bayonne, NJ-1998 Avila Beach, CA)

Born Susanne Noonan, Molly O'Day's father was a judge and her mother was retired opera singer Hannah Kelly. When her father suddenly died, the family was forced to sell their home and move to California. When they arrived in California, O'Day and two of her sisters got into films. The eldest, Isabelle, left films soon after entering the industry, but O'Day and her sister Virginia (renamed Sally O'Neil) became popular ingenues. Both were named WAMPAS Baby Stars—O'Neil in 1926 and O'Day in 1928.

She appeared with her sister in two films—*The Lovelorn* (1927) and *Sisters* (1930). O'Day's breakout role was as Curley Callahan in *The Patent Leather Kid* (1927). However, in 1928 she was ordered by her studio to lose weight (she was by no stretch of the imagination overweight) or be denied roles.

When she was overlooked for some very good roles, O'Day went on the vaudeville circuit and then returned to appear in films until 1935. After her retirement she married comedian Jack Durant and raised four children.

Film Credits

1926	*Forty-five Minutes from Hollywood*
1927	*Hard-Boiled Haggerty; The Patent Leather Kid; The Love-lorn; The Shepherd of the Hills*
1928	*The Little Shepherd of Kingdom Come*
1929	*The Show of Shows*
1930	*Sisters*
1931	*Sea Devils; Sob Sister*
1932	*Devil on Deck*
1933	*Gigolettes of Paris; Get That Venus; Playthings of Denise*
1934	*The Life of Vergie Winters; Hired Wife; Chloe, Love Is Call-ing You*
1935	*Law of the 45s; Lawless Border; Skull and Crown*
1936	*Bars of Hate*

Osborne, "Baby" Marie (1911 Denver, CO-)

Arguably the first child "star," Baby Marie Osborne was born Helen Alice Myers but soon became the foster daughter of Leon and Edith Osborn, who changed her name to Marie. Three years after Marie joined the family, they moved to Long Beach, California, where they worked as actors at the Balboa Amusement Company.

Since the family could not afford to pay someone to watch their child, she always accompanied her parents to the studio. While playing near her parents set, she was discovered by Henry King who was having difficulty finding a boy for a film he was directing. With her Dutch-boy haircut he believed that she could be made to look like a boy.

Her debut was in *Maid of the Wild* (1915), and she was immediately put under contract. King had her second film, *Little Mary Sunshine,* written especially for her, and she was soon Balboa's biggest star. Her association with King continued for five more pictures before her own production company was created.

The first company, Lasalida Film Corporation, was formed in 1917, William Bertram was put in charge of directing her films. The company went out of business only to be followed by Diando Film Corporation which was formed, in part, by Leon Osborn. Between 1918 and 1919 the company capitalized on her popularity by producing no less than twelve "Baby Marie" films. The company was dissolved in 1919, and Osborne appeared in only one other film before she retired at the age of eight.

With an early marriage failing, Osborne decided to return to films in 1934. This time, however, she appeared as an extra or in nonspeaking supporting roles. She served as Ginger Rogers's stand in during the filming of *The Gay Divorcee* (1934) as well as other popular films of the period.

She eventually grew tired of the uncertainty of work as an extra and decided to try a different type of film work. In the early 1950s she went to work at the Western Costume Company where she selected and fitted costumes for actors. By 1954 she was costume supervisor at Twentieth Century Fox Studios. After more than twenty years as a costumer she retired in 1976 and moved to San Clemente, California, where she continues to live.

Film Credits

1914   *Kidnapped in New York*
1915   *Maid of the Wild; Should a Wife Forgive?*
1916   *Little Mary Sunshine; Shadows and Sunshine; Joy and the Dragon*
1917   *Twin Kiddies; Told at Twilight; Sunshine and Gold; When Baby Forgot; Captain Kiddo; Tears and Smiles; The Little Patriot*
1918   *Daddy's Girl; Dolly Does Her Bit; A Daughter of the West; The Voice of Destiny; Cupid By Proxy; Winning Grandma; Dolly's Vacation; Milady o' the Beanstalk*
1919   *Child of M'sieu; The Sawdust Doll; The Little Diplomat; The Old Maid's Baby*
1935   *We're Only Human*
1936   *Swing Time*
1937   *Wise Girl*

1944 *Follow the Boys*
1945 *Here Come the Co-Eds*
1949 *My Own True Love*

Osborne, Vivienne (1896 Des Moines, IA-1961 Los Angeles, CA)

Vivienne Osborne began her career on stage at age five. By the time most teenagers were graduating from high school, she had spent years touring in a stock company throughout Washington State. She was in her early twenties when she made her New York stage debut.

Her screen debut was in *The Gray Brother* (1919), in which she played the steadfast sweetheart of a wrongly convicted man, but the independent film never found a distributor and was never released. She returned to Broadway, but when not performing in a play she continued to appear in films. After appearing in Ziegfeld's musical version of *The Three Musketeers,* Douglas Fairbanks asked her to appear in his Musketeer sequel, *The Iron Mask,* but she decided to remain in New York.

Her forays into film were mostly regrettable until she signed a contract with Paramount in 1931. No longer the ingenue, she was now cast in character roles. Her Hollywood debut, *The Beloved Bachelor* (1931), was a popular melodrama in which Osborne played a woman who married the wrong man and had to give up her true love to another woman.

Osborne moved to Warner Studios after becoming tired of poor roles being given to her by Paramount. Although her first parts were still supporting roles, her later roles had more depth to them. In *Two Seconds* (1932), she played a taxi dancer who leads a man to murder, and in the spoof *The Dark Horse* (1932), she portrayed the brittle former wife of a political advisor.

Unfortunately, bad career choices caused Osborne to become a virtual has-been by 1933. She appeared on the stage for a year before returning to films as a supporting player. She alternated between the stage and films for the rest of her career.

Film Credits

1919 *The Gray Brother*
1920 *In Walked Mary; The Restless Sex; Love's Flame; Over the Hill to The Poorhouse*

1921   *The Right Way; Mother Eternal; Cameron of the Royal Mounted*
1922   *The Good Provider*
1929   *Morgan's Marauders*
1931   *The Beloved Bachelor; Husband's Holiday; Masquerade*
1932   *Two Kinds of Women; The Famous Ferguson Case; Two Seconds; The Dark Horse; Week-End Marriage; Life Begins; Men Are Such Fools*
1933   *Luxury Liner; The Phantom Broadcast; Supernatural; Tomorrow at Seven; The Devil's in Love; Sailor Be Good*
1935   *No More Ladies*
1936   *Follow Your Heart; Let's Sing Again; Sinner Take All; Wives Never Know*
1937   *Champagne Waltz; The Crime Nobody Saw; She Asked for It*
1940   *Primrose Path; Captain Caution; So You Won't Talk*
1944   *I Accuse My Parents*
1946   *Dragonwyck*

The Oscar

One of the first actions that the newly formed Academy of Motion Picture Arts and Sciences took was establish an award for outstanding achievement in various areas of the film industry. Officially named the Academy Award of Merit, a trophy of a knight with a sword standing upon a reel of film was designed by sculptor George Stanley and "Oscar" was born.

Originally the award ceremony was held after a banquet, with the first tickets costing a mere $5. Still considered the most prestigious award an actor can receive, the first best actress Oscar (the only award open to a woman for many years) went to Janet Gaynor for her combined work in *7th Heaven* (1927), *Sunrise* (1927), and *Street Angel* (1928). Although the first ceremony received little attention from the media, since then the program has been broadcast—first on radio then on television.

Voted on by the members of the Academy, being awarded an Oscar had been prized by the film industry because one's peers bestow the honor upon the individual. At first the results were not kept secret. Before 1941 the honorees knew who had won before arriving for the ceremony, but that year the "sealed envelope" was adopted.

In recent years charges have been made that the award is no more than a popularity contest and can be "bought" with enough publicity, but for all its supposed shortcomings, being awarded an Oscar is considered by most to be the height of an actor's career.

Ostriche, Muriel (1896 New York City-1989 St. Petersburg, FL)

Although her tenure as a star was relatively brief, Muriel Ostriche was extremely popular during the height of her fame. She was still a teenager when she entered films and for two years was among the top stars in fan magazine polls.

Her influence during that period was increased by her being chosen as the face of a popular soft drink of the time, and she became known as the "Moxie Girl." At the height of her popularity in 1921, she married and retired to raise a family.

Film Credits

1912   *A Double Misunderstanding; The Passing Parade; That Loving Man; A Tale of the Wilderness; A Blot on the 'Scutcheon; The Letter with the Black Seals; The White Aprons; The Legend of Sleepy Hollow; The Easter Bonnet; Revenge of the Silk Masks; The Raven; Feathertop; The Holy City; Robin Hood; Making Uncle Jealous; Silent Jim; The Honor of the Firm; The Vengeance of the Fakir; Oh, You Ragtime!; Wanted a Wife in a Hurry*

1913   *A Tammany Boarder; An Accidental Servant; The Spectre Bridegroom; The Love Chase; The Crimson Cross; For Better or Worse; The Big Boss; The Bawlerout; Miss Mischief; Frazzled Finance; Flood Tide; The Farmer's Daughters; Lobster Salad and Milk; Algy's Awful Auto; Looking for Trouble; A Campaign Manageress; Bread Upon the Waters; The House in the Tree; Her Right to Happiness; Rick's Re-*

demption; *The Little Church Around the Corner; His Imaginary Family; The Law of Humanity; Cupid's Lieutenant; Helen's Stratagem; Friday the Thirteenth*

1914   *Rural Free Delivery Romance; The Ten of Spades; A Circumstantial Nurse; When the Cat Came Back; The Vacant Chair; The Purse and the Girl; When Paths Diverge; Percy's First Holiday; The Tangled Cat; All's Well That Ends Well; The Hold-Up; Her Way; Billy's Ruse; The Grand Passion; Her First Lesson; Too Much Turkey; Her Awakening; The Strike; Politeness Pays; In Her Sleep; A Circus Romance; Crossed Wires; His Enemy; The Toy Shop; Professor Snaith; The Little Senorita; The Decoy; The Girl of the Seasons; The Veteran's Sword; The Target of Destiny; Her Duty; A Rural Romance; The Belle of the School; The Keeper of the Light; The Varsity Race; The Diamond Disaster; A Madonna of the Poor; The Turning of the Road; Keeping a Husband; Mrs. Van Ruyter's Stratagem; The Amateur Detective; The Reader of Minds; The White Rose*

1915   *When Fate Rebelled; Check No. 130; The Speed King; Pleasing Uncle; An Innocent Burglar; Faces in the Night; When It Strikes Home; Celeste; Mortmain; For the Honor of the Crew; A Daughter of the Sea; What's Ours? The Heart Breaker*

1916   *A Circus Romance; Kennedy Square; Sally in Our Alley; The Men She Married; Who Killed Simon Baird?; The Birth of Character*

1917   *A Square Deal; The Social Leper; Moral Courage; Youth; The Dormant Power; The Good for Nothing; The Volunteer*

1918   *The Way Out; The Purple Lily; Leap to Fame; Journey's End; Tinsel; Merely Players; The Road to France; Hitting the Trail*

1919   *What Love Forgives; The Bluffer; The Moral Deadline; The Hand Invisible*

1920   *Meet Betty's Husband; Betty's Green-Eyed Monster; Betty Sets the Pace; The Sacred Flame*

1921   *The Shadow*

Owen, Seena (1894 Spokane, WA-1966 Hollywood, CA)

Born Signe Auen, Seena Owen made her film debut in 1915 in *A Yankee from the West*. Although she appeared in many films in her fifteen-year career, the two roles for which she received the most attention were Attarea, the Princess Beloved, in *Intolerance* (1916) and the mad Queen Regina in Erich von Stroheim's *Queen Kelly* (1929). She retired from acting and wrote scripts through the 1940s.

Film Credits

1914   *Out of the Air; Environment* (extra)
1915   *A Day That Is Gone; An Image of the Past; The Highbinders; The Fox Woman; Bred in the Bone; The Lamb; The Penitentes; A Yankee from the West; An Old-Fashioned Girl; The Craven*
1916   *Martha's Vindication; Intolerance*
1917   *A Woman's Awakening; Madame Bo-Peep*
1918   *Branding Broadway*
1919   *Breed of Men; The Sheriff's Son; A Man and His Money; One of the Finest; Riders of Vengeance; The City of Comrades; The Fall of Babylon; The Life Line; Victory; A Fugitive from Matrimony*
1920   *The Price of Redemption; Sooner or Later; The House of Toys; The Gift Supreme*
1921   *The Cheater Reformed; Lavender and Old Lace; The Woman God Changed*
1922   *Back Pay; Sisters; The Face in the Fog; At the Crossroads*
1923   *The Go-Getter; Unseeing Eyes; The Leavenworth Case*
1924   *For Woman's Favor; I Am the Man; The Great Well*
1925   *The Hunted Woman; Faint Perfume*
1926   *Shipwrecked; The Flame of the Yukon*
1928   *The Blue Danube; Man-Made Woman; Sinners in Love; His Last Haul; The Rush Hour*
1929   *The Marriage Playground; Queen Kelly*
1932   *Officer Thirteen*

P

Palmer, Corliss (1902 Edison, GA-1952 Camarillo, CA)

Corliss Palmer's career in films began when she was picked as one of the monthly "Honor Roll" winners of Brewster Publications' "Fame and Fortune Contest." Once she was selected as a finalist, she went to New York to appear in several screen tests. In spite of having no theatrical background, she won the contest.

After her selection, the owner of Brewster Publications, Eugene V. Brewster, began a full publicity blitz to promote her to stardom. He funded the development of "Corliss Palmer Face Powder" and hired her to write a beauty column in one of his publications, *Motion Picture Magazine*. He even starred her in films produced by his own film studio from 1921 to1922.

From reading the pages of Brewster's magazines one would think that Palmer was the most popular star of the period, but in reality her films were failures with audiences. When Brewster finally divorced his wife to marry Palmer, the negative publicity did nothing to enhance her career. She continued to appear in films until her divorce from Brewster in 1931. After her divorce she lost her place among Hollywood's social elite. She was eventually committed to a state hospital for the mentally ill.

Film Credits

1921   *Ramon the Sailmaker; In the Blood; Flaming Virtue*
1922   *From Farm to Fame Man; The Disturber; The Thistle and the Rose*
1926   *Her Second Chance; Bromo and Juliet*
1927   *The Return of Boston Blackie; A Man's Past; Polly of the Movies; Honeymoon Hate*
1928   *The Noose; Into the Night; The Night Bird; George Washington Cohen; Trial Marriage; Scarlet Youth; Clothes Make the Woman*
1929   *Broadway Fever; Sex Madness*
1931   *Honeymoon Lane*

Park, Ida May (1880 Los Angeles, CA-1954 Los Angeles, CA)

Ida May Park was one of the most important of Universal's female directors during the silent era. In fact, she wrote an article on the opportunities for women in the field of film directing in *Careers for Women* (1920), but in the 1934 edition her essay was eliminated because, by that time, women had been pushed out of the directing arena.

Park began as a stage actor at the age of fifteen and met her husband, actor Joseph De Grasse, while appearing with him in a play. When he joined Pathe in 1909, Park became a scenario writer. After 1914, the couple formed a production team with Park writing the films and De Grasse directing.

In 1917 Park directed her first solo film, *The Flashlight,* starring Dorothy Phillips, who was Universal's most popular female actor at the time. This began a successful collaboration between director and star which continued through several feature films.

In 1920 Park and De Grasse left Universal, and Park directed three final films that year for her own production company. In 1926 Park wrote the scenario for *The Hidden Way,* directed by De Grasse. Afterward Park retired from films, and nothing is known of her later life except the date of her death.

Directing Credits

1917   *The Flashlight; Fires of Rebellion; The Rescue; Bondage*
1918   *Broadway Love; The Grand Passion; The Risky Road; A Model's Confession; Bread; The Vanity Pool*
1919   *The Amazing Wife*
1920   *The Butterfly Man; Bonnie May; The Midlanders*

Writing Credits

1914   *A Gypsy Romance; The Man Within; Her Bounty*
1915   *All for Peggy; The Girl of the Night; The Grind; Steady Company; Bound on the Wheel; Mountain Justice; Quits; Alas and Alack; A Mother's Atonement; Lon of Lone Mountain; The Millionaire Paupers; Father and the Boys; Betty's Bond-*

age, *The Dancer, A Man and His Money, One Man's Evil, Simple Polly, Unlike Other Girls, Vanity, When Love Is Love*

1916   *Dolly's Scoop; The Grip of Jealousy; Tangled Hearts; The Gilded Spider; Bobbie of the Ballet; The Grasp of Greed; If My Country Should Call; The Place Beyond the Winds; The Price of Silence*

1917   *The Piper's Price; Hell Morgan's Girl; The Girl in the Checkered Coat; The Flashlight; Fires of Rebellion; The Rescue; Bondage*

1918   *The Vanity Pool; Broadway Love; The Grand Passion; The Risky Road; A Model's Confession; Bread*

1919   *The Amazing Wife*

1920   *The Butterfly Man; The Midlanders*

1926   *The Hidden Way*

1930   *Playthings of Hollywood*

Pearson, Virginia (1886 Anchorage, AK-1958 Hollywood, CA)

Virginia Pearson was one of the many actors in the 1920s to rule for a brief period as the leading vamp of Hollywood. Unlike the other actors who let their studio's publicity department rule their personal lives, Pearson refused to pretend to be someone she was not.

Pearson was originally interested in becoming an artist and briefly worked as a newspaper reporter before joining a stock company. After a few years of touring, Pearson moved to Broadway to appear in *A Fool There Was* in 1909. Unfortunately, her success in the role of "vampire" led to her being typecast both on the stage and in the films she later made.

She appeared sporadically in films while focusing on a stage career, but she eventually signed a contract with the Vitagraph Company in 1915. She was soon playing lead roles but always in the same vamp mold, which she felt was limiting and unchallenging. In 1919 she and her actor-husband, Sheldon Lewis, formed the Virginia Pearson Photoplay Company, but the studio lasted through only two productions—*The Bishop's Emeralds* and *Impossible Catherine*.

With the advent of the Jazz Age 1920s, Pearson wisely chose to abandon vamp characters and began to appear in supporting roles. She continued to appear on screen until the early 1930s. She and her husband led a quiet life in retirement until Lewis's death in 1958. Then, slightly less than a year later, Pearson died of uremic poisoning.

Film Credits

1910   *On Her Doorsteps*
1914   *Aftermath; The Stain*
1915   *The Turn of the Road; Thou Art the Man*
1916   *The Hunted Woman; The Vital Question; Blazing Love; Hypocrisy; Daredevil Kate; The Writing on the Wall; The War Bride's Secret; The Tortured Heart; The Kiss of a Vampire*
1917   *The Bitter Truth; Sister Against Sister; All for a Husband; Wrath of Love; When False Tongues Speak; Thou Shalt Not Steal; A Royal Romance*
1918   *A Daughter of France; Her Price; The Liar; The Queen of Hearts; Buchanan's Wife; Stolen Honor; The Firebrand*
1919   *The Love Auction; The Bishop's Emeralds; Impossible Catherine*
1922   *Wilderness of Youth*
1924   *A Prince of a King*
1925   *Wizard of Oz; The Phantom of the Opera; The Red Kimono; What Price Beauty?*
1926   *The Taxi Mystery; Silence; Atta Boy; Lightning Hutch; Mum's the Word*
1927   *Driven from Home*
1928   *The Actress; The Power of Silence; The Big City*
1929   *Smilin' Guns*
1930   *The Danger Man*
1931   *Primrose Path*
1932   *Back Street*

The Perils of Pauline *(1914)*

Perhaps the best remembered of all silent serials, *The Perils of Pauline* was a collaborative effort of Pathe and the Hearst newspaper chain. It was the first hugely successful serial and became the benchmark against which others were measured—rightly or wrongly. It was so popular that a contemporary song, "Poor Pauline," was written soon after its release.

For all its success, it was also the most poorly filmed, badly edited, and absurdly titled. The techniques used in its filming were crude even in the early years of the industry, and when compared to almost any other film from the same time, it is shown to be inept and ludicrous. The titles were often misspelled and commonly used incorrect words; for example, the word "immoral" was used instead of "immortal."

The plot was simple—the villain Koerner (Paul Panzer) wanted to steal an inheritance from the heroine, Pauline (Pearl White). In this prototype serial each chapter, of which there were twenty, was complete unto itself without the cliffhanger endings that serials were later known for using. The stunts and action were what drew the audience to the theaters, and they seemed willing to overlook the technical deficits for the thrills that were displayed on the screen.

The success of this serial ushered in a new genre in which female actors could appear and be independent rather than window dressing for men. Sadly, the female-centered serial ceased to be popular long before the male-centered ones. During the silent era, however, serials starring women were top moneymakers.

Petrova, Olga (1884 Tur Brook, England-1977 Clearwater, FL)

Olga Petrova was a liberated woman before the term was widely used. Born in England of Polish parents, her father was a tyrant who believed female children were no better than unpaid servants. She spent her life in search of true independence for herself from the demands that society placed on women.

Possessed of great talent and a steely determination, Madame Petrova (as she was called) became a prominent British stage actor. She came to the United States to star in a production of the *Folies Bergere,* but the show was not successful. However, Petrova created an act and successfully toured the vaudeville circuit.

Early in 1913 she began touring with the play *Panthea;* while in Chicago she was offered a film contract. Produced by Alice Guy Blaché, her debut film, *The Tigress* (1914), was tremendously successful with critics and the audience. Encouraged by the reviews and the vast exposure that films afforded, Petrova signed a contract with Popular Plays and Players in 1915 to appear in sixteen more films.

After the expiration of her contract, Petrova signed with Famous Players in the spring of 1917. Her first film for them, *The Undying Flame,* was well received if not a complete success. She made two more films for them that were also financially successful.

Late in 1917 she helped to create the Petrova Picture Company. After the company produced five films, however, Petrova decided that she would retire to write and occasionally appear on the stage. Having already written several scenarios, she now wrote poetry, magazine articles, plays, and novels. One of her plays, *Hurricane,* written in 1922, called for access to birth control while her play *What Do We Know?* (1919) dealt critically with the fad of spiritualism.

Film Credits

1914   *The Tigress*
1915   *The Heart of a Painted Woman; The Vampire; My Madonna*
1916   *The Soul Market; Playing with Fire; The Scarlet Woman; The Eternal Question; Extravagance; The Black Butterfly; What Will People Say?*
1917   *Bridges Burned; The Secret of Eve; The Waiting Soul; The Soul of a Magdalen; The Undying Flame; Law of the Land; To the Death; The Silence Sellers; More Truth Than Poetry; Daughter of Destiny; Exile*
1918   *The Life Mask; Tempered Steel; The Panther Woman; The Light Within*

Writing Credits

1917   *Bridges Burned; To the Death; More Truth Than Poetry; Daughter of Destiny*

Philbin, Mary (1903 Chicago, IL-1993 Huntington Beach, CA)

Mary Philbin had a dramatic bent from early childhood, when she reportedly spent her time dressing up and creating stories for her dolls to enact. She set her sights on an acting career while still quite young. However, she decided that she was not attractive enough for films and concentrated on stage work.

She was still a teenager when her mother entered her in a beauty contest sponsored by the local Elks Club and the *Chicago Herald Examiner.* The prize was a chance at a Universal contract and the judge, Erich von Stroheim, recommended that she be tested. Apparently, the studio saw something that she had not—possibly that she epitomized the Victorian ideal of beauty that was still popular at that time.

Her first film was *The Blazing Trail* (1921), and she appeared in several other films following her debut. The following year she was selected as a WAMPAS Baby Star and received full star buildup from her studio. In 1923 she appeared as Agnes, the organ grinder, in *Merry-Go-Round* in a role written especially for her by von Stroheim; some critics cite this film as her best performance. Others feel her best performance was as Christine Daae, the chorus girl-cum-opera singer, in the film for which she best-remembered, Lon Chaney's *The Phantom of the Opera* (1925), citing her unmasking of Erik (the Phantom) as one of the best remembered scenes of the silent era. That year she also appeared in another hit in the remake of the Mary Pickford film *Stella Maris* (1925).

Philbin made the transition to sound in 1929 in the film *The Last Performance*. Her two all-sound films—*The Shannons of Broadway* and *After the Fog*—premiered almost simultaneously. Soon afterward she retired from films and lived modestly in the Los Angeles area until her death.

Film Credits

1921   *Danger Ahead; Red Courage; Sure Fire; False Kisses; The Blazing Trail*
1922   *The Trouper; Human Hearts; His First Job; Foolish Wives*
1923   *Merry-Go-Round; Penrod and Sam; The Temple of Venus; The Thrill Chaser; The Age of Desire; Where Is This West?*
1924   *The Gaiety Girl; The Rose of Paris; Fools' Highway*
1925   *Fifth Avenue Models; The Phantom of the Opera; Stella Maris*
1927   *Surrender*
1928   *Drums of Love; Love Me and the World Is Mine; The Man Who Laughs*
1929   *Port of Dreams; The Last Performance; The Shannons of Broadway; After the Fog*

Phillips, Dorothy (1889 Baltimore, MD-1980 Woodland Hills, CA)

After beginning college in Baltimore, Dorothy Phillips joined the George Fawcett Stock Company and appeared on stage in the Baltimore area before moving to New York to appear on Broadway. When she was not cast in a stage play in the summer of 1911, Phillips signed to appear opposite Francis X. Bushman in a series of films from Essanay. Phillips returned to Broadway in the fall and appeared opposite Allen J. Holubar in *Everywoman*. By the end of the play she had married Holubar and the couple signed a contract with Essanay to ensure that they would be able to work together.

Their work attracted the attention of Carl Laemmle, who signed them to contracts when he created Independent Motion Pictures (IMP). The couple continued to appear together and individually until Holubar became a producer and director. By 1917 the couple had moved to Universal and Holubar directed Phillips in the feature film *Hell Morgan's Girl* (1917).

After several years with Universal, Phillips and Holubar left to create their own production company. Now considered one of Hollywood's golden couples, Phillips and Holubar were at their professional pinnacle. After directing his wife in *Slander the Woman* (1923), Holubar died suddenly of pneumonia at only thirty-three years of age. Grief stricken, Phillips was unable to resume her career until 1925, but by that time she was relegated to mostly supporting roles that became bit parts as the years went on.

Film Credits

1911   *His Friend's Wife; Her Dad the Constable; The New Manager; The Gordian Knot; Fate's Funny Frolic; The Burglarized Burglar; Saved from the Torrents; The Rosary; Love in the Hills; Putting It Over*

1913   *The Coward; Swag of Destiny; The Price of Gold; The Unburied Past; The Prophecy; Two Social Calls; In the North; The Value of Mothers-in-Law; The Final Judgment; The Sign; The Power of Conscience*

1914   *For the People; The Futility of Revenge; Hounded; In All Things Moderation; The Lady of the Island; On the High Seas; The Skull; Tempest and Sunshine; Three Men Who Knew; The Man Who Lost, But Won; Hounded*

1915   *The Affair of the Terrace; The Valley of Silent Men; The Trial of the Upper Yukon; The Springtime of the Spirit; Souls in Pawn; Six to Nine; Six Months to Live; A Shot in the Dark; Don't Wake the Baby; The Proof; Rene Haggard Journeys On; A Seashore Rodeo; Juror Number Seven; The Ladder of Fortune; The Last Act; A Lesson from the Far East; The Adventures of a Seagoing Hack; A Bachelor's Christmas; Children of Chance; A Fireside Realization; A Gentleman of Art; A Happy Pair; The Heart of Sampson; The House with the Drawn Shades; In the Clutch of the Emperor; Jealousy What Are Thou?; Souls in Pawn; The Parson of Pine Mountain; The Phantom Warning; A Photoplay Without a Name; Matty's Decision; The Mystery of the Locked Room; The Mystery of the Man Who Slept*

1916 *Any Youth; Behind the Curtain; Beyond the Trail; Borrowed Plumes; The Cad; The Code of His Ancestors; The Finer Metal; A Gentle Volunteer; Harmony in a Flat; His Brother's Pal; In His Own Trap; The Ivy and the Oak; The Marriage Broker; Mid-Winter Madness; One Who Passed By; Saved by a Song; Shattered Nerves; The Sheriff of Pine Mountain; A Social Outcast; A Wife at Bay; Their Anniversary; The Mark of Cain; If My Country Should Call; The Place Beyond the Winds; The Price of Silence; Her Husband's Honor; Ambition*

1917 *The Piper's Price; Hell Morgan's Girl; The Girl in the Checkered Coat; The Flashlight; A Doll's House; The Fires of Rebellion; The Rescue; Pay Me!; Triumph; Bondage*

1918 *Broadway Love; The Grand Passion; The Risky Road; A Soul for Sale; Mortgaged Wife; The Talk of the Town; The Heart of Humanity*

1919 *Destiny; The Right to Happiness; Paid in Advance*

1920 *Once to Every Woman; The Gorgeous Canary*

1921 *Man, Woman, Marriage*

1922 *The World's a Stage; Hurricane's Girl*

1923 *Slander the Woman; The Unknown Purple*

1925 *Every Man's Wife; Without Mercy; The Sporting Chance*

1926 *The Bar-C Mystery; The Gay Deceiver; Upstage; Remember*

1927 *Women Love Diamonds; The Broken Gate; The Cradle Snatchers; Running Wild*

1930 *The Jazz Cinderella*

1936 *Thank You, Jeeves!*

1940 *And One Was Beautiful*

1942 *My Favorite Spy*

1943 *The Cross of Lorraine*

1944 *Mrs. Parkington*

1946 *The Postman Always Rings Twice*

1949 *The Reckless Moment; A Connecticut Yankee in King Arthur's Court*

1955 *Violent Saturday*

1956 *The Man in the Gray Flannel Suit*

1962 *The Man Who Shot Liberty Valance*

Pickford, Lottie (1894 Toronto, Canada-1936 Los Angeles, CA)

Little is known about Lottie Pickford. Although she lived much of her life with or near her enormously popular older sister, the facts of her life are lost. The world, like her family, seemed interested in only one Pickford daughter.

She was an adequate actor, but she did not have the ambition or interest that her older sister did. She was also the dark opposite of her sister, who was the Victorian blonde ideal. Neither she nor her younger brother, Jack, ever measured up to Mary—and no one let them forget it.

She got her start in show business at the same time as her sister—both appeared in the play *The Silver King* around 1899, when she was six years old. She often appeared in plays with her sister or understudied her as they grew older, but if no job was available for her with the company, she was left at home.

She got her start in films in 1909, appearing in some of the same Biograph films as her sister. Often called "Pickford the Second" in newspapers, her sister was given all the attention. So, perhaps it was in rebellion that Lottie appeared in *The House of Bondage* (1914), an anti-vice film in which she played a prostitute—a role that most audiences found "disgusting."

By 1915 she was married to a New York broker and had signed to star in a serial that her sister had turned down. During the filming it became evident that she was pregnant, making the stunts difficult and dangerous. By the end of the filming she was so big that she had to hide behind props and was unofficially blacklisted.

Once her daughter was born, Pickford returned to the party circuit in Hollywood and was soon divorced. She occasionally appeared in films, mostly ones in which her sister starred. History often dismisses her as a hanger-on, but she never really had a chance to be anyone other than "Mary Pickford's younger sister."

Both her mother and older sister viewed her as inadequate—as an actor and as a person. This is evidenced by the fact that when she was divorced her mother took custody of her daughter and eventually formally adopted the child. With her family thinking she was not a fit mother, Pickford sunk further into a world of alcohol and, probably, drugs.

In 1922 Pickford married again in a lavish wedding supplied by her sister, but her reputation was beyond any amount of rehabilitation. This marriage also ended in divorce. After a few years of parties, in 1929 she again was married—this time to an undertaker-bootlegger from Michigan. This marriage ended in divorce four years later and then she supposedly married a socially prominent man from Pittsburgh. This too ended in divorce.

In 1936, she literally dropped dead in her apartment. Sadly, film historians often ignore her, although her brother, Jack, who was no more successful or influential than she, is cited.

Film Credits

1909 *Two Memories; The Faded Lilies; The Necklace; A Strange Meeting; The Little Darling; 1776; The Broken Locket; His Lost Love; The Light That Came; In the Window Recess; Through the Breakers; The Red Man's View; The Test; To Save Her Soul; What's Your Hurry?; Tender Hearts; The Better Way; The Slave; The Indian Runner's Romance; Getting Even*

1910 *The Woman from Mellon's; The Newlyweds; A Knot in the Plot; A Victim of Jealousy; Serious Sixteen; The Call to Arms; Unexpected Help; A Summer Idyll; The Affair of an Egg; The Oath and the Man; Examination Day at School; A Gold Necklace; Two Little Waifs; A Plain Song; A Child's Stratagem; His Sister-In-Law; White Roses; The Smoker; The Tenderfoot's Triumph; The Broken Doll; Simple Charity; Happy Jack; A Hero; A Golden Supper*

1911 *Fate's Turning; A Wreath of Orange Blossoms; The Midnight Marauder; Little Red Riding Hood* (I); *The Italian Barber; Help Wanted; His Trust; Three Sisters; Sweet Memories; The Toss of a Coin; Who's Who; The Courting of Mary; Love at Cloucester Port*

1912 *A Beast at Bay; Lena and the Geese; A Child's Remorse; Love Finds the Way; The Belle of New Orleans; A Mardi Gras*

Mix-Up; The Pilgrimage; Into the Jungle; The Girl Strikers; Love's Diary

1914   *The House of Bondage*
1915   *The Diamond in the Sky; Franchon the Cricket*
1916   *The Reward of Patience*
1917   *On the Level*
1918   *Mile-A-Minute Kendall; The Man from Funeral Range*
1921   *They Shall Pay*
1924   *Dorothy Vernon of Haddon Hall*
1925   *Don Q Son of Zorro*

Pickford, Mary (1892 Toronto, Canada-1979 Santa Monica, CA)

Courtesy of Silents Are Golden at <SilentsAreGolden.com>

Mary Pickford was *the* most popular film star in the world during the silent era. She was, in a real sense, "America's Sweetheart." During a time when publicity departments christened every actor with grandiose claims, it was actually the filmgoing audience who gave her the nickname. Her response was, "I am a servant of the public. I've never forgotten that."

Perhaps that was her hold over the public—she never forgot, as stars today too often do, that the public made her famous and rich and without them she would be nothing. Still, it is difficult today to understand the immensity of her popularity and hold on the filmgoing public because even the most popular stars today are not as much a part of their fans' lives as "little Mary" was during the early years of film. She was, as many historians have noted, "the industry's most valuable asset."

Gladys Marie Smith, years away from being Mary Pickford, was born into a gentile but poor family with a history of strong women. Her father was an alcoholic who deserted his family when his children were quite young. For appearance's sake, her mother declared herself a "widow" and went about trying to support her family—three children, a mother, and a sister.

Pickford was very sensitive to the undercurrents of emotion in her family and was often sick as a child. After her father's desertion and death, her bond with her mother became unshakable—neither career nor men nor time could break her mother's hold on her. For the rest of her life her family would be *the* most important thing to her.

In 1899 the Smiths rented a room to a couple that worked in the theater. And, although Mrs. Smith was prejudiced against "show people," as were most people of that period, she allowed her daughters to appear in a play, *The Silver King,* for a week. Pickford was eight years old, but she was eager to help support her family—her biggest fear was that the family would be separated.

She soon joined the Valentine Company and became their featured child actor. She continued to move among various stock and touring companies, with her sights on better roles and higher pay. It was a hard life for anyone, and harder still on a child who saw herself as the breadwinner for her entire family.

During this difficult period the Smiths became acquainted with another acting family—the Gishes. Both Pickford and Lillian Gish remarked years later that they could not remember a time when they didn't know each other. In fact, several times the families pooled their finances and shared housing. The girls had much in common, although according to Gish, "when Mary said to do something, we did it!"

Around 1908, Pickford set her sights on working for David Belasco, the most popular Broadway director at that time. Through nerve and subterfuge she worked her way in to see him. It was Belasco who changed her name to Mary Pickford and hired her after she told him that she had been an actress but she wanted "to be a good actress now."

She appeared in several Belasco plays, and in 1909 during a lull in the theatrical season, Pickford followed her mother's suggestion to apply for work with the "flickers" as early movies were called. Although looked down upon by theatrical performers as "not real acting," many supplemented their income with occasional appearances.

Pickford met D. W. Griffith at the Biograph offices in New York. Although he purportedly called her "too little and too fat," he hired her for a week's work. After a day that Pickford felt had been a dismal failure, she was surprised when Griffith asked her back and gave her a $5 increase in salary. With her supporting role in *Her First Biscuits* (1909), "America's Sweetheart" was on her way. In October 1909, the film *Pippa Passes,* starring Pickford and directed by Griffith, was the first film to be noted in *The New York Times.*

Pickford steadily increased her proficiency before the camera and as she became more comfortable with film, she began being featured more often. She became the "Biograph Girl" or simply "the girl with the golden curls" during a time when actors' names were never used. Although she was often at odds with Griffith and never followed his direction blindly, they remained friends for life and later became partners (with Douglas Fairbanks and Charlie Chaplin) in forming United Artists in 1919.

She excelled at the "little girl" roles that made her a star, and she played young girls well into her thirties. Yet beneath her golden curls was a mind for business. She was well known within the film community for her tough contract negotiating style. But her public was very strict with their favor. When she tried to play mature roles, her public expressed their displeasure by staying away from the theaters. By remaining the public's innocent girl, Pickford became the first millionaire actor with a worldwide fan base.

She achieved her first major success in the film *Tess of the Storm Country* (1914), which made her an international star. The Pickford Film Corporation was formed in 1916, and for three years she worked on her own films. She went on to more lucrative contracts and assumed more control over her films until United Artists was formed to distribute her own productions along with those of Fairbanks, Chaplin, and Griffith.

Pickford was consistently named one of the most popular, if not *the* most popular, actors in films into the 1920s. She solidified her popularity in 1920 by marrying filmdom's most dashing male star, Douglas Fairbanks. Together they ruled the world of films from their estate, Pickfair, for sixteen years until their divorce in 1936.

In addition to creating United Artists in 1919, Pickford was instrumental in organizing the Motion Picture Relief Fund in 1921. She was among the thirty-six founding members of the Academy of Motion Picture Arts and Sciences in 1928, when filmmaking was the fourth largest industry in the United States. In the Academy Bulletin (April 2, 1928) Pickford wrote that the "Academy is the League of Nations of the Motion Picture Industry. It is our open forum . . . a common ground. . . ."

As the audiences' tastes changed after World War I, Pickford was able to move slightly away from her little girl persona to more adult roles, but her most popular films of the period always had her as a naive or innocent young woman. The real Mary Pickford was a shrewd businesswoman, a successful scenario writer, and an accomplished producer-director. In a very real way she was "the woman who made Hollywood," as her 1997 biography by Eileen Whitfield states.

In an interview in *Photoplay* in 1931, Pickford stated that she wanted her films destroyed after her death ("I pleased my generation. That is all that matters . . .") because she feared that her films would be ridiculed by succeeding generations. Luckily her longtime friend Lillian Gish convinced her that her films should be enjoyed by future generations and the films were restored.

Pickford retired in 1933 but remained a partner in United Artists and a producer until 1956. A year after her divorce from Fairbanks, Pickford married Buddy Rogers, "America's Boyfriend" and her costar in *My Best Girl* (1927), her last silent film. The marriage lasted until her death in 1979.

In 1929 she received the Academy Award for Best Actress for her role as Norma in *Coquette* (1929), her first sound film. In 1976 she received a Lifetime Achievement Award, with the citation reading, "in recognition of her unique contributions to the film and to the development of film as an artistic medium." In 1961 Pickford was awarded an honorary Doctor of Humanities degree from Middlebury (VT) College—a special honor for the "young girl" who never finished grammar school.

Pickford wrote several books after her retirement. In 1934 she published *Why Not Try God* and a year later wrote *My Rendezvous with Life* (1935). In 1937 she formed the Mary Pickford Cosmetics Company. She finally wrote her autobiography, *Sunshine and Shadow,* in 1955.

Film Credits

1909   *The Fascinating Mrs. Francis; The Deception; The Drive for Life; Two Memories; His Duty; The Violin Maker of Cremona; The Lonely Villa; The Son's Return; The Faded Lilies; Her First Biscuits; The Peachbasket Hat; The Way of Man;*

The Necklace; The Country Doctor; The Cardinal's Conspiracy; Tender Hearts; The Renunciation; Sweet and Twenty; The Slave; They Would Elope; His Wife's Visitor; The Indian Runner's Romance; Oh Uncle; The Seventh Day; The Little Darling; The Sealed Room; 1776; Getting Even; The Broken Locket; In Old Kentucky; The Awakening; The Little Teacher; His Lost Love; In the Watches of the Night; Lines of White on a Sullen Sea; The Gibson Goddess; The Test; The Restoration; The Light That Came; A Midnight Adventure; The Mountaineer's Honor; The Trick That Failed; To Save Her Soul; What's Your Hurry?; Pippa Passes; Mrs. Jones Entertains; What Drink Did; Faded Lilies; The Mexican Sweethearts; A Strange Meeting; The Child's Friend; Wanted: A Child; A Sweet Revenge; The Heart of an Outlaw

1910   *All on Account of the Milk; The Woman from Mellon's; The Englishman and the Girl; The Newlyweds; The Thread of Destiny; The Twisted Trail; The Smoker; As It Is in Life; A Rich Revenge; A Romance of the Western Hills; The Unchanging Sea; Love Among the Roses; The Two Brothers; Ramona; In the Season of Buds; A Victim of Jealousy; Never Again; May and December; A Child's Impulse; Muggsy's First Sweetheart; What the Daisy Said; The Call to Arms; An Arcadian Maid; When We Were in Our Teens; The Sorrows of the Unfaithful; Willful Peggy; Muggsy Becomes a Hero; Examination Day at School; A Gold Necklace; A Lucky Toothache; Waiter No. 5; Simple Charity; The Song of the Wildwood Flute; A Plain Song; White Roses; The Call; His Last Dollar; The Kid; An Affair of Hearts; In the Border States; The Faces at the Window; A Flash of Light; Serious Sixteen; The Userer; Little Angels of Luck; A Summer Tragedy; Iconoclast; That Chink at Golden Gulch; The Masher; Sunshine Sue; A Child's Stratagem*

1911   *When a Man Loves; The Italian Barber; Three Sisters; A Decree of Destiny; Their First Misunderstanding; The Dream; Maid or Man; At the Duke's Command; The Mirror; When the Cat's Away; Her Darkest Hour; Artful Kate; A Manly Man; The Message in the Bottle; The Fisher-Maid; In Old Madrid; Sweet Memories; The Stampede; Second Sight; The Fair Dentist; For Her Brother's Sake; The Master and the*

Man; The Lighthouse Keeper; Back to the Soil; In the Sultan's Garden; For the Queen's Honor; A Gasoline Engagement; At a Quarter of Two; Science; The Skating Bug; The Call of the Song; The Toss of a Coin; 'Tween Two Loves; The Rose's Story; The Sentinel Asleep; The Better Way; His Dress Suit; From the Bottom of the Sea; The Courting of Mary; Love Heeds Not the Showers; Little Red Riding Hood; The Caddy's Dream; On Convert; Pictureland; Conscience; The Temptress; Behind the Stockade; By the House That Jack Built; The Aggressor; The Portrait; A Dog's Tale; The Daddy's Dream

1912　*The Mender of Nets; Iola's Promise; Fate's Interception; The Female of the Species; Just Like a Woman; Won by a Fish; The Old Actor; A Lodging for the Night; A Beast at Bay; Home Folks; Lena and the Geese; The School Teacher and the Waif; An Indian Summer; The Narrow Road; The Inner Circle; With the Enemy's Help; A Pueblo Legend; Friends; So Near Yet So Far; A Feud in the Kentucky Hills; The One She Loved; My Baby; The Informer; The New York Hat; Honor Thy Father; A Siren of Impulse; A Timely Repentance; A Child's Remorse; A Pueblo Legend; Grannie*

1913　*The Unwelcome Guest; In the Bishop's Carriage; Caprice*

1914　*Hearts Adrift; A Good Little Devil; Tess of the Storm Country (I); The Eagle's Mate; Such a Little Queen; Behind the Scenes; Cinderella*

1915　*Mistress Nell; Fanchon the Cricket; The Dawn of Tomorrow; Little Pat; Rags; Esmeralda; A Girl of Yesterday; Madame Butterfly; Broken Hearts; Little Pal; The Foundling (I)*

1916　*The Foundling (II); Poor Little Peppina; The Eternal Grind; Hulda from Holland; Less Than the Dust*

1917　*Pride of the Clan; The Poor Little Rich Girl; A Romance in the Redwoods; The Little American; Rebecca of Sunnybrook Farm; A Little Princess*

1918　*Stella Maris; Amarilly of Clothes-Line Alley; M'Liss; Johanna Enlists; One Hundred Percent American; How Could You Jean?*

1919　*Captain Kidd, Jr.; Daddy-Long-Legs; The Hoodlum; The Heart o' the Hills*

1920　*Pollyanna; Suds*

1921 *The Love Light; Through the Back Door; Little Lord Fauntleroy; The Nut*
1922 *Tess of the Storm Country* (II)
1923 *Rosita; Hollywood*
1924 *Dorothy Vernon of Haddon Hall*
1925 *Little Annie Rooney; Ben-Hur*
1926 *Sparrows; The Black Pirate*
1927 *My Best Girl; The Gaucho*
1929 *Coquette; The Taming of the Shrew*
1930 *Forever Yours*
1931 *Kiki*
1933 *Secrets*

Producing Credits

1915 *The Foundling* (I)
1916 *The Foundling* (II)
1918 *Johanna Enlists*
1919 *Daddy-Long-Legs*
1920 *Pollyanna; Suds*
1921 *The Love Light; Through the Back Door; Little Lord Fauntleroy*
1922 *Tess of the Storm Country*
1923 *Rosita*
1924 *Dorothy Vernon of Haddon Hall*
1925 *Little Annie Rooney*
1926 *Sparrows*
1927 *My Best Girl*
1929 *Coquette; The Taming of the Shrew*
1931 *Kiki*
1933 *Secrets*
1936 *The Gay Desperado; One Rainy Afternoon*
1946 *White Candle Inn; Susie Steps Out; Little Iodine*
1947 *Stork Bites Man; Adventures of Don Coyote*
1948 *Sleep My Love*
1950 *Love Happy*

Writing Credits

1909 *The Awakening; The Little Teacher; The Day After*
1910 *In the Season of Buds; May and December*
1911 *Madame Rex*
1912 *Lena and the Geese*
1913 *When Fate Decrees*
1914 *Hearts Adrift*
1915 *A Girl of Yesterday*
1923 *Garrison's Finish*

Pitts, ZaSu (1898 Parsons, KS-1963 Hollywood, CA)

ZaSu Pitts, who called her popular style "pathetic comedy," was named for both of her maternal aunts—Eliza and Susan. She moved to California with her family, but her father's early death in 1908 left her mother running a boardinghouse. A natural mimic from an early age, Pitts was encouraged by her mother to seek a career in entertainment.

After completing high school, Pitts moved to Hollywood but, because she was not pretty enough, was ignored by film directors. While she waited for her break, she worked as an extra and stuntwoman. Her opportunity came when her friend, famed screenwriter Frances Marion, wrote a part for her in one of her films; Pitts made her screen debut as Becky in *The Little Princess* (1917).

Although called an "ugly duckling," Pitts developed an eccentric persona of a perpetually confused old maid which played well in comedies. After her debut she went on to appear in a series of domestic comedy-dramas in the late 1910s.

Pitts married fellow actor Tom Gallery in 1920 and had her only child, Ann, in 1923. In 1926 when her best friend Barbara LaMarr died, Pitts adopted LaMarr's son, whose name was changed to Donald Michael Gallery. She divorced Gallery in 1932 and the following year married real estate broker John Woodall—a marriage that lasted until her death.

The friends she made—primarily Mary Pickford and Frances Marion—aided her early career. While Pitts was honing her acting skills, her friends made sure that she had roles in their films. Her first lead billing was in King Vidor's *Better Times* (1919), and she went on to make two more films with him.

Although well known as a comedian, Pitts was also an accomplished dramatic actor when allowed to step outside her comedic arena. In fact, her most memorable role during the silent era was the dramatic female lead in Eric von Stroheim's *Greed* (1924). Although the film was a bomb when it was first released, it is often cited as one of the silent era's most impressive films, primarily because of Pitts's excellent performance as the wealthy, but doomed, old maid.

Sadly, although called "the screen's greatest tragediennce" by von Stroheim, after *Greed* failed at the box office, Pitts was stuck in comedy roles where her fluttery-handed spinster alter ego was in demand. Her hands were considered so expressive that studio publicity departments claimed that they could "talk" to the audience by gesture alone.

Although she occasionally appeared in dramas in the silent era and always excelled in her roles, with the advent of sound films Pitts's high-pitched voice did not lend itself to dramatic roles. Also, it became apparent that the viewing audience would not see her in a dramatic role when she had to be replaced in *All Quiet on the Western Front* (1930) because the preview audience laughed during her dramatic scenes. While this was a disappointment to Pitts personally, her voice combined with her hand wringing made her famous during the sound era for her portrayals of zany, always bewildered sidekicks. Between 1930 and 1934 she made sixty films in addition to the seventeen comedy shorts she made with Thelma Todd in an attempt to create a female "Laurel and Hardy" team.

Perhaps tired of her typecasting in films, she toured the vaudeville circuit in 1938 and in the 1940s turned to the stage and radio. However, she remained cast in scatterbrained spinster roles. In the mid-1950s she costarred on the television comedy series *The Gale Storm Show* (1956-1960), as the befuddled beauty shop operator, Esmeralda "Nugey" Nugent. She retired after the series ended except for an infrequent guest appearance or film cameo, bringing an end to a forty-six-year career.

Her successful career proved that her maxim for life was true: "If you believe it, it can be so."

Film Credits

1917   *Uneasy Money; The Little Princess; A Modern Musketeer; Why They Left Home; Tillie of the Nine Lives; O-My the Tent Mover; His Fatal Beauty; He Had 'Em Buffaloed; Canning the Cannibal King; Behind the Map; The Battling Bellboy; Rebecca of Sunnybrook Farm; '49-'17*

1918   *The Pie-Eyed Piper; Good Night Paul; The Talk of the Town; A Society Sensation; A Lady's Name; Who's Your Wife?; How Could You Jean?; Why They Left Home; The Greatest Thing in Life*

1919   *As the Sun Went Down; Men, Women and Money; Better Times; The Other Half; Poor Relations; Sunnyside*

1920   *Bright Skies; Heart of Twenty; Seeing It Through*

1921   *Patsy*

1922   *For the Defense; Youth to Youth; A Daughter of Luxury; Is Matrimony a Failure?*

1923   *Souls for Sale; Mary of the Movies; Three Wise Fools; Poor Men's Wives; Hollywood; The Girl Who Came Back; Tea: What a Kick!*

1924   *West of the Water Tower; Daughters of Today; The Goldfish; Triumph; Changing Husbands; Legend of Hollywood; Wine of Youth; The Fast Set; Sunlight of Paris; Secrets of the Night; Greed*

1925   *The Recreation of Brian Kent; The Great Divide; The Business of Love; A Woman's Faith; Pretty Ladies; Thunder Mountain; Wages for Wives; The Great Love; Old Shoes; Lazybones*

1926   *Mannequin; What Happened to Jones; Monte Carlo; Early to Wed; Sunny Side Up; Risky Business; Her Big Night*

1927   *Casey at Bat*

1928   *Wife Savers; Buck Privates; The Wedding March; Sins of the Fathers; The Honeymoon; 13 Washington Square*

1929   *The Dummy; The Squall; Twin Beds; The Argyle Case; Paris; This Thing Called Love; The Locked Door; Her Private Life; Oh, Yeah!*

1930   *No, No, Nanette; Honey; All Quiet on the Western Front* (replaced); *The Devil's Holiday; The Squealer; Monte Carlo; River's End; War Nurse; The Lottery Bride; Sin Takes a Holiday; Passion Flower; Little Accident; Free Love*

1931   *Finn and Hattie; Bad Sister; Seed; Let's Do Things; Catch As Catch Can; Penrod and Sam; The Pajama Party; The Guardsman; War Mamas; The Silent Witness; On the Loose;*

A Woman of Experience; Their Mad Moment; The Big Gamble; Beyond Victory

1932   *The Unexpected Father; Broken Lullaby; Steady Company; Destry Rides Again; Strangers of the Evening; Westward Passage; Make Me a Star; Roar of the Dragon; Vanishing Frontier; Red Noses; Show Business; Blondie of the Follies; The Crooked Circle; Once in a Lifetime; Madison Square Garden; Back Street; The Trial of Vivienne Ware; Strictly Unreliable; The Soilers; Sneak Easily; Shopworn; Seal Skins; The Old Bull; Alum and Eve; Is My Face Red?*

1933   *Out All Night; Professional Sweetheart; Her First Mate; They Just Had to Get Married; One Track Minds; Mr. Skitch; Meet the Baron; Maids a la Mode; Hello Sister; Bargain of the Century; Asleep in the Feet; Aggie Appleby, Maker of Men; Love, Honor and Oh Baby!*

1934   *The Meanest Gal in Town; Three on a Honeymoon; Dames; Mrs. Wiggs of Cabbage Patch; The Gay Bride; Two Alone; Their Big Moment; Sing and Like It; Private Scandal; Love Birds*

1935   *Ruggles of Red Gap; Hot Tip; The Affair of Susan; Spring Tonic; She Gets Her Man; Going Highbrow*

1936   *Thirteen Hours by Air; The Plot Thickens; Mad Holiday*

1937   *Wanted; Merry Comes to Town; Forty Naughty Girls; 52nd Street; Sing Me a Love Song*

1939   *Naughty But Nice; Nurse Edith Cavell; Mickey the Kid; The Lady's from Kentucky; Eternally Yours*

1940   *It All Came True; No, No, Nanette*

1941   *Weekend for Three; Uncle Joe; Niagara Falls; Miss Polly; Mexican Spitfire's Baby; Broadway Limited; The Bashful Bachelor*

1942   *Tish; Mexican Spitfire at Sea; Meet the Mob; The Bashful Bachelor*

1943   *Let's Face It*

1946   *Breakfast in Hollywood*

1947   *Life with Father; The Perfect Marriage*

1950   *Francis the Talking Mule*

1952   *Denver and Rio Grande*

1954   *Francis Joins the WACs*

1957   *This Could Be the Night*

1959   *The Gazebo*

1962   *The Teenage Millionaire*

1963   *The Thrill of It All; It's a Mad Mad Mad Mad World*

Pretty, Arline (1885 Washington, DC-1978 Hollywood, CA)

Arline Pretty was one of the many female actors who achieved fame as a serial star. A solid and dependable actor, she never achieved stardom and her gentle loveliness belied the active roles she played on film.

After attending finishing school, Pretty joined the Columbia Stock Company and toured for three years. Her screen debut was sometime in 1913, but the studio was a small concern in Florida, so no information on the film is available. Her first verifiable film credits were in 1914 after signing with Universal and appearing opposite King Baggot. In 1915 they made a controversial film titled *An Oriental Romance,* in which she fell in love with an upper-class Chinese man (Baggott).

She moved to Vitagraph in 1916 and appeared in her first serial, *The Secret Kingdom* which took place in both a mythical kingdom and the American West. Later that year she appeared opposite Douglas Fairbanks in the comedy *In Again, Out Again.* She went on to another serial, *The Hidden Hand* (1917), and in 1920 she starred in her final serial, *A Woman in Grey,* one of the best-written serials of that genre. She continued to appear in films, but with the advent of sound she retreated to supporting roles that seldom afforded her billing.

Film Credits

1912　*Human Hearts*
1913　*Love's Justice*
1914　*The Old Guard; The Baited Trap; Human Hearts* (II); *A Mexican Warrior; The Mill Stream; One Best Bet; Shadows; The Silent Valley; The Treasure Train; The Turn of the Tide; The Man Who Misunderstood*
1915　*An All Around Mistake; At the Banquet Table; The City of Terrible Night; The Five Pound Note; A Life in the Balance; The Millionaire Engineer; One Night; An Oriental Romance; Pressing His Suit; The Man Who Found Himself; Three Times and Out*
1916　*The Surprises of an Empty Hotel; The Dawn of Freedom; The Secret Kingdom; The Thirteenth Girl; Beaned by a Beanshooter*
1917　*In Again, Out Again; The Hidden Hand*
1919　*The Challenge of Chance*

1920   *The Valley of Doubt; A Woman in Grey; Life*
1921   *Crossed Currents*
1922   *When the Devil Drives; Love in the Dark; The Wages of Sin; Between Two Husbands*
1923   *Stormswept; The White Flower; Bucking the Barrier; Tipped Off; Rouged Lips*
1924   *A Fool's Awakening*
1925   *Barriers Burned Away; The Primrose Path; The Girl on the Stairs*
1928   *Virgin Lips*
1935   *Shipmates Forever*

Prevost, Marie (1898 Sarnia, Canada-1937 Hollywood, CA)

Courtesy of Silents Are Golden at <SilentsAreGolden.com>

Although born in Canada, Marie Prevost was raised in the United States. She got her start in films in 1916 and made almost 100 films over her career, most of which were comedies. She joined Keystone and was one of Mack Sennett's early "Bathing Beauties."

Prevost continued to work at Keystone as well as freelance with other studios—most notably Universal. Her early work was most often lighthearted farce, but in the mid-1920s she was featured in several of Ernst Lubitsch's stylish social comedies. The late 1920s found Prevost in a string of successful films including *Up in Mabel's Room* (1926) and *Getting Gertie's Garter* (1927).

By the end of the decade, Prevost was having problems with alcohol and her weight. No longer thin enough for leading roles, she was relegated to supporting roles that increased her depression and led to more drinking. She made the transition to sound but only as a supporting player.

After appearing in only a few sound films, the film community believed that she was washed up. While planning a comeback attempt, Prevost died but was not found for several days. In fact, neighbors called the authorities only to complain that she was allowing her dachshund to bark at all hours. Her cause of death was determined to be acute alcoholism and extreme malnutrition—one of the first victims of Hollywood's cult of thinness.

Film Credits

1916 *Unto Those Who Sin; Better Late Than Never*
1917 *Secrets of a Beauty Parlor; Two Crooks; Her Nature Dance*
1918 *The Village Chestnut; She Loved Him Plenty; His Smothered Love; His Hidden Purpose; Hide and Seek Detectives*
1919 *Uncle Tom Without a Cabin; Yankee Doodle in Berlin; Why Beaches Are Popular; When Love Is Blind; Up in Alf's Place; The Speakeasy; Sleuths; Salome vs. Shenandoah; Rip and Stitch Tailors; Reilly's Wash Day; Never Too Old; Love's False Faces; East Lynne with Variations; The Dentist*
1920 *Down on the Farm; Love and Honor and Behave*
1921 *A Small Town Idol; Moonlight Follies; Nobody's Fool; A Parisian Scandal; Call a Cop; Dabbling in Art; Being Respectable*
1922 *Don't Get Personal; The Dangerous Little Demon; The Crossroads of New York; Kissed; Her Night of Nights; The Married Flapper; The Beautiful and the Damned; Heroes of the Street*
1923 *Brass; Red Lights; The Wanters*
1924 *The Marriage Circle; How to Educate a Wife; Daughters of Pleasure; Cornered; Three Women; The Lover of Camille; Tarnish; The Hollywood Kid; The Dark Swan*
1925 *Recompense; Kiss Me Again; Bobbed Hair; Seven Sinners*
1926 *His Jazz Bride; The Caveman; Other's Women's Husbands; Up in Mabel's Room; Almost a Lady; For Wives Only; Nana; Man Bait*
1927 *Getting Gertie's Garter; Night Bride; The Girl in the Pullman; Man Bait*
1928 *On to Reno; A Blonde for a Night; The Racket; The Sideshow; The Rush Hour*

1929   *Divorce Made Easy; The Flying Fool; The Godless Girl*
1930   *Party Girl; Ladies of Leisure; Sweethearts on Parade; War Nurse; Paid*
1931   *Gentleman's Fate; It's a Wise Child; West of the Rockies; Sporting Blood; The Sin of Madelon Claudet; The Runaround; Reckless Living; The Good Bad Girl; Hell Divers*
1932   *Three Wise Girls; Slightly Married; Carnival Boat; Hesitating Love*
1933   *Only Yesterday; Parole Girl; The Eleventh Commandment; Pick Me Up; Rock-a-Bye Cowboy*
1935   *Hands Across the Table; Keystone Hotel*
1936   *Thirteen Hours by Air; Tango; Cain and Mabel; Ten Laps to Go; Bengal Tiger*

Pringle, Aileen (1895 San Francisco, CA-1989 New York City)

Born into a wealthy family in San Francisco, Aileen Pringle appeared on stage in London and New York before divorcing her husband, a low-ranking British nobleman, and moving to Hollywood in 1920. She made her film debut in *The Sport of Kings* (1920).

Her greatest successes were in films based on novels written by Elinor Glyn. Prior to World War I, Glyn's books were popular in Europe for their forbidden romance and stylized sex. Pringle starred in several films based on Glyn's stories of romance among the British aristocracy of a bygone era.

Pringle's studios used her former marriage to a nobleman to legitimize the publicity which claimed that she was a member of the upper classes that she portrayed. Unfortunately, Pringle appeared in so many similar roles that she was stereotyped as the aristocratic woman "driven nearly mad" by unfulfilled desire. When America, too, finally became tired of the contrived "Ruritanian romances" that Glyn produced, Pringle was set adrift.

In the late 1920s Pringle began appearing in comedy roles and found that she enjoyed the freedom of comedy. When she was unable to secure roles in films, she appeared in regional comedy plays such as *Tons of Money* (1928) and *Thin Ice* (1930).

Pringle continued to appear in films through the early 1940s, but she seemed stuck in dramatic roles. In 1944 Pringle married writer James M. Cain, whose novels *Double Indemnity, Mildred Pierce,* and *The Postman Rings Twice* were made into movies. Unfortunately, this marriage, too, did not last and soon Pringle's outspokenness caused her to be overlooked by casting departments. She eventually moved to New York where she lived until her death.

Film Credits

1920   *The Cost; Earthbound; Stolen Moments; The Sport of Kings*
1922   *Oath-Bound; The Strangers' Banquet; My American Wife; The Cost*
1923   *The Christian; Souls for Sale; The Tiger's Claw; Don't Marry for Money; In the Palace of the King*
1924   *Name the Man; Three Weeks; True As Steel; His Hour; Married Flirts; The Wife of the Centaur*
1925   *A Kiss in the Dark; Wildfire; A Thief in Paradise; The Mystic; Soul Mates; One Year to Live*
1926   *The Wilderness Woman; The Great Deception; Tin Gods*
1927   *Adam and Evil; Body and Soul; Tea for Three*
1928   *Wickedness Preferred; Beau Broadway; The Baby Cyclone; Show People; Dream of Love*
1929   *A Single Man; Night Parade; Wall Street*
1930   *Puttin' on the Ritz; Prince of Diamonds; Soldiers and Women*
1931   *Murder at Midnight; The Sin of Madelon Claudet; Subway Express; Convicted*
1932   *Police Court; The Age of Consent; The Phantom of Crestwood; The Bride's Bereavement*
1933   *By Appointment Only*
1934   *Jane Eyre; Once to Every Bachelor; Love Past Thirty; Sons of Steel*
1935   *Vanessa: Her Love Story*
1936   *Wife vs. Secretary; The Unguarded Hour; Piccadilly Jim; Wanted: Jane Turner*
1937   *Thanks for Listening; The Last of Mrs. Cheyney; Nothing Sacred; She's No Lady; John Meade's Woman; Criminal Lawyer*
1938   *Man-Proof; Too Hot to Handle*
1939   *The Hardys Ride High; Calling Dr. Kildare; The Women; The Night of Nights; Should a Girl Marry?*
1942   *They Died with Their Boots On*
1943   *The Youngest Profession; Happy Land; Dr. Gillespie's Criminal Case*
1944   *Since You Went Away, A Wave, a WAC and a Marine; Laura*

Purviance, Edna (1895 Paradise, NV-1958 Hollywood, CA)

Courtesy of Silents Are Golden at
<SilentsAreGolden.com>

Edna Purviance was Charlie Chaplin's first leading lady and remained a nonworking employee of his until her death. Although many contemporary articles praised her talent as a comedian and her attractiveness, viewers seldom remember her today.

Purviance was raised by her mother in a boarding house that the family operated in the rural town of Lovelock, Nevada. She was a talented pianist and played for social occasions in the area. When she graduated in 1913 she immediately left for San Francisco.

She lived with her married sister, Bessie, while she attended business school. To help with expenses she soon found work in an office near Market Street. When she was not working or going to classes, she became known as the girl who walked her pet duck on a leash. After such a sheltered upbringing she delighted in the sights and sounds of the city and embraced the multiculturalism and cosmopolitan atmosphere for which San Francisco was known.

Across the bay from San Francisco was Essanay Studios, where Charlie Chaplin began working in 1914. Soon after his arrival at the studio, Chaplin ventured into San Francisco in search of a leading lady. When the normal venues did not present a likely candidate, a friend of Chaplin's suggested Purviance.

The first picture in which they appeared for Essanay was *A Night Out* (1915). Over the next six years they appeared in about forty films together. She was with him while he perfected his "tramp" character and was credited during this period as his muse and most avid supporter. As often happens in films, she became his leading lady off screen as well as on screen.

Unfortunately, their professional pairing lasted longer than their personal one—Chaplin had a roving eye at the best of times. While he expected to be allowed his indiscretions, he refused to forgive her even a hint of unfaithfulness. Even after they went their separate ways personally, she was his most steadfast friend, offering emotional support throughout his later travails.

Whether from disappointment over the end of their affair or for other reasons, Purviance began to drink, and the signs of overindulgence were evident on film. After Chaplin replaced her in his films, he tried to launch a solo career for her in *A Woman of Paris* (1923), but audiences didn't accept her. Finally, she was dubbed unemployable.

She retired from films and lived quietly near Hollywood. She received a monthly salary from Chaplin until her death. After her death, Chaplin said that he could not have abandoned her because she "was with me when it all began."

Film Credits

1915   *A Night Out; The Champion; In the Park; A Jitney Elopement; The Tramp; By the Sea; Work; A Woman; The Bank; Shanghaied; A Night in the Show; Charlie Chaplin's Burlesque on Carmen*

1916   *The Floorwalker; Police; The Fireman; The Vagabond; The Count; The Pawnshop; The Essanay Revue of 1916; The Rink; Behind the Screen*

1917   *Easy Street; The Cure; The Immigrant; The Adventurer*

1918   *A Dog's Life; Triple Trouble; The Bond; Shoulder Arms; Chase Me Charlie*

1919   *Sunnyside; A Day's Pleasure*

1921   *The Kid; The Idle Class*

1922   *Pay Day*

1923   *The Pilgrim; A Woman of Paris*

1926   *A Woman of the Sea*

1927   *Education of a Prince*

1938   *Charlie Chaplin Festival; Charlie Chaplin Cavalcade*

1947   *Monsieur Verdoux*

1952   *Limelight*

1959   *The Chaplin Revue*

R

Ralston, Esther (1902 Bar Harbor, ME-1994 Ventura, CA)

Courtesy of Silents Are Golden at
<SilentsAreGolden.com>

Called the "American Venus" or "Golden Venus," Esther Ralston is perhaps best remembered as Mrs. Darling in the 1924 version of *Peter Pan*. She was born into a family that could trace its roots back to the notorious Catherine Howard, one of the much-married Henry VIII's wives. In the early years of the twentieth century, her family joined a touring company and soon the entire family—both of her parents, four brothers, and herself—were appearing throughout the United States. When possible she also appeared as an extra in early films such as *Deep Purple* (1916).

When her family moved to California in 1917 to avoid a polio epidemic in New York, Ralston seriously began to pursue a film career. Her first major part was in William Desmond Taylor's *Huckleberry Finn* (1920). She appeared in more than twenty-four films, many of them action serials, before signing a contract with Paramount and being cast as Mrs. Darling. For the rest of the decade she was ranked among the most popular actors in film. She remained with Paramount for six years, with her greatest performance being in the lost film *The Case of Lena Smith* (1929). In 1929 she also ranked as the most popular actor among British moviegoers—surpassing Mary Pickford, Gloria Swanson, and Greta Garbo.

When her option was not picked up by Paramount, Ralston signed with MGM in 1934. After reportedly turning down Louis B. Mayer's romantic overtures, she was indefinitely loaned to Universal. She freelanced for several years before moving into vaudeville, appearing at both The Palace Theater in New York and The Palladium in London.

As film parts became more scarce, Ralston relied on the stage for acting work then moved into radio and, finally, television. In the 1960s she was a regular on the soap opera *Our Five Daughters* before working as vice-president of the Marge Kerr Talent Agency. She wrote her autobiography, *Some Day We'll Laugh* (1985), as well as many poems and short stories.

Film Credits

1916 *Deep Purple*
1918 *For Husbands Only; The Doctor and the Woman*
1920 *Huckleberry Finn; The Peddler of Lies; The Butterfly Man; To Please One Woman; Whispering Devils; Dangerous to Men*
1921 *The Kid; Crossing Trails; The Good Black Sheep; What Do Men Want?*
1922 *Daring Danger; Pals of the West; Remembrance; The Lone Hand; The Test; Pure and Simple; Oliver Twist; The Gypsy Trail; Behind the Mask; Dead Game; The Further Adventures of Yorke Norroy; Timberland Treachery; Unmasked; Tracked Down*
1923 *Under Secret Orders; Railroaded; Blinky; The Wild Party; The Victor; Pure Grit; The Prisoner; The Phantom Fortune*
1924 *The Marriage Circle; The Heart Buster; Peter Pan; Wolves of the North; Jack O'Clubs; Fight and Win; All's Swell on the Ocean; $50,000 Reward*
1925 *The Goose Hangs High; The Lucky Devil; Beggar on Horseback; The Trouble with Wives; The Best People; A Kiss for Cinderella; Womanhandled; The Little French Girl*
1926 *The American Venus; The Blind Goddess; The Quarterback; Old Ironsides*
1927 *Fashions for Women; Children of Divorce; Ten Modern Commandments; Figures Don't Lie; The Spotlight*
1928 *Love and Learn; Something Always Happens; Sawdust Paradise; Half a Bride*
1929 *The Case of Lena Smith; The Wheel of Life; The Mighty; Betrayal*
1931 *Lonely Wives; The Prodigal*
1932 *Rome Express; After the Ball*

1933   *By Candlelight; Black Beauty; To the Last Man*
1934   *Sadie McKee; Romance in the Rain; The Marines are Coming*
1935   *Strange Wives; Mister Dynamite; Ladies Crave Excitement; Together We Live; Streamline Express; Forced Landing; Shadows of the Orient*
1936   *Hollywood Boulevard; Reunion; The Rest Cure; The Girl from Mandalay*
1937   *The Mysterious Pilot; Jungle Menace; As Good As Married*
1938   *The Spy Ring; Slander House; Letter of Introduction*
1940   *Tin Pan Alley*
1941   *San Francisco Docks*
1946   *Child of Divorce*

Rambeau, Marjorie (1889 San Francisco, CA-Palm Springs, CA)

Marjorie Rambeau made her stage debut before she was ten, playing ingenue parts rather than the child parts that her age might suggest. She went on to star in silent films, but none of her films were as adventurous as her real-life childhood.

Her mother, Lillian Burnette, was a doctor—one of the first female doctors in the West. After her separation from Rambeau's father, in 1898 she moved with her two daughters and her mother to Nome, Alaska, to set up a hospital. Sadly, her hospital never became a reality because of the pervasive bias against female doctors in the late Victorian era.

With money tight, Rambeau became the family breadwinner, dressed as a boy and performing in the saloons throughout the region. When it became apparent that the talented "boy" was, in fact, a girl, Rambeau was signed to a vaudeville tour of Alaska during which she performed adult roles in several plays including *Camille, Under Two Flags,* and *The Christian.*

The troupe disbanded in Dawson, and Rambeau, now known as the "Bernhardt of the Klondike," hired a hall in which she gave both dramatic instruction and dance lessons to the culture-hungry miners. When she and her family had saved enough money to return to the States, the miners gave her a farewell gift of a silver-tipped ermine coat, never realizing that Rambeau was only twelve years old.

Upon arriving in San Francisco she joined a theatrical troupe that toured the Pacific Coast before she finally settled in Los Angeles in the spring of 1910. She refused offers to appear on Broadway, content to be a "Coast Defender"—the term for those actors that stayed in the West rather than venture to New York. Finally the offers became too good and she made her Broadway debut in 1913 in *Kick In*.

She married her leading man, but the marriage was stormy and ended after five years. But she was New York's darling and all her plays were long-running hits. Soon films beckoned and she made her film debut in *The Dazzling Miss Davison* (1917). After this success she worked on films during the day and appeared on Broadway for the evening show.

She married a second time, but the marriage again was short-lived, ending in 1923. By now, Rambeau was a much-loved actor but an unhappy person. She started to rely on alcohol to get her through her days, but that crutch affected her performances which, in turn, increased her unhappiness, thereby increasing her alcohol intake in a never-ending cycle. As the talk of her alcohol abuse grew, the roles offered her became fewer and she decided to return to California where she was still thought of as an excellent actor. When she caused a play to be cancelled in mid-performance, she decided that she needed to get control of her drinking problem.

To her credit, she did overcome her addiction and was given a chance to appear on stage again in a revival of her previous hit *Merely Mary Ann*. The success of this play resulted in offers to appear in films—most notably *Her Man* and the Marie Dressler hit *Min and Bill* (both 1930). She had made the transition to sound with ease and appeared in several films in the early 1930s.

With her career reestablished, Rambeau now entered into her third and lasting marriage, to a man she had fallen in love with when she was a teenager. At the time he had been poor and she had to support her family, so they were unable to marry. However, in the intervening years he had made his fortune and proposed to his first love.

After an extended honeymoon, the couple settled in Hollywood, where Rambeau occasionally accepted film roles to please her biggest fan—her husband. She was nominated twice for a Best Supporting Actress Oscar—once in 1940 for *The Primrose Path* and again in 1953 in *Torch Song*.

In 1945 she was involved in a traffic accident that killed her sister and almost killed her. It took three years and innumerable operations for her to be able to walk again aided by a cane. When she was well enough to return to films she signed to appear in *The Walls of Jericho*

(1948) and on the first day of filming the cast gave her a rousing ovation. She continued to appear sporadically in films until she moved with her ailing husband to Palm Springs in 1957.

Film Credits

1917   *The Greater Woman; The Mirror; The Dazzling Miss Davison; Mary Moreland; National Red Cross Pageant; Motherhood; The Debt*
1919   *Common Cause*
1920   *The Fortune Teller*
1926   *Syncopating Sue*
1930   *Her Man; Min and Bill; Her Great Day*
1931   *Inspiration; The Easiest Way; A Tailor Made Man; Strangers May Kiss; The Secret Six; Laughing Sinners; Son of India; This Modern Age; Silence; Leftover Ladies; Hell Divers*
1933   *Strictly Personal; The Warrior's Husband; Man's Castle*
1934   *Palooka; A Modern Hero; Grand Canary; Ready for Love*
1935   *Under Pressure; Dizzy Dames*
1937   *First Lady*
1938   *Merrily We Live; Woman Against Woman*
1939   *The Rains Came; Heaven with a Barbed Wire Fence; Laugh It Off; Sudden Money*
1940   *Santa Fe Marshal; Primrose Path; 20 Mule Team; Tugboat Annie Sails Again; East of the River*
1941   *Tobacco Road; Three Sons o' Guns*
1942   *Broadway*
1943   *In Old Oklahoma*
1944   *Oh, What a Night!*
1945   *Salome, Where She Danced; Army Wives*
1948   *The Walls of Jericho*
1949   *The Lucky Stiff; Any Number Can Play; Abandoned Woman*
1953   *Niagara; Torch Song; Bad for Each Other; Forever Female*
1955   *The View from Pompey's Head; A Man Called Peter*
1956   *Slander*
1957   *Man of a Thousand Faces*

Ray, Allene (1901 San Antonio, TX-1979 Temple City, CA)

Allene Ray won *Motion Picture Classic*'s "Fame and Fortune" beauty contest in 1920 while appearing in a film produced by a Texas-based studio. As a finalist, she went to New York to appear in several screen tests, but because she was under contract in Texas she was not able to move to Hollywood until 1923.

When her contract was complete and after both Mollie King and Juanita Hansen failed in their bid to replace Pearl White, Allene Ray became Pathe's new serial queen who, unlike Pearl's no-romance heroine, could take care of herself but was often more interested in the hero. With the release of her first serial *Way of a Man* (1924), Ray became a hit with the viewing audience.

The next year, she and Walter Miller costarred in the serial *Sunken Silver* and were so popular with the audience that they became a popular team in several serials over the next few years. In addition to being the last big serial queen, Ray appeared in what some historians have cited as the most sophisticated serial of the silent era, *The Green Archer* (1925). When Pathe went out of business, Ray moved to Universal and starred in the last silent serial, *The Indians Are Coming* (1930).

An introvert by nature, Ray was uncomfortable with the attention that her new fame garnered her, but she enjoyed the work. When her natural reserve made it difficult for her to register the proper degree of emotion at tense moments during her films, her directors often had to have stagehands actually scare her with noise-making devises to obtain the proper fear or startled reactions on film.

Because she was a fine athlete and an expert equestrian, Ray never used a double for the many difficult and dangerous stunts that were required during the filming of her many serials. As her value to Pathe increased, her willingness to undertake any stunt necessary caused the studio to devise elaborate measures to ensure her safety. However, since she was just as determined to do her own stunts, these schemes often failed to keep her out of danger.

Unfortunately, Ray entered serials near the end of the silent era and her fame did not last beyond the demise of serials. Since her voice was too high-pitched to register well with the primitive sound equipment, Ray retired with her husband to Northern California.

Film Credits

1919   *Squatter's Right; The Trail's End; A Modern Lochinvar; The Wildcatter*
1920   *Honeymoon Ranch; Crossed Trails; Ramon the Sailmaker*
1921   *West of the Rio Grande; On the High Card*
1922   *Partners of the Sunset*
1923   *Your Friend and Mine; Times Have Changed*
1924   *The Way of a Man; Ten Scars Make a Man; Galloping Hoofs; The Fortieth Door*
1925   *Play Ball; Sunken Silver; The House Without a Key; The Green Archer*
1926   *Snowed In*
1927   *Melting Millions; Hawk of the Hills* (I)
1928   *The Yellow Cameo; The Man Without a Face; The Terrible People*
1929   *Hawk of the Hills* (II); *Overland Bound; The Black Book*
1930   *The Indians Are Coming; Westward Bound*
1931   *The Phantom*
1949   *Gun Cargo*

Revier, Dorothy (1904 San Francisco, CA-1993 Hollywood, CA)

Dorothy Revier was an excellent actor who, like so many, was never really able to reach the heights of stardom that she seemed, at first, destined to achieve. She was born into an entertainment family—her father played with the San Francisco Symphony and her aunt was an opera singer. As a child she studied ballet, spending up to four hours per day practicing.

Upon completing school she began dancing professionally in San Francisco where she met her first husband, director Harry Revier, who took her to Hollywood. Her first film was *Life's Greatest Question* (1921), followed by *The Broadway Madonna* (1922), both of which were directed by her husband. She freelanced among the studios for the next few years, making everything from melodramas to action films.

In 1925 Revier was chosen as a WAMPAS Baby Star and signed a long-term contract with Columbia Pictures, which at that time was considered part of the lesser studios known as Poverty Row. As a result of her association with that studio, Revier became known as "the Queen of Poverty Row." She received star billing for the first time as the secretary that poses as her boss's wife in *Steppin' Out* (1925). With her elegant looks she was often cast as vamps, but for the next few years she was able to exercise her comedic flair in a series of social comedies.

Her most memorable role, and some say her worst performance, was as the immoral Milady de Winter in *The Iron Mask* (1929). Revier made the transition to sound easily and began appearing in a larger variety of roles. When Revier married for the second time, her contract with the Columbia was jeopardized because Columbia head Harry Cohn was supposedly in love with her.

She freelanced for several years after her remarriage but was generally relegated to supporting roles. During this period she lent her name to a line of skin care products sold in department stores. After many mundane, and sometimes just plain bad, films Revier retired in 1936. In later years she said that her one regret in her career was turning down the role of Belle Watling in *Gone with the Wind*.

Film Credits

1921   *Life's Greatest Question*
1922   *The Broadway Madonna*
1923   *The Wild Party; The Supreme Test*
1924   *Marry in Haste; Do It Now; The Martyr Sex; Down by the Rio Grande; The Other Kind of Love; Call of the Mate; The Sword of Valor; Border Women; The Virgin; The Cowboy and the Flapper; Man from God's Country; The Wild West; The Rose of Paris*
1925   *Dangerous Pleasure; Just a Woman; The Danger Signal; An Enemy of Men; Sealed Lips; Steppin' Out; When Husbands Flirt; The Fate of a Flirt*

1926   *The Far Cry; Poker Faces; The False Alarm; When the Wife's Away; The Better Way*

1927   *Stolen Pleasures; Wandering Girls; The Price of Honor; Poor Girls; The Clown; The Drop Kick; The Tigress; The Warning; The Siren*

1928   *The Red Dance; Beware of Blondes; Sinners Parade; Submarine*

1929   *The Iron Mask; The Quitter; The Donovan Affair; Father and Son; The Dance of Life; Light Fingers; Tanned Legs; The Mighty*

1930   *Murder on the Roof; Hold Everything; The Squealer; Vengeance; The Way of All Men; The Bad Man; Call of the West*

1931   *The Black Camel; The Avenger; Graft; Leftover Ladies; Anybody's Blonde*

1932   *Sally of the Subway; Sin's Pay Day; Night World; Arm of the Law; Beauty Parlor; The Widow in Scarlet; The King Murder; No Living Witness; A Scarlet Weekend; The Secret of Wu Sin; The Last Ride*

1933   *Love Is Like That; Thrill Hunter; Above the Clouds; By Candlelight; Love Is Dangerous*

1934   *The Fighting Ranger; Unknown Blonde; Green Eyes; The Curtain Falls; When a Man Sees Red*

1935   *Circus Shadows; Twenty Dollars a Week; Circumstantial Evidence; The Lady in Scarlet; The Eagle's Brood*

1936   *The Cowboy and the Kid*

Reynolds, Vera (1900 Richmond, VA-1962 Beverly Hills, CA)

Courtesy of Silents Are Golden at <SilentsAreGolden.com>

Vera Reynolds trained as a dancer early in her life but moved into one- and two-reel comedies, first with Sennett, and later with Gayety and Christie. Unfortunately, most of the titles of these films have been lost. When she signed with Sennett in 1917 as a comic ingenue, she was paid $20 per week. After several years of comic roles she was given her chance at appearing in dramatic features with Paramount in the 1920s.

While at Paramount she appeared in several of Cecil B. DeMille's society films, including *Prodigal Daughters* (1923) in which she portrayed Gloria Swanson's sister, Marjory. The following year, she received top billing in *Feet of Clay* (1924). She was one of the most popular supporting leading ladies at the end of the silent era and was chosen in 1926 as a WAMPAS Baby Star.

With the advent of sound she was relegated to the minor independent studios known as Poverty Row where she retained her leading lady status, albeit in lesser productions. She made only a handful of sound films before retiring.

Film Credits

1917 *His Hidden Talent; Caught in the End; Luke's Trolley Troubles; That Dawgone Dog; A Self-Made Hero*
1920 *Dry and Thirsty*
1922 *The Pest; Hearts of Oak*
1923 *Prodigal Daughters; Woman-Proof; Chop Suey Louie*
1924 *Flapper Wives; Icebound; For Sale; Broken Barriers; Feet of Clay; Cheap Kisses; Shadows of Paris*
1925 *The Golden Bed; The Million-Dollar Handicap; The Night Club; The Limited Mail; Without Mercy; The Road to Yesterday*
1926 *Steel Preferred; Silence; Sunny Side Up; Risky Business; Corporal Kate; Pride of the Paddock*
1927 *The Little Adventuress; Wedding Bill$; The Main Event; Almost Human*
1928 *Golf Widows; The Divine Sinner; Jazzland*
1929 *Back from Shanghai; Tonight at Twelve*
1930 *The Last Dance; The Lone Rider; Borrowed Wives*
1931 *Neck and Neck; The Lawless Woman; Hell Bent for Frisco; Dragnet Patrol*
1932 *The Monster Walks; Tangled Destinies; Gorilla Ship*

Rhodes, Billie (1894 San Francisco, CA-1988 Los Angeles, CA)

Billie Rhodes began her career on the stage with the Morrison Stock Company. When not working in a play she toured the supper club circuit. A representative of Kalem Company approached her mother during one of her club dates to suggest that Rhodes be tested for a possible film career and her mother reluctantly agreed.

Rhodes's first film was the two-reel drama *Perils at Sea* (1913), followed by several other comedies during the run of her one-year contract—most of the titles of which have been lost. When her contract expired, she returned to the stage and club circuit, but her talent was not forgotten. She was soon offered a contract with Al Christie when he was forming Nestor Studios.

In 1915 Rhodes was the star of Christie's Nestor Comedies. These films were called "polite" or genteel comedies, as opposed to Keystone's slapstick comedies. On average she appeared in one film per week, which meant that she had an extraordinary output of work in her career. When Christie left Nestor, he took Rhodes as one of the stars of his first independent production, *A Seminary Scandal* (1916). Christie next starred her with Jay Belasco in a series of films praised by critics as "clean, wholesome fun."

In 1918 Rhodes moved to feature-length films and began to appear in Capital Comedies for Parsons's National Film Corporation. The following year Rhodes made film history by starring in two features released in the same month—*Hoopla* and *The Lamb and the Lion* (March). Perhaps one of Rhodes's best-remembered roles was as Ruth in *The Blue Bonnet* (1919).

In 1919 Rhodes married her boss, William Parsons, but, sadly, Parson died only seven months later. Rhodes continued her film career, starring in a series of comedies for Special Pictures Corporation, but her style of domestic comedy was no longer popular with the filmgoing public. She retired from films in 1924 and once more returned to the stage and club circuit before eventually retiring to California.

Film Credits

1913   *Perils at Sea; Daughter of the Underworld; The Big Horn Massacre*

1914   *What Could a Poor Girl Do?*

1915   *Almost a King; Wanted . . . a Chaperone; The Tale of His Pants; Saved By A Skirt; The Rise and Fall of Officer 13; Operating on Cupid; A One Cylinder Courtship; On His Wedding Day; Nellie, the Pride of the Fire House; Molly's Malady; A Mixed Up Elopement; All in the Same Boat; And the Best Man Won; The Baby's Fault; Circumstantial Scandal; Dan Cupid-Fixer; Father's Helping Hand; Father's Lucky Escape; Following Father's Footsteps; The Frame-Up on Dad; He Fell in a Cabaret; Her Friend, the Milkman; Her Speedy Affair; His Lucky Vacation; His Nobs, the Duke; His Wife's Husband; It Almost Happened; It Happened on Friday; It Happened While He Fished; Keeping It Dark; Kids and Corsets; A Looney Love Affair; A Maid and a Man; A Maid by Proxy; Wanted: A Leading Lady; When a Man's Fickle; When Cupid Crossed the Bay; When Father Had Gout; When Hubby Grew Jealous; When Their Dads Fell Out; When Three Is a Crowd; With Father's Help; Their Friend, the Burglar; There's Many a Slip; Those Kids and Cupid; Something in Her Eye; When Father Was the Goat*

1916   *The Boy, The Girl and the Auto; Mixed Kids; His Wooden Leg; A Seminary Scandal; The Wrong Bird; Twixt Love and the Iceman; Their Awful Predicament; Some Honeymoon; Never Lie to Your Wife; Never Again, Eddie!; Love and Brass Buttons; The Lion's Breath; The Janitor's Busy Day; How Times Do Change; Her Hero Maid; Henry's Little Kid; He Almost Eloped; Good Night, Nurse; The Disappearing Groom; Across the Hall; The Deacon's Widow; What Could the Girl Do?*

1917   *And in Walked Uncle; Her Hero; A Two-Cylinder Courtship; Mary's Merry Mix-Up; Who's Looney Now?; Putting Her Foot in It*

1918   *The Girl of My Dreams*
1919   *Hoopla; The Lamb and the Lion; The Blue Bonnet; The Love
        Call; She Couldn't Grow Up; In Search of Arcady*
1920   *Miss Nobody; His Pajama Girl*
1921   *The Star Reporter*
1924   *Fires of Youth; Leave It to Gerry; It's a Bear*

Rich, Irene (1891 Buffalo, NY-1988 Hope Ranch, CA)

Courtesy of Silents Are Golden at
<SilentsAreGolden.com>

Irene Rich left a successful career in business to become an actor. During her career she appeared in films, in vaudeville, on stage, and on radio—all successfully. She appeared in more than 100 films over the course of her career, many of which have been lost or have deteriorated so much that viewing is impossible.

She excelled at playing worldly-wise women who had "been around the block." Or, on the other side of the coin, she could portray misunderstood wives who suffered nobly for their family. Her most successful silent films were Lubitsch's sophisticated *Lady Windermere's Fan* (1925) and the first version of *Craig's Wife* (1928).

With the advent of sound her career waned, although she did star opposite Will Rogers as his nagging wife in a series of films in the early 1930s. Deciding to broaden her experience, she turned to radio and hosted an anthology series, *Irene Rich Dramas,* from 1933 to 1944. The series was a mixture of one-episode dramas and serialized dramas that sometimes lasted for several months.

As offers for films came to her, she divided her time between her radio work and the occasional film, until 1948 when she retired from films entirely. Later that year she began a run in the Broadway play *As the Girls Go,* which lasted two years. Late in 1949 she also appeared on television in the dramatic anthology series *The Chevrolet Tele-Theatre* (1948-1950) in the play *Leave It to Mother.* She retired from acting in 1950.

Film Credits

1918　*The Girl in His House; A Law Unto Herself; A Desert Wooing*
1919　*The Silver Girl; Castles in the Air; The Lone Star Ranger; The Sneak; Her Purchase Price; Todd of the Times; A Man in the Open; The Blue Bonnet; The Spite Bride; Wolves of the Night*
1920　*Jes' Call Me Jim; Just Out of College; The Strange Boarder; Water, Water Everywhere; The Street Called Straight; Stop Thief; Godless Men*
1921　*One Man in a Million; A Tale of Two Worlds; Boys Will Be Boys; A Voice in the Dark; Sunset Jones; The Poverty of Riches; The Invisible Power; Desperate Trails; The Ropin' Fool*
1922　*Strength of the Pines; The Call of Home; The Trap; A Fool There Was; The Yosemite Trail; Brawn of the North; While Justice Waits; The Marriage Chance; One Clear Call*
1923　*Dangerous Trails; Brass; Michael O'Halloran; Yesterday's Wife; Rosita; Defying Destiny; Lucretia Lombard; Boy of Mine; Snowdrift*
1924　*Pal o' Mine; Beau Brummel; Cytherea; Being Respectable; Captain January; A Woman Who Sinned; Behold This Woman; A Lost Lady; This Woman; What the Butler Saw*
1925　*My Wife and I; The Man Without a Conscience; Eve's Lover; The Wife Who Wasn't Wanted; Compromise; Lady Windermere's Fan; Pleasure Buyers*
1926　*Silken Shackles; The Honeymoon Express; My Official Wife*
1927　*Don't Tell the Wife; The Climbers; Dearie; The Desired Woman; The Silver Slave*
1928　*Beware of Married Men; Powder My Back; Perfect Crime; Across the Atlantic; Women They Talk About; Craig's Wife; Ned McCobb's Daughter*
1929　*Daughters of Desire; The Exalted Flapper; They Had to See Paris; Shanghai Rose*
1930　*So This Is London; On Your Back; Check and Double Check*
1931　*Strangers May Kiss; Five and Ten; The Mad Parade; The Champ; Wicked; Father's Son; Beau Ideal*
1932　*Manhattan Tower; Her Mad Night; Down to Earth*
1938　*That Certain Age; Hollywood Handicap*
1939　*Everybody's Hobby; The Right Way*
1940　*The Mortal Storm; The Lady in Question; Queen of the Yukon; Keeping Company*
1941　*Three Sons o' Guns*

1942   *This Time for Keeps*
1947   *Angel and the Badman; New Orleans; Calendar Girl*
1948   *Fort Apache; Joan of Arc*

Ricksen, Lucille (1909 Chicago, IL-1925 Los Angeles, CA)

Lucille Ricksen was one the many tragedies of the silent era. She seemed to be on the verge of realizing her dream of film stardom at the early age of fifteen. Having been raised in Chicago, Ricksen had been in the right place to begin a film career with Essanay Company—not an unusual occurrence except that her career started when she was only four years old.

Little is known of her early career with Essanay, but she signed with Goldwyn Company in 1920 as one of the stars of the film versions of Booth Tarkington's *Edgar* stories. With the popularity of the *Edgar* series, Ricksen began appearing in flapper roles as she gained enough experience to graduate to her first adult dramatic role, as Vera in *The Rendezvous* (1923). A year earlier, in 1924, Ricksen was chosen as a WAMPAS Baby Star, and she seemed well on her way to the stardom predicted for her.

Her first role after signing her adult contract with the newly merged Metro-Goldwyn was in the Claire Windsor drama *The Denial* (1925). However, after completing the film Ricksen collapsed from the onset of tuberculosis. Her mother died while caring for her (literally collapsing dead on her daughter), and the shock of this combined with the disease ended Ricksen's life before her sixteenth birthday.

Film Credits

1920   *Edgar and the Teacher's Pet; Edgar Camps Out; Edgar's Little Saw; Edgar Takes the Cake*
1921   *The Old Nest*
1922   *The Married Flapper; Remembrance; The Girl Who Ran Wild; The Stranger's Banquet; Forsaking All Others*
1923   *Trimmed in Scarlet; Human Wreckage; The Rendezvous; The Social Buccaneer; One of Three; Under Secret Orders; The Secret Code; The Radio-Active Bomb; The Showdown*
1924   *The Judgment of the Storm; The Galloping Fish; The Hill Billy; Those Who Dance; Young Ideas; Behind the Curtain; Vanity's Price; The Painted Lady; Idle Tongues*
1925   *The Denial*

Rinehart, Mary Roberts (1876 Pittsburgh, PA-1958 New York City)

Mary Roberts Rinehart was a famous mystery novelist and playwright before she came to Hollywood to write scenarios. During the height of her career she was more famous than her rival Agatha Christie and she was reportedly responsible for coining the phrase "the butler did it."

She was born into a genteel but poor family, and her father was the creator of impractical, nonmarketable inventions. She began writing to escape from her unsettled youth. She graduated from nursing school and in 1896 married a physician who later joined the Army.

In 1903 Rinehart returned to writing to contribute money to the faltering finances of her young family. In 1908 her first novel, *The Circular Staircase,* was published. In addition to working on novels, she became a regular contributor to the *Saturday Evening Post* and other national magazines.

By the beginning of World War I, several of her books had been adapted for the stage and a few had been made into films. During the war she was a newspaper correspondent and one of the only women to report directly from the war zone. She returned to writing and Hollywood at the end of the war.

In 1931 she wrote her autobiography, *My Story.* She continued to write and adapt her work for films when requested until the early 1940s. At that time she decided to concentrate on mystery writing. The last of her novels that was adapted for Broadway and Hollywood was the second version of her novel *The Bat* (1959).

She lived in New York and wrote daily until her death. On a good day she wrote about 4000 words; she left a legacy of more than fifty books, eight plays, more than thirty films, and untold poems, short stories, and articles. She is buried with her husband in Arlington National Cemetery.

Writing Credits

1915　*The Circular Staircase; Affinities* (I); *What Happened to Father* (I); *The Papered Door; Mind Over Motor*
1916　*Acquitted*
1917　*Bab's Diary; Bab's Burglar; Bab's Matinee Idol*
1918　*The Doctor and the Woman; The Street of Seven Stars; Her Country First*

1919   *23 ½ Hours Leave* (I)
1920   *Dangerous Days; It's a Great Life*
1922   *The Glorious Fool; Affinities* (II)
1923   *Long Live the King*
1924   *The Silent Watcher; Her Love Story; K, the Unknown*
1925   *Seven Days*
1926   *The Bat* (I)
1927   *The Unknown; Aflame in the Sky; What Happened to Father?* (II)
1928   *Finders Keepers*
1930   *The Bat Whispers*
1931   *I Take This Woman*
1932   *Miss Pinkerton*
1934   *Elinor Norton*
1936   *Mr. Cohen Takes a Walk*
1937   *23 ½ Hours Leave* (II)
1941   *The Dog in the Orchard; The Nurse's Secret*
1942   *Tish*
1959   *The Bat* (II)

Roland, Ruth (1892 San Francisco, CA-1937 Hollywood, CA)

Courtesy of Silents Are Golden at
<SilentsAreGolden.com>

Second only to Pearl White in serial popularity, Ruth Roland was an astute businesswoman. It was revealed after her retirement that she never did her own stunts, as opposed to White who was known for doing her own stunts. However, this fact was a carefully guarded secret—a serial queen was successful because she *was* the death-defying character she portrayed.

Roland was born into an entertainment family. Her father operated a theater and her mother was a professional singer. She made her stage debut at her father's theater before she was four years old. Her first success was in *Cinderella* followed by an appearance as Little Lord Fauntleroy.

When her parents separated, Roland continued to appear on the stage and on the vaudeville circuit as "Baby Ruth" with her mother as chaperone. After several successful shows, Roland was the first child actor to appear in Honolulu, where she remained for six months appearing in sold-out shows. When she returned to San Francisco, she appeared with the famous Belasco Company.

Her mother died when Roland was eight, which put a temporary end to her acting career. She went to live with an aunt in Los Angeles until she was sixteen and then returned to the stage on her own. Now as an ingenue, Roland toured vaudeville for two years.

While appearing on stage in 1909, a talent scout for the Kalem Company approached Roland and she left immediately for Los Angeles. Although she supposedly made more than 200 shorts while at Kalem, most of these titles have been lost. She excelled at westerns, but Kalem also cast her in comedies and she became their reigning female comic.

However, she tired of comedies and requested different types of films. Soon she was appearing in the "Girl Detective" series in which she played as society girl who worked as a special consultant to the police department. Although the concept bordered on ridiculous, the audience loved the films.

Roland moved to Balboa Feature Film Company in 1915 and was cast in a series of three-reel dramas. Later that year she appeared in her first serial, *The Red Circle,* in which she played a wealthy reformer who, because of a family curse, was also a criminal. Roland excelled at making the audience like her and believe in the exciting, but impossible, situations in which her character always found herself. She was not, however, popular with the people with whom she worked. In fact, she supposedly made an entire serial without talking to her director at all.

For all her lack of people skills, Roland was an excellent horsewoman, a robust swimmer, and a superb shot with any gun or rifle. These talents made her a natural for both serials and westerns. So although she did not do the dangerous stunts in her movies, she was able to hold her own with the other physically challenging requirements of the genre.

In 1918 she was cast in the film that elevated her to the top of the serial world, *Hands Up*. The following year she appeared in arguably her most popular serial, *The Tiger's Trail,* and formed her own production company which released films through Pathe. For the next three years Roland made one serial after another, capitalizing on her popularity. Her final serial was *Haunted Valley* (1923).

In addition to her acting talent, Roland was a shrewd business-woman who often invested her salary in real estate. At the height of her career she was making several thousand dollars per week and, unlike many of her contemporaries, she retired a millionaire. Although she retired from serials, she continued to appear on the vaudeville circuit and play concert dates.

In 1929 she married Ben Bard, a theater owner like her father. She appeared in a few more films, all of which where forgettable. Sadly, after working so that she would be comfortable as she aged, Roland died from cancer at the age of forty-four.

Film Credits

1909   *The Old Soldier's Story; The Cardboard Baby*
1910   *The Indian Scout's Vengeance; Her Indian Mother*
1911   *Arizona Bill; A Chance Shot; The Kidnapped Conductor; Mesquite's Gratitude; He Who Laughs Last*
1912   *The Desert Trail; The Trail of Gold; The Pasadena Peach; Hypnotic Nell; The Bugler of Battery B; The Soldier Brothers of Susanna; The Beauty Parlor of Stone Gulch; Saved from Court Martial; Fat Bill's Wooing; Queen of the Kitchen; A Hospital Hoax; The Belle of the Beach; Death Valley Scotty's Mine; I Saw Him First; Strong Arm Nellie; The Landlubber; The Chaperon Gets a Duckling; Pulque Pete and the Opera Troupe; A Mountain Tragedy; The Peace Offering; Ranch Girls on a Rampage; Ruth Roland, the Kalem Girl; Things Are Seldom What They Seem; Stenographers Wanted; The Schoolma'm of Stone Gulch; The Pugilist and the Girl; The Mummy and the Cowpuncher; How Jim Proposed; The Hoodoo Hat; Walk, You, Walk!; The Romance of a Dry Town; The Dude Cowboy; Accidents Will Happen; The Swimming Party; The Romance of the Town; The Trail Through the Hills; Outwitting Father; A Fish Story; The Chauffeur's Dream; The Girl Bandit's Hoodoo; The Woman Hater; The Loneliness of the Hills; Dr. Skinnem's Wonderful Invention; In Peril of Their Lives; Paying the Board Bill;*

Brave Old Bill; The Bachelor Bride; Something Wrong with Bessie; A California Snipe Hunt

1913 The Manicurist and the Mutt; One on Willie; The Horse That Wouldn't Stay Hitched; Absent Minded Abe; Jones' Jonah Day; The Fired Cook; The Indestructible Mr. Jenks; The Phony Singer; A Coupon Courtship; The Hash House Count; The Black Hand; Why Women Are Police; Percy's Wooing; The Raiders from Double L Ranch; Entertaining Uncle; The Tenderfoot's Luck; Hoodooed on His Wedding Day; The Hobo and the Myth; The Troublesome Telephone; The Speed Limit; Hypnotizing Mamie; The Fickle Freak; The Laundress and the Lady; While Father Telephoned; General Bunco's Victory; Bill's Board Bill; The Good Old Summer Time; Fatty's Deception; The Captivating Widow; Able Minded Abe; The Mission of a Bullet; A Hero Reward; Three Suitors and a Dog; The Matrimonial Venture of the "Bar X" Hands; Trixie and the Press Agent; A Cold Storage Egg; The Sheriff of Stone Gulch; Parcel Post Johnnie; The Cat and the Bonnet; The Bravest Girl in California; Fatty's Busy Day; Pat, the Cowboy; Smoked to a Finish; Cupid's Lariat; Knight of Cyclone Gulch; Curing Her Extravagance; Amateur Burglar; And the Watchman Came Back; The Hobo and the Hobble Skirt

1914 The Joke on Jane; Only One Shirt; The Medicine Show at Stone Gulch; Hiram's Hotel; The Family Skeleton; And the Villain Still Pursued Her; The Confiscated Count; Hubby's Night Off; Gertie Gets the Cash; McBride's Bride; Tight Shoes; Reaping for the Whirlwind; Wanted: An Heir; The Deadly Battle at Hicksville; Don't Monkey with the Buzzsaw; A Substitute for Pants; Sherlock Bonehead; When Men Wear Skirts; The Tattered Duke; The Slavery of Foxicus; Lizzie, the Life Saver; Ham, the Piano Mover; The Peach at the Beach; Bud and Bill and the Waiter; Ham, the Lineman; Ham and the Villain Factory; Cupid Backs the Winners; Wages of Sin; The Indian Maid's Warning; Si's Wonderful Mineral Spring; An Elopement in Rome

1915 The Red Circle; Comrade John; Toil and Tyranny; The Fruit of Folly; The Pomp of Earth; For the Commonwealth; Today and Tomorrow; Blue Blood and Yellow; Houses of Glass; Unto Herself Alone; The Love Liar; When Justice Sleeps;

The Price of Fame; The Pursuit of Pleasure; Jared Fairfax's Millions; Old Isaacson's Diamond; Following a Clue; The Mystery of the Tea Dansant; The House of Glass; The Girl Detective; The Disappearance of Harry Warrington; The Apartment House Mystery; She Would Be a Cowboy; Affair of the Deserted House; The Tip-Off; A Model Wife; Who Pays?; The Price of Fame; Following a Clue

1916   *The Sultana; A Matrimonial Martyr*
1917   *A Message from Reno; The Fringe of Society; The Stolen Play; The Neglected Wife; The Devil's Bait*
1918   *Cupid Angling; Hands Up; The Price of Folly* (eight chapters)
1919   *The Adventures of Ruth; The Tiger's Trail; Love and the Law*
1920   *Ruth of the Rockies*
1921   *The Avenging Arrow*
1922   *The Timber Queen; White Eagle*
1923   *Ruth of the Range; Haunted Valley*
1925   *Where the Worst Begins; Dollar Down*
1927   *The Masked Woman*
1930   *Reno*
1935   *From Nine to Nine*

Royce, Ruth (1893 Versailles, MO-1971 Los Angeles, CA)

One of the most popular villains of silent serials, Ruth Royce made her first film in 1915, *Little Brother of the Rich*. Eventually she turned to the mystery serials that were so popular during the 1920s. She always played the part of an evil, ruthless female who preyed on men and reveled in dominating them and luring them to their doom in the style of the vampire.

She appeared in seven serials during the 1920s. To the viewing audience she epitomized a conniving woman. In addition to these overtly evil characters, she was also often cast as "the other woman." These characters were generally obsessed with success and wealth and were willing to do anything to achieve them.

Film Credits

1915   *Little Brother of the Rich*
1919   *The Splendid Sin*
1920   *The Vanishing Dagger; Blue Streak McCoy; The Girl in Number 29; "If Only" Jim*
1921   *The Man Trackers; All Dolled Up*

1922   *Caught Bluffing; Perils of the Yukon; In the Days of Buffalo Bill*
1923   *The Oregon Trail; In the Days of Daniel Boone; Beasts of Paradise*
1924   *Riders of the Plain; Days of '49; California in '49*
1925   *Action Galore; Warrior Gap; The Power God; Tonio, Son of the Sierras*
1926   *Officer 444; The Gallant Fool; Fort Frayne; Rawhide; Wolves of the Desert; Trooper 77*
1927   *Thunderbolt's Tracks; Code of the Cow Country*

Rubens, Alma (1897 San Francisco, CA-1931 Los Angeles, CA)

Courtesy of Silents Are Golden at
<SilentsAreGolden.com>

Alma Rubens was another of the tragedies of Hollywood and early fame. A star by nineteen, Rubens fell victim to weakness and money which ended a promising career. An early writer compared her beauty to "red roses in an onyx jar," although by the time of her death little of the beauty was still evident.

Like many young girls in the early years of the twentieth century, Rubens dreamed of being a film actor. For her the dream came true with a bit part in D. W. Griffith's infamous epic *The Birth of a Nation* (1915). She appeared in other Griffith films until her breakthrough role as Lemona in Douglas Fairbanks's *Reggie Mixes In* (1916). She appeared with Fairbanks in two other films that year—*The Americano* and *The Half-Breed*—for which she garnered critical acclaim.

For the next few years she appeared in hit after hit and even did some stage work. Despite all her success, she found work harder to find as the decade came to an end due to the ravages of her alcohol and drug addiction. Both her looks and her money wasted away, and she spent time in several asylums in an effort to break heroin's hold on her. Finally, weakened by the drug, she died of pneumonia before her thirty-fourth birthday.

Film Credits

1913   *Benzai*
1914   *Narcotic Spectre; The Gangster and the Girl*
1915   *The Birth of a Nation*
1916   *Reggie Mixes In; The Half-Breed; Intolerance; The Children Pay; Truthful Tulliver; The Americano; The Mystery of Leaping Fish; Judith of the Cumberlands*
1917   *A Woman's Awakening; An Old Fashioned Young Man; The Firefly of Tough Luck; The Regenerates; The Gown of Destiny; Master of His Home; The Cold Deck*
1918   *I Love You; The Answer; The Love Brokers; Madame Sphinx; The Painted Lily; False Ambition; The Ghost Flower*
1919   *Restless Souls; Diane of the Green Van; A Man's Country; The Fall of Babylon*
1920   *Humoresque; The World and His Wife; Thoughtless Woman*
1922   *Find the Woman; The Valley of Silent Men*
1923   *Enemies of Women; Under the Red Robe*
1924   *Week End Husbands; The Rejected Woman; Cytherea; The Price She Paid; Gerald Cranston's Lady; Is Love Everything?*
1925   *The Dancers; She Wolves; A Woman's Faith; Fine Clothes; The Winding Stair; East Lynne*
1926   *The Gilded Butterfly; Siberia; Marriage License?*
1927   *One Increasing Purpose; Heart of Salome*
1928   *The Masks of the Devil*
1929   *Show Boat; She Goes to War*

S

Sagor, Frederica (1900 New York City-)

Frederica Sagor was the only child in her family born after her parents immigrated to the United States from Russia. Her mother was a graduate of Moscow University and had been a student of both Anton Rubinstein and Tchaikovsky at the Moscow Conservatory of Music. Her father was a Jewish businessman; the family left Russia after they were expelled from Moscow because of her father's religion.

Sagor went to Columbia University and studied journalism when it was decided that the family could not "waste money" on sending her to medical school, since it was assumed that she would eventually marry. During her summers she worked at local newspapers—once working for *The Globe* as the first female to be hired as a copyreader. However, she found newspaper work unfulfilling, and in her senior year (1920) she quit school to become assistant to the story editor at the New York office of Universal Pictures.

Before her twenty-third birthday she was made story editor and put in charge of the New York office. As a condition of her acceptance of the position it was agreed that after a year she would be transferred to Hollywood to work as a scenario writer. Although the New York office flourished under her direction, when it came time for her transfer Universal reneged on the agreement, saying no job was available in Hollywood.

Sagor left Universal and moved to Hollywood to become a freelance writer. She wrote the screen adaptation of *The Plastic Age,* which resulted in a three-year contract with MGM. At MGM she was assigned to the newly established Norma Shearer production unit.

While at MGM she met one of their new starlets, Lucille LeSueur, soon to be renamed Joan Crawford. LeSueur, who had been raised in poverty, asked Sagor to help her learn to dress fashionably and behave more "genteelly." With Sagor's help LeSueur became the "Joan Crawford" remembered by film fans.

Meanwhile, Sagor had run into the brick wall of Hollywood politics. In 1926 she decided to return to New York where she could concentrate on novel and short story writing, but while lunching with a friend prior to leaving she met Ernest Maas, a former documentary filmmaker and currently a producer at Fox; Sagor married Maas within the year.

In 1927 the couple both signed contracts with Paramount, but with the onset of the Depression most studios closed their staff writing departments. Sagor was once more freelancing or writing on spec with the hope that the work would be purchased by a studio. To augment her writing income she also did some script editing.

After losing almost everything, the Maases moved back to New York in the hopes of reviving Ernest Maas's documentary film business. When the business failed to materialize, the Maases began writing reviews of Broadway plays in 1934 for *The Hollywood Reporter*—a job that continued until 1937.

Tiring of the uncertainty of writing, Sagor went to work for the Small Agency as a talent agent, but she found that she didn't approve of some the methods used in securing and promoting clients. After leaving this job she used her newfound contract expertise to negotiate a writing contract for herself and her husband with Paramount.

Again in Hollywood, the Maases had several story ideas stolen since there was little protection of intellectual work at this time. Although Sagor was deeply disenchanted with the film industry, when her husband got a job in New York she remained in Hollywood to write. Theirs became a long-distance marriage and they collaborated on projects via letters and telegrams.

Finally one of their scripts, *Miss Pilgrim's Progress,* was purchased, rather than stolen, and went into production starring Betty Grable and Dick Haymes. But what started as the story of women entering the business world with the advent of the typewriter and the social implications of this emancipation was turned into a love story in which the heroine marries her boss and lives happily ever after. Although a huge hit, the film, renamed *The Shocking Miss Pilgrim* (1947), bore little resemblance to the original script.

Late in the 1940s the Maases became involved in one of the darkest chapters of American history—Joseph McCarthy's communist witch hunt. Ardent democrats and the subscribers of various socialist publications, the Maases were labeled communist sympathizers and blacklisted. No longer able to find work, they left the film industry.

Sagor found a job with an insurance company and eventually became an insurance broker while her husband continued as a writer. This enduring collaboration came to an end in 1986 when Maas died as a result of complications of Parkinson's disease.

Writing Credits

1925   *The Plastic Age; His Secretary; The Goose Woman*
1926   *The Model from Paris; The Waning Sex; Flesh and the Devil; Dance Madness*
1927   *The First Night; Rolled Stockings; Silk Legs; It; Hula; The Way of All Flesh*

1928 *The Farmer's Daughter; Red Hair*
1947 *The Shocking Miss Pilgrim*

Sais, Marin (1890 San Rafael, CA-1971 Woodland Hills, CA)

Marin Sais was a descendent of one of the pioneering California families who had been deeded large tracts of land by Spanish kings before California became a state. Educated in convent schools, Sais originally planned a career in opera. While making a triumphant tour of the East Coast, she became ill and was forced to abandon her singing career. She turned to the film industry and signed a contract with Vitagraph in 1910 before moving to Kalem in 1911.

While working with Kalem she appeared in the extremely popular western film series *The American Girl* as Madge King. Each film in the series was centered on the same character but stood alone as a complete work—unlike the later serials in which each film was a continuation of the previous film. Sais starred in several popular serials for Kalem, but when the studio ceased productions in 1917, she freelanced for several years.

In 1920 she appeared in Arrow's popular serial *Thunderbolt Jack*. Not long after this film's release, Sais married her costar, Jack Hoxie, and they appeared together in other westerns. In 1922 she wrote her only scenario, titled *Barbed Wire*.

After having two daughters the couple divorced in 1925. Sais continued to appear in some of Hoxie's films, but in supporting roles rather than as a lead. In addition to her *American Girl* series, Sais is best remembered as Duchess in the *Red Ryder* series and as Calamity Jane in *Deadwood Dick*.

With the advent of sound films, Sais became known as a character actor and continued in films until the early 1950s. Prior to retiring, Sais appeared as Ma Hinshaw in an episode of *The Lone Ranger* television series in 1949. After she retired from films she managed an apartment complex in Hollywood for several years.

Film Credits

1910   *Twelfth Night*
1911   *How Texas Got Left; The Ranger's Stratagem; Mesquite's Gratitude; The Revenue Man and the Girl; He Who Laughs Last*
1912   *The Tenderfoot's Troubles; Death Valley Scotty's Mine; The Chaperon Gets a Ducking; Days of '49; I Saw Him First; Accidents Will Happen; Walk, You, Walk!; The Swimming Party; The Kidnapped Conductor; The Girl Bandit's Hoodoo; The Mine Swindler; Dr. Skinnem's Wonderful Invention; In Peril of Their Lives; Paying the Board Bill; Pat, the Soothsayer; Brave Old Bill; The Bachelor Bride; Something Wrong with Bessie; The Pony Express Girl*
1913   *The Last Blockhouse; The Redemption; The Mountain Witch; The Buckskin Coat; The Attack at Rocky Pass; The California Oil Crooks; The Circle of Fate; The Battle for Freedom; The Scheme of Shiftless Sam Smith; On the Brink of Ruin; The Struggle; The Bandit's Child; The Girl and the Gangster; The Skeleton in the Closet; The Invaders; Trooper Billy; The Big Horn Massacre; Red Sweeney's Mistake; The Boomerang; The Honor System; The Cheyenne Massacre; The Poet and the Soldier; The Fight at Grizzly Gulch; Intemperance; The Chinese Death Horn*
1914   *The Shadow of Guilt; Trapped; The Master Rogue; The Death Sign of High Noon; The Barrier of Ignorance; The Quicksands; The Primitive Instinct; The Rajah's Vow; The Eternal Bond; The Potter and the Clay; King of Chance; The Prison Stain; The Winning Whickers; The Derelict; The Smugglers of Lone Isle; The Fatal Opal; The Boer War; Shannon of the Sixth; The Corsican Sisters*
1915   *Cooky's Adventure; The Tragedy of Bear Mountain; The Waitress and the Boobs; Insurance Nightmare; Ham Among the Redskins; Ham in the Harem; Otta Coin's Ghost; The Social Pirates; The Clairvoyant Swindlers; The Closed Door;*

The Figure in Black; The Money Leeches; The Secret Well; The Vanishing Vases; The Straight and Narrow Path; The Vivisectionist; The Accomplice; The Disappearing Necklace; The Frame-Up; The Strangler's Cord; When Thieves Fall Out; The Man in Irons; The Wolf's Prey; Under Oath; The Dream Seekers; The Pitfall; Stingaree; The Girl Detective; The Barnstormers; The Mysteries of the Grand Hotel

1916   *The Girl from Frisco; Witch of the Dark House; The Darkest Hour*

1917   *The Golden Eagle Trail; The Secret of the Lost Valley; The Lost Legion of the Border; The Vulture of Skull Mountain; The Pot o' Gold; Sagebrush Law; Treasure of Cibola; Hole in the Mountain; False Prophet; Manhunt at San Remo; The Fighting Heiress; Phantom Mine; The Man from Tia Juana; The American Girl*

1918   *The City of Dim Faces; His Birthright; The Vanity Pool; The Further Adventures of Stingaree*

1919   *The Gray Wolf's Ghost; Bonds of Honor*

1920   *Thunderbolt Jack*

1921   *Dead or Alive; The Sheriff of Hope Eternal; The Broken Spur*

1922   *Riders of the Law*

1923   *Good Men and Bad; Wolf's Tracks*

1924   *Behind Two Guns; The Hellion; The Measure of a Man*

1925   *The Roaring Adventure; The Red Rider*

1926   *The Wild Horse Stampede*

1927   *Rough and Ready; Men of Daring; The Fighting Three*

1928   *A Son of the Desert*

1929   *Come and Get It*

1933   *Fighting Cowboy*

1934   *Wheels of Destiny; Rawhide Romance; When Lightning Strikes*

1935   *The Pace That Kills; Circle of Death*

1936   *Heroes of the Range*

1937   *Trailin' Trouble; Renfrew of the Royal Mounted*

1938   *Tell Your Children; Pioneer Trail; Phantom Gold*

1939   *Riders of the Frontier; The Mad Empress; Lone Star Pioneers*

1940   *Deadwood Dick; Wild Horse Range; Five Little Peppers at Home; Two Gun Sheriff; The Shadow; Convicted Woman; One Man's Law; The Durango Kid*
1941   *Billy the Kid in Santa Fe; Cracked Nuts; Sierra Sue; Saddlemates*
1942   *A Tragedy at Midnight*
1943   *Murder at Times Square*
1944   *Frontier Outlaws; Enemy of Women; Oath of Vengeance*
1945   *Bells of Rosarita; Prairie Rustlers; Border Badman; Lightning Raiders; Love, Honor and Goodbye; Along the Navajo Trail; Girls of the Big House*
1946   *Rendezvous 24; Stagecoach to Denver; Terrors on Horseback; King of the Forest Rangers; Colorado Serenade*
1947   *Yankee Fakir; Big Town After Dark*
1949   *Ride, Ryder, Ride!; Roll, Thunder, Roll!; The Fighting Redhead; Cowboy and the Prizefighter*
1953   *The Great Jesse James Raid*

Sedgwick, Eileen (1898 Galveston, TX-1991 Marina del Rey, CA)

Eileen Sedgwick was born with entertaining in her blood, as her entire family was in show business. The family toured in vaudeville as "The Five Sedgwicks." Her brother led the way to the film industry when he became an early silent comedian who later moved into directing Hoot Gibson westerns.

Sedgwick and her sister, Josie, went to work on the Universal lot, appearing in two-reel westerns and short adventure dramas. Sedgwick's big break was in *The Lure of the Circus* (1918), starring opposite Eddie Polo after original star Molly Malone fell ill. This was the first in a string of twelve serials in which she starred which equates to over eighty hours of cliffhangers and thrills.

The locales of her serials included six westerns, one circus setting, two jungle adventures, and three generic mysteries. While appearing in the serials she continued to star in regular feature films. Once serials lost their audience, she continued to appear in dramas and westerns and briefly used the name "Greta Yoltz" to separate herself from her serial past. She retired with the coming of sound and lived in quiet retirement in the Los Angeles area.

Film Credits

1914 *The New Butler*
1915 *The Eagle's Nest; The Mysterious Contragrav; Lone Larry*
1916 *Hired, Tired and Fired; Some Heroes; I'll Get Her Yet; The Town That Tried to Come Back; Kill the Umpire; The Plumbers Waterloo; Room Rent and Romance; The Emerald Pin; Giant Powder; It's Great to Be Married; The Heritage of Hate; The Isle of Life; The Gasoline Habit; The Quitter; When Slim Picked a Peach; When Slim Was Home-Cured; Ain't He Grand?; His Golden Hour; It Sounded Like a Kiss; Number 10 Westbound*
1917 *The Honeymoon Surprise; It's Cheaper to Be Married; The High Cost of Starving; A Bare Living; Good Morning Nurse; A Woman in the Case; The Gasoline Habit; His Family Tree; Swearing Off; The Thousand-Dollar Drop; Flat Harmony; Dropped from the Clouds; Not Too Thin to Fight; Making Monkey Business; Man and Beast; The Paperhanger's Revenge; Money and Mystery; Jungle Treachery; The Lure of the Circus; The Last of the Night Riders; The Lion's Lair; The Temple of Terror; It's Cheaper to Be Single; The Losing Winner*
1918 *Hell's Crater; Watch Your Watch; A Kitchen Hero; Passing the Bomb; Quick Triggers; The Butler's Blunder; Repeating the Honeymoon; Trail of No Return; Roped and Tied; The Human Tiger; Naked Fists; All the Gold; Lure of the Circus (II); The Fickle Blacksmith; The Shifty Shoplifter; The Slow Express; Oh, Man!*
1919 *A Prisoner for Life; A Phantom Fugitive; The Wild Rider; Cyclone Smith's Comeback; A Pistol Point Proposal; Cyclone Smith Plays Trumps; The Great Radium Mystery*
1920 *Love's Battle; Putting It Over; The White Rider*
1921 *The Diamond Queen; The Heart of Arizona; The Girl in the Saddle; The Shadow of Suspicion; Terror Trail; A Woman's Wit; Dream Girl; Arrest Norma MacGregor; A Battle of Wits*
1922 *False Brands; Judgment; Wolf Pack; The Night Attack; Open Wire*
1923 *Making Good; In the Days of Daniel Boone; Scarred Hands; When Law Comes to Hades; Beasts of Paradise*
1924 *The Lone Roundup; The Riddle Rider*

1925   *Dangerous Odds; Fighting Ranger; The Sagebrush Lady; Girl of the West*
1926   *Beyond All Odds; The Winking Idol; Thundering Speed; Strings of Steel; Lightnin' Strikes; Tin Hats; Lure of the West; Temple of Terror*
1927   *When Danger Calls; The Spider's Net*
1928   *A Girl in Every Port; White Flame; Hot Heels; Beautiful but Dumb; The Vanishing West; Yellow Contraband*
1930   *The Jade Box*

Serials

The weekly serials or "chapter plays" were supposedly the result of a circulation war among the newspapers in Chicago. In an effort to increased its readership, the *Chicago Tribune* decided to coordinate a weekly story in the paper with the release of a short film dramatizing that story on film. This was not a new idea—it had been used in 1912 by *McClure's Ladies' World* for the film *What Happened to Mary?*

The difference with this idea was that instead of being a self-contained story every week, the *Tribune* carried a continuing story with a cliff-hanger ending that required the reader/viewer return the next week to see if the heroine survived. With *The Adventures of Kathlyn,* the *Tribune* and writer Harold McGrath created the serial formula—maximum excitement amid unbelievable situations and an uncertain ending every week.

The Adventures of Kathlyn was a tremendous success. It increased *Tribune* readership by 10 percent and made its producer, Selig, a handy profit. It also opened the genre to women. The *Tribune* next sponsored the twenty-three-chapter serial *The Million-Dollar Mystery*. The practice of newspapers sponsoring serials continued for three years.

In addition to giving women a chance to portray active characters, the serial helped the industry transition from two-reel shorts lasting approximately twenty to twenty-five minutes to regular feature-length films. Serials also became a reliable means of making money for the studios. The female-centered serials also brought a sought-after demographic, the middle-class female, into the theaters as regular viewers, which not only increased revenues but also added legitimacy to the industry.

The first internationally popular serial was *The Perils of Pauline* (1914) which starred Pearl White as the intrepid Pauline; it was produced by Pathe. Although not the best serial technically or creatively, it came to represent the genre for succeeding generations. The American-spawned serial eventually moved to Europe and continued there for many years.

After the introduction of sound, serials changed from dramas geared to adults to films aimed at children and the afternoon matinee audience. This change in focus moved women out of leading roles and relegated them once more to supporting roles. These new male-centered adventure serials continued into the 1950s.

By virtue of the genre, serial heroines could do things that "normal" women of the era could not even consider. Their ingenuity and intelligence were celebrated rather than viewed with scorn and disfavor. They gave lie to the accepted belief that women were the "weaker sex" by often exhibiting more "grit" than their male counterparts.

However, even before the advent of sound serial heroines had lost favor with audiences. The audience had grown up and the heroines of the serials became the flappers of the 1920s—both were adventurous and independent. Both character types appealed to women who were trying to push the boundaries of what was acceptable for women within society.

Seymour, Clarine (1898 Brooklyn, NY-1920 New York City)

Courtesy of Silents Are Golden at <SilentsAreGolden.com>

Clarine Seymour, who many believe would have been a talent to equal Lillian Gish, was born into a wealthy family whose situation changed when her father was forced by illness to retire early in 1916 and move his family to New Rochelle, New York. Seymour went to work for the local Thanhouser Company to help with the family finances. Her Thanhouser work brought her a contract with Pathe and appearances in several serials.

In 1917 Seymour moved to Hollywood and joined Hal Roach's Rolin Comedy Company, but she soon left because of "creative differences," which translated to the fact that she didn't like the films or costars assigned to her. From Rolin she went to work with Al Christie as his leading lady. Most of her credits during the period prior to her work with D. W. Griffith have been lost.

In 1919 Seymour costarred in the Griffith film *The Girl Who Stayed at Home,* to rave reviews. Late in 1919 Seymour began work on her first starring film, *The Idol Dancer.* She received enthusiastic reviews with praises for the "vivacity" of her acting and her graceful dancing. She had just signed a four-year contract for $2 million when she died from complications from emergency surgery to repair an intestinal obstruction.

Film Credits

1917	*It Happened to Adele; The Mystery of the Double Cross; Pots-and-Pans Peggy*
1919	*The Girl Who Stayed at Home; True Heart Susie; Scarlet Days*
1920	*The Idol Dancer*

Shearer, Norma (1902 Montreal, Canada-1983 Woodland Hills, CA)

Courtesy of Silents Are Golden at <SilentsAreGolden.com>

Norma Shearer had a middle-class upbringing and was an athletic youngster who enjoyed skiing, swimming, and skating. From the age of nine she knew she wanted a show business career; when she won a beauty contest at the age of fourteen she had the entrée that she needed. When she was eighteen she went to New York to audition for the *Ziegfeld Follies* but was rejected. Not to be dissuaded, Shearer got a job as an extra. In 1923, after several years of working for various studios, she was given a five-year contract with Louis B. Mayer at the urging of Irving Thalberg, who became her husband in 1927. That year she got her chance at stardom when she was cast as Kathi in *The Student Prince in Old Heidelberg.*

After their marriage, Thalberg, who was production chief at MGM, unofficially managed her career and groomed her for stardom. She made the transition to sound easily and continued to be guided by her husband's choices in roles for her. Perhaps her best performances were in 1929 in *The Trial of Mary Dugan* and *Their Own Desire*, for which she was nominated for an Academy Award.

Although she didn't win in 1929, Shearer did win an Oscar for her performance in *The Divorcee* (1930), as a sophisticated modern woman who shows her unfaithful husband that infidelity is not only a male prerogative. The following year she was nominated again for her portrayal of the spoiled socialite who falls for Clark Gable in *A Free Soul* (1931). In 1932 she appeared in two adaptations of plays that Thalberg purchased expressly for her—*Strange Interlude* and *Smilin' Through*.

Shearer received two other Oscar nominations for her performances in *The Barretts of Wimpole Street* (1934) and *Romeo and Juliet* (1936). Thalberg died suddenly in 1936; although her heart wasn't in it, Shearer completed the last project he had developed for her, *Marie Antoinette* (1938), for which she received her final Oscar nomination. She retired from films in 1942.

Film Credits

1920   *The Flapper; Way Down East; The Restless Sex; Torchy's Millions; The Stealers*

1921   *The Sign on the Door*

1922   *Channing of the Northwest; The Man Who Paid; The Leather Pushers; The Bootleggers; The End of the World*

1923   *A Clouded Name; Man and Wife; Pleasure Mad; The Wanters; Lucretia Lombard; The Devil's Partner*

1924   *The Trail of the Law; The Wolf Man; Broadway After Dark; Empty Hands; Broken Barriers; Married Flirts; The Snob; Her Who Gets Slapped; Blue Water*

1925   *Excuse Me; Lady of the Night; Waking Up the Town; A Slave of Fashion; Pretty Ladies; The Tower of Lies; His Secretary*

1926   *The Devil's Circus; The Waning Sex; Upstage*

1927   *The Demi-Bride; After Midnight; The Student Prince in Old Heidelberg*

1928   *The Latest from Paris; The Actress; A Lady of Chance*

1929   *The Trial of Mary Dugan; The Last of Mrs. Cheyney; The Hollywood Revue of 1929; Their Own Desire*
1930   *The Divorcee; Let Us Be Gay*
1931   *Strangers May Kiss; The Slippery Pearls; A Free Soul; Private Lives; The Movie Album; The Christmas Party*
1932   *Smilin' Through; Strange Interlude*
1934   *Riptide; The Barretts of Wimpole Street*
1936   *Romeo and Juliet*
1938   *Marie Antoinette*
1939   *Idiot's Delight; The Women*
1940   *Escape*
1942   *We Were Dancing; Her Cardboard Lover*
1963   *Anniversary*

Shipman, Nell (1892 Victoria, British Columbia-1970 Cabazon, CA)

Nell Shipman worked, for the most part, behind the scenes during the silent film era. Eventually known as "the Queen of the Dogsleds" because of her perchant for including snow scenes in her films, she was still young when she left her middle-class home to join a touring company and work in vaudeville. She took her professional name "Shipman" from the much older man she married while working with a touring company.

She began writing scenarios before she reached her twenties, and her works were produced by several studios, including Selig, Universal, and Vitagraph. She was also a novelist and adapted several of her books for the screen, beginning with *Under the Crescent* (1914) which was made into a series of films by Universal. That same year she made film history when her script *Shepherd of the Southern Cross* was the first film to be shot in Australia.

She received a contract to direct with Universal and also produced and starred in three films for them. Her film *God's Country and the Woman* (1916) was the first feature-length wildlife adventure filmed on location. It was a huge success that established her as a major female director. She kept a large menagerie of animals, in the 1920s estimated at more than 200, to feature in her films, and it was not unusual for her animal stars to get billing equal to that of her human stars.

She was perhaps one of the first feminist film writers insisting that her female characters be independent protagonists and not just women waiting to be saved by a handy man. She also insisted on authenticity in location, which meant she filmed many of her scenes outside the studio. This expensive practice was loosing favor, as filmmaking became a business with an eye on the bottomline.

As the times changed she lost her releasing outlet through Universal and had to close her production company. Unable to care for her animals any longer, she donated them to the San Diego Zoo. As the industry became more male run, Shipman was pushed further out of the mainstream.

She returned to the film industry after the birth of her twins but this time strictly as a writer. She continued to write novels as well, and several of her works were adapted to film. She also worked throughout her life to ensure that animals used in films were treated humanely. In 1969 she wrote her autobiography, *The Silent Screen and My Talking Heart* (1987).

Writing Credits

1913   *One Hundred Years of Mormonism; Outwitted by Billy; The Ball of Yarn*

1915   *The Shepherd of the Southern Cross; The Pine's Revenge; The Widow's Secret; Under the Crescent*

1916   *Son o' the Stars; The Melody of Love*

1917   *My Fighting Gentleman*

1919   *Back to God's Country*

1920   *Something New*

1921   *The Girl from God's Country; A Bear, a Boy, and a Dog*

1923   *The Grub Stake; Trail of the North Wind*

1935   *Wings in the Dark*

Directing Credits

1920   *Something New*

1921   *The Girl from God's Country*

1923   *The Grub Stake; Trail of the North Wind; The Light on the Lookout*

1924   *White Water*

Film Credits

1913   *The Ball of Yarn*
1916   *God's Country and the Woman; The Fires of Conscience; Through the Wall; The Melody of Love*
1917   *The Black Wolf*
1918   *The Wild Strain; Cavanaugh of the Forest Rangers; The Home Trail; The Girl from Beyond; Baree, Son of Kazan; A Gentleman's Agreement*
1919   *Back to God's Country*
1920   *Something New*
1921   *The Girl from God's Country; A Bear, a Boy, and a Dog*
1923   *The Grub Stake; Trail of the North Wind; The Light on the Lookout*
1924   *White Water*

Snow, Marguerite (1889 Salt Lake City, UT-1958 Los Angeles, CA)

Marguerite Snow was one of the serial queens of the 1910s and appeared in Thanhouser's *The Million Dollar Mystery* (1914), a film cited as being the most technically advanced of the genre during that early period. The film cost roughly $125,000 to produce and brought in more than $1.5 million, making it one of the most financially successful serials of all time. Snow played the part of Countess Olga, the evil character bent on stealing the money from Chilton Manor and Stanley Hargreave. Snow followed this success with a sequel called *The Twenty Million Dollar Mystery* (1914).

Snow was raised in Savannah, Georgia, until her father, minstrel comedian William G. Snow, died and her mother moved the family to Denver. She attended the Loretta Heights Academy while appearing in local summer stock productions. Her formal stage debut was in Wichita, Kansas, in 1907 in the play *Monte Cristo*.

Snow was playing lead roles by 1908, and in 1909 she made her Broadway debut as Elsa in *The Devil*. She spent two years touring and then, according to Snow, on a lark appeared in her first movie. She had accompanied a friend to the studio to watch and when asked to participate decided to appear for "the fun of it." However, when the director called for everyone to go outside, in the dead of winter, Snow declined and thought that to be the end of her film effort. However, she was asked back and remained with the studio for about six months before returning temporarily to stage work with the Belasco Company. She returned to films first with the Kinemacolor Company then Thanhouser again. She was cast opposite James Cruze in *She* (1911), a pairing that continued through 1914.

Snow married Cruze in 1913 and together they had a daughter, Julia, the following year. During this period the family moved to Hollywood and Snow began working with the Metro studio. In 1918 Snow appeared in her final serial, *The Eagle's Eye*, enacted amid World War I intrigues. However, before the film was released the war ended and audiences lost interest in spies.

Snow divorced Cruze in 1923 and made her last film, *Kit Carson over the Great Divide*, in 1925. That same year she remarried and settled down with her second husband, actor Neely Edwards. She died in 1958 from complications of an earlier kidney operation.

Film Credits

1911   *Baseball and Bloomers; The Old Curiosity Shop; His Younger Brother; Lorna Doane; The Pied Piper of Hamelin; The Honeymooners; The Lady from the Sea; The Tomboy; She; Get Rich Quick; The Railroad Builder; The Stepmother; Motoring; Little Old New York; Back to Nature; Cupid the Conquerer; The Romance of Lonely Island; The Moth; Count Ivan and the Waitress; The Buddhist Priestess; In the Chorus; Young Lachinvar; The Five Rose Sisters; The Tempter and Dan Cupid; Their Burglar; The Missing Heir*

1912   *Flying to Fortune; My Baby's Voice; For Sale—a Life; Into the Desert; The Saleslady; Love's Miracle; Jilted; The Ring of a Spanish Grandee; Whom God Hath Joined; Dottie's New Doll; Under Two Flags; Lucile; The Mail Clerk's Temptation; And the Greatest of These Is Charity; Undine; Put Yourself in His Place; Forest Rose; Brains vs. Brawn; The Star of Bethlehem; Dr. Jekyll and Mr. Hyde; A Militant Suffragette; A Niagara Honeymoon; East Lynne; The Girl of the Grove; Jess; Nursie and the Knight; The Woman in White*

1913   *The Dove in the Eagle's Nest; When the Studio Burned; The Idol of the Hour; For Her Boy's Sake; When Ghost Meets Ghost; The Marble Heart; The Caged Bird; Tannhauser; The Girl at the Cabaret; Peggy's Invitation; Carmen; The Tiniest Star*

1914   *The Dancer; Joseph in the Land of Egypt; Their Best Friend; A Woman's Loyalty; The Dog of Flanders; The Million Dollar Mystery* (I); *From Wash to Washington; The Twenty Million Dollar Mystery*

1915   *The Heart of the Princess Marsari; The Angel in the Mask; Daughter of Kings; The Patriot and the Spy; The Second in Command; The Silent Voice; Rosemary*

1916   *A Corner in Cotton; The Half Million Bribe; The Faded Flower; The Upstart; The Marble Heart; His Great Triumph; Her Great Triumph*

1917   *Broadway Jones; The Hunting of the Hawk*

1918   *The First Law; The Eagle's Eye; Mission of the War Chest; The Million Dollar Mystery* (II); *The Marriage Trap*

1919   *In His Brother's Place*

1920   *The Woman in Room 13; Felix O'Day; The Great Shadow; Rouge and Riches*

1921   *Lavender and Old Lace*

1922   *The Veiled Woman*

1924   *Chalk Marks*

1925   *Savages of the Sea; Kit Carson over the Great Divide*

St. Johns, Adela Rogers (1894 Los Angeles, CA-1988 Arroyo Grande, CA)

Adela Rogers St. Johns came from a well-to-do family whose father was the famous criminal lawyer Earl Rogers. Although she eventually became a screenwriter, her first career was as a journalist and fiction writer. She went to work for the *San Francisco Examiner* in 1913 and moved to the *Los Angeles Herald Examiner* a few years later.

She left newspapers for magazines when she began writing a column for *Photoplay* in 1919. She collected her works into books and three of them were made into movies—*The Skyrocket* (1923), *The Single Standard* (1925), and *A Free Soul* (1931). She continued to write occasionally for films through the early 1950s, during which time several of her short stories were adapted into films.

St. Johns was supposedly the inspiration for the character Hildie, played by Rosalind Russell, in *His Girl Friday* (1940). She also influenced several early writers, including Frances Marion and June Mathis. When she died, her obituary noted that she had been a "tough, hard newspaper woman."

Writing Credits

1918   *Old Love for New; Marked Cards; The Secret Code*
1924   *Broken Laws; Inez from Hollywood*
1925   *Lady of the Night; The Red Kimona*
1926   *The Wise Guy; The Skyrocket*
1927   *The Broncho Twister; Children of Divorce; Singed; The Patent Leather Kid; The Arizona Wildcat*
1928   *The Heart of a Follies Girl; Lilac Time*
1929   *Scandal; The Single Standard*
1931   *A Free Soul*
1932   *The Animal Kingdom; What Price Hollywood?*
1934   *Miss Fane's Baby Is Stolen; A Woman's Man*
1937   *A Star Is Born; Back in Circulation*
1942   *The Great Man's Lady*
1943   *Government Girl*
1946   *That Brennan Girl*
1948   *Smart Woman*
1953   *The Girl Who Had Everything*

Starke, Pauline (1901 Joplin, MO-1977 Santa Monica, CA)

Little is known of Pauline Starke's childhood and life before she started in films. Called the "Glad-Sad Girl" because of the heavy melodramas in which she appeared, contemporary articles characterized her as being somber and reflective in person. It is known that she started her career with Triangle Films and that she claimed to have been an extra in D. W. Griffith's *The Birth of a Nation* (1915).

Her first verifiable appearance was as a dancing girl in Griffith's epic *Intolerance* (1916). She continued to play small supporting roles until she signed with Fine Arts, where she received star recognition and promotion. Her breakout films are considered to be *A Connecticut Yankee in King Arthur's Court* and *Salvation Nell* (both 1921).

She was chosen as a WAMPAS Baby Star in 1922, the first year the title was awarded. No longer cast as the innocent girl, she now assumed an alluring persona with an air of mystery and tragedy. One of her most successful films of this period was *Women Love Diamonds* (1927).

Starke made the transition to sound, but not successfully. She began appearing in Poverty Row productions, and then in smaller and smaller parts. After her film career ended, she did some stage work in New York before she moved with her husband to Europe and eventually sailed with him around the world several times. She apparently attempted suicide in 1948 due to ill health then lived quietly in the beach town of Santa Monica in California.

Film Credits

1915	*The Birth of a Nation*
1916	*Intolerance; The Rummy; The Wharf Rat; Puppets*
1917	*Cheerful Givers; Madame Bo-Peep; The Regenerates; Until They Get Me*
1918	*The Argument; Innocent's Progress; The Shoes That Danced; The Man Who Woke Up; Alias Mary Brown; Daughter Angele; The Atom; Irish Eyes*
1919	*Whom the Gods Would Destroy; The Fall of Babylon; Eyes of Youth; The Life Line; The Broken Butterfly; Soldiers of Fortune*
1920	*The Little Shepherd of Kingdom Come; Dangerous Days; The Courage of Marge O'Doone; Seeds of Vengeance; The Untamed*
1921	*Snowblind; Salvation Nell; Wife Against Wife; Flower of the North; A Connecticut Yankee in King Arthur's Court; The Forgotten Woman*
1922	*My Wild Irish Rose; If You Believe It, It's So; The Kingdom Within*
1923	*Lost and Found on a South Sea Island; The Little Church Around the Corner; The Little Girl Next Door; His Last Race; In the Palace of the King; Eyes of the Forest*

1924   *Arizona Express; Missing Daughters; Dante's Inferno; Hearts of Oak; Forbidden Paradise*

1925   *The Man Without a Country; The Devil's Cargo; Adventure; Sun-Up; Bright Lights*

1926   *Honesty—the Best Policy; War Paint; Love's Blindness; Dance Madness*

1927   *Women Love Diamonds; Captain Salvation; Dance Magic; Streets of Shanghai*

1929   *Man, Woman and Wife; The Viking; The Mysterious Island*

1930   *The Royal Romance; What Men Want*

1935   *Twenty Dollars a Week*

1941   *She Knew All the Answers*

1944   *Lost Angel*

Stars

When films first started being exhibited, little attention was given to the individual actors who appeared in them. Most studios had what they called their troupe or company of actors who appeared interchangeably in the films. This was the policy of the studios to avoid having to pay their lead actors more money as they became more popular.

However, as more people went to see films and the films themselves became more narrative in nature, the audience began to choose their favorite stars and demanded to know more about the individual actors. In answer to the audience preferences, the film exhibitors were one of the first groups to try to differentiate performers in their effort to publicize that the films that they were showing were "better" than their competition's films.

In January 1910, Kalem began issuing portraits of their actors and posters with the pictures and names of their troupe. Not long after this Carl Laemmle pulled off the famous publicity stunt of declaring that his newly acquired star, Florence Lawrence, was not dead as reported (anonymously by him) and thus began the first star buildup, including personal appearances and interviews. From originally being identified with the studio as "The Biograph Girl," for example, the actors increasingly became known by their names. By the mid-1910s the star system was in full swing, complete with diva behavior and outrageous salaries.

Stedman, Myrtle (1885 Chicago, IL-1938 Hollywood, CA)

One of the busiest actors of the silent era, Myrtle Stedman was twenty-eight when she entered films. She generally appeared in supporting roles and, although she was never a star, her career outlasted many of the silent film industry's so-called luminaries.

She began her career in one-reelers for Selig in 1910 and by 1913 was appearing in features. Her final silent film was *The Sin Sister* (1929), and she also appeared in the part-sound film *The Jazz Age* that year. She made the transition to sound easily and continued to appear in films until her sudden death in 1938.

Film Credits

1910   *The Range Riders*
1911   *The Two Orphans; The Bully of Bingo Gulch; A Fair Exchange; A New York Cowboy; A Tennessee Love Story; Told in Colorado; Why the Sheriff Is a Bachelor; Western Hearts; The Telltale; A Romance of the Rio Grande*
1912   *Why Jim Reformed; The Whiskey Runners; When Women Ruled; A Wartime Romance; The Saint and the Siwash; A Rough Ride with Nitroglycerine; Roped In; The Ranger and His Horse; The Opium Smugglers; The Mantle of Red Evans; The Fighting Instinct; Exposed by the Dictograph; An Equine Hero; The Dynamiters; Driftwood; The Double Cross; Circumstantial Evidence; The Cattle Rustlers; Buck's Romance; The Brotherhood of Man; The Brand Blotter; The Boob; Between Love and the Law; A Cowboy's Best Girl; The Scapegoat; When the Heart Calls; His Father's Bugle; His Chance to Make Good*
1913   *The Range Law; The Jealousy of Miguel and Isabella; The Stolen Moccasins; The Capture of Bad Brown; The Escape of*

Jim Dolan; Sallie's Sure Shot; The Suffragette; The Sheriff of Yawapai County; Mother Love vs. Gold; A Matrimonial Deluge; The Lonely Heart; The Life Timer; The Law and the Outlaw; Juggling with Fate; Howlin' Jones; How It Happened; How Betty Made Good; The Gunfighter's Son; Good Resolutions; Dishwash Dick's Counterfeit; The Deputy's Sweetheart; The Cattle Thief's Escape; Buster's Little Game; Billy's Birthday Present; The Bank's Messenger; An Apache's Gratitude; The Shotgun Man and the Stage Driver; That Mail Order Suit; Religion and Gun Practice; Taming the Tenderfoot; The Marshal's Captive; Made a Coward; The Taming of Texas Pete; The Good Indian; The Rejected Lover's Luck; Saved from the Vigilantes; The Silver Grindstone; The Schoolmarm's Shooting Match; The Child of the Prairies; Cupid in the Cow Camp; Physical Culture on the Quarter Circle V Bar

1914 *Martin Eden; The Country Mouse; The Valley of the Moon; The Chechako; Burning Daylight; By Unseen Hand*

1915 *The Hypocrites; The Caprices of Kitty; Help Wanted; The Wild Olive; Kilmeny; Nearly a Lady; The Majesty of the Law; Peer Gynt; 'Twas Ever Thus; Jane; The Reform Candidate; It's No Laughing Matter*

1916 *The Call of the Cumberlands; Pasquale; The American Beauty; The Soul of Kura San*

1917 *Happiness of Three Women; The Prison Without Walls; As Men Love; The World Apart*

1918 *In the Hollow of Her Hand*

1919 *In Honor's Web; The Teeth of the Tiger*

1920 *The Silver Horde; Harriet and the Piper; The Tiger's Coat; Sex; Old Dad*

1921 *The Concert; Black Roses; The Whistle; Sowing the Wind*

1922 *Nancy from Nowhere; Ashes; Reckless Youth; The Hands of Nara; Rich Men's Wives*

1923 *The Dangerous Age; The Famous Mrs. Fair; Crashin' Throu; Temporary Marriage; Six Days; Flaming Youth; The Age of Desire*

1924 *The Judgment of the Storm; Lilies of the Field; Bread; Wine; The Breath of Scandal; The Woman of the Jury*

1925   *If I Marry Again; The Mad Whirl; Sally; The Goose Hangs High; Chickie; Tessie*

1926   *The Far Cry; The Prince of Pilsen; Don Juan's Three Nights; The Man in the Shadow*

1927   *The Black Diamond Express; The Life of Riley; Woman's Wares; The Irresistible Lover; No Place to Go*

1928   *Alias the Deacon; Sporting Goods; Their Hour*

1929   *Sin Sister; The Jazz Age; The Wheel of Life; The Love Racket*

1930   *Lummox; The Truth About Youth; Little Accident; Go to Blazes*

1931   *Beau Ideal*

1932   *The Widow in Scarlet; Klondike; Forbidden Company; Alias Mary Smith*

1933   *One Year Later*

1934   *Beggars in Ermine; School for Girls*

1935   *Here's to Romance*

1936   *Song of the Saddle; Gold Diggers of 1937; Give Me Liberty; San Francisco; Polo Joe*

1937   *The Green Light; That Certain Woman; Back in Circulation; Over the Goal; Alcatraz Island; Ready, Willing and Able; The Go-Getter; Under Southern Stars; She Loved a Fireman; That Man's Here Again; The Case of the Stuttering Bishop; Confession; Expensive Husbands*

1938   *A Slight Case of Murder; Love, Honor and Behave; Penrod and His Twin Brother; Accidents Will Happen*

Stella Maris *(1918)*

Produced by the Pickford Film Corporation, Mary Pickford's own production unit within Famous Players, *Stella Maris* was directed by Marshall Neilan and written by Frances Marion. The film involved two very different women in love with the same man. Some critics view it as Pickford's best work.

Pickford played both women—the beautiful invalid Stella and the plain, hunchbacked Unity Blake. Stella's life had been blessed, while Unity had known only cruelty and despair. The man both women loved, John Risca, was married to the alcoholic for whom Unity worked.

In despair because she realizes that she will never be loved, Unity kills the wife and then shoots herself. John is then free to turn to Stella and they live "happily ever after." Although some of Pickford's fans objected to her appearance as Unity, the film was a critical and popular success.

Stewart, Anita (1895 Brooklyn, NY-1961 Beverly Hills, CA)

Courtesy of Silents Are Golden at <SilentsAreGolden.com>

Anita Stewart entered the film industry in 1911 at the urging of her brother-in-law, Ralph Ince, the brother of Thomas Ince. She worked as an extra and played bit parts while still in high school. Her father was a successful businessman, so the family lived comfortably and there was no pressure put on her to work.

She found she enjoyed the work, so once she graduated she signed with Vitagraph and was elevated to leading lady status between 1912 and 1917. She received top billing for the first time in *Her Choice* (1912) under her real name, Anna M. Stewart. She used her real name for her first few films, but after it was printed incorrectly as "Anita Stewart," the name stuck.

The film that brought her firmly into the limelight was *The Wood Violet* (1912), which showcased not only her beauty but also her acting ability. Two years later, after appearing in *A Million Bid* (1914), Stewart was officially a hot property. She appeared in a successful serial, *The Goddess* (1915), before the studio established her own production company.

Her contract had not expired with Vitagraph when she decided she wanted to move to Metro Studios. She was sued when she conveniently became too ill to fulfill her last few months with Vitagraph. She lost the case and the judgment added her "sick days" onto the length of the contract. This judgment is still used as precedent in actor-studio court cases today.

When her contract with Metro expired, she worked for William Randolph Hearst's Cosmopolitan Productions. However, when she married millionaire George Converse in 1929, she retired from films and the couple traveled extensively. After their divorce, Stewart served as president of the Film Welfare League and became a successful painter.

Film Credits

1911   *The Battle Hymn of the Republic; A Tale of Two Cities; Prejudice of Pierre Marie*

1912   *The Godmother; The Wood Violet; Song of the Shell; Her Choice; Red Cross Martyr; Billy's Pipe Dream*

1913   *Papa Puts One Over; The Tiger; The Wreck; Why Am I Here; The Web; Treasure of Desert Island; Sweet Deception; The Swan Girl; Song Bird of the North; A Regiment of Two; The Prince of Evil; The Moulding; Love Finds a Way; The Lost Millionaire; His Second Wife; His Last Fight; The Forgotten Latchkey; A Fighting Chance; The Classmates Frolic; The Bringing out of Papa; Belinda the Slavey; Two's Company, Three's a Crowd*

1914   *The Lucky Elopement; Wife Wanted; Uncle Bill; Shadows of the Past; The Right and the Wrong of It; The Painted World; A Million Bid; Lincoln the Lover; He Never Knew; The Girl from Prosperity; Four Thirteen; Diana's Dress Reform; Back to Broadway; 'Midst Woodland Shadows*

1915   *Two Women; From Headquarters; The Juggernaut; The Sins of the Mothers; The Sort-of-Girl-That-Came-from-Heaven; The Rich Girl; His Phantom Sweetheart; The Goddess; Count 'Em; The Awakening*

1916   *My Lady's Slipper; The Suspect; The Daring of Diana; The Combat*

1917   *The Glory of Yolanda; The More Excellent Way; Clover's Rebellion; The Message of the Mouse; The Girl Philippa*

1918   *Virtuous Wives*

1919   *A Midnight Romance; Mary Regan; The Painted World; Her Kingdom of Dreams; In Old Kentucky; Two Women; Shad-*

ows of the Past; The Human Desire; The Mind-the-Paint
Girl; The Wreck

1920   *The Fighting Shepherdess; The Yellow Typhoon; Harriet and the Piper*

1921   *The Invisible Fear; Her Mad Bargain; Sowing the Wind; Playthings of Destiny*

1922   *The Woman He Married; Rose o' the Sea; A Question of Honor*

1923   *Souls for Sale; Mary of the Movies; The Love Piker; Hollywood*

1924   *The Great White Way*

1925   *The Boomerang; Baree, Son of Kazan; Go Straight; Never the Twain Shall Meet*

1926   *Rustling for Cupid; The Prince of Pilsen; Lodge in the Wilderness; Whispering Wires; Morganson's Finish*

1927   *Wild Geese; Isle of Sunken Gold*

1928   *Name the Woman; Romance of a Rogue; Sisters of Eve*

1932   *The Hollywood Handicap*

Stonehouse, Ruth (1892 Denver, CO-1941 Hollywood, CA)

Ruth Stonehouse began her entertainment career as a dancer at the age of eight. Her first credit in a film was in 1911 with Essanay Studios. While with the studio she made more than 100 films in six years.

In 1916 she signed with Universal where she wrote and directed some of the films in which she appeared. She became a regular in the serial genre; the first serial in which she starred was *The Masked Rider* (1919). By the mid-1920s she was in supporting roles and with the advent of sound she retired from films. During her retirement she devoted herself to charity work and served as chairman of the Women's Auxiliary Council of the Children's Home Society. She died suddenly in 1941.

Film Credits

1911   *Mr. Wise, Investigator*
1912   *Neptune's Daughter; Twilight; The End of the Feud; Chains; The Virtue of Rags; Sunshine; The Shadow of the Cross; Giuseppe's Good Fortune; From the Submerged; Billy McGrath's Love Letters; The Stain; Mr. Hubby's Wife; Requited Love; An Adamless Eden; Billy McGrath's Art Career; His Birthday Jacket*
1913   *The Thirteenth Man; The Broken Heart; An Old, Old Song; A Bottle of Musk; The Pathway of Years; The Spy's Defeat; A Wolf Among Lambs; The Little Mother; The Unknown; A Woman's Way; Easy Payments; Homespun; The World Above; Broken Threads United; In Convict Garb; A Ray of God's Sunshine; Three Scraps of Paper; Thy Will Be Done; The Man Outside; The Heart of the Law; Let No Man Put Asunder; The Laird of McGillicuddy; The Ghost of Self; When Soul Meets Soul; The Good in the Worst of Us; The Brand of Evil*
1914   *The Hour and the Man; The Other Girl; The Man for A' That; Ashes of Hope; Trinkets of Tragedy; The Night Hawks; The Fable of Lutie; Sparks of Fate; A Splendid Dishonor; Blood Will Tell; The Battle of Love; The Unplanned Elopement; The Long Cold Night; Let No Man Escape; The Hand That Rocks the Cradle; The Grip of Circumstance; Fires of Fate; The Daring Young Person; The Counter-Melody; An Angel Unaware; Hearts and Flowers; The Conqueror; The Price of His Honor; No. 28 Diplomat; White Lies; The Real Agatha; Mother O' Dreams; The Servant Question; The Girl from Thunder Mountain; Surgeon Warren's Ward; The Masked Wrestler; Nearly Married; One Wonderful Night; The Motor Buccaneers; Mongrel and Master*
1915   *The Lieutenant Governor; Misjudged Mr. Hartley; The Creed of the Klan; Third Hand High; A Romance of the Night; An Amateur Prodigal; The Surprise of My Life; The Dance at Aleck Fontaine's; Man in Motley; The Fable of the Divine Spark That Had a Short Circuit; The Fable of the Galumptious Girl; The Wood Nymph; The Conflict; The Profligate; A Night in Kentucky; The Romance of an American Duchess;*

The Fable of the Highroller and the Buzzing Blondine; Otherwise Bill Harrison; The Fable of the Two Sensational Failures; Above Abyss; The Slim Princess; The Gilded Cage; A Dignified Family; Temper; The Call of Yesterday; When My Lady Smiles; The Fable of Hazel's Two Husbands and What Became of Them; Darling Dandy; A Phantom Husband; Inheritance; The Spider; Miss Freckles; The Crimson Wing; The Papered Door; The Alster Case; Brought Home; Does the Woman Forget?; The Conflict

1916   *The Phone Message; Love Never Dies; Kinkaid, Gambler; The Winning Pair; The Law and the Lady; Angels Unaware; Adventures of Peg o' the Ring; Destiny*

1917   *A Limb of Satan; Mary Ann in Society; The Stolen Actress; Tacky Sue's Romance; A Walloping Time; Fighting for Love; Love Aflame; The Saintly Sinner; Follow the Girl; The Edge of the Law; The Heart of Mary Ann; Dorothy Dares; Daredevil Dan; Puppy Love; A Phantom Husband*

1919   *Rosalind at Redgate; The Four-Flusher; The Red Viper; The Master Mystery; The Masked Rider*

1920   *Parlor, Bedroom and Bath; The Hope; Conrad in Quest of His Youth; Cinderella's Twin; The Land of Jazz; Are All Men Alike?*

1921   *I Am Guilty; Don't Call Me Little Girl*

1923   *Lights Out; The Way of the Transgressor; The Flash; Flames of Passion*

1924   *A Girl From Limberlost; Broken Barriers*

1925   *Straight Through; A Two-Fisted Sheriff; Fifth Avenue Models; The Fugitive; Blood and Steel; The Scarlet West; Ermine and Rhinestones; False Pride*

1926   *The Wives of the Prophet; Broken Homes*

1927   *The Ladybird; Poor Girls; The Satin Woman*

1928   *The Ape; The Devil's Cage*

Writing Credits

1917   *A Walloping Time; Puppy Love; The Heart of Mary Ann; Dorothy Dares; Daredevil Dan*

1925   *Rough Going*

Directing Credits

1917   *A Walloping Time; Tacky Sue's Romance; Puppy Love; The
        Heart of Mary Ann; Mary Ann in Society; A Limb of Satan;
        Dorothy Dares; Daredevil Dan; The Stolen Actress*
1919   *Rosalind at Redgate*

Storey, Edith (1892 New York City-1967 Northport, NY)

Edith Storey began her show business career while still a child, appearing on the stage and with touring companies. She traveled to Australia to appear in the original production of *Mrs. Wiggs of the Cabbage Patch,* but she left the production during the play's second season to enter films.

She signed with the newly formed Vitagraph Company in 1908 and appeared in a variety of roles in every conceivable type of film. After appearing in films ranging from horse dramas to period melodramas, Storey filmed a series of western dramas during 1911 in which she perfected her cowhand skills, leading a director to comment that she could "ride anything with hair and four legs, throw a rope and shoot with the best of the cowpunchers."

After being recalled to Brooklyn, Storey appeared in period dramas for the next few years, resulting in her becoming one of Vitagraph's top stars. In 1917, Storey left Vitagraph and signed with the Metro Company. Unfortunately, Metro was unable to showcase her talents properly and, discouraged, Storey retired from the screen in 1921.

During World War I Storey drove an ambulance, but after the war she returned to her quiet life on Long Island. Although film fans had forgotten her by the time of her death, her star can be found at 1523 Vine on the Hollywood Walk of Fame.

Film Credits

1908   *Barbara Fritchie: The Story of a Patriotic American Woman; Francesca di Rimini*

1909   *Cure for Bashfulness; Mogg Megone: An Indian Romance; A Brave Irish Lass; King Lear; The Gift of Youth; The Way of the Cross; Onawanda; The Life of Moses; Oliver Twist; Les Miserables* (Part I)

1910   *Twelfth Night; Saved by the Flag; Auld Robin Gray; Drumsticks; Love's C.O.D.; A Western Welcome*

1911   *A Tale of Two Cities; The Immortal Alamo; The Battle Hymn of the Republic; A Geranium; Billy the Kid; The Child Crusoes; Beyond the Law; The Tired, Absent-Minded Man; A Western Heroine; A Fighting Schoolmaster; Her Cowboy Lover; An Aeroplane Elopement; The Military Air-Scout; Mary's Strategem; The Kiss of Mary Jane; In the Hot Lands; Bessie's Ride; When the Table Turned; Tested by the Flag; Wages of War; How Betty Won the School; A Western Girl*

1912   *The Heart of the King's Jester; The Star Reporter; Old Love Letters; The Serpents; Yellow Bird; The Troublesome Step-Daughters; The Barrier That Was Burned; The Godmother; The Scoop; Two Women and Two Men; The Victoria Cross; The Telephone Girl; On Her Wedding Day; A Marriage of Convenience; The Love Sick Maidens of Cuddleton; Lincoln's Gettysburg Address; The Lady of the Lake; In the Furnace Fire; His Lordship, the Valet; The Heart of Esmeralda; The Governor Who Had a Heart; Following the Star; Mr. Dawson Turns the Tables; Coronets and Hearts; The Caveman; The French Spy; A Spanish Love Song; Never Again; A Vitagraph Romance; Nothing to Wear; None But the Brave Deserve the Fair; A Modern Atlanta; The Reincarnation of Karma*

1913   *Vengeance of Durand, or The Two Portraits; Sisters All; The Strength of Men; The Still Voice; The Next Generation; Peggy's Burglar; The Trap; A Regiment of Two; Red and White Roses; The Prince of Evil; The Leading Lady; A Homespun Tragedy; Hearts of the First Empire; The Delayed Letter; The Cure; The Classmates Frolic; The Chains*

*of an Oath; The Call; Brother Bill; 'Mid Kentucky Hills;
When Bobby Forgot*

1914   *The Christian; Warfare in the Skies; Steve O'Grady's Chance;
How Cissy Made Good; The Old Flute Player; The Mischief
Maker; In the Latin Quarter; Hope Foster's Mother; A Flor-
ida Enchantment; Children of the Feud; Captain Alvarez*

1915   *The Silent Plea; The Island of Regeneration; A Queen for an
Hour; The Dust of Egypt; The Ruling Power; A Price for
Folly; On Her Wedding Night; The Quality of Mercy;
O'Garry of the Royal Mounted; A Man's Sacrifice; Love's
Way; Jane Was Worth It; The Enemies; The Night of the
Wedding*

1916   *Jane's Bashful Hero; The Two Edged Sword; Jane's Husband; The Shop Girl; The Tarantula; An Enemy of the King;
Susie the Sleuth; She Won the Prize*

1917   *Money Magic; Aladdin from Broadway; Captain of the Gray
Horse Troop*

1918   *The Eyes of Mystery; Revenge; The Claim; The Treasure of
the Sea; The Demon; The Silent Woman; The Legion of
Death; Edith's Victory for Democracy*

1919   *As the Sun Went Down*

1920   *Moon Madness*

1921   *Beach of Dreams; The Greater Profit*

1930   *The Movie Album* (documentary)

Suffrage Films

From the advent of films, producers used the medium to perpetuate
the accepted view of the social order. This meant that women should
remain in the home and care for husband and family. As a result of
this view, several films were produced that satirized the campaign to
secure the vote for women. In these films the female suffragists were
masculinized and played by men, as in *A Busy Day* (1914) in which
Charlie Chaplin played an aggressive suffragette who attempts to
dominate men.

During the early 1910s the National American Woman Suffrage
Association (NAWSA) and the Women's Political Union (WPU) produced four films that supported their views. In their films, the suffragettes were attractive women who combined political activity with in-
volvement with family and romantic interests. Sadly, only two of

these films survived—*Votes for Women* (1912) and *80 Million Women Want–?* (1913).

In the NAWSA-sponsored melodrama *Votes for Women,* the appealing suffragist characters combat the corrupt senator who stands against progressive reform. The film received added attention because of the appearance of two prominent suffragists: Jane Addams and Anna Howard Shaw. The film presented suffragists as the caretakers of higher ideals and the logical impetus of social reform.

In 1913, with the success of NAWSA's film, WPU produced *80 Million Women Want–?* The film also presented an attractive, socially conscious suffragist who, this time, reforms her fiancé who is involved in corrupt politics. After the corrupt politicians are forced from power and the women win the vote, the final scene shows the now-reformed fiancé bestowing a marriage license on the suffragist. This film also presented two prominent suffragists—Emmeline Pankhurst and Harriet Stanton Blatch.

By 1915 suffragists had abandoned the use of films to promote votes for women. They found that the cost of making films was not offset by the revenues or publicity generated by them. Although other films were made that either supported or criticized the campaign to win the vote for women, suffragist organizations did not produce a film after 1915.

Partial Listing of Films About Suffrage

1898 *The Lady Barber*
1908 *A Day in the Life of a Suffragette*
1909 *When Women Vote; When Women Win; For the Cause of Suffrage*
1910 *A Determined Woman*
1911 *The Reformation of the Suffragettes; A Suffragette in Spite of Himself; Suffrage and the Man; Will It Ever Come to This?; Oh; You Suffragette!*
1912 *A Cure for Suffragettes; Votes for Women; Was He a Suffragette?*
1913 *How They Got the Vote; 80 Million Women Want–?; Suffragettes Again*
1914 *A Busy Day; The Suffragettes' Revenge; Your Girl and Mine*

1916   *The Woman in Politics*
1917   *One Law for Both*
1918   *Woman*
1919   *Experimental Marriage*

Sul-Te-Wan, Madame (1873 Kentucky-1959 Woodland Hills, CA)

Madame Sul-Te-Wan, whose real name was Nellie Conley, was the first black actor, male or female, to sign a film contract and be a featured performer. She appeared in mainstream films and eschewed the films made by black filmmakers. Sadly, although she was a true pioneer in the film industry, virtually nothing is available about her life.

She was the daughter of a laundress and delivered the clean laundry to actors at the theater, often being allowed to watch the shows from the wings. It was there that she decided to become an actor herself. Her career spanned over forty years and she appeared in some of the classic films of her time. Like many performers who got their start in silent films, by the end of her career she was playing supporting, often uncredited, roles and bit parts. In 1986, Wan was honored with the Oscar Micheaux Award and inducted into the Black Filmmakers' Hall of Fame.

Once thought to have been Dorothy Dandridge's grandmother, in his definitive biography of Dandridge, Donald Bogle disproved this rumor, stating that he believed it originated because Wan played Dandridge's grandmother in *Carmen Jones* (1954).

Film Credits

1915   *The Birth of a Nation*
1916   *Hoodoo Ann; Intolerance; The Children Pay*
1917   *Stage Struck*
1918   *Who's Your Father?*
1922   *Manslaughter*
1924   *The Lightning Rider*
1925   *The Narrow Street*
1927   *Uncle Tom's Cabin*
1929   *Queen Kelly; Thunderbolt*
1930   *Sarah and Son; The Thoroughbred*
1931   *Pagan Lady; Heaven on Earth*

1933 *King Kong; Ladies They Talk About*
1934 *A Modern Hero; Imitation of Life; Black Moon*
1937 *Maid of Salem; In Old Chicago*
1938 *The Toy Wife; Kentucky*
1939 *Tell No Tales; Torchy Plays with Dynamite*
1940 *Safari; Maryland*
1941 *King of the Zombies; Sullivan's Travels*
1943 *Revenge of the Zombies*
1954 *Carmen Jones*
1957 *Something of Value; Band of Angels*
1958 *Buccaneer; Tarzan and the Trappers*

Swanson, Gloria (1899 Chicago, IL-1983 New York City)

Courtesy of Silents Are Golden at
<SilentsAreGolden.com>

Gloria Swanson was the civilian equivalent of a military brat and lived in various locations including Chicago; Key West, Florida; and San Juan, Puerto Rico. She entered films at the age of sixteen with Essanay Studio in Chicago as an extra in *The Fable of Elvira and Farina and the Meal Ticket* (1915). She worked between studios—first Keystone then Triangle—and was eventually elevated to star status while at Triangle in 1918 following a string of successful dramas.

After Triangle went bankrupt she signed a contract with Cecile B. DeMille, whose films added impetus to her rise to stardom. He carefully groomed her and the roles she played for maximum impact on the audience, ensuring her success and increasing salary. She excelled at playing misunderstood or wronged wives and sophisticated women of the world. In 1922 she took over the management of her career and was known for her hard-driving ambition. When she left DeMille and Paramount in 1926, she was the highest-paid actor at the studio, but she decided that she wanted more control over her films so she went to United Artists.

During this period her chief supporter and film backer was Joseph P. Kennedy, with whom she was having an affair. However, her choices in films were not good and she went into personal debt to complete *Queen Kelly* (1929). Supposedly she remained in debt until she made *Sunset Boulevard* in 1950.

When film roles became scarce in the 1930s and 1940s, she turned to stage work. It was believed by some that she lost audience approval because of her extravagant lifestyle while the country reeled from the Depression. She made two comebacks in films—*Father Takes a Wife* (1941), which was quickly forgotten, and *Sunset Boulevard,* which was named twelfth on the list of the top 100 movies of the twentieth century by the American Film Institute. She also made guest appearances on television during the 1950s and 1960s.

Even though she stopped making movies in the early 1950s, Swanson always conducted herself as a star. She said in an early interview, "When I am a star, I will be every inch and every moment the star!" Someone once noted that she was the "second woman in Hollywood to make a million [but] the first to spend it." The rumor in Hollywood was that she had made and spent over $8 million during the height of her career.

When not working, her favorite pastime was collecting husbands. She was married seven times and was the first Hollywood star to marry into the European aristocracy with her marriage to the Marquis de la Falaise de la Coudraye in 1925. Sadly, she was not wise in her choice of husbands; after her seventh divorce in 1981 she remained single.

She wrote her autobiography, *Swanson on Swanson,* in 1980. Of this book she said, "I've given my memoirs far more thought than any of my marriages. You can't divorce a book." Her acting style was called "simple and straight-forward" and earned her, during her career, three Oscar nominations for best actress.

After her retirement she remained available for interviews and let it be known that she would return to film for the right role. However, she did not remain idle. She became involved in several business ventures that were relatively successful. She had her own line of designer clothes—a logical direction in which to go since she was known for her fashion sense, perhaps more than for her acting. She also created a line of cosmetics called "Essence of Nature."

Film Credits

1915   *The Fable of Elvira and Farina and the Meal Ticket; His New Job; Sweedie Goes to College; The Romance of an American Duchess; The Broken Pledge; At the End of a Perfect Day; The Ambition of the Baron*

1916   *A Social Club; The Nick of Time Baby; Hearts and Sparks; Haystacks and Steeples; A Dash of Courage; The Danger Girl*

1917   *Teddy at the Throttle; The Sultan's Wife; A Pullman Bride; Dangers of a Bride; Whose Baby?; Baseball Madness*

1918   *Society for Sale; Everywoman's Husband; The Secret Code; You Can't Believe Everything; Wife or Country; Station Content; Shifting Sands; Her Decision; Till I Come Back to You*

1919   *Don't Change Your Husband; For Better, for Worse; Male and Female*

1920   *Something to Think About; Why Change Your Wife?*

1921   *The Great Moment; The Affairs of Anatol; Under the Lash; Don't Tell Everything*

1922   *Beyond the Rocks; The Impossible Mrs. Bellew; My American Wife; Her Husband's Trademark; Her Gilded Cage*

1923   *Prodigal Daughters; Bluebeard's Eighth Wife; Zara; Hollywood*

1924   *The Humming Bird; A Society Scandal; Manhandled; Her Love Story; Wages of Virtue*

1925   *Madame Sans-Gêne; Stage Struck; The Coast of Folly*

1926   *Untamed Lady; Fine Manners*

1927   *The Love of Sunya*

1928   *Sadie Thompson*

1929   *The Trespasser; Queen Kelly*

1930   *What a Widow!*

1931   *Indiscreet; Tonight or Never*

1933   *Perfect Understanding*

1934   *Music in the Air*

1941   *Father Takes a Wife*

1949   *Down Memory Lane*

1950   *Sunset Boulevard*
1952   *Three for Bedroom C*
1962   *Nero's Mistress*
1974   *Airport 1975*

Producing Credits

1927   *The Love of Sunya*
1928   *Sadie Thompson*
1929   *Queen Kelly*
1930   *What a Widow!*
1933   *Perfect Understanding*

Sweet, Blanche (1896 Chicago, IL-1986 New York City)

Blanche Sweet, called "one of the greatest emotional actresses in the silent drama," was one of D. W. Griffith's favorite female stars even though she did not fit his idealized Victorian woman. She was neither frail nor dependent, and Griffith showcased her talent in roles as determined and resourceful women.

She was born into a show business family and made her stage debut at eighteen months when she was carried on stage in the drama *Blue Jeans,* with the Pollard Stock Company in Cincinnati. She was a veteran stage actor when she decided to apply for a film job during the slow theatrical season of 1909. She worked with Edison on a few films before applying at Biograph.

She met D. W. Griffith and he put her in *A Corner in Wheat* (1909) the same day. Although Sweet said that Griffith did not initially impress her, she developed tremendous respect for him—personally and professionally. In her time at Biograph she became one of their most important players and appeared in over seventy one- and two-reel films.

However, when Biograph moved to California, Sweet left the company to become a dancer with the Gertrude Hoffman troupe; she returned to films when she realized she was a better actor than dancer. She came to California and starred in the classic *The Lonedale Operator* (1911). She left Biograph in 1914 and freelanced among the early Hollywood studios before signing with Famous Players-Lasky in 1915. She worked with several well-known directors including Cecil B. DeMille, William de Mille, Frank Reicher, and, the man she eventually married, Marshall Neilan.

Sweet and Neilan created their own production company in 1918 and released their films through Pathe. The company was dissolved in 1921, but Sweet continued to appear in quality productions. One of her most memorable was the first film version of Eugene O'Neill's *Anna Christie* (1923).

After a five-year courtship, in 1922 she finally married Neilan, but the marriage ended in divorce in 1929. During the marriage the two collaborated on some of Sweet's best films, including *Tess of the D'Urbervilles* (1924).

Although she made the transition to sound, she appeared in only a few films before announcing her retirement from film to concentrate on the stage. She starred on Broadway and toured in several productions in addition to appearing on the radio during the 1930s. In 1936 she married actor Raymond Hackett—a marriage that lasted until his death in 1958.

The Hacketts returned to California and Sweet continued to appear on the stage when a role appealed to her. During the 1950s Red Scare in the United States, Sweet was listed as a member of the Communist party and blacklisted. This made getting any entertainment job virtually impossible.

After her husband's death, Sweet returned to New York and worked as a saleswoman in a department store before finding her niche as a film historian. Until her death she worked tirelessly to aid writers interested in the silent era and the film industry's infancy. She also served as a director of the National Board of Review of Motion Pictures and as consultant to the Department of Film at The Museum of Modern Art.

Film Credits

1909   *A Corner in Wheat; To Save Her Soul; Choosing a Husband; A Man with Three Wives; The Day After; In Little Italy*

1910   *The Rocky Road; All on Account of the Milk; A Romance of a Western Hills; A Flash of Light; Love in Quarantine*

1911   *The Two Paths; Heart Beats of Long Ago; His Daughter; Lily of the Tenements; A Decree of Destiny; The Lonedale Operator; The Spanish Gypsy; The Broken Cross; How She Triumphed; The White Rose of the Wilds; The Smile of a Child; The Primal Call; Fighting Blood; A Country Cupid; The Last Drop of Water; Out from the Shadow; The Blind Princess and the Poet; The Stuff Heroes Are Made Of; The Making of a Man; The Long Road; Love in the Hills; A Woman Scorned; The Voice of a Child; Winning the Heiress; The Country Lovers; The Battle; Through Darkened Vales; Was He a Coward?; Priscilla's April Fool Joke; Priscilla and the Umbrella; The New Dress; Enoch Arden* (Part I); *The Indian Brothers; The Miser's Heart*

1912   *The Eternal Mother; The Transformation of Mike; A Sister's Love; For His Son; Under Burning Skies; The Goddess of Sagebrush Gulch; The Punishment; One Is Business, the Other Crime; The Lesser Evil; An Outcast Among Outcasts; A Temporary Truce; The Spirit Awakened; Man's Lust for Gold; The Inner Circle; With the Enemy's Help; A Change of Spirit; Blind Love; The Chief's Blanket; The Painted Lady* (I); *The God Within; A Sailor's Heart; The Old Bookkeeper; A String of Pearls; A Pueblo Romance*

1913   *Three Friends; Pirate Gold; Oil and Water; A Chance Deception; The Massacre; Love in an Apartment Hotel; Broken Ways; Near to Earth; The Hero of Little Italy; If Only We Knew; Death's Marathon; The Mistake; The Coming of Angelo; Two Men of a Desert; The Vengeance of Galora; The Stolen Bride; The House of Discord; Her Wedding Bell*

1914   *Classmates; Judith of Bethulia; The Battle at Elderbush Gulch; Brute Force; Home Sweet Home; The Escape; The Avenging Conscience; The Tear That Burned; Strongheart; The Soul of Honor; The Sentimental Sister; The Second Mrs. Roebuck; The Old Maid; The Odalisque; Men and Women;*

The Little Country Mouse; Her Awakening; For Those Un-born; For Her Father's Sins; Ashes of the Past

1915   *The Warrens of Virginia; The Captive; Stolen Goods; The Clue; The Secret Orchard; The Case of Becky; The Secret Sin*

1916   *The Ragamuffin; The Blacklist; The Sowers; The Thousand-Dollar Husband; The Dupe; Public Opinion; The Storm; Un-protected*

1917   *The Evil Eye; Those Without Sin; The Tides of Barnegat; The Silent Partner*

1919   *The Hushed Hour; A Woman of Pleasure; The Unpardonable Sin; Fighting Cressy*

1920   *The Deadlier Sex; The Girl in the Web; Help Wanted—Male; Her Unwilling Husband; Simple Souls*

1921   *That Girl Montana*

1922   *Quincy Adams Sawyer*

1923   *Souls for Sale; The Meanest Man in the World; In the Palace of the King; Anna Christie*

1924   *Those Who Dance; Tess of the D'Urbervilles*

1925   *The Sporting Venus; His Supreme Moment; Why Women Love; The New Commandment*

1926   *The Lady from Hell; Bluebeard's Seven Wives; The Far Cry; Diplomacy*

1927   *Singed*

1929   *The Woman in White; Always Faithful*

1930   *Woman Racket; Show Girl in Hollywood; The Silver Horde*

1959   *The Five Pennies*

Takagi, Tokuko Nagai (1891 Tokyo, Japan-1919)

Tokuko Nagai Takagi had a brief career in silent films in the United States but was a tremendous star of Japanese operettas in her own country. Her films can be viewed as historical documents of the time, reflecting Japanese-American relations and cultural attitudes.

Takagi married at fifteen and came to the United States with her new husband. After trying several businesses, the couple created a magic act and began touring Canada and the New England area. While in New York, Takagi started taking dance lessons and was recommended to appear in a Thanhouser Company film.

During the next two years Takagi appeared in four films for Thanhouser which ran the gambit from romantic tragedy to not-too-subtle political agendas of "beware of the Japanese expansionist tendencies." By the late 1910s, the anti-Japanese feelings as reflected in films made it impossible for Takagi to continue in a film career in the United States.

Takagi and her husband left the United States to tour Europe and Russia, but they returned to Japan when World War I broke out. In Japan she became renown as a dancer of European operettas that she adapted for Japanese tastes. In her native country she was viewed as an innovator and pioneer.

Film Credits

1911   *The East and the West*
1912   *The Birth of the Lotus Blossom; For the Mikado; Miss Taqu of Tokyo*

Taliaferro, Mabel (1887 New York City-1979 Honolulu, Hawaii)

Known as "the Sweetheart of American Movies" before Mary Pickford laid claim to "America's Sweetheart," Mabel Taliaferro made her career playing naive innocents. Taliaferro began her show business career appearing on the stage while still a child. As she grew older she moved into juvenile leads and eventually made her film debut as the lead in *Cinderella* (1911).

Although she was extremely popular with film audiences, Taliaferro retired in 1921. She returned to films to make a final appearance in *My Love Come Back* in 1940.

Film Credits

1911	*Cinderella*
1912	*The Sunbeam*
1914	*The Three of Us*
1916	*Her Great Price; God's Half Acre; The Dawn of Love; Snowbird; The Sunbeam* (II)
1917	*The Barricade; Magdalene of the Hills; Peggy, the Will o' the Wisp; Peggy Leads the Way; Draft 258; A Wife by Proxy; The Jury of Fate*
1919	*The Mite of Love*
1921	*Sentimental Tommy; The Rich Slave*
1924	*Alexander Hamilton*
1940	*My Love Come Back*

Talmadge, Constance (1898 Brooklyn, NY-1973 Los Angeles, CA)

Courtesy of Silents Are Golden at <SilentsAreGolden.com>

The youngest of the three Talmadge sisters who entered show business during the silent era, Constance Talmadge was a talented comedian. Her exact year of birth is uncertain because she, like many silent stars, changed her birth date regularly. Her tombstone, which historians doubt is correct, has 1903-1973 carved on it.

Called "Dutch" from an early age because her short blonde hairstyle made her look like "a little Dutch boy," Talmadge was a rough-and-ready tomboy who once announced she wouldn't play with a neighbor child because the neighbor was "afraid to risk her life." With the help of sister Norma, she entered films in 1914 as an extra at Vitagraph at $5 a day.

She eventually graduated to her own films and appeared for several years opposite Billy Quirk in comedy shorts. She became one of the studio's favorite players and was known as "the Vitagraph Tomboy."

Her big break came as the Mountain Girl in the Babylonian segment of D. W. Griffith's *Intolerance* (1916).

After her sister Norma married Joseph Schenck, she benefited from his assistance with her career and was soon one of the top silent comedians. For a few years she even had her own production company which gave her additional control over her films. She retired from films with the advent of sound and lived comfortably on the money she had made from films and from her several advantageous marriages.

Her sense of humor and attitude toward acting might be summed up by the cable she sent to Norma in response to a particularly bad review that her sister had received: "Quit pressing your luck, baby. The critics can't knock those trust funds Momma set up for us." Although Peg Talmadge was called "the original stage mother," she did make sure that her daughters' futures were secure.

When she received her star on the Walk of Fame, rather than just put her feet in the cement, she walked across it, leaving five footprints in her wake. Her star remains the only one with more than two footprints. The sisters' influence is still felt in Hollywood, where Talmadge Street is named for both Constance and Norma. The street ran along the west side of the old Vitagraph Studio but now borders the ABC Television Center.

She was considered the best businesswoman of the three sisters. With the help of their mother, the Talmadge sisters made sure to invest their earnings and alimony settlements wisely. In 1927 the sisters opened Talmadge Park, a real estate development in San Diego now known as the Talmadge District, which has streets named after each of the sisters.

Film Credits

1914   *Uncle Bill; The Peacemaker; Our Fairy Play; The Mysterious Lodger; The Moonstone of Fez; The Maid from Sweden; In the Latin Quarter; In Bridal Attire; Forcing Dad's Consent; Fixing Their Dads; Father's Timepiece; The Evolution of Percival; The Egyptian Mummy; Buddy's First Call; Buddy's Downfall*

1915   *The Young Man Who Figgered; The Vanishing Vault; A Study in Trumps; Spades Are Trumps; The Master of His House;*

The Little Puritan; The Lady of Shalott; A Keyboard Strategy; The Green Cat; Captivating Mary Carstairs; Burglarious Billy; The Boarding House Feud; Billy's Wager; Billy the Bear Tamer; Bertie's Stratagem; Beached and Bleached; In the Latin Quarter; Can You Beat It?; Georgia Pearce

1916   *The Missing Links; Intolerance; The Microscope Mystery; The Matrimaniac; The She-Devil*

1917   *A Girl of the Timber Claims; Betsy's Burglar; Scandal; The Honeymoon*

1918   *Good Night, Paul; A Pair of Silk Stockings; Up the Road with Sallie; The Studio Girl; The Shuttle; Sauce for the Goose; Mrs. Leffingwell's Boots; The Lesson; A Lady's Name*

1919   *Romance and Arabella; Experimental Marriage; Happiness a la Mode; The Veiled Adventure; The Fall of Babylon; A Virtuous Vamp; A Temperamental Wife; Who Cares?*

1920   *Two Weeks; In Search of a Sinner; The Love Expert; Dangerous Business; The Perfect Woman; Good References*

1921   *Mama's Affair; Woman's Place; Wedding Bells; Lessons in Love*

1922   *Polly of the Follies; East Is West; The Primitive Lover*

1923   *Dulcy; The Dangerous Maid*

1924   *The Goldfish; In Hollywood with Potash and Perlmutter; Her Night of Romance*

1925   *Learning to Love; Her Sister from Paris; Seven Chances; Heart Trouble*

1926   *The Duchess of Buffalo*

1927   *Venus of Venice; Breakfast at Sunrise*

1929   *Venus*

Talmadge, Natalie (1896 Brooklyn, NY-1969 Santa Monica, CA)

The middle sister of the Talmadge trio, Natalie Talmadge was the least interested in being in films and left the industry as soon as possible. In fact, while her sisters appeared in films, she worked as a secretary to famous comedian Roscoe "Fatty" Arbuckle.

She made her first credited film appearance in 1917, although she had appeared as an uncredited extra in films before that time. She received her only writing credit for the scenario for *Out West* in 1918. But any career in films was forgotten when she married comedian

Buster Keaton in 1921. It was said that while her mother helped both Norma and Constance with their careers because they were talented, she could only help Natalie make a good marriage.

She appeared in one film after her marriage, Keaton's *Our Hospitality* (1923), although after her divorce she sometimes appeared in bit parts in Norma's later films. She lived in a beach house after her divorce and slowly drank herself to death.

Film Credits

1916	*Intolerance*
1917	*A Country Hero*
1919	*The Isle of Conquest*
1920	*The Love Expert; Yes or No*
1921	*Passion Flower; The Haunted House*
1923	*Our Hospitality*

Talmadge, Norma (1893 Jersey City, NJ-1957 Las Vegas, NV)

Courtesy of Silents Are Golden at <SilentsAreGolden.com>

The eldest of the three Talmadge sisters, Norma Talmadge was modeling by the time she was thirteen to help her mother support the family after their alcoholic father deserted them. Her modeling brought her to the attention of film producers, and her first bit part was in *The Household Pest* (1910). She continued to appear in other small roles throughout 1910.

Her first substantial role was in *A Tale of Two Cities* (1911) as Mimi, a seamstress that goes to the guillotine. By 1913 she was being touted as Vitagraph's most promising young actress. In five years at Vitagraph she made more than 250 films and was able to hone her acting talent.

She traveled west to appear in a film, but the film flopped and the studio went bankrupt, leaving her unemployed. She eventually signed on with sister Constance's studio, run by the legendary D. W. Griffith, and appeared in seven features.

The family remained in California for several months then returned east where Norma married producer Joseph Schenck and opened her own production company. The first film produced was *Panthea* (1917) which established Norma as a first-rate tragedienne. She continued to appear in films that focused on quiet suffering and womanly sacrifice through most of the 1920s, but by 1928 her popularity with audiences had waned. With the advent of sound films it was discovered that her voice did not record well, so she retired after appearing in *Du Barry; Woman of Passion* (1930).

She divorced Schenck in 1934, after being separated from him for seven years, and within days married vaudevillian George Jessel. At the time Jessel had a radio show, and Talmadge was added to the cast in the hopes of improving the show's ratings and reviving her career. Neither hope was realized.

By 1939 she divorced Jessel and married for the final time in 1946—a marriage that lasted until her death in 1957. She developed arthritis in her final years and was completely bedridden.

It is said that she started the trend to included footprints on the Walk of Fame when she accidentally stepped into the wet cement in front of Grauman's Chinese Theatre. In West Hollywood is a street called Norma Place near where her studio used to be which recognizes her importance to the heritage of Hollywood, the film industry, and the towns that sprang up around the film capital.

She is often remembered as an imperious diva who once remarked to a fan that approached her for her autograph after she retired from films, "Go away. I don't need you anymore." But she was also a loyal friend who thought nothing of standing by those she cared about, either publicly amid rumors and scandal or privately.

Film Credits

1910   *Love of Chrysanthemum; Uncle Tom's Cabin; A Dixie Mother; In Neighboring Kingdoms; The Household Pest; A Broken Spell*

1911   *A Tale of Two Cities; The Sky Pilot; The General's Daughter; The Thumb Print; The Child Crusoes; Forgotten, or an An-*

swered Prayer; Her Hero; Paola and Francesca; The Four Poster Pest; The Stumbling Block; His Last Cent

1912   *Captain Barnacle's Messmates; The First Violin; Mrs. Carter's Necklace; Mrs. 'enry 'awkins; Counsel for the Defense; The Troublesome Step-Daughters; Captain Barnacle's Waif; Captain Barnacle, Reformer; Mr. Butler Buttles; The Love Sick Maidens of Cuddleton; Fortunes of a Composer; A Fortune in a Teacup; The Extension Table; A Romance of Wall Street; Wanted . . . A Grandmother; The Higher Mercy; Father's Hot Toddy; Faithful Unto Death; His Official Appointment; The Model for St. John; O'Hara, Squatter and Philosopher; His Official Appointment*

1913   *Just Show People; The Silver Cigarette Case; An Old Man's Love Story; The Other Woman; The Doctor's Secret; Father's Hatband; His Silver Bachelorhood; An Elopement at Home; The Blue Rose; The Honorable Algernon; Wanted: A Strong Hand; Under the Daisies; The Solitaires; Omens and Oracles; O'Hara As a Guardian Angel; The Midget's Revenge; Fanny's Conspiracy; Extremities; 'Arriet's Baby; The Tables Turned; O'Hara Helps Cupid; Stenographer Troubles; O'Hara's Godchild; Belinda the Slavey; The Lady and Her Maid; Casey at Bat*

1914   *The Vavasour Ball; The Sacrifice of Kathleen; A Helpful Sisterhood; Cupid versus Money; Miser Murray's Wedding Present; A Wayward Daughter; Fogg's Millions; Memories in Men's Souls; The Loan Shark King; The Wooing of Myra May; A Question of Clothes; Under False Colors; Sunshine and Shadows; Sawdust and Salome; The Right of Way; Politics and the Press; The Peacemaker; Old Reliable; Officer John Donovan; The Mill of Life; John Rance, Gentleman; His Little Page; The Hidden Letters; The Hero; Goodbye Summer; The Salvation of Kathleen*

1915   *The Barrier of Faith; Janet of the Chorus; Elsa's Brother; The Criminal; The Battle Cry of Peace; The Crown Prince's Double; A Pillar of Flame; A Daughter's Strange Inheritance; Captivating Mary Carstairs; Dust of Desire; A Daughter of Israel*

1916   *The Missing Links; Martha's Vindication; The Children in the House; Going Straight; The Devil's Needle; The Social Secretary; Fifty-Fifty*

1917   *Panthea; Poppy; The Secret of Storm Country; The Moth; The Law of Compensation*

1918   *The Ghosts of Yesterday; De Luxe Annie; The Safety Curtain; Her Only Way; The Forbidden City; The Right of Purchase*

1919   *The Heart of Wetona; The New Moon; The Probation Wife; The Way of a Woman; The Isle of Conquest; Girl of Gold*

1920   *A Daughter of Two Worlds; The Woman Gives; Yes or No; The Branded Woman; She Loves and Lies*

1921   *Passion Flower; The Wonderful Thing; Love's Redemption; The Sign on the Door*

1922   *Smilin' Through; The Eternal Flame*

1923   *The Voice from the Minaret; Within the Law; The Song of Love; Ashes of Vengeance*

1924   *Secrets; The Only Woman; In Hollywood with Potash and Perlmutter*

1925   *The Lady; Graustark*

1926   *Kiki; Camille*

1927   *The Dove*

1928   *Show People; The Woman Disputed*

1929   *New York Nights*

1930   *Du Barry; Woman of Passion*

Tashman, Lilyan (1899 Brooklyn, NY-1934 New York City)

Remembered more as a fashion icon than as a talented actor, Lilyan Tashman greatly influenced the viewing public's views on what was fashionable and chic. When she died she was mourned with almost as much fanfare and angst as Valentino.

Born into a middle-class family, Tashman was the tenth and youngest child. While in her teens, she began modeling and posing for artists. She appeared on the vaudeville circuit and made her stage debut in 1914 in the chorus of *The Lilac Domino*.

By 1916 she was regularly appearing in Ziegfeld's productions, wearing the most outlandish outfits with style and grace. She continued to appear in "legitimate" theater, and her breakthrough role was as Trixie in *The Gold Diggers* (1921). The play was a hit and soon women were clamoring for the Lilyan Tashman look in clothes and hairstyles.

Film companies began vying to capitalize on her popularity. Soon she signed with Paramount to make her film debut in *Experience* (1921), but she did not care for films and returned to the stage. While working in New York, Hollywood kept offering supporting roles that were little more than elegant walk-ons.

When the film rights to a play she was appearing in, *The Garden of Weeds,* were sold, she agreed to revive her role for the film. By now she had been typed as a bad girl and she continued to appear in this type of role for the remainder of her silent film career. Married to actor Edmund Lowe, in 1925 Tashman now became known as a Hollywood hostess. Although after her death rumors surfaced about her sexual preference, she apparently enjoyed a loving and companionable marriage.

Her sound debut was *The Trial of Mary Dugan* (1929) in which she had a critically acclaimed dramatic courtroom scene. Unlike many silent stars, sound was an advantage to Tashman because now not only could she look good, she could deliver the type of one-liners she was famous for off screen. Her performance in supporting roles often stole scenes from the supposed stars of the films in which she appeared.

Her career slowed considerably after surgery for acute appendicitis in 1932, from which Tashman never fully recovered. She continued to appear in films, but her ill health became noticeable. In 1934 she underwent another emergency operation—this time to remove cancerous tumors—but died while in surgery. After her death, Lexington Avenue in New York City had to be blocked off to allow the crowd of more than 3,000 mourners to pay their final respects. Her funeral almost turned into a riot, as a crowd of nearly 10,000 swarmed Washington Cemetery and several onlookers were injured.

In a strange turn of events, her final film, *Frankie and Johnny,* was released two years after her death, giving her a posthumous screen credit.

Film Credits

1921   *Experience*
1922   *Head Over Heels*
1924   *Manhandled; Winner Takes All; The Garden of Weeds; Nellie, the Beautiful Cloak Model; The Dark Swan; Is Love Everything?*
1925   *Ports of Call; The Parasite; A Broadway Butterfly; Déclassée; I'll Show You the Town; The Girl Who Wouldn't Work; Pretty Ladies; Seven Days; Bright Lights*
1926   *Rocking Moon; The Skyrocket; Whispering Smith; Siberia; So This Is Paris; For Alimony Only; Love's Blindness*
1927   *Don't Tell the Wife; Evening Clothes; Camille; The Woman Who Did Not Care; The Prince of Headwaiters; The Stolen Bride; A Texas Steer; French Dressing*
1928   *Happiness Ahead; Craig's Wife; Take Me Home; Manhattan Cocktail; Phyllis of the Follies; Lady Raffles*
1929   *The Lone Wolf's Daughter; The Trial of Mary Dugan; Gold Diggers of Broadway; The Marriage Playground; New York Nights; Hardboiled; Bulldog Drummond*
1930   *No, No, Nannette; Puttin' on the Ritz; On the Level; The Matrimonial Bed; Leathernecking; The Cat Creeps*
1931   *Millie; Finn and Hattie; The Mad Parade; Girls About Town; Up Pops the Devil; The Road to Reno; One Heavenly Night; Murder by the Clock*
1932   *Scarlet Dawn; The Wiser Sex; Those We Love*
1933   *Too Much Harmony; Wine; Women and Song; Mama Loves Papa*
1934   *Riptide*
1936   *Frankie and Johnnie*

Terry, Alice (1899 Vincennes, IN-1987 Burbank, CA)

It would be impossible to write about Alice Terry without also writing about director Rex Ingram, her husband for twenty-nine years. Their careers, almost more than their personal lives, are indelibly intertwined.

Born Alice Frances Taaffe, Alice Terry moved to Los Angeles with her family when she was fifteen. Soon after arriving she met Enid Markey, an actor living in her building who convinced her to apply for a job in films at Thomas Ince's studio, known as Inceville. She was hired and soon appeared in several of his films including his production *Civilization* (1916).

While at Inceville Terry did everything from acting to editing, but it was not until she met Ingram that her talent was fully utilized. Although she worked only as an extra in their first films together, after he recovered from an illness acquired during World War I and returned to film production, Ingram offered Terry the first of many lead roles in his film *Hearts Are Trumps* (1920). This success was followed by the role of Marguerite in *The Four Horsemen of the Apocalypse* (1921) which established Ingram as one of the best directors of the silent era and propelled Terry to major stardom.

The friendship that became a successful working collaboration eventually became love. The couple secretly married in November 1921. The couple was so involved in their work that they married on a Saturday and returned to the studio to complete the film on which they were working on Monday—delaying their honeymoon until the film was complete.

Although Terry continued to appear in films, she was more devoted to Ingram's career than her own. In her mind she was first and foremost "a housewife" who promoted her husband's work unceasingly. Ingram, who readily admitted that his wife was vital to his creativity, recognized Terry's many contributions and abilities in his final film by listing her as co-director.

In 1925 Ingram bought Victorine Studios in Nice, France, and Terry appeared in his first independent production, *Our Sea* (1926). Since Ingram often became completely absorbed in his projects, Terry was the acknowledged family business manager and the person who made life go smoothly so that Ingram could create. Although Terry occasionally returned to the United States to appear in a film while Ingram had his studio in France, she was always quick to return to her husband's side. Neither Terry nor Ingram were comfortable with the new sound medium, so when Ingram lost his studio the couple retired to Cairo.

After their retirement, the couple did not see each other for almost two years while Ingram wrote his first novel and Terry returned to California after her mother's death. When Ingram completed his novel and followed his wife to California, they purchased two adjacent houses—one as a residence and one for Ingram as an escape or work area depending on his mood. The couple continued happily until Ingram's sudden death in 1950.

Film Credits

1915 *Strictly Business*
1916 *Not My Sister; Civilization; A Corner in Colleens*
1917 *Wild Winship's Widow; The Bottom of the Well; Alimony; Tillie's Terrible Tumbles*
1918 *A Bachelor's Children; Old Wives for New; Love Watches; The Trimmed Lamp; The Song and the Sergeant; Sisters of the Golden Circle; The Brief Debut of Tildy*
1919 *Thin Ice; The Love Burglar; The Valley of the Giants; The Day She Paid*
1920 *Shore Acres; The Devil's Passkey; Hearts Are Trumps*
1921 *The Four Horsemen of the Apocalypse; The Conquering Power*
1922 *Turn to the Right; The Prisoner of Zenda*
1923 *Where the Pavement Ends; Scaramouche*
1924 *The Arab*
1925 *The Great Divide; Sackcloth and Scarlet; Confessions of a Queen; Any Woman*
1926 *Our Sea; The Magician*
1927 *The Garden of Allah; Lovers?*
1928 *The Three Passions*
1932 *Baroud*

Theby, Rosemary (1892 St Louis, MO-1973 Los Angeles, CA)

One of the members of Hollywood's "in" crowd during the silent era, Rosemary Theby began her career by attending the Sergent Dramatic School in New York. She joined the Vitagraph stock company of players in 1910 and debuted in *The Sacrifice* that year.

She played vamps before Theda Bara made a career of it, but Theby luckily avoided being typecast in that role. She spent the remainder of the decade appearing in a variety of starring roles. In 1924 she married director Harry Myers. Although by this time she was appearing more often in supporting roles, as a couple they were still part of the elite group of pioneers and stars that held court in Hollywood.

Sadly, by the 1930s she was appearing in uncredited or extra roles. After Myers's death in 1934, Theby married again and retired to Kansas City. She eventually returned to California. When she died in 1973, neither the press nor the film community acknowledged her death.

Film Credits

1910   *The Sacrifice; The Wager*
1911   *A Geranium*
1912   *A Red Cross Martyr; The Two Battles; As You Like It; The Godmother; The Reincarnation of Karma; Irene's Infatuation; The Illumination; His Father's Son; A Fortune in a Teacup; Mr. Bolter's Infatuation; Love in the Ghetto; An Eventful Elopement; Rock of Ages; Wanted, a Sister; The Light of St. Bernard; A Juvenile Love Affair; Written in Sand; Father's Hot Toddy; The Mills of the Gods; The Hand Bag*
1913   *How It All Happened; The Silver Cigarette Case; Better Days; His Silver Bachelorhood; The Web; A Soul in Bondage; A Fighting Chance; The Classmates Frolic; Ashes; Fight for the Right; Betty's Baby; The Ambassador's Disappearance; The Little Minister; Off Road; The Weapon; The Glow Worm; The Heart of a Rose; Her Rosary; Maria Rosa; The Missing Ring*
1914   *The Bride of Marblehead; The Little Gray Home; The Rock of Hope; The Accusation; Thumb Prints and Diamonds; The Attorney's Decision; The Double Life; The Hopeless Game; The Price of a Ruby*
1915   *Baby; The Man of Shame; The Earl of Pawtucket; Men at Their Best; The House of a Thousand Relations; The Artist and the Vengeful One; The Cards Never Lie; The Cheval Mystery; The Danger Line; Father's Child; Father's Money; Fathers Three; The Hard Road; He Was Only a Bathing Suit Salesman; Mumps; My Tomboy Girl; Playing with Fire; The Prize Story; A Romance of the Backwoods; Saved by a Dream; We Should Worry for Auntie*

1916   *Artistic Atmosphere; The Pipe Dream; Baby's Toofs; High Fliers; In the Night; The Latest in Vampires; Lathered Truth; Love Spasms; Man and Morality; The Model Husband; Housekeeping; Gertie's Garter; The Good Stenographer; Green Eyes; His Wedding Promise; Their Dream House; A Financial Frenzy*

1917   *The Winged Mystery; The Hash House Mystery*

1918   *The Rogue; The Straight and Narrow; The Great Love; Boston Blackie's Little Pal; Unexpected Places; Love's Pay Day; The Silent Mystery; The Midnight Patrol; Bright and Early*

1919   *The Spender; Faith; Peggy Does Her Darndest; The Hushed Hour; The Amateur Adventuress; Upstairs and Down; Tangled Threads; Yvonne from Paris; Heartsease; When a Woman Strikes; Are You Legally Married?*

1920   *Butterfly Man; Rio Grande; A Splendid Hazard; Whispering Devils; Married to Order; The Little Gray Mouse; Kismet; Unseen Forces; Dice of Destiny; Terror Island; The Mystery of 13*

1921   *A Connecticut Yankee in King Arthur's Court; Good Woman; Shame; Hicksville to Broadway; Across the Divide; Fightin' Mad; Partners of Fate; The Last Trail*

1922   *Yellow Men and Gold; I Am the Law; More to Be Pitied Than Scorned; Rich Men's Wives; The Eternal Flame*

1923   *Your Friend and Mine; Slander the Woman; The Girl of the Golden West; The Rip Tide; Mary of the Movies; Tea: With a Kick; In Search of a Thrill; Long Live the King; Lost and Found on a South Seas Island*

1924   *The Son of the Sahara; Behold the Woman; The Red Lily; Secrets of the Night; So Big; Pagan Passions*

1925   *As Man Desires; The Re-Creation of Brian Kent; Fifth Avenue Models; Wreckage; One Year to Live*

1926   *The Truthful Sex*

1927   *The Second Hundred Years; A Bowery Cinderella; Riding to Fame*

1928   *A Woman Against the World; The Port of Missing Girls; The Chinatown Mystery*

1929   *Girls Who Dare; The Dream Melody; Trial Marriage; Montmartre Rose; The Peacock Fan*

1930   *Sugar Plum Papa; Bulls and Bears; Midnight Daddies; Scotch; He Trumped Her Ace*
1931   *Taxi Troubles; Ten Nights in a Barroom*
1932   *Doctor's Orders*
1933   *The Fatal Glass of Beer*
1935   *Man on the Flying Trapeze; The Drunkard; Wings in the Dark*
1936   *San Francisco; His Brother's Wife; Yours for the Asking; Our Relations; Neighborhood House*
1937   *The Devil Is Driving; Vogues of 1938; Rich Relations; Make Way for Tomorrow*
1938   *You Can't Take It with You*
1939   *One Million B. C.*

Thomas, Olive (1894 Charleroi, PA-1920 Neuilly-sur-Seine, France)

Born Oliveretta Elaine Duffy, like many silent era stars the correct year of her birth is not known. Although generally acknowledged as having been a promising actor, Olive Thomas is best remembered today as the doomed wife of Jack Pickford, Mary Pickford's younger brother.

After getting married at thirteen (a relatively common practice at that time) and divorced two years later, Thomas moved to New York and began working in a department store. Soon after arriving, on a dare, she entered a "most beautiful girl in New York" contest and won.

She then started modeling for artists such as Harrison Fisher and Howard Chandler Christy. Fisher introduced her to Florenz Ziegfeld and she began appearing on Broadway in Ziegfeld's famous *Follies*. Her success on Broadway resulted in a contract with International Film Company in 1916.

Soon after coming to California, Thomas met Jack Pickford at a dance at Nat Goodwin's on the Santa Monica pier. Commenting on her upcoming marriage after a courtship of only eight months, Thomas said, "We got along so well on the dance floor that we decided that we would be able to get along together for the rest of our lives." Whether this quote is an example of Thomas's naïveté or studio public relations expertise, the film audience loved the romance and the couple was married in October 1916.

Thomas continued to make films that were extremely popular with film audiences, and the marriage, though reported as rocky at times in various fan magazines, survived. The couple sailed to France for a second honeymoon in early August 1920 and took up residence at the Ritz.

On September 9, after spending the night out, Pickford called the front desk requesting a doctor for his wife. When the doctor arrived, Thomas was "writhing in pain." Although the death was ruled as accidental, many theories have been put forth regarding the circumstances of her death. One theory suggests that Thomas accidentally took a lethal dose of the mercury bichloride that she took to combat the venereal disease (thought to have been syphilis) she contracted from her husband. Another supposes that she accidentally took the bichloride instead of the sleeping pills she expected to find on the nightstand. Another theory states that she committed suicide because she couldn't live with her drug addiction anymore. Many other theories involve Pickford killing her for various reasons.

Her death brought an abrupt end to a promising career. Over 4,000 people attended her funeral, but she was soon forgotten by both her fans and her husband, who married again barely a year later.

Film Credits

1916 *Beatrice Fairfax* (episode ten)
1917 *A Girl Like That; Madcap Madge; An Even Break; Broadway Arizona; Indiscreet Corinne; Tom Sawyer*
1918 *Betty Takes a Hand; Limousine Life; Heiress for a Day*
1919 *Toton the Apache; The Follies Girl; Upstairs and Down; Love's Prisoner; Prudence on Broadway; The Glorious Lady; Out Yonder; The Spite Bride*
1920 *The Flapper; Darling Mine; Everybody's Sweetheart; Youthful Folly; Footlights and Shadows*

Thurman, Mary (1895 Richfield, UT-1925 New York City)

A versatile actor that never found an audience, Mary Thurman starred in Sennett comedies as well as Allan Dwan melodramas. Thurman originally taught school after graduating from the University of Utah, but her life changed in 1916 when she took a vacation to Los Angeles and was lured into acting. She first worked for D. W.

Griffith and that year appeared in a small role in DeWolf Hopper's
Sunshine Dad (1916).

She signed with Mack Sennett and was given the complete "bathing beauty" promotion. She was very successful in comedy, but she soon decided that to be taken seriously as an actor she had to appear in dramatic films and therefore asked to be released from her contract.

She freelanced for several studios while she honed her dramatic talent. She was soon in demand as a leading lady, appearing opposite such male stars as Richard Barthelmess, William S. Hart, and Monte Blue.

However, by 1925 her career had stalled and while in New York she was hospitalized for a lingering illness contracted while filming in Florida. While in the hospital she suddenly died of pneumonia.

Film Credits

1916   *His First False Step; A Scoundrel's Toll; Bombs!; Sunshine Dad*

1917   *Mabel's First False Step; Pinched in the Finish; The Betrayal of Maggie; A Dog Catcher's Love; That Night; Her Fame and Shame; The Stone Age; The Late Lamented; A Bedroom Blunder*

1918   *Watch Your Neighbor; Love Loops the Loop; Beward of Boarders; Ladies First*

1919   *This Hero Stuff; Spotlight Sadie; The Poor Boob; The Prince and Betty*

1920   *Sand; The Valley of Tomorrow; In the Heart of a Fool; The Scoffer*

1921   *The Primal Law; Bare Knuckles; A Broken Doll; The Lady from Longacre; The Sin of Martha Queed; Leap Year*

1922   *The Green Temptation; The Bond Boy*

1923   *The Tents of Allah; Wife in Name Only; Zara; A Bride for a Knight; Does It Pay?*

1924   *Love of Women; The Truth About Women; Trouping with Ellen; Those Who Judge; For Another Woman; Greater Than Marriage; Playthings of Desire; The Law and the Lady*

1925   *Back to Life; The Necessary Evil; The Fool; The Mad Marriage; A Little Girl in a Big City; Down On the Suwannee River; The Wives Of the Prophet*

Tincher, Fay (1884 Topeka, KS-1983 Brooklyn, NY)

Described as "the female Charlie Chaplin," Fay Tincher became immortalized in film history as the star of Al Christie's first two-reel comedy.

Born into a well-to-do family, Tincher was given a well-rounded and progressive education by her parents. After high school she moved to Chicago to attend the Chicago Musical College, enrolling in 1898. She appeared in many of the school's theatrical productions and joined the Shogun Stock Company before graduating.

After the tour ended, she moved to New York and in 1901 began appearing at the Weber Music Hall. But after the death of her father, Tincher and her sister left for Europe for a three-year "Grand Tour." Upon her return she began appearing on the vaudeville circuit and became a success in musical comedy.

Although she had appeared in a few films as an extra, Tincher's first billed role was in D. W. Griffith's 1914 drama *The Battle of the Sexes,* as the vampish Cleo who made Lillian Gish's character miserable. After appearing in more Griffith films, it became apparent that comedy rather than dramas was her forte. She began appearing in a succession of comedies for various studios, most notably in the "Ethel and Bill" series in which she created her trademark character—the gum-chewing secretary in black-and-white outfits. Considering herself to be plain and unattractive, she chose black-and-white outfits to be her signature so that the audience would remember her; but no matter what she wore, the audience loved her.

Her success in appearing as Dulcinea in DeWolf Hopper's production of *Don Quixote* (1915) led to starring roles in other Hopper films as well as several Keystone comedies. After appearing in several Christie films, including the first two-reel comedy, Tincher signed to appear as Min in the *Gumps* series of comedies opposite Joe Murphy from 1923 to 1928.

With the advent of sound films, Tincher retired from films. She lived in Chicago for several years before moving to New York. But what she did after leaving films is a mystery—all that is known is that according to her death certificate, she never married.

Film Credits

1909 *Ethel's Luncheon*
1913 *Private Box 23; A Puritan Episode*

1914   *After Her Dough; The Battle of the Sexes; Adventures in Diplomacy; The Right Dope; Nearly a Burglar's Bride; The Quicksands; The Scene of His Crime; A Race for a Bride; Home Sweet Home; The Escape; The White Slave Catchers; A Physical Culture Romance; Out Again, in Again; The Last Drink of Whiskey; Ethel Has a Steady; The Deceiver; Casey's Vendetta; Bill Takes a Lady Out to Lunch . . . Never Again; Bill Manages a Prize Fighter; Bill Joins the W. W. W.s; Bill and Ethel at the Ball; Ethel's Roof Party*

1915   *Ethel Gets the Evidence; Don Quixote; Where Breezes Blow; Unwinding It; Shocking Stockings; Safety First; The Record Breaker; Over and Back; Music Hat Charms; Mr. Wallack's Wallet; Mixed Values; The Love Pirate; Home Again; Gasoline Gus; A Flyer in Spring Water; Father Love; The Fatal Finger Prints; Faithful to the Finish; Ethel's New Dress; Ethel's Doggone Luck; Ethel's Disguise; Ethel's Deadly Alarm Clock; The Deacon's Whiskers; Cupid and the Pest; A Chase of Moonlight; Caught by the Handle; By Fair Means or Foul; Brave and Bold; Bill Turns Valet; Bill Gives a Smoker; Beppo the Barber; Beautiful Love*

1916   *Sunshine Dad; Mr. Goode, Samaritan; Bedelia's Bluff; Skirts; The French Milliner; A Calico Vampire; The Lady Drummer; The Two O'Clock Train; Rough Knight; Loves Getaway; Laundry Liz*

1918   *O Susie Beware; Main 1-2-3*

1919   *The Fire Flingers; Sally's Blighted Career; Rowdy Ann; Mary Moves In; Dangerous Nan McGrew*

1920   *A Seaside Siren; Go West, Young Woman*

1922   *The Leather Pushers*

1923   *Aggravatin' Mama; Oh! Min!; Uncle Bim's Gifts; Watch Papa; Oh! What a Day!*

1924   *Excitement; Andy in Hollywood; Andy's Hats in the Ring; Andy's Stump Speech; Andy's Temptation; A Day of Rest; Westbound; Swing Bad the Sailor; That Kid from Madrid; A Tough Tenderfoot; What's the Use?*

1925   *Andy Takes a Flyer; Andy's Lion Tale; Chester's Donkey Party; Dynamited; The Smash Up*

1926   *Tow Service; Better Luck; The Big Surprise; California Here We Come; A Close Call; Dumb Luck; I Told You So; Lots of Grief; Min Walks in Her Sleep; Min's Away; Min's Home on the Cliff; Never Again; Shady Rest*

1927   *All Wet; Andy Nose His Onions; A Battle Scarred Hero; Broke Again; Circus Daze; The Mild West; I'm the Sheriff; Rooms for Rent; Ocean Bruises; Too Much Sleep; A Total Loss; Up Against It; When Greek Meets Greek; Youth and Beauty; And How!*

1928   *Any Old Count; A Case of Scotch; The Cloud Buster; Out in the Rain*

1924   *All Wet* (II)

Writing Credit

1918   *Main 1-2-3*

Todd, Thelma (1905 Lawrence, MA-1935 Pacific Palisades, CA)

Thelma Todd was a member of two comedy teams that were created to rival and match the success of Laurel and Hardy. Her entry into films was not the culmination of a long-held dream; although she worked her way through school as an illustrator's model, her first career was as a sixth grade teacher. After teaching for two years, Todd won the title "Miss Massachusetts" in 1924 and went on to the Miss America pageant.

Although she didn't win the Miss America title, talent scouts saw her and Paramount signed her to a contract. Rather than put her in films immediately, they sent her to New York to their newly opened six-month acting school with twenty-four other film hopefuls. After a few months in the school she began to receive bits parts and only a year later she appeared opposite Ed Wynn in the film that made her a comedy star, *Rubber Heels* (1927).

When her Paramount contract was not renewed, Todd moved to Hollywood. She freelanced briefly before signing with the Hal Roach Company where she worked for the remainder of her career. In 1929 she became a recording artist as well as a comedian when she recorded three songs—"Let Me Call You Sweetheart," "If I Had You," and "Honey." Described as "stunningly beautiful," she costarred with many of the great comics of the period, making more than twenty feature films in one year.

In 1931 she started her own multifilm comedy series for Roach which added to her popularity. She was paired with ZaSu Pitts in an effort to create a female comedy team, and they made seventeen comedy shorts in a two-year period. Todd played a character that was street-smart while Pitts played one that naively got them into outlandish scrapes. After Pitts left the studio, Todd was paired with wise-cracking Patsy Kelly and their team made twenty-one film shorts, but neither teaming made the impact of their male counterparts.

Todd appeared in two successive Marx Brothers films—*Monkey Business* (1931) and *Horse Feathers* (1932). The following year she made her British film debut in *You Made Me Love You* (1933), a musical version of *The Taming of the Shrew*.

As her career waned, she opened Thelma Todd's Sidewalk Café in 1935; her clientele were mostly show-business people. Todd's career was virtually over before she was found dead from carbon monoxide poisoning in her parked car in her garage. Surrounded by inconsistencies, her death remains unsolved to this day.

Film Credits

1926   *God Gave Me Twenty Cents; Fascinating Youth*
1927   *Rubber Heels; Fireman, Save My Child; The Shield of Honor; The Gay Defender; Nevada*
1928   *The Haunted House; The Crash; Heart to Heart; Vamping Venus; The Noose; Naughty Baby; Abie's Irish Rose*
1929   *Seven Footprints to Satan; Trial Marriage; Unaccustomed As We Are; Bachelor Girl; Careers; Snappy Sneezer; Hotter Than Hot; Crazy Feet; Sky Boy; Stepping Out; House of Horror; Her Private Life; Hurdy Gurdy; Look Out Below*
1930   *Command Performance; The Real McCoy; The Fighting Parson; Whispering Whoopee; All Teed Up; The Shrimp; The King; Her Man; Follow Thru; The Head Guy; Looser Than Loose; Another Fine Mess; High C's; Dollar Dizzy*
1931   *No Limit; Love Business; Chickens Come Home; The Pip from Pittsburgh; The Hot Heiress; Love Fever; Rough Seas; Aloha; Let's Do Things; The Maltese Falcon; Catch As Catch*

Can; Monkey Business; The Pajama Game; War Mamas; On
the Loose; Swanee River; Corsair; Broadminded
1932   *Voice of Hollywood No. 13; Seal Skins; The Big Timer; The
Nickel Nurser; Red Noses; This Is the Night; Strictly Unreliable; The Old Bull; Horse Feathers; Speak Easily; Show
Business; Klondike; Alum and Eve; The Soilers; Deception;
Sneak Easily; Call Her Savage*
1933   *Air Hostess; Asleep in the Feet; Maids a la Mode; The Bargain of the Century; Cheating Blondes; The Devil's Brother;
One Track Minds; Beauty and the Bus; Backs to Nature; Sit-
ting Pretty; Counselor at Law; Son of a Sailor; Air Fright;
You Made Me Love You; Mary Stevens, M.D.*
1934   *Palooka; Babes in the Goods; The Poor Rich; Soup and Fish;
Bottoms Up; Maid in Hollywood; I'll Be Suing You; Cock-
eyed Cavaliers; Three Chumps Ahead; One Horse Farmers;
Opened by Mistake; Done in Oil; Lightning Strikes Twice;
Bum Voyage; Take the Stand; Hips, Hips, Hooray!*
1935   *Treasure Blues; Sing, Sister, Sing; The Tin Man; The Misses
Stooge; After the Dance; Slightly Static; Two for Tonight;
Twin Triplets; Hot Money; Top Flat*
1936   *All-American Toothache; The Bohemian Girl* (released after
her death)

Trunnelle, Mabel (1879 Dwight, IL-1981 Glendale, CA)

Born and raised in rural Illinois, Mabel Trunnelle first appeared on
the stage and in touring companies throughout the United States before turning to films. After marrying fellow stage actor Herbert Prior,
they both joined Edison's Stock Company as early as 1907.

Trunnelle usually appeared opposite her husband, and between
1909 and 1911 they appeared in numerous short films for Edison. In
the latter part of 1911 they left to appear in a series of comedy-dramas
for the Majestic Company, but the association was brief. They returned to Edison in 1912 and Trunnelle became one the company's
major stars, appearing in the *Olive* series and other one- and two-reelers. Trunnelle transitioned into the longer feature format easily and
began appearing in every type of film from historical drama to western.

When Edison stopped producing films, Trunnelle joined the Vitagraph Company. Virtually retired by the end of the decade, she ap-

peared in only two films in the early 1920s. Her husband continued to occasionally appear as a character actor until his death in 1954, and Trunnelle lived in the home they had shared until she died at the age of 101.

Film Credits

1908   *A Women's Way*
1909   *Nursing a Viper; The Light That Came; Two Women and a Man; The Prince and the Pauper*
1910   *The Princess and the Peasant; The Big Dam*
1911   *The Battle of Bunker Hill; Three of a Kind; The Doomed Ship; The Star Spangled Banner; A Modern Cinderella; In the Days of Chivalry; The Doctor; Silver Threads Among the Gold; The Haunted Sentinel Tower; The Quarrel on the Cliff; Van Bidder's Experiment; Venom of the Poppy; At Jones' Ferry; Under the Tropical Sun; The Lighthouse by the Sea; The Sheriff; The Sailor's Love Letter; Mary's Masquerade; A Perilous Ride; Pull for Shore, Sailor!; Keeping Mabel Home; The Signs of the Three Labels; How Sir Andrew Lost His Vote; The Actress; Will You Marry Me?*
1912   *His Fate's Rehearsal; Next; Spare the Rod; A Mother's Sacrifice; An Old Lady of Twenty; Lucky Man; Arresting Father; His Step-Mother; Petticoat Perfidy; Strip Poker; Does Your Wife Love You?; The Best Man Wins?; The Closed Bible; The Unwilling Bigamist; The Better Influence; Leap Year; The Eternal Masculine; The Return of Life; Not on the Programme; Down and Out; Buncoed; Dogs; Stage Struck Mamie; The Little Quakeress; Papa's Double; Getting Rich Quick; The Flat Upstairs; The Lost Messenger; Farmer Allen's Daughter; A Higher Thought; A Game of Chess; The New Butler; A Disputed Claim; Mabel's Beau; Mary's Chauffeur; The Butterfly; A Garrison Joke; The Winner and the Spoils; All for Jim; All for Him; Captain Ben's Yarn; A Woman Alone; Hazel Kirke; Two of a Kind; The Crime of Carelessness; The Silent Call; A Game for Two; Thorns of Success; Willie's Dog; The Duke's Dilemma; Washington Crosses the Delaware*

1913   *The Running Away of Doris; The Maid of Honor; The Day That Is Dead; The Governess; The Doctor's Photograph; The Ranch Owner's Love-Making; Ann; The Lost Deed; The Unprofitable Boarder; The New Pupil; Two Little Kittens; An Unsullied Shield; The Tree Imp; Janet of the Dunes*

1914   *Across the Burning Trestle; A Night at the Inn; The Mexican's Gratitude; Meg o' the Mountains; The Lost Melody; The Everlasting Triangle; Bottle's Baby; Young Mrs. Winthrop; A Question of Identity*

1915   *The Tragedies of the Crystal Globe; Out of the Ruins; Eugene Aram; Shadows from the Past; Ransom's Folly; The Magic Skin; The Destroying Angel*

1916   *The Heart of the Hills; The Martyrdom of Philip Strong; A Message to Garcia*

1917   *The Master Passion; Where Love Is; The Ghost of Old Morro; The Grell Mystery*

1918   *Power*

1922   *Singed Wings*

1923   *The Love Trap*

Turner, Florence (1885 New York City-1946 Woodland Hills, CA)

Although the audience knew her only as "the Vitagraph Girl," Florence Turner was one of the first film performers to become a star and the first performer to be signed to an exclusive contract. Norma Talmadge once said of her, "I would rather have touched the hem of her skirt than to have shaken hands with Saint Peter."

She began her career on the stage at the age of three, later touring the vaudeville circuit doing impersonations of well-known people of the period. Turner joined Vitagraph in 1907 and worked as bookkeeper, payroll clerk, and cashier as well as an actor. In 1910 she began making personal appearances to promote Vitagraph and a new song titled "The Vitagraph Girl." It was as a result of these appearances that an article was written about her using, possibly for the first time, the words *motion picture star.*

Turner left Vitagraph for a vaudeville tour and in 1913 went on to tour England, appearing in music halls and theaters. While in England, she formed her own production company, Turner Films, Ltd. Her company made more than thirty films in a two-year period which were distributed in the United States as well as England.

She returned to the United States after World War I broke out, but she was not successful in reviving her film career. After the war ended, she returned to England to play lead roles in British films, but these films were not released in the United States. When not appearing in films, she continued touring music halls with her vaudeville act.

Turner was briefly stranded in England when all British studios closed in 1924. Luckily Marion Davies paid for her and her mother's return fares and helped Turner find film work. Turner appeared in small roles for several years as a member of MGM's stock company before retiring to the Motion Picture Country Home.

Film Credits

1907   *Athletic American Girls; Bargain Fiend, or Shopping a la Mode; How to Cure a Cold; Cast Up by the Sea; Gypsy Warning*

1908   *Romance of a War Nurse; An Unexpected Santa Claus; The Two Brothers; MacBeth; Romeo and Juliet; Richard III; The Merchant of Venice; Ex-convict No. 900; The New Stenographer* (Edison)

1909   *Kenilworth; King Lear; A Midsummer's Night Dream; A Daughter of the Sun; Fuss and Feathers; Launcelot and Elaine; The Heart of a Clown*

1910   *Twelfth Night; Sisters; For Her Sister's Sake; A Dixie Mother; Uncle Tom's Cabin; St. Elmo; How Championships Are Won and Lost; Over the Garden Wall; Auld Robin Gray; A Pair of Schemers; Sisters; Wilson's Wife's Countenance; Dairy Jones and Captain Bragg; Peg Woffington; Her Mother's Wedding Gown; Back to Nature; Rose Leaves; Jean, the Matchmaker; Renunciation; Brother Man; In the*

Mountains of Kentucky; Jean Goes Fishing; Love, Luck and Gasoline; A Tin-Type Romance; Jean and the Calico Doll

1911 *A Tale of Two Cities; The Sacrifice; Intrepid Davy; The Thumb Print; Forgotten; Auld Lang Syne; One Touch of Nature; Jealousy; The Discarded Favourite; Show Girl; Jean Rescues; Cherry Blossoms; Answer of the Roses; Prejudice of Pierre Marie; Birds of a Feather; Captain Barnacle's Courtship; For His Sake; Spirit of Light; Proving His Love; The Stumbling Block; The Wrong Patient; Wig Wag; The New Stenographer* (Vitagraph)

1912 *Mrs. Carter's Necklace; Flirt or Heroine; A Vitagraph Romance; Jean Intervenes; The Irony of Fate; Indian Romeo and Juliet; Aunty's Romance; A Red Cross Martyr; She Cried; Wanted: A Grandmother; How Mr. Bullington Ran the House; Her Diary; Two Cinders; The Loyalty of Sylvia; When Persistency and Obstinacy Meet; The Face or the Voice; Una of the Sierras; Susie to Susanne; Hypnotizing the Hypnotist; The Signal of Distress; While She Powdered Her Nose; The Path of True Love*

1913 *Sisters All; What a Change of Clothes Did; The Harper Mystery; Rose of Surray; Checkmated; The House in Suburbia; Under the Make-Up; Jean's Evidence; The Wings of the Moth; Everybody's Doing It; Cutey and the Twins; The Skull; Stenographer Troubles; One Good Turn; Deerslayer*

1914 *The Murdock Trial; Creatures of Habit; Snobs; Polly's Progress; Flotilla the Flirt; For Her People; Through the Valley of Shadows; Daisy's Doodad's Dial; The Shepherd Lassie of Argyle; Shopgirls*

1915 *My Old Dutch; As Ye Repent; Alone in London; A Welsh Singer; Lost and Won; Far from the Madding Crowd*

1916 *Doorsteps; Grim Justice; East Is East*

1919 *Fool's Gold*

1920 *Blackmail; The Ugly Duckling; The Brand of Lopez; Three Men in a Boat*

1921 *Passion Fruit; The Old Wives' Tale; All Dolled Up*

1922 *The Little Mother; Was She Justified?*

1923 *Hornet's Nest*

1924 *Janice Meredith; Women and Diamonds; Film Favourites; The Boatswain's Mate; Sally Bishop*

1925   *The Price of Success; Never the Twain Shall Meet; The Dark Angel; The Mad Marriage*

1926   *The Gilded Highway; Padlocked; The Last Alarm; The Flame of the Argentine*

1927   *The Overland Stage; The Broken Gates; Stranded; The Cancelled Debt; Sally in Our Alley; College; The Chinese Parrot*

1928   *Marry the Girl; Walking Back; Jazzland; The Road to Ruin; The Pace That Kills; The Law and the Man; Jean and the Calico Doll*

1929   *Kid's Clever; The Iron Mask*

1930   *The Rampant Age*

1931   *The Ridin' Fool*

1932   *The Animal Kingdom; The Sign of the Cross; The Trial of Vivienne Ware*

1933   *He Couldn't Take It*

1936   *One Rainy Afternoon*

1943   *Thousands Cheer*

An Unseen Enemy *(1912)*

An Unseen Enemy was the first film in which Lillian and Dorothy Gish appeared. Directed by D. W. Griffith, the short concerned two sisters, recently orphaned, who were trapped in a room by their unscrupulous housekeeper. The housekeeper, aware that the girls' brother had locked money from their father's small estate in the household safe, had a criminal acquaintance try to break into the safe.

The drunken housekeeper then threatens the girls with a gun that she waves through a hole in the wall. However, the incompetent thieves lock the girls in a room with a telephone, so the girls contact their brother in town and he brings a rescue party that apprehends the would-be thieves.

Lillian Gish went on to be one of Griffith's favorite actors and had a career that lasted over seventy years. Dorothy Gish, who did not appear in films for as long as her sister, became recognized as a fine comedienne.

Vale, Vola (1897 Buffalo, NY-1970 Hawthorne, CA)

Considered one of the great beauties of her day, Violet Irene Smith had only appeared in amateur productions prior to joining Biograph in 1913. Appearing as Vola Smith in a variety of two- and three-reelers, she changed her last name to Vale in 1916 when she moved to Universal Company. While at Universal she appeared as the female lead in several William S. Hart films, before marrying Albert Russell and starring in several western productions directed by her husband and his brother, William. After her divorce she went back to social melodramas, but her career had started to decline. In 1926 she married writer and director John Gorman and retired from the screen after appearing in his production *Black Tears* (1927). This marriage also ended in divorce. Her third marriage, to Lawrence McDougal, lasted thirty-eight years, until his death in 1970. Vale died eight months later.

Film Credits

1914   *Masks and Faces; A Scrap of Paper; Captain Fracasse; Frederick Holme's Ward; Heart Trouble; His Emergency Wife; The Passing Storm; The Inevitable; Cupid Entangled; His Romany Wife; The Smugglers Ward; Alias Jimmie Barton; The Iron Master*

1915   *The Black Sheep; The Harvest; Love's Enduring Flame; The Soul of Pierre; The Girl He Brought Home; Merry Mary; Paths That Crossed; Felix Holt; What Happened to Peggy; Lorna Doone*

1916   *The Price of Silence; Chain of Evidence; Celeste; The Cry of Conscience; The Eternal Way; For Her Mother's Sake; From the Rogues; A Great Love; Hired and Fired; The Sody Clerk;*

Song of the Woods; A Thousand a Week; Weapons of Love; The Woman He Feared; It Sounded Like a Kiss; The Eagle's Wings

1917   *Each to His Kind; The Secret of Black Mountain; Mentioned in Confidence; The Silent Man; The Son of His Father; The Winning of Sally Temple; Zollenstein; The Bond Between; The Lady in the Library; Topsy Turvy Twins*

1918   *The Wolves of the Rail; The Locked Heart*

1919   *Happy Though Married; A Heart in Pawn; Hearts Asleep; Six Feet Four; The Hornet's Nest; Someone Must Pay*

1920   *Overland Red; The Purple Cipher; Someone in the House; The Iron Rider; A Master Stroke; Common Sense; Alias Jimmy Valentine*

1921   *Singing River; White Oak; Duke of Chimney Butte*

1922   *Good Men and True*

1923   *Crashin' Thru; Soul of the Beast; The Man Between; Mothers-in-Law; The Midnight Flower*

1924   *The Mirage*

1925   *Who Cares; Heartless Husbands; Little Annie Rooney; The Phantom of the Opera*

1926   *Her Big Adventure; Two Can Play; The Sky Pirate*

1927   *Black Tears*

Valkyrien, Valda (1895 Reykjavik, Iceland-1956 Los Angeles, CA)

Adele Frede originally tried to get into films in Europe, but the ranks were closed to all but "legitimate" stage stars. So Frede changed her name to Valkyrien (the "Valda" was added later when producers decided one name was not enough), enhanced her past, and arrived in New York in 1914 on the arm of her fiancé, a noble of dubious lineage, Baron Hrolf von DeWitz.

Now, rather than an actress-wannabe born in Iceland, Valkyrien was a former "premiere danseuse" at the Danish Royal Ballet who had been crowned "the most beautiful girl of her race" before leaving Denmark. The American public embraced the beautiful royal (she and her fiancé were quickly married by the production company who signed her) and she became the "baroness of acting" and "Brunhilde from Denmark."

Little was ever written about her acting talent, but she became a notorious personality who appeared more often in society and gossip columns than in any film. Her final show business appearance was in Ziegfeld's *Follies* (1919) before retiring from acting and marrying her second husband, a successful import-export merchant.

Film Credits

1912   *The Great Circus Catastrophe; The New Shoeshine Boy; Unlucky Suitors; The Story of Mother; Vanquished*
1914   *Baroness* (fifteen one-reelers)
1915   *Youth; The Valkyrie*
1916   *Silas Marner; The Cruise of Fate; Diana; The Unwelcome Mother; The Hidden Valley*
1917   *The Image Maker; Magda; The Crusher*
1918   *The Commercial Pirates; T'Other Dear Charmer; Huns Within Our Gates*
1919   *Bolshevism on Trial*

Valli, Virginia (1895 Chicago, IL-1968 Palm Springs, CA)

Courtesy of Silents Are Golden at
<SilentsAreGolden.com>

Virginia Valli began her career in stock companies in addition to doing some work with local film companies in the Chicago area. By 1917 she was appearing in films for Essanay Studios, and in 1920 she traveled to Hollywood.

She was an established film presence by the mid-1920s. Her most active period was from 1924 to 1927, but she did make the transition to sound. However, by then her popularity was waning under the onslaught of younger talent because she had reached the "advanced" age of thirty-one.

Soon after her transition to sound, Valli announced that she was retiring to marry fellow actor Charles Farrell. This action saved her from the indignity of being relegated to appearing with minor studios for less money and in smaller roles.

Film Credits

1917   *Skinner's Dress Suit; Satan's Private Door; Filling His Own Shoes; The Golden Idiot; Efficiency Edgar's Courtship; The Fable of Speedy Sprite; The Fibbers*

1918   *Ruggles of Red Gap; The Midnight Bride; Uneasy Money*

1919   *His Father's Wife; The Black Circle*

1920   *The Dead Line; The Plunger; The Very Idea; The Common Sin*

1921   *Sentimental Tommy; The Man Who; A Trip to Paradise; The Devil Within; The Idle Rich; The Silver Lining; Love's Penalty*

1922   *The Right That Failed; Tracked to Earth; His Back Against the Wall; The Black Bag; Storm; The Village Blacksmith*

1923   *Shock*

1924   *A Lady of Quality; Wild Oranges; The Confidence Man; In Every Woman's Life; K: The Unknown; The Signal Tower*

1925   *The Price of Pleasure; Up the Ladder; The Lady Who Lied; The Man Who Found Himself; The Pleasure Garden; Siege*

1926   *Watch Your Wife; The Family Upstairs; Flames*

1927   *Stage Madness; Marriage; Evening Clothes; Judgment of the Hills; East Side, West Side; Ladies Must Dress; Paid to Love*

1928   *The Escape; The Street of Illusion*

1929   *Behind Closed Doors; The Isle of Lost Ships; The Lost Zeppelin; Mister Antonio*

1930   *Guilty?*

1931   *Night Life in Reno*

Velez, Lupe (1908 San Luis Potosi, Mexico-1944 Beverly Hills, CA)

Courtesy of Silents Are Golden at
<SilentsAreGolden.com>

Lupe Velez was called "Whoopee Lupe" or "the Mexican Spitfire" for good reason. She was known for her extremely volatile off-screen behavior rather that her acting ability. Her fans found her love of life and, often, excessive emotional displays as entertaining as any film role.

Velez took singing and dancing lessons while working to help support her family after moving to the United States. After appearing in local clubs and variety shows, she was encouraged to go to Hollywood to try getting into movies. Once there she did not immediately find work in films, but she was cast in the 1927 *Music Box Revue*. This stage engagement led to a small part in Laurel and Hardy's *Sailors Beware* (1927).

Her next part was in Douglas Fairbanks's *The Gaucho* (1927) as the fiery but sensitive "Mountain Girl." This role resulted in a five-year contract with United Artists and being selected as a WAMPAS Baby Star in 1929. The following year she starred in *Lady of the Pavements* (1929), a film produced by D. W. Griffith.

About this time she embarked on the first of her well-publicized affairs—this time with Gary Cooper. Although they were together for several years, they never married because of Cooper's family's objections. After this rejection, her behavior became, at times, more wild and excessive.

With the advent of sound, Velez's strong accent limited the types of characters that she could convincingly play. Rather than end her contract, her studio decided to make all her films in both English and Spanish. This allowed the studio to capitalize on her fan base among Spanish-speaking audiences both domestically and overseas.

After several years of similar roles, Velez went to Broadway in 1933 to star in a musical revue where her "incendiary" personality was more discussed than the show. It was at this time that her romance and marriage to Johnny Weissmuller became another headline-grabbing event. But her attempt to play a dramatic role was greeted with near failure and she retreated to the comedic roles that were popular with her fans. She made a vaudeville tour in 1935 while the first of many divorce proceedings were started to end her union with Weissmuller.

Velez then traveled to England where she appeared in three films and a musical revue at the Adelphi Theatre. She returned to the United States to appear in *High Flyers* (1937) before making her first movie produced in Mexico. Her divorce was finalized in 1939, and afterward she starred in the first of eight films featuring a recurring character, Carmelita Lindsay.

In 1944, after several well-publicized romances, Velez took an overdose of Seconal because she feared the scandal that would ensue when it became known that she was four months pregnant and that the father refused to marry her.

Film Credits

1927	*What Women Did for Me; Sailors Beware; The Gaucho*
1928	*Stand and Deliver*
1929	*Lady of the Pavements; Wolf Song; Where East Is East; Tiger Rose*
1930	*Hell Harbor; The Storm; East Is West*
1931	*Resurrection; The Squaw Man; The Cuban Love Song*
1932	*Kongo; Men in My Life; The Naked Half Truth; The Broken Wing*
1933	*Mr. Broadway; Hot Pepper*
1934	*Hollywood Party; Strictly Dynamite; Palooka; Laughing Boy*
1935	*The Morals of Marcus*
1936	*Gypsy Melody*
1937	*Stardust; High Flyers*
1938	*The Zandunga*
1939	*The Girl from Mexico*
1940	*Mexican Spitfire; The Mexican Spitfire Out West*
1941	*Six Lessons from Madame La Zonga; Playmates; Mexican Spitfire's Baby; Honolulu Lu*

1942 *Mexican Spitfire's Elephant; Mexican Spitfire Sees a Ghost; Mexican Spitfire at Sea*
1943 *Redhead from Manhattan; Mexican Spitfire's Blessed Event; Ladies' Day*
1944 *Nana*

Vidor, Florence (1895 Houston, TX-1977 Pacific Palisades, CA)

Florence Vidor was a talent in her own right, although the young man she married in 1915 who went on to become a renowned director, King Vidor, gets most of the coverage in film histories. During her career she worked for almost all the studios in existence during the 1910s and 1920s.

She first worked for Vitagraph Studios in small supporting roles. Her breakthrough role was in *A Tale of Two Cities* (1917), and she had her first lead role that year while working at Famous Players-Lasky in *Hashimura Togo* opposite Sessue Hayakawa. While Vidor was comfortable in any genre of film, she preferred to appear in comedies, particularly the light social comedies that were prevalent during the 1920s.

Although she never achieved the heights of stardom, she was one of the most sought-after supporting actors of her era because no matter what the role she delivered a solid performance. During the early years of films, there were two methods of acting—the often flamboyant overdone style that originated on the stage and the more naturalistic style of realistic actions. Depending on the role, Vidor was either melodramatic in the theatrical style or down-to-earth in the realistic style.

Sadly the Vidors' success brought about the demise of their marriage. They separated in 1923 and were divorced as few years later. In 1928, Vidor married Jascha Heifetz, a concert violinist, and retired from films after her voice proved unsuitable for sound films. Vidor traveled with her husband on tours and during the course of their marriage had two children. Although theirs seemed the perfect marriage to outsiders, the couple divorced in 1945.

Film Credits

1916   *The Intrigue; The Yellow Girl; Bill Peter's Kid; Curfew at Simpton Center*

1917   *A Tale of Two Cities; American Methods; The Cook of Canyon Camp; Hashimura Togo; The Countess Charming; The Secret Game*

1918   *The Widow's Might; The Hidden Pearls; The Honor of His House; The White Man's Law; Old Wives for New; The Bravest Way; Till I Come Back to You*

1919   *The Other Half; Poor Relations*

1920   *The Family Honor; The Jack-Knife Man*

1921   *Lying Lips; Beau Revel; Hail the Woman*

1922   *Woman, Wake Up; Real Adventure; Dusk to Dawn; Conquering the Woman; Skin Deep*

1923   *Souls for Sale; Alice Adams; Main Street; The Virginian*

1924   *The Marriage Circle; Borrowed Husbands; Welcome Stranger; Barbara Frietchie; Christine of the Hungry Heart; Husbands and Lovers; The Mirage*

1925   *The Girl of Gold; Marry Me; Grounds for Divorce; The Trouble with Wives; Are Parents People?*

1926   *The Enchanted Hill; The Grand Duchess and the Waiter; Sea Horses; You Never Know Women; The Eagle of the Sea; The Popular Sin*

1927   *Afraid to Love; The World at Her Feet; One Woman to Another; Honeymoon Hate*

1928   *Doomsday; The Magnificent Flirt; The Patriot*

1929   *Chinatown Nights*

W

Walcamp, Marie (1894 Dennison, OH-1936 Los Angeles, CA)

Known as the "daredevil of the movies" and the "adventuress of the screen" during a time when perilous exploits were commonplace, Marie Walcamp achieved stardom as a serial star. She began her career on stage and in vaudeville before accepting a film contract and moving west.

She signed with Universal in 1913 and began appearing in the light comedies popular in the 1910s. In 1914, she appeared in her first melodrama with an exotic locale and continued that formula for several movies. Then, in 1916, she appeared in what some believe to be the first serial western, *Liberty.*

After the release of *Liberty,* she appeared in several of Lois Weber's social dramas such as *The Flirt* (1916) and *Where Are My Children?* (1916). Soon she was again appearing in wilderness dramas that relied on the action to draw audiences, and her serial career was born. She made several films featuring the character "Tempest Cody" for Universal, a studio known for its serials.

After the decline of serials in popularity, Walcamp appeared sporadically in films after the early 1920s, but she could never achieve the success she had enjoyed as a serial star. Sadly, in November 1936, Walcamp committed suicide while suffering from depression.

Film Credits

1913   Memories; The Werewolf; By Fate's Decree; The Doctor's Orders; The Girl and the Tiger; The Girl Ranchers; The Village Blacksmith; What the Wild Waves Did

1914   Won in the Clouds; A Redskin Reckoning; The Phantom Light; Our Enemy's Spy; The Option; Olana of the South Seas; A Nation's Peril; The Brand of His Tribe; Cast Adrift in the South Seas; A Daughter of the Plains; The Flash of Fate; The Great Universal Mystery; The Half-Breed; Hiram and Zeke Masquerade; In the Wolves' Fangs; The Isle of Abandoned Hope; Johnnie from Jonesboro; The Jungle Master; The Law of the Lumberjack; The Law of the Range; The Legion of the Phantom Tribe; The Lure of the Geisha; A Mexican Spy in America; Rescued by Wireless; A Romance of Hawaii; The Silent Peril; The Trial Breakers; The Vagabond Soldier; Tempest Cody; Kidnapper

1915   Terrors of the Jungle; The Test of a Man; The Toll of the Sea; The Torrent; The War of the Wild; The Yellow Star; The Awaited Hour; The Blood of His Brother; The Blood of the Children; The Broken Toy; The Circus Girl's Romance; The Crime of Thought; Custer's Last Scout; A Daughter of the Jungles; A Fight to a Finish; The Governor Maker; The Heart of a Tigress; In Jungle Wilds; The Jungle Queen; The Lost Ledge; The Oaklawn Handicap; Ridgeway of Montana; Surrender; Coral; A Double Deal in Pork; From the Lion's Jaws; Chasing the Limited; The Mysterious Contragrav

1916   Hop, the Devil's Brew; The Flirt; John Needham's Double; Liberty; Discontent; The Human Pendulum; The Iron Rivals; A Railroad Bandit; The Money Lenders; Onda of the Orient; The State Witness; Tammany's Tiger; The Silent Terror; The Quest of Virginia; Where Are My Children?; The Leap; Liberty; Who Pulled the Trigger?

1917   Her Great Mistake; The Indian's Lament; A Jungle Tragedy; The Star Witness; Steel Hearts; The Red Ace; Patria; The Kidnapped Bride

1918   The Lion's Claw; Tongues of Flame; The Whirlwind Finish

1919   The Red Glove; Tempest Cody Bucks the Trust; Tempest Cody Flirts with Death; Tempest Cody Gets Her Man; Tempest Cody

Hits the Trail; Tempest Cody Plays Detective; Tempest Cody Rides Wild; Tempest Cody Turns the Tables; Tempest Cody's Man Hunt

1920   *The Dragon's Net*
1921   *The Blot*
1924   *Western Vengeance; Treasure Canyon; A Desperate Adventure*
1927   *In a Moment of Temptation*

WAMPAS Baby Stars

Before the era of sound, the most prestigious honor a young female actor could receive was to be chosen as a WAMPAS Baby Star. The award was the brainchild of the newly formed Western Associated Motion Picture Advertisers (WAMPAS) as a means to publicize their organization, but it soon became *the* way to publicize new female actors that the studios hoped would become stars.

WAMPAS was formed in 1920 by a group of professional publicists from the film industry. Before the advent of the Academy Awards the industry had no organized means to honor great performances, but the title WAMPAS Baby Star acknowledged a young female actor's potential to become a star.

The award's most prestigious period was the 1920s, when studios vied to have their ingenue of the year selected as one of the thirteen yearly Baby Stars. The term *baby* did not denote age, but merely film experience in an era before the term starlet was coined. Once selected, the honorees were publicized and touted endlessly for their one-year reign.

Not all Baby Stars went on to have successful careers in films. In fact, some were never really heard from after their initial publicity, while others remained only supporting actors. But some choices were *golden.*

Some of the successes include Joan Crawford, Fay Wray, Clara Bow, and Delores Del Rio. As further tribute to their careers, two WAMPAS silent film recipients later received special awards for career achievement—Clara Bow and Delores Del Rio.

A complete listing of those selected between 1922 and 1929 can be found in Appendix B.

Ward, Fannie (1871 St. Louis, MO-1952 New York City)

Called "America's Peter Pan," Fannie Ward was an early actor who never seemed to age and, therefore, appeared in youthful roles long after her contemporaries. In fact, she was in her forties when she was appearing as liberated flappers in the late 1910s.

Ward knew she wanted to be an actor from an early age; after winning both a local talent contest and a beauty contest her ambition was set. This determination caused her father to disown her when she went to New York to pursue a show business career. Interestingly, her mother assisted her in her goals and even traveled with her to New York.

She had a solid career on the stage in New York for nearly twenty years before moving into films in 1913. She appeared in supporting roles when not appearing on Broadway until she appeared in Cecil B. DeMille's production of *The Cheat* (1915), opposite Sessue Hayakawa. The film was a smash hit and elevated Ward to star status. Her films were well received by both men and women, and she spent several years making films before returning to the stage.

Ward was no stranger to celebrity, as she had become a headliner of the society pages after marrying a wealthy London financier and being adopted by the European aristocracy. However, extended separations brought about an eventual divorce, and she later married actor Jack Dean whom she remained married to until his death in 1950.

Although Ward enjoyed light comic roles, she excelled at drama and tragedy, perhaps because of her background on the stage. Being extremely fond of fashion, she especially enjoyed costume or historical dramas that allowed her several wardrobe changes.

She retired from films in the 1920s and concentrated on her stage career. She retired from public life completely after her daughter's death in a plane crash in 1938. After her retirement, Ward opened a beauty shop in Paris aptly named The Fountain of Youth. Anita Loos immortalized her in her 1925 novel *Gentleman Prefer Blondes,* when Lorelei Lee encountered the still-youthful Ward in London saying, "when a girl is cute for fifty years it really begins to get historical."

Film Credits

1915	*The Marriage of Kitty; The Cheat*
1916	*Tennessee's Pardner; For the Defense; A Gutter Magdalene; Each Pearl a Tear; Witchcraft; The Years of the Locust*
1917	*The Winning of Sally Temple; A School for Husbands; Unconquered; Her Strange Wedding; The Crystal Gazer; On the Level; Betty to the Rescue*
1918	*The Yellow Ticket; The Narrow Path; A Japanese Nightingale; Innocent*
1919	*Common Clay; The Cry of the Weak; The Profiteers; Our Better Selves; The Only Way*
1920	*La Rafale* (France); *Le Secret du Lone Star* (France)

Warrenton, Lule (1862 Flint, MI-1932 Laguna Beach, CA)

Lule Warrenton began her career as a stage actor and moved into films in her forties. She became known as "Mother" Warrenton because of the many maternal roles she appeared in throughout her film career.

In 1916 she was given her own production company within Universal to produce short films centered on children. A year later she left Universal to start her own company, Frieder Film Corporation. Her first, and only, production was *A Bit o' Heaven* (1917), and it was both a critical and popular success. Although the studio announced two other films that were in development, production on these never began. By the end of the year Warrenton was back at Universal as an actor; the reason was never revealed.

She continued as an actor until 1922, when she retired from films. She is remembered not only as a pioneering film producer but also as the founder of the Hollywood Girls' Club.

Directing Credits

1916   *When Little Lindy Sang; Us Kids*
1917   *The Valley of Beautiful Things; A Bit o' Heaven*

Film Credits

1913   *The Pretender; White Squaw; Genesis: 4-9; His Brand; Memories; Under the Black Flag; The Werewolf; The Mask; The Jew's Christmas*
1914   *The Man Who Slept; Samson; A Bad Egg; Cast Adrift in the South Seas; The Eleventh Hour; For the Family Honor; The Great Universal Mystery; The Jungle Master; The Law and the Lumberjack; The Law of the Range; The Lure of the Geisha; A Mexican Spy in America; Rescued by Wireless; The Silent Peril; Some Boy; Too Much Married; Isle of Abandoned Hope*
1915   *Bound on the Wheel; Jewel; The College Orphan; The Frame-Up; The Lion's Ward; A Double Deal in Pork; Across the Footlights; The Burden Bearer; The Great Fear; His Real Character; The Queen of Jungle Land; Simple Polly; Terrors of the Jungle; From the Lion's Jaws*
1916   *Bobbie of the Ballet; The Gilded Spider; Her Bitter Cup; Drugged Waters; Eleanor's Catch; A Family Affair; The Human Cactus; A Soul Enslaved; Under the Spell; It Happened in Honolulu; Secret Love; The Secret of the Swamp*
1917   *The Silent Lady; The Girl Who Couldn't Grow Up; Princess Virtue*
1918   *More Trouble; $5,000 Reward; Daughter Angele*
1919   *Molly of the Follies; Be a Little Sport; Broken Commandments; The Merry-Go-Round; The Wilderness Trail; A Fugitive from Matrimony; When a Man Rides Alone*
1920   *White Lies; The Sin That Was His; Rose of Nome*
1921   *Blind Hearts; The Jolt; Ladies Must Live; The Dangerous Moment*
1922   *Strength of the Pines; Calvert's Valley; Shirley of the Circus*

Weber, Lois (1879 Allegheny, PA-1939 Hollywood, CA)

Born Florence Lois Weber, she was arguably the most important female director of silent films as well as the first native-born female director. She used the films she directed to impart messages that upheld her strict religious upbringing and social conscience.

Weber was a concert pianist at sixteen years of age and appeared in town halls and community centers. She suffered from severe stage fright to the point that she almost became ill before each performance, so she quit the concert circuit to work in a rescue mission of the Church Army workers, an organization similar to the Salvation Army.

However, after her father's death she was forced to return to performing to support herself and her mother. She was again stricken with the debilitating stage fright that had plagued her earlier concerts. Luckily she found that she did not become ill when others were on stage with her, so she turned to acting and achieved some success with various small touring companies.

During her touring days she met and married theatrical manager Phillips Smalley. He was initially very supportive of Weber's creative efforts and she gave him partial credit for much of her work, although historians now believe that his contributions were emotional rather than creative.

When the film industry began she moved into the new medium as a writer, director, and actor with Gaumont's American-based Chronophone Company. While working there Weber began experimenting with synchronizing sound to film action. She was the second person to work seriously with this concept—the first pioneer being another female director, Alice Guy.

She moved to Reliance Motion Picture Company in 1910, then moved to Rex Company where she completed an average of one film per week. When Rex was absorbed into Universal Pictures in 1912, she became head of production. At that time she was the highest-paid director—$5,000 per week.

In 1914 Weber left Universal for the newly formed Bosworth Studios. After a year she returned to Universal and, with its help, founded her own production studio, Lois Weber Productions, in 1917. Her studio concentrated on domestic dramas and films that disseminated her views on social issues.

Weber was deeply committed to using films to explore social issues in an effort to influence the audience. From the beginning of her career in films, she believed that huge potential existed for the use of film as an educational tool; with her own company she was able to exert this educational force. She did not work on a film if she did not believe in its message and seldom worked in any genre other than drama because of her preference for such social messages. Her films always dealt with controversial subjects such as religious hypocrisy (*The Hypocrites,* 1915), the evil of gossip (*Scandal,* 1915), birth control (*The Hand That Rocks the Cradle,* 1917), and abortion (*Where Are My Children?,* 1916).

In 1916 she became the first and only woman asked to become a member of the Motion Picture Directors Association, the precursor to the Directors Guild of America. Although her films were sometimes seen as message heavy, they were always acknowledged as finely crafted and equal or superior to the productions of her male peers.

Her films lost their appeal to audiences in the early 1920s and her company was dissolved. However, her reputation was still such that in 1921 Paramount offered her a contract at $50,000 per film plus half the profits. Within two years, however, she was back with Universal, which employed more women as directors than any other studio during the silent era. It was also during this period that she went through a personal and professional crisis after her divorce from Smalley. Evidently she needed the emotional stability of marriage to allow her to feel the freedom to be creative; it wasn't until her remarriage to Harry Gantz that she was able to regain some of her former success.

For a few years she moved between projects at United Artists and Universal, but soon her career was once more stagnating. The audience for her liberal, message-laden movies was gone, and the types of freewheeling films being produced did not appeal to her. By the late 1920s, where once a female director had been almost a common sight, Weber was now a curiosity.

After she retired from directing, she wrote freelance scenarios while she tried to interest the educational community in the use of films as learning tools and visual aids, but it would be years before educators began using films as teaching aids. It was reported that she managed an apartment building in the 1930s. By the end of her life often the only work she could find was polishing other writers' scripts.

Although the film industry virtually forgot Weber, years before his death Carl Laemmle had said, "I would trust Miss Weber with any sum of money that she needed to make any picture that she wanted to make. . . .She knows the motion picture business as few people do."

Not only was her career exceptional, but she also helped other women get started in the industry. Directors Lule Warrenton, Elsie Jane Wilson, Cleo Madison, and Jeannie Macpherson all started their careers with Weber. Frances Marion, perhaps the most prominent writer of the silent era, began her career with Weber in 1914 at Bosworth Studios.

Directing Credits

1911   *A Heroine of '76; On the Brink; A Breach of Faith; The Martyr; The Heiress; The Realization; Fate*

1912   *Angels Unaware; The Final Pardon; Eyes That See Not; The Price of Peace; Power of Thought; The Greater Love; The Troubadour's Triumph; An Old Fashioned Girl; A Japanese Idyll; Faraway Fields; Fine Feathers; The Bargain; The Greater Christian*

1913   *His Sister; Two Thieves; In the Blood; Troubled Waters; An Empty Box; The Peacemaker; Bobby's Baby; Until Death; The Dragon's Breath; The Cap of Destiny; The King Can Do No Wrong; How Men Propose; Through Strife; Civilized and Savage; The Heart of Jewess; Just in Time; The Light Woman; His Brand; Shadows of Life; Memories; The Thumb Print; The Clue; The Haunted Bride; The Blood Brotherhood; James Lee's Wife; The Mask; The Jew's Christmas; The Wife's Deceit; The Rosary; The Pretender; Thieves and the Cross*

1914   *The Female of the Species; A Fool and His Money; The Leper's Coat; The Coward Hater; Woman's Burden; The Weaker Sister; A Modern Fairy Tale; The Spider and Her Web; In the Days of His Youth; The Babies' Doll; The Man Who Slept; On Suspicion; An Episode; Career of Waterloo Peterson; The Triumph of Mind; The Stone in the Road; Closed Gates; The Pursuit of Hate; Lost by a Hair; Mary Plain; Behind the Veil; The Traitor; Helping Mother; The Merchant of Venice; An Old Locke; Avenged; Daisies*

1915   *It's No Laughing Matter; The Hypocrites; Sunshine Molly;*
        Captain Courtesy; Betty in Search of a Thrill; Scandal;
        Jewel; A Cigarette—That's All
1916   *Hop, The Devil's Brew; The Flirt; The Dumb Girl of Portici;*
        John Needham's Double; The Eye of God; Shoes; Saving the
        Family Name; The People vs. John Doe; Wanted: A Home;
        Idle Wives; Discontent; Where Are My Children?; There Is
        No Place Like Home; Under the Spell; The Rock of Riches;
        The Gilded Life
1917   *The Mysterious Mrs. Musselwhite; Hand That Rocks the Cra-*
        dle; The Price of a Good Time; Even As You and I; The Face
        Downstairs
1918   *The Doctor and the Woman; For Husbands Only; Borrowed*
        Clothes
1919   *When a Girl Loves; A Midnight Romance; Mary Regan;*
        Home; Forbidden
1920   *To Please One Woman; Mum's the Word; Life's Mirror*
1921   *Too Wise Wives; The Blot; What Do Men Want?; What's*
        Worth While?
1923   *A Chapter in Her Life*
1926   *The Marriage Clause*
1927   *Sensation Seekers; The Angel of Broadway; Topsy and Eva*
1934   *White Heat*

Producing Credits

1913   *How Men Propose*
1915   *Jewel; Hypocrites*
1916   *Shoes; The People vs. John Doe; Wanted: A Home; Where*
        Are My Children?
1917   *The Hand That Rocks the Cradle*
1918   *For Husbands Only; Borrowed Clothes*
1921   *Too Wise Wives; The Blot; What's Worth While?; What Do*
        Men Want?

Writing Credits

1911   *The Martyr*
1912   *The Price of Peace; Power of Thought; The Troubadour's*
        Triumph; An Old Fashioned Girl; Faraway Fields

1913　*His Sister; Two Thieves; In the Blood; Bobby's Baby; Until Death; The Cap of Destiny; The King Can Do No Wrong; How Men Propose; The Heart of Jewess; Just in Time; The Call; The Light Woman; Genesis: 4-9; His Brand; Shadows of Life; Thieves and the Cross; The Haunted Bride; James Lee's Wife; The Jew's Christmas; The Rosary; The Wife's Deceit*

1914　*The Female of the Species; A Fool and His Money; The Weaker Sister; A Modern Fairy Tale; The Spider and Her Web; In the Days of His Youth; The Babies' Doll; The Man Who Slept; The Triumph of Mind; Closed Gates; Lost by a Hair; Behind the Veil; Helping Mother; The Opened Shutters; False Colors; The Merchant of Venice; An Old Locke; The Traitor*

1915　*It's No Laughing Matter; The Hypocrites; Sunshine Molly; Scandal; Jewel; A Cigarette, That's All*

1916　*Hop, The Devil's Brew; The Flirt; The Dumb Girl of Portici; The Eye of God; Shoes; Saving the Family Name; The People vs. John Doe; Idle Wives; Discontent; Where Are My Children?; There Is No Place Like Home; Under the Spell; Wanted: A Home; The Rock of Riches; The Gilded Life*

1917　*The Mysterious Mrs. Musselwhite; Hand That Rocks the Cradle; The Price of a Good Time; The Face Downstairs; The Boyhood He Forgot*

1918　*Tarzan of the Apes; The Doctor and the Woman; For Husbands Only; Borrowed Clothes*

1919　*When A Girl Loves; A Midnight Romance; Mary Regan; Home; Forbidden*

1920　*To Please One Woman*

1921　*What's Worth While?; The Blot; What Do Men Want?; Too Wise Wives*

1923　*A Chapter in Her Life*

1926　*The Marriage Clause*

1927　*Sensation Seekers; Topsy and Eva*

1934　*White Heat*

Film Credits (As Actor)

1911　*A Heroine of '76; On the Brink; A Breach of Faith; The Martyr; Lost Illusions; The Heiress; The Realization; Fate*

1912　*Angels Unaware; The Final Pardon; Eyes That See Not; Power of Thought; The Greater Love; An Old Fashioned*

Girl; A Japanese Idyll; Faraway Fields; The Greater Christian; The Bargain; Fine Feathers

1913   *His Sister; Two Thieves; In the Blood; Troubled Waters; An Empty Box; The Peacemaker; Bobby's Baby; Until Death; The Dragon's Breath; The Cap of Destiny; The King Can Do No Wrong; How Men Propose; Suspense; Through Strife; Civilized and Savage; The Heart of Jewess; Just in Time; The Call; The Light Woman; His Brand; Shadows of Life; Memories; The Clue; Thieves and the Cross; The Haunted Bride; The Blood Brotherhood; James Lee's Wife; The Mask; The Jew's Christmas; The Wife's Deceit; The Picture of Dorian Gray; The Pretender; The Rosary*

1914   *The Female of the Species; A Fool and His Money; The Leper's Coat; The Coward Hater; Woman's Burden; The Spider and Her Web; The Babies' Doll; On Suspicion; The Triumph of Mind; Avenged; The Stone in the Road; Closed Gates; The Pursuit of Hate; Lost by a Hair; The Great Universal Mystery; Mary Plain; Behind the Veil; Helping Mother; False Colors; The Merchant of Venice; Daisies; An Old Locke*

1915   *Sunshine Molly; Scandal*

1916   *Hop, The Devil's Brew; The Eye of God; Idle Wives; The Gilded Life; The Rock of Riches; Under the Spell*

1917   *Hand That Rocks The Cradle; The Boyhood He Forgot; The Face Downstairs; Alone in the World*

West, Claire (1893-1980)

Little is known about Claire West's life even though she was the first female costume designer in the film industry. She was interested in drawing and fashion from an early age. In fact, she was so talented that she was selling her fashion sketches to women's magazines while still in high school.

Unlike most women of the era, West graduated from college around 1915. She went to Paris where she became a successful fashion artist. When she returned to the United States, she found a job designing costumes for films. One of her first assignments was to design the costumes for D. W. Griffith's classic *Intolerance* (1916), which required her to design costumes for several different time periods. After several years working in films she became designer for Cecil B. DeMille and worked almost exclusively for him.

Design Credits

1915	*The Birth of a Nation*
1916	*Intolerance*
1919	*Male and Female*
1921	*The Affairs of Anatol*
1922	*Saturday Night*
1923	*Adam's Rib; Bella Donna*
1924	*Flirting with Love; For Sale; The Goldfish; The Lady; The Ten Commandments; Sherlock, Jr.*
1925	*The Golden Bed; The Merry Widow*

What Happened to Mary? *(1912)*

What Happened to Mary? was the first film serial written to appeal to working women, in an effort to bring more women and, thus, legitimacy into film theaters. The series was a joint venture between the Edison Kinetoscope Company and *The Ladies World,* one of the most popular women's magazines of the day.

Starting with the story's second chapter, Edison produced a one-reel film to coincide with the story that appeared each month in the magazine. The series lasted through the summer of 1913 and was the start of the serial craze which led many women to stardom during the silent era.

White, Pearl (1889 Green Ridge, MO-1938 Neuilly-sur-Seine, France)

Since Pearl White, called "the lady daredevil of films," never told the same story twice about her early life, it is uncertain which of her stories, if any, were true. It is generally believed that her mother died when she was still a toddler and her father raised her along with her siblings (the number of siblings varies). Although very strict, her father allowed White to join an acting company after she turned eighteen as long as she gave her earnings to him.

Eventually she began to tour. In 1907 she married, but the marriage was not a success (although she didn't initiate a divorce until 1914). When the company disbanded in the South, White continued to travel throughout Central and South America as a singer in dance halls and casinos.

Although she tried to settle down after returning from South America, performing and traveling were in her blood. When her voice began to give out, White turned to films and signed with the Powers Film Company in New Jersey around 1910. In 1911 she appeared in films for Lubin and in 1912 she worked for Crystal Film Company and then Pathe. Interestingly, White never made a film in Hollywood, spending her entire career in the East.

In 1913 White took an extended tour of Europe and upon her return was introduced to Louis Gasnier who was preparing to film *The Perils of Pauline.* As they say, it was the start of something very big. After *The Perils of Pauline* (1914) proved successful, White embarked on a serial career that included *The Exploits of Elaine* (1914), *The New Exploits of Elaine* (1915), *The Romance of Elaine* (1915), *The Iron Claw* (1916), *The Fatal Ring* (1917), and *The House of Hate* (1918). She was Pathe's biggest moneymaker, and the audiences for her serials, estimated at more than 15 million in the United States alone, loved her.

In 1918 White married Major Wallace McCutcheon only to have him disappear in 1920. He was later found in a Washington, DC, sanitarium. Mentally and emotionally destroyed by his experiences in World War I and his divorce from White, he eventually committed suicide.

In 1919 White authorized the release of what was supposed to be her autobiography, *Just Me,* although it is thought that she had little to do with the actual writing of the book; it is generally believed that little in the book is true. In the early 1920s White moved to Fox Studios to make feature films, but her fans did not accept this transition and she moved to France to enjoy the fruits of her film career. While in Europe she appeared in some musical revues and made a final serial, *Plunder* (1923), for her old friend George Seitz.

White had originally gained fame for doing all the dangerous stunts in her serials without a double. However, during the filming of *Plunder* a stunt double was used and was killed doing one of the stunts. This caused a minor scandal, and the negative publicity and White's guilt over the accident caused her to suffer a breakdown.

She remained in France after she recovered, buying the Hotel de Parisin Biarritz and operating a casino for many years. She also acquired a nightclub and a stable of racing horses. Always good at handling her money, she left a small fortune when she died.

Film Credits

1910   *The Girl from Arizona; The Missing Bridegroom; Her Photograph; The Hoodoo; A Summer Flirtation; The New Magdalene; The Woman Hater; The Maid of Niagara; When the World Sleeps; The Yankee Girl; Motor Fiend; How Rastus Gets His Turkey; Sunshine in Poverty Row; Tommy Gets His Sister Married; The Horse Shoer's Girl; The Burlesque Queen; The Matinee Idol; The Music Teacher; A Woman's Wit; The Sheriff and Miss Jones*

1911   *The Count of Monte Cristo; Home, Sweet Home; Helping Him Out; Angel of the Slums; His Birthday; Memories of the Past; Through the Window; The Reporter; The Lost Necklace; The Power of Love; For the Honor of the Name; The Stepsisters; Prisoner of the Mohican; For Massa's Sake; Love Molds Labor; Her Little Slipper; Love's Renunciation; The Unseen Complication; The Terms of the Will*

1912   *The Blonde Lady; Her Old Love; The Man from the North Pole; McQuick the Sleuth; The Only Woman in Town; The Quarrel; A Pair of Fools; The Mind Cure; The Mad Lover; Locked Out; His Wife's Stratagem; His Visitor; Her Kid Sister; Her Dressmaker's Bills; The Gypsy Flirt; The Girl in the Next Room; The Chorus Girl; Bella's Beaus; The Arrow Maker's Daughter; Mayblossom (I); A Tangled Marriage; For the Honor of the Name; Pals; At the Burglar's Command; The Spendthrift's Reform; The Life of Buffalo Bill; The Hand of Destiny; Oh, Such a Night!*

1913   *Accident Insurance; A Woman's Revenge; The Woman and the Law; With Her Rival's Help; Willie's Great Scheme; Will Power; Where Charity Begins; Who Is the Goat?; Who Is in the Box?; When Love Is Young; When Duty Calls; What Papa Got; The Veiled Lady; Two Lunatics; True Chivalry; Toodleums; Through Fire and Air; That Other Girl; That Crying*

Baby; Strictly Business; Starving for Love; The Soubrette; Robert's Lesson; The Rich Uncle; Pleasing Her Husband; Pearl's Mistake; Pearl's Hero; Pearl's Dilemma; Pearl's Admirers; Pearl As a Detective; Pearl As a Clairvoyant; Pearl and the Lamp; Pearl and the Poet; The Paper Doll; Out of the Grave; Out Parent-in-Law; Oh! You Scotch Lassie!; Oh! You Pearl; A Night in Town; A News Item; The New Typist; Muchly Engaged; Much Ado About Nothing; Misplaced Love; Mary's Romance; The Lure of the Stage; Lovers Three; Lost in the Night; Knights and Ladies; The Kitchen Mechanic; Hubby's New Coat; An Hour of Terror; Homlock Shermes; His Last Gamble; His Awful Daughter; His Aunt Emma; A Hidden Love; Heroic Harold; Her Secretaries; Her Lady Friend; Hearts Entangled; The Heart of an Artist; The Hand of Providence; The Hall-Room Girls; The Greater Influence; Girls Will Be Boys; The Girl Reporter; Forgetful Flossie; First Love; A Supper for Three; Some Luck; The Smuggled Laces; Schultz's Lottery Ticket; Our Willie; Oh! Whiskers!; Ma and the Boys; A Joke on the Sheriff; An Innocent Bridegroom; His Twin Brother; His Romantic Wife; Her Joke on Belmont; False Love and True; The False Alarm; The Fake Gas-Man; Box and Cox; An Awful Scene; The Drummer's Notebook; Dress Reform; A Dip into Society; The Convict's Daughter; College Chums; A Child's Influence; Caught in the Act; A Call from Home; The Cabaret Singer; The Broken Spell; The Fatal Plunge; Out of the Grove; Daisy Wins the Day; At the Burglar's Command; A Night at the Club; Pals; The Lass That Loved a Sailor

1914   *The Lifted Veil; The Perils of Pauline; Willie's Disguise; What Pearl's Pearls Did; What Didn't Happen to Mary; A Telephone Engagement; A Sure Cure; Some Collectors; Shadowed; The Shadow of a Crime; The Ring; Oh! You Mummy; Oh! You Puppy; McSweeney's Masterpiece; The Mashers; Lizzie and the Iceman; The Lady Doctor; It May Come to This; Her New Hat; A Grateful Outcast; Going Some; The Girl in Pants; Getting Reuben Back; Get Out and Get Under; For a Woman; A Father's Devotion; The Exploits of Elaine; Easy Money; East Lynne in Bugville; The Dancing Craze; Was He a Hero?*

1915 *The Romance of Elaine; The New Exploits of Elaine; A Lady in Distress*
1916 *Hazel Kirke; Pearl of the Army; The Iron Claw; The King's Game*
1917 *The Fatal Ring; Mayblossom* (II)
1918 *The House of Hate*
1919 *The Lightning Raider; The Black Secret*
1920 *The White Moll; The Tiger's Cub; The Thief*
1921 *The Mountain Woman; Know Your Men; Beyond Price; A Virgin Paradise*
1922 *The Broadway Peacock; Without Fear; Any Wife*
1923 *Plunder*
1924 *The Perils of Paris; Terror*

Williams, Kathlyn (1888 Butte, MT-1960 Hollywood, CA)

Courtesy of Silents Are Golden at
<SilentsAreGolden.com>

Kathlyn Williams was an academic actor, having studied drama at both Wesleyan University and the Empire School of Acting in New York as a protégé of Senator W. A. Clarke. She went on to become one of the most successful serial stars of the period; for her many successful dramatic roles she was promoted as "the Bernhardt of the screen."

After appearing on stage and with touring companies, her first screen appearances were for the Biograph Company during 1910 while the company was wintering in California. Later that year she moved to the Selig company and became their leading lady. Since no actors were identified at the time, she became known as the "Selig Girl."

In December 1913 Williams starred in Selig's first serial, *The Adventures of Kathlyn*. *The Adventures of Kathlyn* was a joint venture between Selig and *The Chicago Tribune,* with the newspaper printing each weekly installment as the film was released. Although serialized adventures were not new, Selig added many wild animals (called the "Selig Zoo" which eventually helped to start the famed San Diego Zoo), more thrills, and abundant adventure.

The concept was a hit; not only did the newspaper's circulation go up, but Williams became the reigning queen of serials. Her popularity was evidenced by the fact that a contemporary hesitation waltz and a cocktail were named after her. Women copied her hairstyle and style of dress. Men were not immune, buying more than 60,000 postcards featuring her likeness in less than a week.

In addition to her serial fame, she also starred as Cherry Malotte in one of Selig's most famous productions, *The Spoilers* (1914), which has been remade four times in the succeeding years. This performance is generally cited as the best of her career.

That year Williams wrote, directed, and starred in *The Leopard's Foundling*. Although she was quoted in contemporary publications as saying, " Women can direct just as well as men and . . .they often have a keener artistic sense . . ." she never directed again. The film was only a moderate success.

By 1916 Selig was having financial difficulties, so Williams moved to the Oliver Morosco Photoplay Company which released films through Paramount. Once again she became one of the company's most popular stars. In 1917 she had a dual role as both mother and daughter in *The Cost of Hatred*.

By the 1920s Williams, no longer young enough to portray ingenues, was appearing in character roles. In 1922 her only son, Victor, died—a blow she never fully recovered from. Although she made the transition to sound, Williams retired from films in 1935. In 1950 Williams was involved in a serious traffic accident that resulted in her right leg being amputated. The actor, now confined to a wheelchair most of the time, went into a deep depression from which she never truly recovered. She passed away ten years later.

Film Credits

1909   *The Politician's Love Story; Lines of White on a Sullen Sea; On Thanksgiving Day*
1910   *Gold Is Not All; A Romance of the Western Hills; Thou Shalt Not; The Queen of Hearts; The Merry Wives of Windsor;*

Mezeppa, or the Wild Horse of Tatary; The Fire Chief's Daughter; Dora Thorne; Blasted Hopes

1911   *Back to the Primitive; Captain Kate; The Totem Mark; Dad's Girls; Lost in the Arctic; Maud Muller; How They Stopped the Run on the Bank; Lost in the Jungle; The Witch of the Everglades; The Wheels of Justice; The Two Orphans; Ten Nights in a Bar Room; The Rose of Old St. Augustine; Paid Back; The Ne'er Do Well; Life on the Border; Jim and Joe; Jealous George; The Inner Mind; In Old California When the Gringos Came; Getting Married; The Curse of the Redman; Rescued by Her Lions; The Survival of the Fittest; The Man from the East; 1861; The Girl and the Judge*

1912   *The Coming of Columbus; Harbor Island; When the Heart Rules; When Memory Calls; An Unexpected Fortune; The Turning Point; The Stronger Mind; Sons of the North Woods; The Prosecuting Attorney; On the Trail of the Germs; The House of His Master; The Horseshoe; The Girl with the Lantern; The Girl at the Cupola; Driftwood; The Brotherhood of Man; As the Fates Decree; The Adopted Son; The Last Dance; The Governor's Daughter*

1913   *Two Men and a Woman; With Love's Eyes; A Welded Friendship; Women: Past and Present; A Mansion of Misery; The Young Mrs. Eames; The Adventures of Kathlyn (I); A Wise Old Elephant; When May Weds December; Two Too Many; The Tree and the Chaff; The Tide of Destiny; Thor, Lord of the Jungle; Their Stepmother; The Stolen Melody; Songs of Truce; Mrs. Hamilton's Jewels; Man and His Other Self; The Love of Penelope; A Little Child Shall Lead Them; The Lipton Cup; Lieutenant Jones; In the Midst of the Jungle; I Hear Her Calling Me; The Flight of the Crow; The Child of the Sea; The Burglar Who Robbed Death; The Artist and the Brute; The Young Hunter; The Shuttle of Faith; The Conscience Fund*

1914   *The Spoilers; The Losing Fight; The Woman of It; A Woman Laughs; The Tragedy That Lived; Till Death Us Do Part; The Story of the Blood Red Rose; The Speck on the Wall; The Leopard's Foundling; The Lady or the Tigers; In Tune with the Wild; Hearts and Masks; Chip of the Flying U; Caryl of the Mountains; His Fight; The Lonesome Trail; Her Sacrifice; The Soul Mate; The Flower of Faith*

1915   *The Carpet from Bagdad; The Rosary; Sweet Alyssum; The Vision of the Shepherd; A Sultana of the Desert; The Strange Case of Talmai Lind; Ebb Tide; The Coquette's Awakening*

1916   *Thou Shalt Not Covet; The Adventures of Kathlyn (II); The Ne'er Do Well; Into the Primitive; The Valiants of Virginia; Redeeming Love; The Temptation of Adam; The Return; Number 13 Westbound; The Brand of Cain; The Black Orchid; The Devil Stone; Sweet Lady Peggy; The Devil, the Servant, and the Man (I)*

1917   *Out of the Wreck; The Cost of Hatred; The Highway of Hope; Big Timber; Pioneer Days; A Man, a Girl, and a Lion; In the African Jungle*

1918   *The Whispering Chorus; We Can't Have Everything; The Thing We Love*

1919   *The Better Wife; Her Purchase Price; Her Kingdom of Dreams; A Girl Named Mary*

1920   *The Tree of Knowledge; Conrad in Quest of His Youth; The U.P. Trail; The Prince Chap; Just a Wife; Double Speed*

1921   *Forbidden Fruit; Hush; A Private Scandal; Everything for Sale; A Virginia Courtship; Morals; A Man's Home*

1922   *Clarence*

1923   *The World's Applause; Souls for Sale; Trimmed in Scarlet; Broadway Gold; The Spanish Dancer*

1924   *When a Girl Loves; Wanderer of the Wasteland; Single Wives; The Enemy Sex; The City That Never Sleeps; The Painted Flapper*

1925   *Locked Doors; The Best People; The Wanderer*

1927   *Sally in Our Alley*

1928   *We Americans; Our Dancing Daughters; Honeymoon Flats*

1929   *A Single Man; The Single Standard; Wedding Rings; Her Husband's Women*

1930   *Road to Paradise*

1931   *Daddy Long Legs*

1932   *Unholy Love*

1933   *Blood Money; The Big Race*

1935   *Rendezvous at Midnight*

Wilson, Elsie Jane (1890 New Zealand-1965 Los Angeles, CA)

Elsie Jane Wilson, like many women who directed films during the silent era, has been virtually ignored by film historians. Wilson began her acting career at the age of two and was in her early twenties when she immigrated to the United States with her husband, fellow actor Rupert Julian. They appeared on the stage until joining Universal's Rex Company in 1914.

She first began directing with her husband and then began her solo directing career in 1917 with a series of films starring child actor Zoe Rae, who was known as the "Universal Baby." Her films were not often critical successes and were considered appropriate for only women and children, since they dealt with "soft" topics. Although her final film, *The Game's Up* (1919), received good reviews and was touted as "simply a scream," she hung up her director megaphone and declared that directing was a man's job. Little is known about Wilson after she retired, but her husband continued to direct throughout the silent era.

Directing Credits

1917 *The Little Pirate; The Cricket; The Silent Lady; My Little Boy*
1918 *New Love for Old; Beauty in Chains; The Dream Lady; The Lure of Luxury; The City of Tears*
1919 *The Game's Up*

Film Credits

1914 *The Imp Abroad; The Triumph of Mind; The Midnight Visitor; The Hole in the Garden Wall; Out of the Depths; Daisies; A Law Unto Herself*
1915 *The Lure of the Mask; Bound on the Wheel; Mountain Justice; A White Feather Volunteer; Gilded Youth; The Water Clue; One Hundred Years Ago; The Evil Suspicion; Temptation*
1916 *The Underworld; The Red Lie; Arthur's Last Fling; As Fate Decides; John Pellet's Dream; The Blackmailer; The Eyes of Fear; The Marriage of Arthur; The Fur Trimmed Coat; False Gems; Romance at Random; The Human Cactus; Little Boy*

Blue; Bettina Loved a Soldier; The Evil Women Do; Oliver Twist

1917   *The Circus of Life; A Kentucky Cinderella; Mother o' Mine; The Mystery Ship*

1920   *Officer, Call a Cop*

Wilson, Lois (1894 Pittsburgh, PA-1988 Reno, NV)

Prior to winning the Miss Alabama title "as Alabama's most beautiful daughter" in a contest sponsored by Universal in 1915 and beginning a successful career as an actor, Lois Wilson worked as a schoolteacher. But her first love was acting. Her dedication to her art and her expressive eyes started her on a career that spanned nearly sixty years.

Upon winning the Alabama title, Wilson and several other state winners traveled by train across the United States on "The American Beauty Special." The entire trip was a huge publicity stunt for the newly opened Universal Studios, with frequent updates as to the train's progress across the country. Still, Wilson remembered the trip as "three weeks of absolute joy."

She began her career with Universal at $25 per week doing bit roles and extra work. Dissatisfied at Universal, she moved to the California Motion Picture Company, but she made only three films there. Deciding against committing herself to one studio, she freelanced among several of the smaller production companies before going to Famous Players in 1919.

Her personal favorite film was *Miss Lulu Betts* (1921). Although she appeared in several leading roles, she preferred character parts. Unlike many of her peers, she was willing to downplay her attractiveness and appear dowdy for a good supporting role. In 1922 she was one of the first young women to be selected as a WAMPAS Baby Star. In 1924 she represented the American film industry at the British Empire Exposition.

As she became more comfortable with film work, Wilson began working in plays and local stock companies. Her theater work made the transition to sound easier for her than for some of her peers. Although she was well respected in her profession, she never became a star. After she moved back East in 1937 she spent most of her time working in theater until the early 1950s, when she became involved in television.

During the 1949-1950 season she appeared as Mrs. Aldrich in *The Aldrich Family.* She also appeared on several of the live dramatic series of the early years such as *Studio One* (1948-1958) and *Ford Theatre Hour* (1949-1951, 1952-1957). Later she appeared in recurring roles on several of the early soap operas, including *The Guiding Light* (1952-) and *The Secret Storm* (1954-1974).

Her roles in films engendered an awareness and concern for social issues, such as the preservation of the environment and Native American rights, that continued after her retirement. She was also one of the first members of Actors' Equity, an organization dealing with actors' rights.

Film Credits

1915   *When the Queen Loved O'Rourke; The Road to Paradise; The Palace of Dust; The Hypocrite*

1916   *Married on a Wing; The Gay Lord Waring; Hulda the Silent; A Son of the Immortals; The Decoy; The Silent Battle; The Pool of Flame; The Beckoning Trail; The Morals of Hilda; Green Eyes; The White Man's Law; Her Chance; He Wrote a Book; Arthur's Desperate Resolve; Langdon's Legacy; The Dumb Girl of Portici*

1917   *Won by Grit; Black Evidence; Alimony; Treason; Flames of Treachery; The Whispered Name*

1918   *His Robe of Honor; The Turn of a Card; One Dollar Bid; Parentage; Maid o' the Storm; A Burglar for a Night; The Bells; Prisoners of the Pines; Three X Gordon; A Man's Man* (I)

1919   *The Drifters; Come Again Smith; The End of the Game; Gates of Brass; The Best Man; A Man's Fight; Love Insurance; Why Smith Left Home; It Pays to Advertise; The Price Woman Pays*

1920   *Too Much Johnson; Thou Art the Man; The City of Masks; What's Your Hurry?; Who's Your Servant?; A Full House; Burglar Proof; Midsummer Madness*

1921   *What Every Woman Knows; The City of Silent Men; The Lost Romance; The Hell Diggers; Miss Lulu Betts*

1922   *The World's Champion; Our Leading Citizen; Manslaughter; Without Compromise; Broad Daylight; Is Matrimony a Failure?*

1923   *The Covered Wagon; Bella Donna; Only 38; To the Last Man; Ruggles of Red Gap; The Call of the Canyon; A Man's Man* (II); *Hollywood*

1924   *Piped Piper Malone; Another Scandal; Icebound; Monsieur Beaucaire; The Man Who Fights Alone; North of 36*

1925   *Contraband; The Thundering Herd; Welcome Home; Rugged Water; The Vanishing American; Irish Luck; The King of Main Street*

1926   *Bluebeard's Seven Wives; Let's Get Married; Fascinating Youth; The Show Off; The Great Gatsby*

1927   *New York; Broadway Nights; The Gingham Girl; Alias the Lone Wolf; French Dressing*

1928   *Coney Island; Ransom; Sally's Shoulders; On Trial; Object: Alimony; Conquest; Miss Information*

1929   *A Bird in Hand; Kid Gloves; Her Husband's Women; The Gamblers; The Show of Shows; Wedding Rings*

1930   *The Furies; Lovin' the Ladies; Once a Gentleman; Temptation; For Love or Money*

1931   *Seed; The Age for Love*

1932   *The Expert; The Secrets of Wu Sin; The Crash; Rider of Death Valley; Law and Order; Divorce in the Family; Drifting; The Devil Is Driving*

1933   *Obey the Law; Laughing at Life; The Deluge; Female; In the Money*

1934   *The Show Off; No Greater Glory; There's Always Tomorrow; School for Girls; Bright Eyes; Ticket to a Crime*

1935   *Your Uncle Dudley; Public Opinion; Cappy Rick Returns; Born to Gamble; Society Fever; Life Returns*

1936   *The Return of Jimmy Valentine; Wedding Present; Laughing at Trouble*

1939   *Bad Little Angel*

1940   *Nobody's Children*
1941   *For Beauty's Sake*
1949   *The Girl from Jones Beach*

Wilson, Margery (1896 Gracey, KY-1986 Arcadia, CA)

Margery Wilson entered show business at the age of eleven as a diseuse, a reciter of dramatic monologues. Considered a child prodigy, Wilson was a popular attraction at churches and social clubs. At fourteen she signed with a touring company and began appearing in plays throughout the United States. While appearing in Seattle both Wilson and her sister traveled to Hollywood to investigate the jobs available in the film industry.

The first studio that Wilson checked was Reliance-Mutual, where she met director D. W. Griffith. Her first major role was as "Brown Eyes," the bride-to-be in the French Huguenots segment of *Intolerance* (1916). Although under contract with Griffith, Wilson was loaned to other studios during this time; when Griffith left for Europe late in 1916 to film *Hearts of the World* (1918), her contract was transferred to Thomas Ince's Triangle Company.

In 1919 Wilson left Triangle and freelanced for a few months before trying her hand at producing and directing films. She used her experience staging plays for her first film production, *That Something,* which concerned "that something" that made a man either a success or a failure. The film, which was released a year after it was produced, was not a popular hit but did receive favorable notices.

Wilson then wrote a series of two-reel comedies, the first being *Two of a Kind* (1920), which concerned two identical-looking boys. She directed only two other films—*Insinuation* (1922) and *The Offenders* (1924). Wilson later claimed that she was the first director to film an entire film "on location" without using any studio scenes.

Wilson spent three years touring the United States and Canada promoting *Insinuation.* In 1927 she married and retired from films because her husband (she later said) "didn't want me to do anything." After her marriage, she began a writing career and wrote thirteen non-fiction books on self-improvement topics including *Charm* (1930), *Your Personality and God* (1938), *Make Up Your Mind* (1940), *The Woman You Want to Be* (1942), *How to Live Beyond Your Means* (1945), and *Believe in Yourself* (1949). She published her autobiography, *I Found My Way,* in 1956.

Film Credits

1914   *Jane Eyre*
1915   *The Lucky Transfer; Bred in the Bone; Double Trouble*
1916   *Intolerance; Eye of the Night; The Primal Lure; The Return of Draw Egan; A Corner in Colleens; The Honorable Algy; The Sin Ye Do; The Habit of Happiness*
1917   *The Bride of Hate; The Gun Fighter; The Last of the Ingrahams; The Desert Man; Wolf Lowry; The Clodhopper; The Mother Instinct; Mountain Dew; Wild Sumac*
1918   *Without Honor; The Flames of Chance; The Hard Rock Breed; The Law of the Great Northwest; The Hand at the Window; Old Love for New; Marked Cards*
1919   *Venus in the East; Crooked Straight; Desert Gold*
1920   *The Blooming Angel; That Something; The House of Whispers*
1922   *Insinuation; Why Not Marry?*

Directing Credits

1920   *That Something*
1922   *Insinuation; The Offenders*

Writing Credit

1922   *Insinuation*

Windsor, Claire (1897 Cawker City, KS-1972 Hollywood, CA)

Courtesy of Silents Are Golden at
<SilentsAreGolden.com>

Called the "Patrician Beauty" as well as the "Perfect American Beauty," Claire Windsor was a single mother when she entered films after winning a beauty contest in Washington. The success of films brought a demand for attractive women to populate them, and this need made earning a living as an actor seem possible to the many would-be actors that flocked to Hollywood.

Like many hopefuls before and after her, she worked as an extra and bit player when she first arrived in Hollywood. Then she caught the attention of director Lois Weber who signed her to a contract. Windsor's classic features and refined manners made her a natural for the melodramas that Weber favored.

In 1921 Windsor was the center of a publicity stunt aimed at publicizing both her and Charlie Chaplin, one of her frequent escorts. Headlines screamed: "Chaplin Offers $1000 Reward for Missing Star." She was supposedly found thirty-six hours later "semiconscious." This maneuver guaranteed a good turnout for the couple's films released later in the year.

In 1922 Windsor was one of the first actors chosen as a WAMPAS Baby Star. Later in 1922 Windsor signed a contract with Goldwyn Pictures. However, the death of director William Desmond Taylor that year cast a shadow over her rising star. She had been Taylor's dinner date the night he was killed and was questioned by the police. Luckily, the fervor died down and Windsor was able to continue with her career.

In 1924, during the filming of *A Son of the Sahara,* Windsor fell in love with her leading man, Bert Lytell. After a turbulent courtship the couple married in Mexico at the home of writer Jaime Del Rio and his wife, Delores, who had yet to be discovered by Hollywood. The marriage lasted only three years and was Windsor's final attempt at matrimony, although newspapers were filled with her subsequent affairs.

Windsor was one of the first stars signed by the newly merged Metro-Goldwyn-Mayer Studio. As the years passed Windsor became known for her attractive style of dress, but it was not generally known that she designed and made many of her own clothes both on and off screen. In the 1920s, as one of Hollywood's "beautiful people," Windsor was a regular at William Randolph Hearst's estate on the California coast.

The advent of sound films brought an end to Windsor's star days, but she continued to appear in character roles. In 1931 as she was beginning a successful run in the play *The Wonder Bar* (1931-1933) with Al Jolson, she was named in an "alienation of affections" suit brought by the wife of a wealthy stockbroker. The case made headlines for weeks, but luckily for Windsor it was eventually settled for $1,200 rather than the $75,000 originally awarded.

As her film career waned, Windsor concentrated on stage work. She appeared in several plays with varying success throughout the

1940s, but she remained a member of Hollywood's social elite even though her star had faded.

Once she retired, Windsor began exhibiting paintings she had done as a hobby for years. In 1968 she served as president of the American Institute of Fine Arts, a group founded by Mary Pickford and others to foster an appreciation for traditional art.

In April 1972 the newly refurbished Alexandria Hotel named one of its suites in her honor. In the summer of that year Windsor represented her longtime friend Mary Pickford at a special screening of *Rebecca of Sunnybrook Farm* (1917) in Pleasanton, California, where the film had been made. Sadly, a few months later Windsor died of a massive heart attack.

Film Credits

1919	*Eyes of Youth*
1920	*To Please One Woman; The Luck of the Irish*
1921	*The Blot; What Do Men Want?; What's Worth While?; Too Wise Wives; Dr. Jim; The Raiders*
1922	*Grand Larceny; One Clear Call; Fools First; Rich Men's Wives; Brothers Under the Skin; The Strangers' Banquet; Broken Chains*
1923	*The Eternal Three; The Little Church Around the Corner; Rupert of Hentzau; The Acquittal; Souls for Sale*
1924	*Nellie, the Beautiful Cloak Model; A Son of the Sahara; For Sale; Born Rich*
1925	*The Denial; Just a Woman; The White Desert; Souls for Sables; The Dixie Handicap*
1926	*Dance Madness; Money Talks; Tin Hats*
1927	*A Little Journey; The Claw; The Bugle Call; Foreign Devils; The Frontiersman; Blondes by Choice; Opening Night*
1928	*Nameless Men; Fashion Madness; Satan and the Woman; The Grain of Dust; Domestic Meddlers; Show People*
1929	*Captain Lash; Midstream*
1932	*Self Defense; Sister to Judas*
1933	*The Constant Woman; Kiss of Araby*
1934	*Cross Streets*
1937	*Topper*
1938	*Barefoot Boy*
1946	*How Do You Do?*

Wong, Anna May (1905 Los Angeles, CA-1961 Santa Monica, CA)

Courtesy of Silents Are Golden at
<SilentsAreGolden.com>

Anna May Wong was the most successful female actor of Asian ancestry during the silent film era. Her parents ran a laundry in Los Angeles and Wong became a photographer's model while attending Los Angeles High School. Living so near the film capital allowed her to "study" filmmaking from an early age.

When she was fourteen, James Wang, a friend of her father's who was an actor, helped her get a job as a lantern bearer in Alla Nazimova's film *The Red Lantern* (1919). Her father, who wanted his daughter to follow Chinese customs, locked her in her room to keep her from getting additional jobs when he learned she had cut school to work on the film. However, he was eventually convinced that the money would be useful at home, so he relented on the condition that she be chaperoned at the studios.

Upon her return to the film studio, she was offered a bit part in *Dinty* (1920). As soon as she was able to support herself with her film work she moved out of her father's house, causing a complete estrangement from her family. She continued to appear in small roles and bit parts, including a role in the first Technicolor feature filmed in Hollywood, *The Toll of the Sea* (1922). Finally she got her big break when she was cast as the Mongol slave girl in *The Thief of Bagdad* (1924).

Wong became a popular actor when she worked in films made with Asian themes. She played both heroines and evil adventurers and became, to the filmgoing audience, a symbol of the "mysterious" East. Soon her trademark eyebrow-length bangs and ethnic Asian dress were instantly recognizable to her many fans.

She made the transition to sound and became recognized the world over, spending several years in Europe making films and appearing in European stage plays. While in Europe she wrote a musical play, *Tschun-Tshi,* which was produced in Vienna in 1928. When she returned to the United States, she appeared on Broadway as a gangster's moll in *On The Spot*. She signed with Paramount and made two of her most popular films, *Daughter of the Dragon* (1931) and, perhaps her most famous, *Shanghai Express* (1932) with Marlene Dietrich.

Wong next embarked on a coast-to-coast vaudeville tour that lasted until 1933. She then returned to Europe to tour in a one-woman show. In the late 1930s, as she found roles becoming more scarce, Wong turned to writing; articles that she wrote about her impressions of her parents' homeland after a 1935 visit appeared in *The New York Tribune*.

Sadly, with the advent of World War II film audiences wanted escapist films, not the heavy melodramas in which Wong excelled. As the war progressed, Asians were also looked upon with suspicion. Although she found occasional work, for the remainder of the war she devoted her time to the USO and to raising money for Chinese war relief.

Wong worked briefly in television in the series *The Gallery of Madame Liu-Tsong* (1951) on the DuMont Network. She played an art gallery owner and amateur detective, but the series ran for only eleven episodes. After the demise of her series she appeared on several of the dramatic anthologies of the 1950s. In 1960, the year before her death, Wong tried a comeback in two films—*Portrait in Black* and *The Savage Innocents,* but neither was well received by the public.

Film Credits

1919   *The Red Lantern*
1920   *Dinty*
1921   *Shame; Bits of Life; The First Born*
1922   *The Toll of the Sea*
1923   *Mary of the Movies; Drifting; Thundering Dawn*
1924   *The Thief of Bagdad; Peter Pan; The Fortieth Door; The Alaskan; Lilies of the Field*
1925   *Forty Winks; His Supreme Moment*
1926   *Fifth Avenue; A Trip to Chinatown; The Silk Bouquet; The Desert's Toll*
1927   *Driven from Home; Mr. Wu; Old San Francisco; The Chinese Parrot; The Devil Dancer; Streets of Shanghai; The Honorable Mr. Buggs; Why Girls Love Sailors*

1928   *The Crimson City; Chinatown Charlie; Across to Singapore; Wasted Love*
1929   *City Butterfly; Piccadilly*
1930   *Hai-Tang; The Flame of Life; Elstree Calling; The Flame of Love*
1931   *Daughter of the Dragon*
1932   *Shanghai Express; Hollywood on Parade*
1933   *A Study in Scarlet*
1934   *Tiger Bay; Limehouse Blues; Java Head; Chu Chin Chow*
1937   *Daughter of Shanghai; Hollywood Party*
1938   *Dangerous to Know; When Were You Born?*
1939   *King of Chinatown; Island of Lost Men*
1940   *Chinese Garden Festival*
1941   *Ellery Queen's Penthouse Mystery*
1942   *The Lady from Chungking*
1943   *Bombs over Burma*
1949   *Impact*
1959   *The Savage Innocents*
1960   *Portrait in Black*

Woodruff, Eleanor (1891 Towanda, PA-1980 Princeton, NJ)

Eleanor Woodruff, like so many silent film actors, was extremely popular for a brief period and then faded from the limelight, but during her heyday, she was one of the most prominent actors in films.

She was born into a wealthy family and educated at the National School of Oratory. She joined a touring stock company in 1909 and began a successful acting career. Two years later she made her Broadway debut in *The Five Frankfurters* (1911).

In 1912 Woodruff made her film debut for Pathe and became one of the studio's leading dramatic actors. After three years at Pathe, she joined the Vitagraph Company where she appeared in two- and three-reelers as well as the newly established feature film.

Woodruff was persuaded to leave films for the opportunity to star in Booth Tarkington's *Mister Antonio* (1916). She continued to appear on the stage in both the United States and Europe until her final appearance in Somerset Maugham's *The Breadwinner* (1931).

After her 1931 marriage to stockbroker Dorsey Richardson, she retired completely from show business. For many years she concentrated on doing charity and political work as her husband rose in the ranks of politics to become an economic advisor to Presidents Kennedy and Johnson. As her children grew older, she started an interior decorating business and taught speech in schools near her home of Princeton, New Jersey.

Film Credits

1913   *The Two Mothers; The Bomb Boys; The Finger of Fate; In the Mesh of Her Hair*

1914   *The Second Generation; Rods of Wrath; The Sword of Damocles; The Winning Hand; The Perils of Pauline; The Last Volunteer; The Stain; All Love Excelling; The Ticket-of-Leave Man; A Leech of Industry*

1915   *His Rinkie; The West Wind; From the Dregs; The Heights of Hazard*

1916   *The Island of Surprise; Britton of the Seventh; The Hero of Submarine D-2; The Weakness of Man; Jaffrey; Big Jim Garrity*

1922   *The Pasteboard Crown*

Wray, Fay (1907 Cardston, Alberta, Canada-2004 New York City)

Courtesy of Silents Are Golden at <SilentsAreGolden.com>

Fay Wray, best remembered as the woman who brought about King Kong's destruction, was raised in Arizona and Utah. After the influenza epidemic of 1918 claimed her older sister, Wray moved with her family to California and began to look for work in the film industry. Her first jobs were in the comedy shorts with Hal Roach's studio. Soon she moved to Universal to play leads in westerns while she honed her talents and learned the industry in which she worked.

Her big break came when she was chosen to play Mitzi Schrammell, the female lead in Erich von Stroheim's classic *The Wedding March* (1928). Two years earlier she had been chosen as a WAMPAS Baby Star and became Paramount's most publicized new star.

After her marriage in 1928, she continued her heavy filming schedule, appearing in twenty-five features in three years. In 1933 she appeared in the film that secured her place in film history, *King Kong*. As Ann Darrow in one of the most famous films of all time, *King Kong* was a variation of the "Beauty and the Beast" theme. It grossed $90,000 in its first four days. In 1998, *King Kong* was named one of "100 greatest films of all time" by the American Film Institute.

Wray starred in *Viva Villa!* opposite Wallace Beery in 1934; the film was nominated for Best Picture later that year. In 1938 Wray divorced her husband and began the task of raising their daughter, Susan, alone. Two years later her ex-husband killed himself and Wray was truly a single parent. In 1942 Wray again married, and this marriage proved happier than her first.

After a decade of retirement, Wray returned to films when her husband became too ill to work. When her second husband died in 1955, Wray again retired from films. By this time, however, she had already started working in television. In 1953 she was cast as the mother in the situation comedy *The Pride of the Family* (1953-1955). After the end of this series, she continued to appear in several episodes of both *Perry Mason* (1957-1966) and *Alfred Hitchcock Presents* (1955-1965).

In 1989 she published her autobiography, *On the Other Hand*. In August 1997, an autobiographical play that she had written, *The Meadowlark,* dealing with life in a copper-mining town in Utah was presented in New Hampshire and directed by her daughter.

She made a special appearance at the seventieth anniversary presentation of The Academy Awards in 1998 and was introduced by Billy Crystal as "the legendary Fay Wray."

Film Credits

1923   *Gasoline Love*
1925   *Your Own Back Yard; Chasing the Chaser; Unfriendly Enemies; Moonlight and Noses; What Price Goofy; The Coast*

Patrol; Isn't Life Terrible?; Should Sailors Marry?; Madame Sans Jane; No Father to Guide Him

1926   *The Man in the Saddle; Don't Shoot; One Wild Time; Don Key, a Son of Burro; The Wild Horse Stampede; Lazy Lightning*

1927   *Loco Luck; A One Man Game; Spurs and Saddles*

1928   *The Legion of the Condemned; Street of Sin; The First Kiss; The Wedding March; The Honeymoon*

1929   *Thunderbolt; Pointed Heels; The Four Feathers*

1930   *Paramount on Parade; The Texan; The Border Legion; The Sea God; Captain Thunder; Behind the Make-Up*

1931   *The Conquering Horde; Three Rogues; Dirigible; The Lawyer's Secret; The Unholy Garden; The Slippery Pearls; The Finger Points*

1932   *Stowaway; Doctor X; The Most Dangerous Game*

1933   *Mystery of the Wax Museum; King Kong; Shanghai Madness; One Sunday Afternoon; The Woman I Stole; The Vampire Bat, Master of Men, The Bowery, The Big Brain, Below the Sea, Ann Carver's Profession*

1934   *The Countess of Monte Cristo; The Affair of Cellini; The Richest Girl in the World; Cheating Cheaters; Woman in the Dark; Once to Every Woman; Madame Spy; The Clairvoyant; Black Moon; Viva Villa!*

1935   *White Lies; Mills of the Gods; Come Out of the Pantry; Bulldog Jack*

1936   *When Knights Were Bold; They Met in a Taxi; Roaming Lady*

1937   *It Happened in Hollywood; Murder in Greenwich Village*

1938   *The Jury's Secret*

1939   *Navy Secrets; Smashing the Spy Ring*

1940   *Wildcat Bus*

1941   *Adam Had Four Sons; Melody for Three*

1942   *Not a Ladies' Man*

1953   *Treasure of the Golden Condor; Small Town Girl*

1955   *Queen Bee; Hell on Frisco Bay; The Cobweb*

1956   *Rock Pretty Baby*

1957   *Crime of Passion; Tammy and the Bachelor*

1958   *Summer Love; Dragstrip Riot*

𝒴

Young, Clara Kimball (1890 Chicago, IL-1960 Woodland Hills, CA)

Born into a show business family, Clara Kimball Young became a popular actor and a pioneering producer. Called "the Dark Madonna," she never reached the heights of fame that some of her peers achieved, but she was a reliable actor who always gave her best performance and enhanced the films in which she appeared.

She made her stage debut at three years of age and appeared in vaudeville and stock before entering films in 1909, when she signed a contract with Vitagraph. In 1915 she moved to World Film Corporation as their main leading lady. The next year she and Lewis J. Selznick formed the Clara Kimball Young Film Corporation devoted to producing only her own films. She was a top box-office draw between 1918 and 1921.

Courtesy of Silents Are Golden at <SilentsAreGolden.com>

She excelled at the social satires popular during the late 1910s and frequently starred with Maurice Costello early in her career. She was graceful enough to also be believable in the costume melodramas popular during the early years of the film industry, but her best roles were in emotionally charged dramas.

Sadly, in 1922 she allowed her second husband to take charge of her films and their quality deteriorated sharply. This forced her to retire from films and return to vaudeville. When she returned to films in the 1930s, it was as a supporting player in mostly low-budget films.

Film Credits

1909   *Washington Under the American Flag; A Midsummer Night's Dream*

1910   *Uncle Tom's Cabin; The Sepoy's Wife; Ransomed or, A Prisoner of War; Richelieu, or the Conspiracy*

1911   *Lady Godiva*

1912   *The Old Kent Road; Dr. LaFleur's Theory; The Troublesome Step-Daughters; Mrs. Lirriper's Lodgers; Lord Browning and Cinderella; When Roses Wither; Wanted: A Sister; A Vitagraph Romance; Popular Betty; Poet and Peasant; The Picture Idol; A Mistake in Spelling; Lulu's Doctor; A Lively Affair; Lincoln's Gettysburg Address; The Jocular Winds of Fate; The Irony of Fate; In the Flat Above; The Haunted Rocker; Half a Hero; The Eavesdropper; Cardinal Woolsey; The Pipe; Professor Optimo; Mockery; The Money Kings; Rock of Ages*

1913   *Beau Brummel; The Old Guard; The Hindoo Charm; Betty in the Lion's Den; Up in a Balloon; The White Slave; When Mary Grew Up; What a Change of Clothes Did; The Way Out; The Test; The Taming of Betty; The Spirit of the Orient; Put Yourself in Their Place; The Pirates; On Their Wedding Eve; Mystery of the Stolen Jewels; Mystery of the Stolen Child; Mr. Mintern's Misadventures; A Maid of Mandalay; Love's Sunset; Love Hath Wrought a Miracle; The Lonely Princess; The Little Minister; A Lesson in Jealousy; Jerry's Mother-in-Law; Delayed Proposals; Jack's Chrysanthemum; The Interrupted Honeymoon; Getting Up a Practice; Fellow Voyagers; A Faithful Servant; Cupid versus Women's Rights; Beauty Unadorned; The Volunteer; Strike Breakers*

1914   *Sonny Jim in Search of a Mother; My Official Wife; David Garrick; Lola; The Violin of Monsieur; Taken by Storm; Some Steamer Scooping; The Silver Snuff Box; The Perplexed Bridegroom; Her Husband; Happy-Go-Lucky; Goodness Gracious; The Fates and Flora Fourflush; The Awakening of Barbara Dare*

1915   *The Deep Purple; Hearts in Exile; Marrying Money; Trilby; The Heart of the Blue Ridge; Camille*

1916   *The Feast of Life; The Dark Silence; The Common Law; The Rise of Susan; The Yellow Passport; The Foolish Virgin*

1917   *Shirley Kaye; The Price She Paid; Magda; The Easiest Way*

1918   *The Reason Why; The Claw; The Savage Woman; The Road Through the Dark; The Marionettes; The House of Glass*

1919   *Cheating Cheaters; The Better Wife; Soldiers of Fortune; Eyes of Youth*

1920   *The Forbidden Woman; For the Soul of Rafael; Mid-Channel*

1921	*Hush; Charge It; What No Man Knows; Straight from Paris*
1922	*The Worldly Madonna; The Hands of Nara; Enter Madame*
1923	*Cordelia the Magnificent; A Wife's Romance; The Woman of Bronze*
1925	*Lying Wives*
1931	*Kept Husbands; Mother and Son; Women Go on Forever*
1932	*Probation; Love Bound; File 113*
1934	*Romance in the Rain; The Return of Chandu* (I and II); *I Can't Escape*
1935	*She Married Her Boss; His Night Out; Fighting Youth; Hollywood Extra Girl; The Drunkard; Chandu on the Magic Island; Atlantic Adventure*
1936	*Ants in the Pantry; Three on the Trail; Oh Susanna; The Rogue's Tavern; The Last Assignment; The Black Coin; The Fighting Coward; Dangerous Waters*
1937	*New News; Hills of Old Wyoming; Dangerously Yours; The Mysterious Pilot*
1938	*The Frontiersman; The Wages of Sin; The Secret of Treasure Island*
1941	*The Roundup*
1942	*Mr. Celebrity; Confessions of a Vice Baron*

Young, Loretta (1913 Salt Lake City, UT-2000 Palm Springs, CA)

Loretta Young grew up in Hollywood, where her mother ran a boarding house. She was a child extra by the time she was four years old, aided by her uncle who was an assistant director. During this time, Mae Murray, the lead in Young's first film, *The Primrose Ring,* became so enchanted by the four-year-old that she tried to adopt Young, but her mother would not allow it. Young did, however, live with Murray for more than a year. Although she took a break from films to attend a local convent school, she did appear in small roles in *The Sheik* (1921) and *Naughty but Nice* (1927). While in school, Young helped her mother at the boarding house but dreamed of returning to films.

Her performance as Denise Laverne in *The Magnificent Flirt* (1928) was the first role she played after deciding to work at being an actor. She quickly advanced from bit parts to featured roles and inge-nue leads. In 1929 her career was further aided by her selection as a WAMPAS Baby Star and the resulting publicity she received in mag-azines and newspapers. In 1930 she made headlines of a different type when she eloped to Yuma, Arizona, with divorced actor Grant Withers, who was nine years her senior. Withers had costarred with her in *The Second Floor Mystery* (1930). The marriage was annulled within the year.

Although two of her three sisters (Polly Ann Young and Sally Blane) were also in films, Young's career soon outpaced those of her sisters. The three appeared together in only one film, *The Story of Al-exander Graham Bell* (1939), in which they played sisters along with a fourth sister, Georgiana Young.

It was after Young signed with Fox Studios that she really came into her own as an actor. While she always managed to appear elegant and refined in her screen appearances, she was now given roles that demanded acting ability. She became known as one of the most tal-ented and beautiful women in Hollywood.

After years of credible performances, Young was awarded a Best Actress Oscar for her portrayal of Katrin Holstrom in *The Farmer's Daughter* (1947). The film was incredibly popular, and she went from that success to *The Bishop's Wife* (1947), also an enormous hit. Both films remain classics of that era. In 1949 Young was again nom-inated for an Academy Award for her portrayal of Sister Margaret in *Come to the Stable*. In 1953 she appeared in her final film, *It Happens Every Thursday*.

Although she had retired from the silver screen, Young only moved her talents to a new medium. Her dramatic anthology televi-sion series *The Loretta Young Show* ran from 1953 to 1961; she is of-ten remembered for her beautiful gowns and dramatic stairway en-trances. Her appearances in plays on the show garnered her three Emmy awards as Best Actress in a Dramatic Series. More than a de-cade later, Young sued NBC for violating her previous contract when it scheduled reruns of *The Loretta Young Show* in 1972, charging that since some of the episodes were almost twenty years old the viewing audience might ridicule her. She was awarded more than a half-million dollars.

In 1962 she created a new series, *The New Loretta Young Show,* but this show was not a success. She did not appear on any screen for twenty-four years. Then, in 1989, she made one final appearance in a TV movie, *Lady in the Corner.*

Young spent her retirement working for and endowing Catholic charities. In 1961 she wrote a book, *The Things I Had to Learn.* After years of rumors, it was revealed that her "adopted" daughter, Judy Lewis, was actually Young's illegitimate daughter by Clark Gable.

Film Credits

1917 *The Primrose Ring; Sirens of the Sea*
1919 *The Only Way*
1921 *The Sheik; White and Unmarried*
1927 *Naughty but Nice; Her Wild Oat*
1928 *The Whip Woman; The Magnificent Flirt; The Head Man; Laugh, Clown, Laugh; Scarlet Seas*
1929 *Seven Footprints to Satan; The Squall; The Girl in the Glass Cage; Fast Life; The Careless Age; The Forward Pass; The Show of Shows*
1930 *Loose Ankles; The Man from Blankley's; Show Girl in Holly-wood; The Second Floor Mystery; Road to Paradise; Kismet (I); The Truth About Youth; The Devil to Pay!*
1931 *The Right of Way; Three Girls Lost; Big Business Girl; Platinum Blonde; The Ruling Voice; Too Young to Marry; The Slippery Pearls; I Like Your Nerve; Beau Ideal; How I Play Golf*
1932 *The Hatchet Man; Week-end Marriage; Life Begins; They Call It Sin; Play Girl; Taxi!*
1933 *Grand Slam; Zoo in Budapest; The Life of Jimmy Dolan; Midnight Mary; Man's Castle; She Had to Say Yes; Heroes for Sale; Employees' Entrance; The Devil's in Love*
1934 *Born to Be Bad; Bulldog Drummond Strikes Back; The White Parade; The House of Rothschild; Caravan*
1935 *The Call of the Wild; Clive of India; Shanghai; The Crusades*
1936 *The Unguarded Hour; Ramona; Private Number; Ladies in Love*
1937 *Love Is News; Café Metropole; Wife, Doctor, and Nurse; Second Honeymoon; Love Under Fire*

1938 *Three Blind Mice; Suez; Kentucky; Four Men and a Prayer*
1939 *Eternally Yours; The Story of Alexander Graham Bell; Wife; Husband and Friend*
1940 *He Stayed for Breakfast; The Doctor Takes a Wife*
1941 *The Lady from Cheyenne; The Men in Her Life; Bedtime Story*
1943 *China; A Night to Remember; Show Business at War*
1944 *Ladies Courageous; And Now Tomorrow*
1945 *Along Came Jones*
1946 *The Stranger*
1947 *The Farmer's Daughter; The Bishop's Wife; The Perfect Marriage*
1948 *Rachel and the Stranger*
1949 *Come to the Stable; Mother Is a Freshman; The Accused*
1950 *Key to the City*
1951 *Half Angel; Cause for Alarm*
1952 *Paula; Because of You*
1953 *It Happens Every Thursday*

Appendix A

The Longest Acting Careers
of Female Silent Actors

75 years   Lillian Gish (1893-1993)
            An Unseen Enemy (1912) ~ *The Whales of August* (1987)

68 years   Bessie Love (1898-1986)
            Birth of a Nation (1915) ~ *The Hunger* (1983)

59 years   Gloria Swanson (1899-1983)
            At The End of a Perfect Day (1915) ~ *Airport 1975* (1974)

59 years   Madge Kennedy (1891-1987)
            Baby Mine (1917) ~ *Marathon Man* (1976)

58 years   Minta Durfee (1891-1975)
            Fatty's Day Off (1913) ~ *Willard* (1971)

54 years   Mae Marsh (1895-1968)
            Ramona (1910) ~ *Cheyenne Autumn* (1964)

51 years   Dorothy Gish (1898-1968)
            An Unseen Enemy (1912) ~ *The Cardinal* (1963)

50 years   Pola Negri (1894-1987)
            Love and Passion (1914) ~ *The Moon-Spinners* (1964)

Appendix B

WAMPAS (Western Associated Motion Picture Advertisers) Baby Stars (1922-1929) and Sisters

BABY STARS

1922

Marion Aye
Lila Lee
Louise Lorraine
Kathryn McGuire
Colleen Moore
Pauline Starke
Claire Windsor

Helen Ferguson
Jacqueline Logan
Bessie Love
Patsy Ruth Miller
Mary Philbin
Lois Wilson

1923

Eleanor Boardman
Dorothy Devore
Betty Francisco
Kathleen Key
Margaret Leahy
Derelys Perdue
Ethel Shannon

Evelyn Brent
Virginia Brown Faire
Pauline Garon
Laura LaPlante
Helen Lynch
Jobyna Ralston

1924

Clara Bow
Carmelita Geraghty
Ruth Hiatt
Hazel Keener
Blanche Mehaffey
Marion Nixon
Alberta Vaughn

Elinor Fair
Gloria Grey
Julanne Johnston
Dorothy Mackaill
Margaret Morris
Lucille Ricksen

1925

Betty Arlen	Violet (LaPlante) Avon
Olive Borden	Anne Cornwall
Ena Gregory	Madeline Hurlock
Natalie Joyce	June Marlowe
Joan Meredith	Evelyn Pierce
Dorothy Revier	Duane Thompson
Lola Todd	

1926

Mary Astor	Mary Brian
Joyce Compton	Delores Costello
Joan Crawford	Marceline Day
Delores Del Rio	Janet Gaynor
Sally Long	Edna Marion
Sally O'Neil	Vera Reynolds
Fay Wray	

1927

Patricia Avery	Rita Carewe
Helen Costello	Barbara Kent
Natalie Kingston	Frances Lee
Mary McAlister	Gladys McConnell
Sally Phipps	Sally Rand
Martha Sleeper	Iris Stuart
Adamae Vaughn	

1928

Lina Basquette	Flora Bramley
Sue Carol	Ann Christy
June Collyer	Alice Day
Sally Eilers	Audrey Ferris
Dorothy Gulliver	Gwen Lee
Molly O'Day	Ruth Taylor
Lupe Velez	

1929

Jean Arthur	Sally Blane
Betty Boyd	Ethlyne Claire

Doris Dawson
Helen Foster
Caryl Lincoln
Mona Rico
Loretta Young

Josephine Dunn
Doris Hill
Anita Page
Helen Twelvetrees

WAMPAS SISTERS

Laura LaPlante	1924	Alberta Vaughn	1924
Violet Avon	1925	Adamae Vaughn	1927
Delores Costello	1926	Marceline Day	1926
Helen Costello	1927	Alice Day	1928
Sally O'Neil	1926	Sally Blane	1929
Molly O'Day	1928	Loretta Young	1929

Appendix C

Grauman's Chinese Theatre
Forecourt of the Stars

Grauman's Chinese Theatre was built and opened in 1927; it was declared a historic-cultural landmark in 1968. The tradition of stars putting footprints and handprints in cement accompanied by their signature started unintentionally when Norma Talmadge visited the new theater and accidentally stepped into wet cement. The idea of intentionally leaving footprints was developed and the tradition continues today.

Forecourt of the Stars

Ceremony #1	Mary Pickford	April 1927
Ceremony #2	Norma Talmadge	May 1927
Ceremony #3	Norma Shearer	August 1927
Ceremony #7	Colleen Moore	December 1927
Ceremony #8	Gloria Swanson	December 1927
Ceremony #9	Constance Talmadge	December 1927
Ceremony #11	Pola Negri	April 1928
Ceremony #12	Bebe Daniels	May 1929
Ceremony #13	Marion Davies	May 1929
Ceremony #14	Janet Gaynor	May 1929
Ceremony #15	Joan Crawford	September 1929
Ceremony #78	Louella O. Parsons	September 1946

Appendix D

Female Pioneers Behind the Scenes in the Film Industry (1895-1930)

Zoe Akins	writer
Dorothy Arzner	writer/director/editor
Ruth Ann Baldwin	writer/director
Clara Beranger	writer
Ouida Bergere	writer/actor
Marguerite Bertsch	writer/director
Adele Buffington	writer
Mrs. George R. Chester	writer/editor
Lenore Coffee	writer
Grace Cunard	writer/director/actor
BeBe Daniels	actor/producer
Dorothy Davenport	writer/director/actor/producer
Beulah Marie Dix	writer
Lillian Ducey	writer
Marion Fairfax	writer/director
Dorothy Farnum	writer
Gene Gauntier	writer/director/actor/producer
Lillian Gish	director/actor
Elinor Glyn	writer/director/producer
Alice Guy	director
Julia Crawford Ivers	writer/director
Osa Johnson	producer
Sonya Levien	writer
Anita Loos	writer/producer
Jeannie Macpherson	writer/director/actor

Cleo Madison	director/actor
Frances Marion	writer/director/actor
Sarah Y. Mason	writer
June Mathis	writer
Lucille McVey	writer/director/actor
Bess Meredyth	writer/director
Jane Murfin	writer/director
Mary Murillo	writer
Alla Nazimova	director/actor/producer
Mabel Normand	director/actor/producer
Ida May Park	writer/director/producer
Elizabeth Pickett	writer
Mary Pickford	actor/producer
Olga Printzlau	writer
Frederica Sagor Maas	writer
Blanche Sewell	editor
Nell Shipman	writer/director/actor
Ruth Stonehouse	writer/director/actor/producer
Alice Terry	director/actor
May Tully	writer/director
Florence Turner	writer/director/actor/producer
Eve Unsell	writer/editor
Beatrice Van	writer/actor
Virginia Van Upp	writer/producer
Lule Warrenton	writer/director/actor/producer
Lois Weber	writer/director/actor/producer
Kathlyn Williams	writer/director/actor
Elsie Jane Wilson	director/actor
Margery Wilson	director/actor/producer
Dorothy Yost	writer

Author's note: Not all of these women's stories have survived the years. The individuals that have a significant body of work and reliable biographical information available have been included in the book.

Appendix E

Locations of Early Women Stars on the Hollywood Walk of Fame

Anchoring the west end of the Walk is a silver gazebo with four life-size statues of silver screen "goddesses":

Mae West	Delores Del Rio
Dorothy Dandridge	Anna May Wong

6901 Hollywood Boulevard	Greta Garbo
6821 Hollywood Boulevard	Mabel Normand
6801 Hollywood Boulevard	Alice Calhoun
	Louise Fazenda
	Olive Borden
6777 Hollywood Boulevard	Bessie Love
6761 Hollywood Boulevard	Katherine MacDonald
6737 Hollywood Boulevard	Jane Darwell
6723 Hollywood Boulevard	Aileen Pringle
6701 Hollywood Boulevard	Mary Astor
6685 Hollywood Boulevard	Myrna Loy
6673 Hollywood Boulevard	Flora Finch
6655 Hollywood Boulevard	Dorothy Sebastian
6617 Hollywood Boulevard	Billie Burke
6563 Hollywood Boulevard	Ruth Etting
6541 Hollywood Boulevard	Viola Dana
6525 Hollywood Boulevard	Miriam Cooper
6517 Hollywood Boulevard	Madge Bellamy
6519 Hollywood Boulevard	Leatrice Joy

6513 Hollywood Boulevard	Clara Kimball Young
6501 Hollywood Boulevard	Julia Faye
6385 Hollywood Boulevard	Dorothy Gish
6351 Hollywood Boulevard	Billie Dove
6349 Hollywood Boulevard	Fay Wray
6333 Hollywood Boulevard	Jetta Goudal
	Jean Arthur
6315 Hollywood Boulevard	Hedda Hopper
6307 Hollywood Boulevard	Theda Bara
6305 Hollywood Boulevard	Mildred Harris
6301 Hollywood Boulevard	Constance Binney
	Gloria Swanson
6263 Hollywood Boulevard	Ruth Chatterton
	Helen Parrish (Our Gang)
6245 Hollywood Boulevard	Sylvia Sidney
6231 Hollywood Boulevard	Constance Collier
6225 Hollywood Boulevard	Bette Davis
	Irene Rich
6201 Hollywood Boulevard	Marie Prevost
6161 Hollywood Boulevard	Helen Ferguson
6141 Hollywood Boulevard	Tallulah Bankhead
6135 Hollywood Boulevard	Loretta Young (II)
6125 Hollywood Boulevard	Virginia Valli
	Pauline Starke
6927 Hollywood Boulevard	Lupe Velez
6933 Hollywood Boulevard	Lois Wilson
6935 Hollywood Boulevard	(Alla) Nazimova
7001 Hollywood Boulevard	Ethel Barrymore
7021 Hollywood Boulevard	Claire Windsor
	Vilma Banky
	Mae Busch
6100 Hollywood Boulevard	Loretta Young (I)
6140 Hollywood Boulevard	Pola Negri

6150 Hollywood Boulevard	Anna Q. Nilsson
	Mary Boland
	Jeanie Macpherson
6250 Hollywood Boulevard	Constance Bennett
6260 Hollywood Boulevard	Ruth Roland
6262 Hollywood Boulevard	Thelma Todd
6280 Hollywood Boulevard	Mary Pickford
	Janet Gaynor
6300 Hollywood Boulevard	Polly Moran
	Louella O. Parsons (I)
6304 Hollywood Boulevard	Marguerite Clark
6316 Hollywood Boulevard	Nita Naldi
6318 Hollywood Boulevard	Mae Murray
6326 Hollywood Boulevard	Marion Davies
6336 Hollywood Boulevard	Marjorie Rambeau
6358 Hollywood Boulevard	Dorothy Phillips
6376 Hollywood Boulevard	Laura LaPlante
6400 Hollywood Boulevard	Marlene Dietrich
6404 Hollywood Boulevard	Beatrice Lillie
6408 ½ Hollywood Boulevard	Alma Rubens
6418 Hollywood Boulevard	Louella O. Parsons (II)
6504 Hollywood Boulevard	Agnes Ayres
6518 Hollywood Boulevard	Lois Weber
6538 Hollywood Boulevard	Marie Dresser
6548 Hollywood Boulevard	Evelyn Brent
6554 Hollywood Boulevard	Zasu Pitts
6562 Hollywood Boulevard	Olga Petrova
6608 Hollywood Boulevard	Annette Kellerman
6620 Hollywood Boulevard	Gilda Gray
6626 Hollywood Boulevard	Alice Terry
6636 Hollywood Boulevard	Norma Shearer
6652 Hollywood Boulevard	Bessie Barriscale
6664 Hollywood Boulevard	Esther Ralston

6669 Hollywood Boulevard	Patsy Kelly
6720 Hollywood Boulevard	Mabel Taliaferro
6724 Hollywood Boulevard	Anita Stewart
6750 Hollywood Boulevard	Gloria Swanson (II)
6776 Hollywood Boulevard	Elsie Janis
6834 Hollywood Boulevard	Louise Glaum
6838 Hollywood Boulevard	Pearl White
6904 Hollywood Boulevard	Marguerite De La Motte
6928 Hollywood Boulevard	Eleanor Boardman
6936 Hollywood Boulevard	Ethel Clayton
7000 Hollywood Boulevard	Pauline Frederick
7038 Hollywood Boulevard	Kathlyn Williams
1501 Vine Street	Alice White
1511 Vine Street	Belle Bennett
1523 Vine Street	Edith Storey
1529 Vine Street	Lina Basquette
1549 Vine Street	Colleen Moore
1559 Vine Street	Mary Brian
1601 Vine Street	Renee Adoree
1627 Vine Street	Barbara LaMarr
1639 Vine Street	Sue Carol Ladd
1645 Vine Street	Delores Costello
S/W Corner Hollywood and Vine	Constance Talmadge
1709 Vine Street	Miriam Hopkins
	Geraldine Farrar (II)
1719 Vine Street	Hattie McDaniel
1731 Vine Street	May McAvoy
	Marie Dressler
1751 Vine Street	Betty Compson
	Sarah Bernhardt
1779 Vine Street	Texas Guinan
1752 Vine Street	Beverly Bayne
	Joan Crawford

	Madge Evans
	Marion Nixon
1750 Vine Street	Carmel Myers
	Blanche Sweet
1724 Vine Street	Mary Miles Minter
	Mrs. Sidney Drew
1720 Vine Street	Lillian Gish
1718 Vine Street	Lila Lee
1716 Vine Street	BeBe Daniels
1708 Vine Street	Betty Blythe
Hollywood and Vine	Anna May Wong
	Molly O'Day
1630 Vine Street	Delores Del Rio
1620 Vine Street	Estelle Taylor
	Geraldine Ferrar (II)
1600 Vine Street	Mae Marsh
	Madge Kennedy
1560 Vine Street	Dorothy Dalton
	Mae West
	Corinne Griffith
1500 Vine Street	Clara Bow
	Norma Talmadge
Sunset and Vine	Helene Costello
6300 Vine Street	Marguerite Clark
1500 N. Vine Street	Dorothy Arzner

Bibliography

Abel, Richard. *The Red Rooster Scare: Making Cinema American 1900-1910*. Los Angeles: University of California Press, 1999.

——. *Silent Film*. New Brunswick, NJ: Rutgers University Press, 1995.

Acker, Ally. *Reel Women: Pioneers of the Cinema 1896-Present*. New York: Continuum Publishing Company, 1991.

Ardmore, Jane Kesner Morris. *The Self-Enchanted: Mae Murray, Image of an Era*. New York: McGraw-Hill, 1959.

Arvidson, Linda. *When Movies Were Young*. Mineola, NY: Dover Publications, 1968.

Astor, Mary. *My Story: An Autobiography*. New York: Doubleday and Co., 1959.

——. *A Life on Film*. New York: Delacorte, 1971.

Baker, Roger. *Drag: A History of Female Impersonation in the Performing Arts*. New York: New York University Press, 1994.

Bankhead, Tallulah. *Tallulah: My Autobiography*. New York: Harper and Brothers, 1952.

Barrymore, Ethel. *Memories*. London: Hulton Press Ltd., 1956.

Basinger, Jeanine. *Silent Stars*. Hanover, NH: Wesleyan University Press, 1999.

Basquette, Lina. *Lina, DeMille's Godless Girl*. Edgewater, FL: Denlinger's Publishers, Ltd., 1990.

Batille, Gretchen M. and Charles L. P. Silet, Eds. *The Pretend Indians: Images of Native Americans in the Movies*. Ames: Iowa State University Press, 1980.

Beck, Calvin Thomas. *Scream Queens: Heroines of the Horrors*. New York: MacMillan Publishing Company, Inc., 1978.

Bellamy, Madge. *A Darling of the Twenties: The Autobiography of Madge Bellamy*. Vestal, NY: Vestal Press, 1989.

Beranger, Clara. *Writing for the Screen*. Dubuque, IO: Wm. C. Brown. Co., 1950.

Bertsch, Marguerite. *How to Write for Moving Pictures: A Manual of Instruction and Information*. New York: Doran, 1917.

Blum, Daniel. *A Pictorial History of the Silent Film*. New York: Grosset and Dunlap, 1953.

Bodeen, DeWitt. *From Hollywood*. New York: A.S. Barnes and Company, 1976.

Bogle, Donald. *Dorothy Dandrige: A Biography*. New York: Amistad Press, 1997.

——. *Toms, Coons, Mulattoes, Mammies and Bucks: An Interpretative History of Blacks in American Films*. New York: Continuum Publishing Company, 1996.

Bowser, Eileen. *The Transformation of Cinema: 1907-1915.* Los Angeles: University of California Press, 1990.

Braff, Richard E. *The Universal Silents (1912-1929).* Jefferson, NC: McFarland and Company, 1999.

Brooks, Louise. *Lulu in Hollywood.* New York: Knopf, 1983.

Brown, Gene. *Movie Time: A Chronology of Hollywood and the Movie Industry from Its Beginnings to the Present.* New York: MacMillan Publishing Company, 1995.

Brown, Kelly R. *Florence Lawrence; the Biograph Girl: America's First Movie Star.* Jefferson, NC: McFarland and Company, 1999.

Brownlow, Kevin. *Behind the Mask of Innocence.* Los Angeles: University of California Press, 1990.

———. *Hollywood: The Pioneers.* New York: Alfred A. Knopf, 1979.

———. *The Parade's Gone By.* New York: Alfred A. Knopf, 1968.

Burke, Billie. *With a Feather on My Nose.* New York: Appleton-Century, 1949.

Butler, Ivan. *Silent Magic: Rediscovering the Silent Film Era.* New York: Ungar Publishing Company, 1988.

Card, James. *Seductive Cinema: The Art of Silent Film.* Minneapolis: University of Minnesota Press, 1999.

Cary, Diana Serra (Baby Peggy Montgomery). *Hollywood Posse: The Story of a Galland Band of Horsemen Who Made Movie History.* Boston: Houghton Mifflin, 1975.

———. *Hollywood's Children: An Inside account of the Child Star Era.* Dallas, TX: Southern Methodist University Press, 1978.

———. *Jackie Coogan, The World's Boy King: A Biography of Hollywood's Legendary Child Star.* Scarecrow Press, 2003.

———. *Whatever Happened to Baby Peggy?* New York: St. Martins, 1996.

Castle, Irene. *Castles in the Air.* New York: Doubleday, 1958.

———. *My Husband.* New York: New Library Press, 1919.

Castle, Vernon and Irene Castle. *Modern Dancing.* New York: Harper and Bros., 1917.

Cooper, Miriam. *Dark Lady of the Silents: My Life in Early Hollywood.* Indianapolis, IN: Bobbs-Merrill, 1973.

Cowie, Peter. *Seventy Years of Cinema.* New York: A.S. Barnes and Company, 1969.

Crafton, Donald. *The Talkies: American Cinema's Transition to Sound 1926-1931.* Los Angeles: University of California Press, 1997.

Crawford, Christina. *Mommy Dearest.* New York: William Morrow, 1978.

Cripps, Thomas. *Slow Fade to Black: The Negro in American Film 1900-1942.* New York: Oxford University Press, 1977.

Da, Lottie and Jan Alexander. *Bad Girls of the Silver Screen.* New York: Carroll and Graf Publishers, Inc., 1989.

Davies, Marion. *The Times We Had: Life with William Randolph Hearst.* Indianapolis, IN: Bobbs-Merrill Company, 1975.

deCordova, Richard. *Picture Personalities: The Emergence of the Star System in America.* Champaign: University of Illinois Press, 2001.

Douglas, George H. *Women of the 20s.* Dallas, TX: Saybrook Publishers, 1986.

Doyle, Billy H. *The Ultimate Directory of Silent Screen Performers.* Metuchen, NJ: Scarecrow Press, Inc., 1995.

Dressler, Marie. *The Life Story of an Ugly Duckling.* New York: Robert M. McBride and Co., 1924.

———. *My Own Story.* Boston: Little, Brown and Co., 1934.

Drew, William M. *Speaking of Silents: First Ladies of the Screen.* Vestal, NY: The Vestal Press, Ltd., 1989.

Edmonds, I.G. *Big U: Universal in the Silent Days.* New York: A.S. Barnes and Company, 1977.

Emerson, John and Anita Loos. *Breaking into Movies.* New York, 1921.

———. *How to Write Photoplays.* Philadelphia: George W. Jacobs, 1920.

Etherington-Smith, Meredith and Jeremy Pilcher. *The "IT" Girls: Elinor Glyn, Novelist and Her Sister, Lucile, Couturiere.* New York: Harcourt, Brace and Jovanovich, 1986.

Everson, William K. *American Silent Film.* New York: Da Capo Press, 1998.

Eyman, Scott. *The Speed of Sound: Hollywood and the Talkie Revolution: 1926-1930.* New York: Simon and Schuster, 1997.

Farrar, Geraldine. *The Autobiography of Geraldine Farrar: Such Sweet Compulsion.* New York: Graystone Press, 1938.

Fass, Paula S. *The Damned and the Beautiful.* New York: Oxford University Press, 1977.

Finler, Joel W. *Silent Cinema.* London: B.T. Batsford, Ltd., 1997.

Fowler, Marion. *The Way She Looks Tonight.* New York: St. Martin's Press, 1996.

Francke, Lizzie. *Script Girls: Screenwriters in Hollywood.* London: British Film Institute, 1994.

Franklin, Joe. *Classics of the Silent Screen: A Pictorial Treasury.* New York: Citadel Press, 1959.

Fuller, Kathryn H. *At the Picture Show.* Washington, DC: Smithsonian Institution Press, 1996.

Fussell, Betty Harper. *Mabel: Hollywood's First I-Don't-Care Girl.* New York: Ticknor and Fields, 1982.

Gish, Lillian. *Dorothy and Lillian Gish.* New York: Scribners, 1973.

Gish, Lillian with Ann Pinchot. *The Movies, Mr. Griffith, and Me.* Englewood Cliffs, NJ: Prentice-Hall, Inc., 1969.

Glyn, Elinor. *Romantic Adventure.* New York: E.P. Dutton, 1936.

Griffith, Corinne. *Papa's Delicate Condition.* Boston: Houghton Mifflin, 1952.

———. *This You Won't Believe!* New York: F. Fell, 1972.

Griffith, Richard and Arthur Mayer. *The Movies: The Sixty-Year Story.* New York: Bonanza Books, 1957.

Hadley-Garcia, George. *Hispanic Hollywood.* New York: Carol Publishing Company, 1990.

Hanson, Steve and Patrick King Hanson. *Lights, Camera, Action: A History of the Movies in the Twentieth Century.* Los Angeles: LA Times, 2000.

Harmon, Jim and Donald F. Glut. *The Great Movie Serials: Their Sound and Fury.* Garden City, NY: Doubleday and Company, 1972.

Higashi, Sumiko. *Virgins, Vamps, and Flappers: American Silent Movie Heroines.* New York: Eden Press, 1978.

Hopper, Hedda. *From Under My Hat.* Garden City, NY: Doubleday, 1964.

Hopper, Hedda with James Brough. *The Whole Truth and Nothing But.* New York: Doubleday, 1963.

Jones, G. William. *Black Cinema Treasures.* Denton: University of Texas Press, 1991.

Jones, Ken D., Arthur F. McClure, and Alfred E. Twomey. *Character People: Stalwarts of the Cinema.* New York: A.S. Barnes and Company, 1976.

Karney, Robyn, Ed. *Cinema Year-by-Year 1984-2001.* New York: Dorling Kindersley Limited, 2001.

———. *The Movie Stars' Story.* New York: Crown Publisher, Inc., 1984.

Keller, Helen. *The Story of My Life.* New York: The Century Company, 1904.

Kellerman, Annette. *Physical Beauty: How to Keep It.* New York: Doran, 1918.

Keylin, Arleen and Suri Fleischer. *Hollywood Album.* New York: Arno Press, 1979.

Kinnard, Roy. *Fifty Years of Serial Thrills.* Metuchen, NJ: Scarecrow Press, 1983.

Klotman, Phyllis Rauch. *Frame-by-Frame: A Black Filmography.* Bloomington: Indiana University Press, 1979.

Koszarski, Richard. *An Evening's Entertainment: The Age of Silent Feature Pictures: 1915-1928.* Los Angeles: University of California Press, 1990.

———. *Hollywood Directors 1914-1940.* New York: Oxford University Press, 1976.

Kotsilibas-Davis, James and Myrna Loy. *Myrna Loy: Being and Becoming.* New York: Knopf, 1987.

Kuhns, William. *Movies in America.* Dayton, OH: Pflaum/Standard, 1972.

Lahue, Kalton C. *Bound and Gagged: The Story of the Silent Serials.* New York: Castle Books, 1968.

———. *Ladies in Distress.* New York: A.S. Barnes and Company, 1971.

———. *Continued Next Week: A History of the Moving Picture Serial.* Norman: University of Oklahoma Press, 1964.

Lahue, Kalton C., Ed. *Motion Picture Pioneer: The Selig Polyscope Company.* New York: A.S. Barnes and Company, 1973.

Lahue, Kalton C. and Terry Brewer. *Kops and Custards: The Legend of Keystone Films.* Norman: University of Oklahoma Press, 1968.

Lahue, Kalton C. and Samuel Gill. *Clown Princes and Court Jesters.* New York: A.S. Barnes and Company, 1970.

LaSalle, Mick. *Complicated Women*. New York: St. Martin's Press, 2000.

Lee, Betty. *Marie Dressler: The Unlikeliest Star*. Lexington: University Press of Kentucky, 1997.

Lee, Raymond. *The Films of Mary Pickford*. New York: Castle Books, 1970.

Levin, Martin, Ed. *Hollywood and the Great Fan Magazines*. New York: Arbor House Publishing Company, 1970.

Liebman, Roy. *From Silents to Sound*. Jefferson, NC: McFarland and Company, 1998.

———. *Silent Film Performers*. Jefferson, NC: McFarland and Company, 1996.

———. *The W.A.M.P.A.S. Baby Stars: 1922-1934*. Jefferson, NC: McFarland and Company, 2000.

Lloyd, Ann, Ed. *The Illustrated History of the Cinema*. New York: MacMillan Publishing Company, 1986.

Loos, Anita. *Cast of Thousands*. New York: Grosset and Dunlap, 1977.

———. *Gentlemen Prefer Blondes: The Illuminating Diary of a Professional Lady*. New York: Boni and Liveright, 1925.

———. *A Girl Like I*. New York: Viking Penguin, 1966.

———. *Kiss Hollywood Good-Bye*. New York: Viking Penguin, 1974.

———. *The Talmadge Girls*. New York: Viking Press, 1978.

Love, Bessie. *From Hollywood with Love*. North Pomfret, VT: David and Charles, 1977.

Maltin, Leonard. *The Great Movie Comedians*. New York: Crown Publishers, Inc., 1978.

Manchel, Frank. *Women on the Hollywood Screen*. New York: Franklin Watts, 1977.

Mapp, Edward. *Directory of Blacks in the Performing Arts*. Metuchen, NJ: Scarecrow Press, 1978.

Marion, Frances. *Off with Their Heads*. New York: Macmillan, 1972.

Marsh, Mae. *Screen Acting*. Los Angeles: Photo-Star Publishing Co., 1921.

Martin, Linda and Kerry Segrave. *Women in Comedy: The Funny Ladies from the Turn of the Century to the Present*. Secaucus, NJ: Citadel Press, 1986.

May, Lary. *Screening Out the Past: The Birth of Mass Culture and the Motion Picture Industry*. Chicago: University of Chicago Press, 1983.

Mayne, Judith. *Directed by Dorothy Arzner*. Indianapolis: Indiana University Press, 1994.

McCreadie, Marsha. *The Women Who Write the Movies*. New York: Birchlane Press, 1994.

Miller, Patsy Ruth. *My Hollywood: When Both of Us Were Young*. Atlantic City, NJ: O'Raghailligh Ltd. Publishers, 1988.

Mitchell, Glenn. *A-Z of Silent Film Comedy*. London: B.T. Batsford, Ltd., 1998.

Moore, Colleen. *Silent Star: Colleen Moore Talks About Her Hollywood*. New York: Doubleday, 1968.

Mordden, Ethan. *Movie Star: A Look at the Woman Who Made Hollywood.* New York: St. Martin's Press, 1983.

Murray, James P. *To Find an Image: Black Films from Uncle Tom to Superfly.* New York: The Bobbs-Merrill Company, Inc., 1973.

Negri, Pola. *Memoirs of a Star.* Garden City, NY: Doubleday, 1970.

Neseby, James R. *Black Images in American Film: 1896-1954.* Washington, DC: University Press of America, 1982.

Null, Gary. *Black Hollywood from 1910 to Today.* New York: Citadel Press, 1993.

Nunn, Curtis. *Marguerite Clark: American Darling of Broadway and the Silent Screen.* Fort Worth: Texas Christian University Press, 1981.

O'Leary, Liam. *The Silent Cinema.* London: Studio Vista, 1965.

Paine, Albert Bigelow. *Life and Lillian Gish.* New York: Macmillan, 1932.

Parish, James Robert. *The Paramount Pretties.* New Rochelle, NY: Arlington House, 1972.

Parkinson, David. *History of Film.* New York: Thames and Hudson, Inc., 1996.

Patterson, Lindsay. *Black Films and Film-Makers.* New York: Dodd, Mead and Company, 1975.

Peary, Danny, Ed. *Close-Ups: Intimate Portraits of Movie Stars.* New York: Workman Publishing, 1978.

Pickford, Mary. *My Rendezvous with Life.* New York: H.C. Kinsey and Co. Inc., 1935.

———. *Sunshine and Shadow.* Garden City, NY: Doubleday and Co. Inc, 1955.

———. *Why Not Try God?* New York: H.C. Kinsey and Co. Inc., 1934.

Pratt, George C. *Spellbound in Darkness: A History of Silent Film.* Greenwich, CT: New York Graphic Society, Ltd., 1973.

Rainey, Buck. *Those Fabulous Serial Heroines: Their Lives and Films.* Metuchen, NJ: Scarecrow Press, 1990.

Ralston, Esther. *Some Day We'll Laugh: An Autobiography.* Metuchen, NJ: Scarecrow Press, 1985.

Ramsaye, Terry. *A Million and One Nights: A History of the Motion Picture Through 1925.* New York: Simon and Schuster, Inc., (1926) 1986.

Rhinehart, Mary Roberts. *My Story.* New York: Farrar and Rinehart, 1931.

Rhines, Jesse Algeron. *Black Film, White Money.* New Brunswick, NJ: Rutgers University Press, 1996.

Richards, Larry. *African American Films Through 1959.* Jefferson, NC: McFarland and Company, 1998.

Robertson, Patrick. *The Guinness Movie Facts and Feats.* Enfield, Middlesex, UK: Guiness Books, 1988.

Rosen, Marjorie. *Popcorn Venus: Women, Movies and the American Dream.* New York: Coward, McCann and Geoghegan, 1973.

Ross, Steven J. *Working Class Hollywood: Silent Film and the Shaping of Class in America.* Princeton, NJ: Princeton University Press, 1998.

Sagor Maas, Frederica. *The Shocking Miss Pilgrim: A Writer in Early Hollywood.* Lexington: University Press of Kentucky, 1999.

Sarris, Andrew. *You Ain't Heard Nothing Yet.* New York: Oxford University Press. 1998.

Sennett, Robert S. *Hollywood Hoopla: Creating Stars and Selling Movies in the Golden Age of Hollywood.* New York: Billboard Books, 1998.

Shipman, David. *The Great Movie Stars: The Golden Years.* New York: Crown Publishers, Inc., 1970.

Shipman, Nell. *The Silent Screen and My Talking Heart.* Boise, ID: Boise State University, 1987.

Sinyard, Neil. *Silent Movies.* New York: Smithmark Publishers, 1995.

Slide, Anthony. *Aspects of American Film History Prior to 1920.* Metuchen, NJ: Scarecrow Press, 1978.

——. *Early American Cinema.* New York: A.S. Barnes and Company, 1970.

——. *Early Women Directors.* New York: A.S. Barnes and Company, 1977.

——. *The Griffith Actresses.* New York: A.S. Barnes and Company, 1973.

——. *The Idols of Silence.* New York: A.S. Barnes and Company, 1978.

Smith, Scott. *The Film 100.* Secaucus, NJ: Carol Publishing Group, 1998.

Spears, Jack. *Hollywood: The Golden Era.* New York: Castle Books, 1971.

Stamp, Shelley. *Movie Struck Girls: Women and Motion Picture Culture After the Nickelodeon.* Princeton, NJ: Princeton University Press, 2000.

Stedman, Raymond Wm. *The Serials: Suspense and Drama by Installment.* Norman: University of Oklahoma Press, 1971.

Stenn, David. *Clara Bow: Runnin' Wild.* New York: Penguin Books, 1990.

Swanson, Gloria. *Swanson on Swanson.* New York: Random House, 1980.

Tapert, Annette. *The Power of Glamour: The Women Who Defined the Magic of Stardom.* New York: Crown Publishers, Inc., 1998.

Unterburger, Amy L. *The St. Martin's Women Filmmakers Encyclopedia: Women on the Other Side of the Camera.* Farmington Hills, MI: Invisible Ink Press, 1999.

Weaver, John T. *Twenty Years of Silents; 1908-1928.* Metuchen, NJ: Scarecrow Press, 1971.

White, Pearl. *Just Me.* New York: GH Doran Cie, 1919.

Whitfield, Eileen. *Pickford: The Woman Who Made Hollywood.* Lexington: University Press of Kentucky, 1997.

Wilson, Margery. *Believe in Yourself.* Philadelphia: J.B. Lippincott, 1949.

——. *Charm.* New York: Frederick A. Stokes Company, 1930.

——. *How to Live Beyond Your Means.* Philadelphia: J.B. Lippincott, 1945.

——. *I Found My Way.* Philadelphia: J.B. Lippincott, 1956.

——. *Make Up Your Mind.* New York: Frederick A. Stokes Company, 1940.

——. *The Woman You Want to Be.* Philadelphia: J.B. Lippincott, 1942.

——. *Your Personality and God.* New York: Frederick A. Stokes, 1938.

Wogenknecht, Edward. *Stars of the Silents.* Metuchen, NJ: Scarecrow Press, 1987.

Wollstein, Hans J. *Vixens; Floozies and Molls.* Jefferson, NC: McFarland and Company, 1999.

Wray, Fay. *On the Other Hand.* New York: St. Martin's, 1989.

Young, Loretta, as told to Helen Ferguson. *The Things I Had To Learn.* Indianapolis, IN: Bobbs-Merrill, 1961.

Zierold, Norman. *Sex Goddesses of the Silent Screen.* Chicago: Henry Regnery Company, 1973.

Index

Order a copy of this book with this form or online at:
http://www.haworthpress.com/store/product.asp?sku=5077

An Encyclopedic Dictionary of Women in Early American Films 1895-1930

_____ in hardbound at $69.95 ((ISBN: 0-7890-1842-X)

_____ in softbound at $49.95 (ISBN: 0-7890-1843-8)

Or order online and use special offer code HEC25 in the shopping cart.

COST OF BOOKS_____

☐ **BILL ME LATER:** (Bill-me option is good on US/Canada/Mexico orders only; not good to jobbers, wholesalers, or subscription agencies.)

☐ Check here if billing address is different from shipping address and attach purchase order and billing address information.

POSTAGE & HANDLING_____
(US: $4.00 for first book & $1.50 for each additional book)
(Outside US: $5.00 for first book & $2.00 for each additional book)

Signature_____

SUBTOTAL_____

☐ **PAYMENT ENCLOSED: $_____**

IN CANADA: ADD 7% GST_____

☐ **PLEASE CHARGE TO MY CREDIT CARD.**

STATE TAX_____
(NJ, NY, OH, MN, CA, IL, IN, & SD residents, add appropriate local sales tax)

☐ Visa ☐ MasterCard ☐ AmEx ☐ Discover
☐ Diner's Club ☐ Eurocard ☐ JCB

Account # _____

FINAL TOTAL_____
(If paying in Canadian funds, convert using the current exchange rate, UNESCO coupons welcome)

Exp. Date_____

Signature_____

Prices in US dollars and subject to change without notice.

NAME_____

INSTITUTION_____

ADDRESS_____

CITY_____

STATE/ZIP_____

COUNTRY_____ COUNTY (NY residents only)_____

TEL_____ FAX_____

E-MAIL_____

May we use your e-mail address for confirmations and other types of information? ☐ Yes ☐ No
We appreciate receiving your e-mail address and fax number. Haworth would like to e-mail or fax special discount offers to you, as a preferred customer. **We will never share, rent, or exchange your e-mail address or fax number.** We regard such actions as an invasion of your privacy.

Order From Your Local Bookstore or Directly From
The Haworth Press, Inc.
10 Alice Street, Binghamton, New York 13904-1580 • USA
TELEPHONE: 1-800-HAWORTH (1-800-429-6784) / Outside US/Canada: (607) 722-5857
FAX: 1-800-895-0582 / Outside US/Canada: (607) 771-0012
E-mailto: orders@haworthpress.com

For orders outside US and Canada, you may wish to order through your local
sales representative, distributor, or bookseller.
For information, see http://haworthpress.com/distributors

(Discounts are available for individual orders in US and Canada only, not booksellers/distributors.)
PLEASE PHOTOCOPY THIS FORM FOR YOUR PERSONAL USE.
http://www.HaworthPress.com   BOF04